MW00813322

X-O MANOWAR

BOOK THREE

ROBERT VENDITTI | DOUG BRAITHWAITE | DIEGO BERNARD
LAURA MARTIN | BRIAN REBER

CONTENTS

PRELUDE TO ARMOR HUNTERS

Writers: Robert Venditti (Origin, X-O MANOWAR #23-24, "Burial," "The Fate of Kings") and Justin Jordan ("Bar Fight")
Writer-Artists: Andy Runton ("Owly & Wormy in... Shanhara's Day Off") and Tom Fowler ("Battle for the Ages")
Artists: J.G. Jones (Origin), Rafer Roberts ("Bar Fight"), and Bryan Hitch ("The Fate of Kings")
Penciler: Diego Bernard (X-O MANOWAR #23-24, "Burial")
Inkers: Alejandro Sicat (X-O MANOWAR #23) and Allison Rodrigues (X-O MANOWAR #24, "Burial")
Colorists: Matt Hollingsworth (Origin), Brian Reber (X-O MANOWAR #23-24, "Burial"), and David Baron ("The Fate of Kings")
Letterer: Dave Sharpe (Origin, X-O MANOWAR #23-24, "Burial," "The Fate of Kings")
Cover Artists: CAFU (X-O MANOWAR #23); Diego Bernard with Alejandro Sicat (X-O MANOWAR #24); and Jelena Kevic-Djurdjevic (X-O MANOWAR #25)

ARMOR HUNTERS

Collection Cover Art: Clayton Henry

CREDITS

X-O MANOWAR

Writer: Robert Venditti
Penciler: Diego Bernard (#26-29)
Inker: Allison Rodrigues (#26-29)
Colorists: Brian Reber (#26-27) and Romulo
Fajardo (#28-29)
Letterer: Dave Sharpe
Cover Artists: Clayton Crain (#26), Miguel
Sepúlveda (#27), Diego Bernard (#28), and
CAFU (#29)

ARMOR HUNTERS

Writer: Robert Venditti
Artist: Doug Braithwaite
Colorist: Laura Martin
Letterer: Dave Sharpe
Cover Artists: Jorge Molina (#1) and
Doug Braithwaite (#2-4)

GALLERY

Diego Bernard
CAFU
Clayton Crain
Trevor Hairsine
Bryan Hitch
Lewis LaRosa
Arturo Lozzi

Cary Nord
Brian Reber
Allison Rodrigues
Bart Sears
Miguel Sepúlveda
Alejandro Sicat
Robert Venditti

Assistant Editor: Josh Johns
Editor: Warren Simons

VALIANT

Peter Cuneo
Chairman

Dinesh Shamdasani
CEO & Chief Creative Officer

Gavin Cuneo
Chief Operating Officer & CFO

Fred Pierce
Publisher

Warren Simons
VP Editor-in-Chief

Walter Black
VP Operations

Hunter Gorinson
Director of Marketing,
Communications & Digital Media

Atom! Freeman
Director of Sales

Matthew Klein
Andy Liegl
John Petrie
Sales Managers

Josh Johns
Associate Director of Digital Media and Development

Travis Escarfullery
Jeff Walker
Production & Design Managers

Tom Brennan
Editor

Kyle Andrukiewicz
Editor and Creative Executive

Peter Stern
Publishing & Operations Manager

Andrew Steinbeiser
Marketing & Communications Manager

Danny Khazem
Editorial Operations Manager

Ivan Cohen
Collection Editor

Steve Blackwell
Collection Designer

Lauren Hitzhusen
Editorial Assistant

Rian Hughes/Device
Trade Dress & Book Design

Russell Brown
President, Consumer Products,
Promotions and Ad Sales

Geeta Singh
Licensing Manager

X-O Manowar® Deluxe Edition Book 3. Published by Valiant Entertainment LLC. Office of Publication: 350 Seventh Avenue, New York, NY 10001. Compilation copyright © 2016 Valiant Entertainment LLC. All rights reserved. Contains materials originally published in single magazine form as X-O Manowar #23-29 and Armor Hunters® #1-4. Copyright © 2014 Valiant Entertainment LLC.

Printed in Canada. First Printing. ISBN: 9781682151310.

PRELUDE TO ARMOR HUNTERS

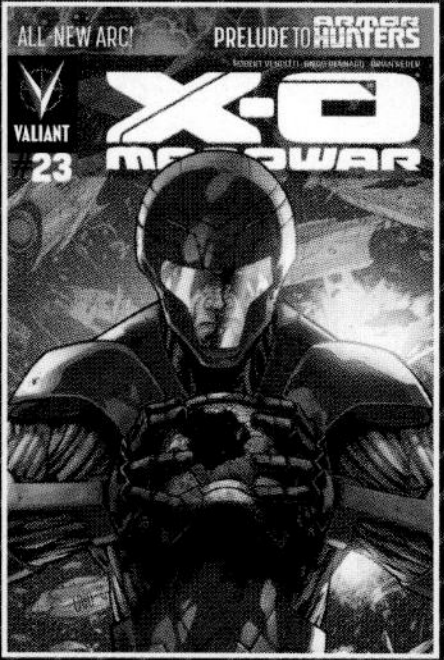

ALL-NEW ARC!
PRELUDE TO ARMOR HUNTERS
VALIANT
X-O MANOWAR
#23

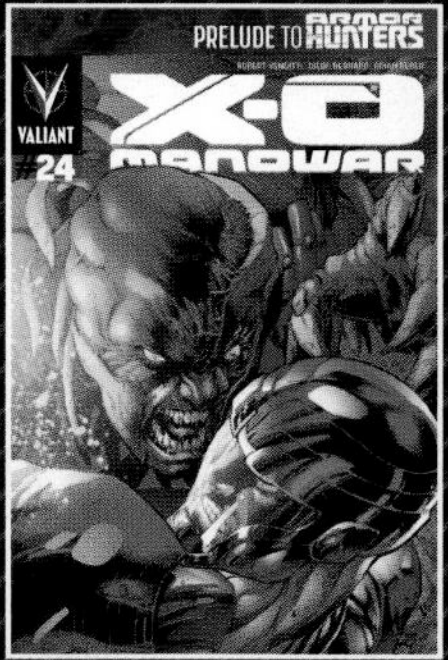

PRELUDE TO ARMOR HUNTERS
VALIANT
X-O MANOWAR
#24

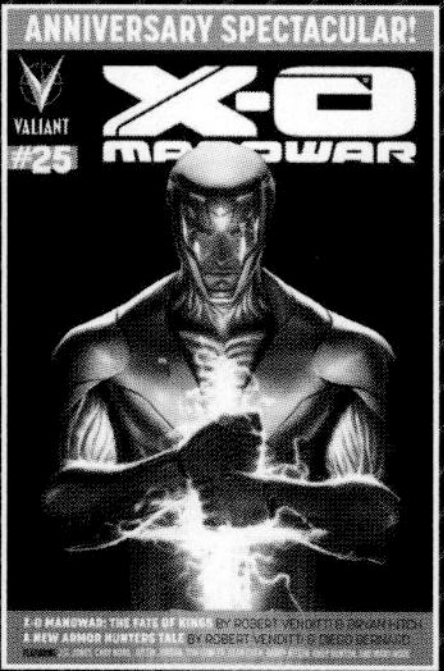

ANNIVERSARY SPECTACULAR!
VALIANT
X-O MANOWAR
#25

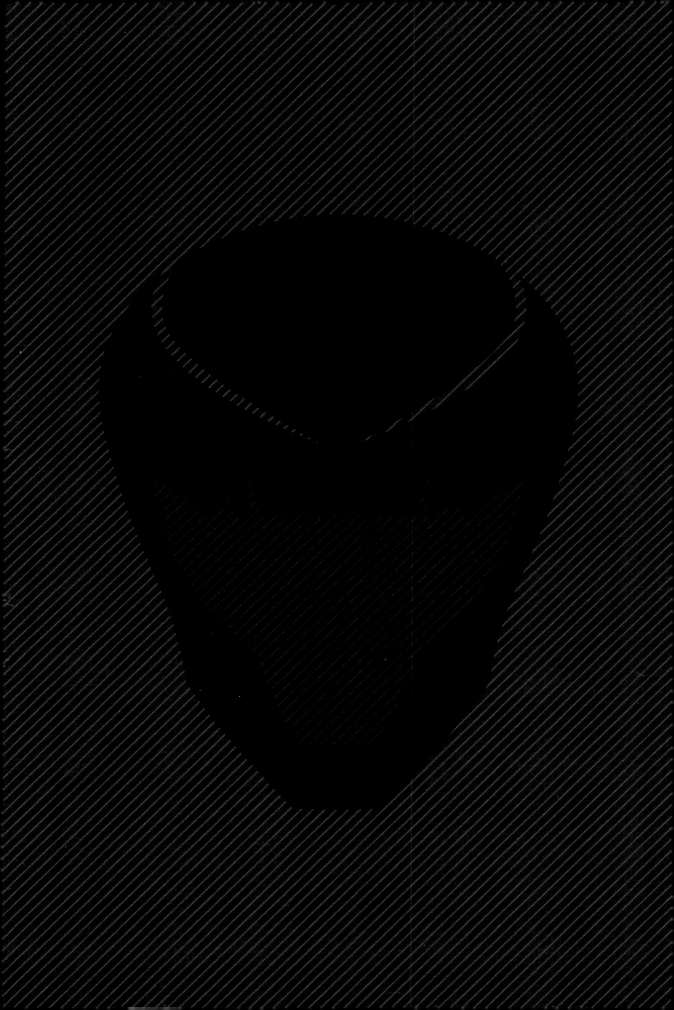

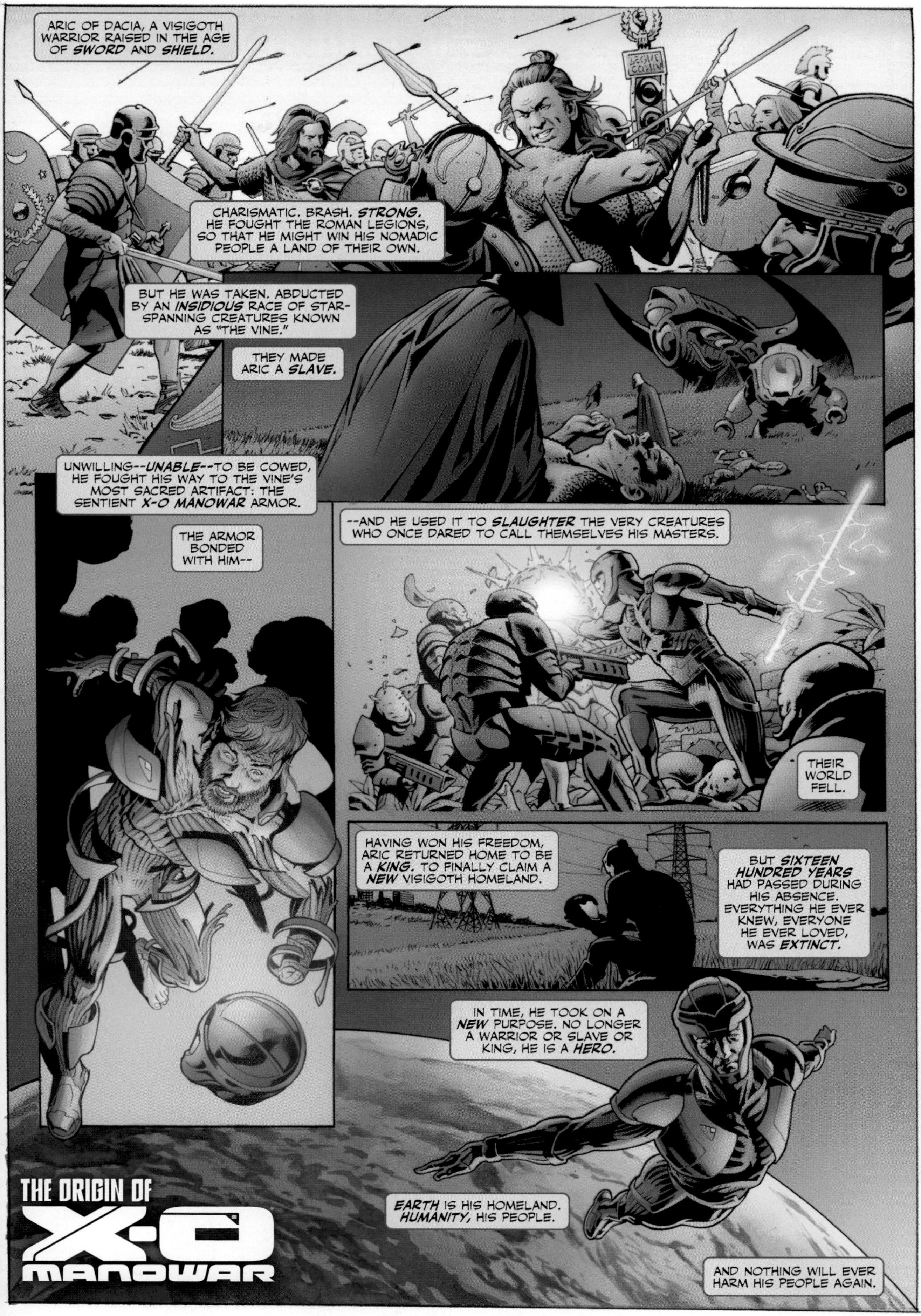

ARIC OF DACIA, A VISIGOTH WARRIOR RAISED IN THE AGE OF SWORD AND SHIELD.
LEGIO COHM
CHARISMATIC. BRASH. STRONG. HE FOUGHT THE ROMAN LEGIONS, SO THAT HE MIGHT WIN HIS NOMADIC PEOPLE A LAND OF THEIR OWN.
BUT HE WAS TAKEN. ABDUCTED BY AN INSIDIOUS RACE OF STAR-SPANNING CREATURES KNOWN AS "THE VINE."
THEY MADE ARIC A SLAVE.
UNWILLING--UNABLE--TO BE COWED, HE FOUGHT HIS WAY TO THE VINE'S MOST SACRED ARTIFACT: THE SENTIENT X-O MANOWAR ARMOR.
THE ARMOR BONDED WITH HIM--
--AND HE USED IT TO SLAUGHTER THE VERY CREATURES WHO ONCE DARED TO CALL THEMSELVES HIS MASTERS.
THEIR WORLD FELL.
HAVING WON HIS FREEDOM, ARIC RETURNED HOME TO BE A KING. TO FINALLY CLAIM A NEW VISIGOTH HOMELAND.
BUT SIXTEEN HUNDRED YEARS HAD PASSED DURING HIS ABSENCE. EVERYTHING HE EVER KNEW, EVERYONE HE EVER LOVED, WAS EXTINCT.
IN TIME, HE TOOK ON A NEW PURPOSE. NO LONGER A WARRIOR OR SLAVE OR KING, HE IS A HERO.
THE ORIGIN OF X-O MANOWAR
EARTH IS HIS HOMELAND. HUMANITY, HIS PEOPLE.
AND NOTHING WILL EVER HARM HIS PEOPLE AGAIN.

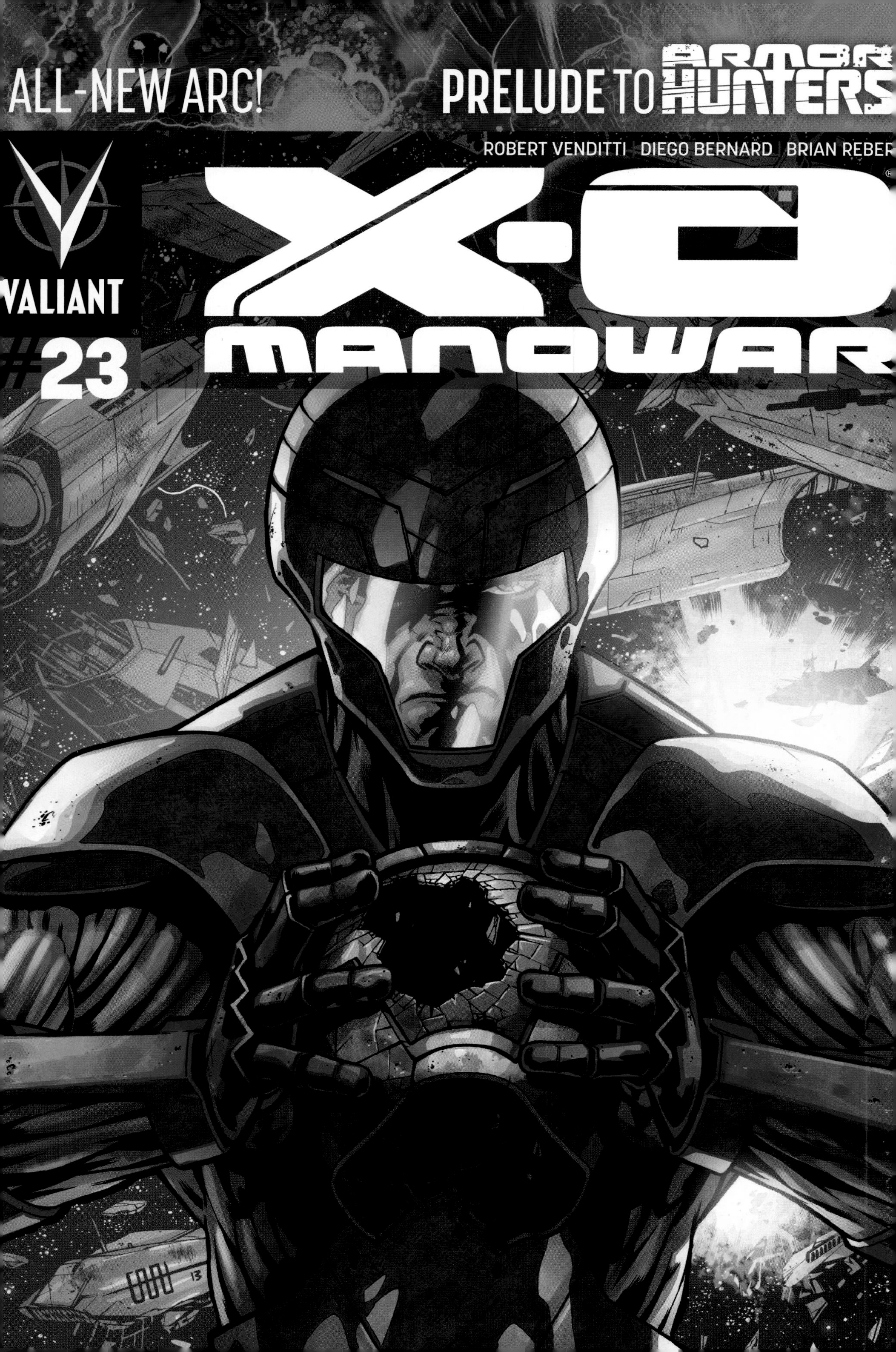
ALL-NEW ARC!
PRELUDE TO ARMOR HUNTERS
ROBERT VENDITTI | DIEGO BERNARD | BRIAN REBER
VALIANT
#23
X-O MANOWAR

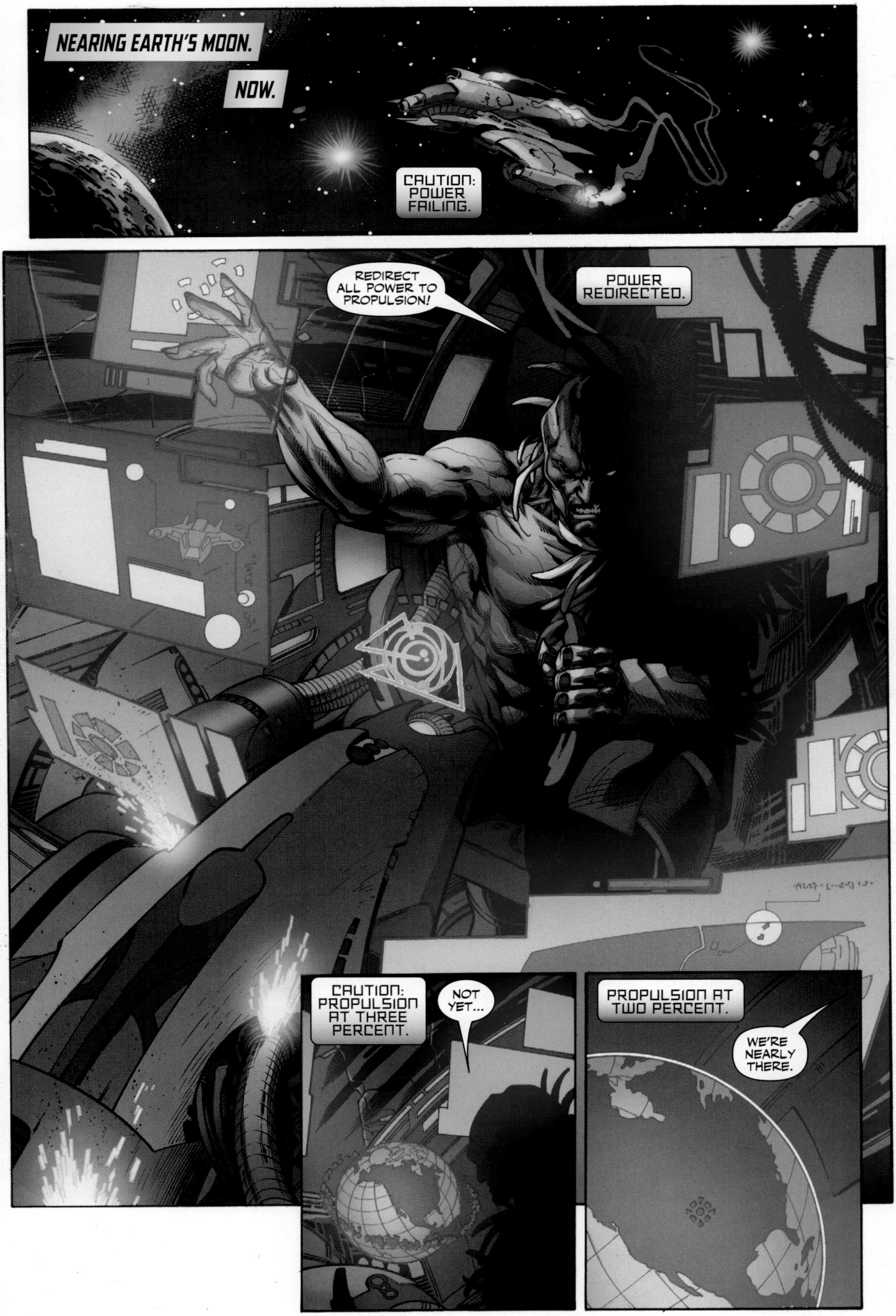
NEARING EARTH'S MOON.
NOW.
CAUTION: POWER FAILING.
REDIRECT ALL POWER TO PROPULSION!
POWER REDIRECTED.
CAUTION: PROPULSION AT THREE PERCENT.
NOT YET...
PROPULSION AT TWO PERCENT.
WE'RE NEARLY THERE.

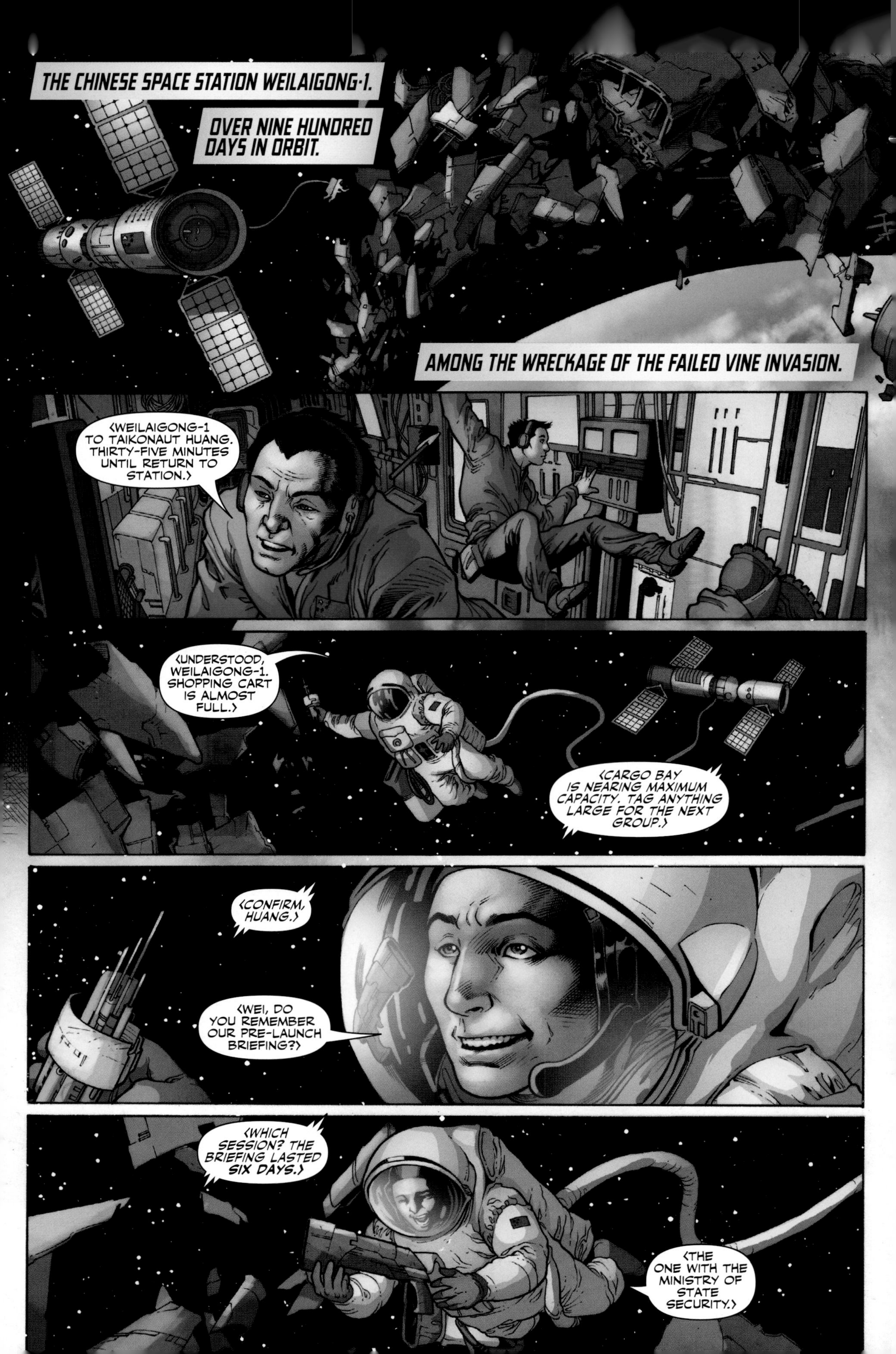
THE CHINESE SPACE STATION WEILAIGONG-1.
OVER NINE HUNDRED DAYS IN ORBIT.
AMONG THE WRECKAGE OF THE FAILED VINE INVASION.
<WEILAIGONG-1 TO TAIKONAUT HUANG. THIRTY-FIVE MINUTES UNTIL RETURN TO STATION.>
<UNDERSTOOD, WEILAIGONG-1. SHOPPING CART IS ALMOST FULL.>
<CARGO BAY IS NEARING MAXIMUM CAPACITY. TAG ANYTHING LARGE FOR THE NEXT GROUP.>
<CONFIRM, HUANG.>
<WEI, DO YOU REMEMBER OUR PRE-LAUNCH BRIEFING?>
<WHICH SESSION? THE BRIEFING LASTED SIX DAYS.>
<THE ONE WITH THE MINISTRY OF STATE SECURITY.>

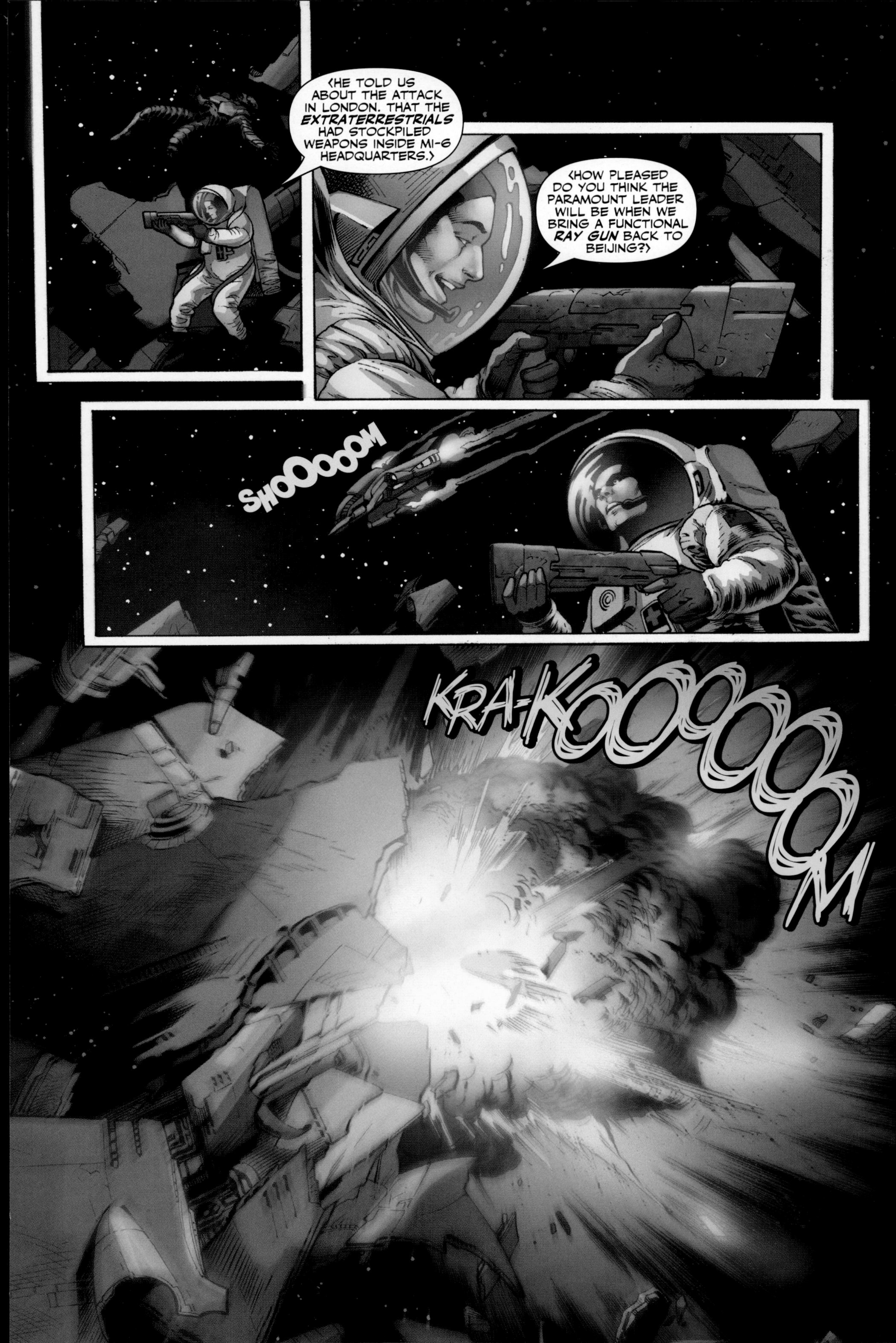
<HE TOLD US ABOUT THE ATTACK IN LONDON. THAT THE EXTRATERRESTRIALS HAD STOCKPILED WEAPONS INSIDE MI-6 HEADQUARTERS.>
<HOW PLEASED DO YOU THINK THE PARAMOUNT LEADER WILL BE WHEN WE BRING A FUNCTIONAL RAY GUN BACK TO BEIJING?>
SHOOOOOOM
KRA-KOOOOOOOOM

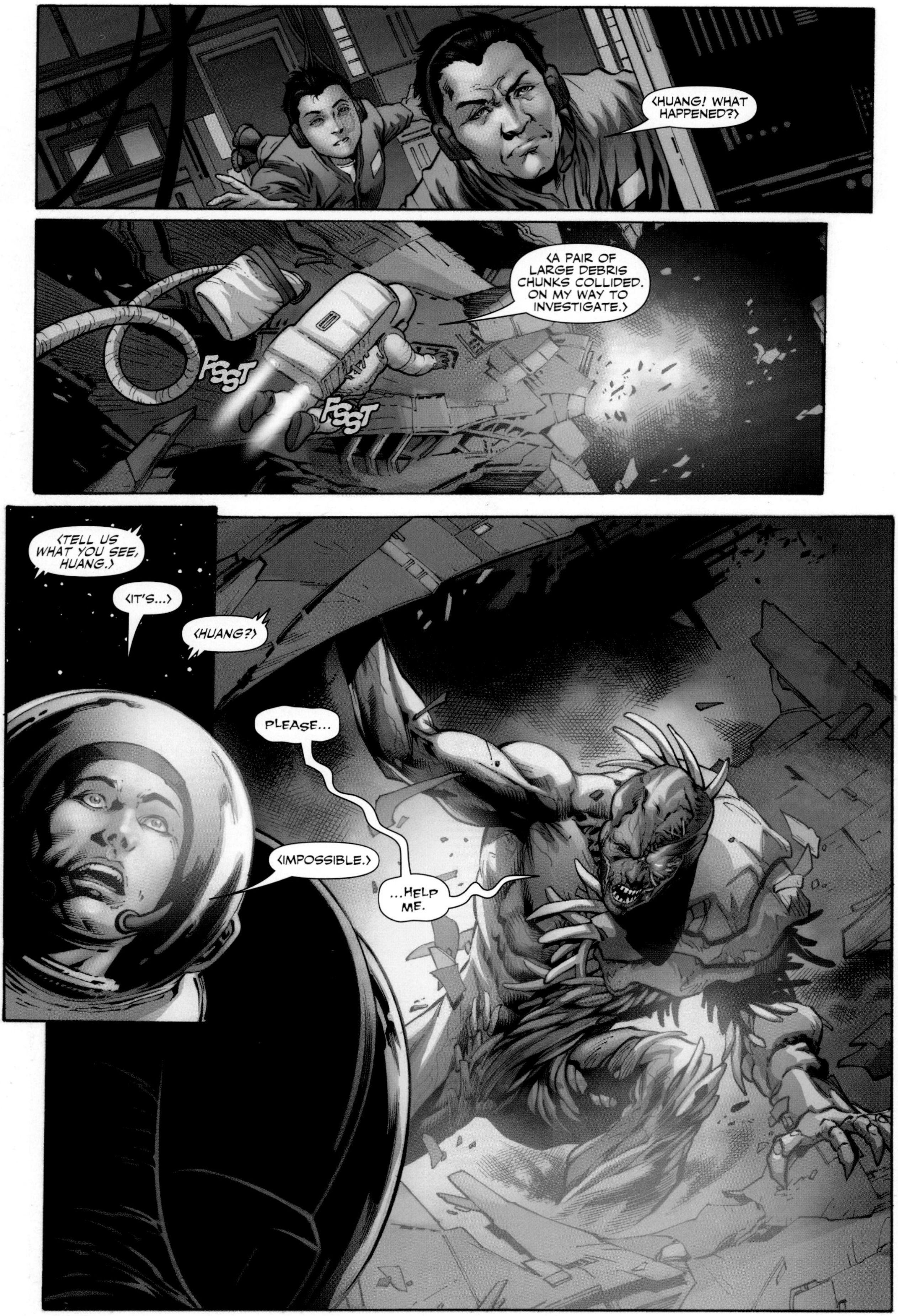
<HUANG! WHAT HAPPENED?>
<A PAIR OF LARGE DEBRIS CHUNKS COLLIDED. ON MY WAY TO INVESTIGATE.>
FSST
FSST
<TELL US WHAT YOU SEE, HUANG.>
<IT'S...>
<HUANG?>
PLEASE...
<IMPOSSIBLE.>
...HELP ME.

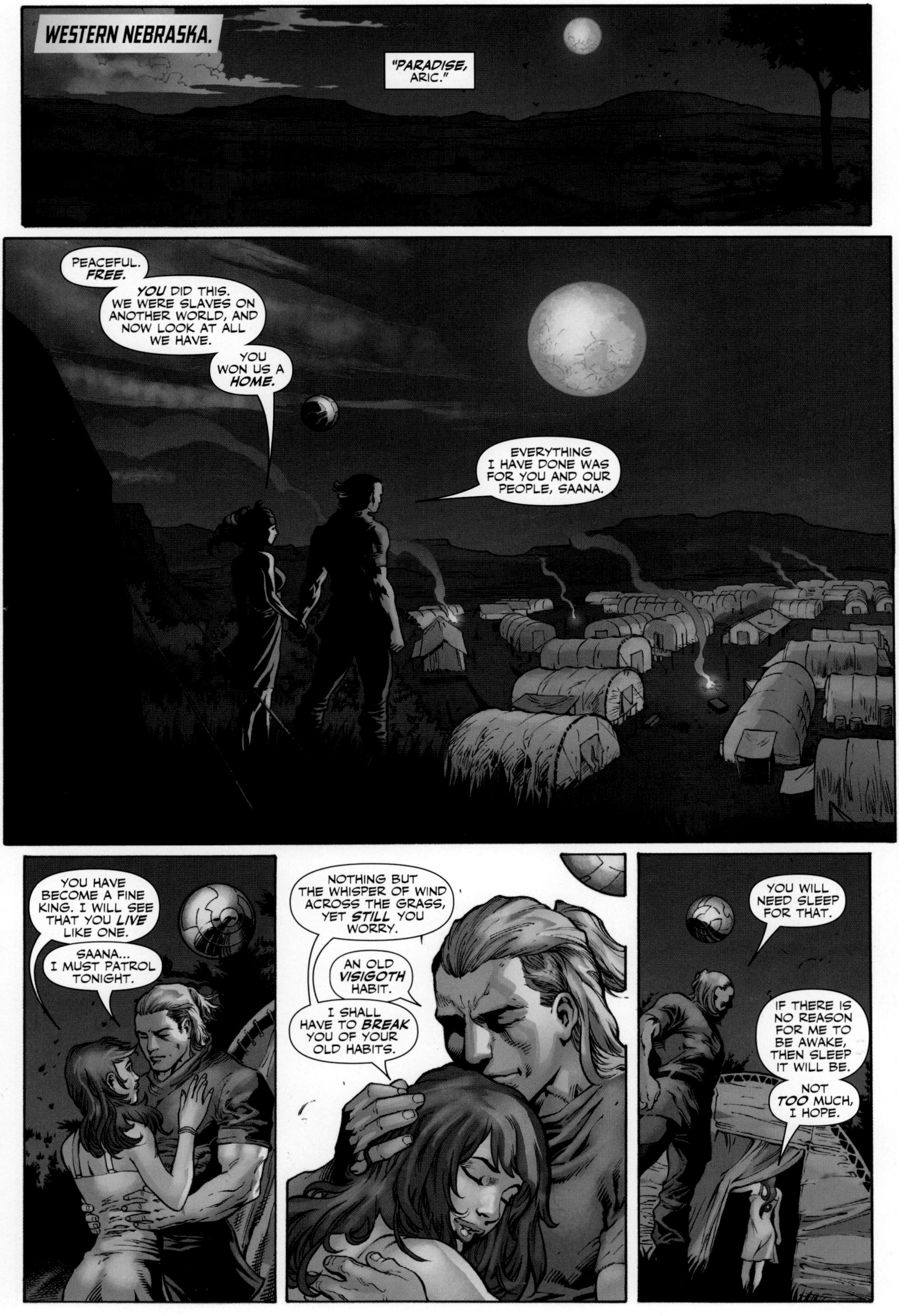
WESTERN NEBRASKA.
"PARADISE, ARIC."
PEACEFUL. FREE.
YOU DID THIS. WE WERE SLAVES ON ANOTHER WORLD, AND NOW LOOK AT ALL WE HAVE.
YOU WON US A HOME.
EVERYTHING I HAVE DONE WAS FOR YOU AND OUR PEOPLE, SAANA.
YOU HAVE BECOME A FINE KING. I WILL SEE THAT YOU LIVE LIKE ONE.
SAANA... I MUST PATROL TONIGHT.
NOTHING BUT THE WHISPER OF WIND ACROSS THE GRASS, YET STILL YOU WORRY.
AN OLD VISIGOTH HABIT.
I SHALL HAVE TO BREAK YOU OF YOUR OLD HABITS.
YOU WILL NEED SLEEP FOR THAT.
IF THERE IS NO REASON FOR ME TO BE AWAKE, THEN SLEEP IT WILL BE.
NOT TOO MUCH, I HOPE.

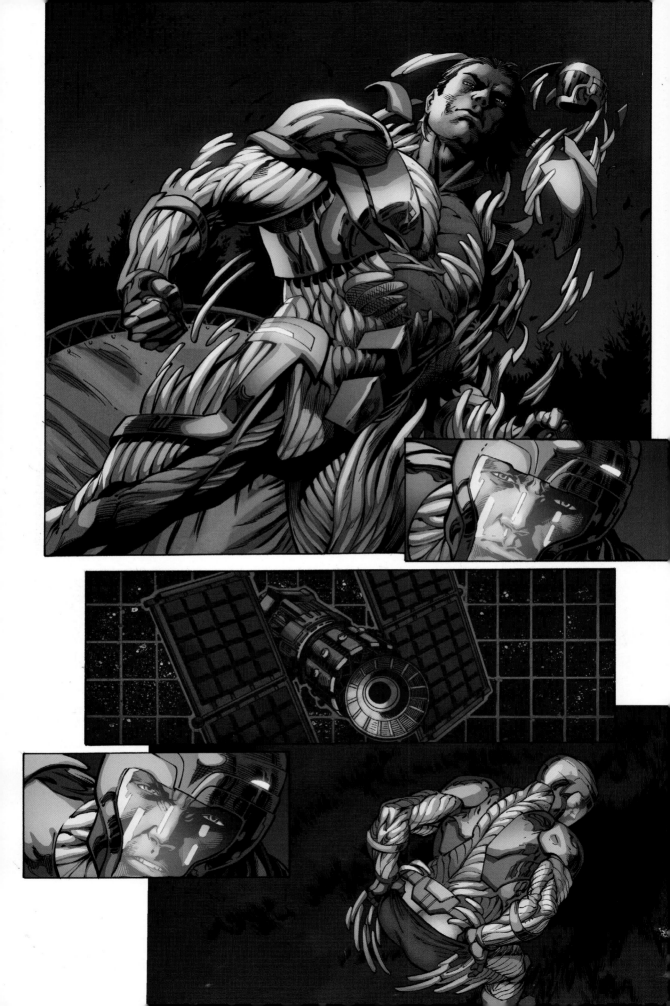

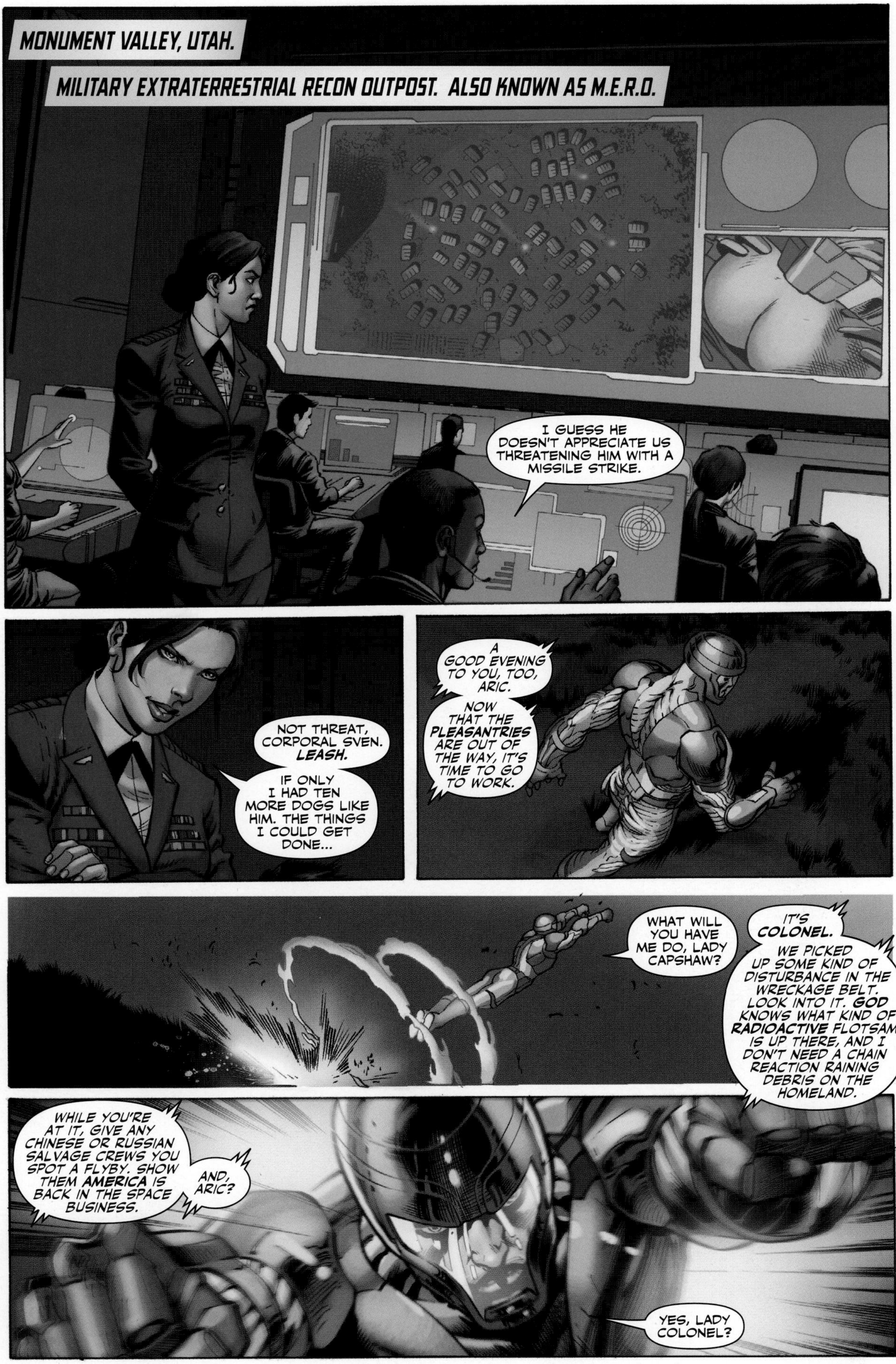
MONUMENT VALLEY, UTAH.
MILITARY EXTRATERRESTRIAL RECON OUTPOST. ALSO KNOWN AS M.E.R.O.
I GUESS HE DOESN'T APPRECIATE US THREATENING HIM WITH A MISSILE STRIKE.
NOT THREAT, CORPORAL SVEN. LEASH.
IF ONLY I HAD TEN MORE DOGS LIKE HIM. THE THINGS I COULD GET DONE...
A GOOD EVENING TO YOU, TOO, ARIC.
NOW THAT THE PLEASANTRIES ARE OUT OF THE WAY, IT'S TIME TO GO TO WORK.
WHAT WILL YOU HAVE ME DO, LADY CAPSHAW?
IT'S COLONEL.
WE PICKED UP SOME KIND OF DISTURBANCE IN THE WRECKAGE BELT. LOOK INTO IT. GOD KNOWS WHAT KIND OF RADIOACTIVE FLOTSAM IS UP THERE, AND I DON'T NEED A CHAIN REACTION RAINING DEBRIS ON THE HOMELAND.
WHILE YOU'RE AT IT, GIVE ANY CHINESE OR RUSSIAN SALVAGE CREWS YOU SPOT A FLYBY. SHOW THEM AMERICA IS BACK IN THE SPACE BUSINESS.
AND, ARIC?
YES, LADY COLONEL?

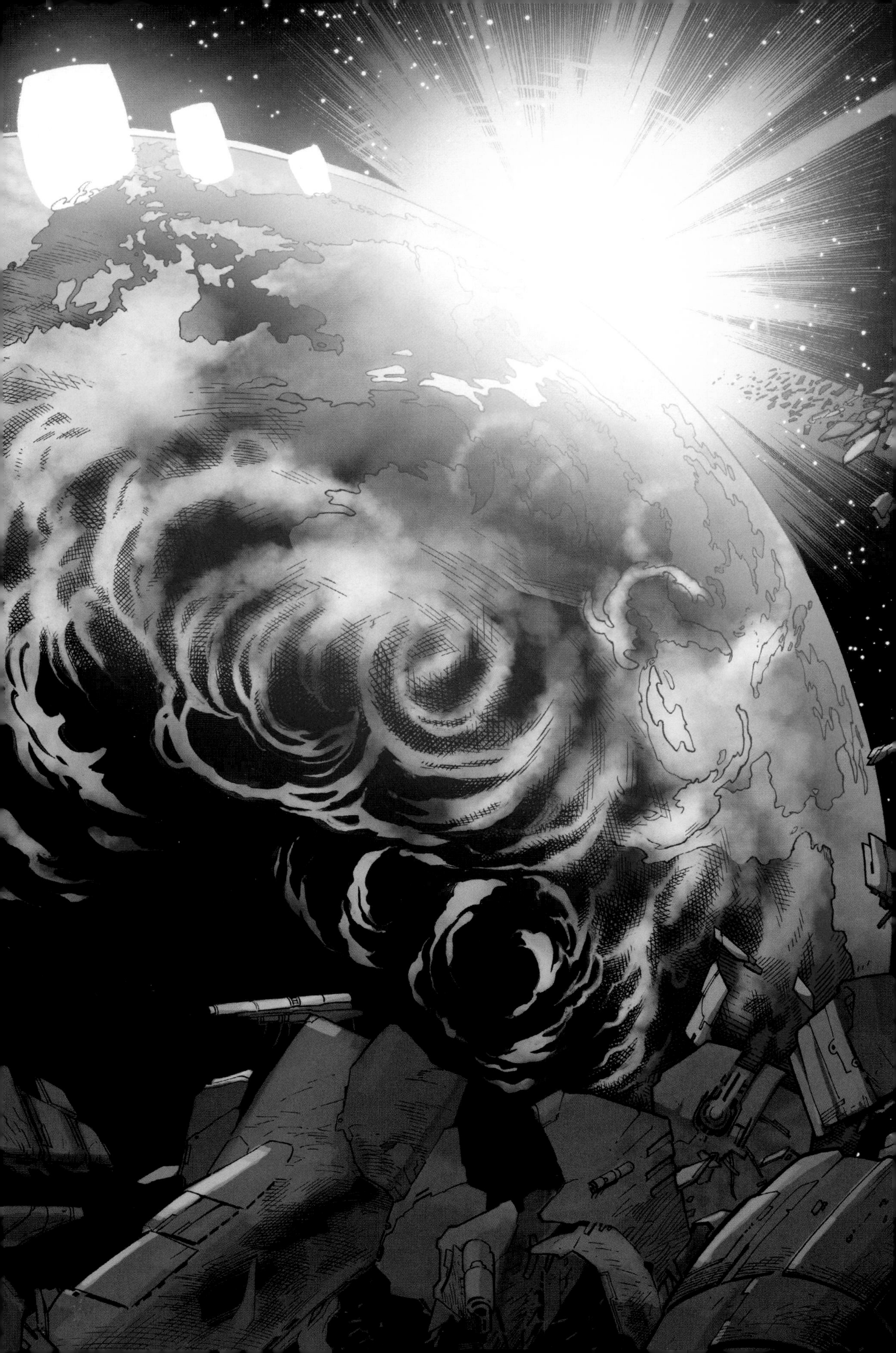

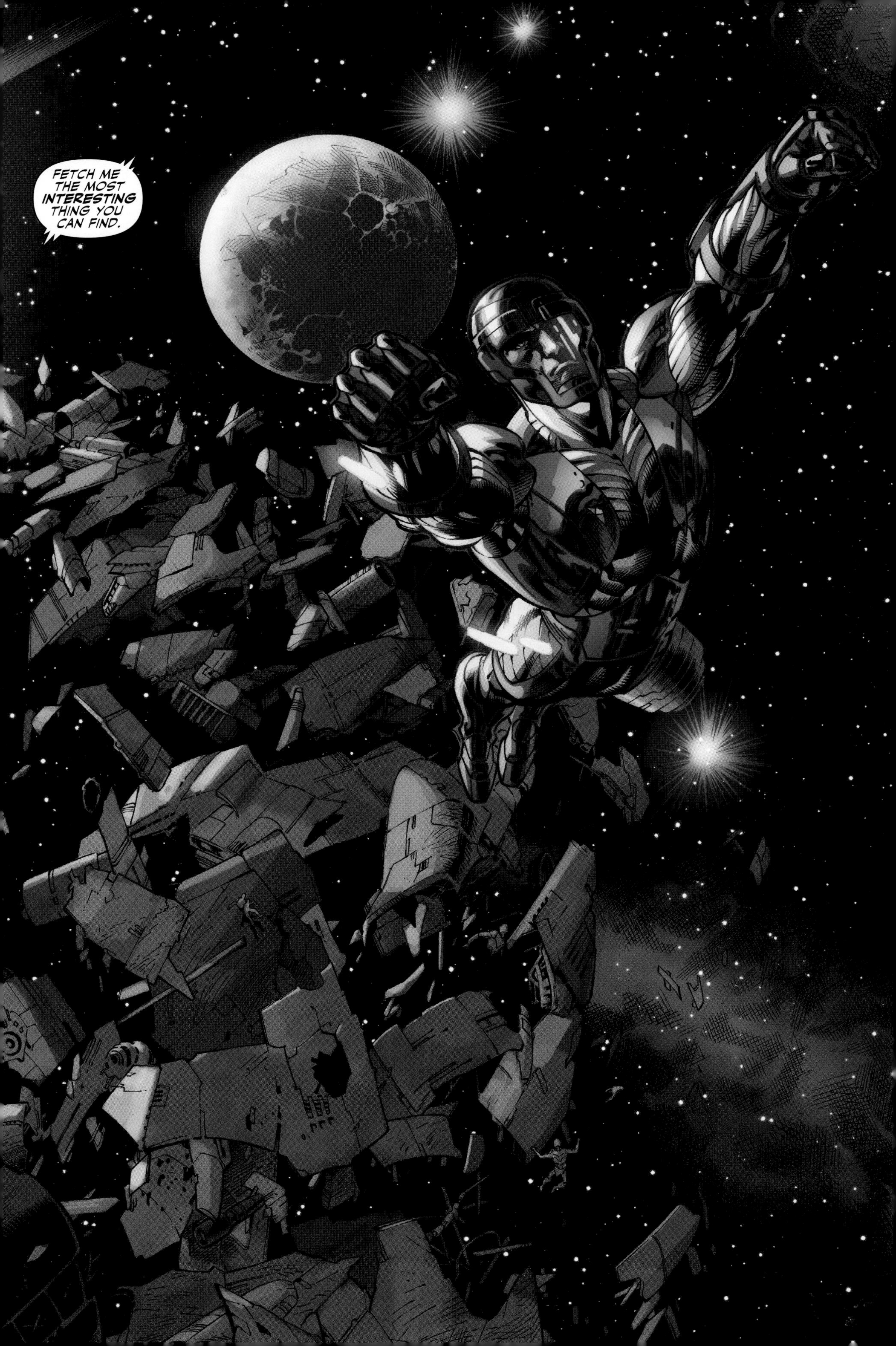
FETCH ME THE MOST INTERESTING THING YOU CAN FIND.

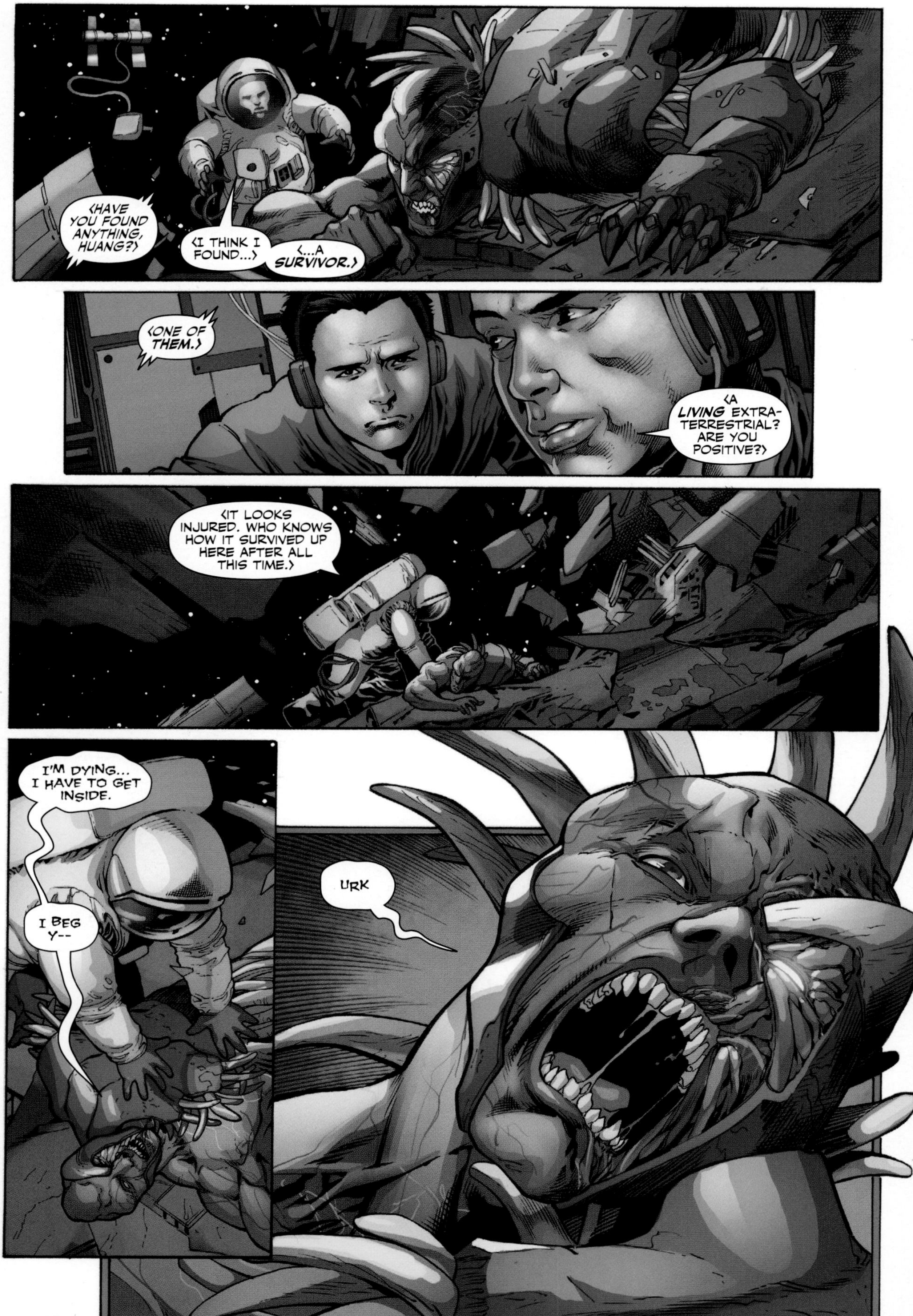
‹HAVE YOU FOUND ANYTHING, HUANG?›
‹I THINK I FOUND...›
‹...A *SURVIVOR.*›
‹ONE OF *THEM.*›
‹A *LIVING* EXTRA-TERRESTRIAL? ARE YOU POSITIVE?›
‹IT LOOKS INJURED. WHO KNOWS HOW IT SURVIVED UP HERE AFTER ALL THIS TIME.›
I'M DYING... I HAVE TO GET INSIDE.
I BEG Y--
URK

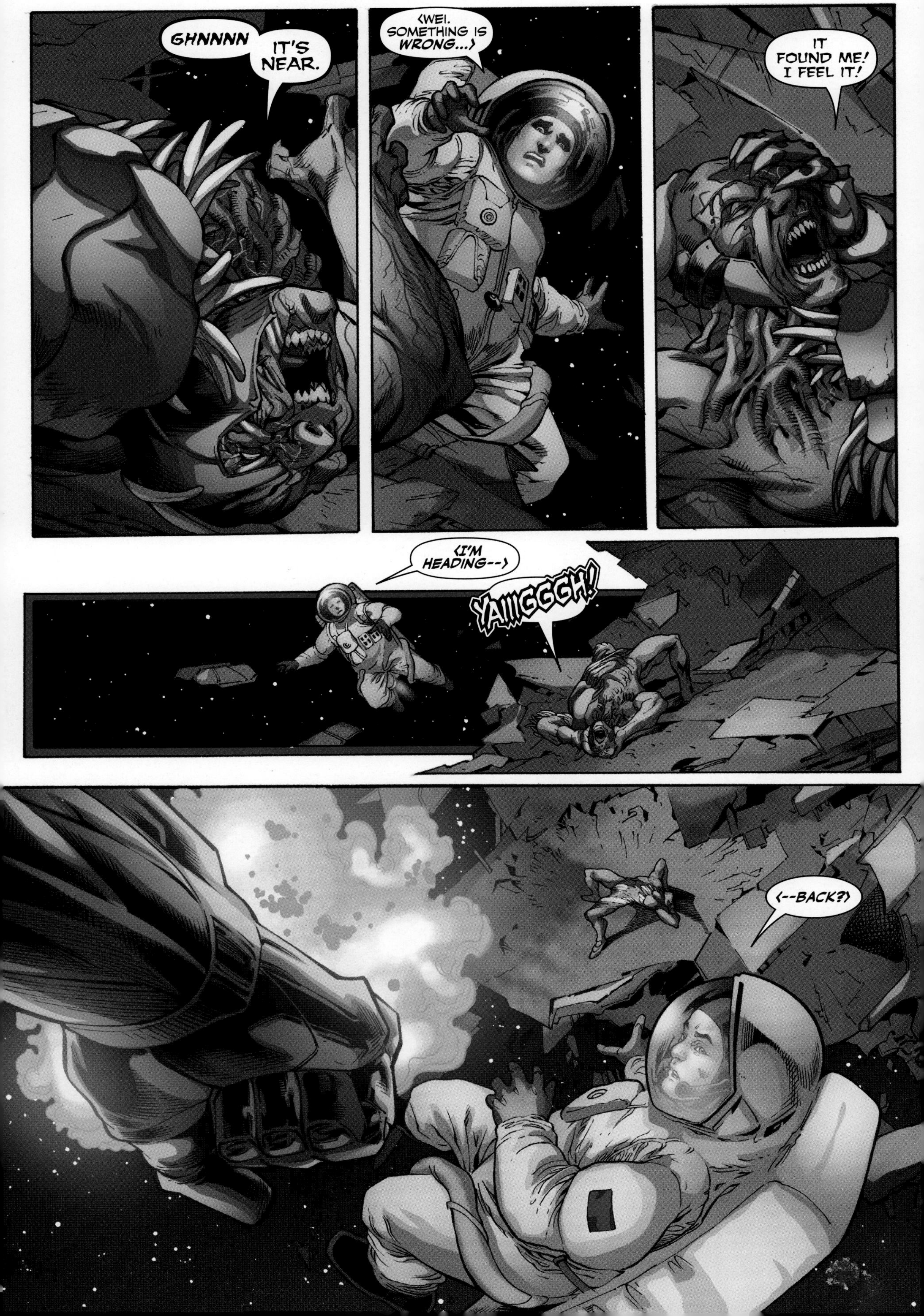
GHNNNN
IT'S NEAR.
<WEI. SOMETHING IS WRONG...>
IT FOUND ME! I FEEL IT!
<I'M HEADING-->
YAIIIGGGH!
<--BACK?>

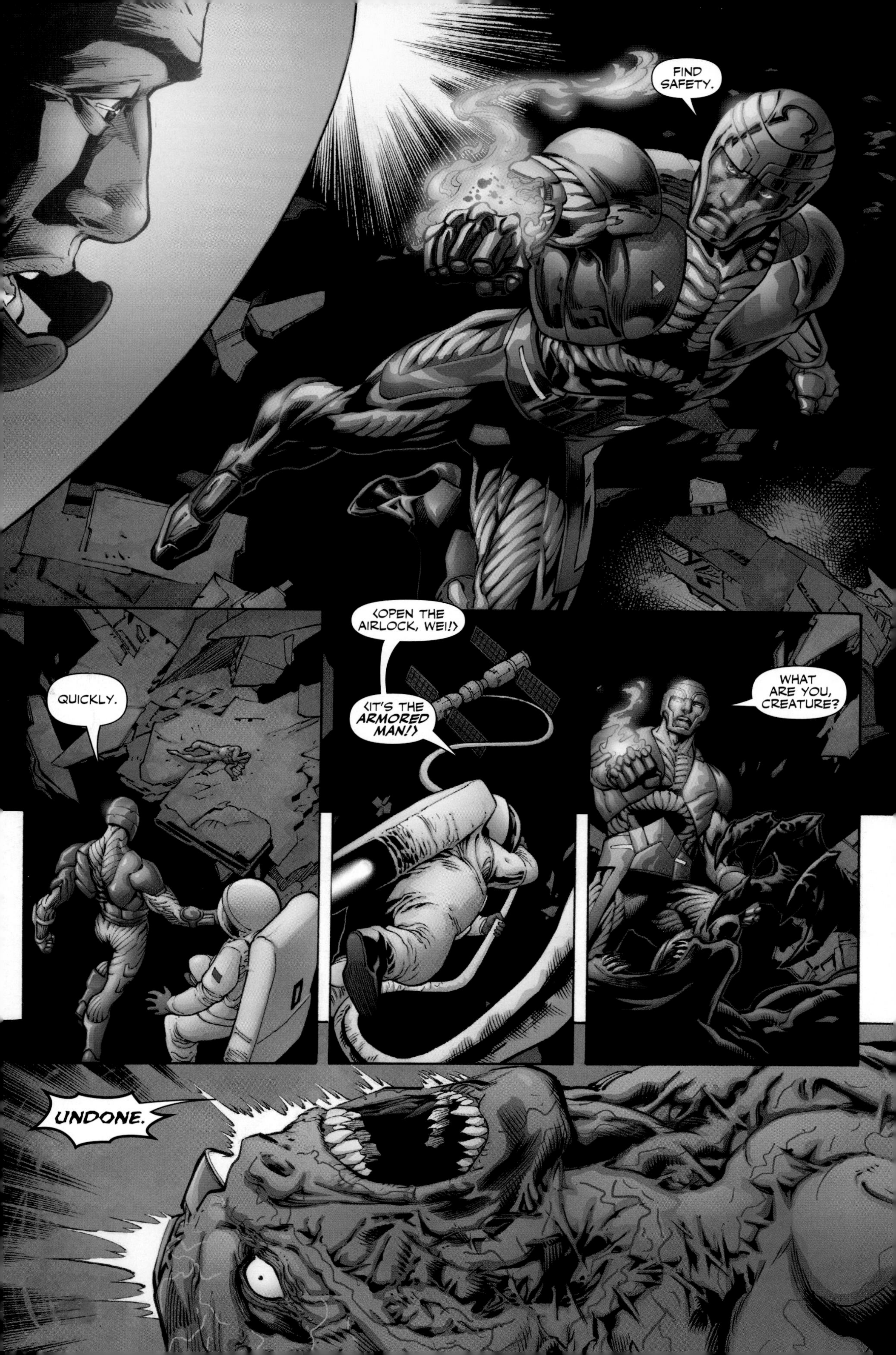

FIND SAFETY.
QUICKLY.
<OPEN THE AIRLOCK, WEI!>
<IT'S THE *ARMORED MAN!*>
WHAT ARE YOU, CREATURE?
UNDONE.

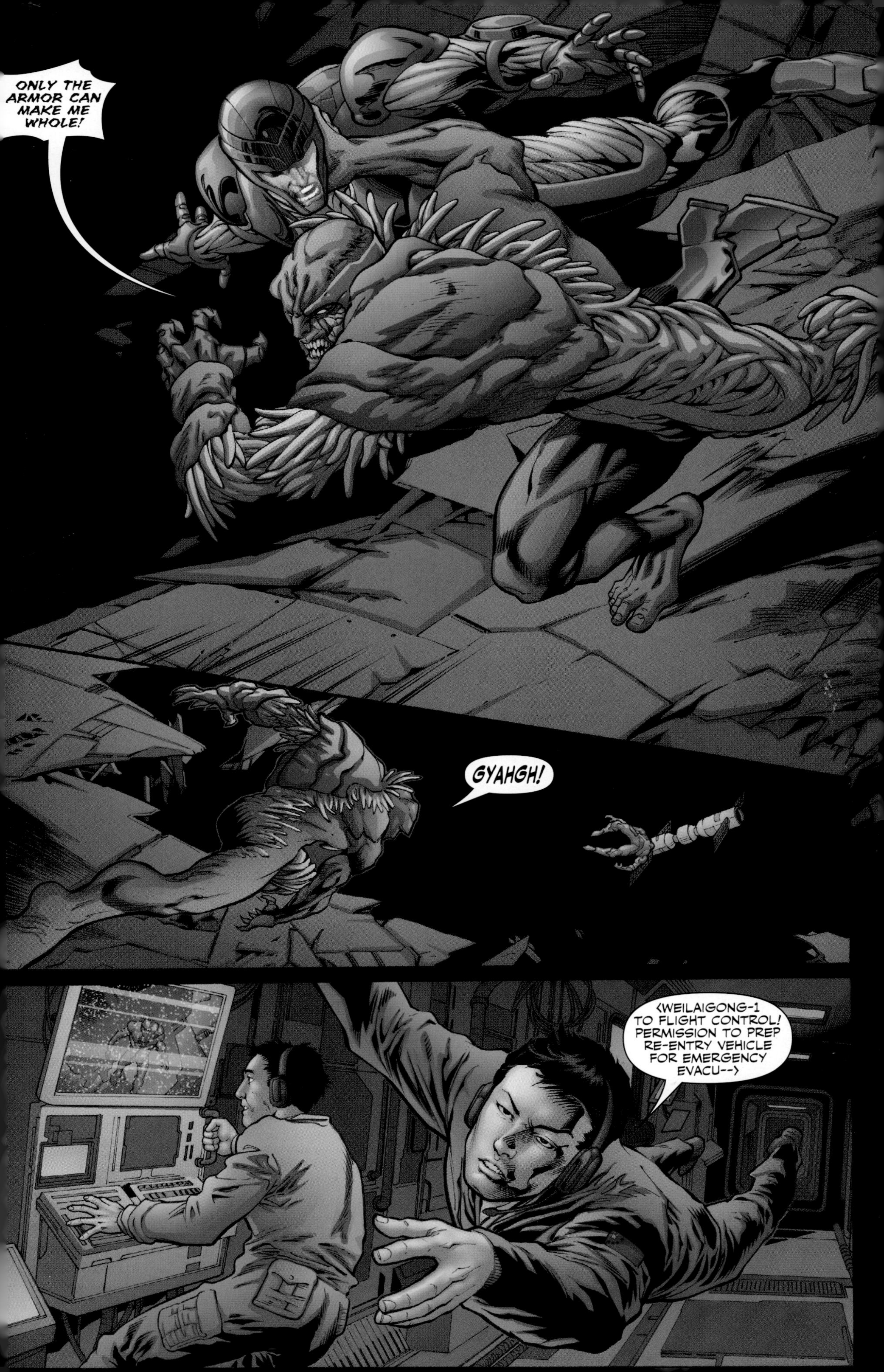

ONLY THE ARMOR CAN MAKE ME WHOLE!
GYAHGH!
<WEILAIGONG-1 TO FLIGHT CONTROL! PERMISSION TO PREP RE-ENTRY VEHICLE FOR EMERGENCY EVACU-->

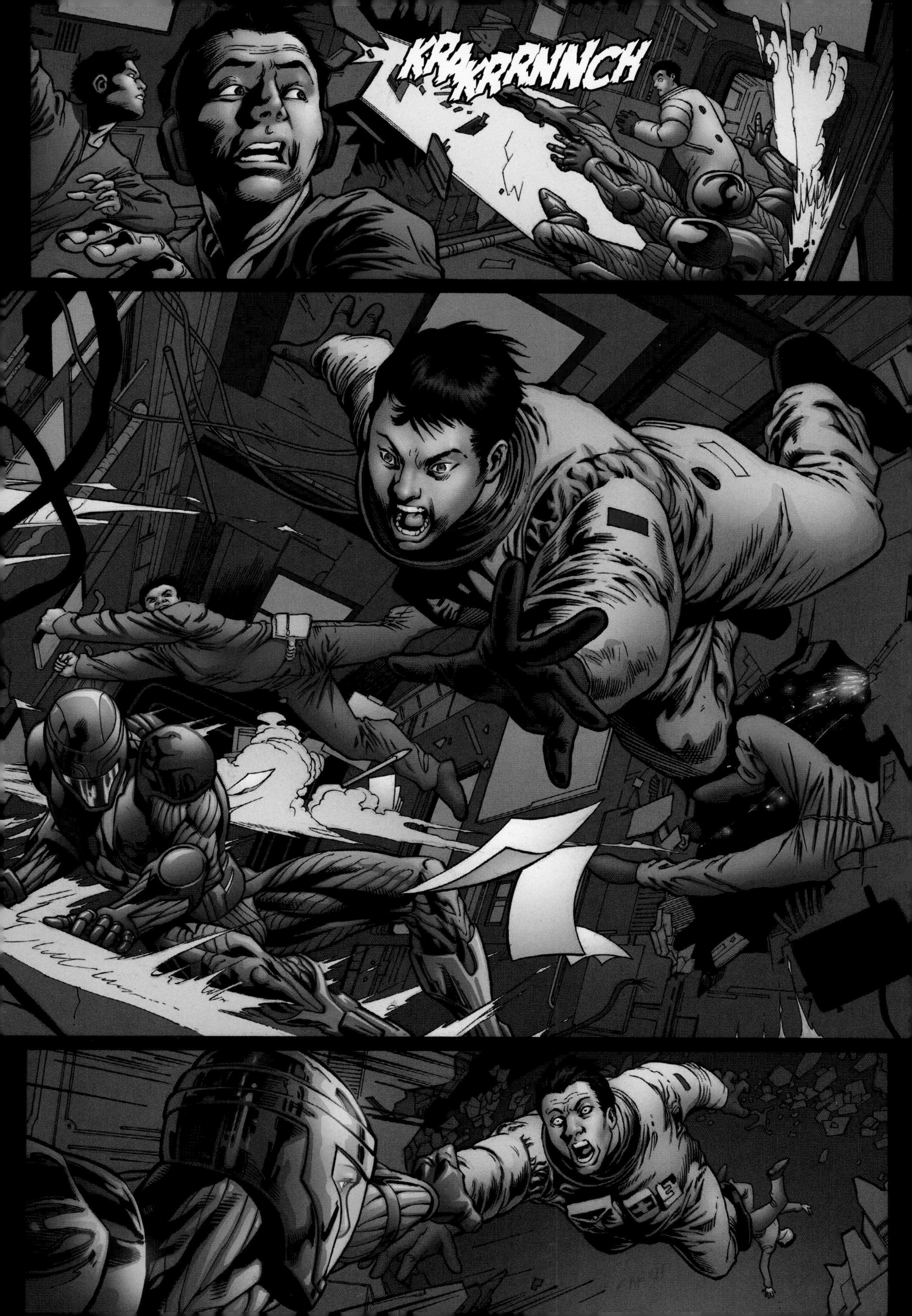
KRAKRRNNCH

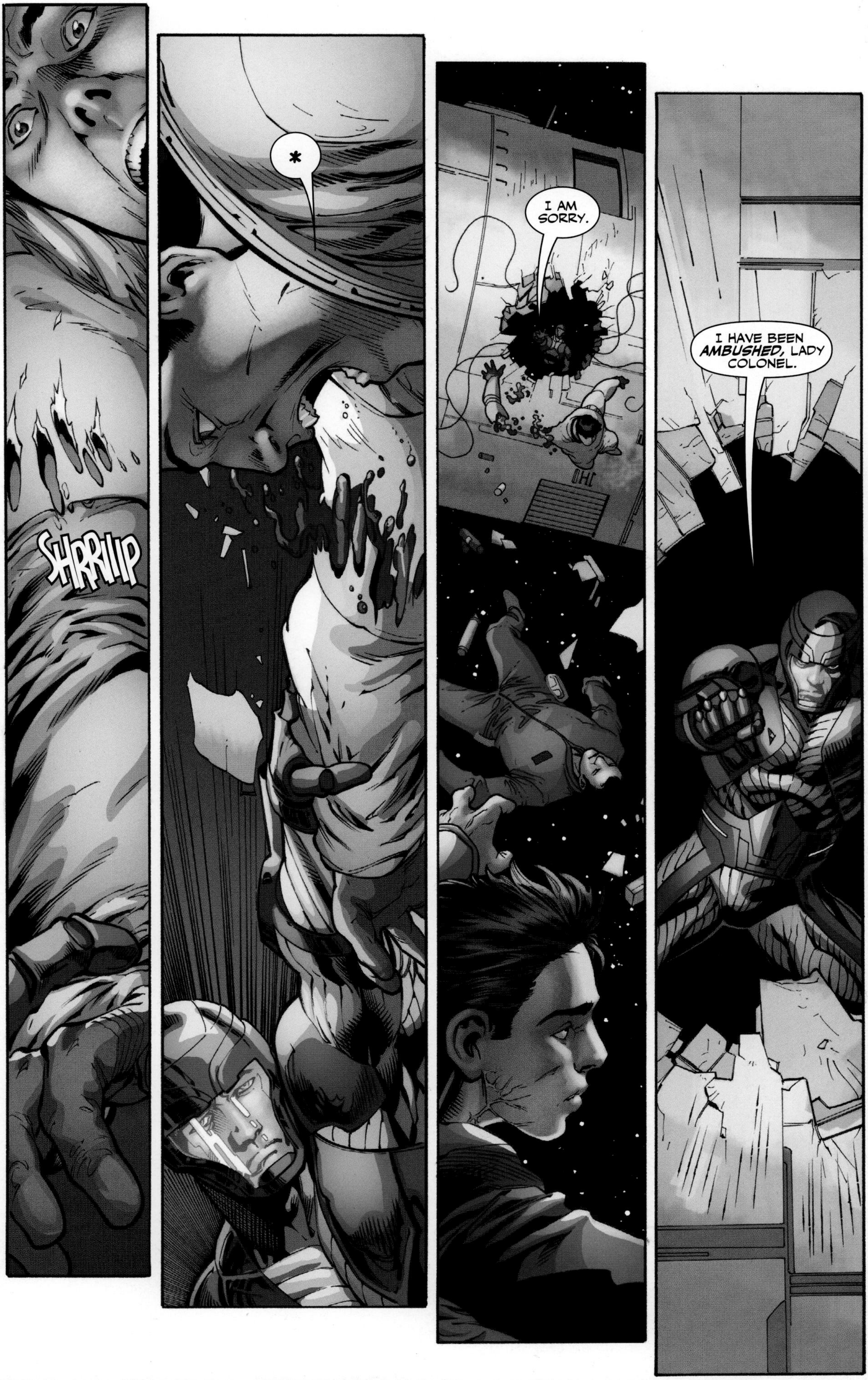
SHRRIIIP
*
I AM SORRY.
I HAVE BEEN AMBUSHED, LADY COLONEL.

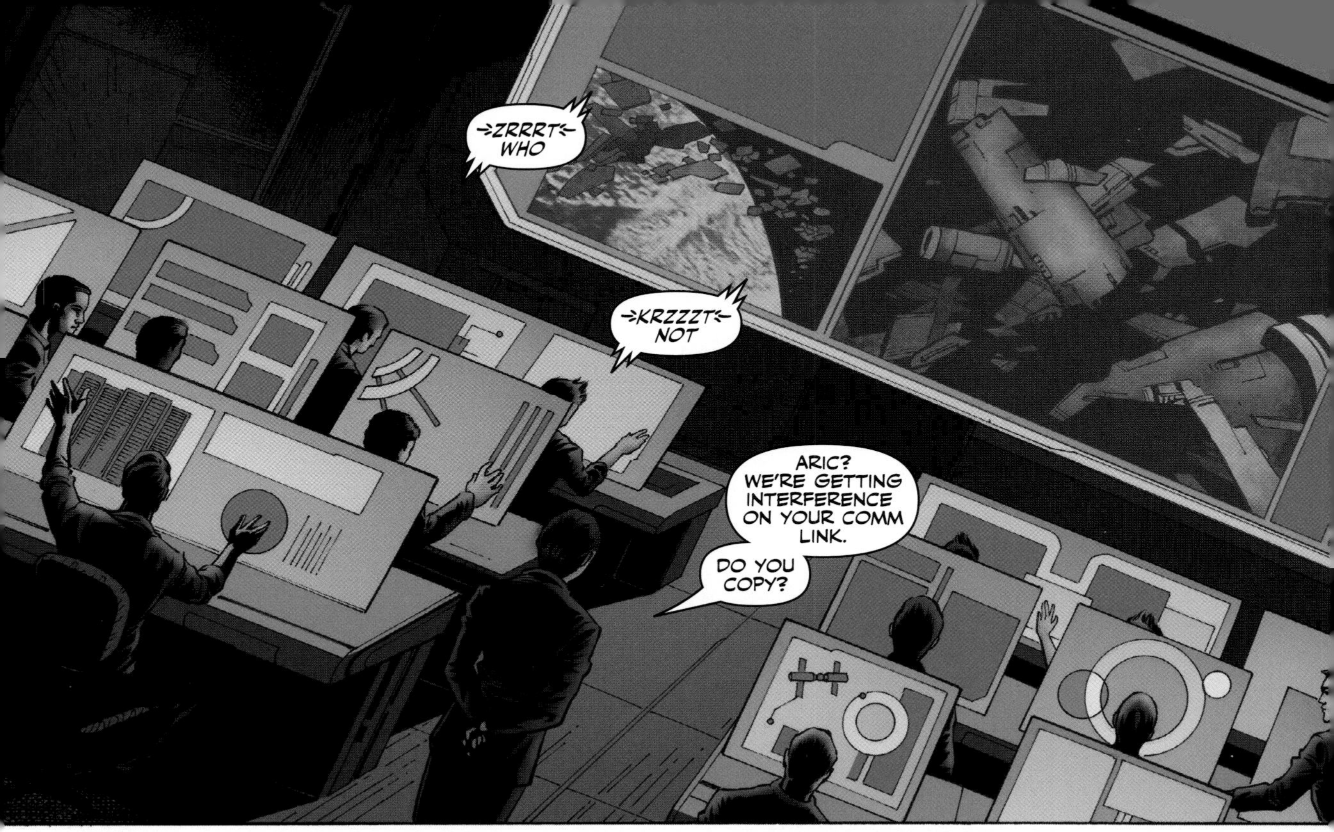

-ZRRRT- WHO
-KRZZZT- NOT
ARIC? WE'RE GETTING INTERFERENCE ON YOUR COMM LINK.
DO YOU COPY?

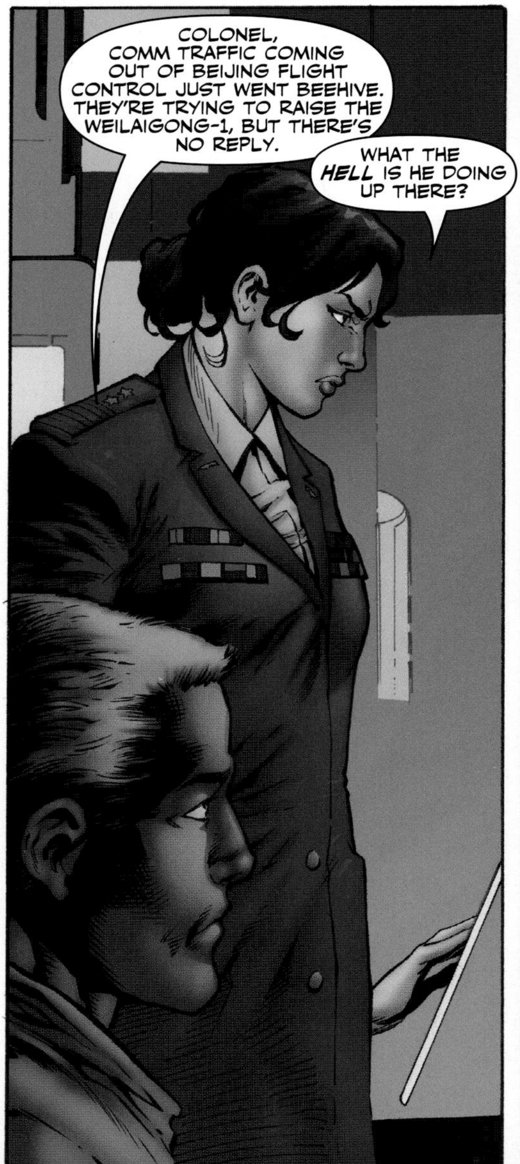

COLONEL, COMM TRAFFIC COMING OUT OF BEIJING FLIGHT CONTROL JUST WENT BEEHIVE. THEY'RE TRYING TO RAISE THE WEILAIGONG-1, BUT THERE'S NO REPLY.
WHAT THE **HELL** IS HE DOING UP THERE?

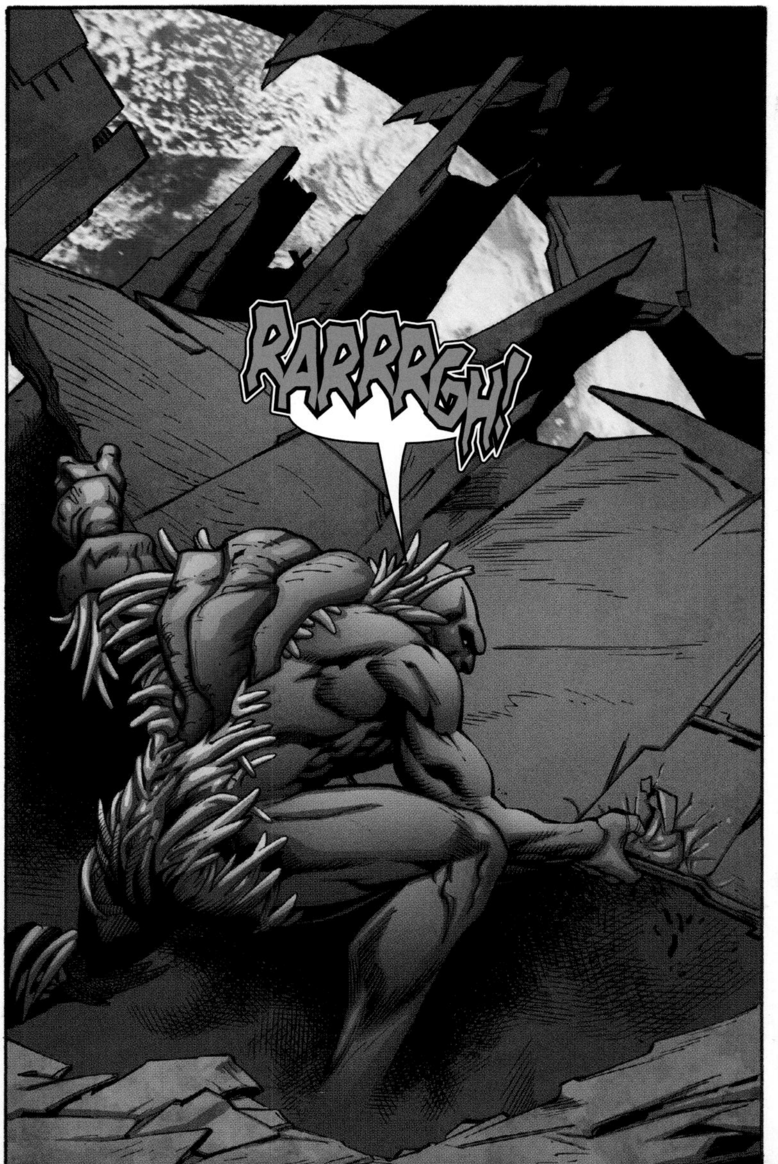

RARRRGH!

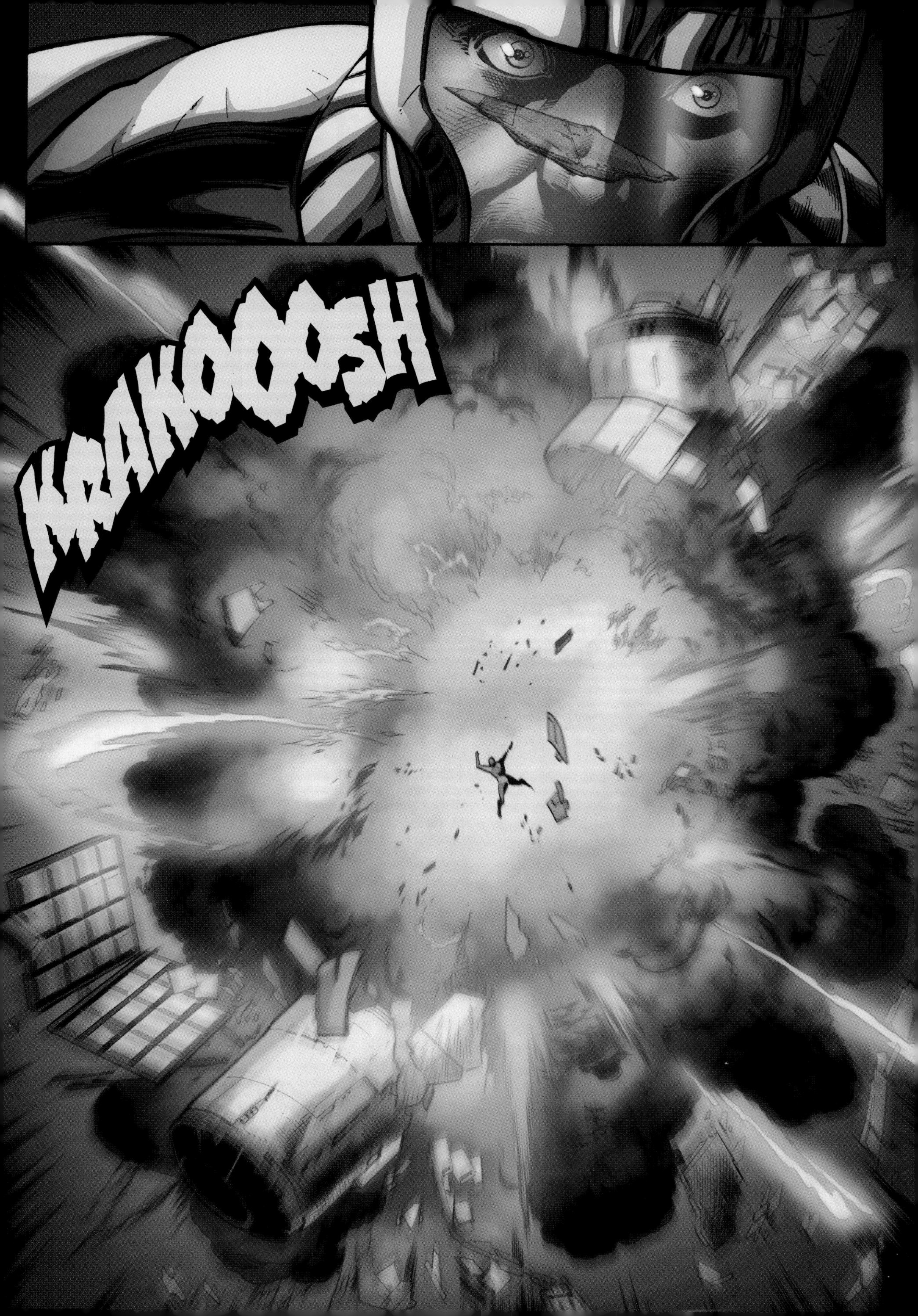
KRAKOOOSH

UHNN

YOU'LL NEVER DEFEAT THEM!

≈GFF≈

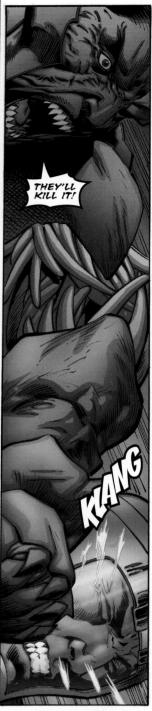

THEY'LL KILL IT!

KLANG

KOOOOM

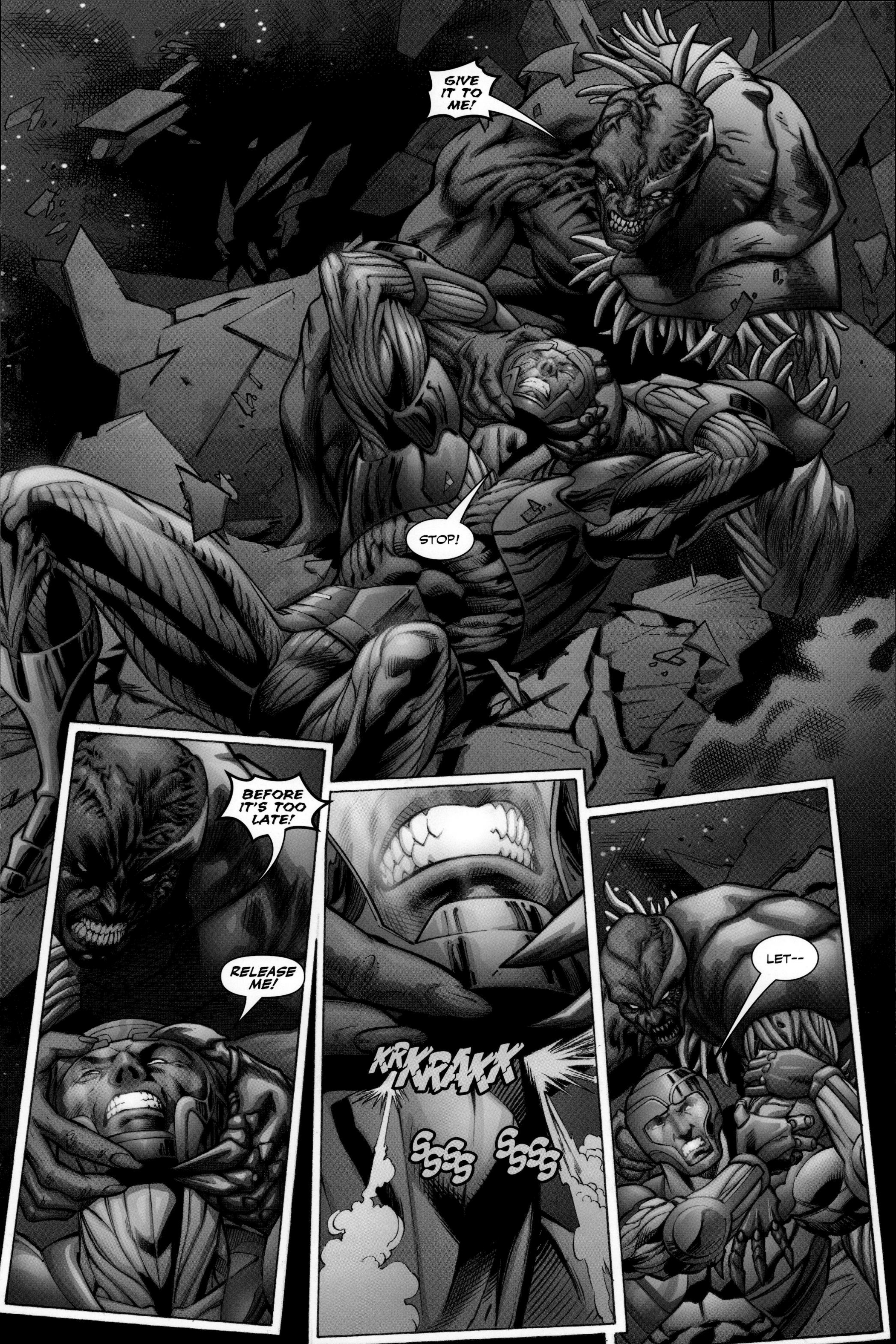
GIVE IT TO ME!
STOP!
BEFORE IT'S TOO LATE!
RELEASE ME!
KRKRAKK
SSSS
SSSS
LET--

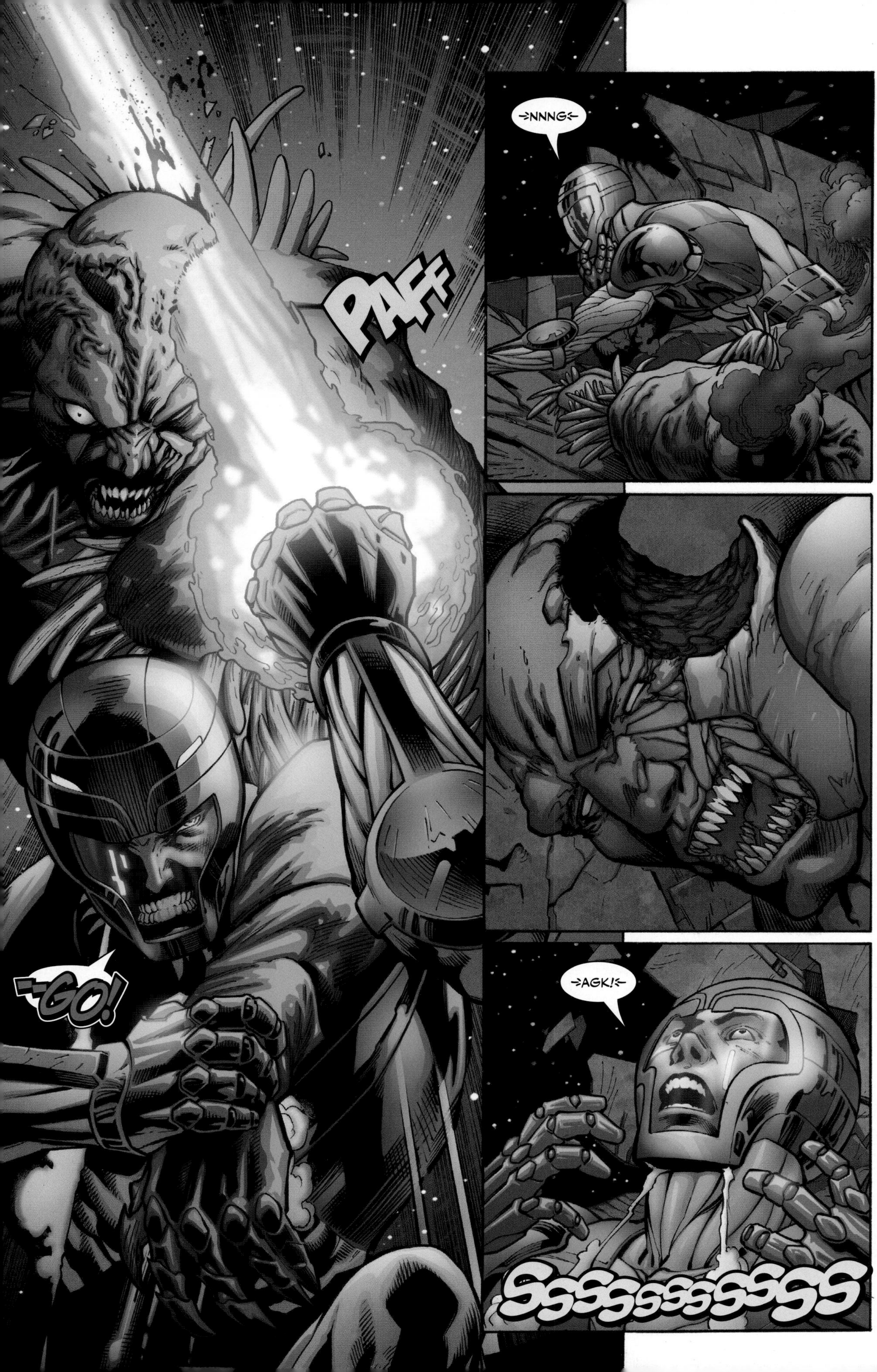
PAFF
--GO!
-NNNG-
-AGK!-
SSSSSSSSSSSS

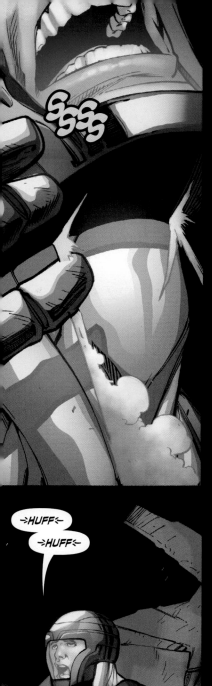

SSSS

SSSS

GASP!

HUFF
HUFF

ULLLG

GRRGLK

MU*SSH*T
HAVE IT*K*

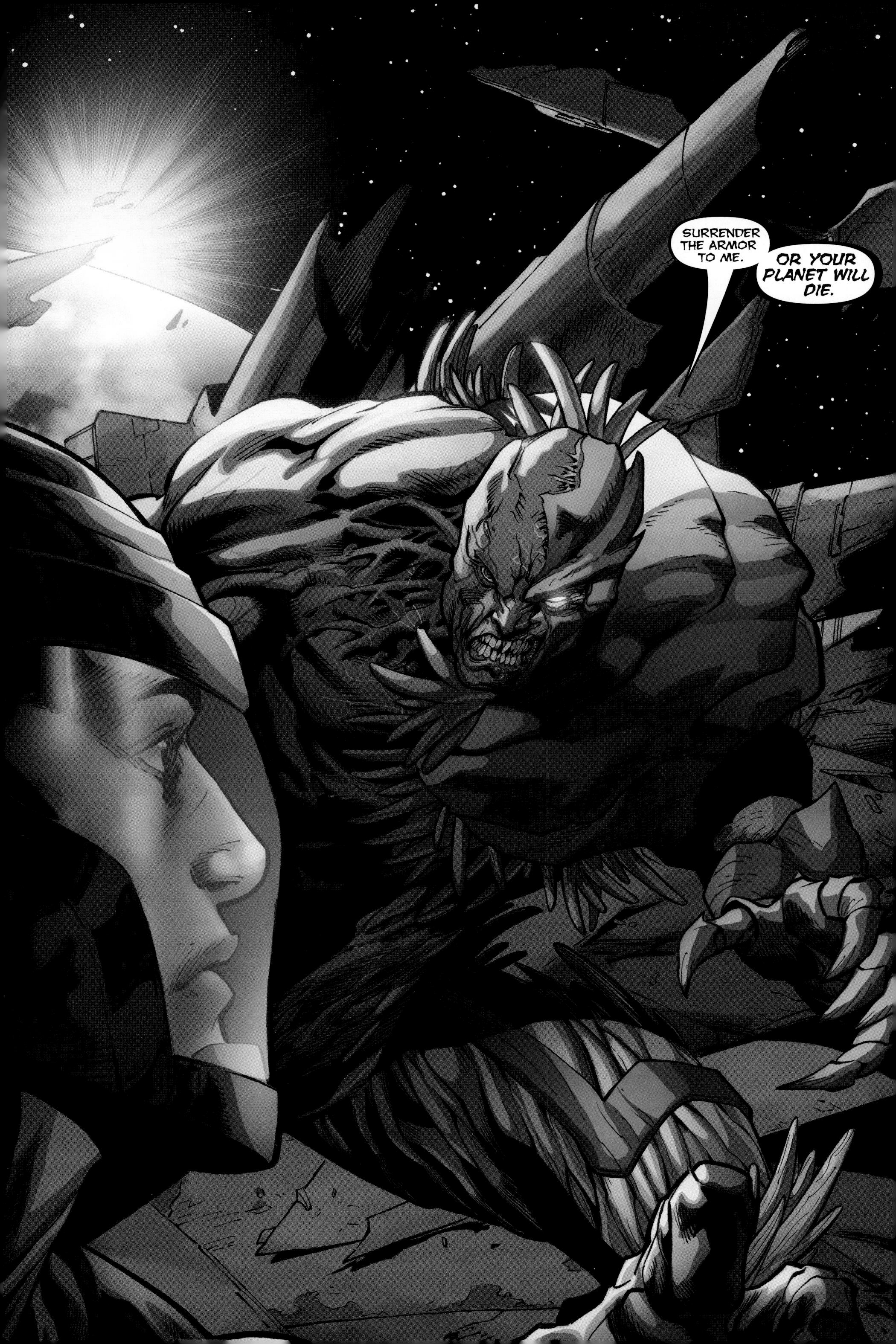
SURRENDER THE ARMOR TO ME.
OR YOUR PLANET WILL DIE.

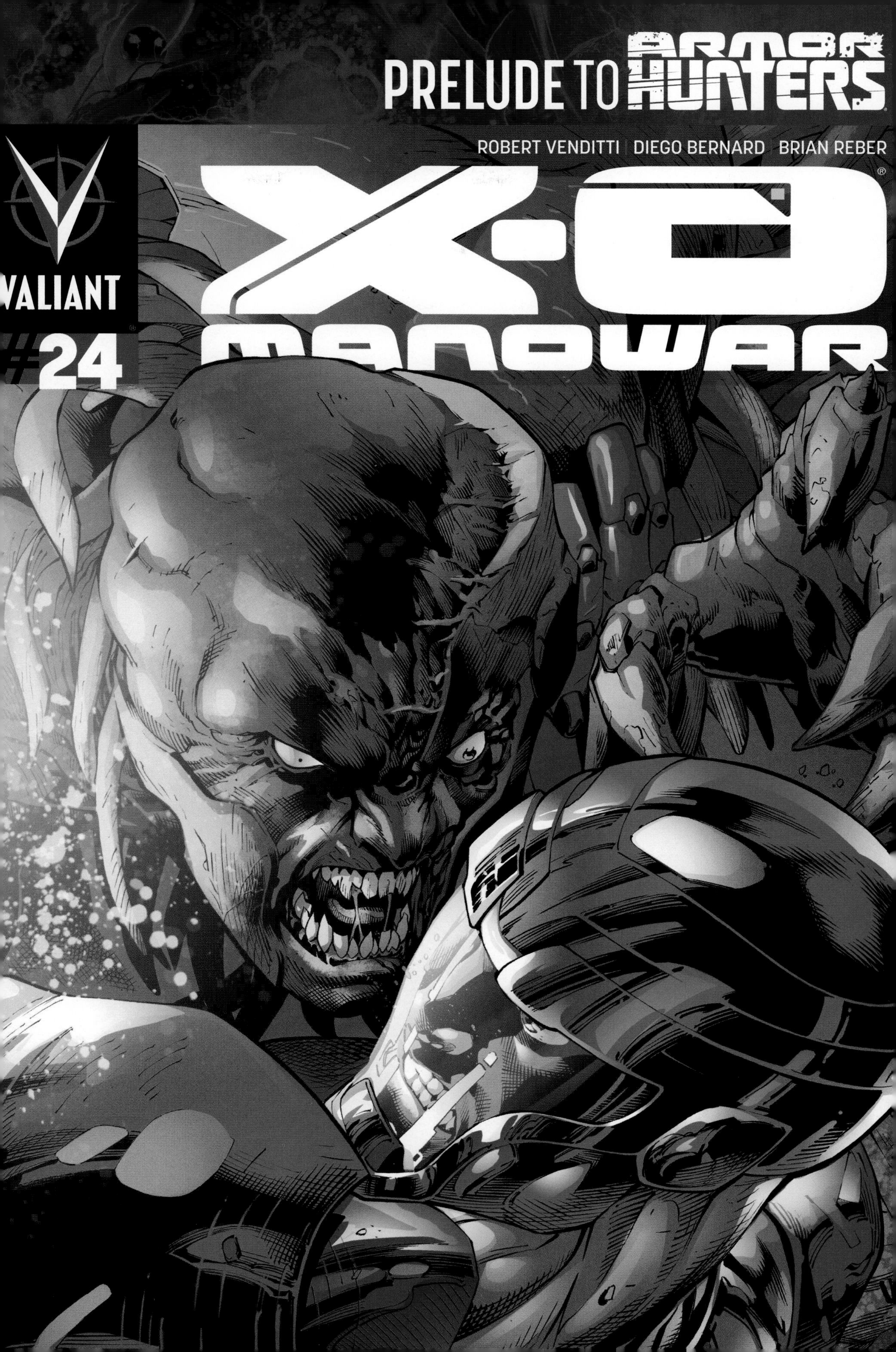
PRELUDE TO ARMOR HUNTERS
ROBERT VENDITTI | DIEGO BERNARD | BRIAN REBER
VALIANT
X-O MANOWAR
#24

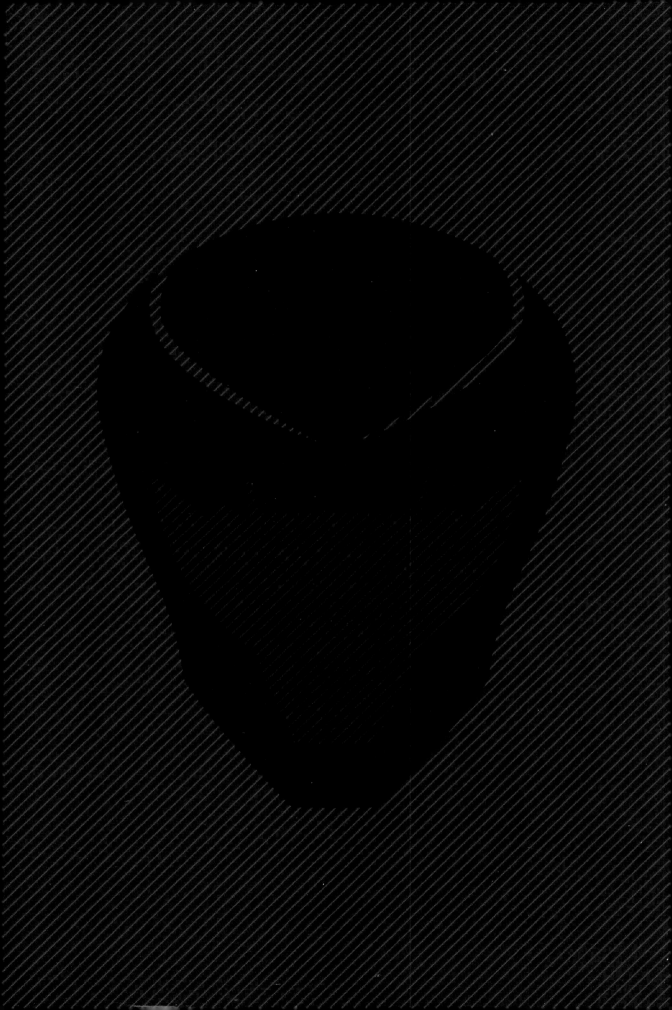

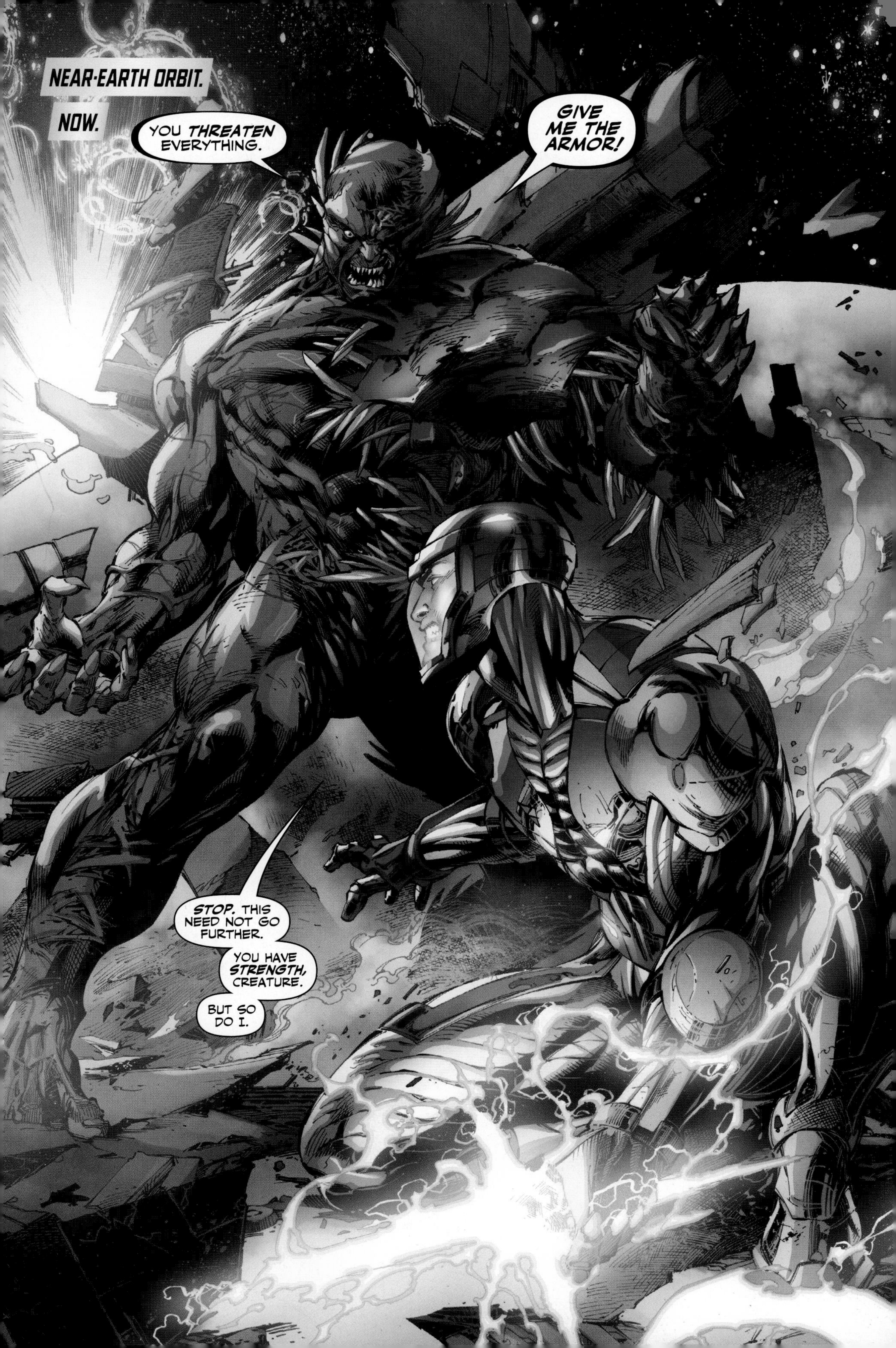
NEAR-EARTH ORBIT.
NOW.
YOU THREATEN EVERYTHING.
GIVE ME THE ARMOR!
STOP. THIS NEED NOT GO FURTHER.
YOU HAVE STRENGTH, CREATURE.
BUT SO DO I.

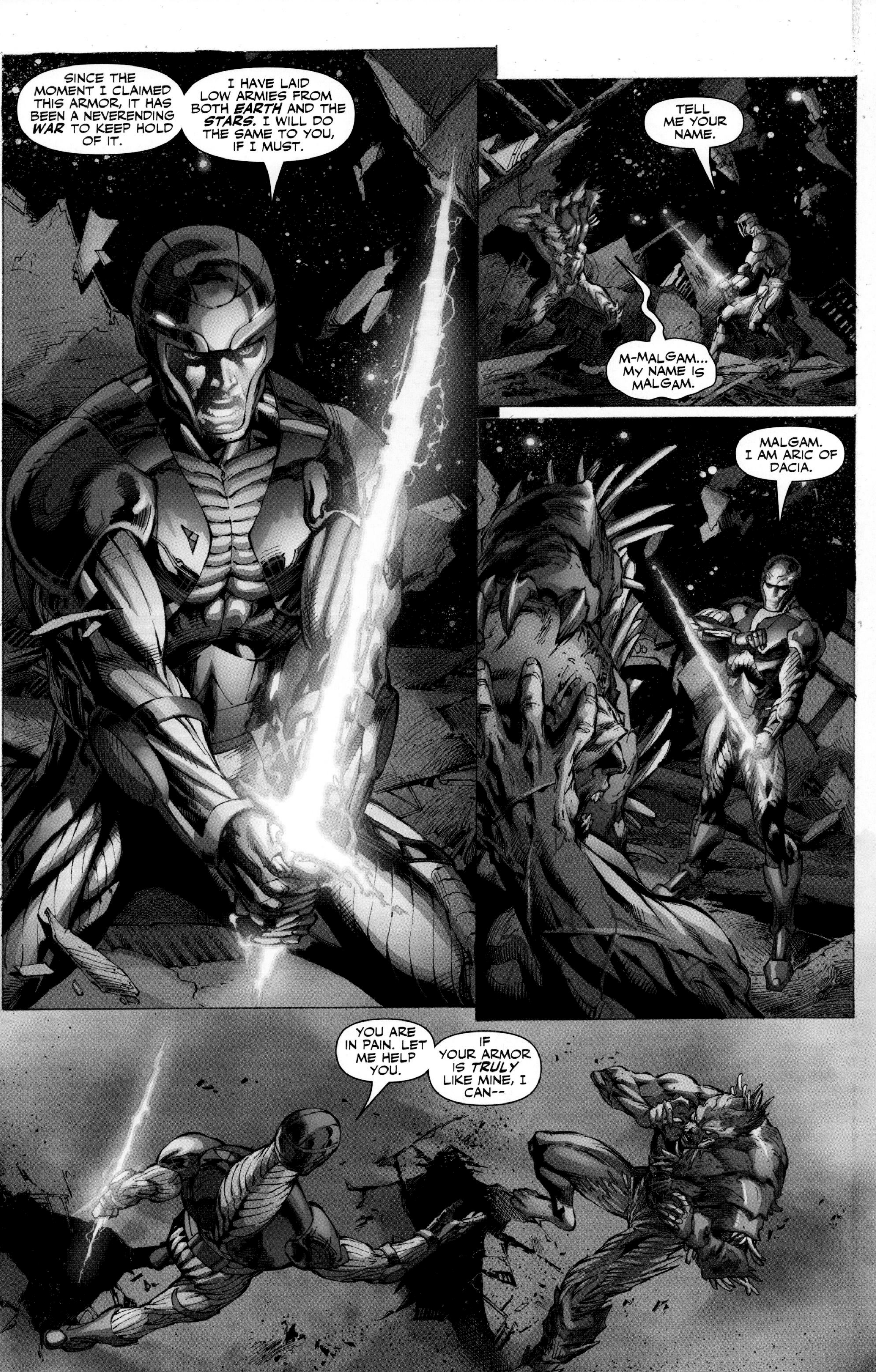
SINCE THE MOMENT I CLAIMED THIS ARMOR, IT HAS BEEN A NEVERENDING WAR TO KEEP HOLD OF IT.
I HAVE LAID LOW ARMIES FROM BOTH EARTH AND THE STARS. I WILL DO THE SAME TO YOU, IF I MUST.
TELL ME YOUR NAME.
M-MALGAM... MY NAME IS MALGAM.
MALGAM. I AM ARIC OF DACIA.
YOU ARE IN PAIN. LET ME HELP YOU.
IF YOUR ARMOR IS TRULY LIKE MINE, I CAN--

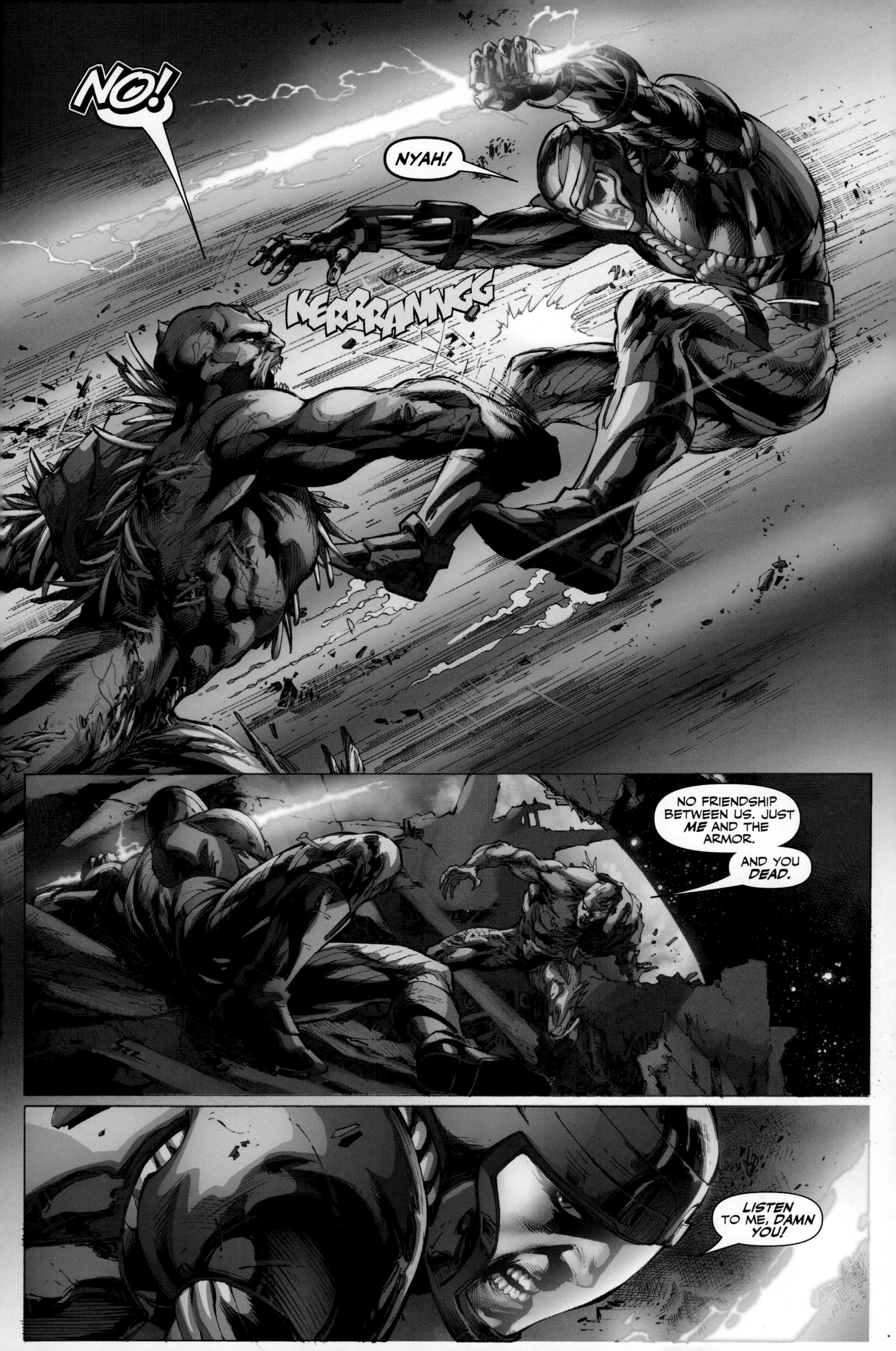
NO!
NYAH!
KERRRANNGG
NO FRIENDSHIP BETWEEN US. JUST ME AND THE ARMOR.
AND YOU DEAD.
LISTEN TO ME, DAMN YOU!

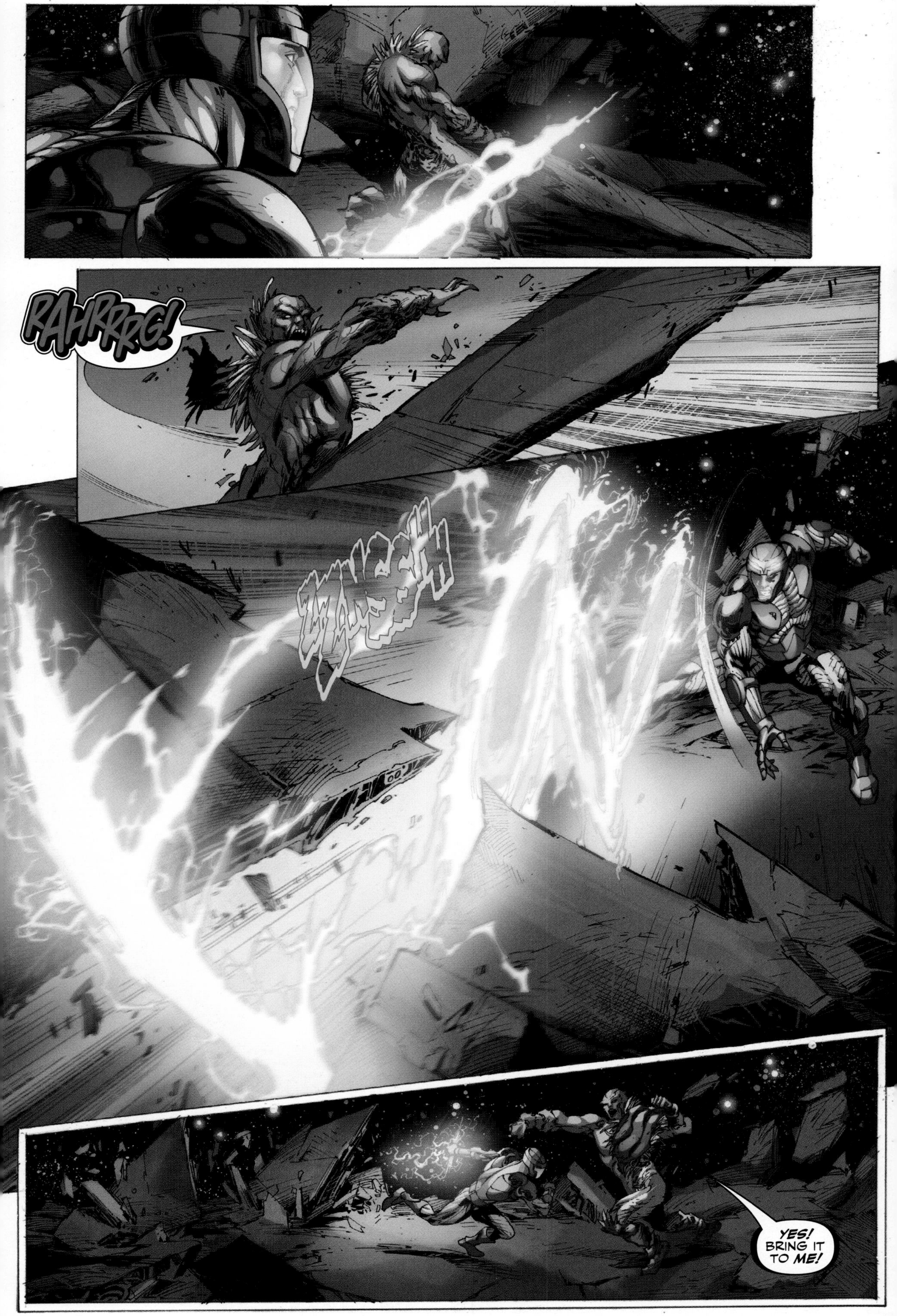
RAHRRRG!
YES! BRING IT TO *ME!*

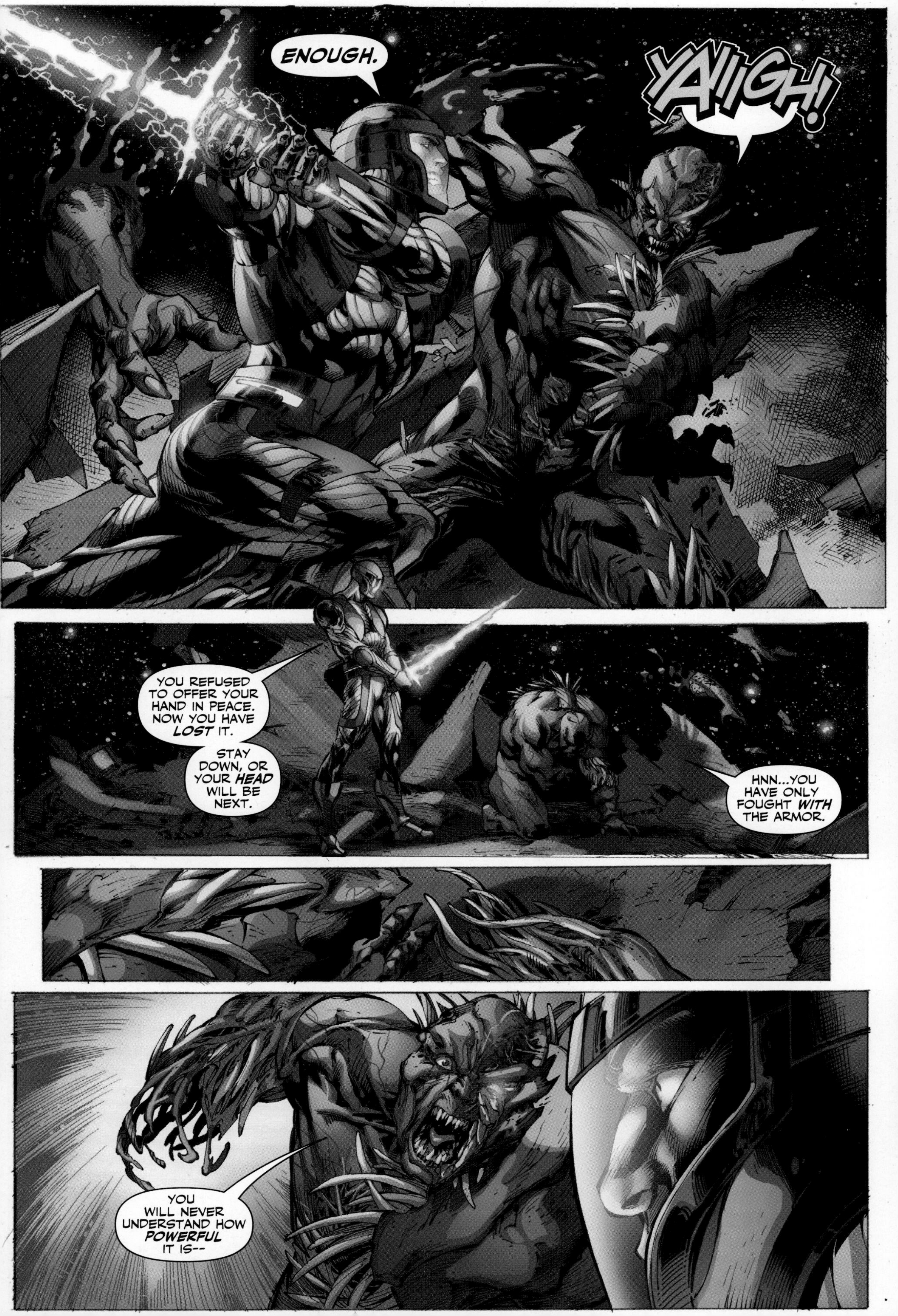

ENOUGH.
YAIIIGH!
YOU REFUSED TO OFFER YOUR HAND IN PEACE. NOW YOU HAVE LOST IT.
STAY DOWN, OR YOUR HEAD WILL BE NEXT.
HNN...YOU HAVE ONLY FOUGHT WITH THE ARMOR.
YOU WILL NEVER UNDERSTAND HOW POWERFUL IT IS--

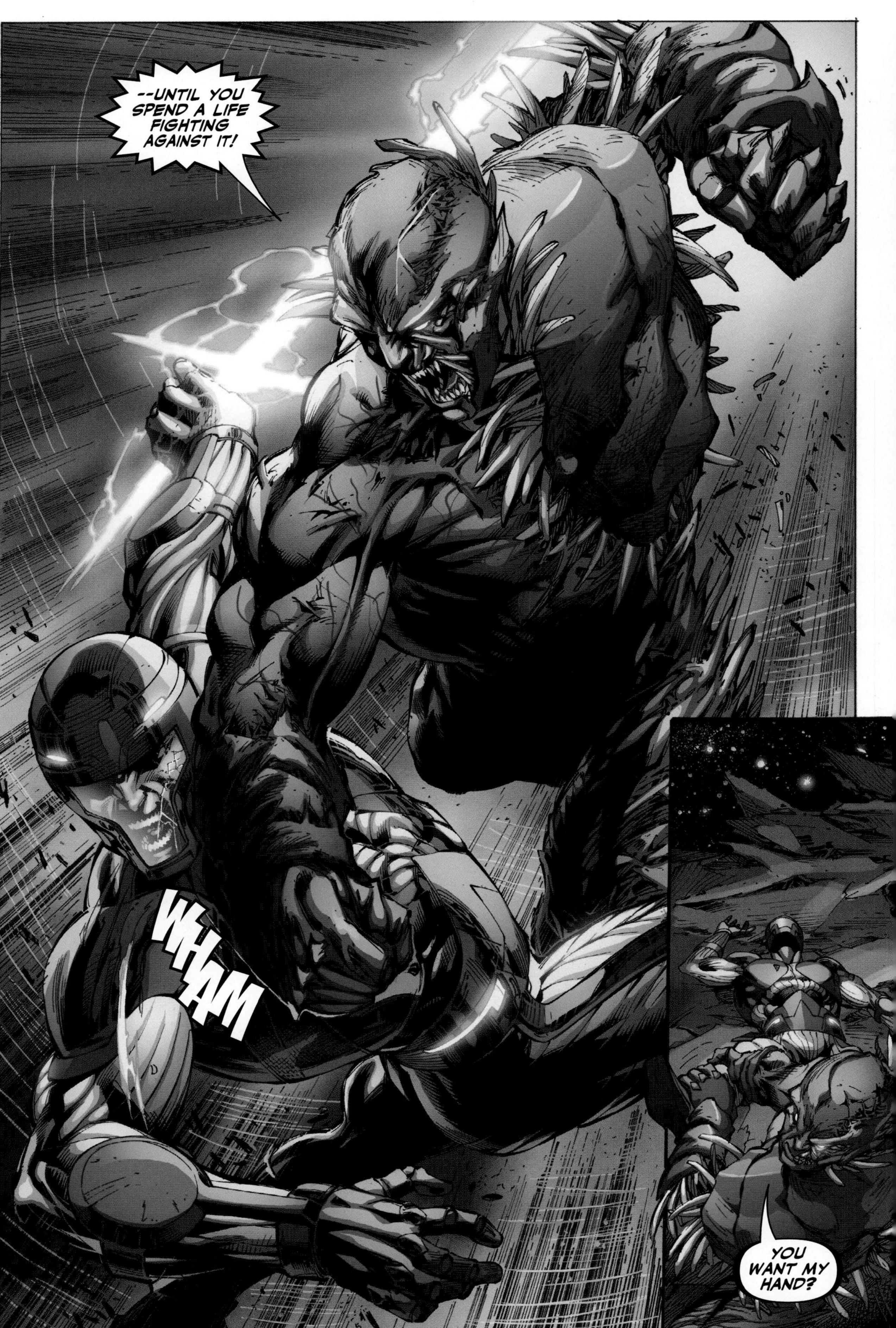
--UNTIL YOU SPEND A LIFE FIGHTING AGAINST IT!
WHAM
YOU WANT MY HAND?

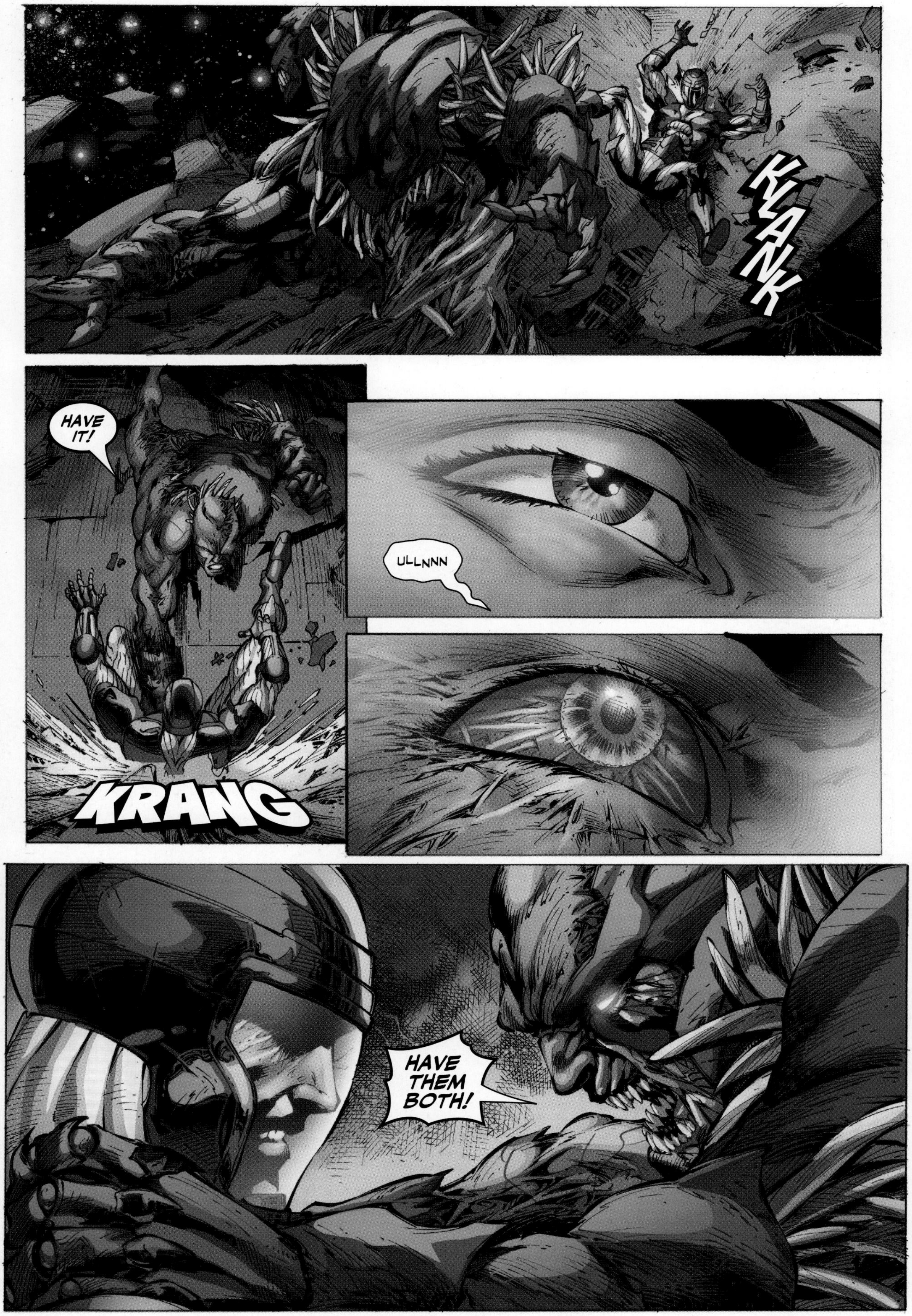
KLANK
HAVE IT!
KRANG
ULLNNN
HAVE THEM BOTH!

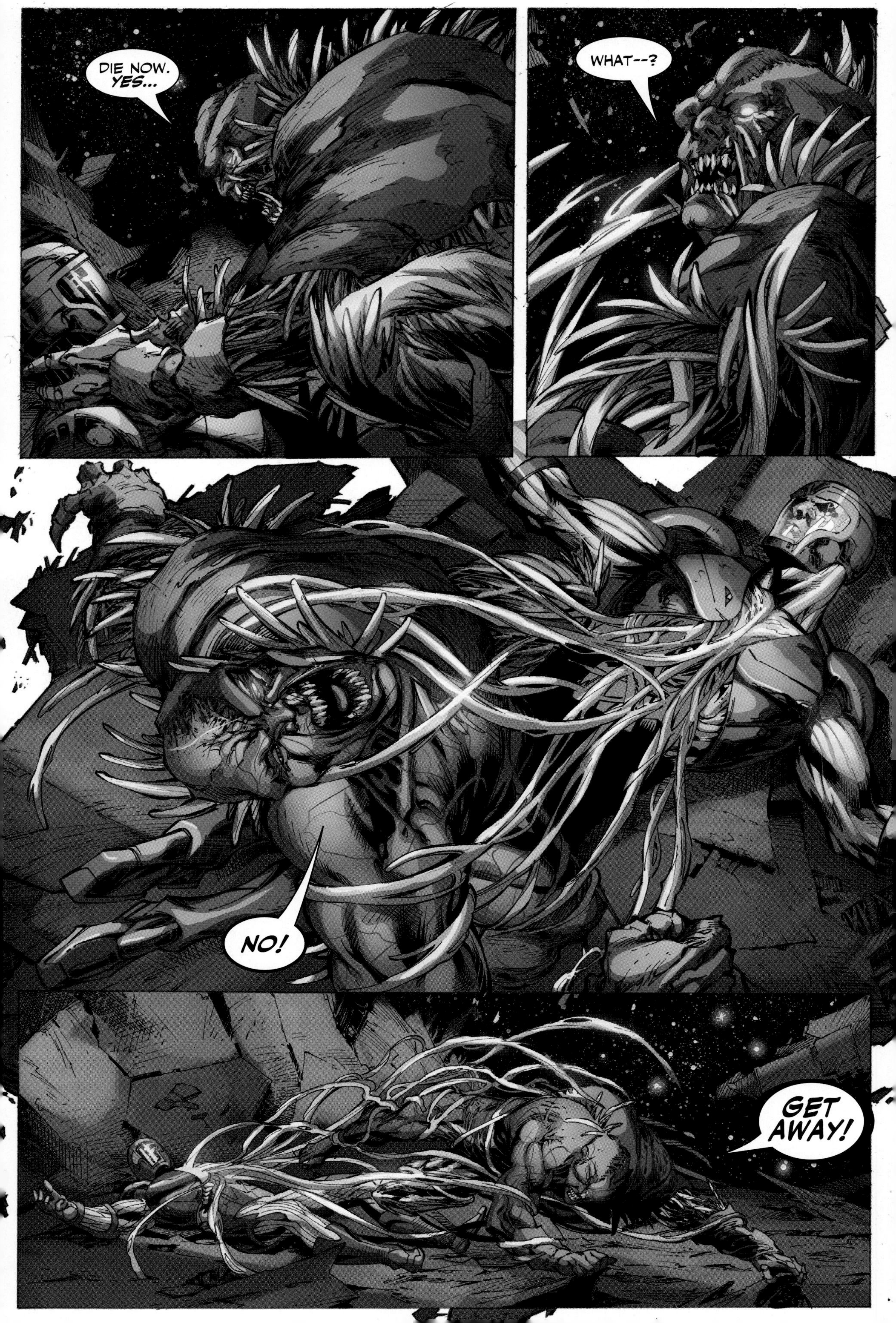
DIE NOW.
YES...
WHAT--?
NO!
GET AWAY!

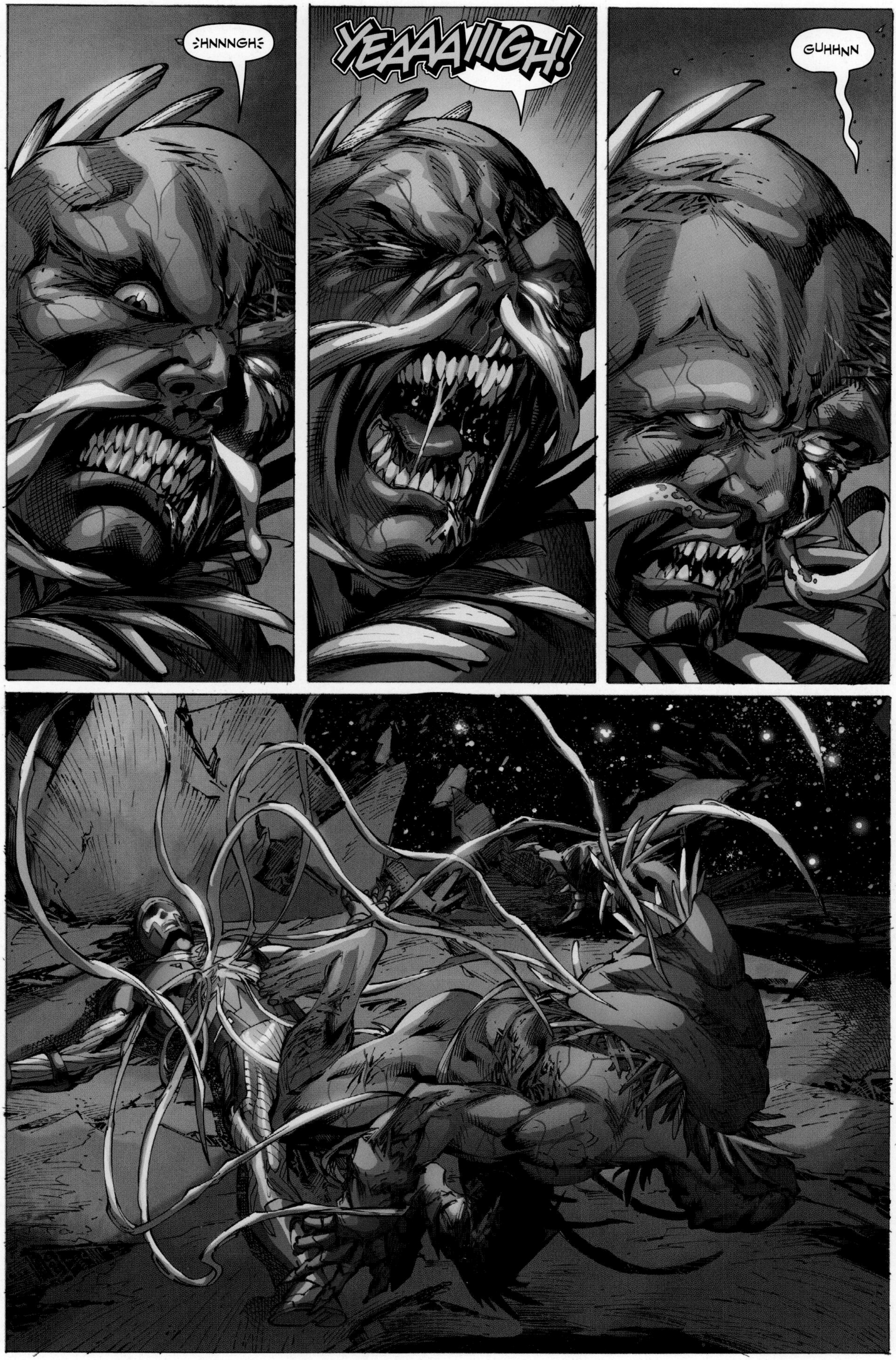
HNNNGH
YEAAAIIIGH!
GUHHNN

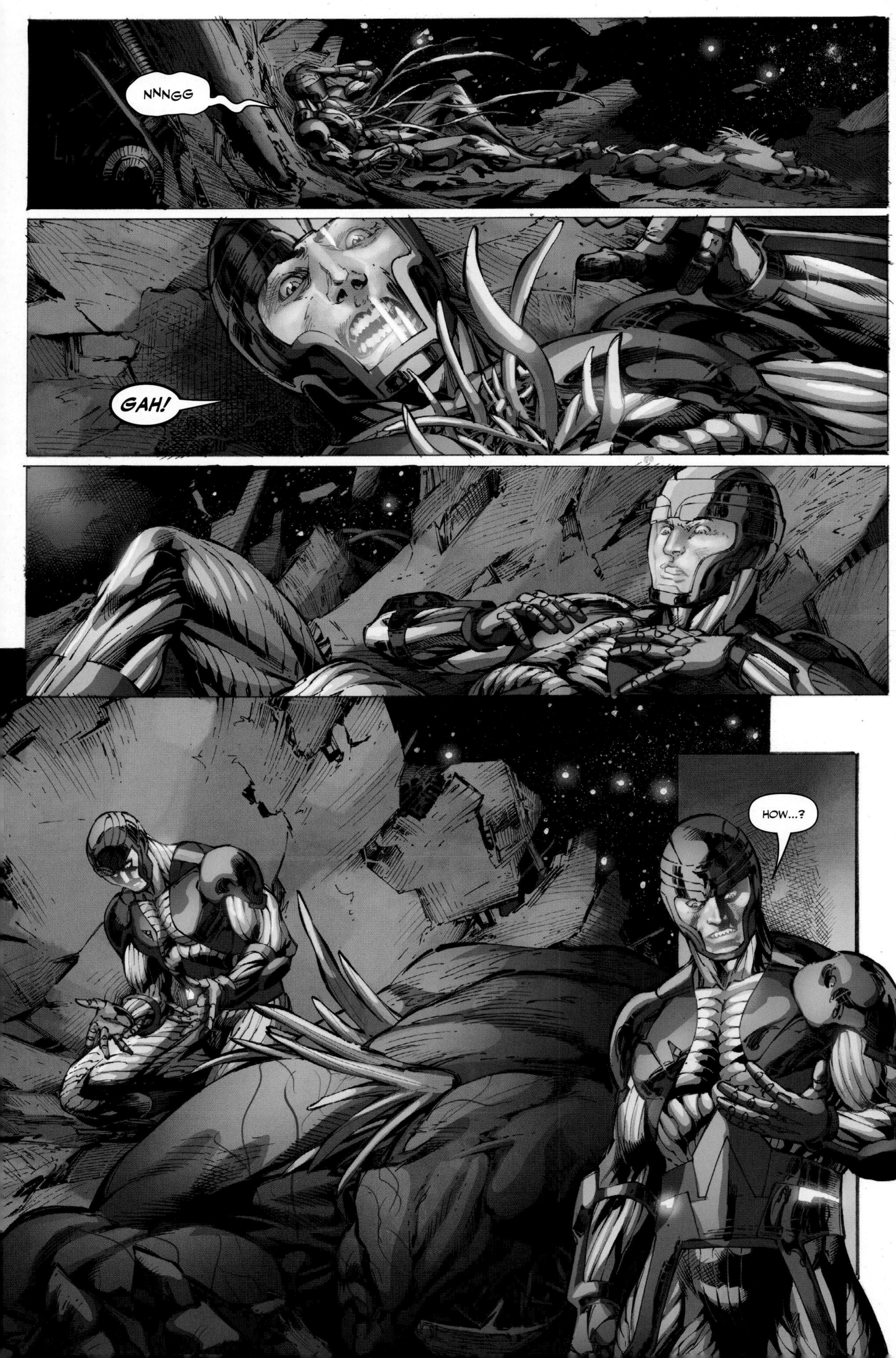
NNNGG
GAH!
HOW...?

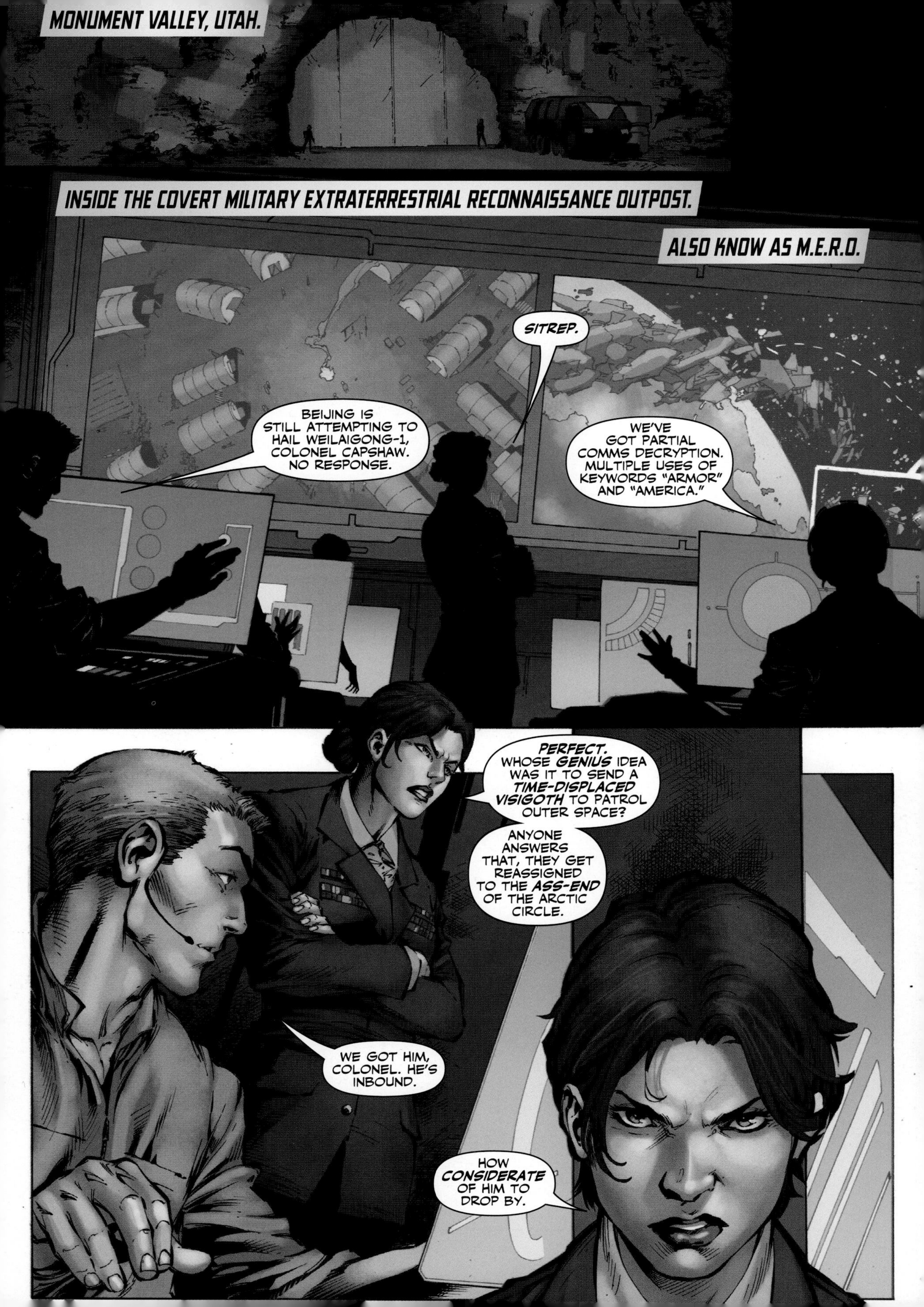
MONUMENT VALLEY, UTAH.
INSIDE THE COVERT MILITARY EXTRATERRESTRIAL RECONNAISSANCE OUTPOST.
ALSO KNOW AS M.E.R.O.
SITREP.
BEIJING IS STILL ATTEMPTING TO HAIL WEILAIGONG-1, COLONEL CAPSHAW. NO RESPONSE.
WE'VE GOT PARTIAL COMMS DECRYPTION. MULTIPLE USES OF KEYWORDS "ARMOR" AND "AMERICA."
PERFECT. WHOSE GENIUS IDEA WAS IT TO SEND A TIME-DISPLACED VISIGOTH TO PATROL OUTER SPACE?
ANYONE ANSWERS THAT, THEY GET REASSIGNED TO THE ASS-END OF THE ARCTIC CIRCLE.
WE GOT HIM, COLONEL. HE'S INBOUND.
HOW CONSIDERATE OF HIM TO DROP BY.

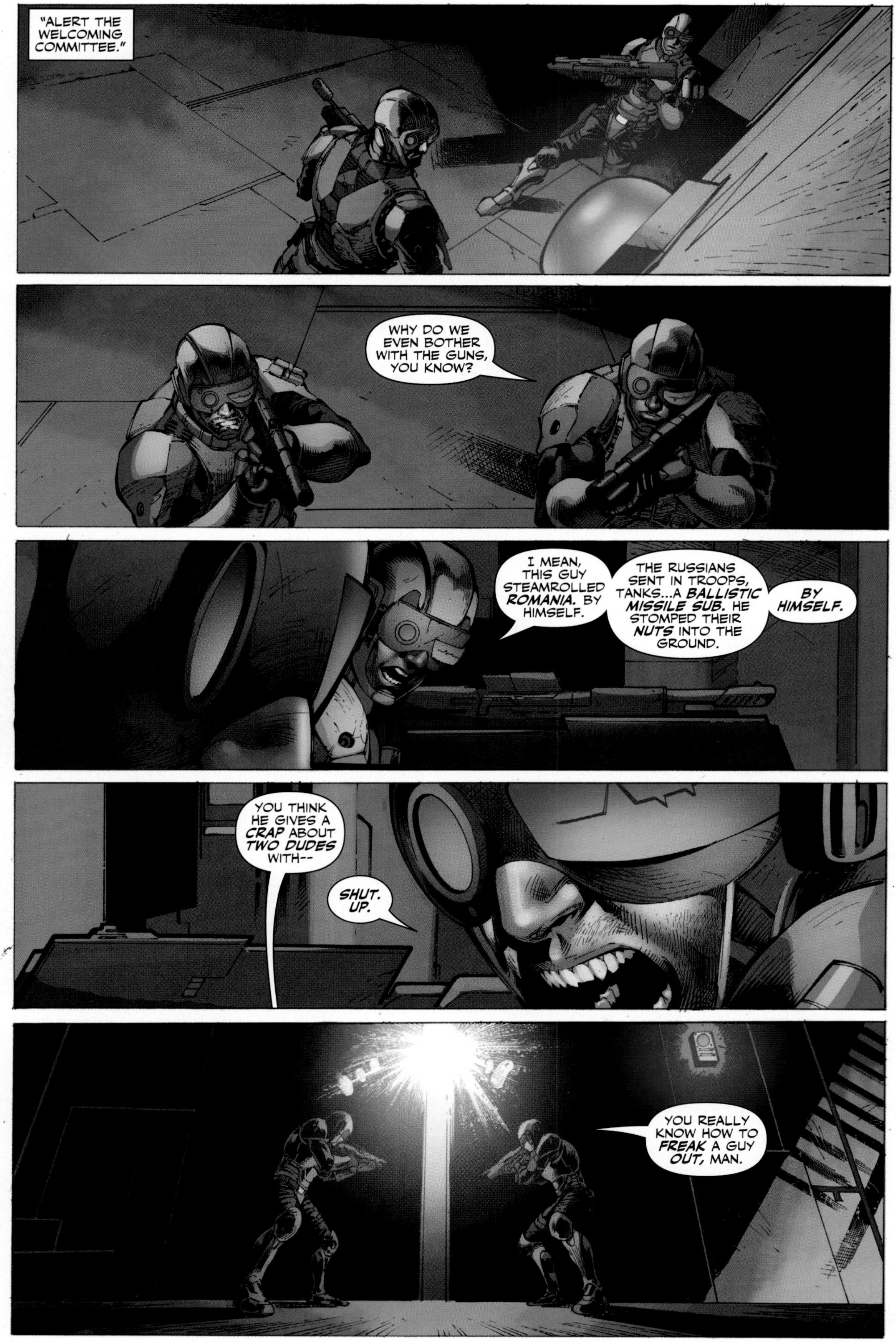
"ALERT THE WELCOMING COMMITTEE."
WHY DO WE EVEN BOTHER WITH THE GUNS, YOU KNOW?
I MEAN, THIS GUY STEAMROLLED ROMANIA. BY HIMSELF.
THE RUSSIANS SENT IN TROOPS, TANKS...A BALLISTIC MISSILE SUB. HE STOMPED THEIR NUTS INTO THE GROUND.
BY HIMSELF.
YOU THINK HE GIVES A CRAP ABOUT TWO DUDES WITH--
SHUT. UP.
YOU REALLY KNOW HOW TO FREAK A GUY OUT, MAN.

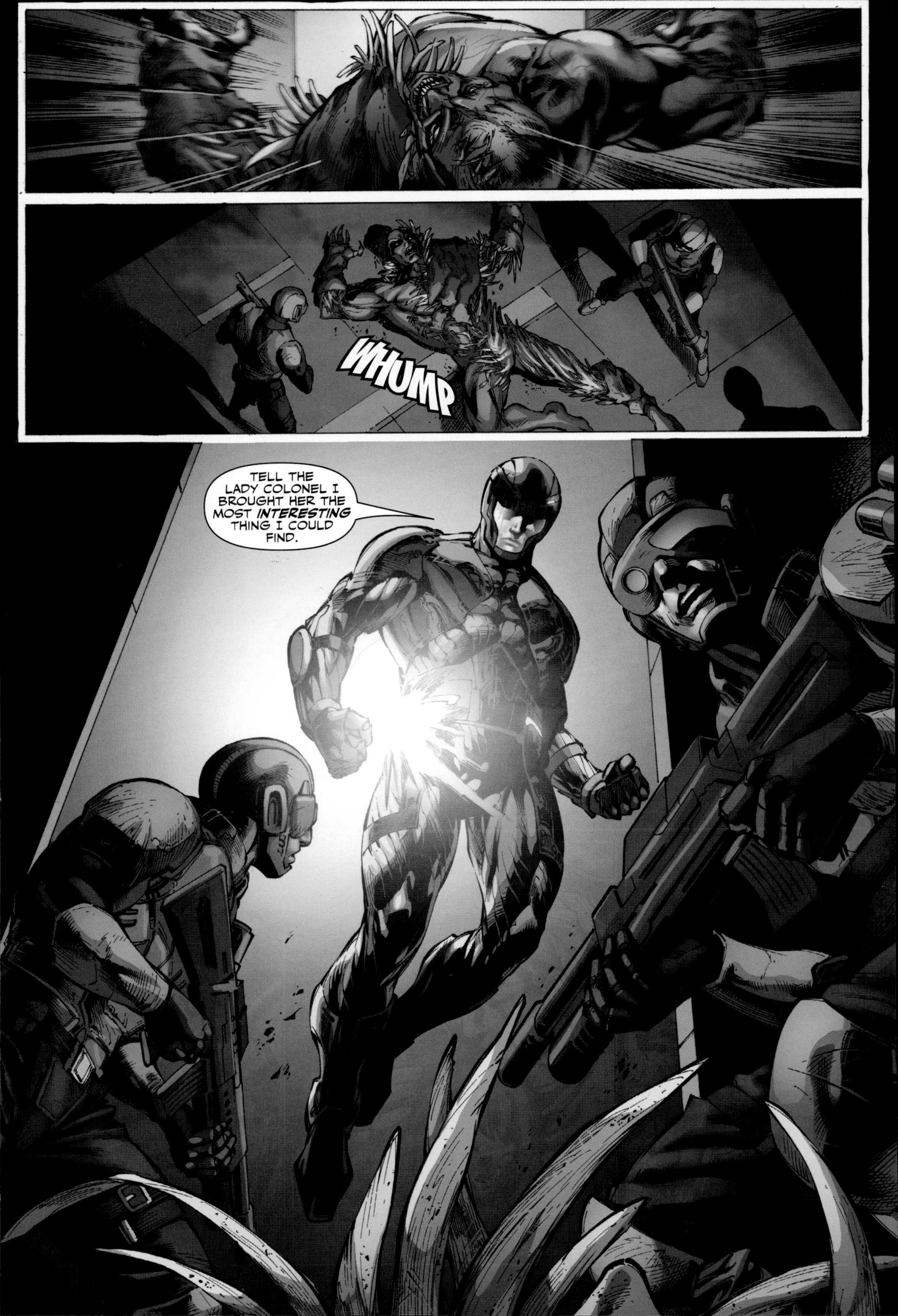
WHUMP
TELL THE LADY COLONEL I BROUGHT HER THE MOST *INTERESTING* THING I COULD FIND.

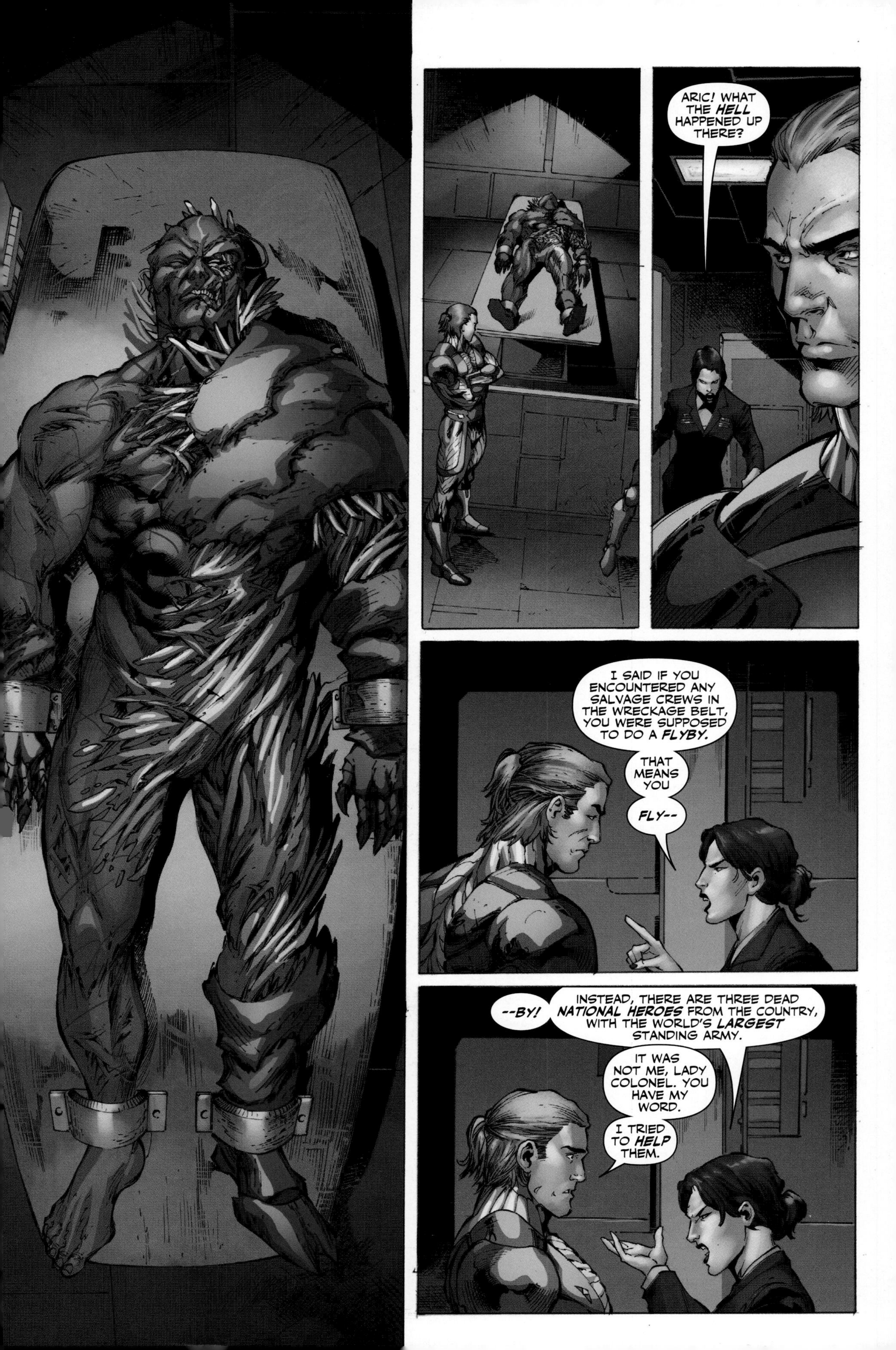
ARIC! WHAT THE HELL HAPPENED UP THERE?
I SAID IF YOU ENCOUNTERED ANY SALVAGE CREWS IN THE WRECKAGE BELT, YOU WERE SUPPOSED TO DO A FLYBY.
THAT MEANS YOU
FLY--
--BY!
INSTEAD, THERE ARE THREE DEAD NATIONAL HEROES FROM THE COUNTRY, WITH THE WORLD'S LARGEST STANDING ARMY.
IT WAS NOT ME, LADY COLONEL. YOU HAVE MY WORD.
I TRIED TO HELP THEM.

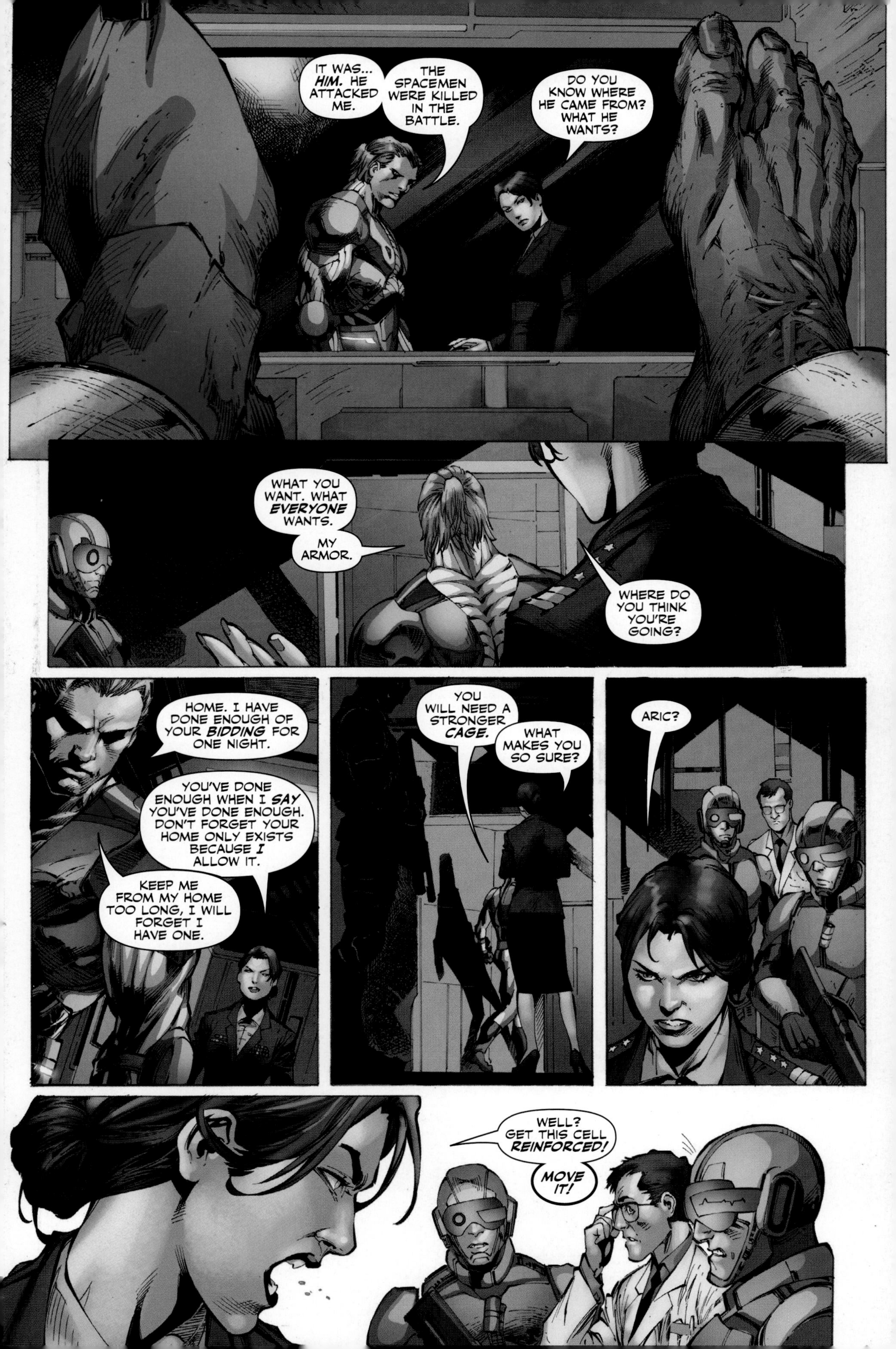
IT WAS... HIM. HE ATTACKED ME.
THE SPACEMEN WERE KILLED IN THE BATTLE.
DO YOU KNOW WHERE HE CAME FROM? WHAT HE WANTS?
WHAT YOU WANT. WHAT EVERYONE WANTS.
MY ARMOR.
WHERE DO YOU THINK YOU'RE GOING?
HOME. I HAVE DONE ENOUGH OF YOUR BIDDING FOR ONE NIGHT.
YOU'VE DONE ENOUGH WHEN I SAY YOU'VE DONE ENOUGH. DON'T FORGET YOUR HOME ONLY EXISTS BECAUSE I ALLOW IT.
KEEP ME FROM MY HOME TOO LONG, I WILL FORGET I HAVE ONE.
YOU WILL NEED A STRONGER CAGE.
WHAT MAKES YOU SO SURE?
ARIC?
WELL? GET THIS CELL REINFORCED!
MOVE IT!

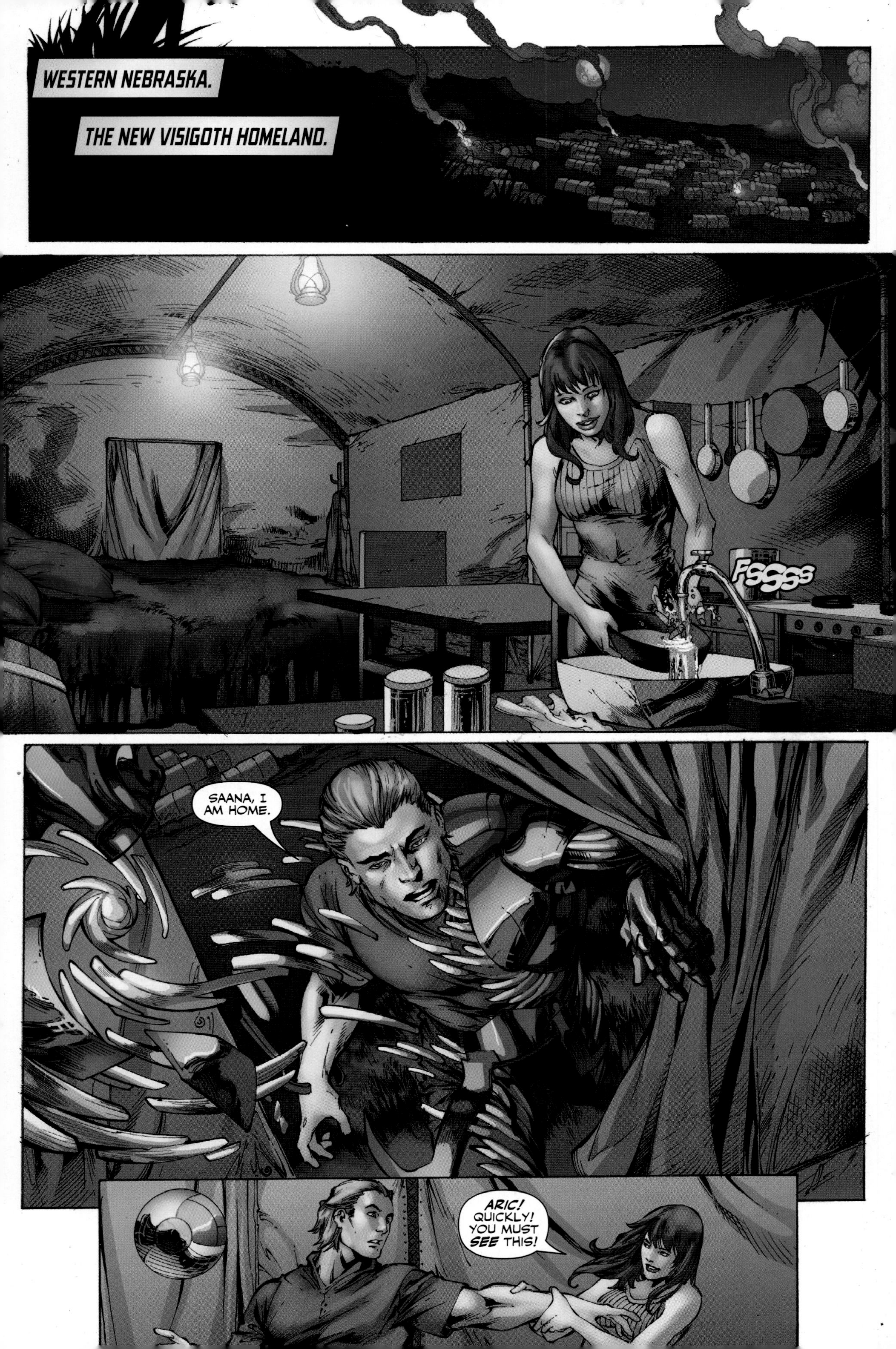

WESTERN NEBRASKA.
THE NEW VISIGOTH HOMELAND.
FSSSS
SAANA, I AM HOME.
ARIC! QUICKLY! YOU MUST SEE THIS!

TURN IT. I HAD A DIFFICULT DAY. I--

JUST *TURN* IT!

NO, NO. *HERE.*

HOW DID THIS HAPPEN?

THE SOLDIER-BUILDERS DID SOMETHING WHILE YOU WERE GONE. *ALL* THE TENTS ARE LIKE THIS NOW.

IT JUST FLOWS AND FLOWS AND FLOWS...

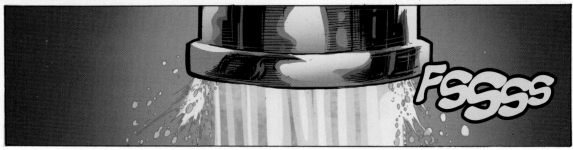

FSSSS

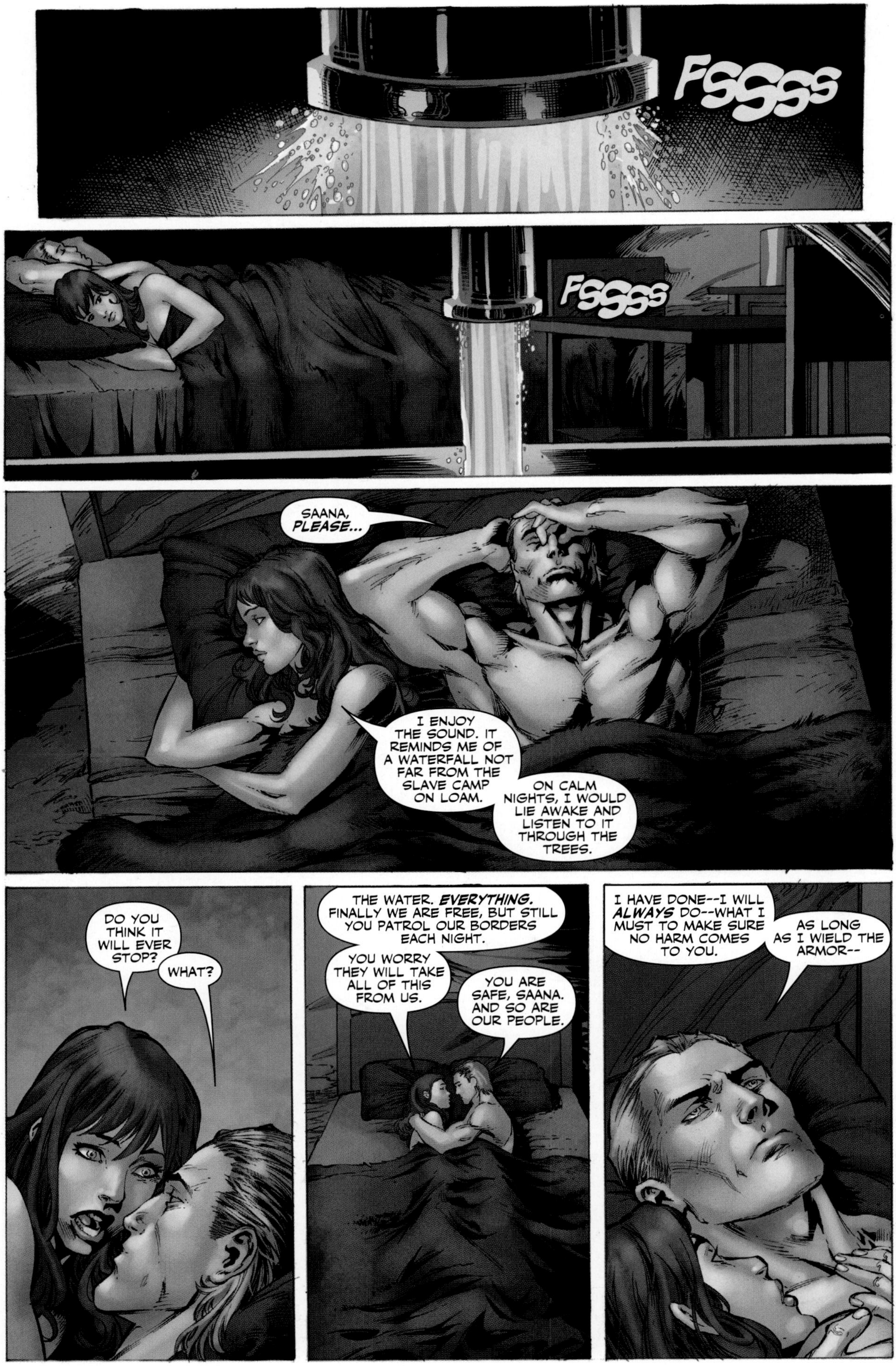
FSSSS
FSSSS
SAANA, PLEASE...
I ENJOY THE SOUND. IT REMINDS ME OF A WATERFALL NOT FAR FROM THE SLAVE CAMP ON LOAM.
ON CALM NIGHTS, I WOULD LIE AWAKE AND LISTEN TO IT THROUGH THE TREES.
DO YOU THINK IT WILL EVER STOP?
WHAT?
THE WATER. EVERYTHING. FINALLY WE ARE FREE, BUT STILL YOU PATROL OUR BORDERS EACH NIGHT.
YOU WORRY THEY WILL TAKE ALL OF THIS FROM US.
YOU ARE SAFE, SAANA. AND SO ARE OUR PEOPLE.
I HAVE DONE--I WILL ALWAYS DO--WHAT I MUST TO MAKE SURE NO HARM COMES TO YOU.
AS LONG AS I WIELD THE ARMOR--

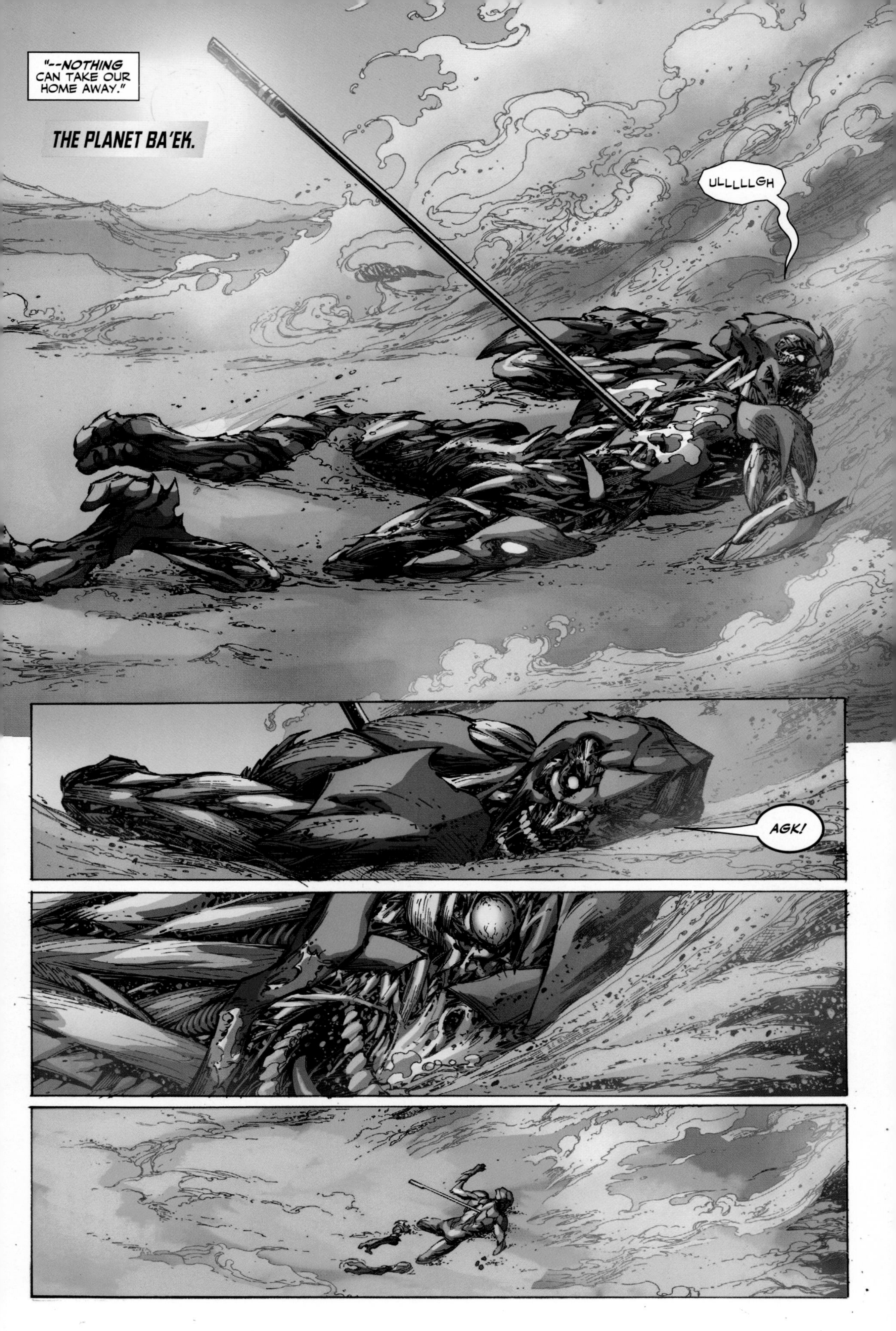
"--NOTHING CAN TAKE OUR HOME AWAY."
THE PLANET BA'EK.
ULLLLLGH
AGK!

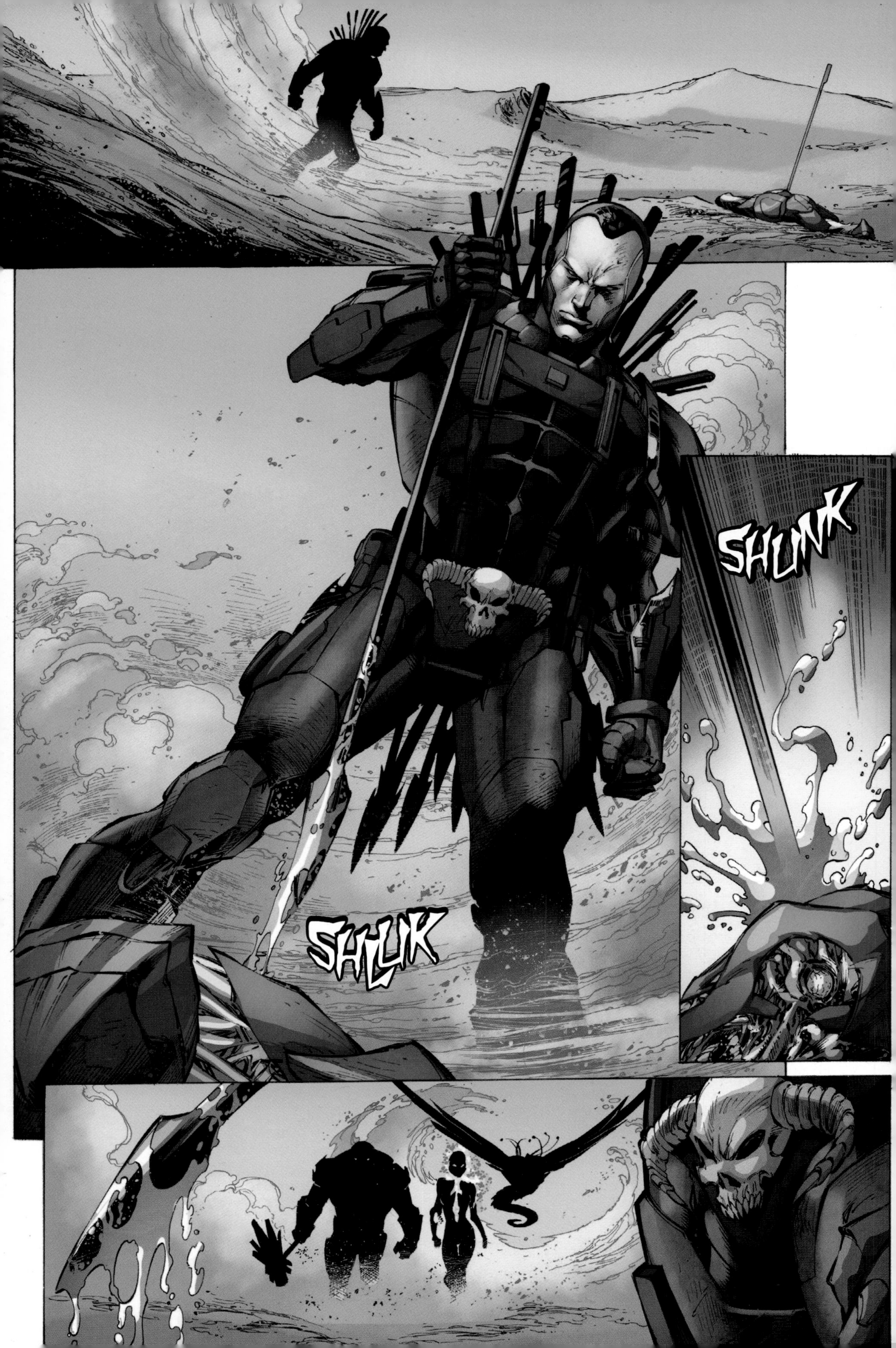
SHUNK
SHLUK

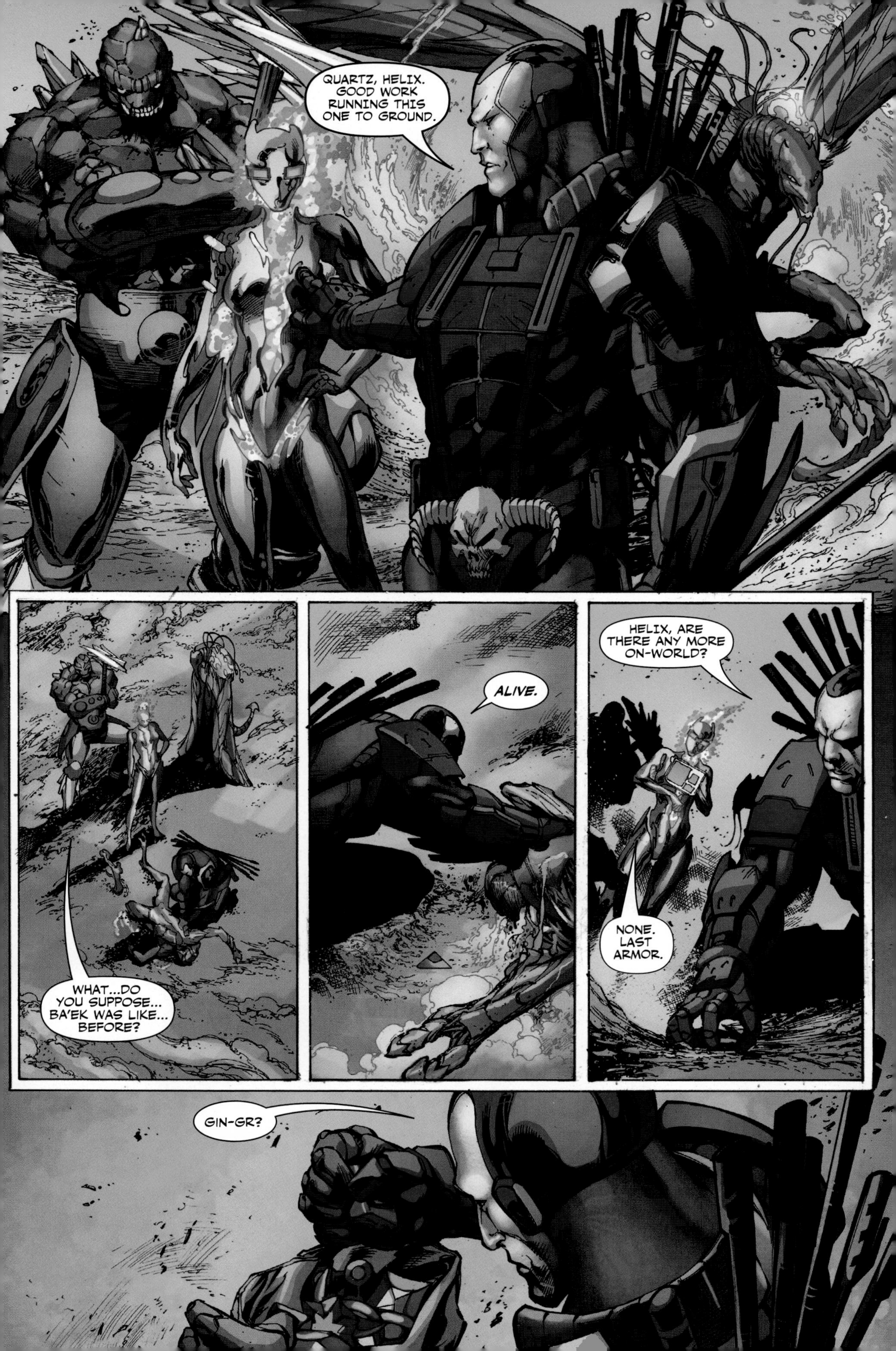
QUARTZ, HELIX. GOOD WORK RUNNING THIS ONE TO GROUND.
WHAT...DO YOU SUPPOSE... BA'EK WAS LIKE... BEFORE?
ALIVE.
HELIX, ARE THERE ANY MORE ON-WORLD?
NONE. LAST ARMOR.
GIN-GR?

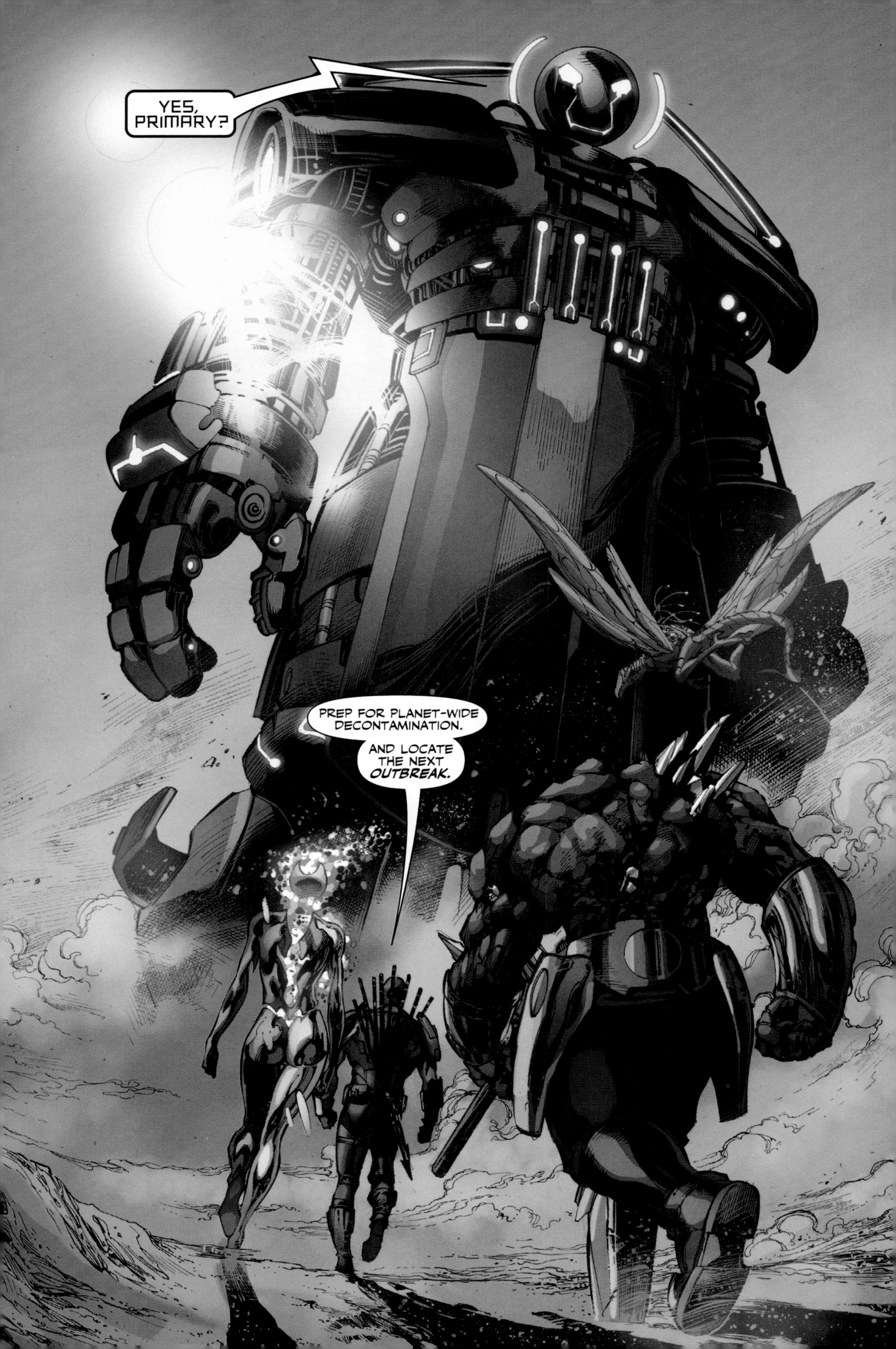
YES, PRIMARY?
PREP FOR PLANET-WIDE DECONTAMINATION.
AND LOCATE THE NEXT *OUTBREAK.*

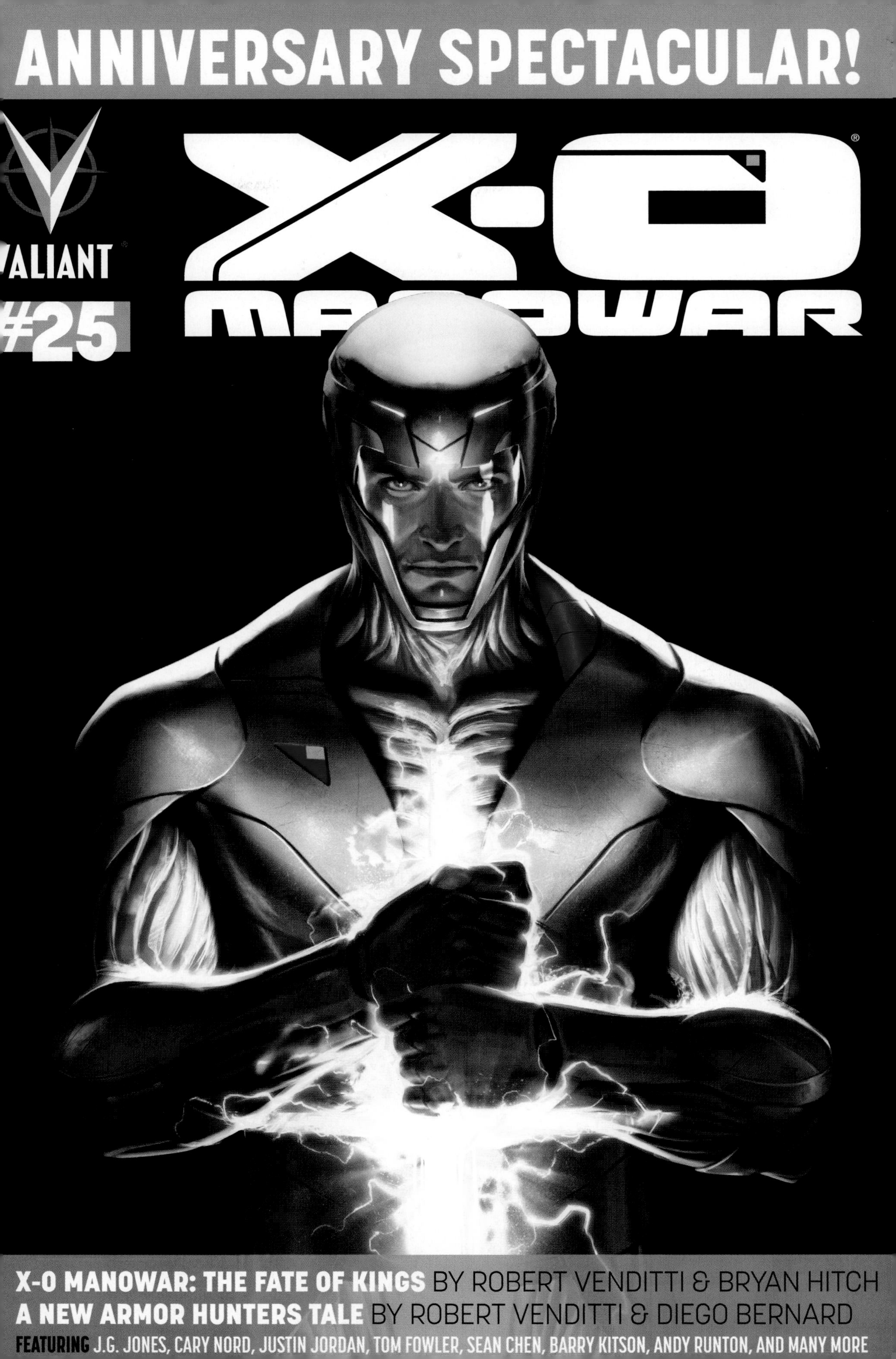
ANNIVERSARY SPECTACULAR!
VALIANT
#25
X-O MANOWAR
X-O MANOWAR: THE FATE OF KINGS BY ROBERT VENDITTI & BRYAN HITCH
A NEW ARMOR HUNTERS TALE BY ROBERT VENDITTI & DIEGO BERNARD
FEATURING J.G. JONES, CARY NORD, JUSTIN JORDAN, TOM FOWLER, SEAN CHEN, BARRY KITSON, ANDY RUNTON, AND MANY MORE

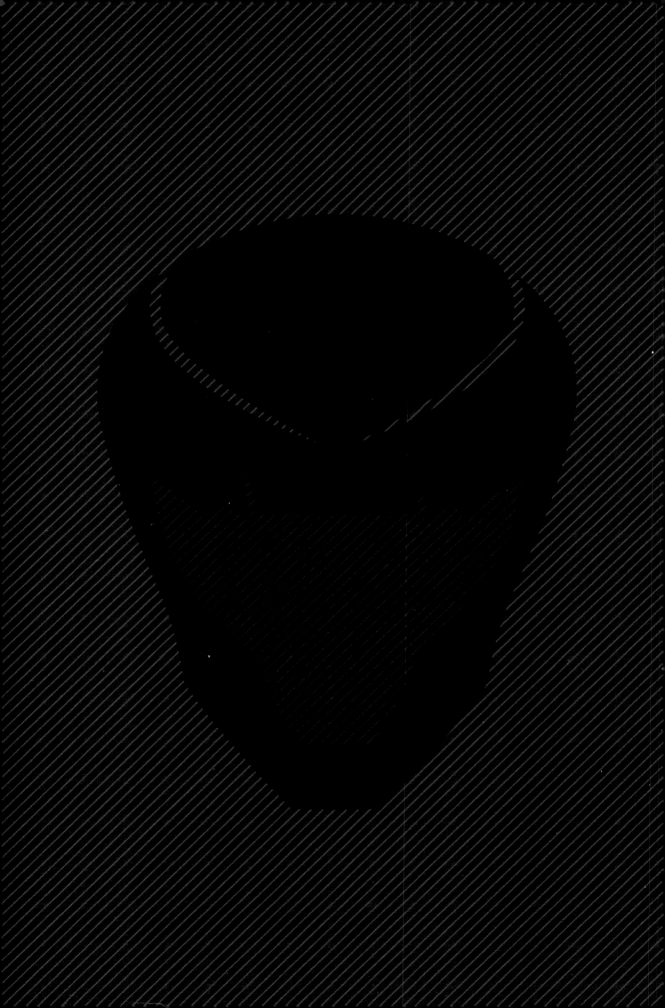

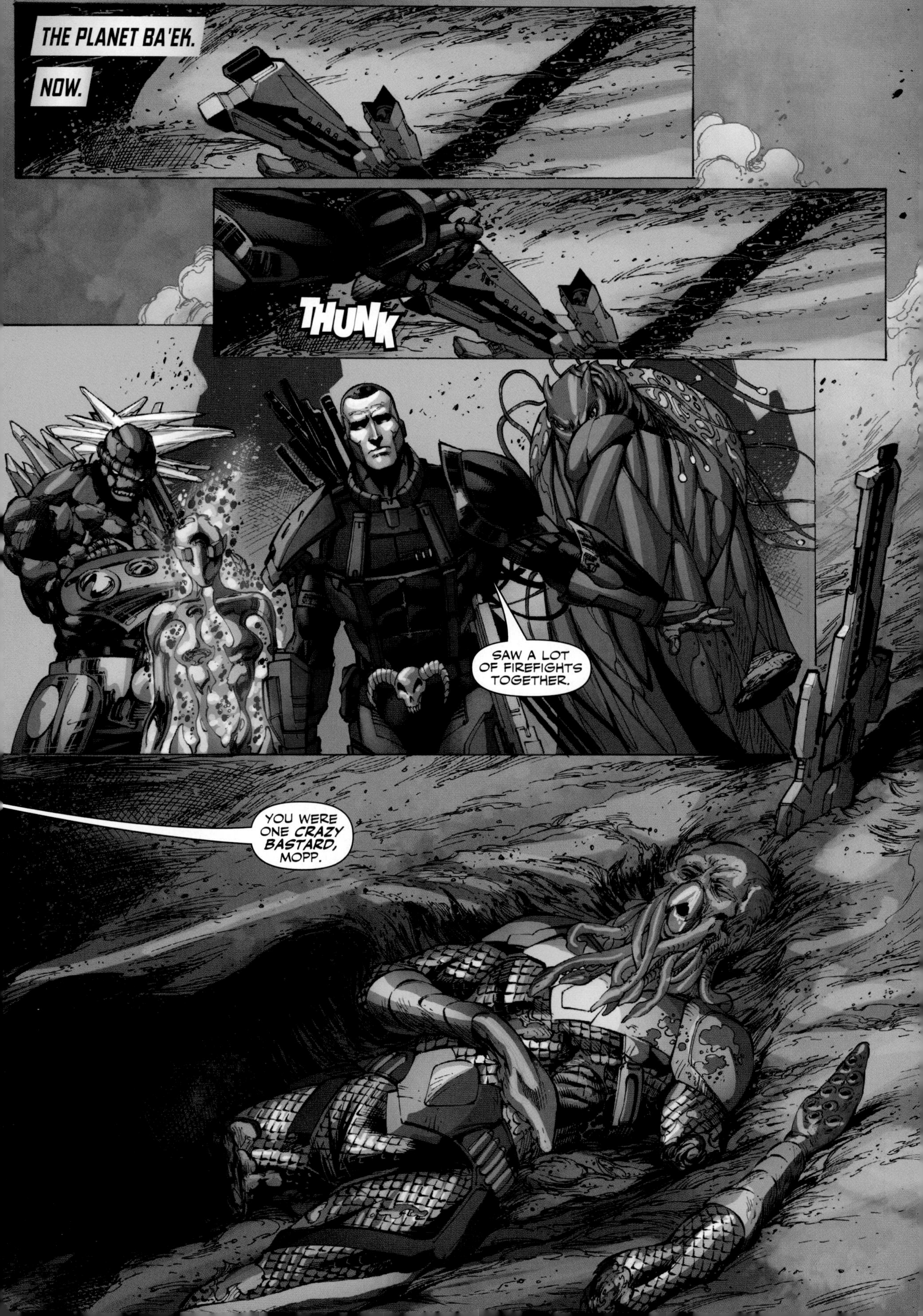
THE PLANET BA'EK.
NOW.
THUNK
SAW A LOT OF FIREFIGHTS TOGETHER.
YOU WERE ONE *CRAZY BASTARD,* MOPP.

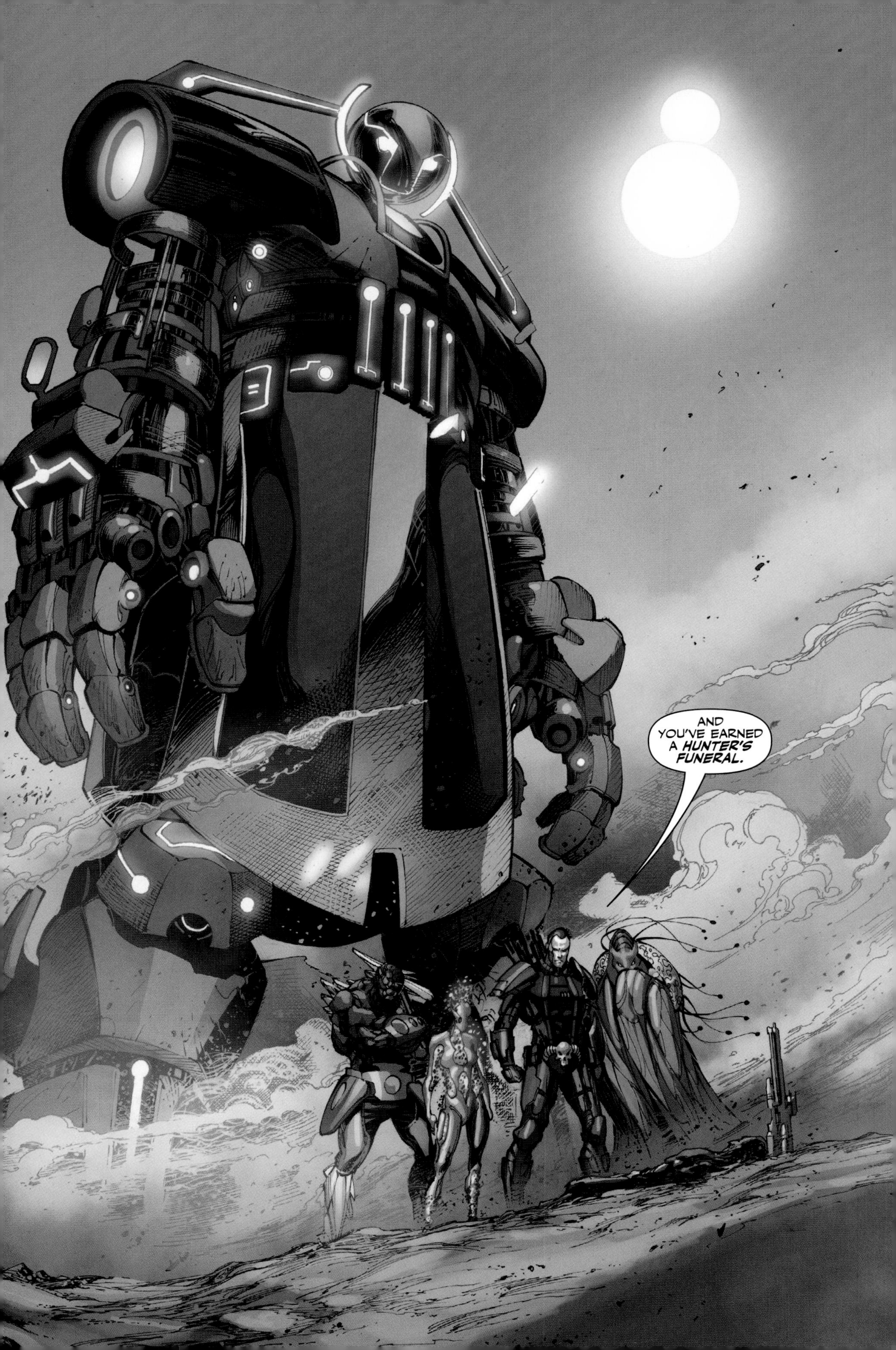
AND YOU'VE EARNED A *HUNTER'S FUNERAL.*

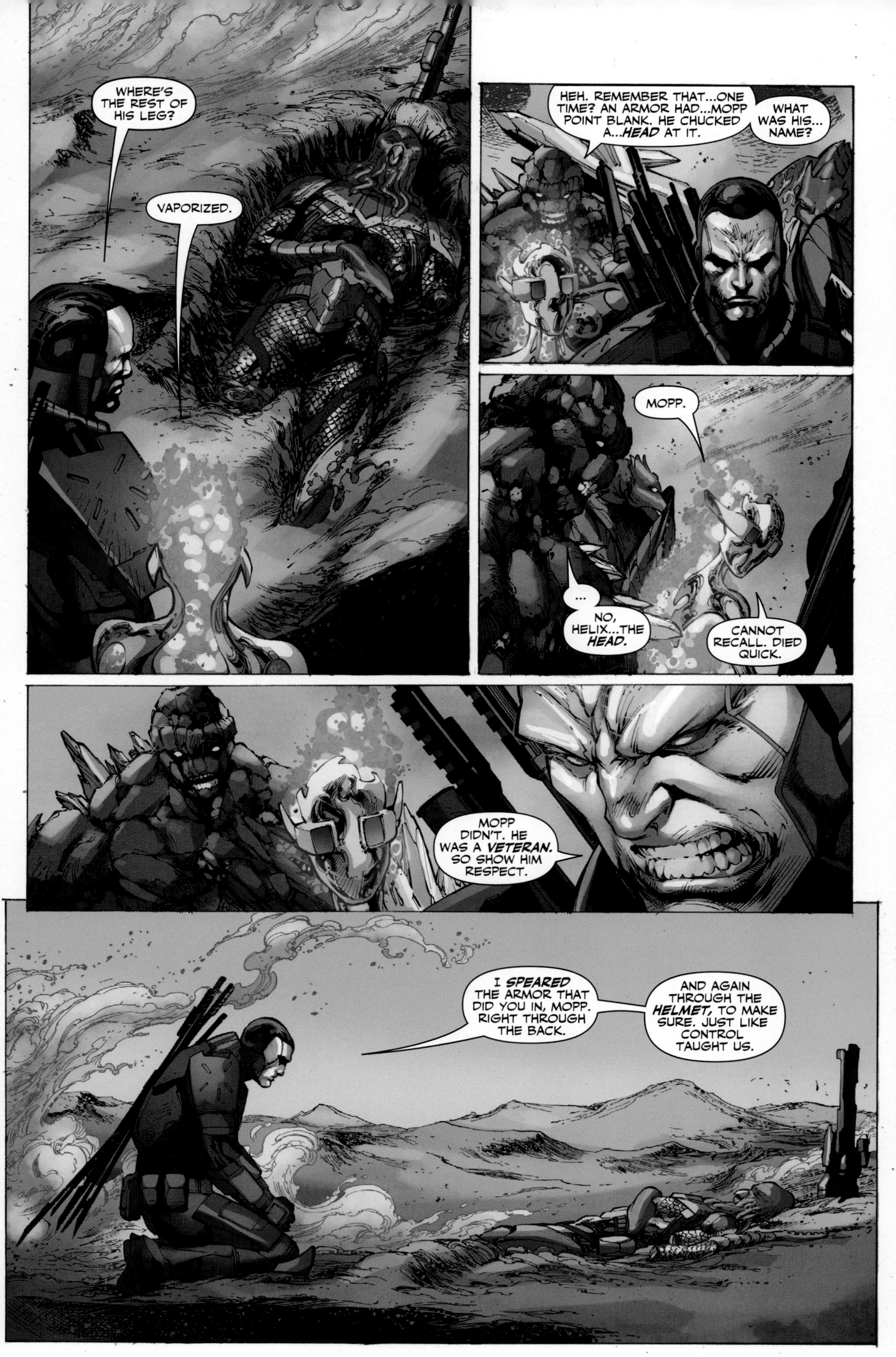
WHERE'S THE REST OF HIS LEG?
VAPORIZED.
HEH. REMEMBER THAT...ONE TIME? AN ARMOR HAD...MOPP POINT BLANK. HE CHUCKED A...HEAD AT IT.
WHAT WAS HIS... NAME?
MOPP.
...
NO, HELIX...THE HEAD.
CANNOT RECALL. DIED QUICK.
MOPP DIDN'T. HE WAS A VETERAN. SO SHOW HIM RESPECT.
I SPEARED THE ARMOR THAT DID YOU IN, MOPP. RIGHT THROUGH THE BACK.
AND AGAIN THROUGH THE HELMET, TO MAKE SURE. JUST LIKE CONTROL TAUGHT US.

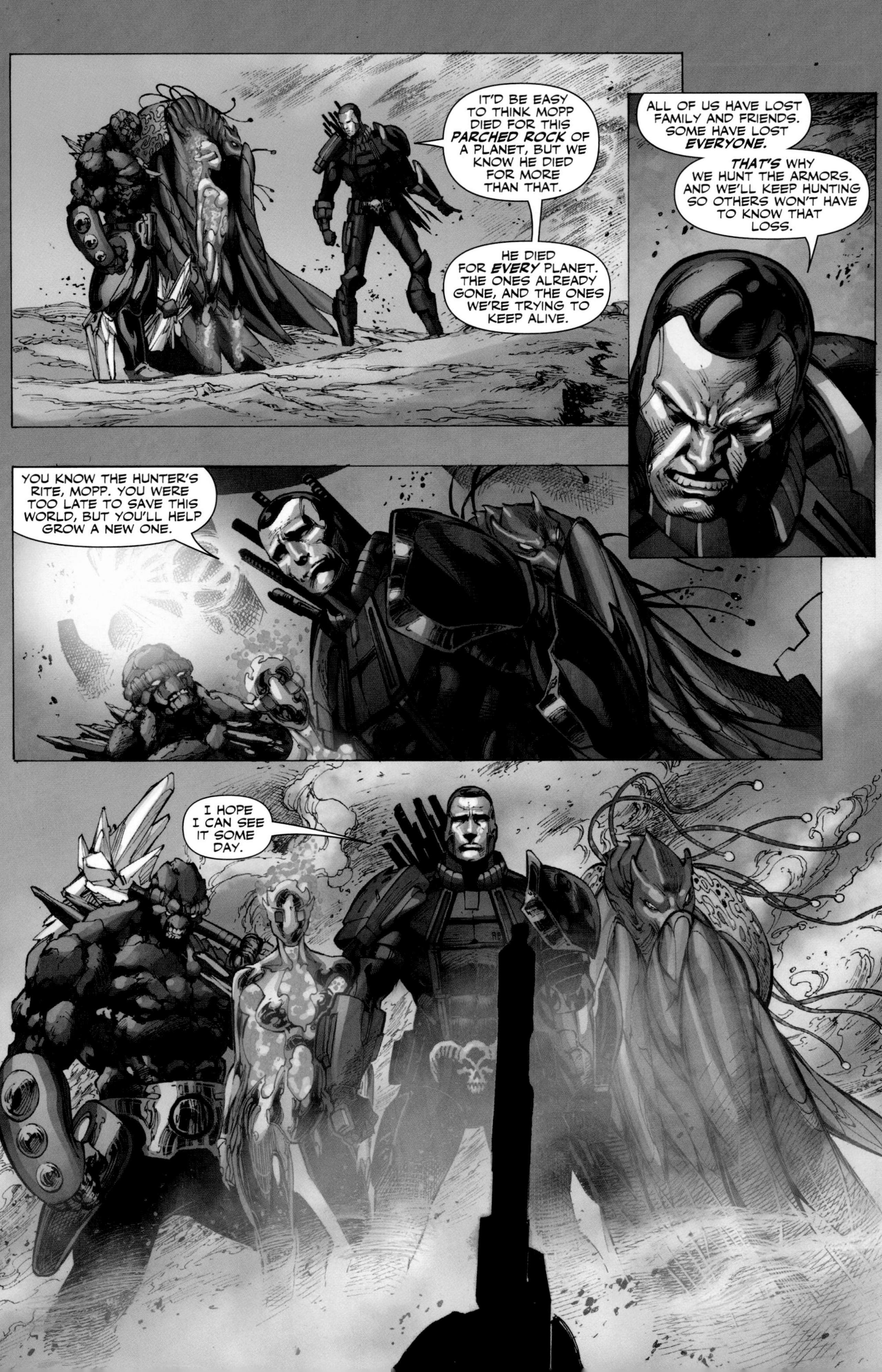
IT'D BE EASY TO THINK MOPP DIED FOR THIS PARCHED ROCK OF A PLANET, BUT WE KNOW HE DIED FOR MORE THAN THAT.
HE DIED FOR EVERY PLANET. THE ONES ALREADY GONE, AND THE ONES WE'RE TRYING TO KEEP ALIVE.
ALL OF US HAVE LOST FAMILY AND FRIENDS. SOME HAVE LOST EVERYONE.
THAT'S WHY WE HUNT THE ARMORS. AND WE'LL KEEP HUNTING SO OTHERS WON'T HAVE TO KNOW THAT LOSS.
YOU KNOW THE HUNTER'S RITE, MOPP. YOU WERE TOO LATE TO SAVE THIS WORLD, BUT YOU'LL HELP GROW A NEW ONE.
I HOPE I CAN SEE IT SOME DAY.

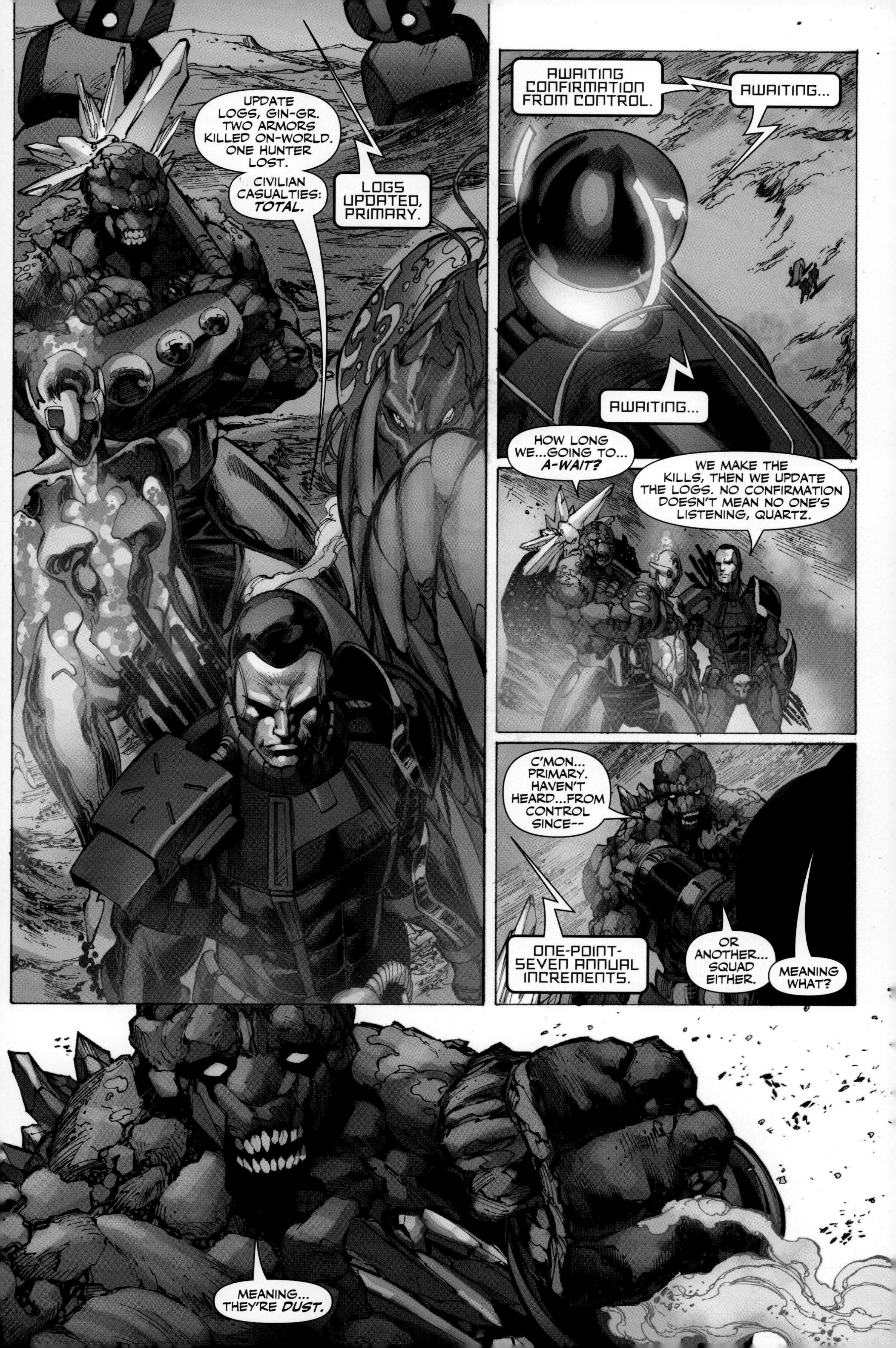
UPDATE LOGS, GIN-GR. TWO ARMORS KILLED ON-WORLD. ONE HUNTER LOST.
CIVILIAN CASUALTIES: *TOTAL.*
LOGS UPDATED, PRIMARY.
AWAITING CONFIRMATION FROM CONTROL.
AWAITING...
AWAITING...
HOW LONG WE...GOING TO... *A-WAIT?*
WE MAKE THE KILLS, THEN WE UPDATE THE LOGS. NO CONFIRMATION DOESN'T MEAN NO ONE'S LISTENING, QUARTZ.
C'MON... PRIMARY. HAVEN'T HEARD...FROM CONTROL SINCE--
ONE-POINT-SEVEN ANNUAL INCREMENTS.
OR ANOTHER... SQUAD EITHER.
MEANING WHAT?
MEANING... THEY'RE *DUST.*

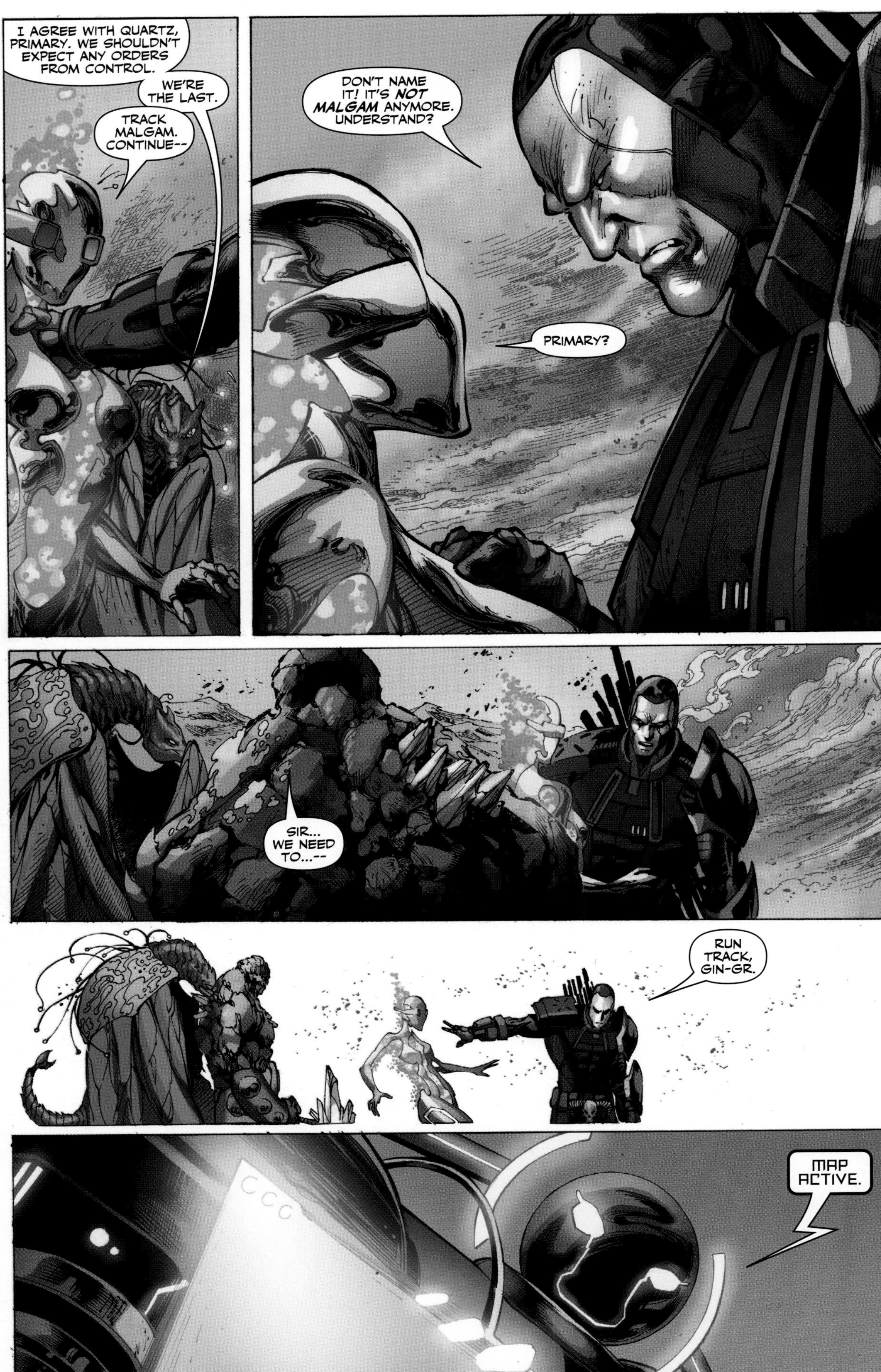
I AGREE WITH QUARTZ, PRIMARY. WE SHOULDN'T EXPECT ANY ORDERS FROM CONTROL.
WE'RE THE LAST.
TRACK MALGAM. CONTINUE--
DON'T NAME IT! IT'S NOT MALGAM ANYMORE. UNDERSTAND?
PRIMARY?
SIR... WE NEED TO...--
RUN TRACK, GIN-GR.
MAP ACTIVE.

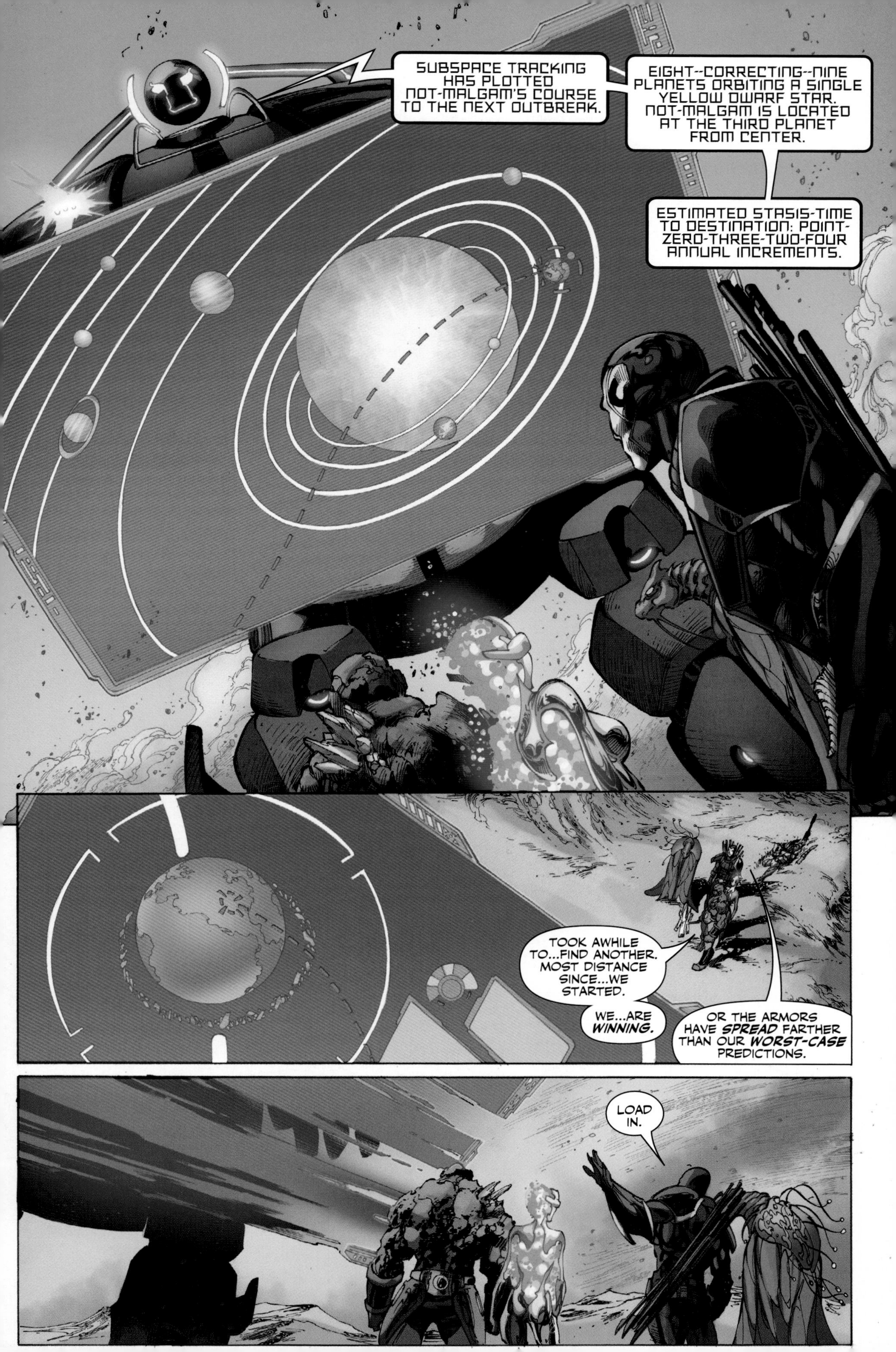
SUBSPACE TRACKING HAS PLOTTED NOT-MALGAM'S COURSE TO THE NEXT OUTBREAK.
EIGHT--CORRECTING--NINE PLANETS ORBITING A SINGLE YELLOW DWARF STAR. NOT-MALGAM IS LOCATED AT THE THIRD PLANET FROM CENTER.
ESTIMATED STASIS-TIME TO DESTINATION: POINT-ZERO-THREE-TWO-FOUR ANNUAL INCREMENTS.
TOOK AWHILE TO...FIND ANOTHER. MOST DISTANCE SINCE...WE STARTED.
WE...ARE *WINNING.*
OR THE ARMORS HAVE *SPREAD* FARTHER THAN OUR *WORST-CASE* PREDICTIONS.
LOAD IN.

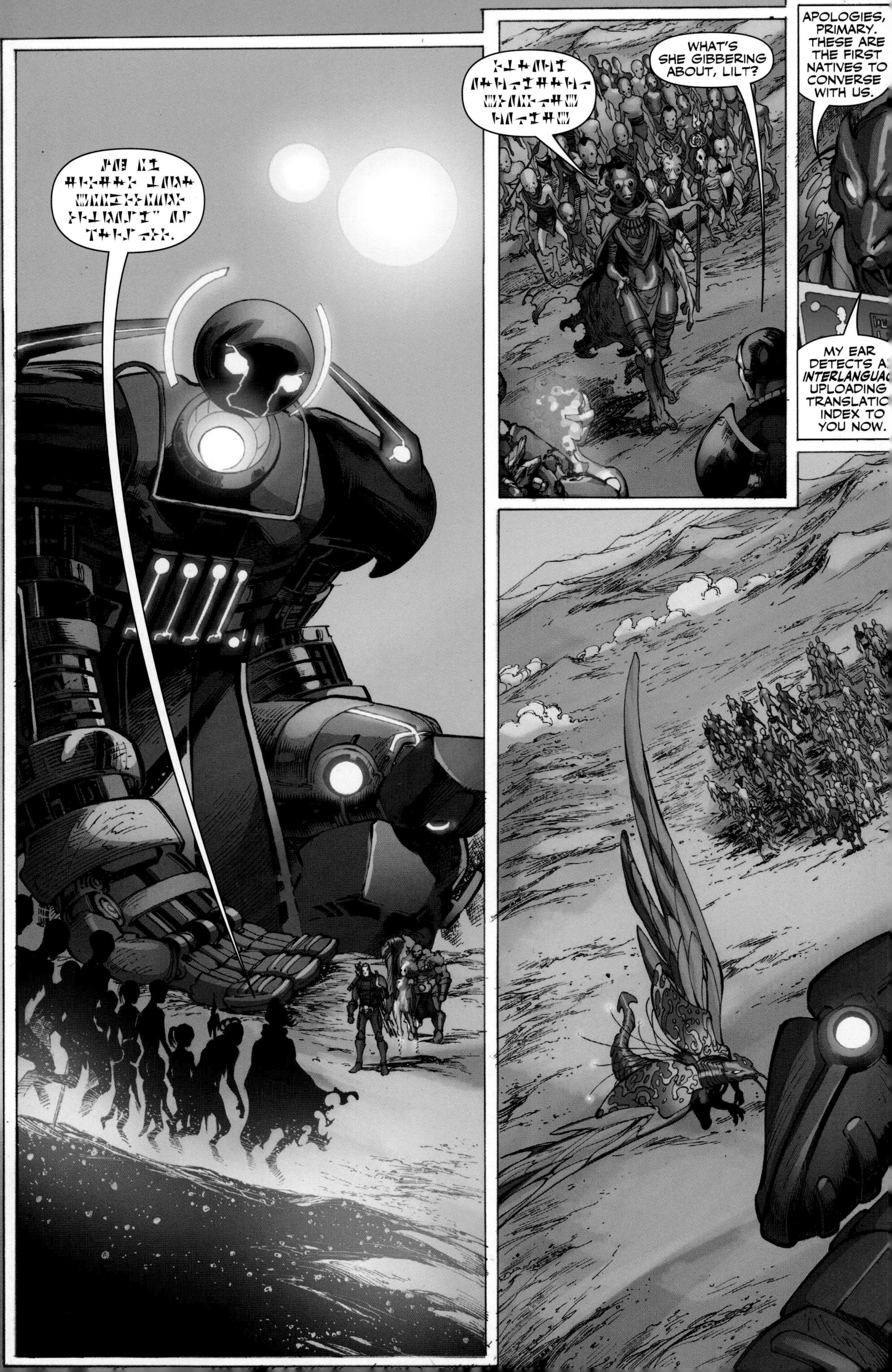
WHAT'S SHE GIBBERING ABOUT, LILT?
APOLOGIES, PRIMARY. THESE ARE THE FIRST NATIVES TO CONVERSE WITH US.
MY EAR DETECTS A *INTERLANGUA* UPLOADING TRANSLATI INDEX TO YOU NOW.

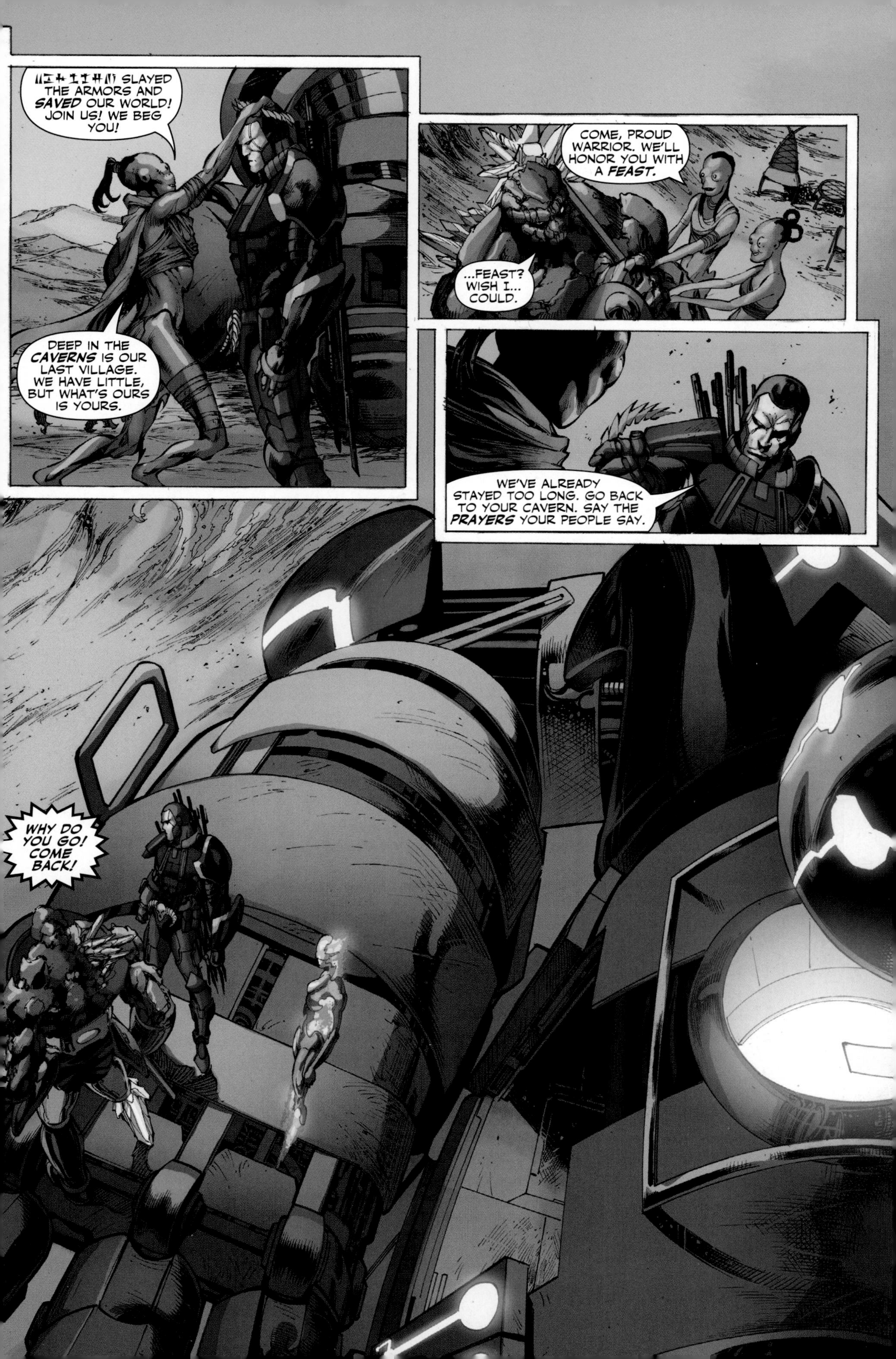
SLAYED THE ARMORS AND SAVED OUR WORLD! JOIN US! WE BEG YOU!
DEEP IN THE CAVERNS IS OUR LAST VILLAGE. WE HAVE LITTLE, BUT WHAT'S OURS IS YOURS.
COME, PROUD WARRIOR. WE'LL HONOR YOU WITH A FEAST.
...FEAST? WISH I... COULD.
WE'VE ALREADY STAYED TOO LONG. GO BACK TO YOUR CAVERN. SAY THE PRAYERS YOUR PEOPLE SAY.
WHY DO YOU GO! COME BACK!

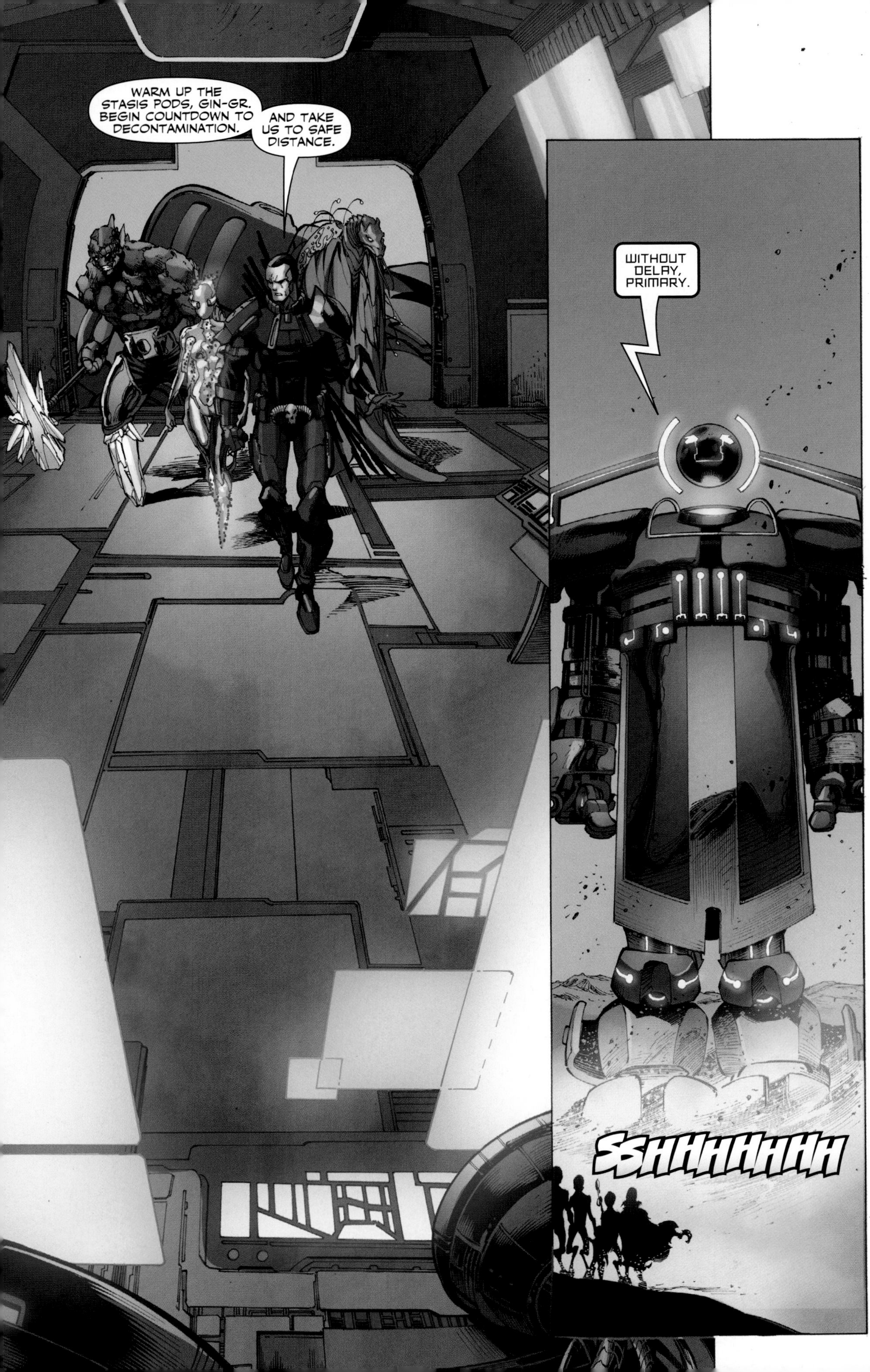

WARM UP THE STASIS PODS, GIN-GR. BEGIN COUNTDOWN TO DECONTAMINATION.
AND TAKE US TO SAFE DISTANCE.
WITHOUT DELAY, PRIMARY.
SSHHHHHHH

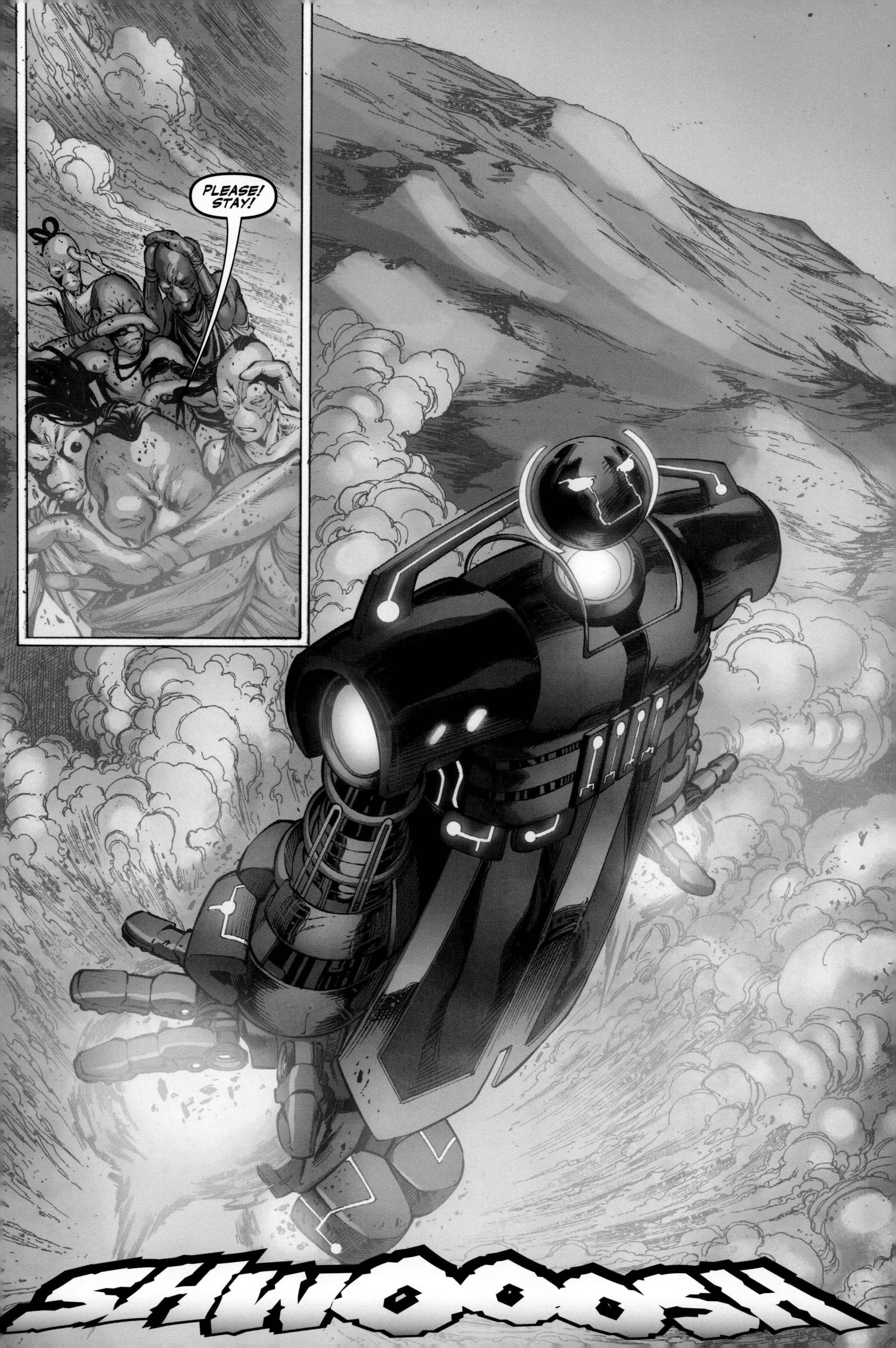
PLEASE! STAY!
SHWOOOSH

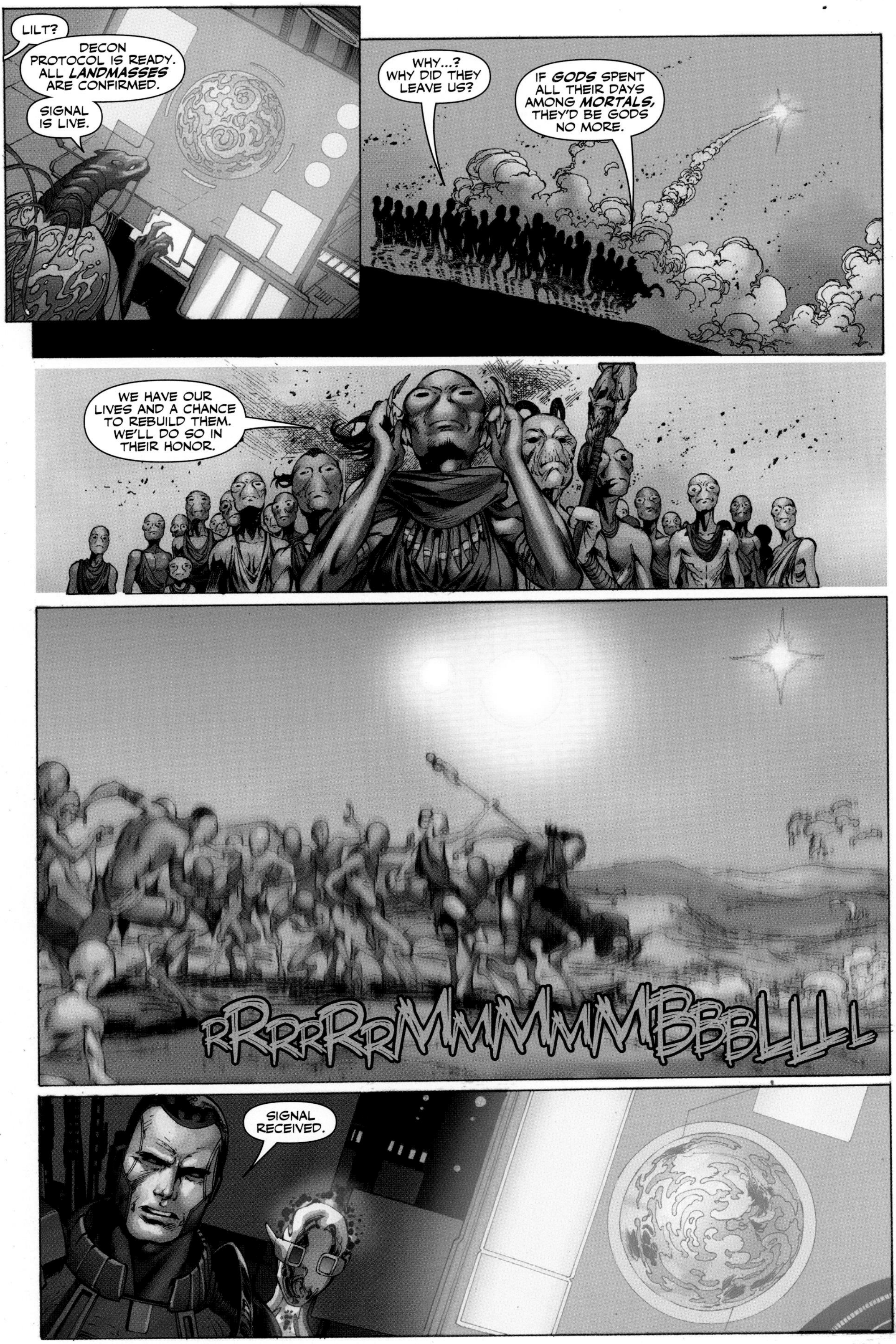

LILT?
DECON PROTOCOL IS READY. ALL *LANDMASSES* ARE CONFIRMED.
SIGNAL IS LIVE.
WHY...? WHY DID THEY LEAVE US?
IF *GODS* SPENT ALL THEIR DAYS AMONG *MORTALS,* THEY'D BE GODS NO MORE.
WE HAVE OUR LIVES AND A CHANCE TO REBUILD THEM. WE'LL DO SO IN THEIR HONOR.
RRRRRRRMMMMMMBBBLLLL
SIGNAL RECEIVED.

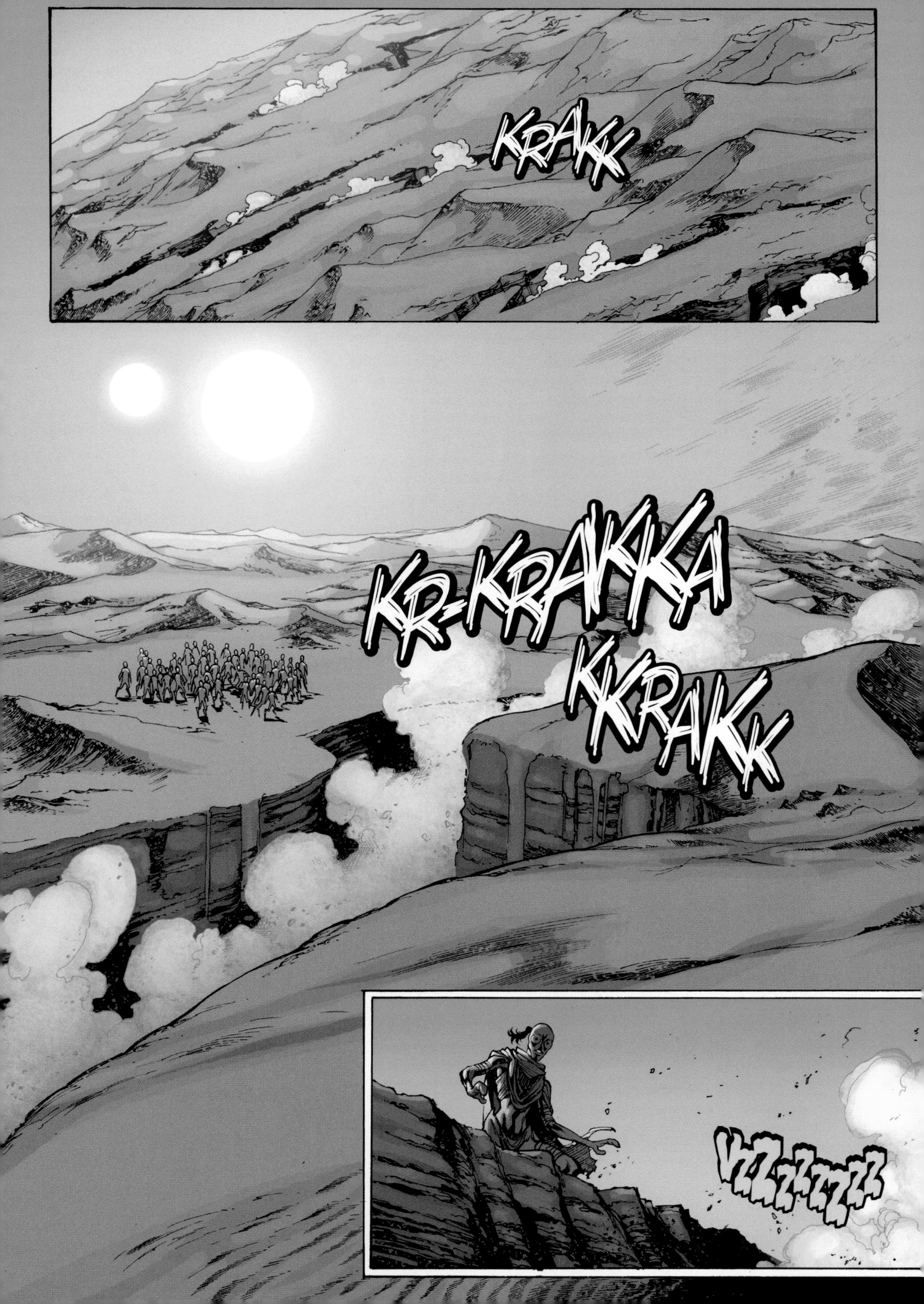
KRAKK
KR-KRAKKA
KKRAKK
VZZZZZZZZZ

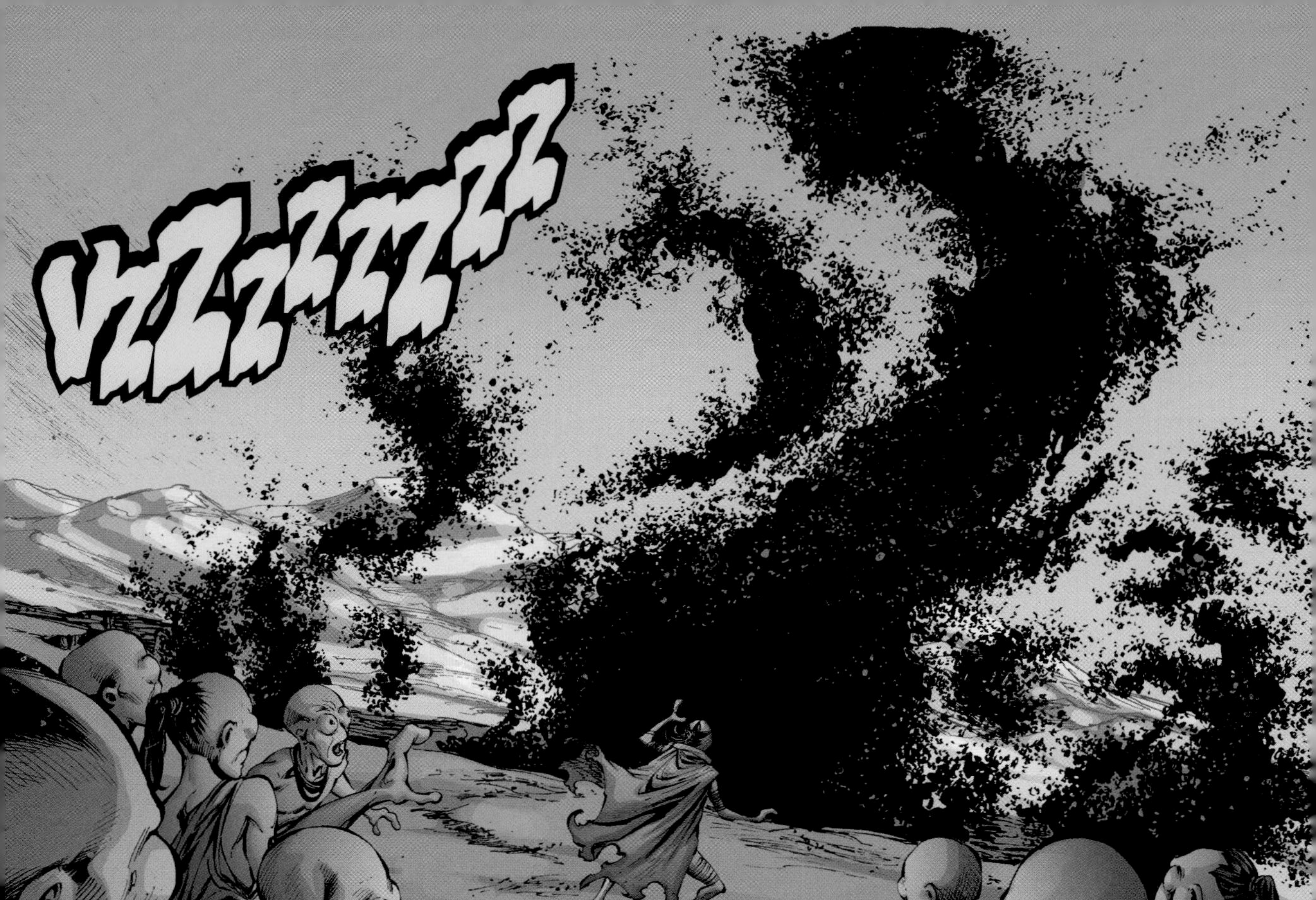
VZZZZZZZZZZ
THE GODS HAVE FORSAKEN US!
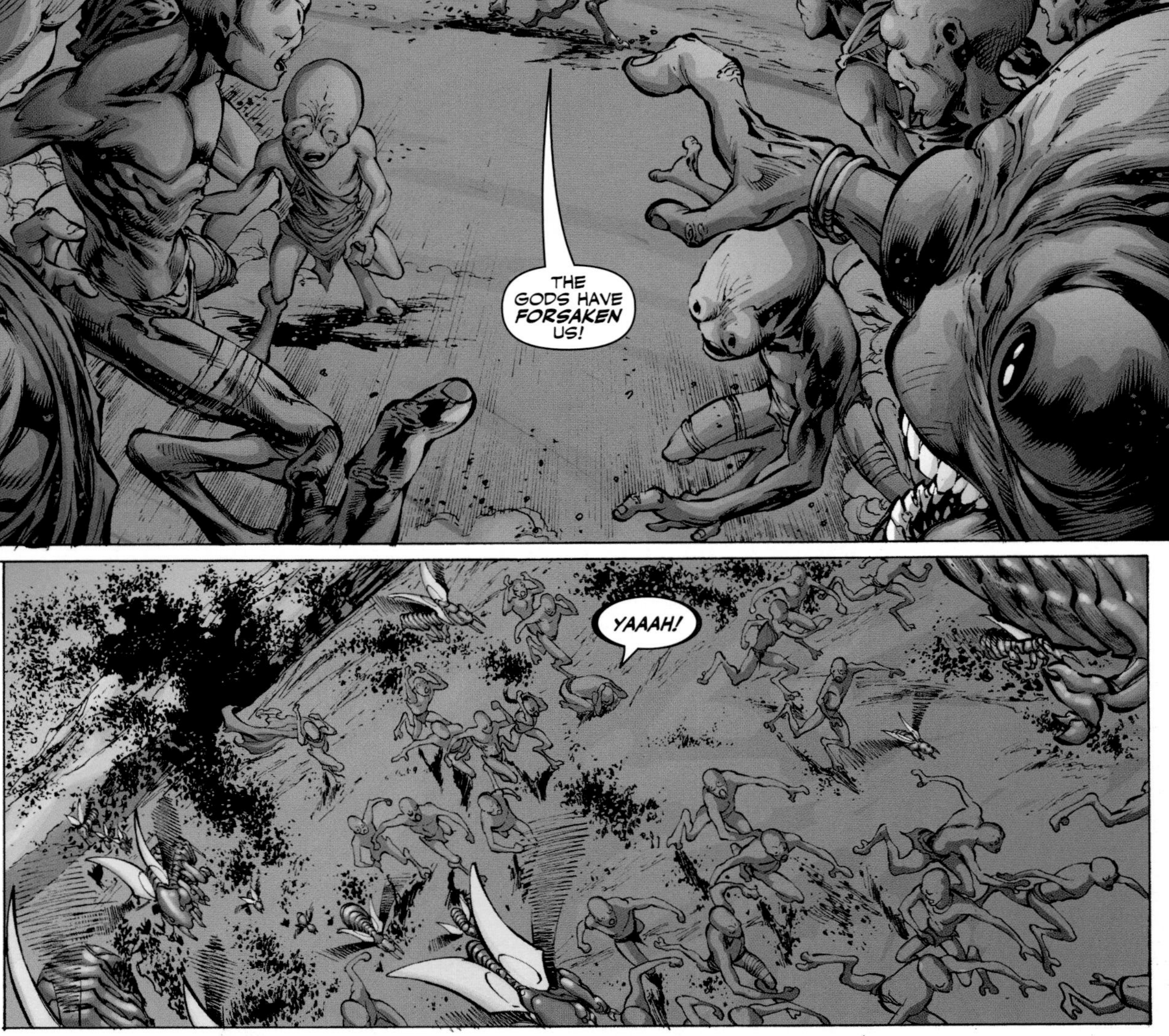
YAAAH!

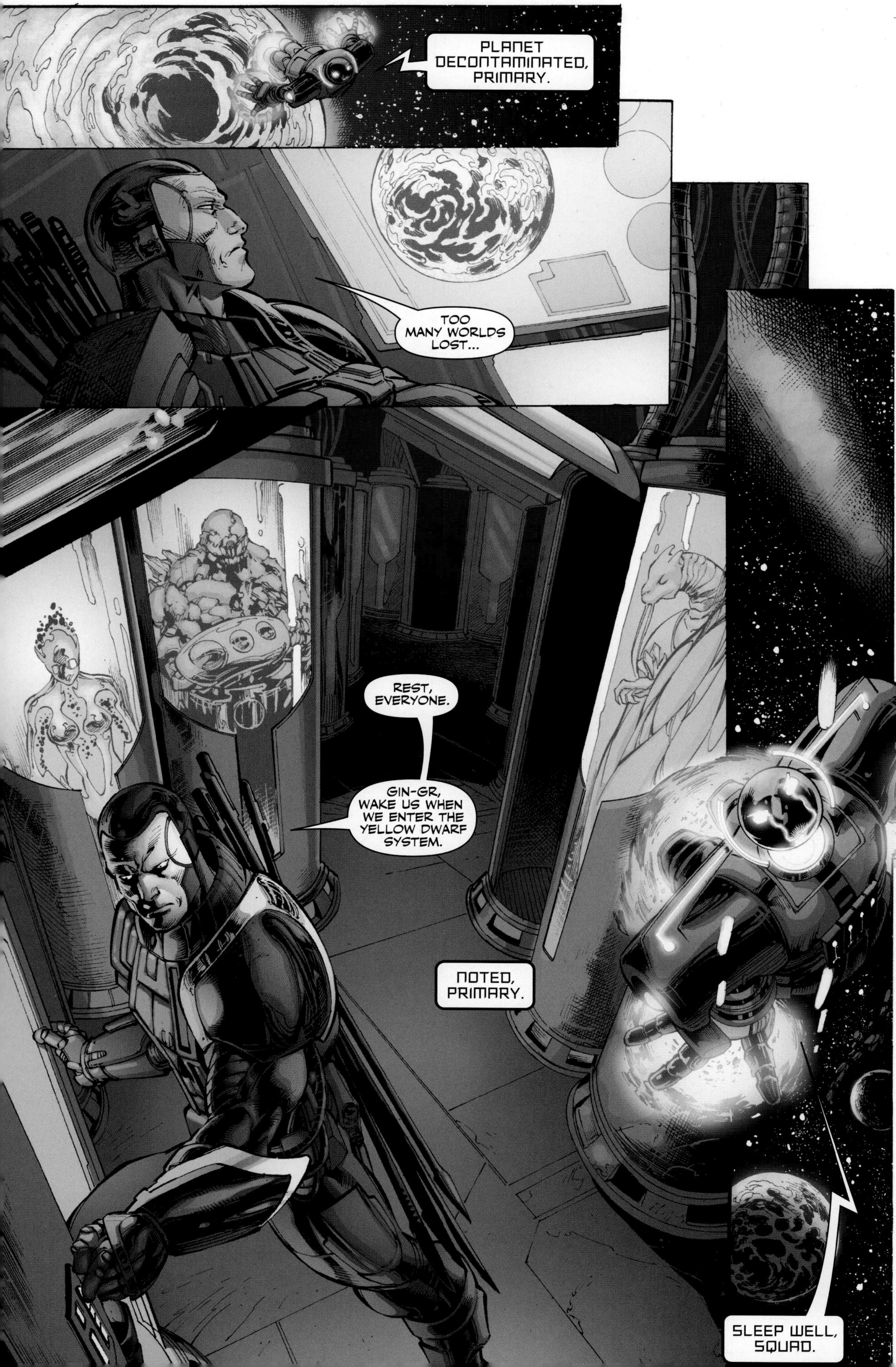

PLANET DECONTAMINATED, PRIMARY.
TOO MANY WORLDS LOST...
REST, EVERYONE.
GIN-GR, WAKE US WHEN WE ENTER THE YELLOW DWARF SYSTEM.
NOTED, PRIMARY.
SLEEP WELL, SQUAD.

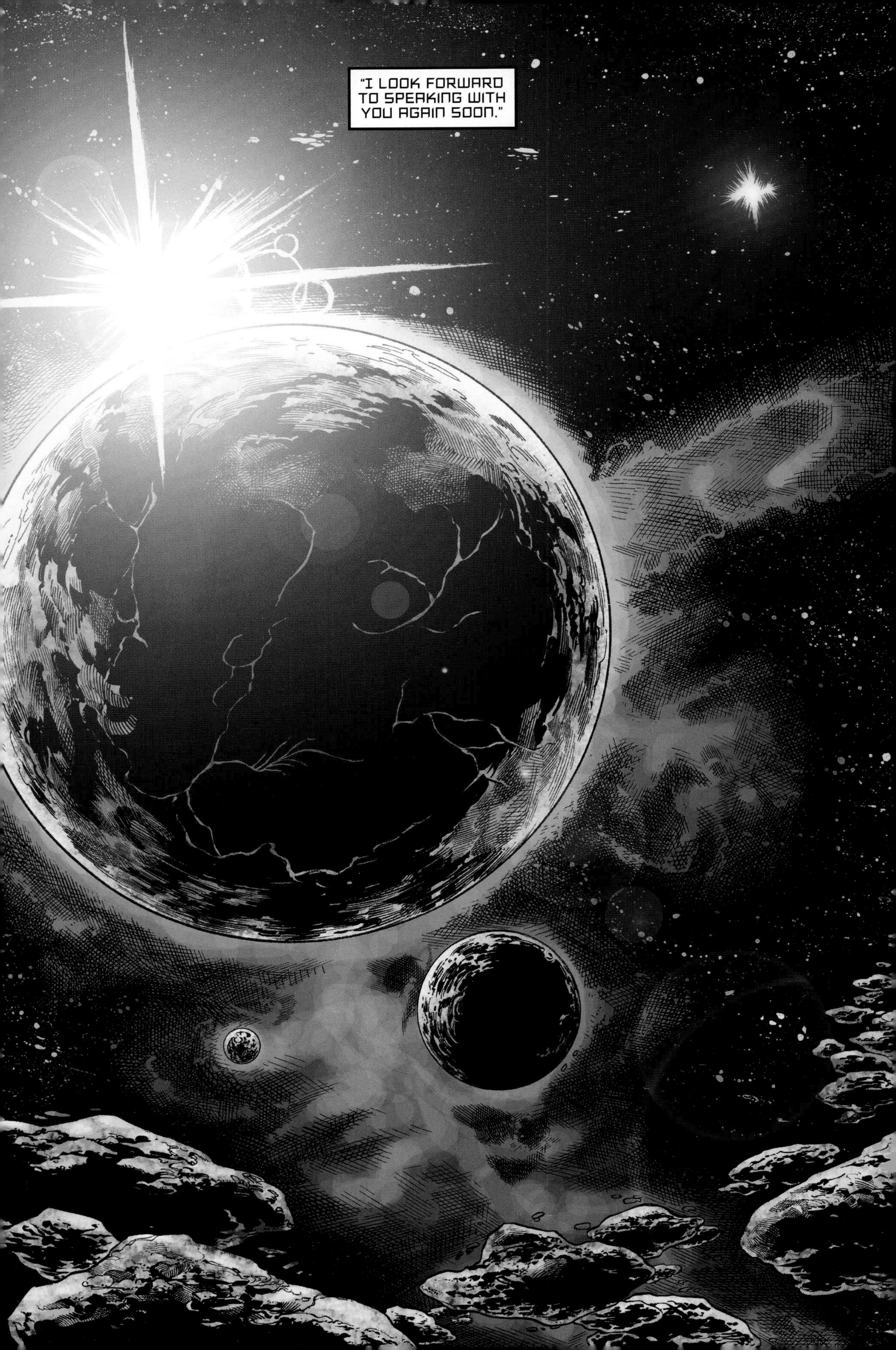
"I LOOK FORWARD TO SPEAKING WITH YOU AGAIN SOON."

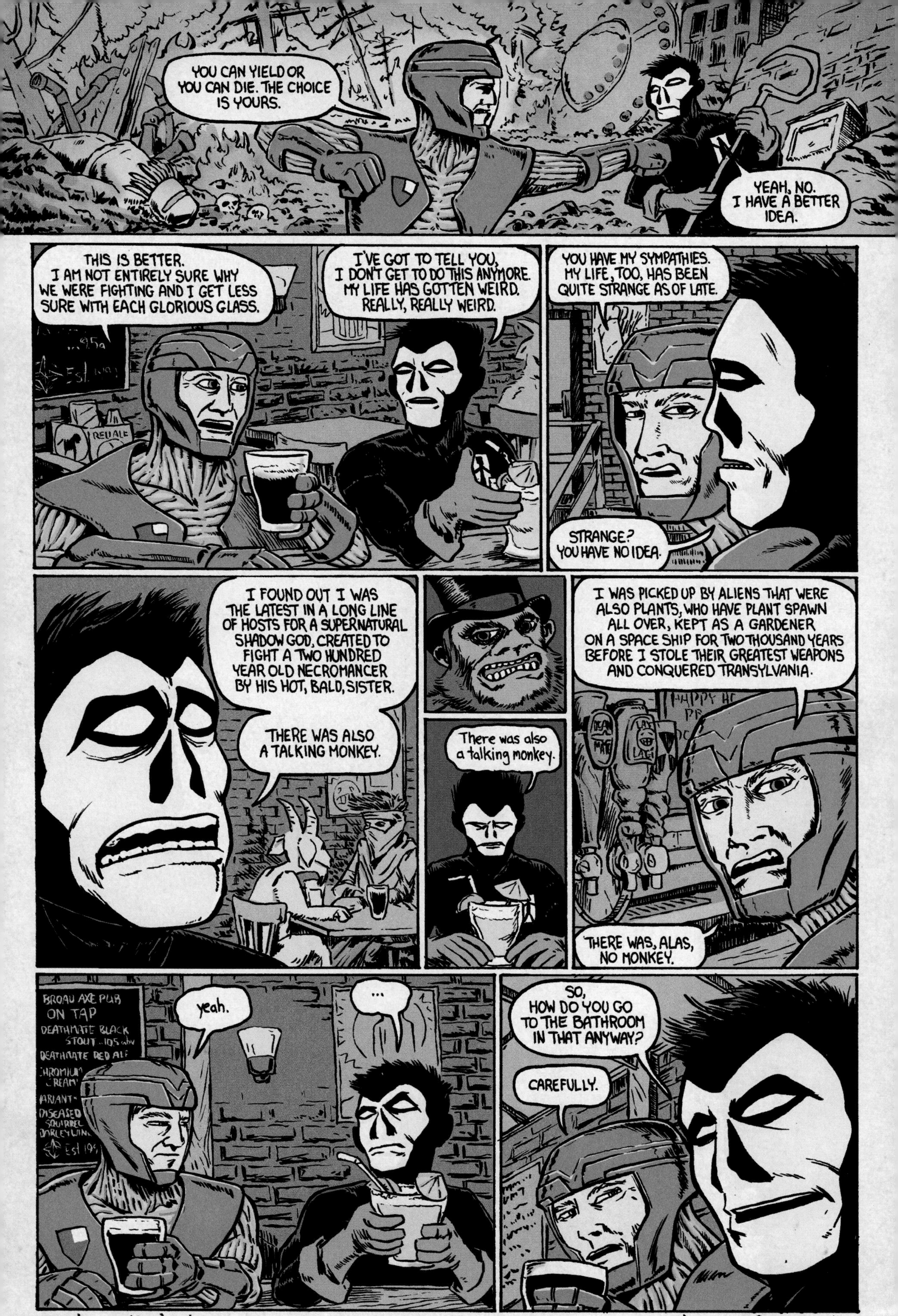
YOU CAN YIELD OR YOU CAN DIE. THE CHOICE IS YOURS.
YEAH, NO. I HAVE A BETTER IDEA.
THIS IS BETTER. I AM NOT ENTIRELY SURE WHY WE WERE FIGHTING AND I GET LESS SURE WITH EACH GLORIOUS GLASS.
I'VE GOT TO TELL YOU, I DON'T GET TO DO THIS ANYMORE. MY LIFE HAS GOTTEN WEIRD. REALLY, REALLY WEIRD.
YOU HAVE MY SYMPATHIES. MY LIFE, TOO, HAS BEEN QUITE STRANGE AS OF LATE.
STRANGE? YOU HAVE NO IDEA.
I FOUND OUT I WAS THE LATEST IN A LONG LINE OF HOSTS FOR A SUPERNATURAL SHADOW GOD, CREATED TO FIGHT A TWO HUNDRED YEAR OLD NECROMANCER BY HIS HOT, BALD, SISTER.
THERE WAS ALSO A TALKING MONKEY.
There was also a talking monkey.
I WAS PICKED UP BY ALIENS THAT WERE ALSO PLANTS, WHO HAVE PLANT SPAWN ALL OVER, KEPT AS A GARDENER ON A SPACE SHIP FOR TWO THOUSAND YEARS BEFORE I STOLE THEIR GREATEST WEAPONS AND CONQUERED TRANSYLVANIA.
THERE WAS, ALAS, NO MONKEY.
BROAD AXE PUB
ON TAP
DEATHMATE BLACK STOUT
DEATHMATE RED ALE
yeah.
...
SO, HOW DO YOU GO TO THE BATHROOM IN THAT ANYWAY?
CAREFULLY.

words: justin jordan

pictures: rafer roberts

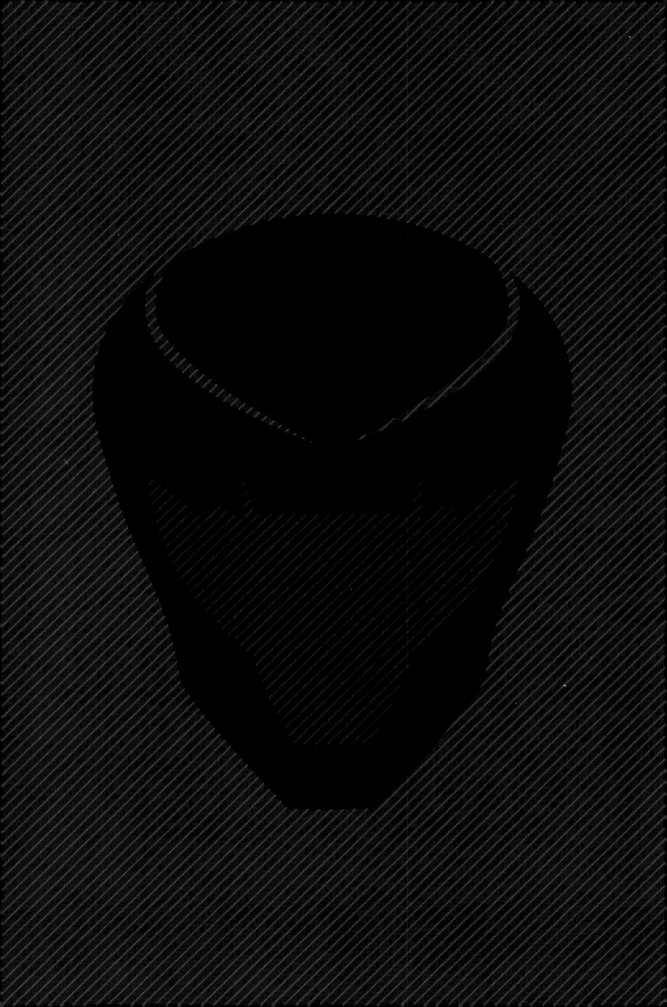

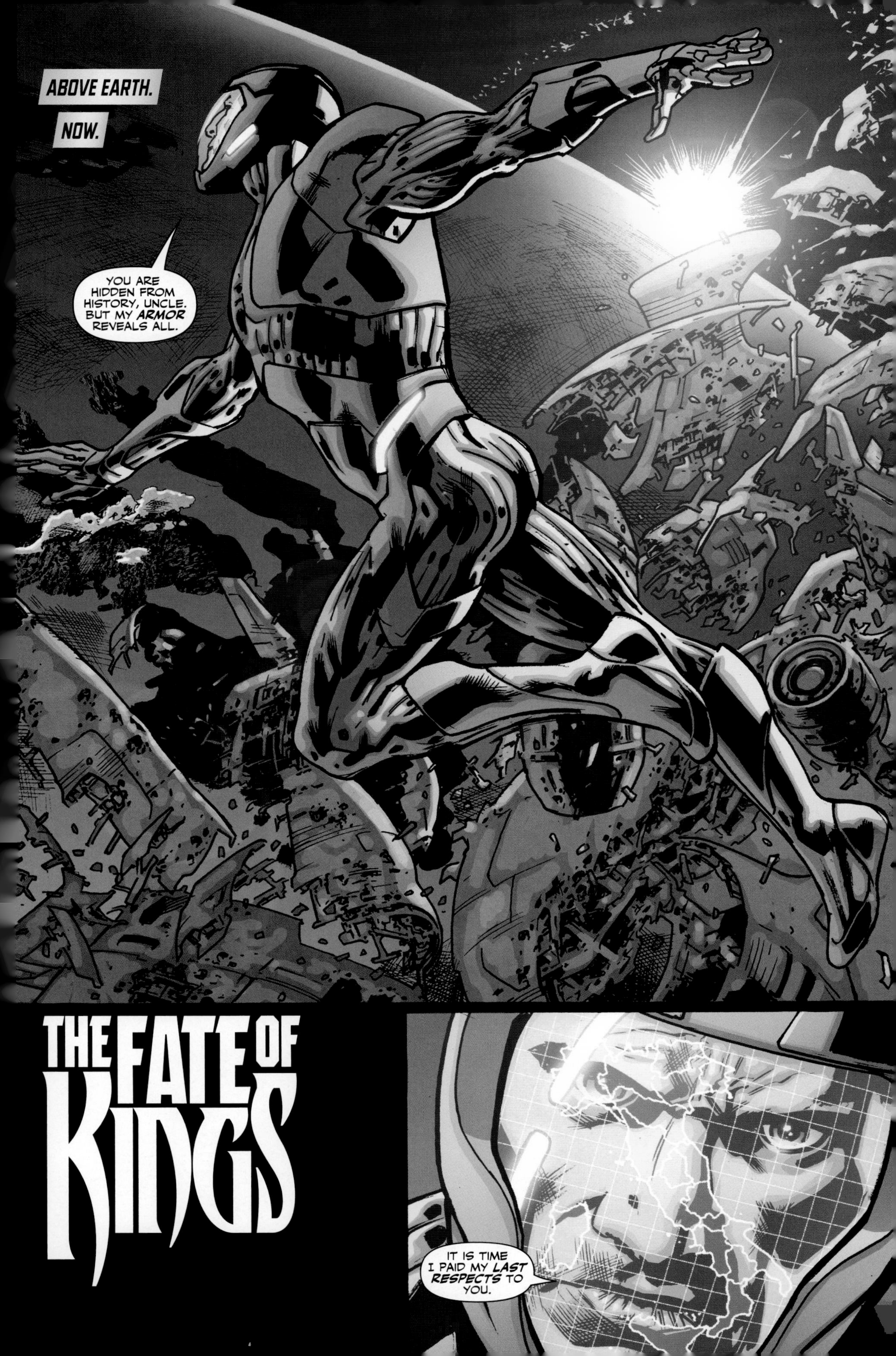
ABOVE EARTH.
NOW.
YOU ARE HIDDEN FROM HISTORY, UNCLE. BUT MY ARMOR REVEALS ALL.
THE FATE OF KINGS
IT IS TIME I PAID MY LAST RESPECTS TO YOU.

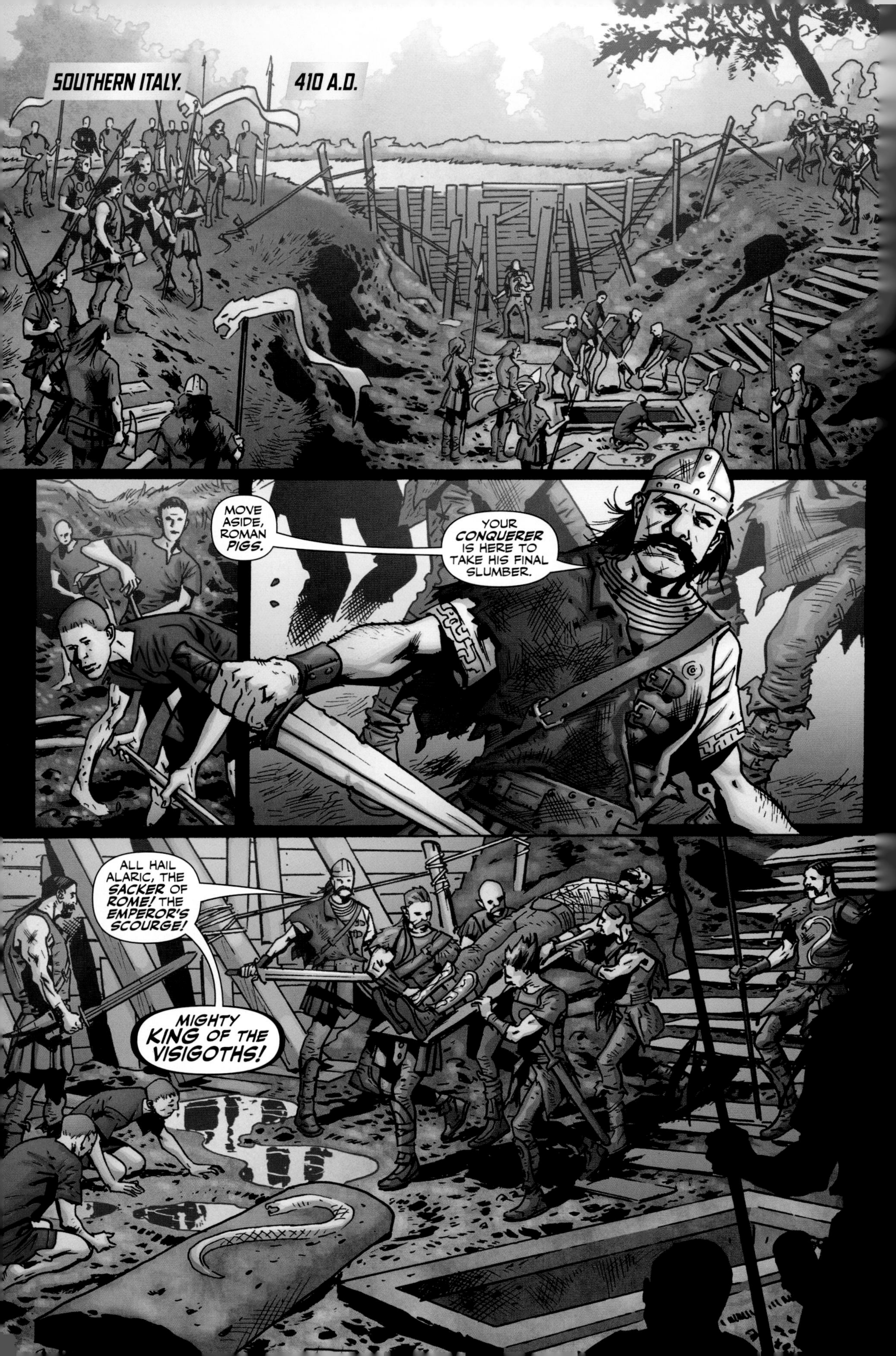
SOUTHERN ITALY.
410 A.D.
MOVE ASIDE, ROMAN PIGS.
YOUR CONQUERER IS HERE TO TAKE HIS FINAL SLUMBER.
ALL HAIL ALARIC, THE SACKER OF ROME! THE EMPEROR'S SCOURGE!
MIGHTY KING OF THE VISIGOTHS!

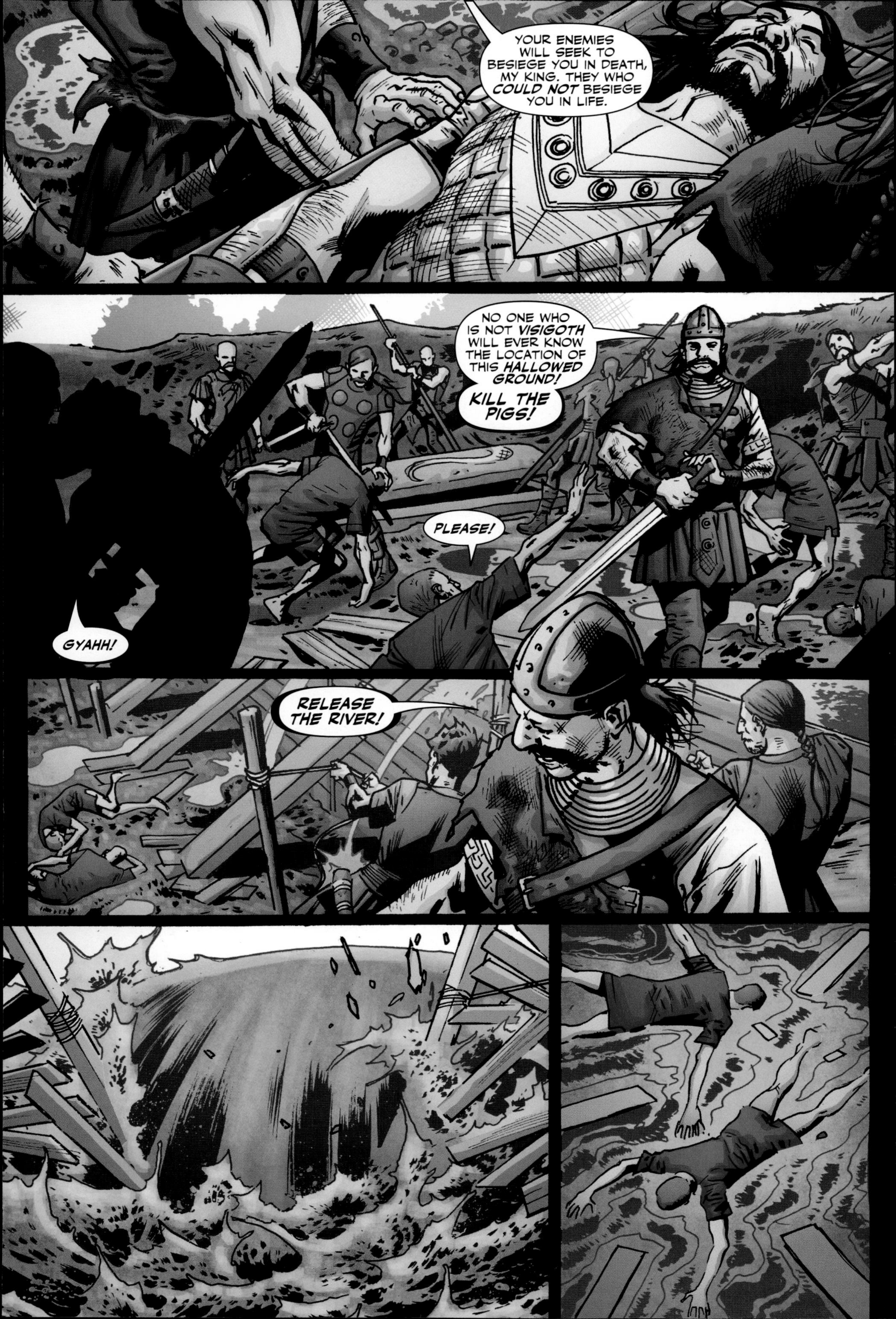
YOUR ENEMIES WILL SEEK TO BESIEGE YOU IN DEATH, MY KING. THEY WHO *COULD NOT* BESIEGE YOU IN LIFE.
NO ONE WHO IS NOT *VISIGOTH* WILL EVER KNOW THE LOCATION OF THIS *HALLOWED GROUND!*
KILL THE PIGS!
PLEASE!
GYAHH!
RELEASE THE RIVER!

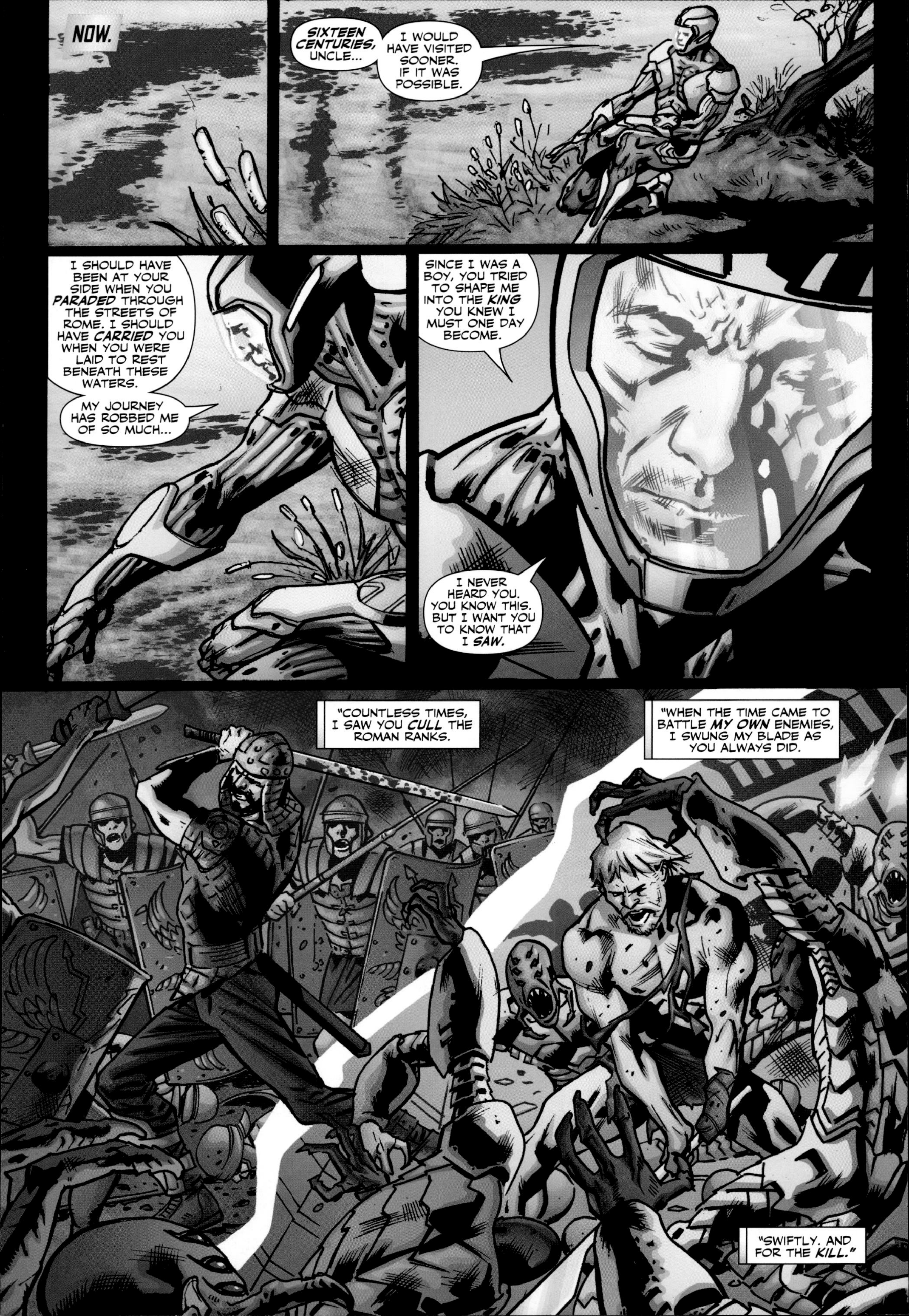
NOW.
SIXTEEN CENTURIES, UNCLE...
I WOULD HAVE VISITED SOONER. IF IT WAS POSSIBLE.
I SHOULD HAVE BEEN AT YOUR SIDE WHEN YOU PARADED THROUGH THE STREETS OF ROME. I SHOULD HAVE CARRIED YOU WHEN YOU WERE LAID TO REST BENEATH THESE WATERS.
MY JOURNEY HAS ROBBED ME OF SO MUCH...
SINCE I WAS A BOY, YOU TRIED TO SHAPE ME INTO THE KING YOU KNEW I MUST ONE DAY BECOME.
I NEVER HEARD YOU. YOU KNOW THIS. BUT I WANT YOU TO KNOW THAT I SAW.
"COUNTLESS TIMES, I SAW YOU CULL THE ROMAN RANKS.
"WHEN THE TIME CAME TO BATTLE MY OWN ENEMIES, I SWUNG MY BLADE AS YOU ALWAYS DID.
"SWIFTLY. AND FOR THE KILL."

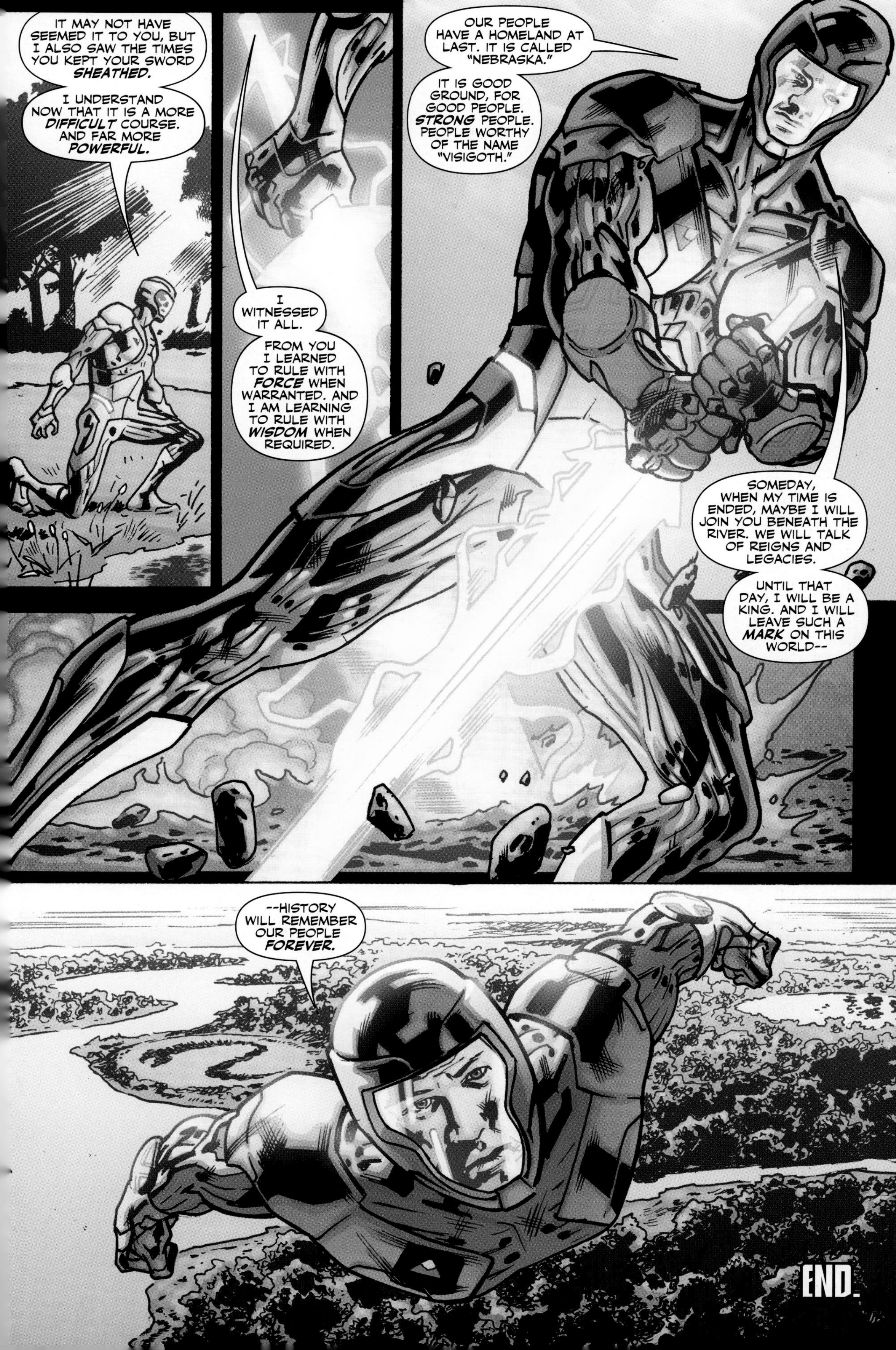
IT MAY NOT HAVE SEEMED IT TO YOU, BUT I ALSO SAW THE TIMES YOU KEPT YOUR SWORD SHEATHED.
I UNDERSTAND NOW THAT IT IS A MORE DIFFICULT COURSE. AND FAR MORE POWERFUL.
I WITNESSED IT ALL.
FROM YOU I LEARNED TO RULE WITH FORCE WHEN WARRANTED. AND I AM LEARNING TO RULE WITH WISDOM WHEN REQUIRED.
OUR PEOPLE HAVE A HOMELAND AT LAST. IT IS CALLED "NEBRASKA."
IT IS GOOD GROUND, FOR GOOD PEOPLE. STRONG PEOPLE. PEOPLE WORTHY OF THE NAME "VISIGOTH."
SOMEDAY, WHEN MY TIME IS ENDED, MAYBE I WILL JOIN YOU BENEATH THE RIVER. WE WILL TALK OF REIGNS AND LEGACIES.
UNTIL THAT DAY, I WILL BE A KING. AND I WILL LEAVE SUCH A MARK ON THIS WORLD--
--HISTORY WILL REMEMBER OUR PEOPLE FOREVER.
END.

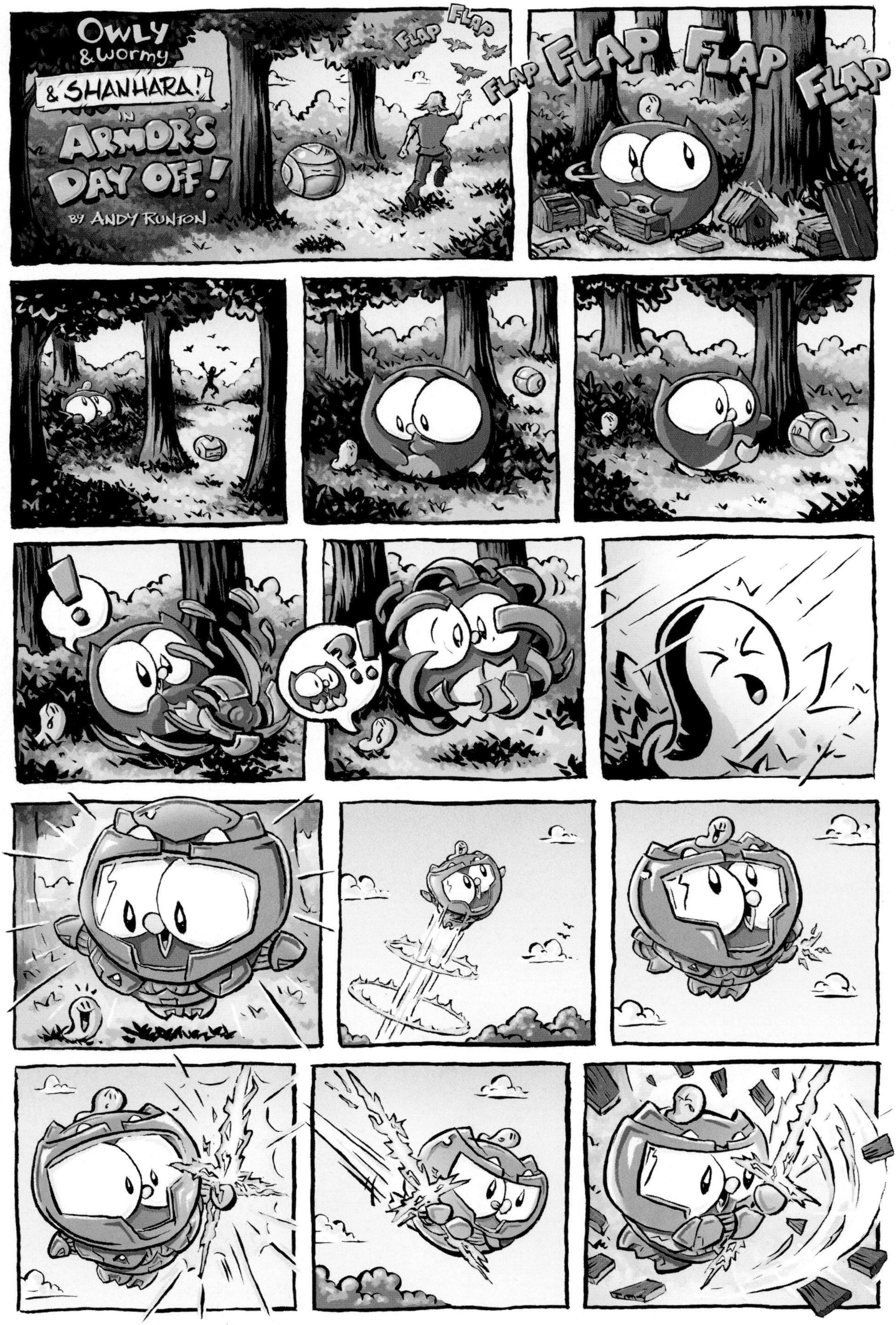

OWLY
& Wormy
& SHANHARA!
IN
ARMOR'S DAY OFF!
BY ANDY RUNTON
FLAP FLAP
FLAP FLAP FLAP FLAP FLAP

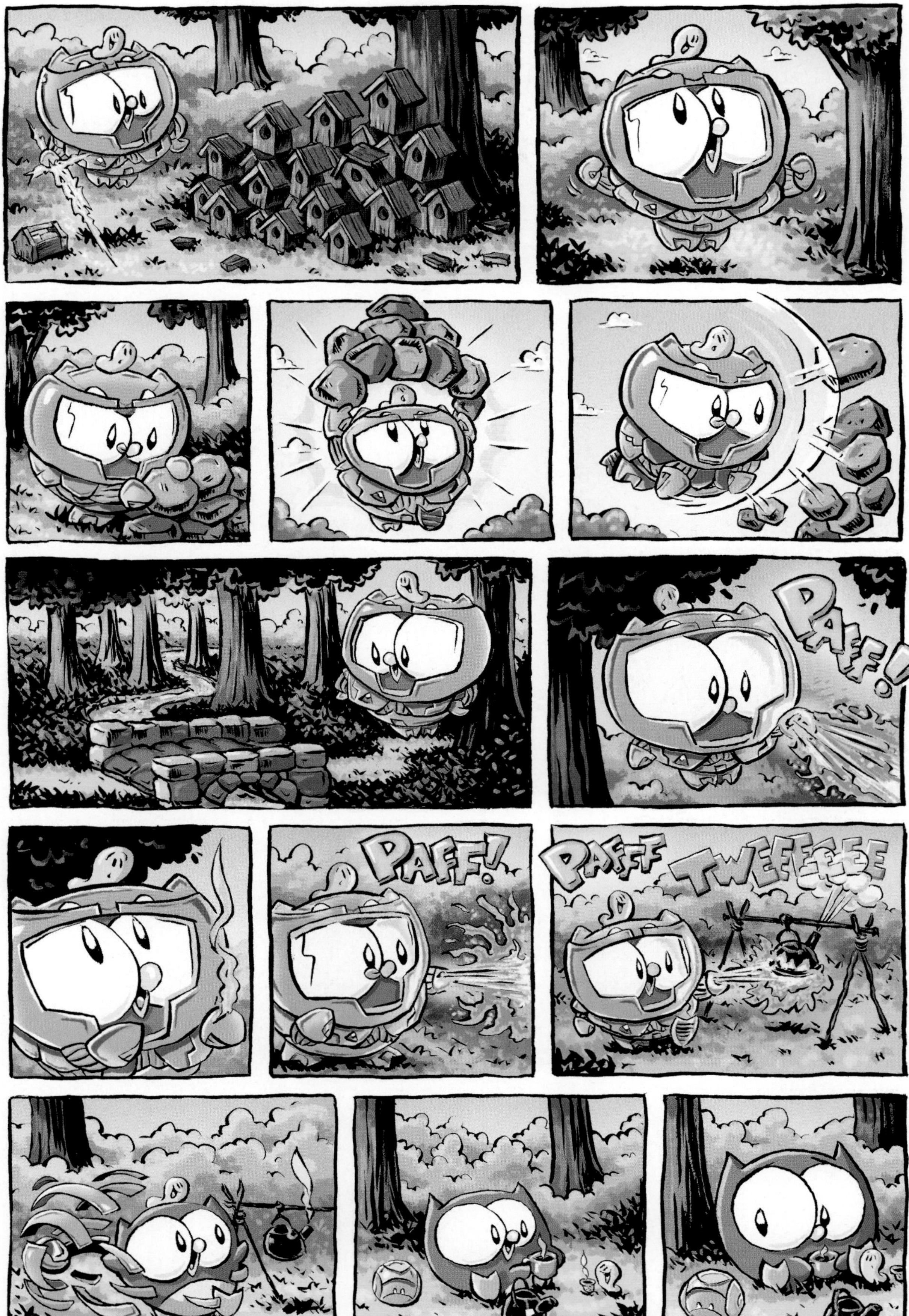
PAFF!
PAFF!
PAFFF
TWEEEEEE

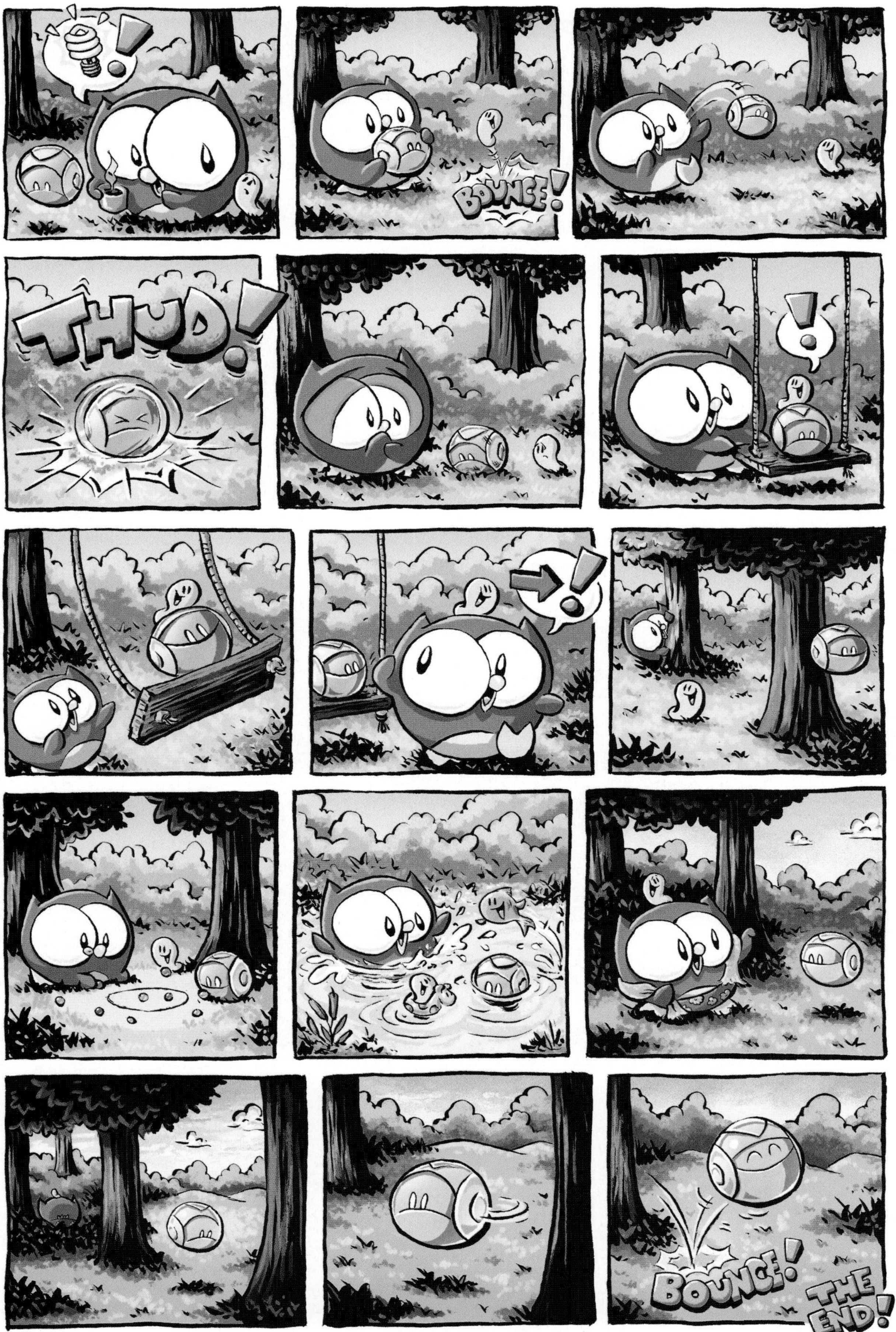
BOUNCE!
THUD!
BOUNCE!
THE END!

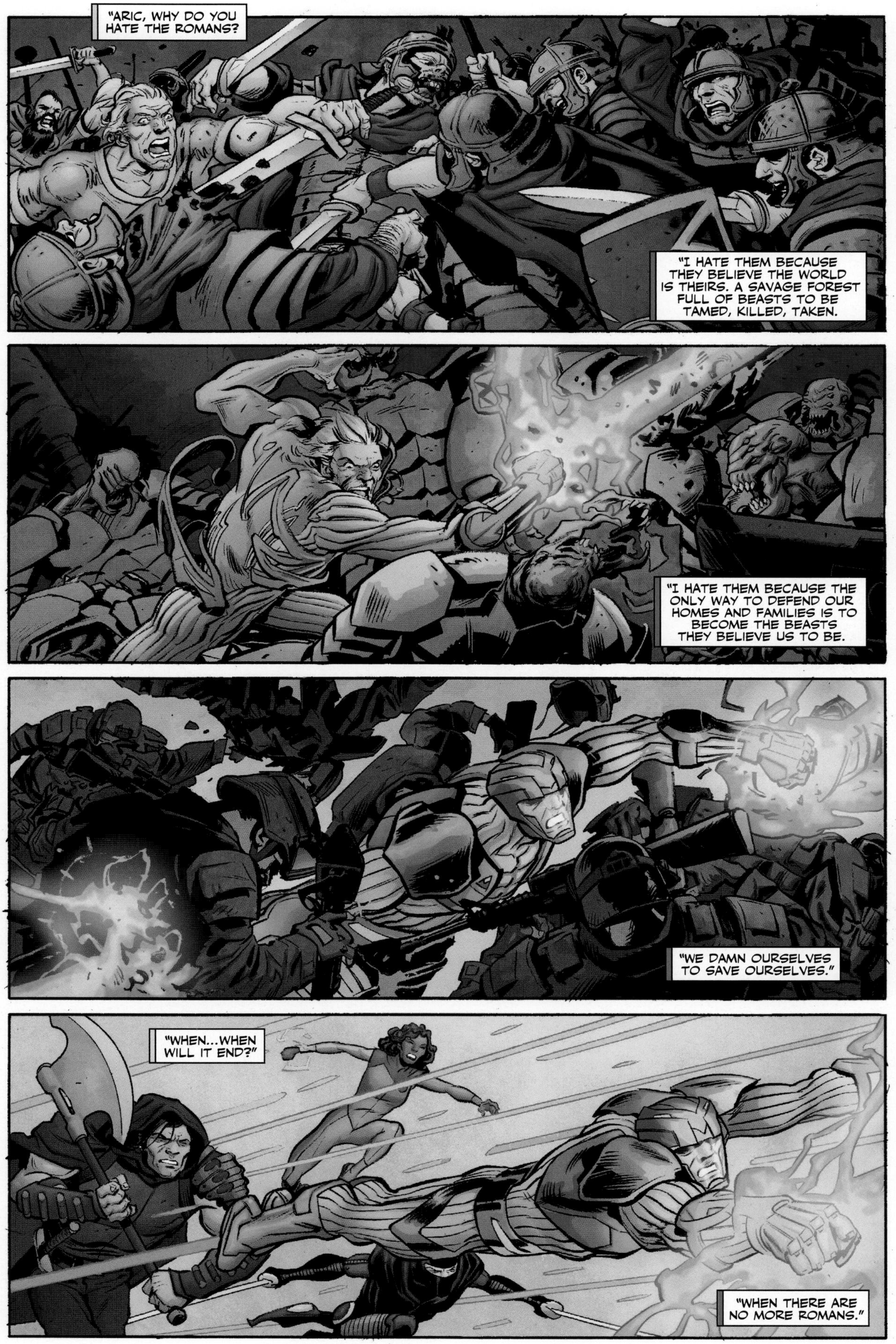
"ARIC, WHY DO YOU HATE THE ROMANS?
"I HATE THEM BECAUSE THEY BELIEVE THE WORLD IS THEIRS. A SAVAGE FOREST FULL OF BEASTS TO BE TAMED, KILLED, TAKEN.
"I HATE THEM BECAUSE THE ONLY WAY TO DEFEND OUR HOMES AND FAMILIES IS TO BECOME THE BEASTS THEY BELIEVE US TO BE.
"WE DAMN OURSELVES TO SAVE OURSELVES."
"WHEN...WHEN WILL IT END?"
"WHEN THERE ARE NO MORE ROMANS."

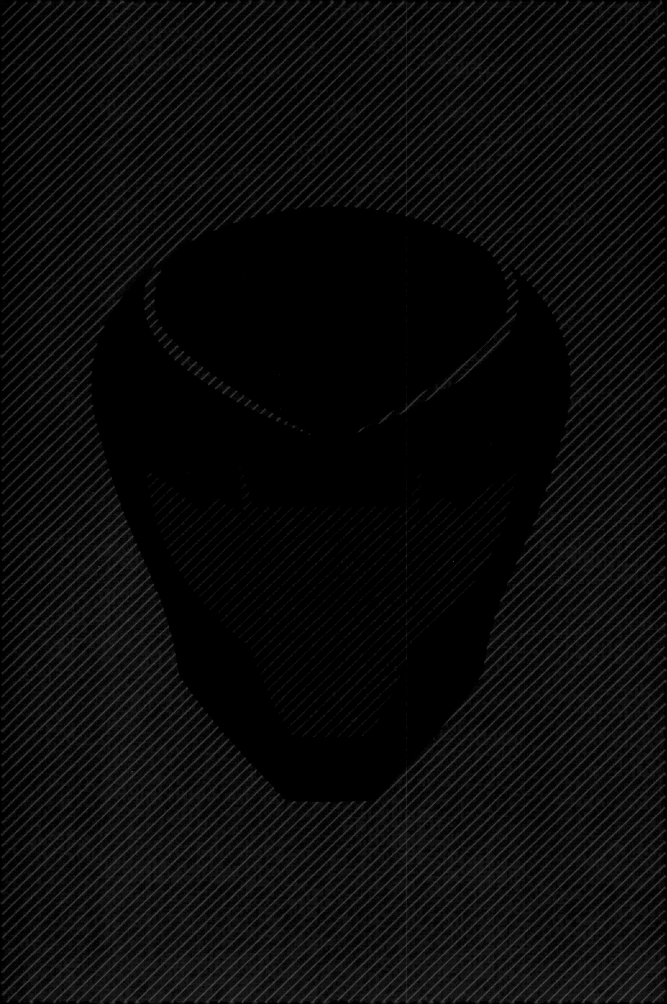

ARMOR HUNTERS

VALIANT
#1
ARMOR HUNTERS

VALIANT
ROBERT VENDITTI | DIEGO BERNARDO
#26
X-O MANOWAR
ARMOR HUNTERS

VALIANT
#2
ARMOR HUNTERS

VALIANT
#27
X-O MANOWAR
ARMOR HUNTERS

VALIANT
#3
ARMOR HUNTERS

VALIANT
#28
X-O MANOWAR
ARMOR HUNTERS

VALIANT
#4
ARMOR HUNTERS
THE EPIC CONCLUSION!

VALIANT
#29
X-O MANOWAR
ARMOR HUNTERS

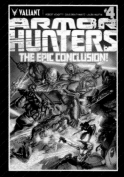

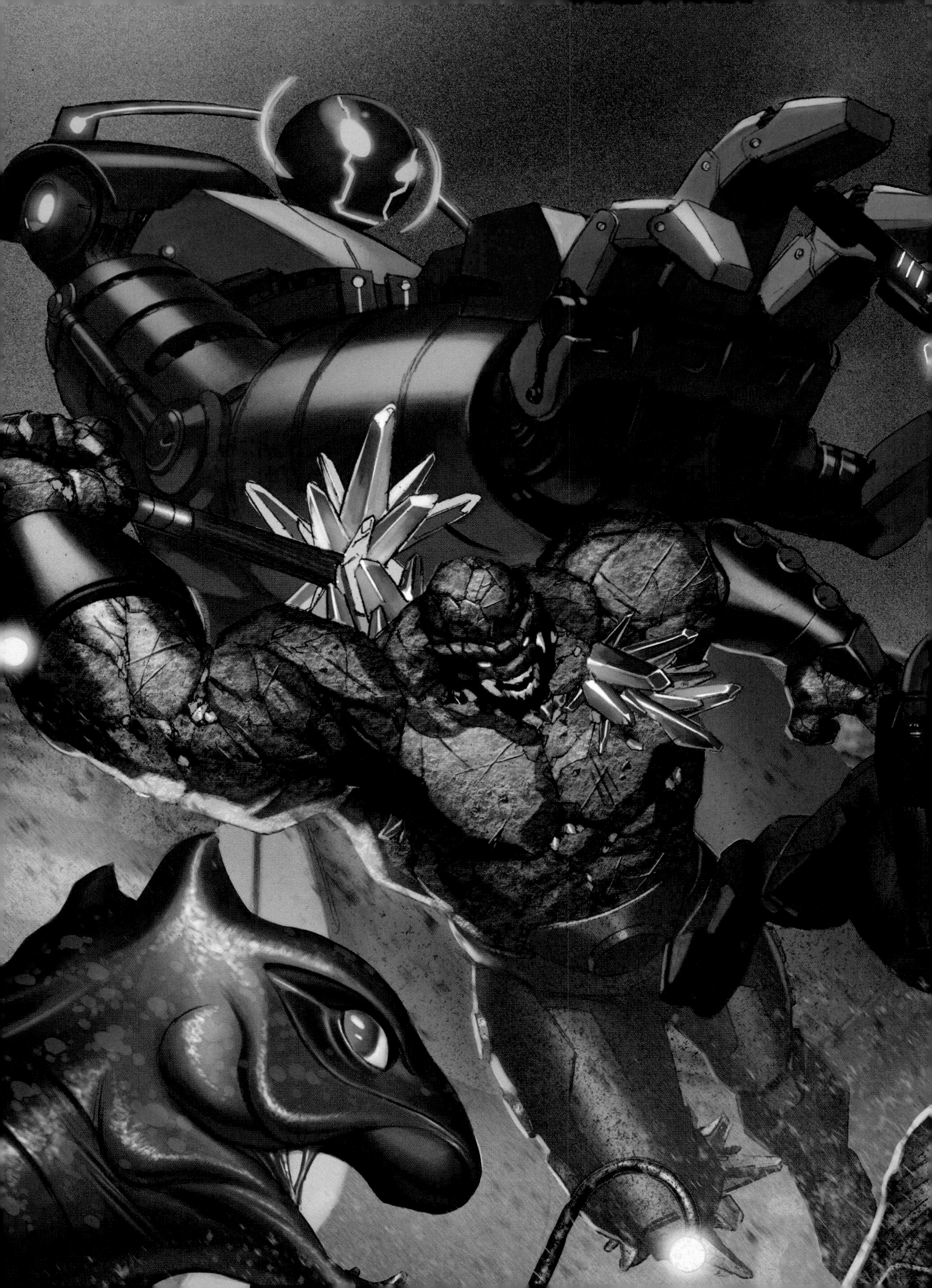

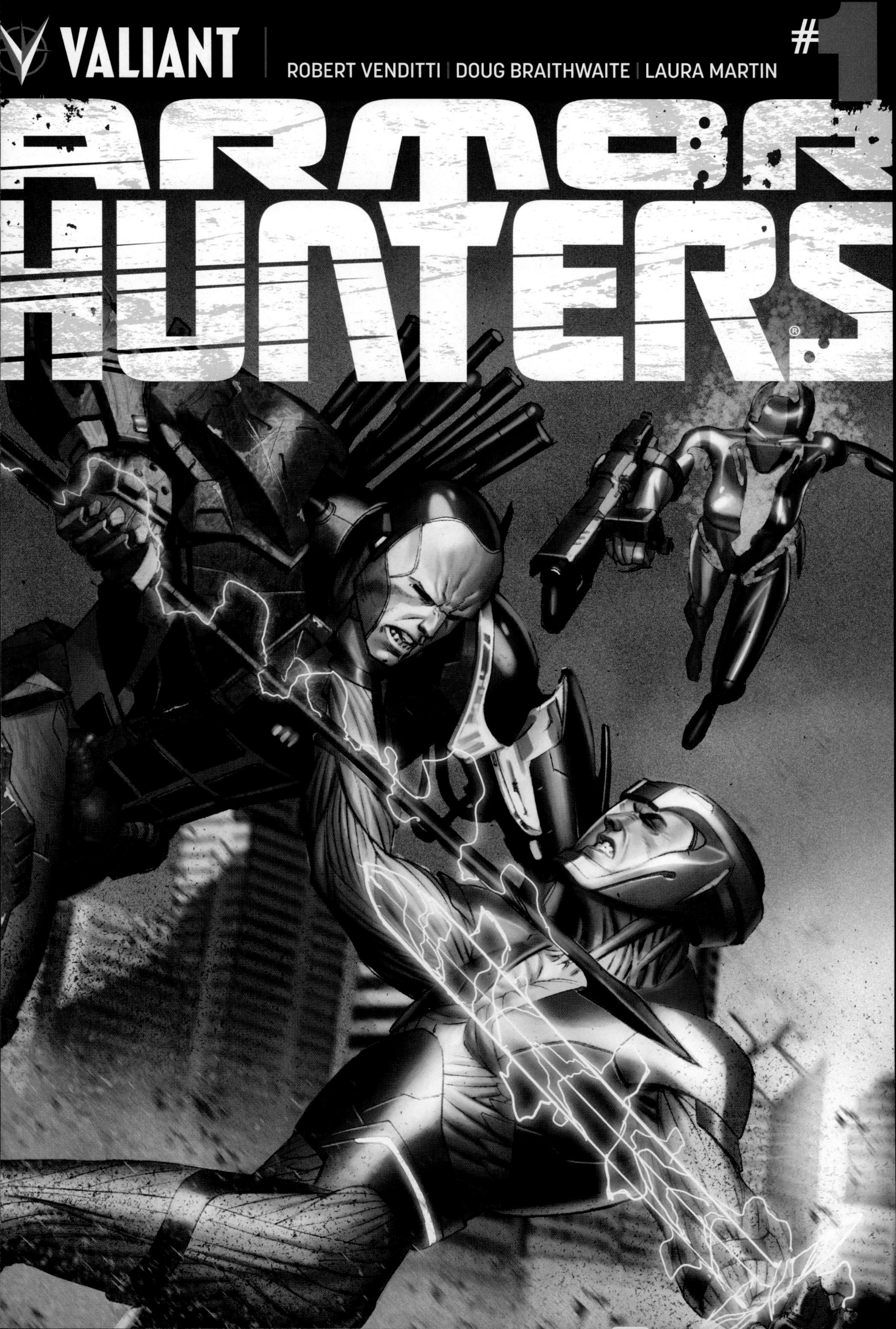
VALIANT
#1
ROBERT VENDITTI | DOUG BRAITHWAITE | LAURA MARTIN
ARMOR HUNTERS®

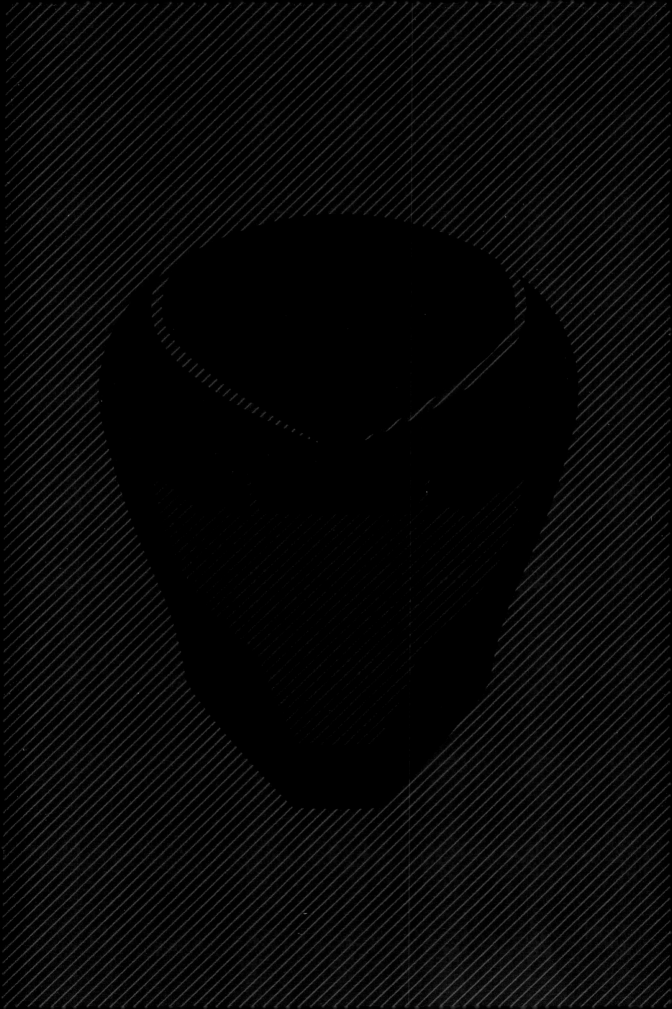

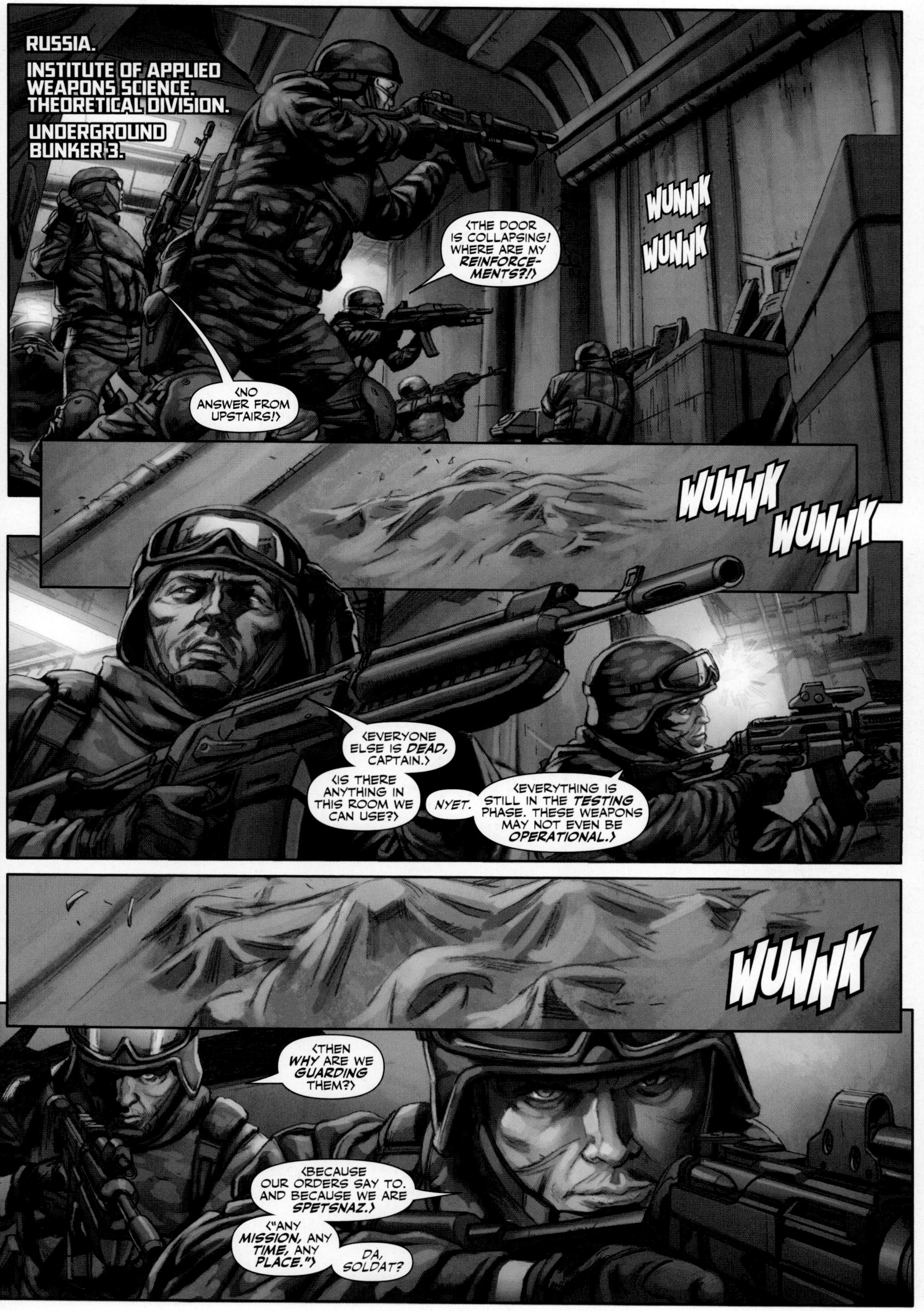
RUSSIA.
INSTITUTE OF APPLIED WEAPONS SCIENCE. THEORETICAL DIVISION.
UNDERGROUND BUNKER 3.
WUNNK WUNNK
<THE DOOR IS COLLAPSING! WHERE ARE MY REINFORCEMENTS?!>
<NO ANSWER FROM UPSTAIRS!>
WUNNK WUNNK
<EVERYONE ELSE IS DEAD, CAPTAIN.>
<IS THERE ANYTHING IN THIS ROOM WE CAN USE?>
NYET.
<EVERYTHING IS STILL IN THE TESTING PHASE. THESE WEAPONS MAY NOT EVEN BE OPERATIONAL.>
WUNNK
<THEN WHY ARE WE GUARDING THEM?>
<BECAUSE OUR ORDERS SAY TO. AND BECAUSE WE ARE SPETSNAZ.>
<"ANY MISSION, ANY TIME, ANY PLACE.">
DA, SOLDAT?

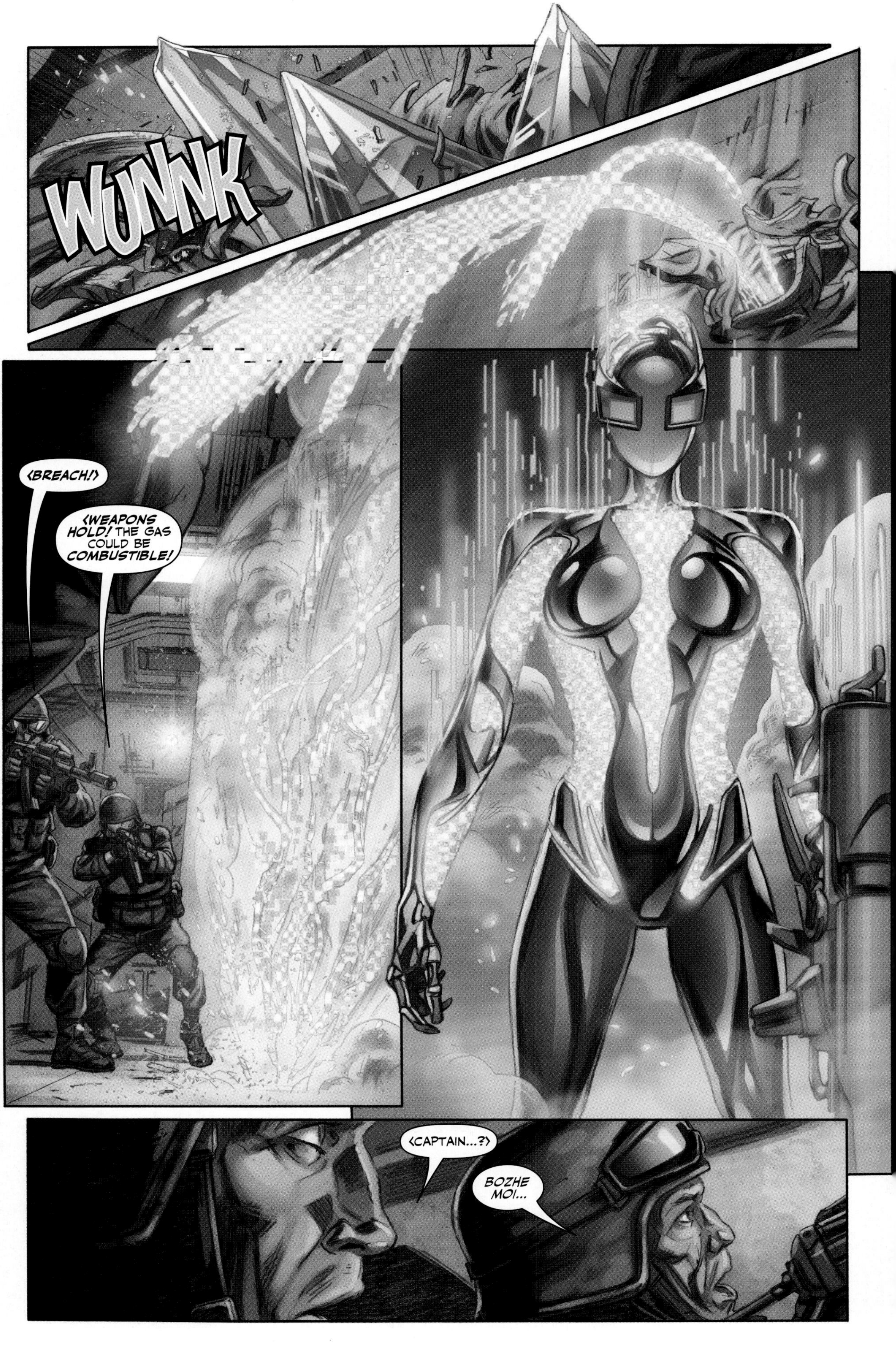
WUNNK
<BREACH!>
<WEAPONS HOLD! THE GAS COULD BE COMBUSTIBLE!>
<CAPTAIN...?>
BOZHE MOI...

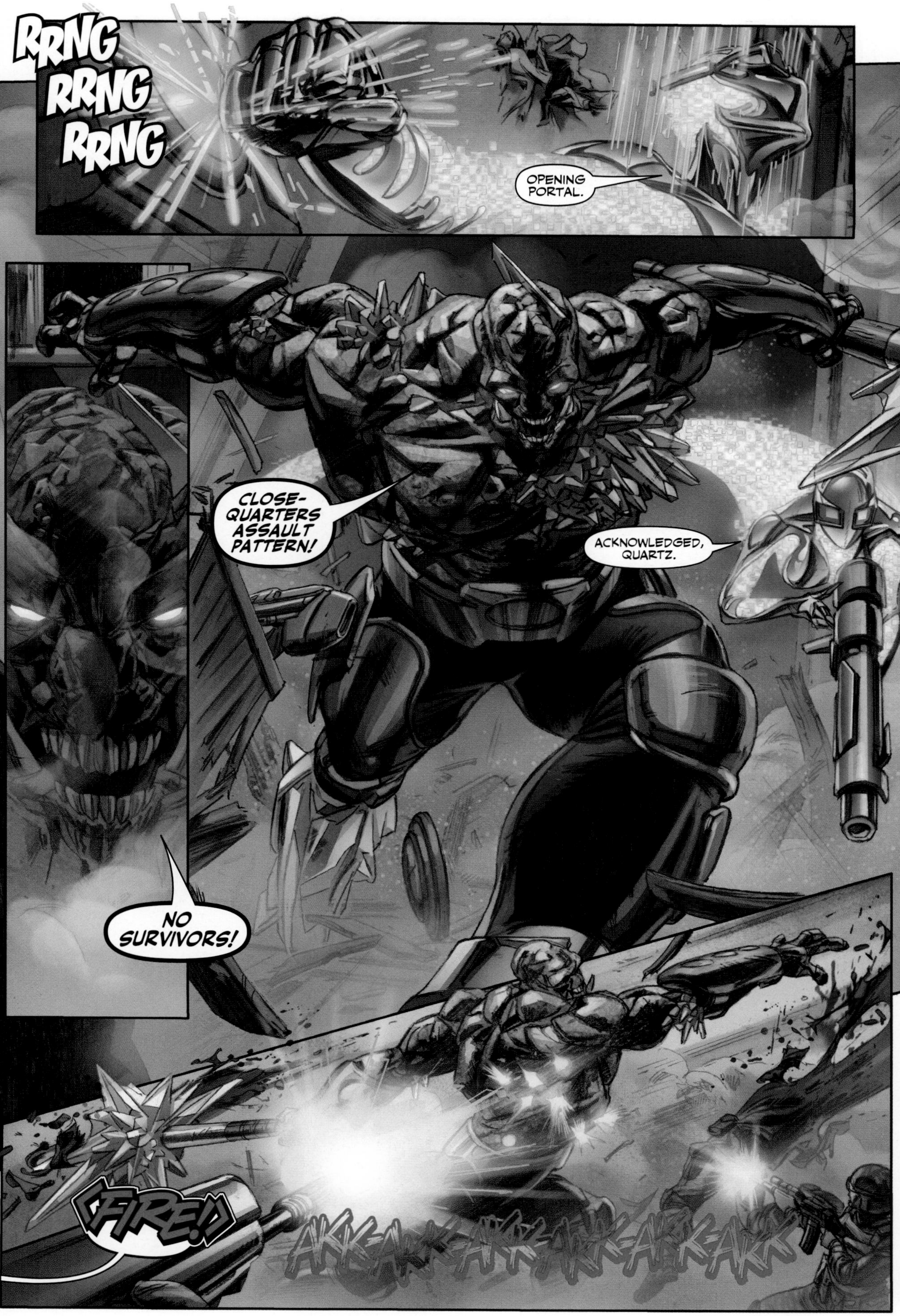
RRNG
RRNG
RRNG
OPENING PORTAL.
CLOSE-QUARTERS ASSAULT PATTERN!
ACKNOWLEDGED, QUARTZ.
NO SURVIVORS!
FIRE!
AKKAKKAKKAKKAKKAKKAKK

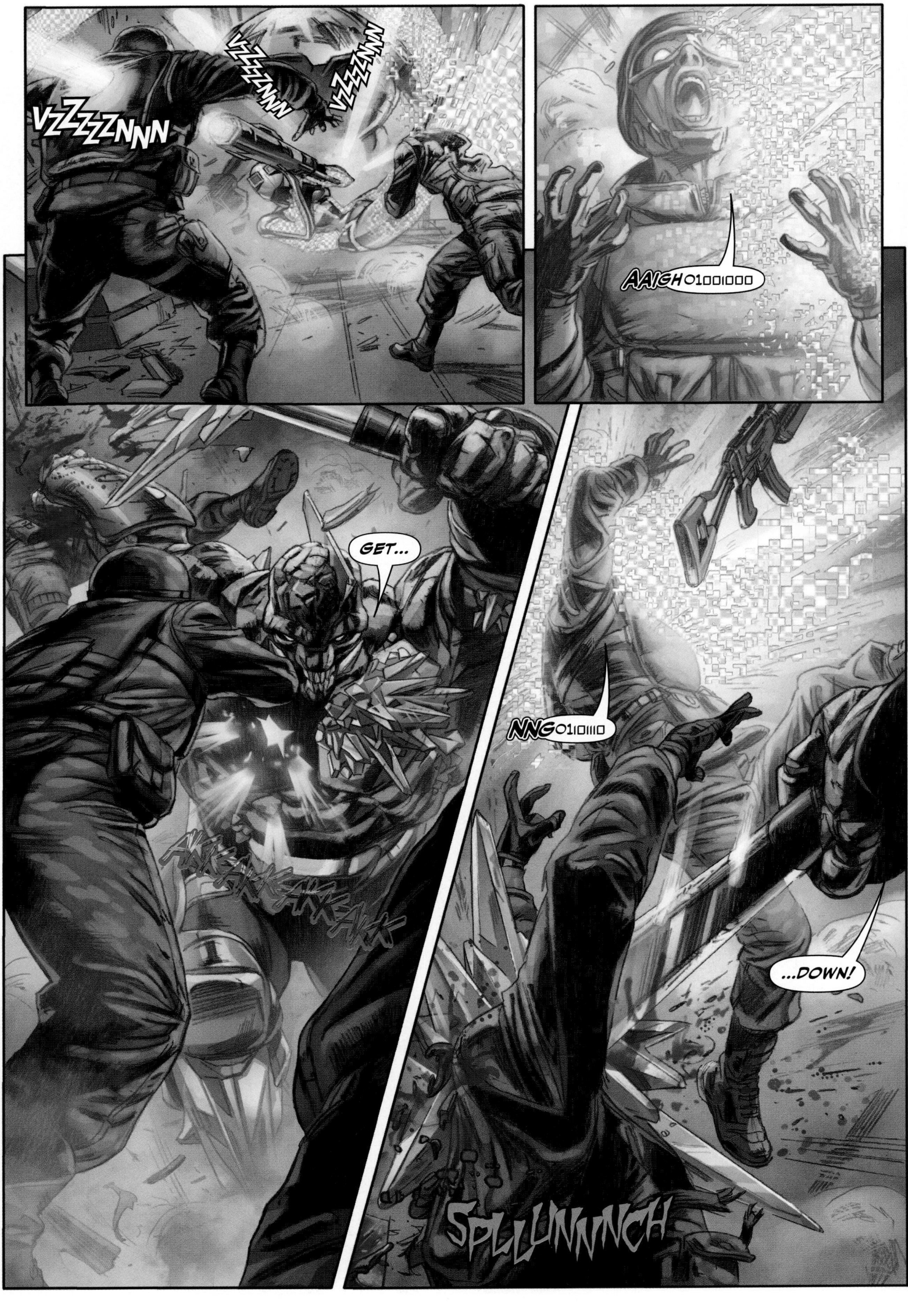
VZZZZZNNN
VZZZZZNNN
VZZZZZNNN
AAIGH01001000
GET...
NNG01101110
...DOWN!
SPLLUNNNCH

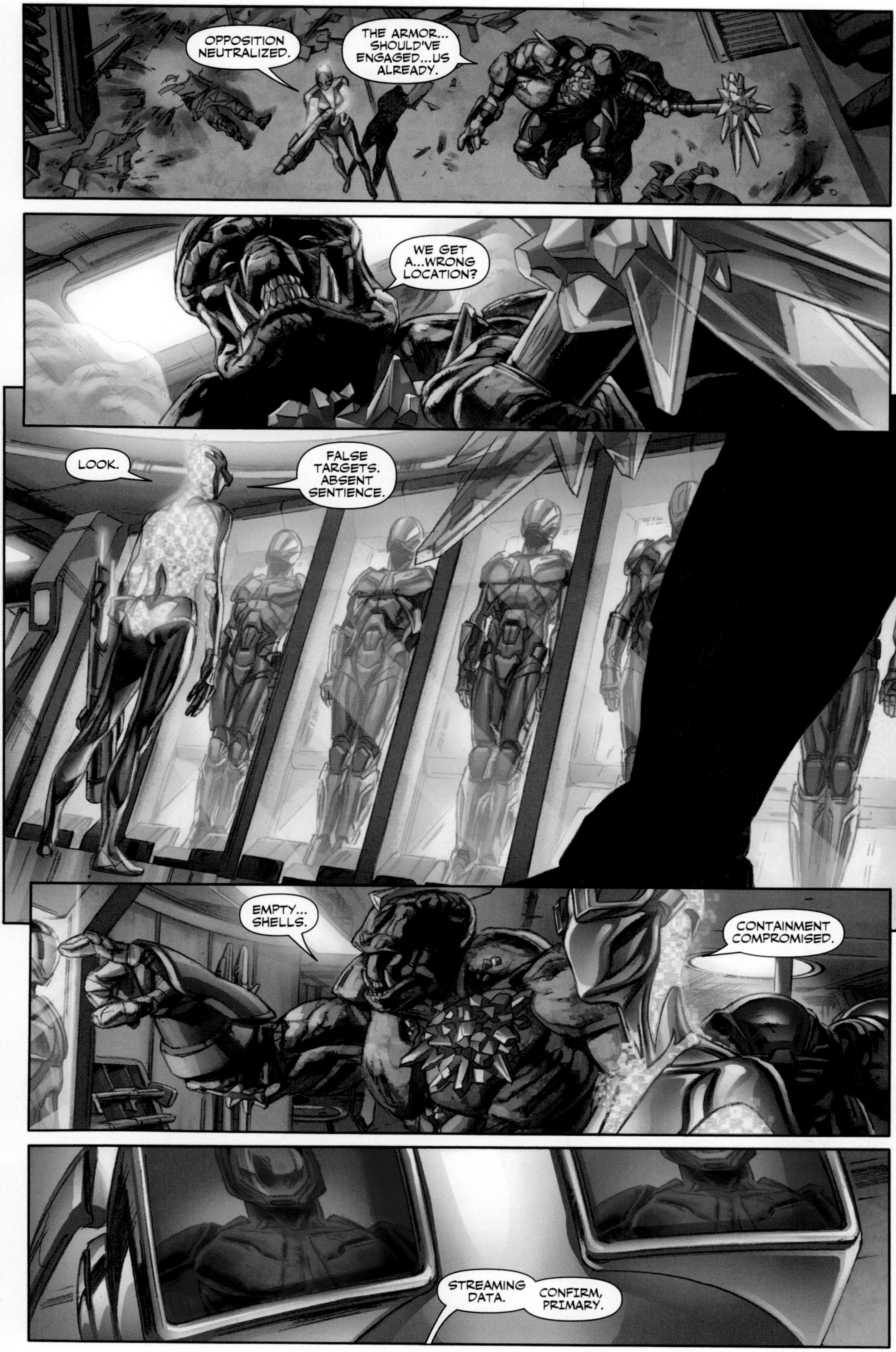
OPPOSITION NEUTRALIZED.
THE ARMOR... SHOULD'VE ENGAGED...US ALREADY.
WE GET A...WRONG LOCATION?
LOOK.
FALSE TARGETS. ABSENT SENTIENCE.
EMPTY... SHELLS.
CONTAINMENT COMPROMISED.
STREAMING DATA.
CONFIRM, PRIMARY.

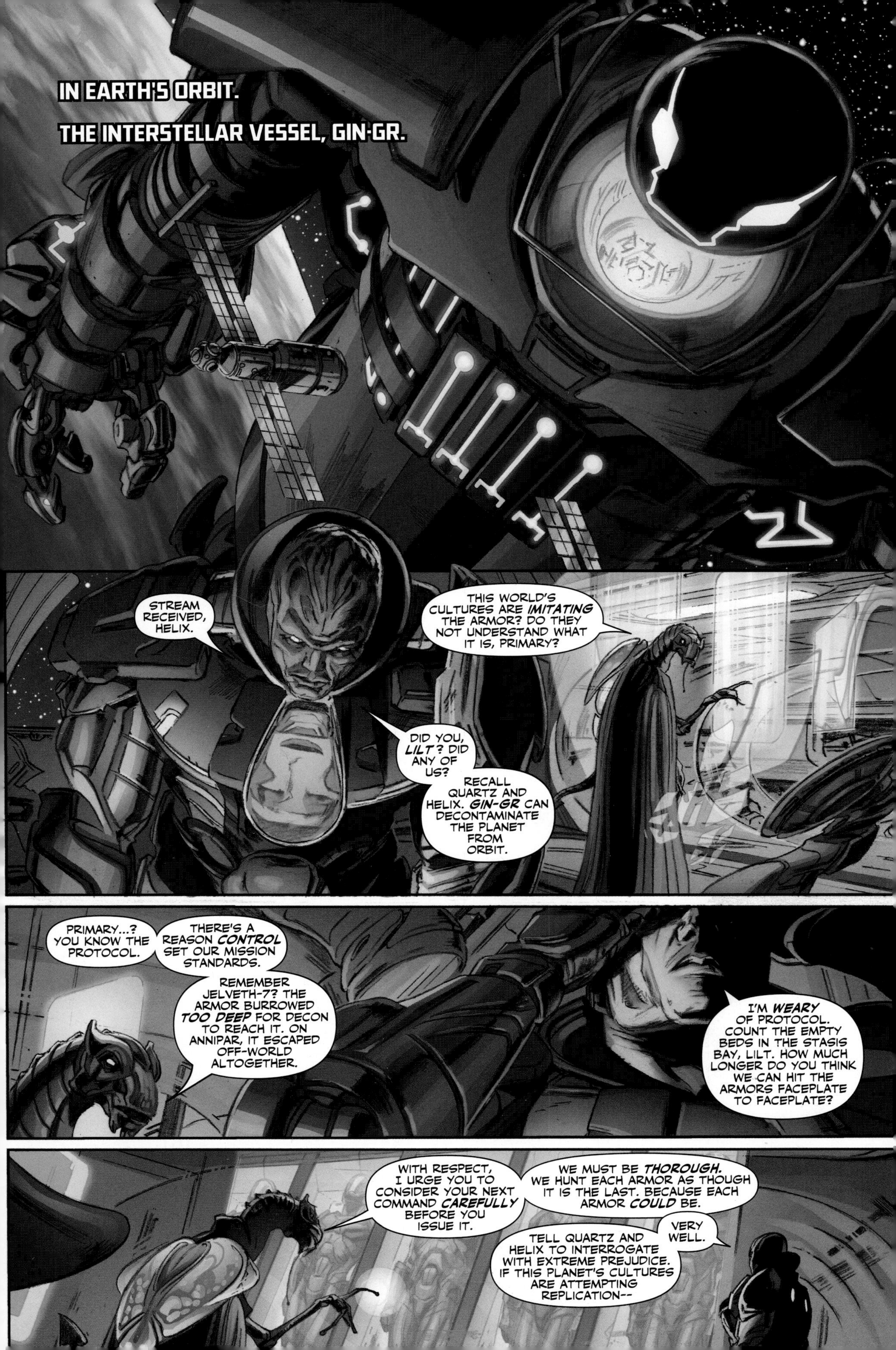

IN EARTH'S ORBIT.
THE INTERSTELLAR VESSEL, GIN-GR.
STREAM RECEIVED, HELIX.
THIS WORLD'S CULTURES ARE *IMITATING* THE ARMOR? DO THEY NOT UNDERSTAND WHAT IT IS, PRIMARY?
DID YOU, *LILT*? DID ANY OF US?
RECALL QUARTZ AND HELIX. *GIN-GR* CAN DECONTAMINATE THE PLANET FROM ORBIT.
PRIMARY...? YOU KNOW THE PROTOCOL.
THERE'S A REASON *CONTROL* SET OUR MISSION STANDARDS.
REMEMBER JELVETH-7? THE ARMOR BURROWED *TOO DEEP* FOR DECON TO REACH IT. ON ANNIPAR, IT ESCAPED OFF-WORLD ALTOGETHER.
I'M *WEARY* OF PROTOCOL. COUNT THE EMPTY BEDS IN THE STASIS BAY, LILT. HOW MUCH LONGER DO YOU THINK WE CAN HIT THE ARMORS FACEPLATE TO FACEPLATE?
WITH RESPECT, I URGE YOU TO CONSIDER YOUR NEXT COMMAND *CAREFULLY* BEFORE YOU ISSUE IT.
WE MUST BE *THOROUGH.* WE HUNT EACH ARMOR AS THOUGH IT IS THE LAST. BECAUSE EACH ARMOR *COULD* BE.
VERY WELL.
TELL QUARTZ AND HELIX TO INTERROGATE WITH EXTREME PREJUDICE. IF THIS PLANET'S CULTURES ARE ATTEMPTING REPLICATION--

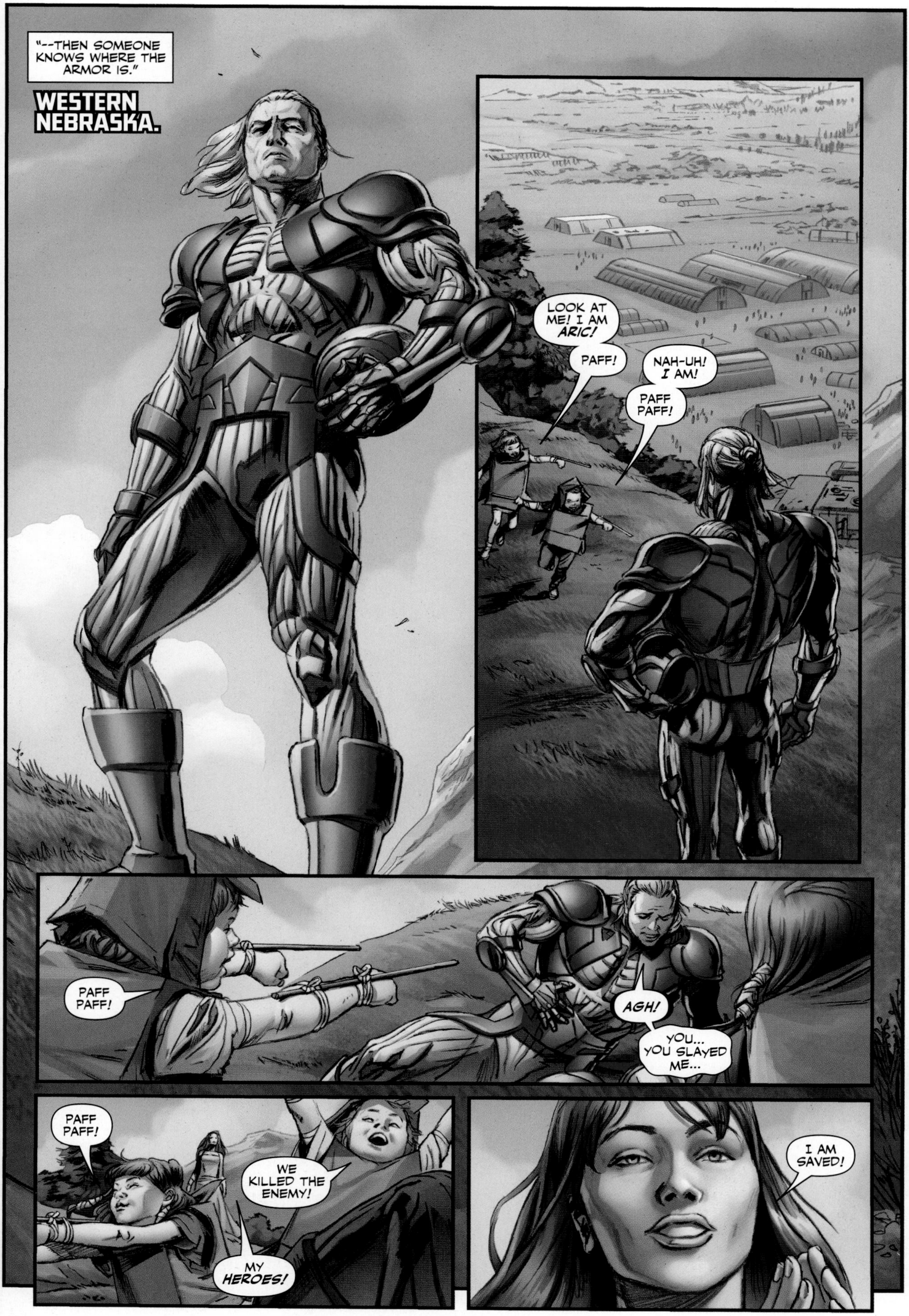
"--THEN SOMEONE KNOWS WHERE THE ARMOR IS."
WESTERN NEBRASKA.
LOOK AT ME! I AM ARIC!
PAFF!
NAH-UH! I AM!
PAFF PAFF!
PAFF PAFF!
AGH!
YOU... YOU SLAYED ME...
PAFF PAFF!
WE KILLED THE ENEMY!
MY HEROES!
I AM SAVED!

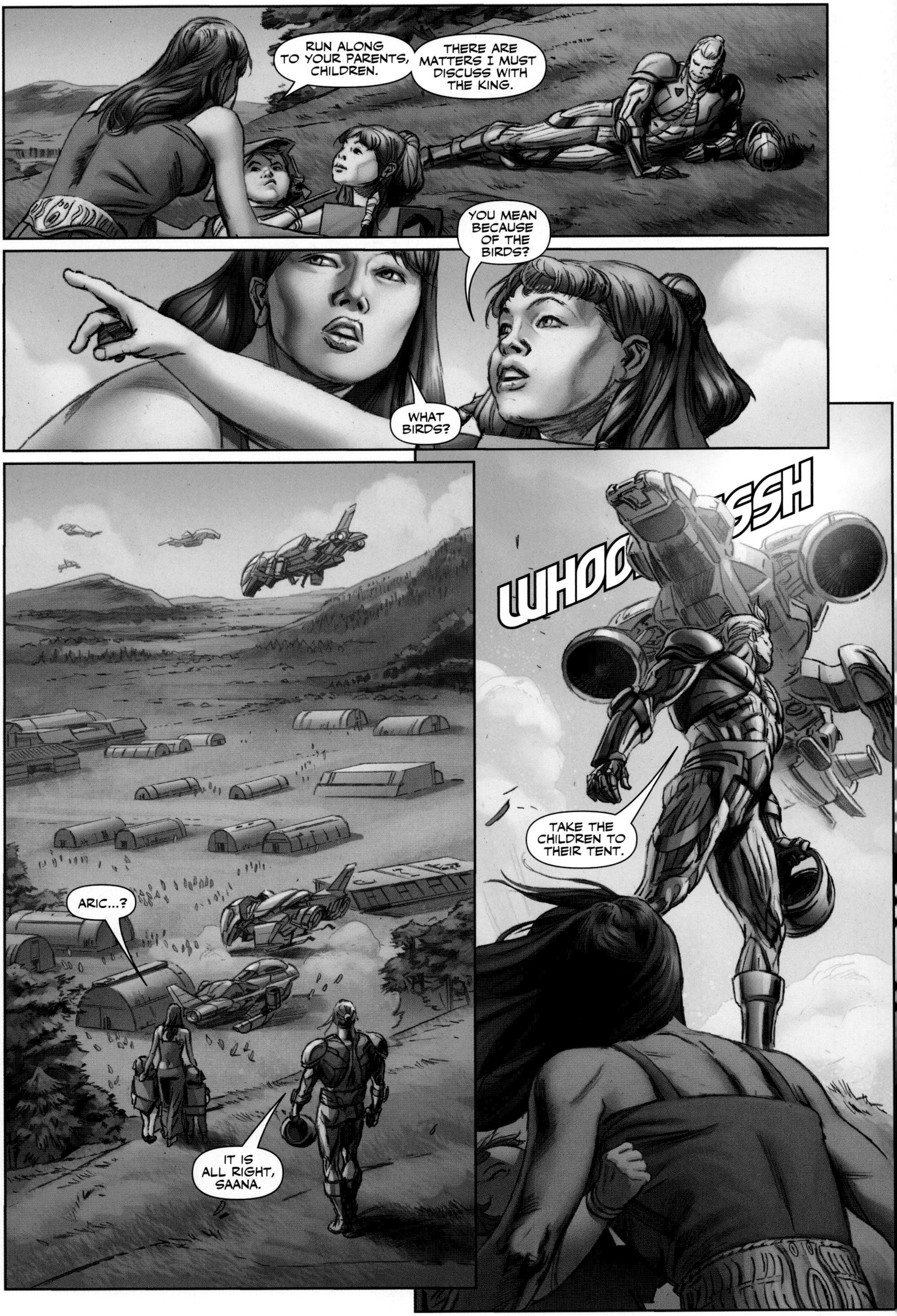
RUN ALONG TO YOUR PARENTS, CHILDREN.
THERE ARE MATTERS I MUST DISCUSS WITH THE KING.
YOU MEAN BECAUSE OF THE BIRDS?
WHAT BIRDS?
ARIC...?
IT IS ALL RIGHT, SAANA.
WHOO
SSH
TAKE THE CHILDREN TO THEIR TENT.

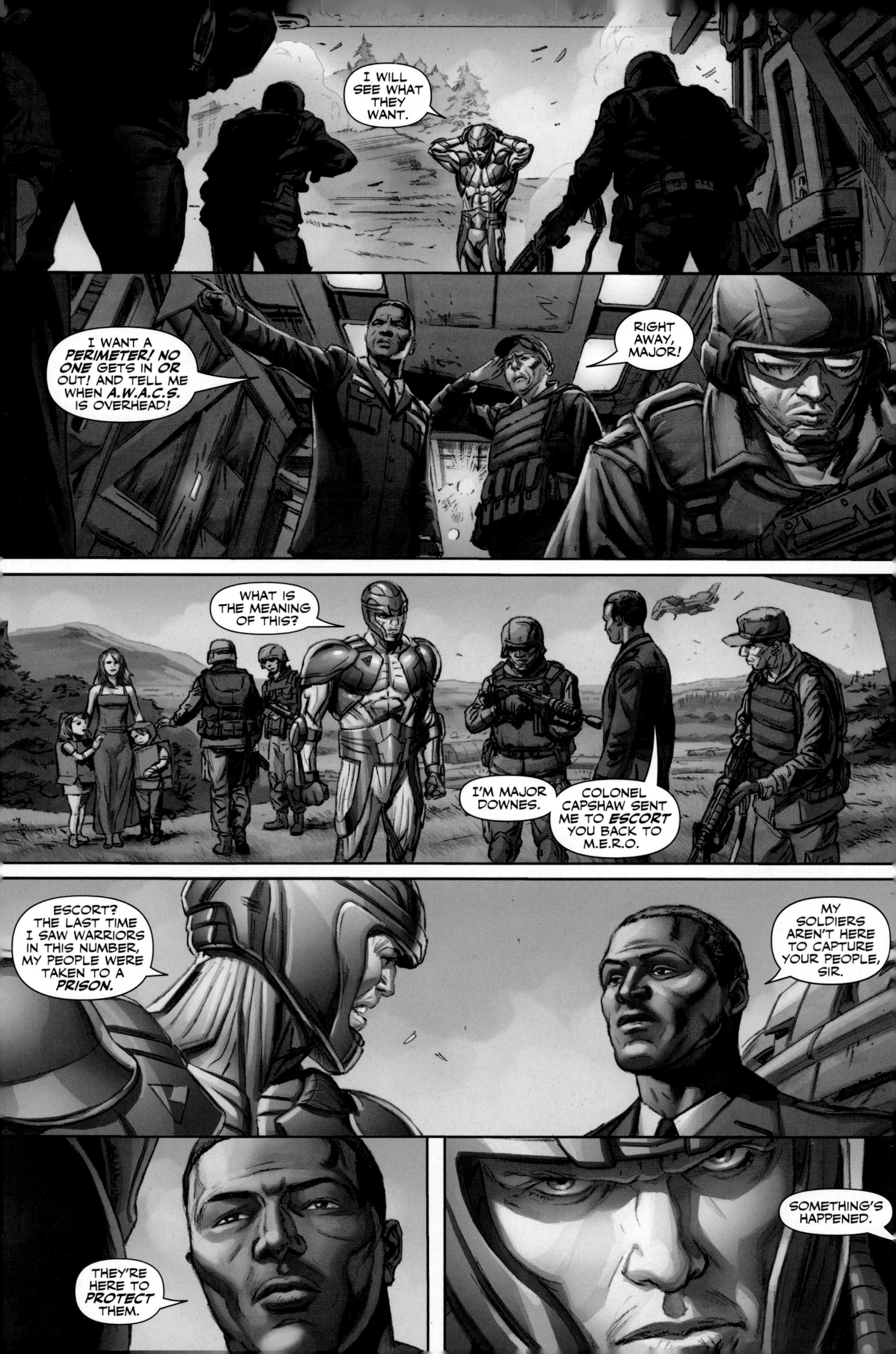

I WILL SEE WHAT THEY WANT.
I WANT A PERIMETER! NO ONE GETS IN OR OUT! AND TELL ME WHEN A.W.A.C.S. IS OVERHEAD!
RIGHT AWAY, MAJOR!
WHAT IS THE MEANING OF THIS?
I'M MAJOR DOWNES.
COLONEL CAPSHAW SENT ME TO ESCORT YOU BACK TO M.E.R.O.
ESCORT? THE LAST TIME I SAW WARRIORS IN THIS NUMBER, MY PEOPLE WERE TAKEN TO A PRISON.
MY SOLDIERS AREN'T HERE TO CAPTURE YOUR PEOPLE, SIR.
THEY'RE HERE TO PROTECT THEM.
SOMETHING'S HAPPENED.

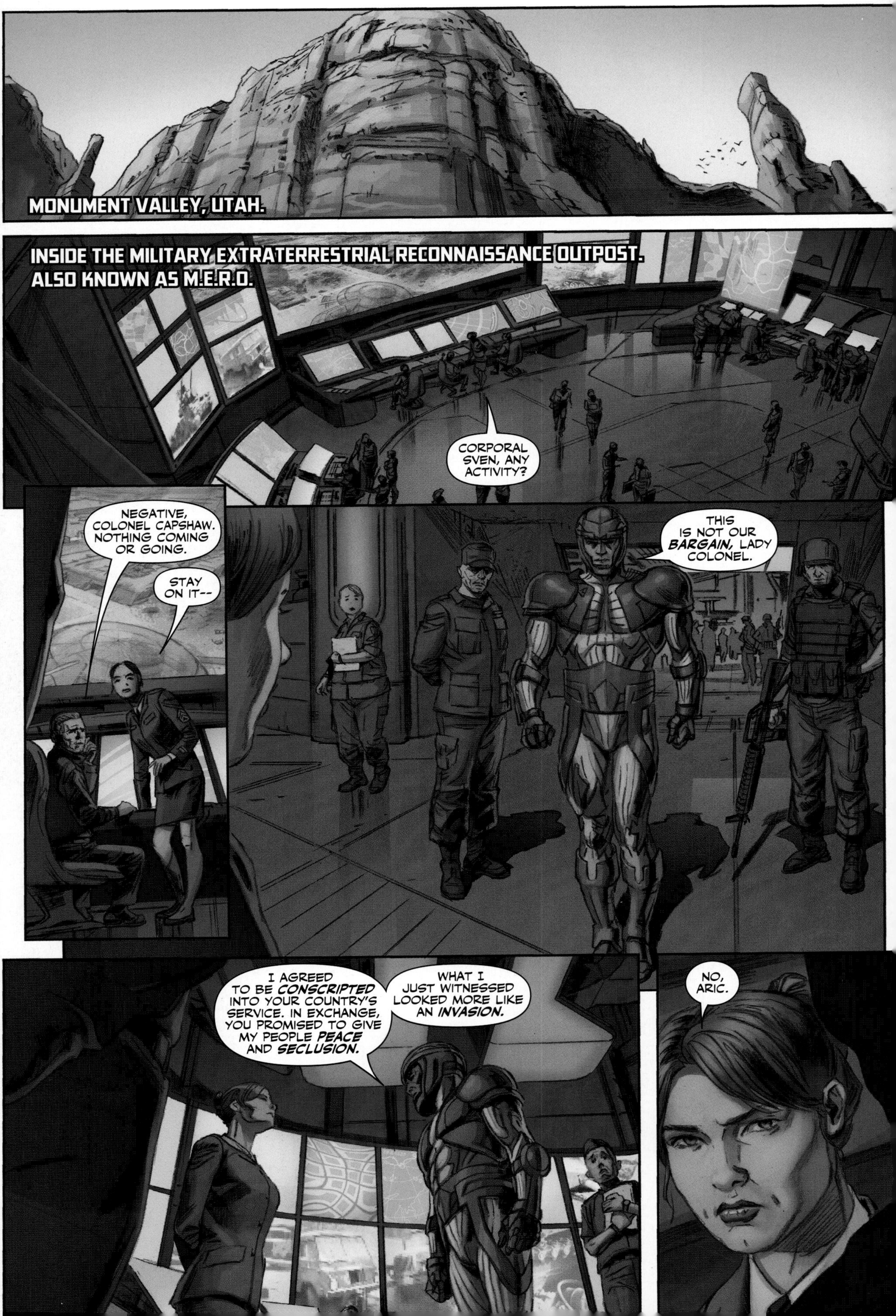
MONUMENT VALLEY, UTAH.
INSIDE THE MILITARY EXTRATERRESTRIAL RECONNAISSANCE OUTPOST. ALSO KNOWN AS M.E.R.O.
CORPORAL SVEN, ANY ACTIVITY?
NEGATIVE, COLONEL CAPSHAW. NOTHING COMING OR GOING.
STAY ON IT--
THIS IS NOT OUR BARGAIN, LADY COLONEL.
I AGREED TO BE CONSCRIPTED INTO YOUR COUNTRY'S SERVICE. IN EXCHANGE, YOU PROMISED TO GIVE MY PEOPLE PEACE AND SECLUSION.
WHAT I JUST WITNESSED LOOKED MORE LIKE AN INVASION.
NO, ARIC.

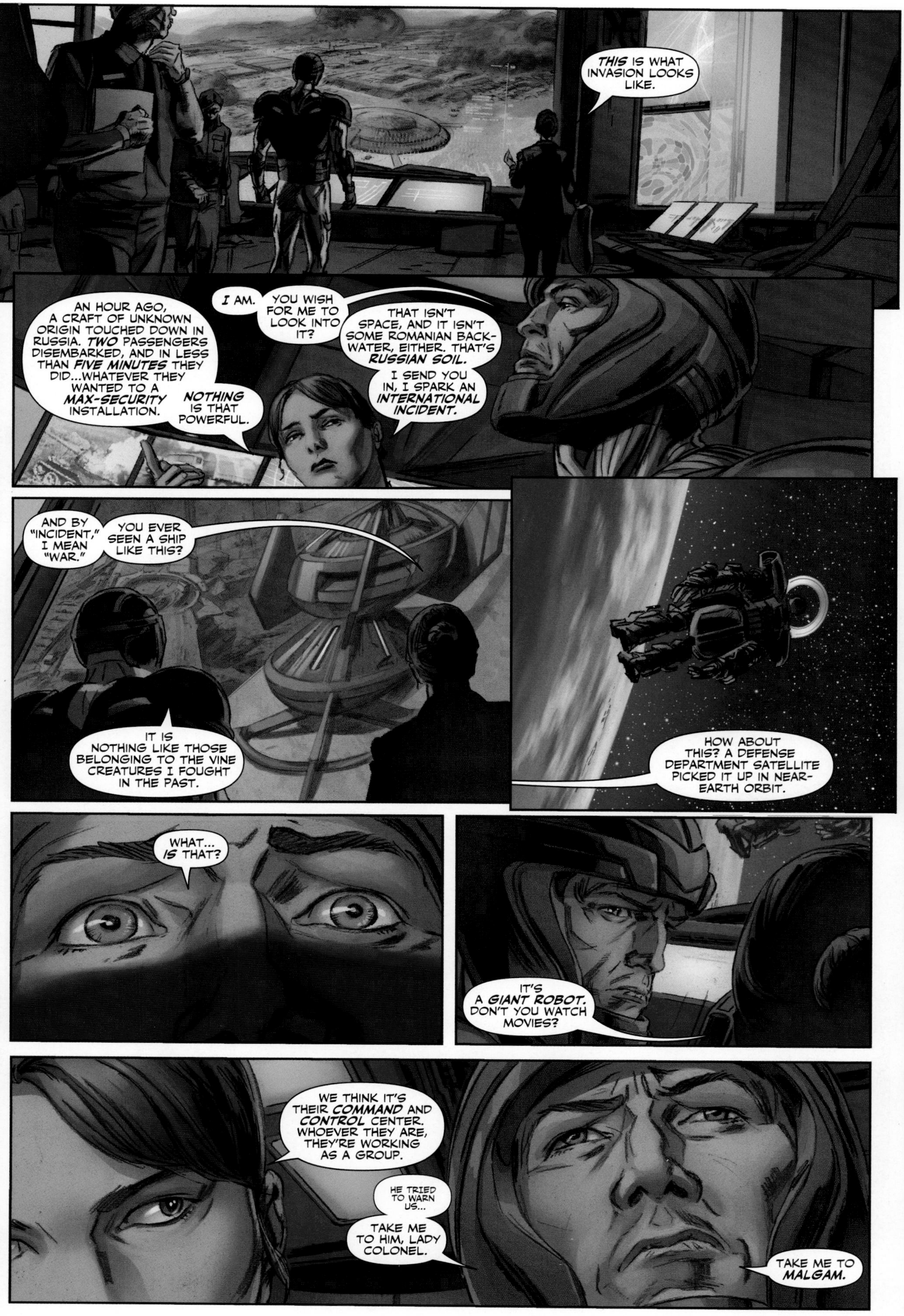
THIS IS WHAT INVASION LOOKS LIKE.
AN HOUR AGO, A CRAFT OF UNKNOWN ORIGIN TOUCHED DOWN IN RUSSIA. TWO PASSENGERS DISEMBARKED, AND IN LESS THAN FIVE MINUTES THEY DID...WHATEVER THEY WANTED TO A MAX-SECURITY INSTALLATION.
NOTHING IS THAT POWERFUL.
I AM.
YOU WISH FOR ME TO LOOK INTO IT?
THAT ISN'T SPACE, AND IT ISN'T SOME ROMANIAN BACKWATER, EITHER. THAT'S RUSSIAN SOIL.
I SEND YOU IN, I SPARK AN INTERNATIONAL INCIDENT.
AND BY "INCIDENT," I MEAN "WAR."
YOU EVER SEEN A SHIP LIKE THIS?
IT IS NOTHING LIKE THOSE BELONGING TO THE VINE CREATURES I FOUGHT IN THE PAST.
HOW ABOUT THIS? A DEFENSE DEPARTMENT SATELLITE PICKED IT UP IN NEAR-EARTH ORBIT.
WHAT... IS THAT?
IT'S A GIANT ROBOT. DON'T YOU WATCH MOVIES?
WE THINK IT'S THEIR COMMAND AND CONTROL CENTER. WHOEVER THEY ARE, THEY'RE WORKING AS A GROUP.
HE TRIED TO WARN US...
TAKE ME TO HIM, LADY COLONEL.
TAKE ME TO MALGAM.

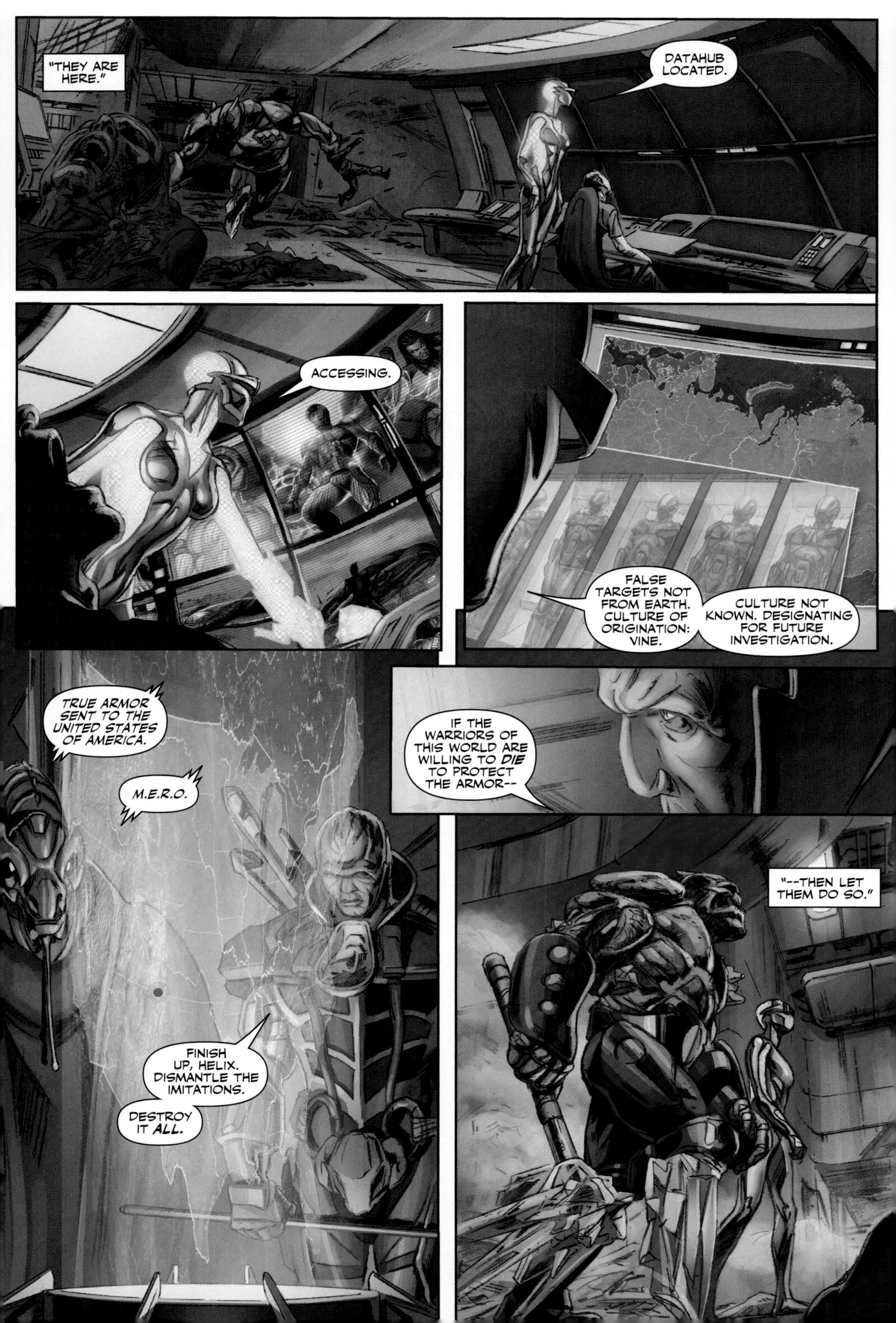
"THEY ARE HERE."
DATAHUB LOCATED.
ACCESSING.
FALSE TARGETS NOT FROM EARTH. CULTURE OF ORIGINATION: VINE.
CULTURE NOT KNOWN. DESIGNATING FOR FUTURE INVESTIGATION.
TRUE ARMOR SENT TO THE UNITED STATES OF AMERICA.
M.E.R.O.
IF THE WARRIORS OF THIS WORLD ARE WILLING TO *DIE* TO PROTECT THE ARMOR--
FINISH UP, HELIX. DISMANTLE THE IMITATIONS.
DESTROY IT *ALL.*
"--THEN LET THEM DO SO."

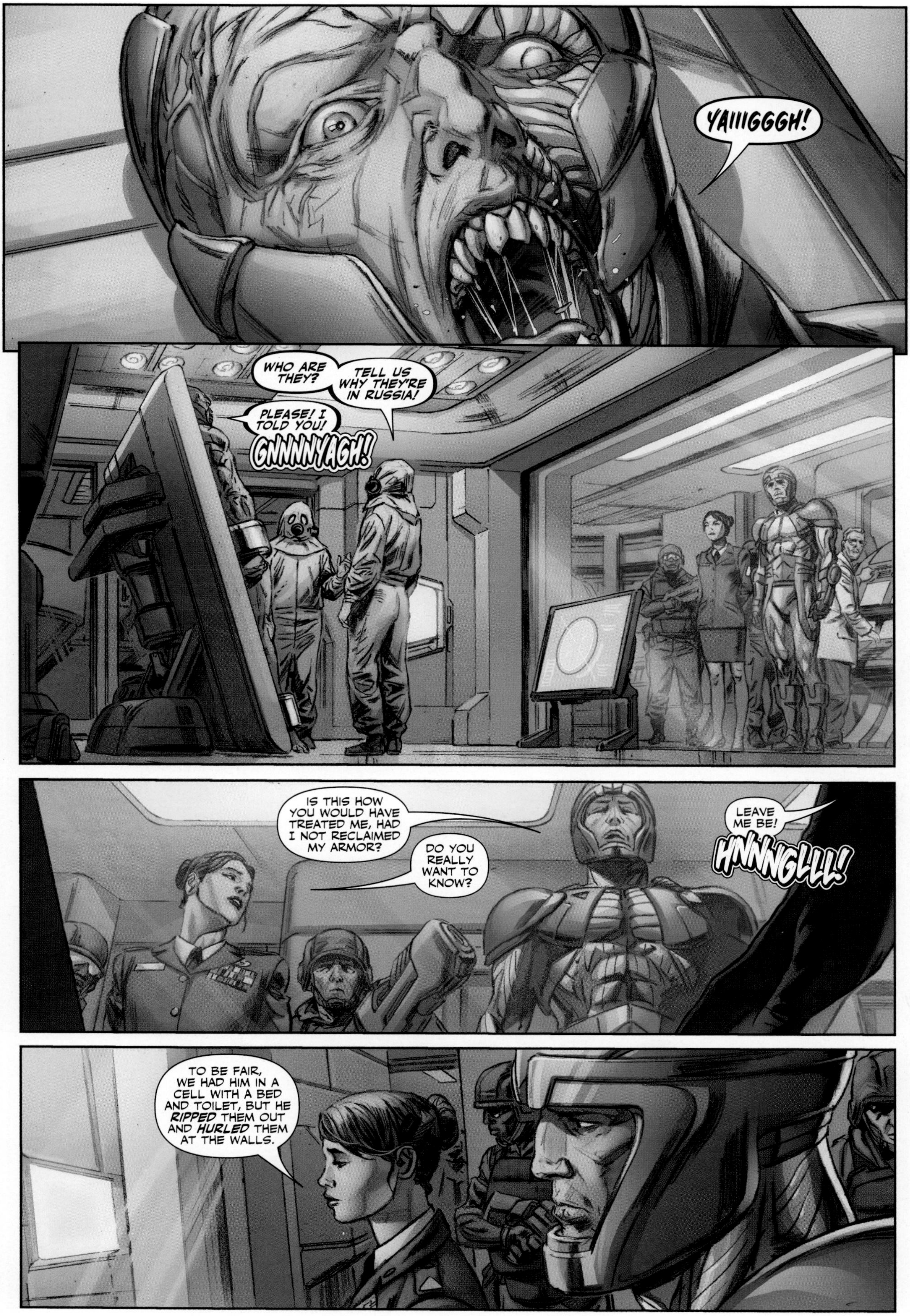
YAIIIGGGH!
WHO ARE THEY?
TELL US WHY THEY'RE IN RUSSIA!
PLEASE! I TOLD YOU!
GNNNNYAGH!
IS THIS HOW YOU WOULD HAVE TREATED ME, HAD I NOT RECLAIMED MY ARMOR?
DO YOU REALLY WANT TO KNOW?
LEAVE ME BE!
HNNNGLLL!
TO BE FAIR, WE HAD HIM IN A CELL WITH A BED AND TOILET, BUT HE *RIPPED* THEM OUT AND *HURLED* THEM AT THE WALLS.

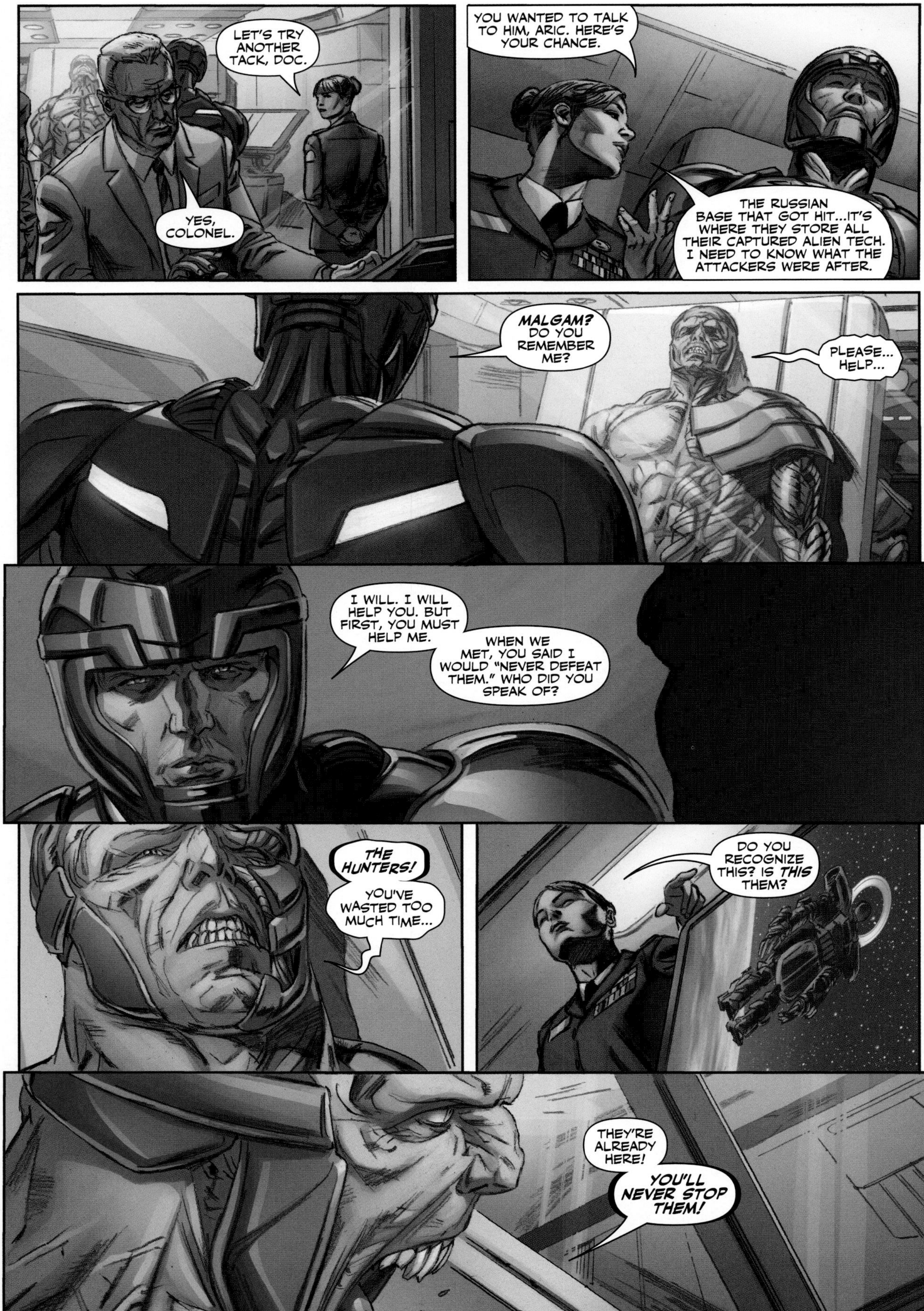
LET'S TRY ANOTHER TACK, DOC.
YES, COLONEL.
YOU WANTED TO TALK TO HIM, ARIC. HERE'S YOUR CHANCE.
THE RUSSIAN BASE THAT GOT HIT...IT'S WHERE THEY STORE ALL THEIR CAPTURED ALIEN TECH. I NEED TO KNOW WHAT THE ATTACKERS WERE AFTER.
MALGAM? DO YOU REMEMBER ME?
PLEASE... HELP...
I WILL. I WILL HELP YOU. BUT FIRST, YOU MUST HELP ME.
WHEN WE MET, YOU SAID I WOULD "NEVER DEFEAT THEM." WHO DID YOU SPEAK OF?
THE HUNTERS!
YOU'VE WASTED TOO MUCH TIME...
DO YOU RECOGNIZE THIS? IS THIS THEM?
THEY'RE ALREADY HERE!
YOU'LL NEVER STOP THEM!

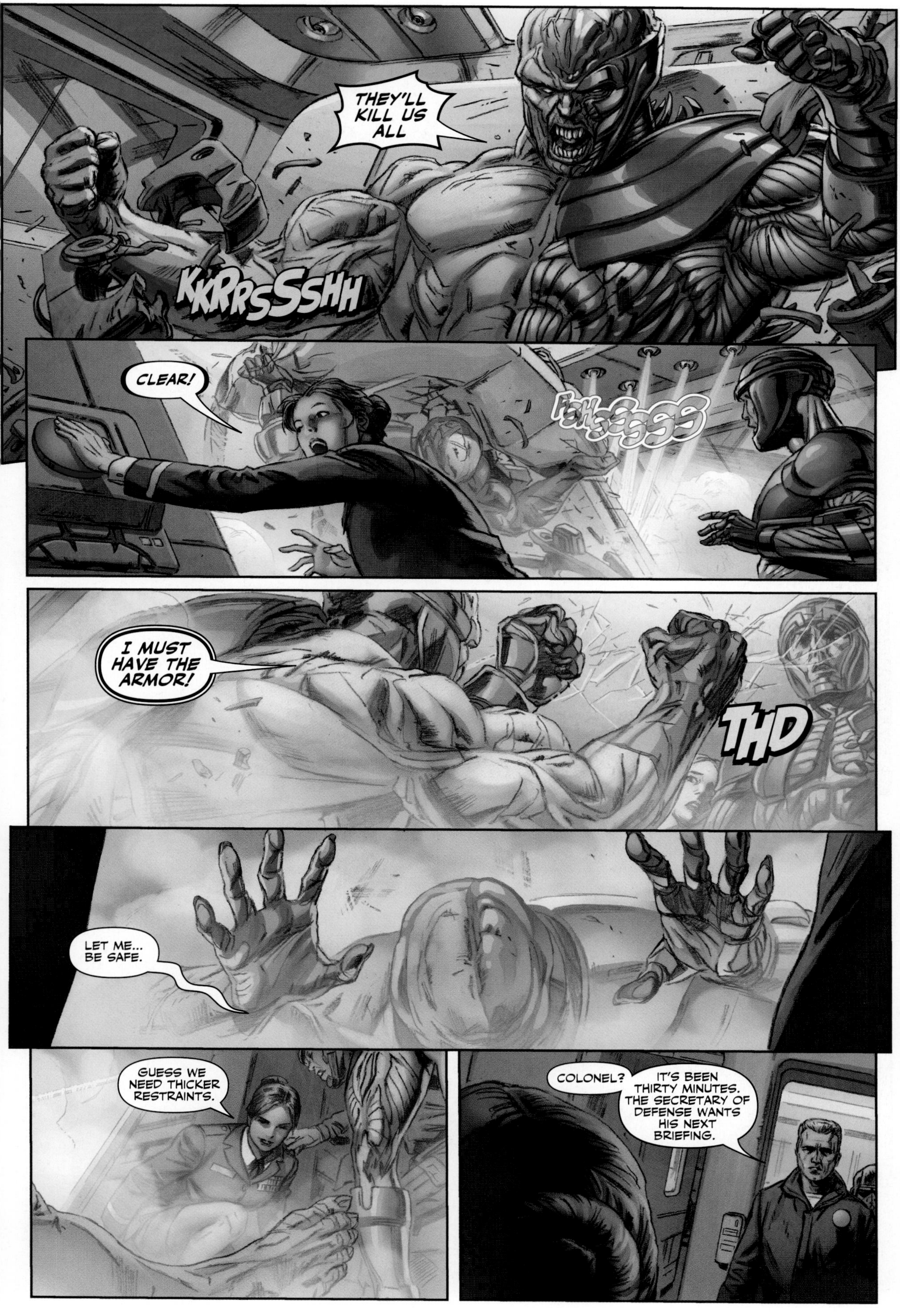
THEY'LL KILL US ALL
KKRRSSSHH
CLEAR!
FSHSSSS
I MUST HAVE THE ARMOR!
THD
LET ME... BE SAFE.
GUESS WE NEED THICKER RESTRAINTS.
COLONEL?
IT'S BEEN THIRTY MINUTES. THE SECRETARY OF DEFENSE WANTS HIS NEXT BRIEFING.

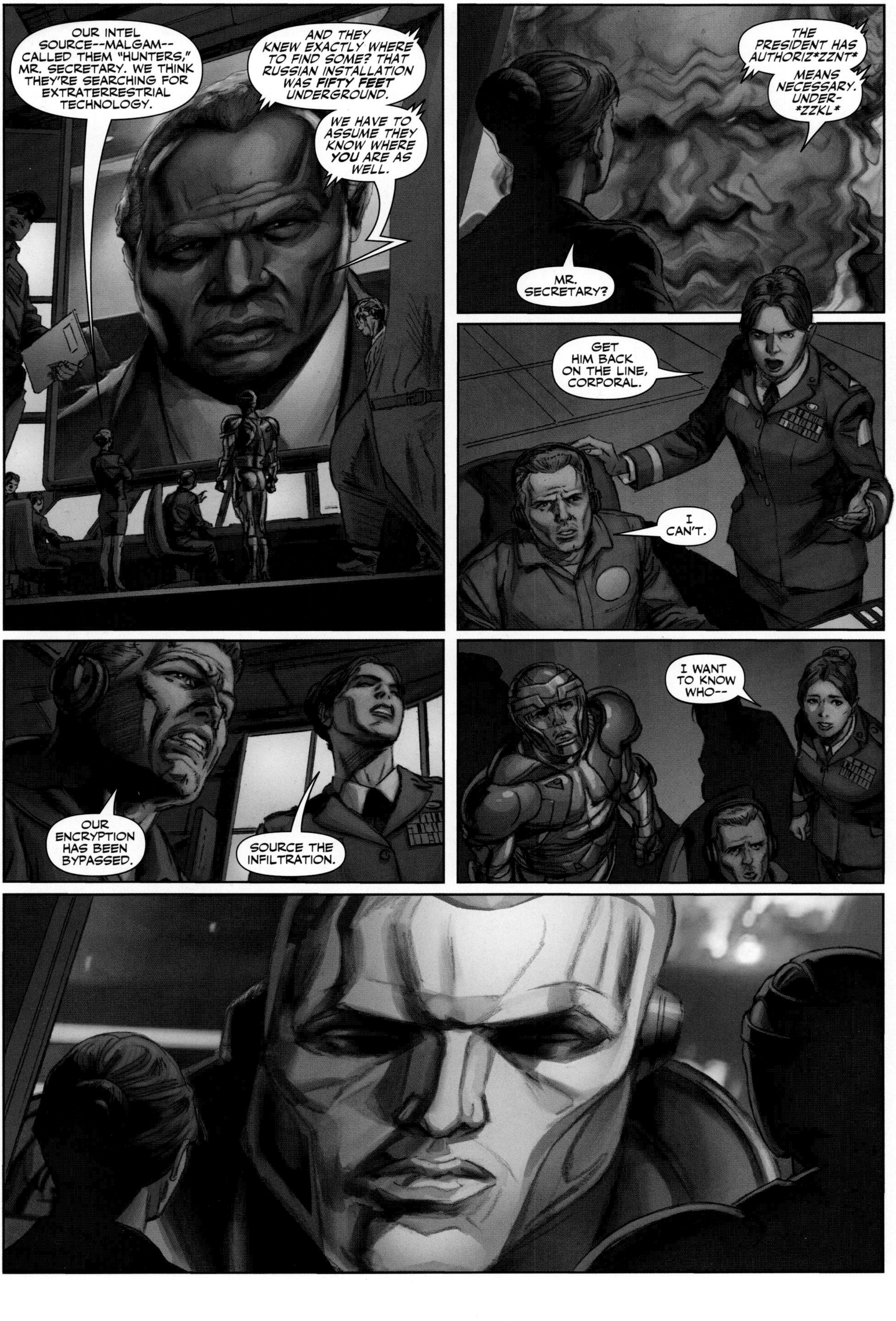
OUR INTEL SOURCE--MALGAM--CALLED THEM "HUNTERS," MR. SECRETARY. WE THINK THEY'RE SEARCHING FOR EXTRATERRESTRIAL TECHNOLOGY.
AND THEY KNEW EXACTLY WHERE TO FIND SOME? THAT RUSSIAN INSTALLATION WAS **FIFTY FEET** UNDERGROUND.
WE HAVE TO ASSUME THEY KNOW WHERE **YOU** ARE AS WELL.
THE PRESIDENT HAS AUTHORIZ*ZZNT*
MEANS NECESSARY. UNDER-*ZZKL*
MR. SECRETARY?
GET HIM BACK ON THE LINE, CORPORAL.
I CAN'T.
OUR ENCRYPTION HAS BEEN BYPASSED.
SOURCE THE INFILTRATION.
I WANT TO KNOW WHO--

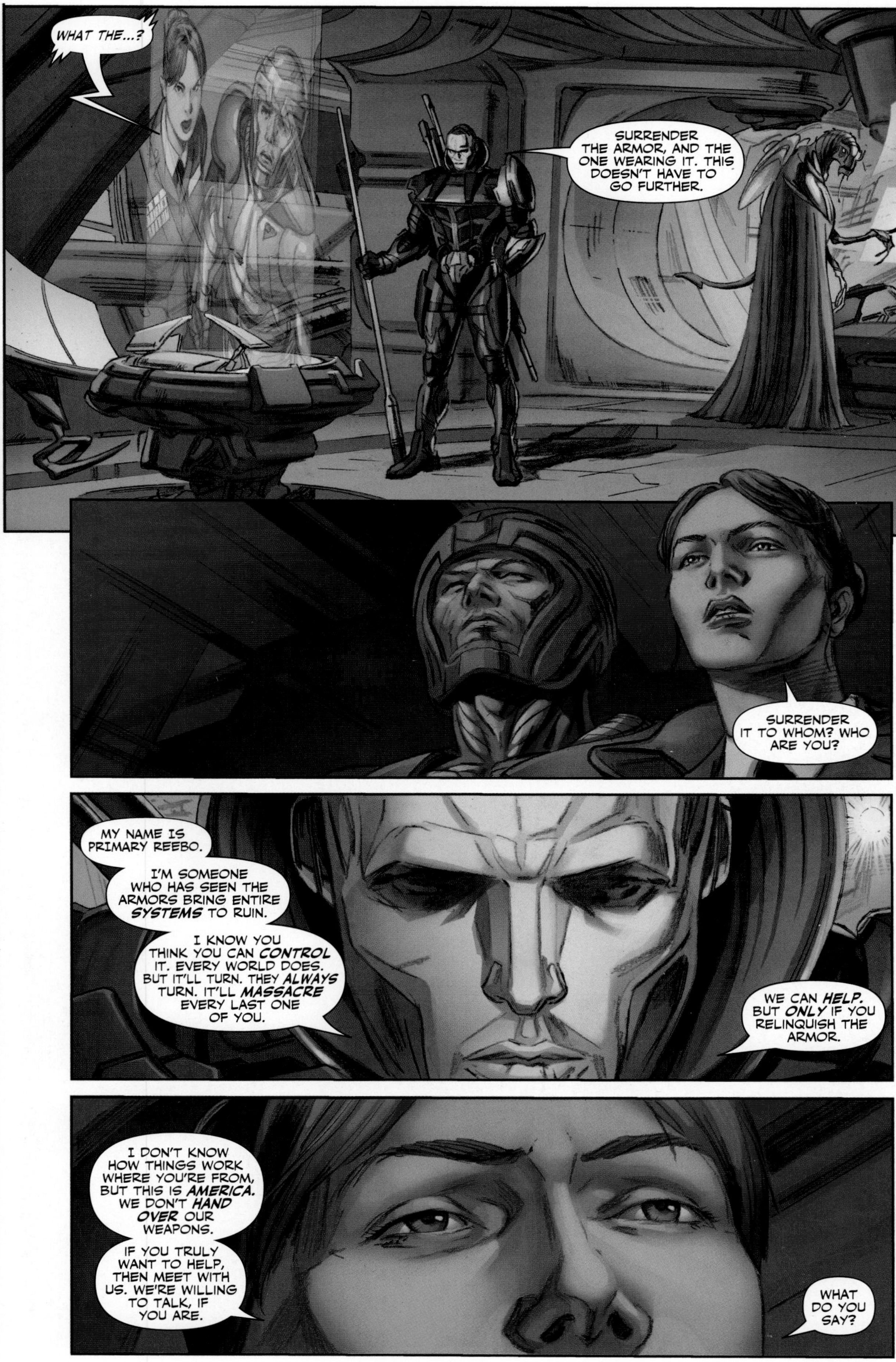
WHAT THE...?
SURRENDER THE ARMOR, AND THE ONE WEARING IT. THIS DOESN'T HAVE TO GO FURTHER.
SURRENDER IT TO WHOM? WHO ARE YOU?
MY NAME IS PRIMARY REEBO.
I'M SOMEONE WHO HAS SEEN THE ARMORS BRING ENTIRE SYSTEMS TO RUIN.
I KNOW YOU THINK YOU CAN CONTROL IT. EVERY WORLD DOES. BUT IT'LL TURN. THEY ALWAYS TURN. IT'LL MASSACRE EVERY LAST ONE OF YOU.
WE CAN HELP. BUT ONLY IF YOU RELINQUISH THE ARMOR.
I DON'T KNOW HOW THINGS WORK WHERE YOU'RE FROM, BUT THIS IS AMERICA. WE DON'T HAND OVER OUR WEAPONS.
IF YOU TRULY WANT TO HELP, THEN MEET WITH US. WE'RE WILLING TO TALK, IF YOU ARE.
WHAT DO YOU SAY?

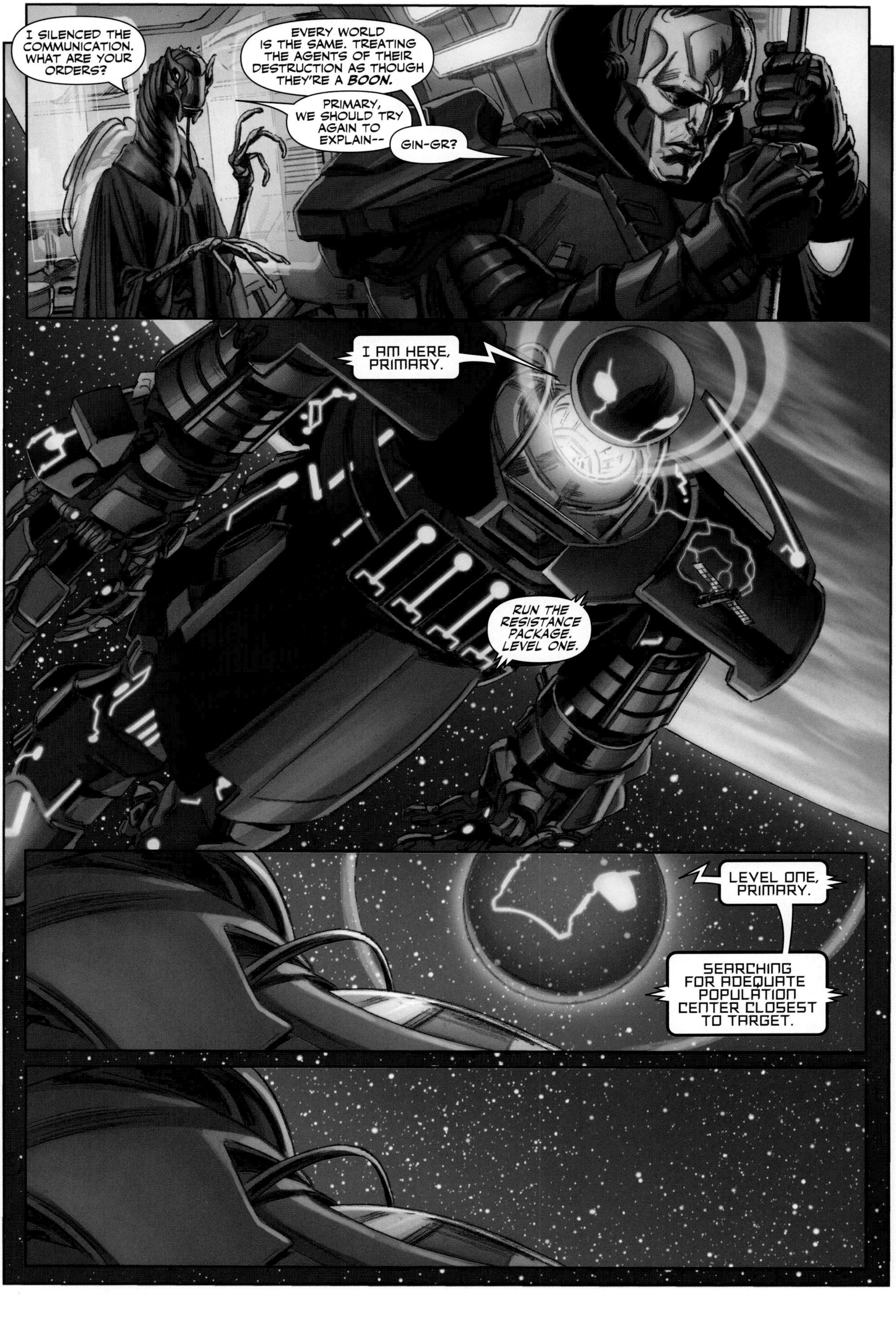

I SILENCED THE COMMUNICATION. WHAT ARE YOUR ORDERS?
EVERY WORLD IS THE SAME. TREATING THE AGENTS OF THEIR DESTRUCTION AS THOUGH THEY'RE A *BOON.*
PRIMARY, WE SHOULD TRY AGAIN TO EXPLAIN--
GIN-GR?
I AM HERE, PRIMARY.
RUN THE RESISTANCE PACKAGE. LEVEL ONE.
LEVEL ONE, PRIMARY.
SEARCHING FOR ADEQUATE POPULATION CENTER CLOSEST TO TARGET.

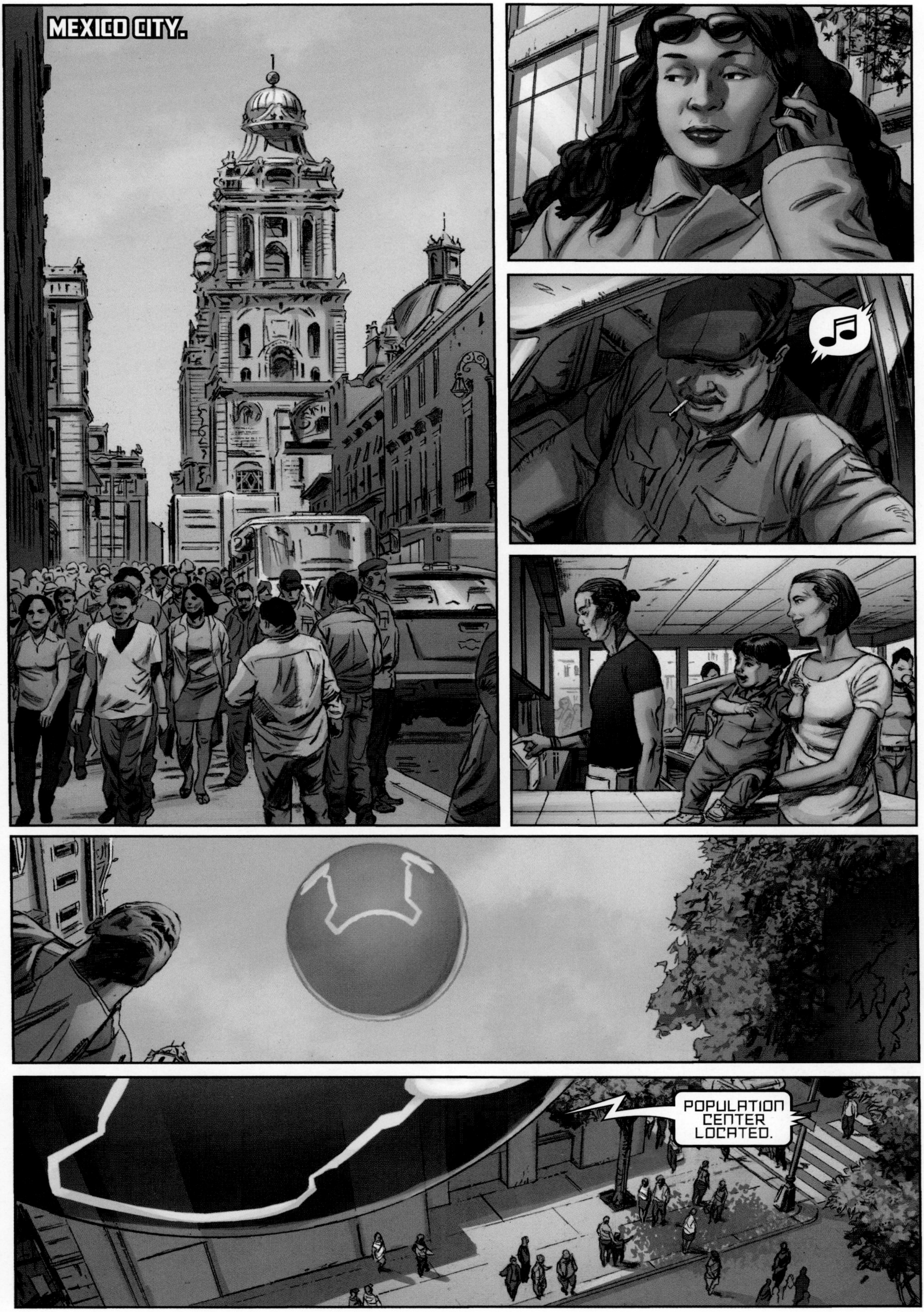
MEXICO CITY.
♫
POPULATION CENTER LOCATED.

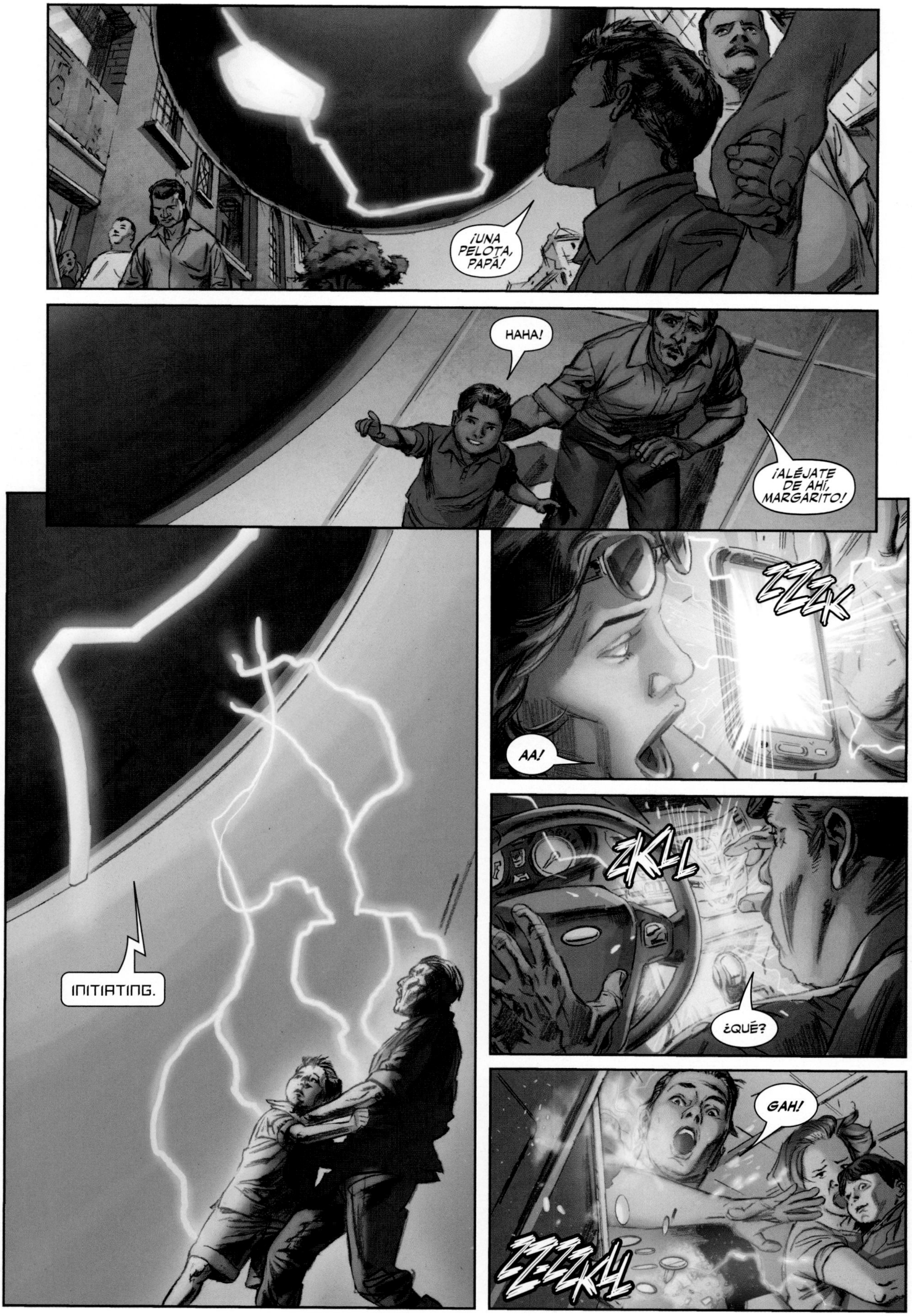
¡UNA PELOTA, PAPÁ!
HAHA!
¡ALÉJATE DE AHÍ, MARGARITO!
INITIATING.
ZZZK
AA!
ZKLL
¿QUÉ?
GAH!
ZZZZKL

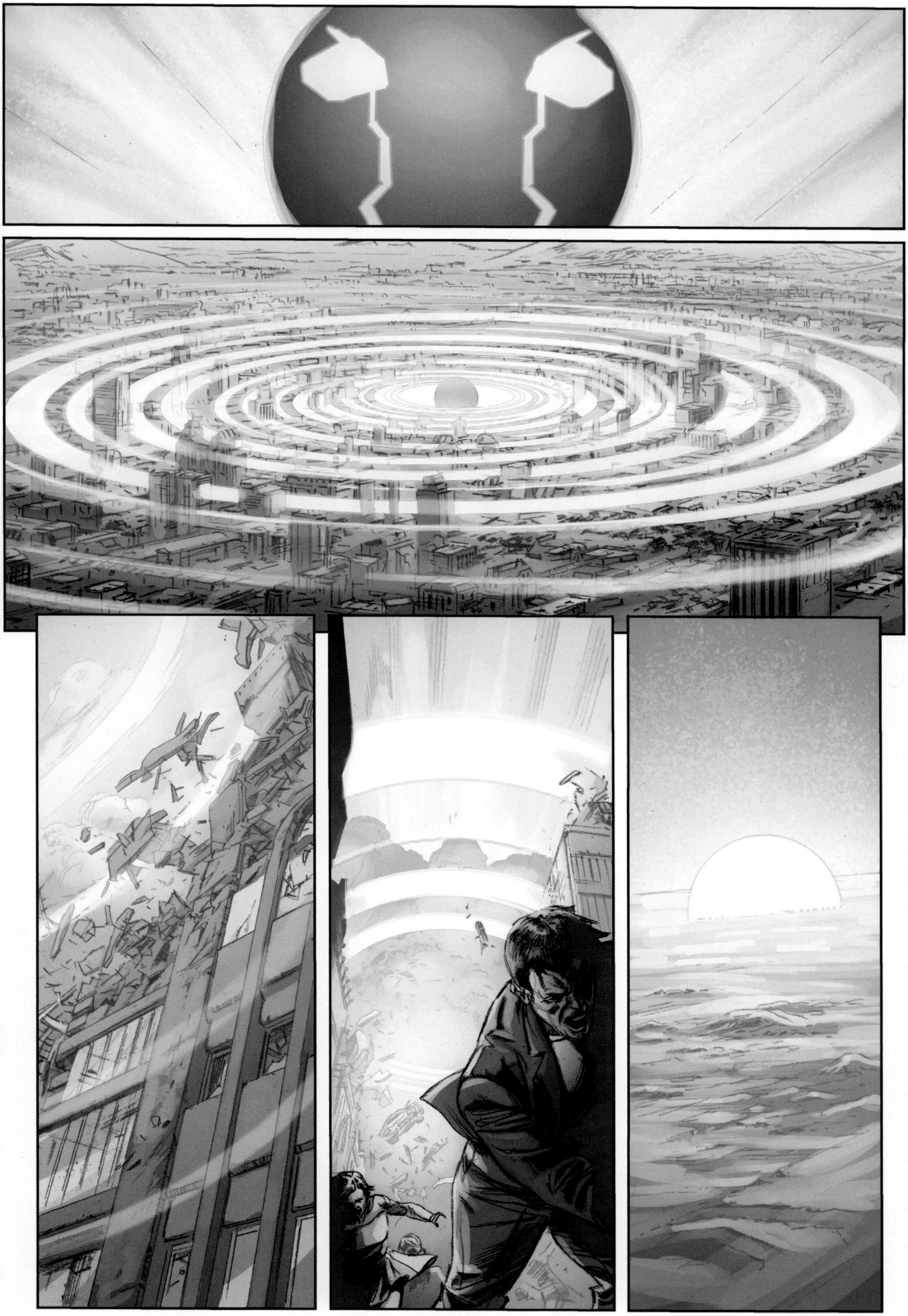

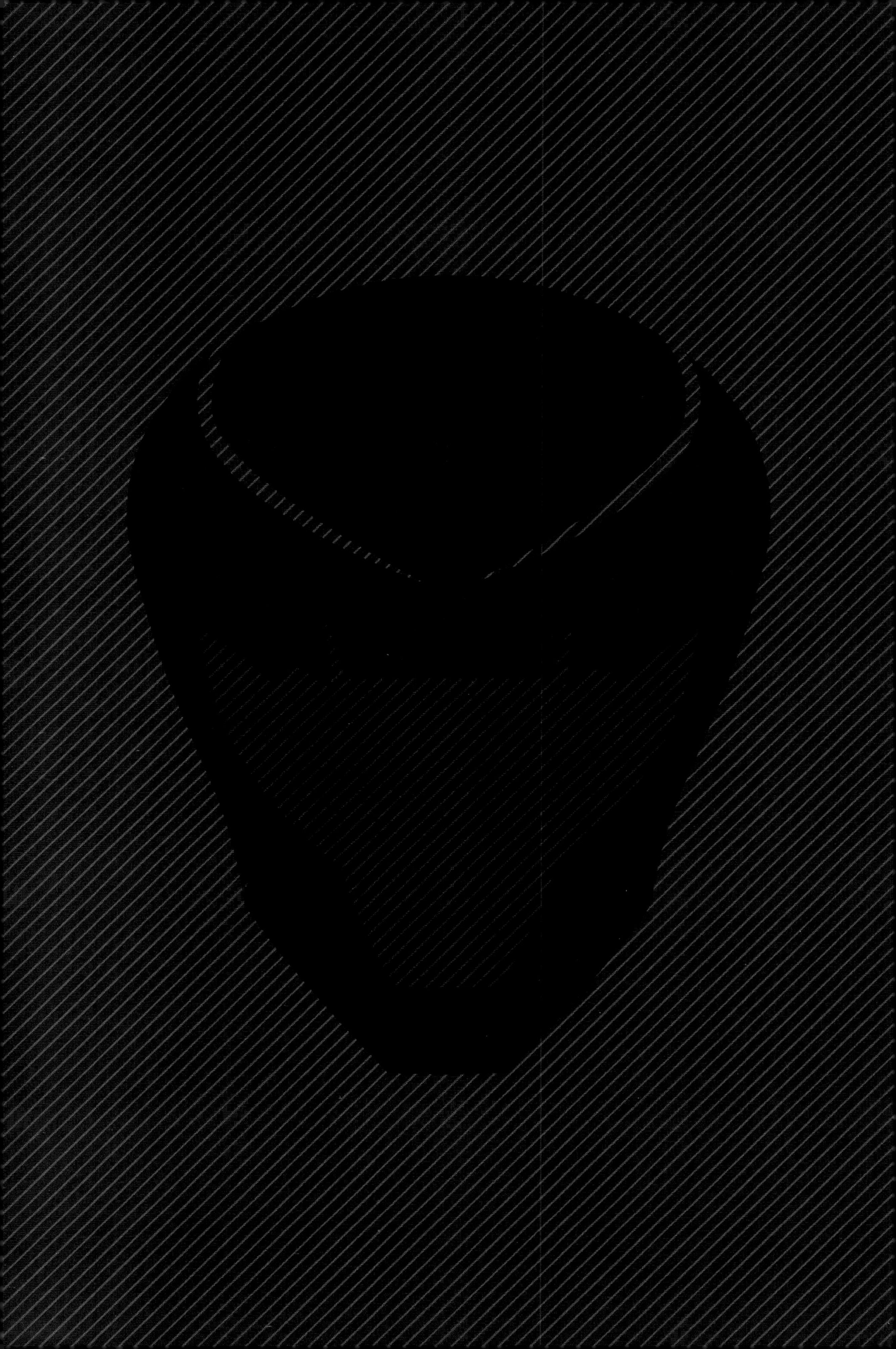

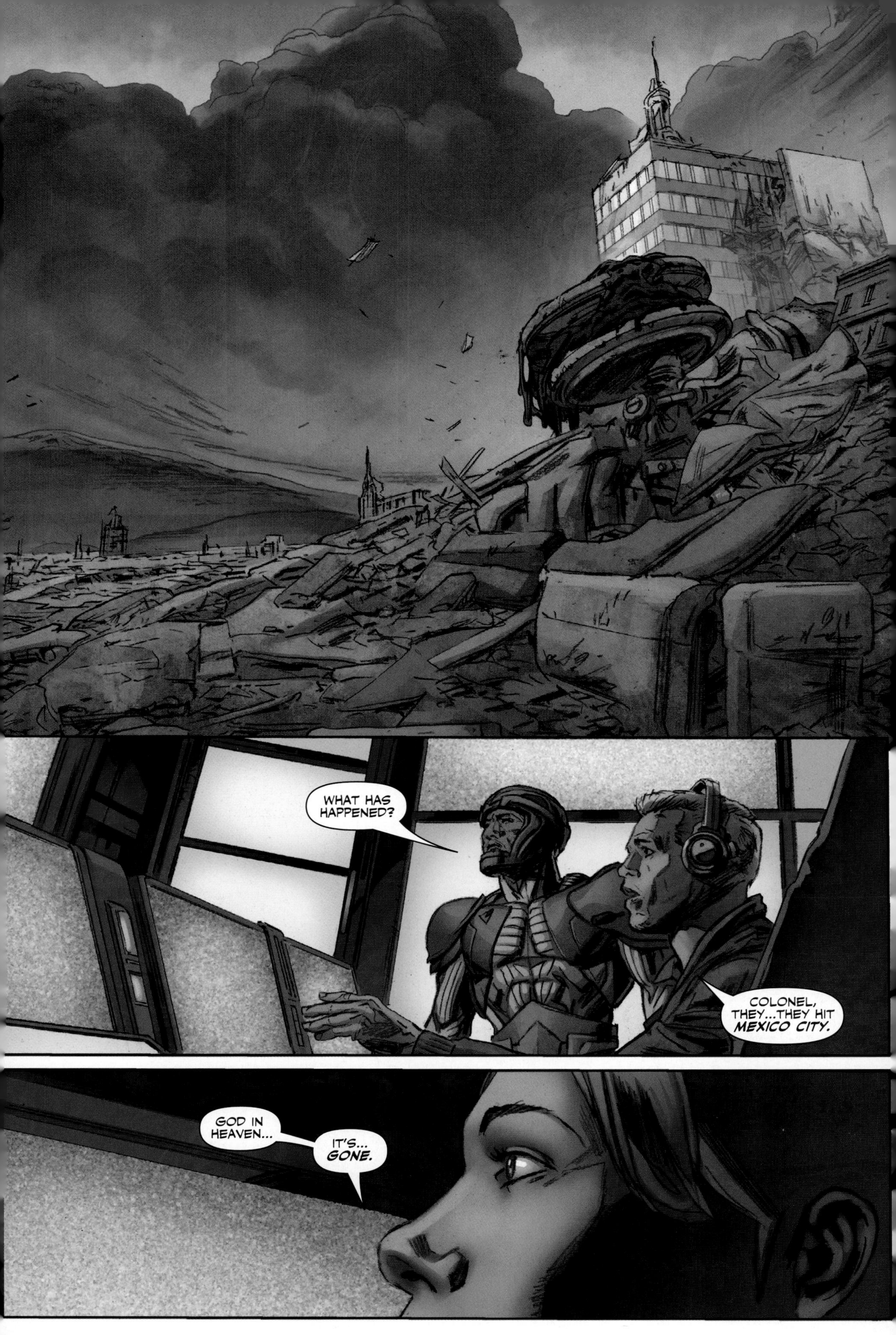
WHAT HAS HAPPENED?
COLONEL, THEY...THEY HIT *MEXICO CITY.*
GOD IN HEAVEN...
IT'S... *GONE.*

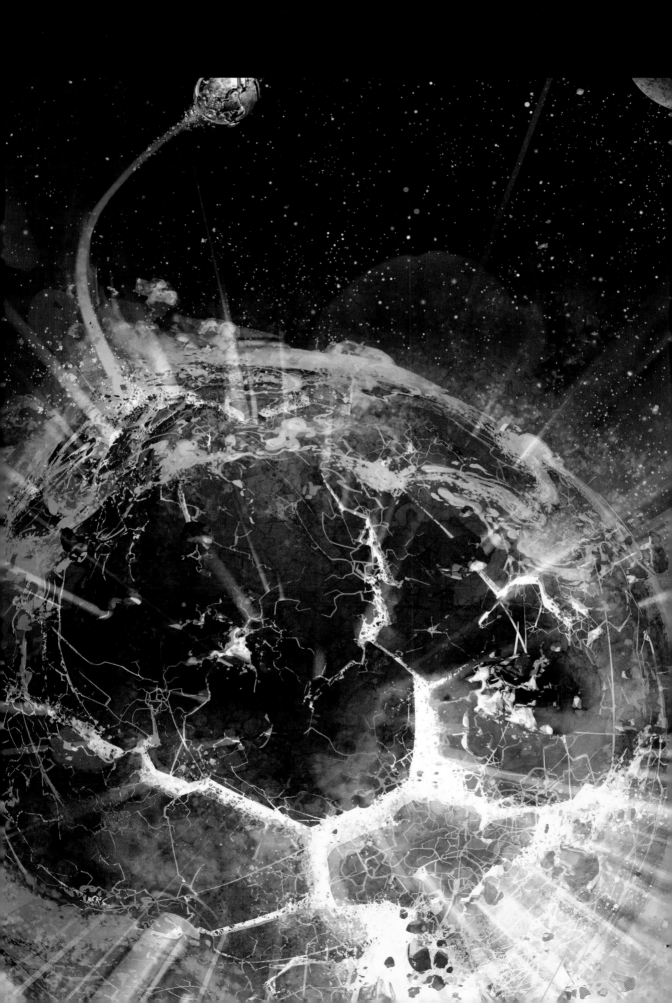

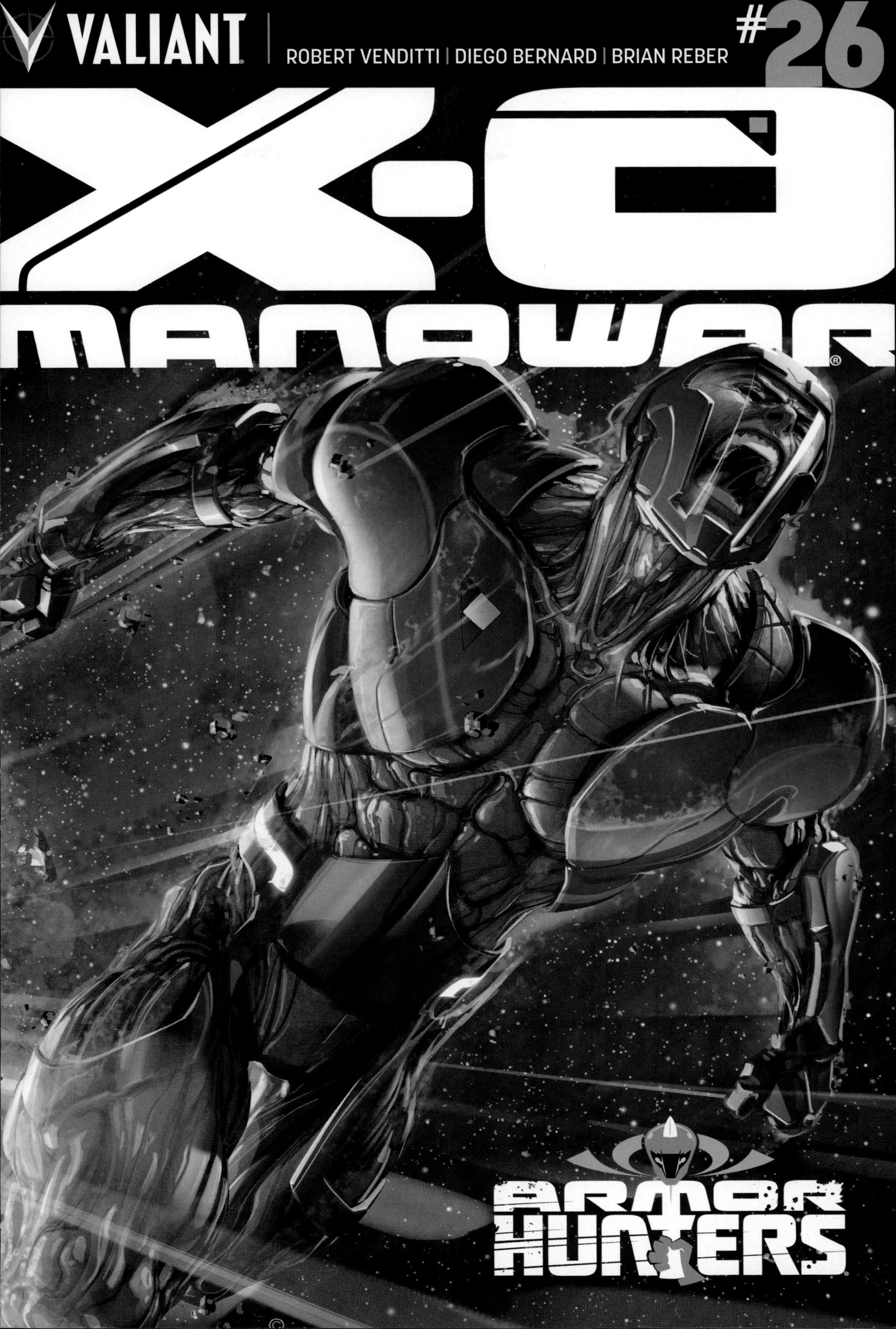
VALIANT
ROBERT VENDITTI | DIEGO BERNARD | BRIAN REBER
#26
X-O MANOWAR
ARMOR HUNTERS

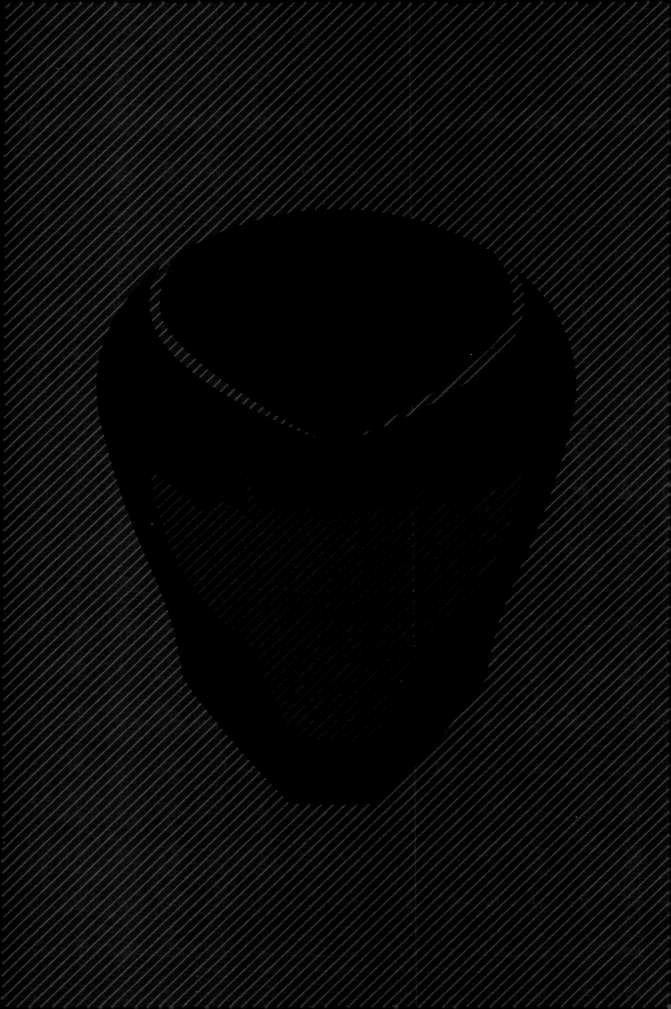

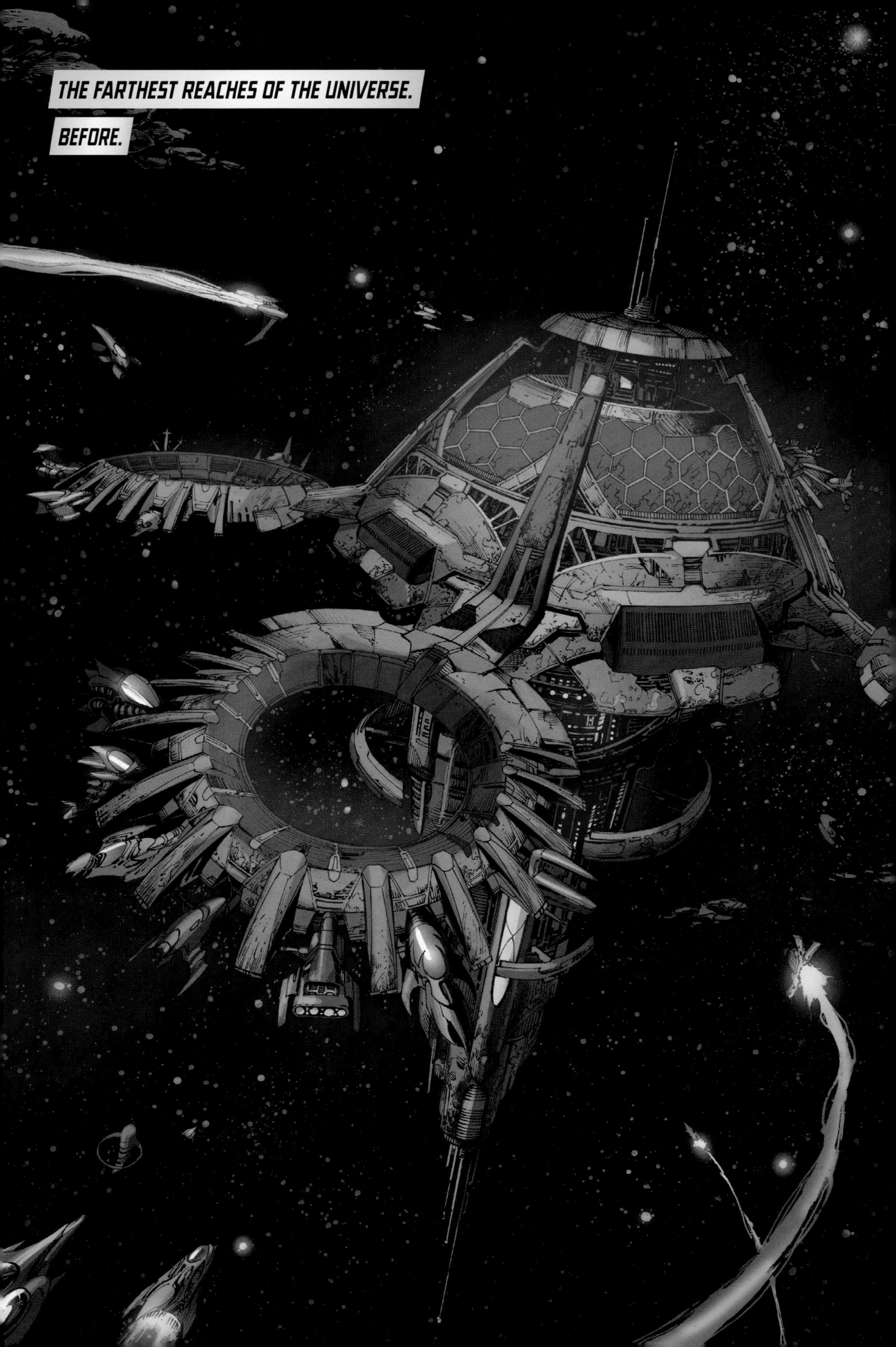
THE FARTHEST REACHES OF THE UNIVERSE.
BEFORE.

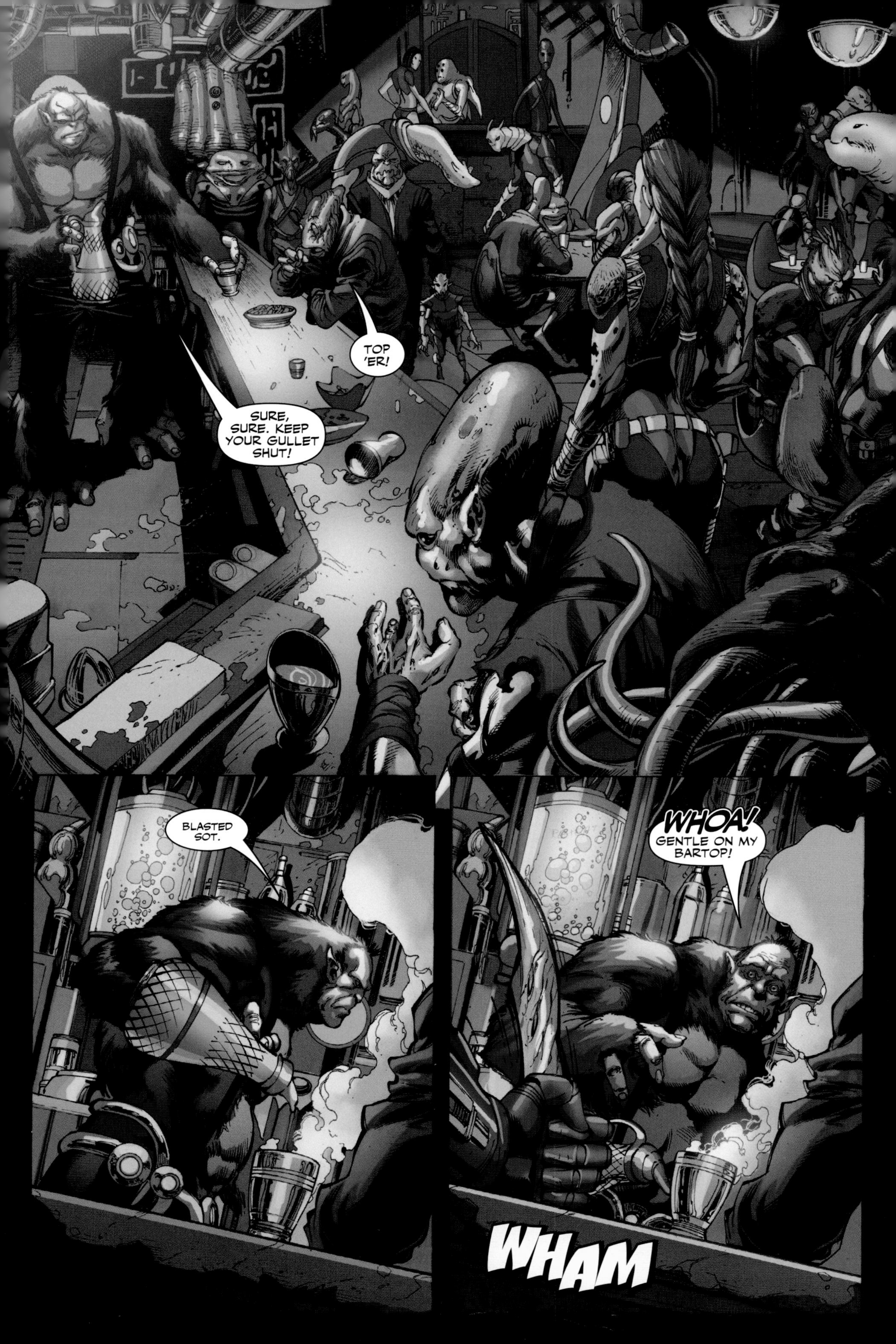
TOP 'ER!
SURE, SURE. KEEP YOUR GULLET SHUT!
BLASTED SOT.
WHOA! GENTLE ON MY BARTOP!
WHAM

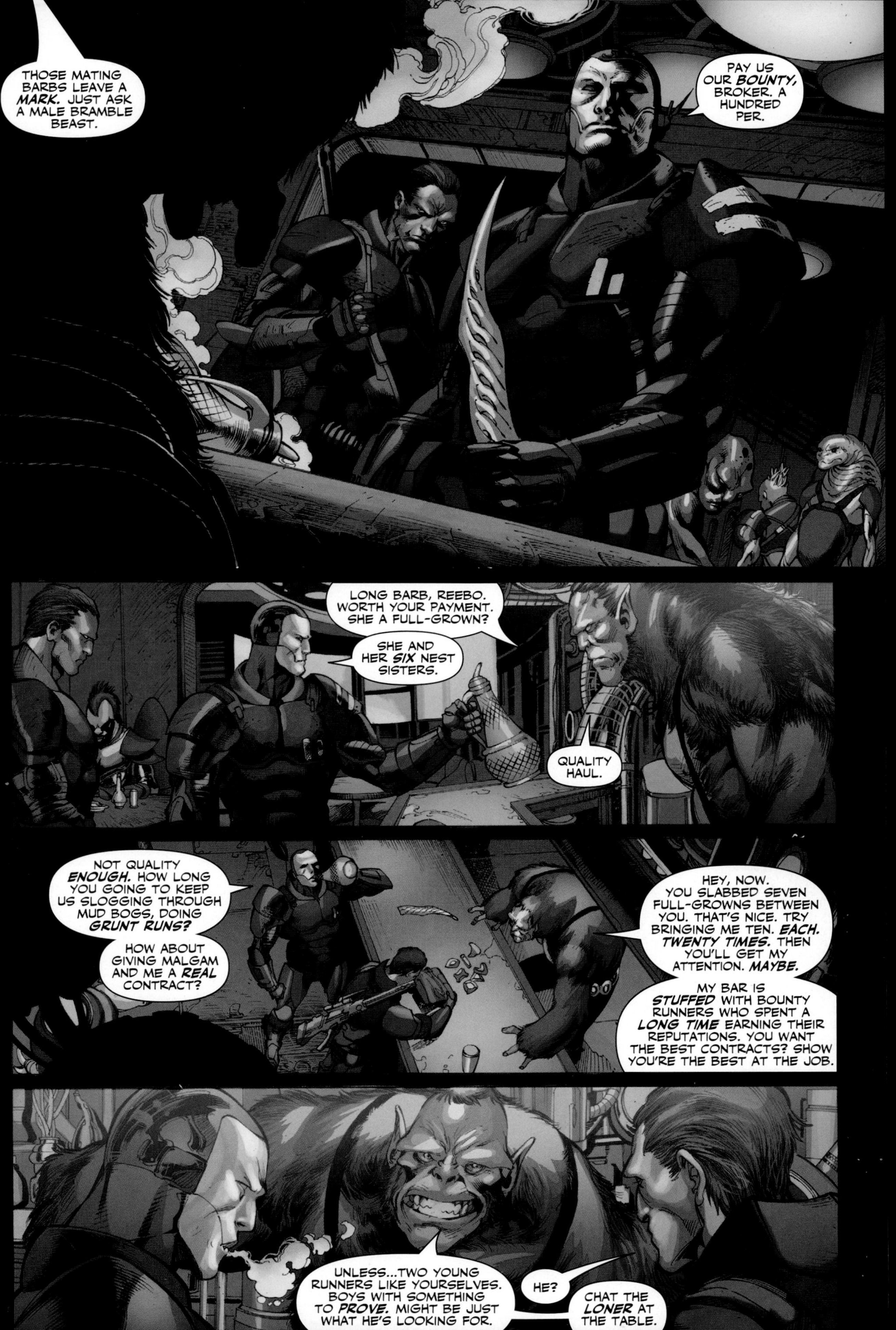
THOSE MATING BARBS LEAVE A MARK. JUST ASK A MALE BRAMBLE BEAST.
PAY US OUR BOUNTY, BROKER. A HUNDRED PER.
LONG BARB, REEBO. WORTH YOUR PAYMENT. SHE A FULL-GROWN?
SHE AND HER SIX NEST SISTERS.
QUALITY HAUL.
NOT QUALITY ENOUGH. HOW LONG YOU GOING TO KEEP US SLOGGING THROUGH MUD BOGS, DOING GRUNT RUNS?
HOW ABOUT GIVING MALGAM AND ME A REAL CONTRACT?
HEY, NOW. YOU SLABBED SEVEN FULL-GROWNS BETWEEN YOU. THAT'S NICE. TRY BRINGING ME TEN. EACH. TWENTY TIMES. THEN YOU'LL GET MY ATTENTION. MAYBE.
MY BAR IS STUFFED WITH BOUNTY RUNNERS WHO SPENT A LONG TIME EARNING THEIR REPUTATIONS. YOU WANT THE BEST CONTRACTS? SHOW YOU'RE THE BEST AT THE JOB.
UNLESS...TWO YOUNG RUNNERS LIKE YOURSELVES. BOYS WITH SOMETHING TO PROVE. MIGHT BE JUST WHAT HE'S LOOKING FOR.
HE?
CHAT THE LONER AT THE TABLE.

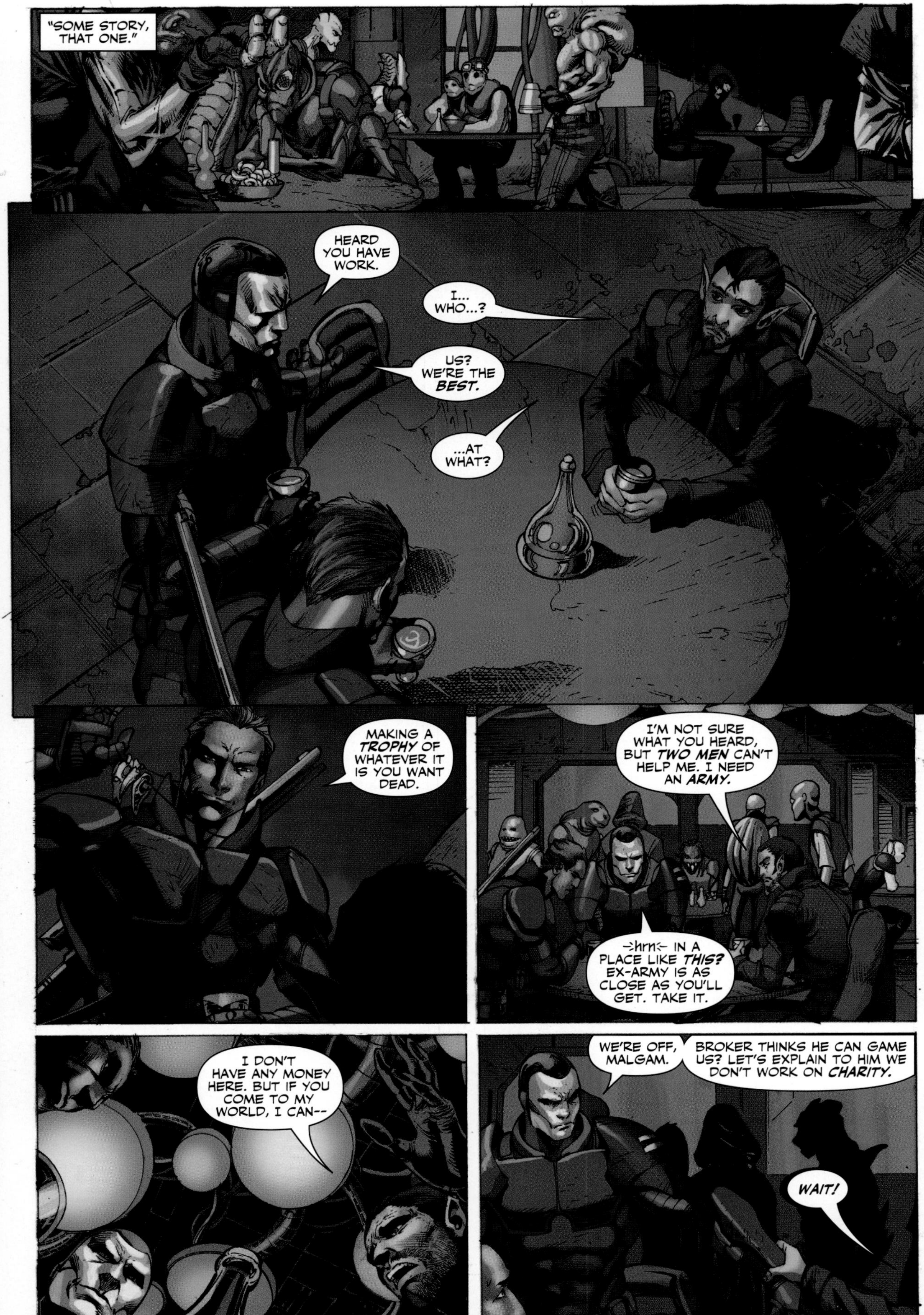
"SOME STORY, THAT ONE."
HEARD YOU HAVE WORK.
I... WHO...?
US? WE'RE THE BEST.
...AT WHAT?
MAKING A TROPHY OF WHATEVER IT IS YOU WANT DEAD.
I'M NOT SURE WHAT YOU HEARD, BUT TWO MEN CAN'T HELP ME. I NEED AN ARMY.
hrn IN A PLACE LIKE THIS? EX-ARMY IS AS CLOSE AS YOU'LL GET. TAKE IT.
I DON'T HAVE ANY MONEY HERE. BUT IF YOU COME TO MY WORLD, I CAN--
WE'RE OFF, MALGAM.
BROKER THINKS HE CAN GAME US? LET'S EXPLAIN TO HIM WE DON'T WORK ON CHARITY.
WAIT!

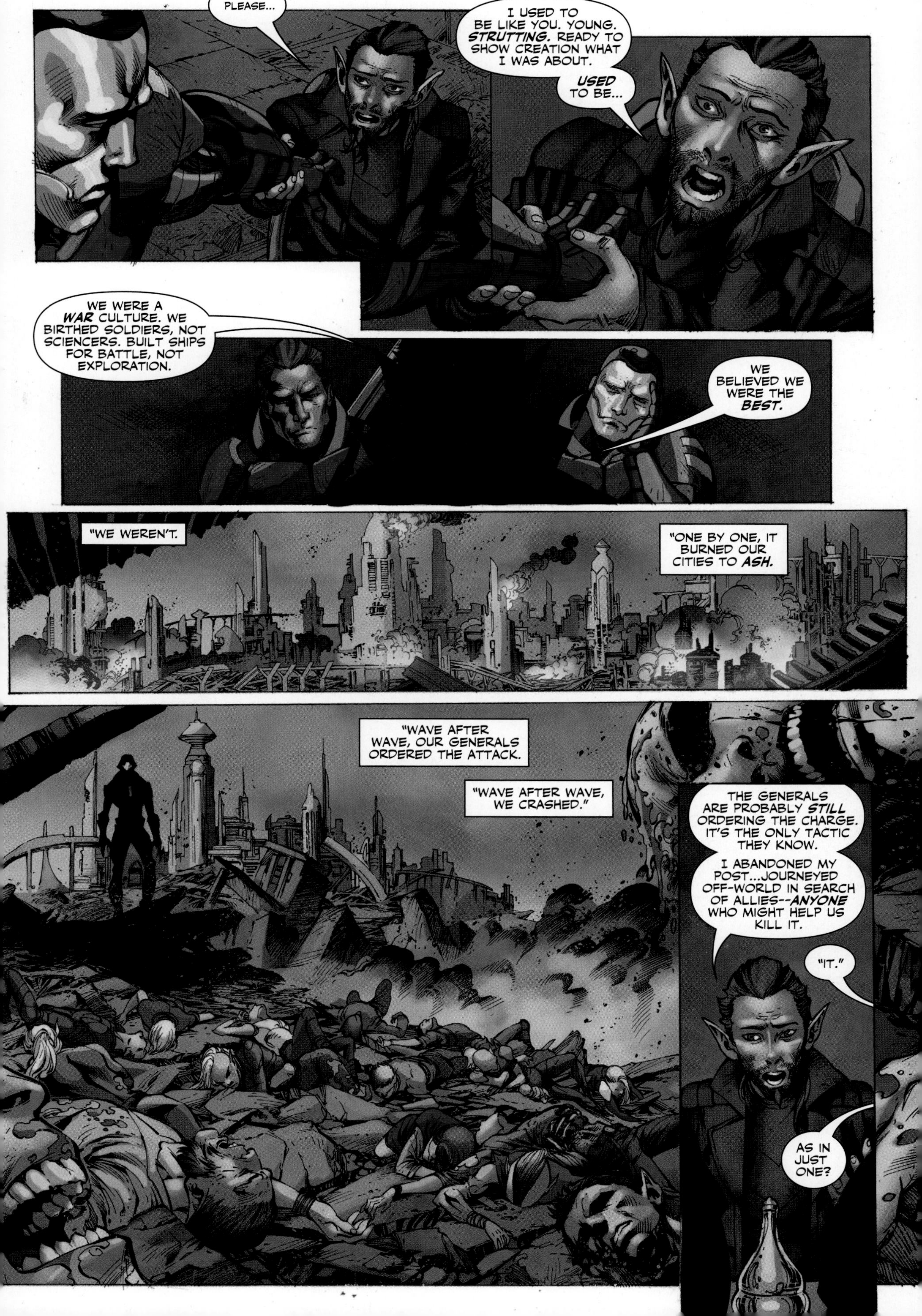
PLEASE...
I USED TO BE LIKE YOU. YOUNG. STRUTTING. READY TO SHOW CREATION WHAT I WAS ABOUT.
USED TO BE...
WE WERE A WAR CULTURE. WE BIRTHED SOLDIERS, NOT SCIENCERS. BUILT SHIPS FOR BATTLE, NOT EXPLORATION.
WE BELIEVED WE WERE THE BEST.
"WE WEREN'T.
"ONE BY ONE, IT BURNED OUR CITIES TO ASH.
"WAVE AFTER WAVE, OUR GENERALS ORDERED THE ATTACK.
"WAVE AFTER WAVE, WE CRASHED."
THE GENERALS ARE PROBABLY STILL ORDERING THE CHARGE. IT'S THE ONLY TACTIC THEY KNOW.
I ABANDONED MY POST...JOURNEYED OFF-WORLD IN SEARCH OF ALLIES--ANYONE WHO MIGHT HELP US KILL IT.
"IT."
AS IN JUST ONE?

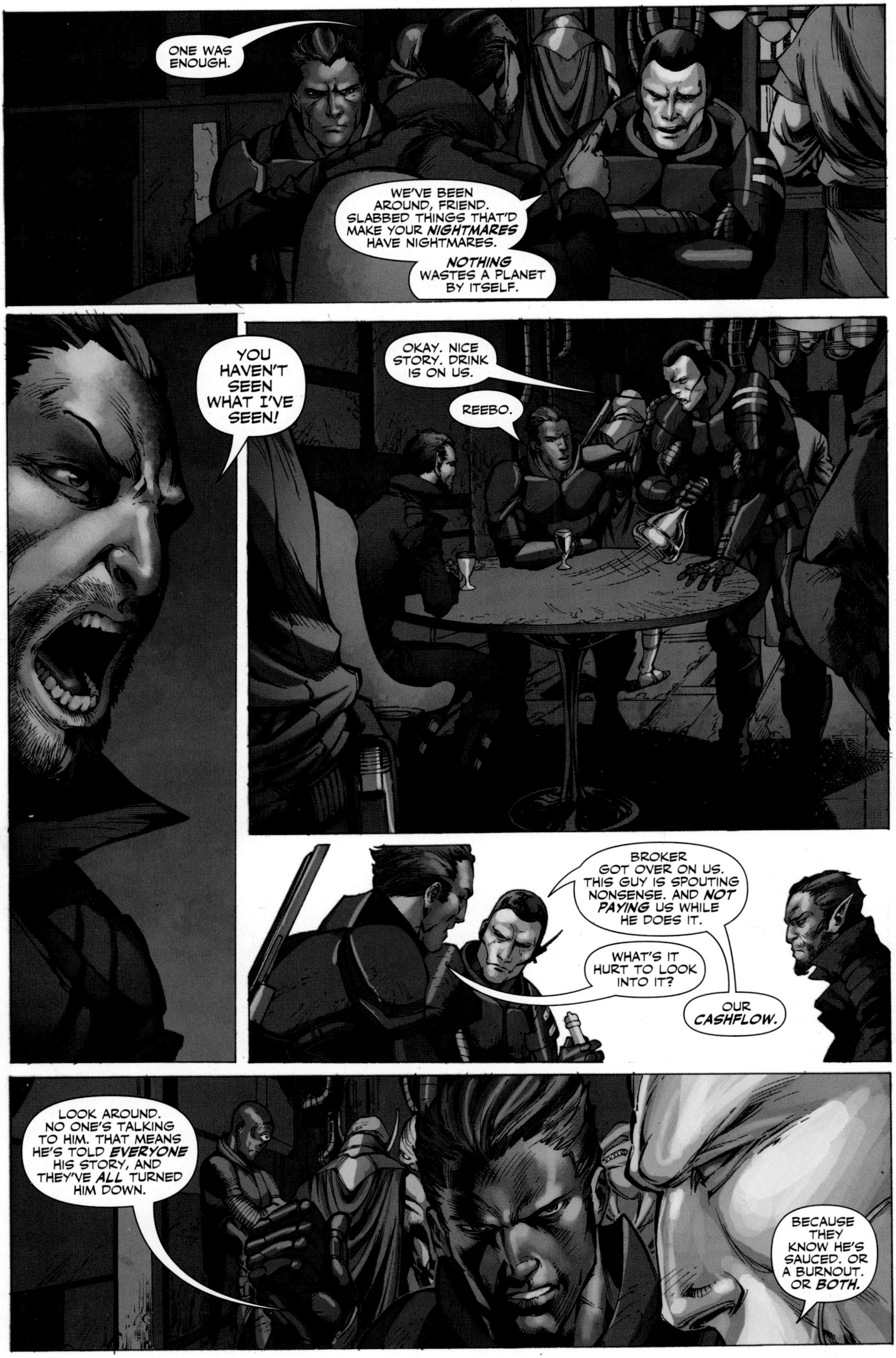

ONE WAS ENOUGH.
WE'VE BEEN AROUND, FRIEND. SLABBED THINGS THAT'D MAKE YOUR *NIGHTMARES* HAVE NIGHTMARES.
NOTHING WASTES A PLANET BY ITSELF.
YOU HAVEN'T SEEN WHAT I'VE SEEN!
OKAY. NICE STORY. DRINK IS ON US.
REEBO.
BROKER GOT OVER ON US. THIS GUY IS SPOUTING NONSENSE. AND *NOT PAYING* US WHILE HE DOES IT.
WHAT'S IT HURT TO LOOK INTO IT?
OUR *CASHFLOW.*
LOOK AROUND. NO ONE'S TALKING TO HIM. THAT MEANS HE'S TOLD *EVERYONE* HIS STORY, AND THEY'VE *ALL* TURNED HIM DOWN.
BECAUSE THEY KNOW HE'S SAUCED. OR A BURNOUT. OR *BOTH.*

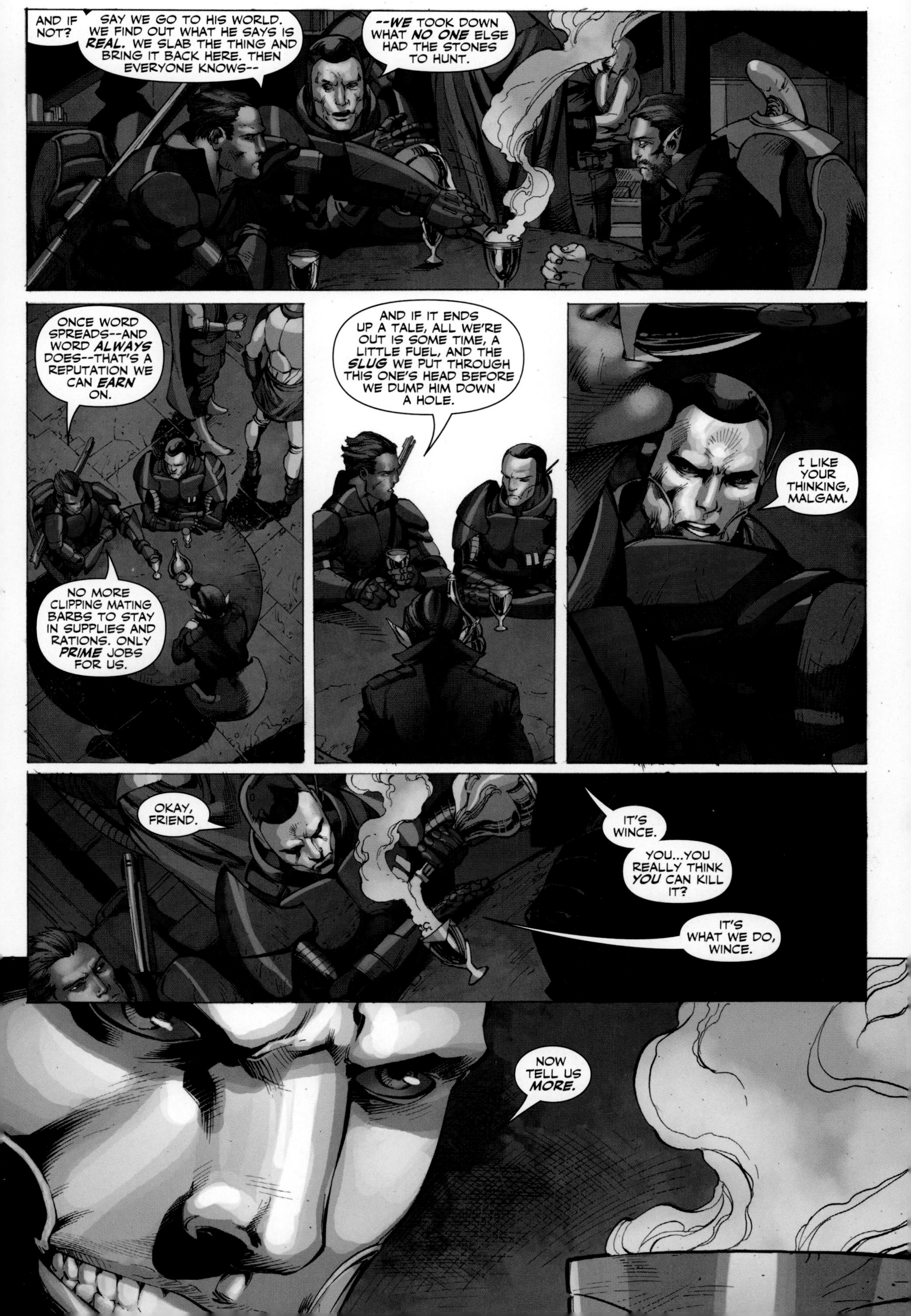

AND IF NOT?
SAY WE GO TO HIS WORLD. WE FIND OUT WHAT HE SAYS IS REAL. WE SLAB THE THING AND BRING IT BACK HERE. THEN EVERYONE KNOWS--
--WE TOOK DOWN WHAT NO ONE ELSE HAD THE STONES TO HUNT.
ONCE WORD SPREADS--AND WORD ALWAYS DOES--THAT'S A REPUTATION WE CAN EARN ON.
NO MORE CLIPPING MATING BARBS TO STAY IN SUPPLIES AND RATIONS. ONLY PRIME JOBS FOR US.
AND IF IT ENDS UP A TALE, ALL WE'RE OUT IS SOME TIME, A LITTLE FUEL, AND THE SLUG WE PUT THROUGH THIS ONE'S HEAD BEFORE WE DUMP HIM DOWN A HOLE.
I LIKE YOUR THINKING, MALGAM.
OKAY, FRIEND.
IT'S WINCE.
YOU...YOU REALLY THINK YOU CAN KILL IT?
IT'S WHAT WE DO, WINCE.
NOW TELL US MORE.

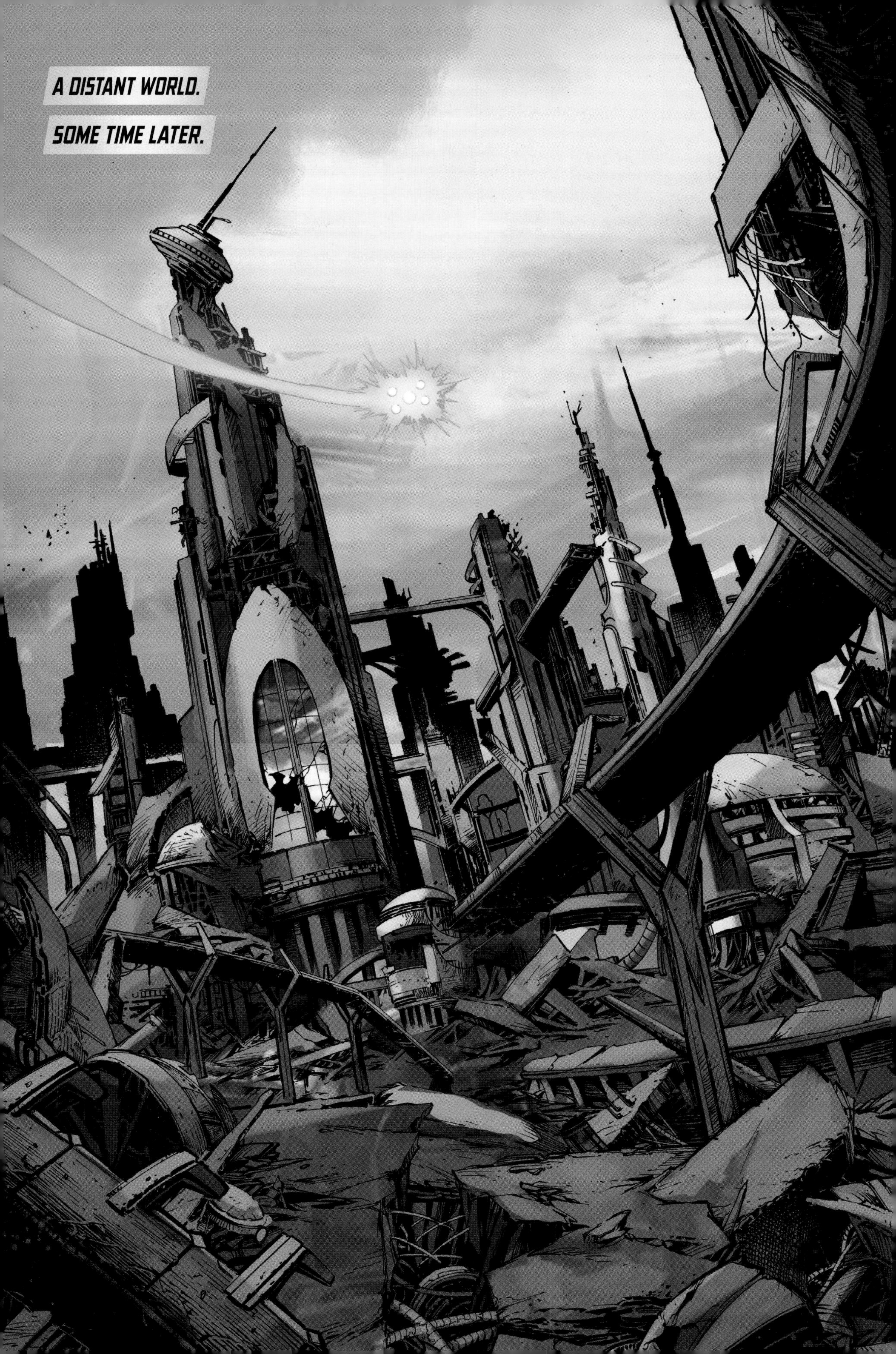
A DISTANT WORLD.
SOME TIME LATER.

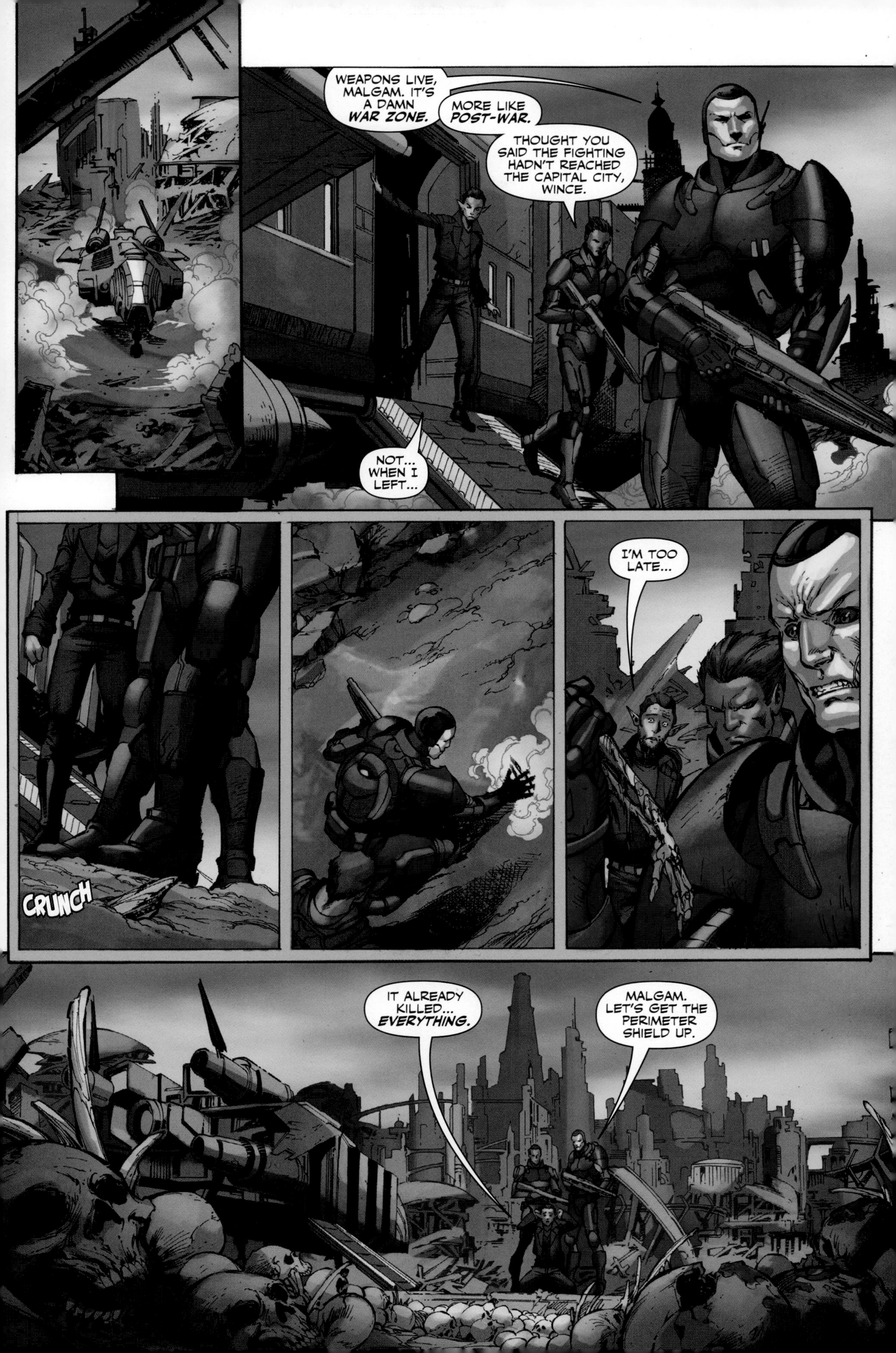
WEAPONS LIVE, MALGAM. IT'S A DAMN *WAR ZONE.*
MORE LIKE *POST-WAR.*
THOUGHT YOU SAID THE FIGHTING HADN'T REACHED THE CAPITAL CITY, WINCE.
NOT... WHEN I LEFT...
CRUNCH
I'M TOO LATE...
IT ALREADY KILLED... *EVERYTHING.*
MALGAM. LET'S GET THE PERIMETER SHIELD UP.

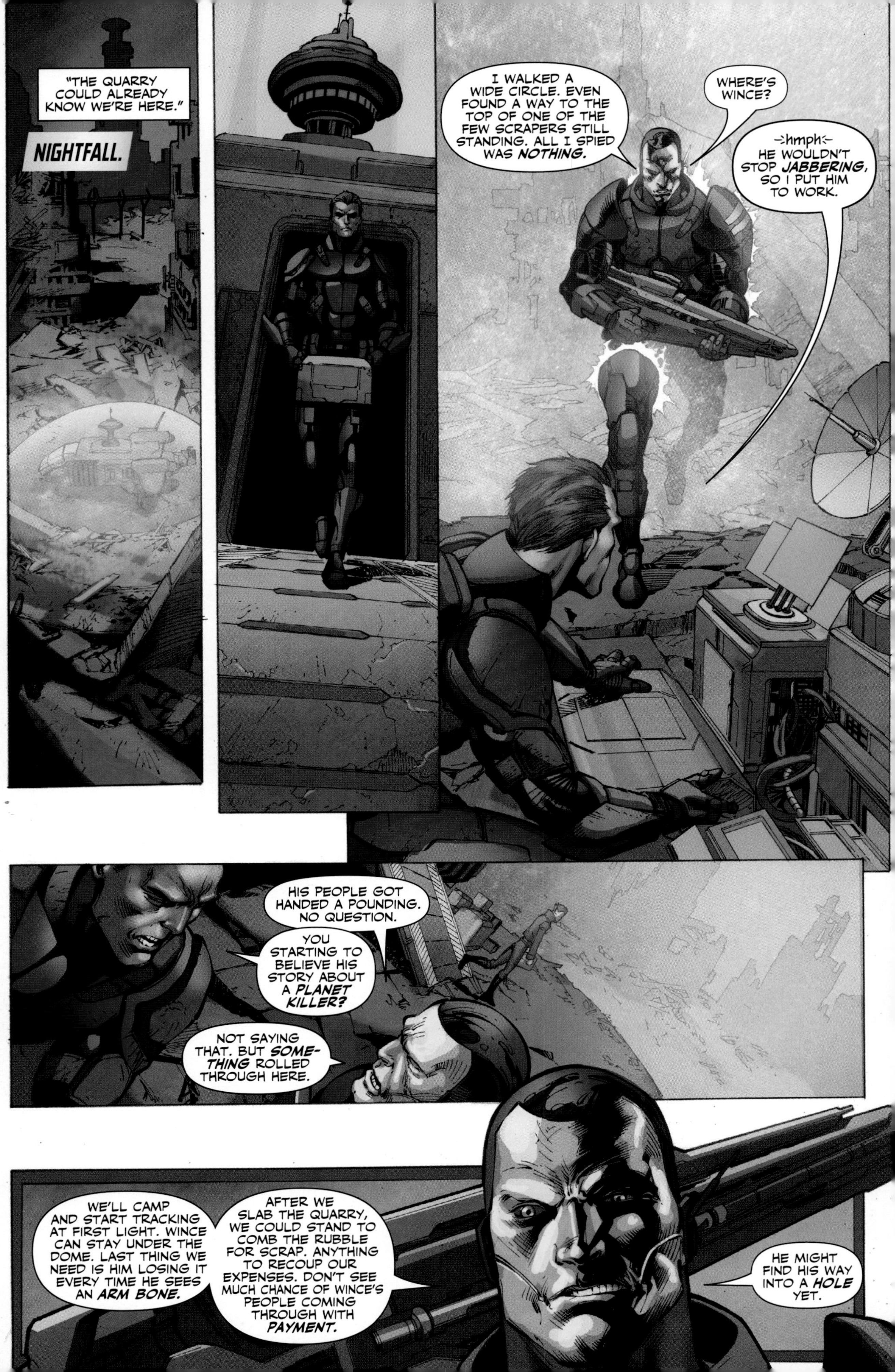
"THE QUARRY COULD ALREADY KNOW WE'RE HERE."
NIGHTFALL.
I WALKED A WIDE CIRCLE. EVEN FOUND A WAY TO THE TOP OF ONE OF THE FEW SCRAPERS STILL STANDING. ALL I SPIED WAS NOTHING.
WHERE'S WINCE?
-hmph- HE WOULDN'T STOP JABBERING, SO I PUT HIM TO WORK.
HIS PEOPLE GOT HANDED A POUNDING. NO QUESTION.
YOU STARTING TO BELIEVE HIS STORY ABOUT A PLANET KILLER?
NOT SAYING THAT. BUT SOMETHING ROLLED THROUGH HERE.
WE'LL CAMP AND START TRACKING AT FIRST LIGHT. WINCE CAN STAY UNDER THE DOME. LAST THING WE NEED IS HIM LOSING IT EVERY TIME HE SEES AN ARM BONE.
AFTER WE SLAB THE QUARRY, WE COULD STAND TO COMB THE RUBBLE FOR SCRAP. ANYTHING TO RECOUP OUR EXPENSES. DON'T SEE MUCH CHANCE OF WINCE'S PEOPLE COMING THROUGH WITH PAYMENT.
HE MIGHT FIND HIS WAY INTO A HOLE YET.

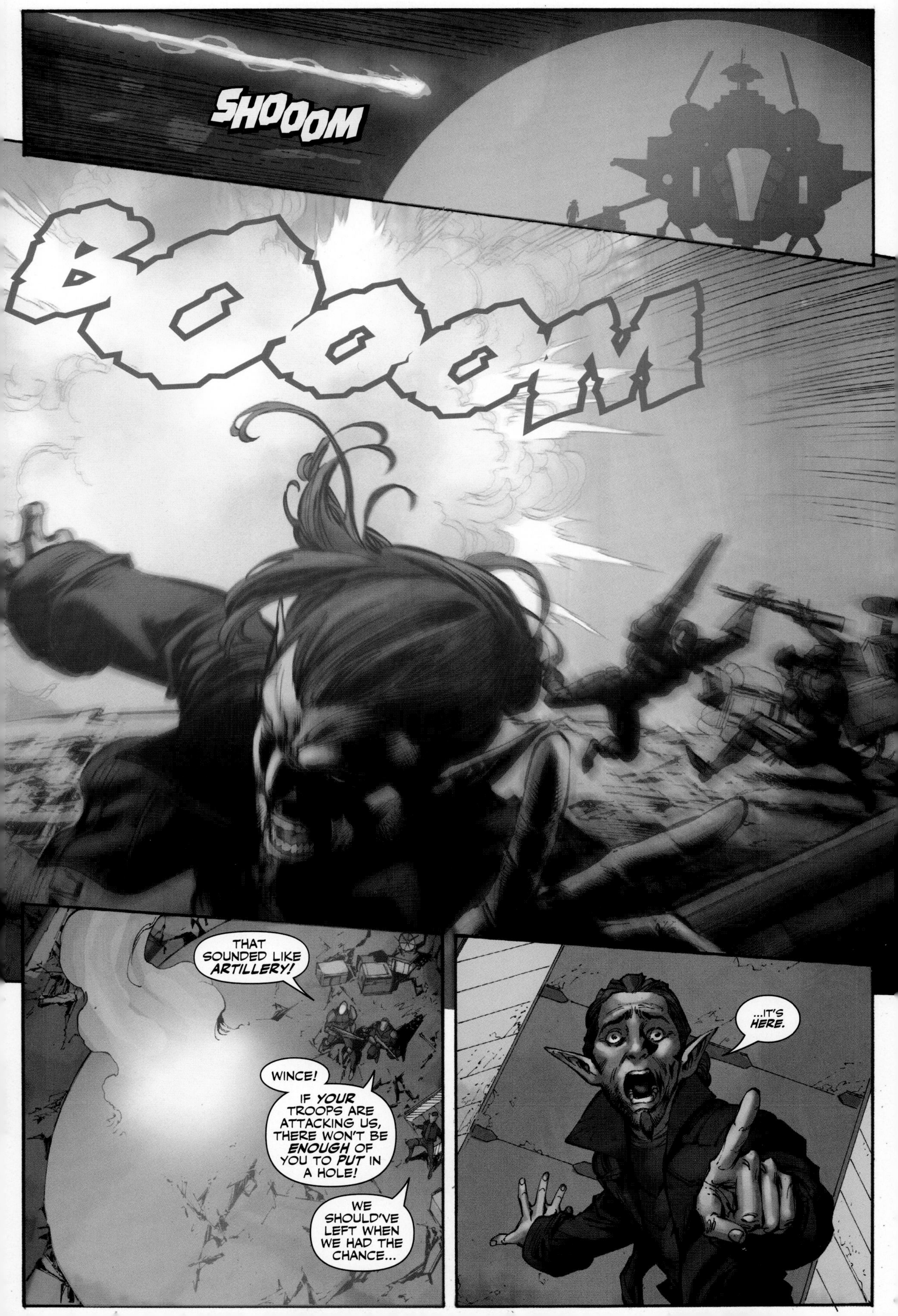
SHOOOM
BOOOOM
THAT SOUNDED LIKE ARTILLERY!
WINCE!
IF YOUR TROOPS ARE ATTACKING US, THERE WON'T BE ENOUGH OF YOU TO PUT IN A HOLE!
WE SHOULD'VE LEFT WHEN WE HAD THE CHANCE...
...IT'S HERE.

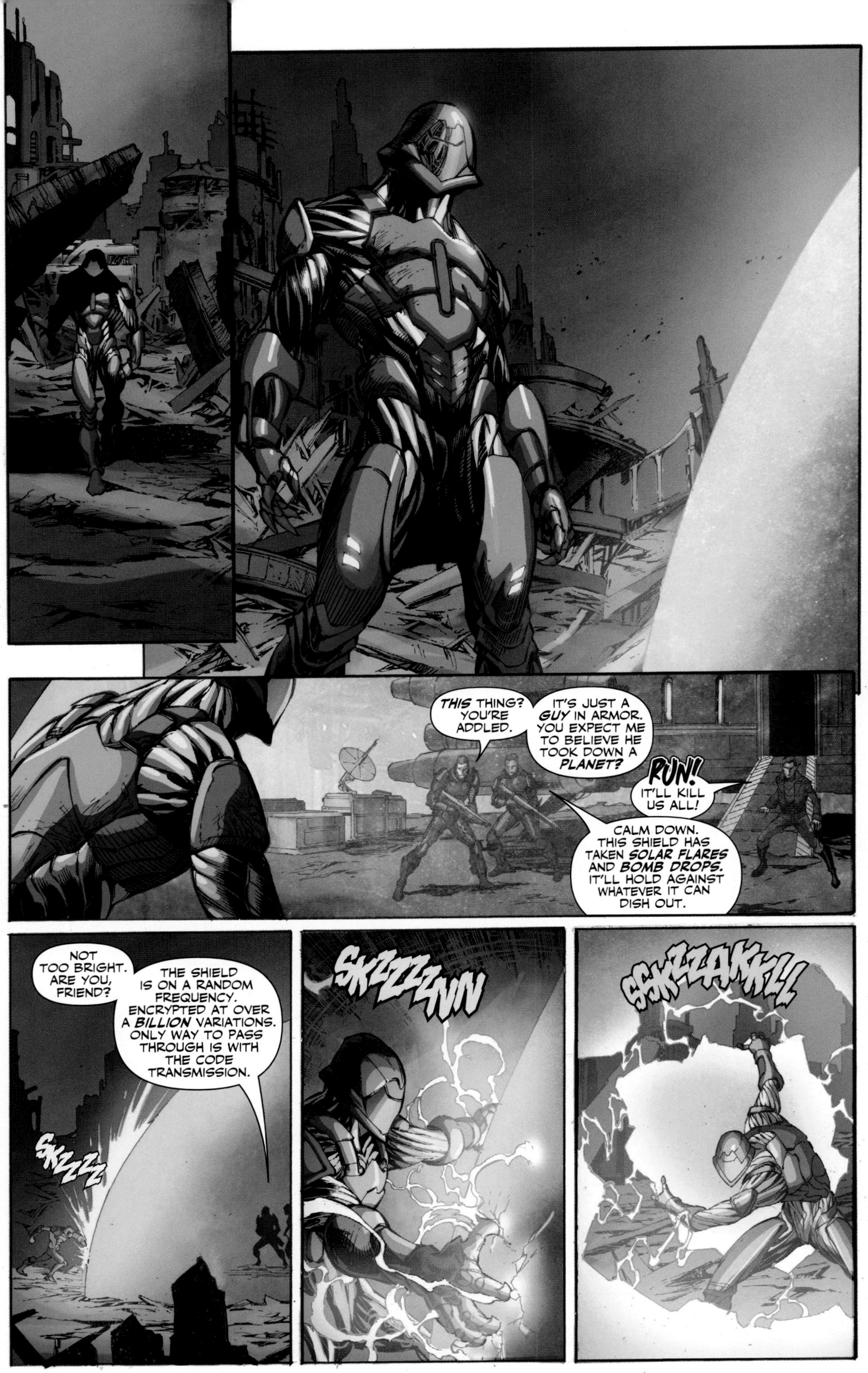
THIS THING? YOU'RE ADDLED.
IT'S JUST A GUY IN ARMOR. YOU EXPECT ME TO BELIEVE HE TOOK DOWN A PLANET?
RUN! IT'LL KILL US ALL!
CALM DOWN. THIS SHIELD HAS TAKEN SOLAR FLARES AND BOMB DROPS. IT'LL HOLD AGAINST WHATEVER IT CAN DISH OUT.
NOT TOO BRIGHT. ARE YOU, FRIEND?
THE SHIELD IS ON A RANDOM FREQUENCY. ENCRYPTED AT OVER A BILLION VARIATIONS. ONLY WAY TO PASS THROUGH IS WITH THE CODE TRANSMISSION.
SKZZZZ
SKZZZZNN
SSKZZAKKL!

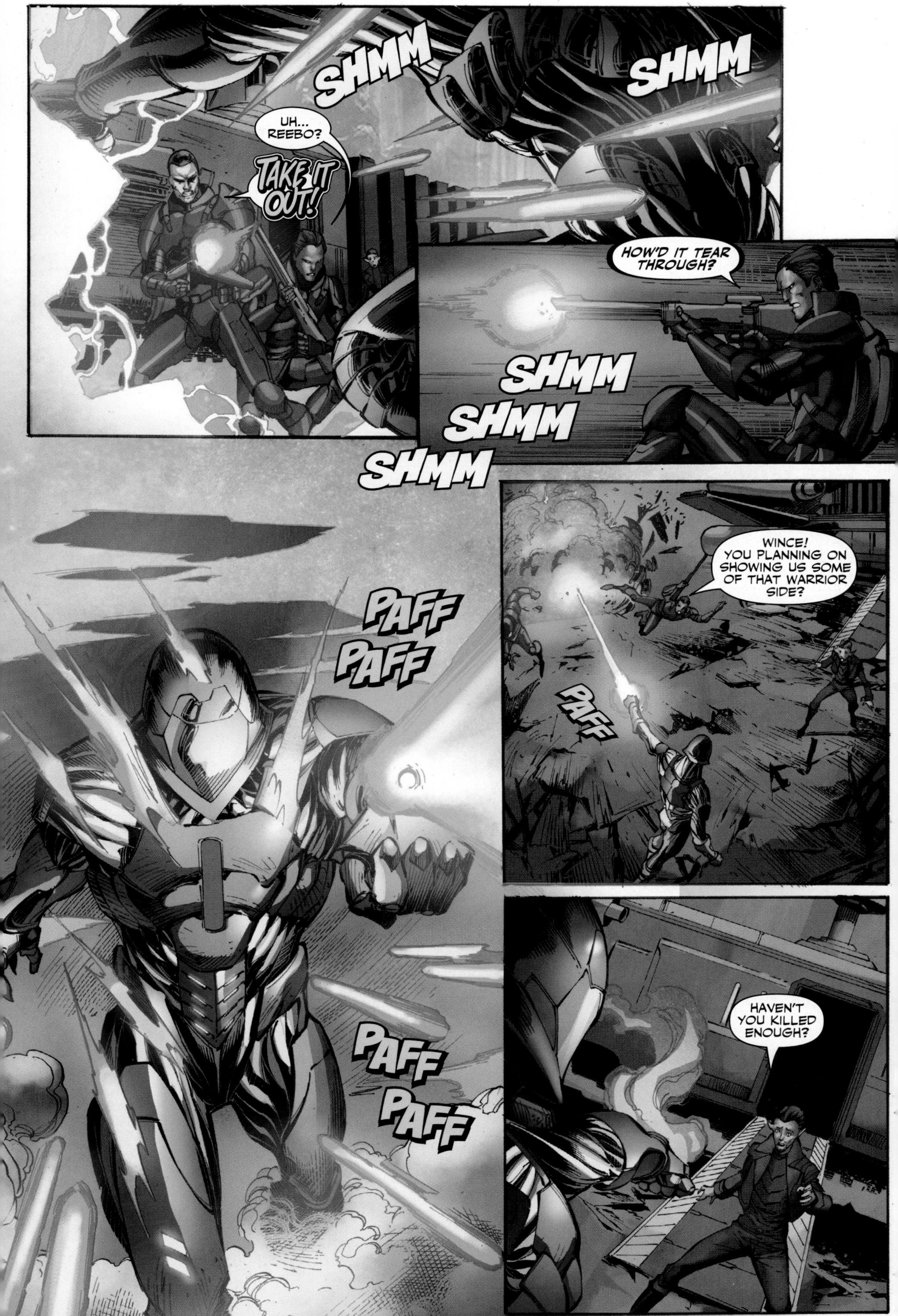

SHMM
SHMM
UH... REEBO?
TAKE IT OUT!
HOW'D IT TEAR THROUGH?
SHMM
SHMM
SHMM
WINCE! YOU PLANNING ON SHOWING US SOME OF THAT WARRIOR SIDE?
PAFF
PAFF
PAFF
PAFF
PAFF
HAVEN'T YOU KILLED ENOUGH?

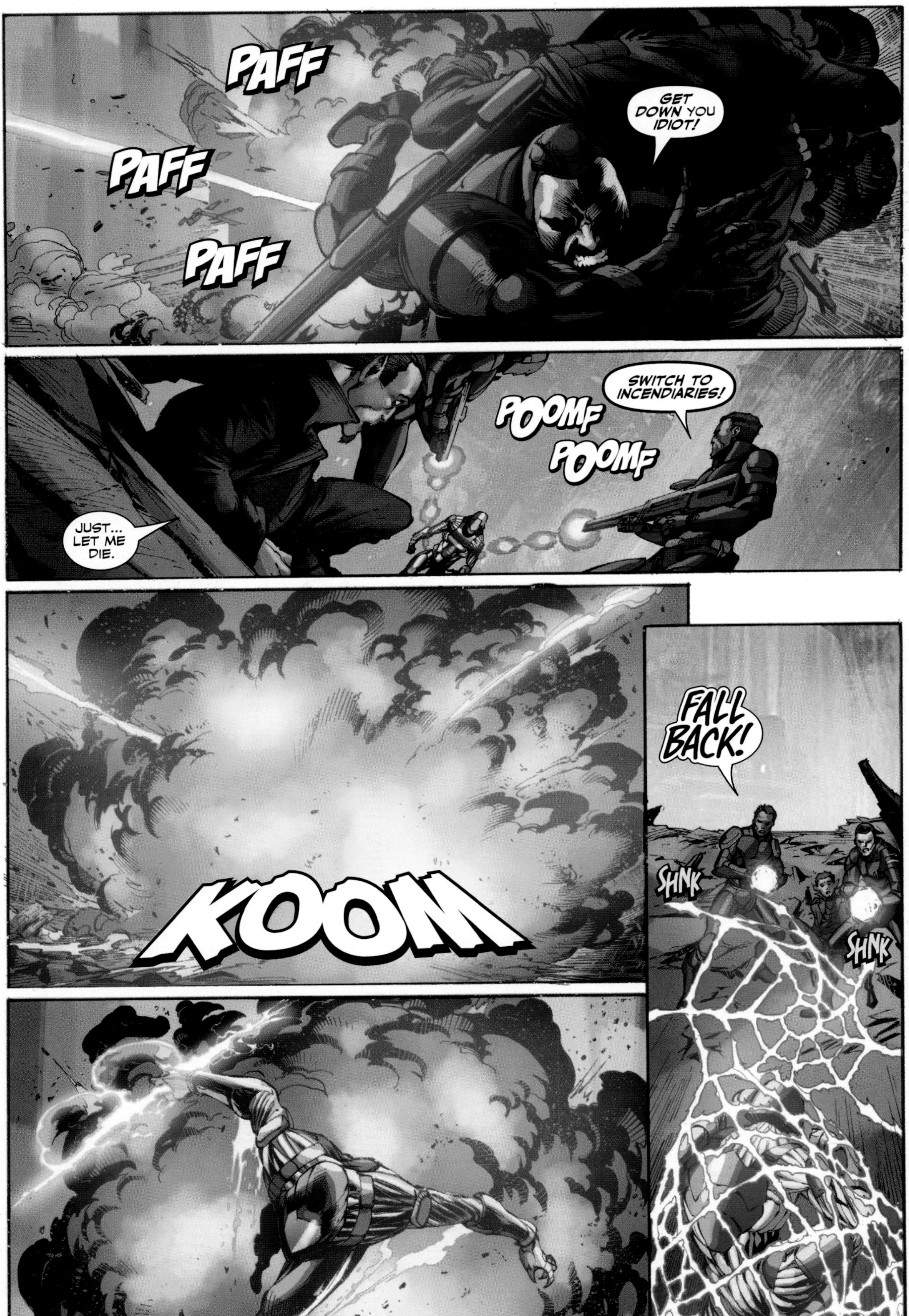
PAFF
PAFF
PAFF
GET DOWN YOU IDIOT!
SWITCH TO INCENDIARIES!
POOMF
POOMF
JUST... LET ME DIE.
KOOM
FALL BACK!
SHNK
SHNK

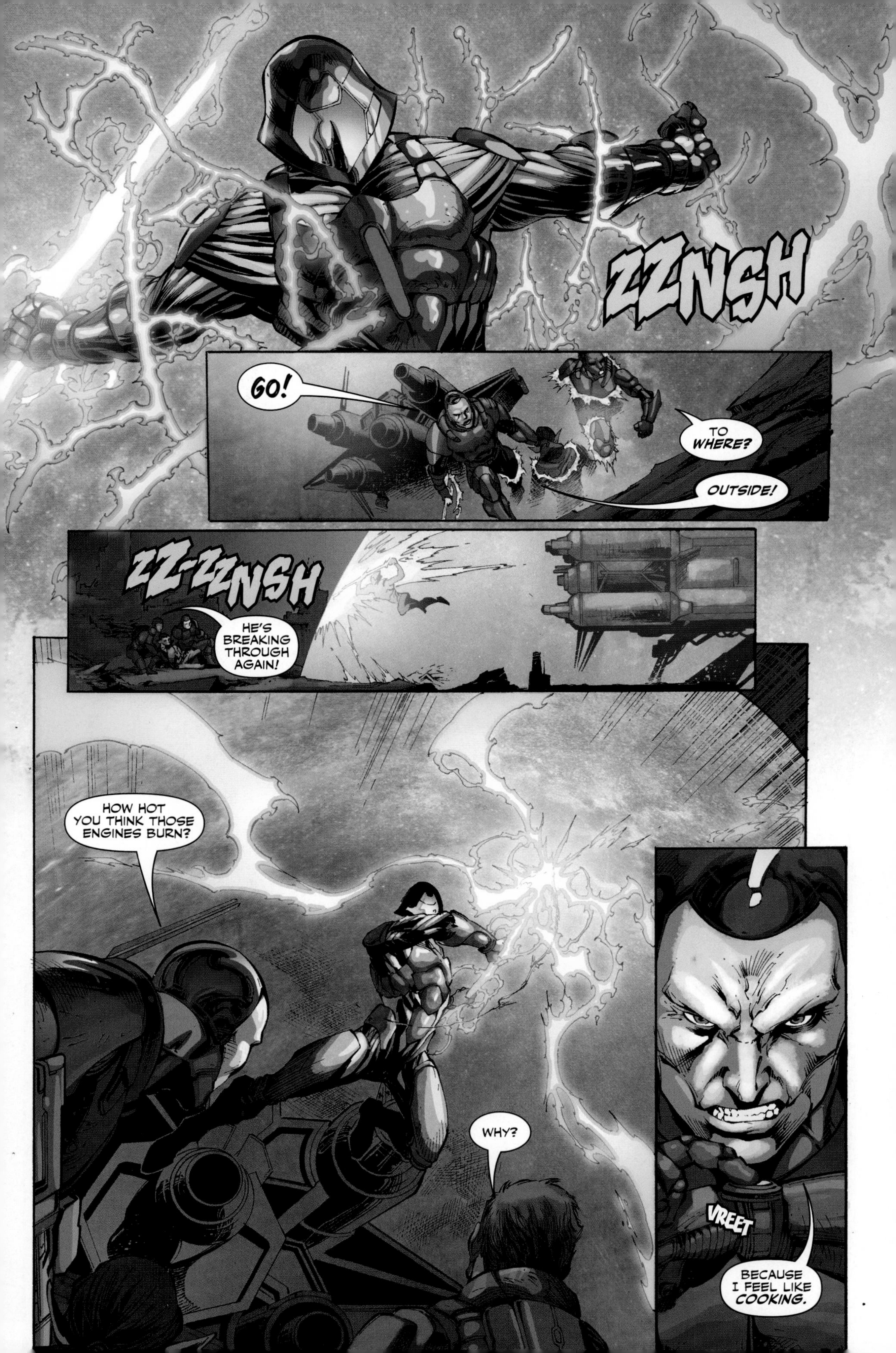

ZZNSH
GO!
TO WHERE?
OUTSIDE!
ZZ-ZZNSH
HE'S BREAKING THROUGH AGAIN!
HOW HOT YOU THINK THOSE ENGINES BURN?
WHY?
!
VREET
BECAUSE I FEEL LIKE COOKING.

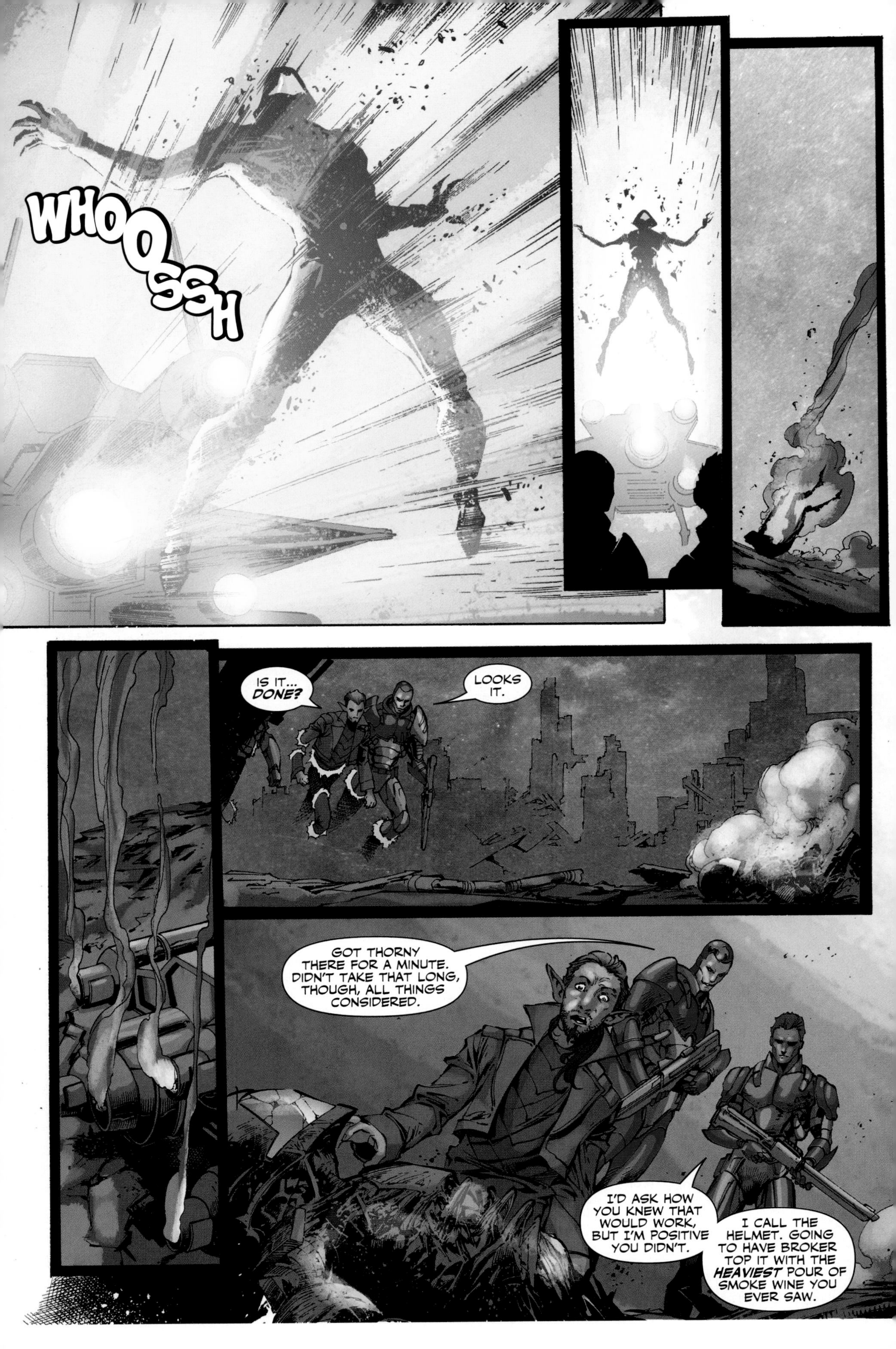
WHOOOSSH
IS IT... DONE?
LOOKS IT.
GOT THORNY THERE FOR A MINUTE. DIDN'T TAKE THAT LONG, THOUGH, ALL THINGS CONSIDERED.
I'D ASK HOW YOU KNEW THAT WOULD WORK, BUT I'M POSITIVE YOU DIDN'T.
I CALL THE HELMET. GOING TO HAVE BROKER TOP IT WITH THE *HEAVIEST* POUR OF SMOKE WINE YOU EVER SAW.

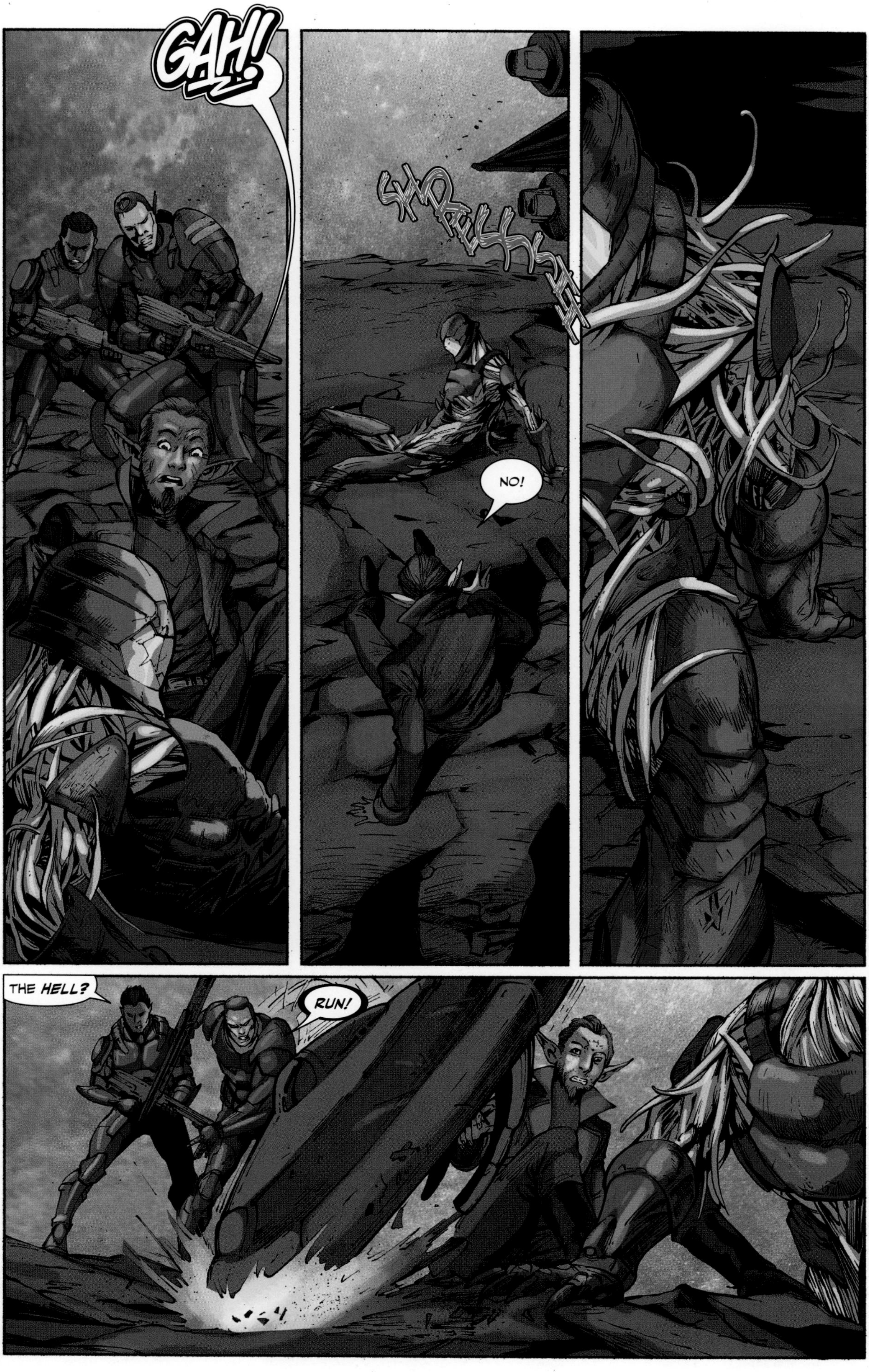
GAH!
NO!
THE HELL?
RUN!

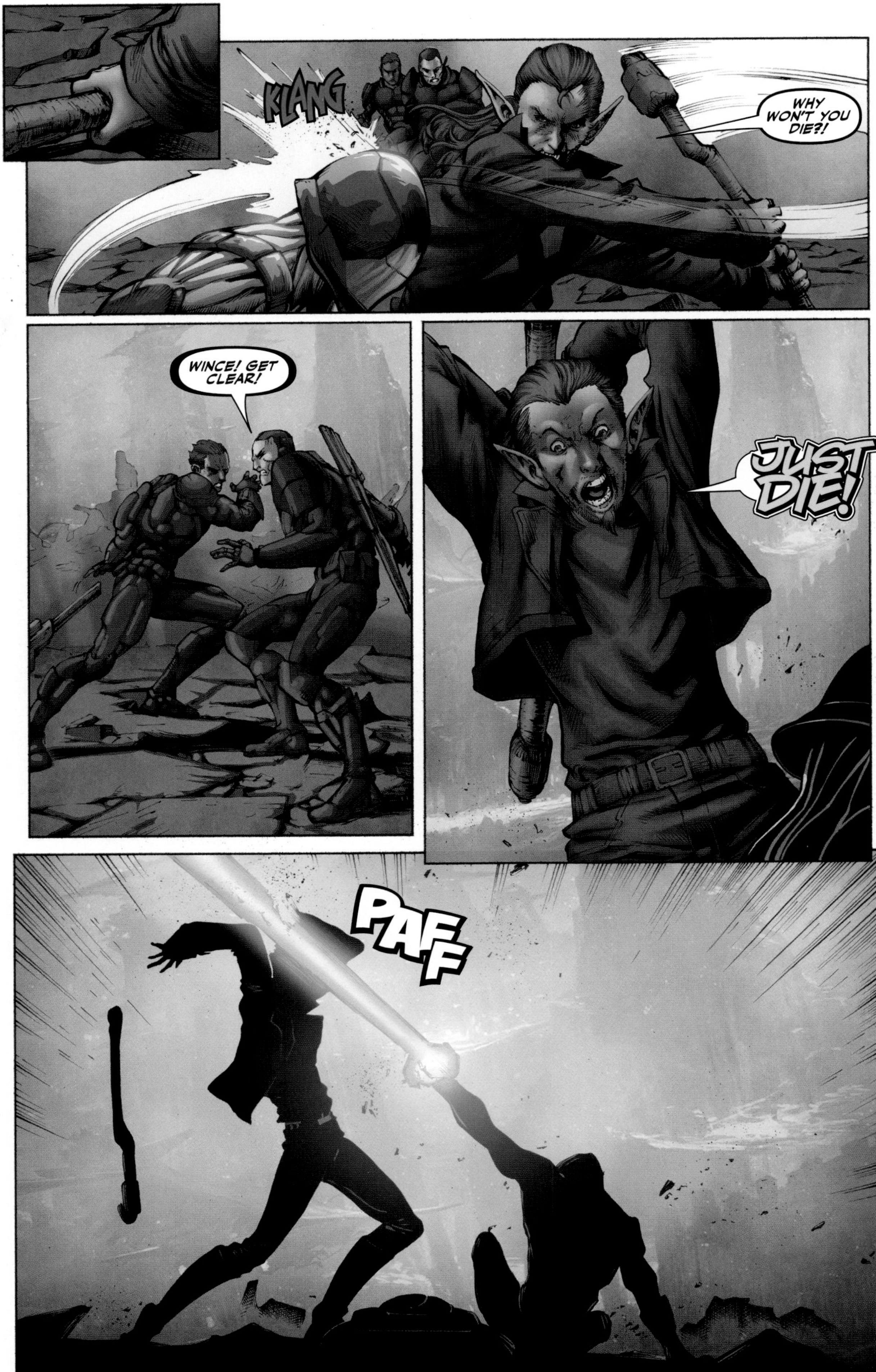
KLANG
WHY WON'T YOU DIE?!
WINCE! GET CLEAR!
JUST DIE!
PAFF

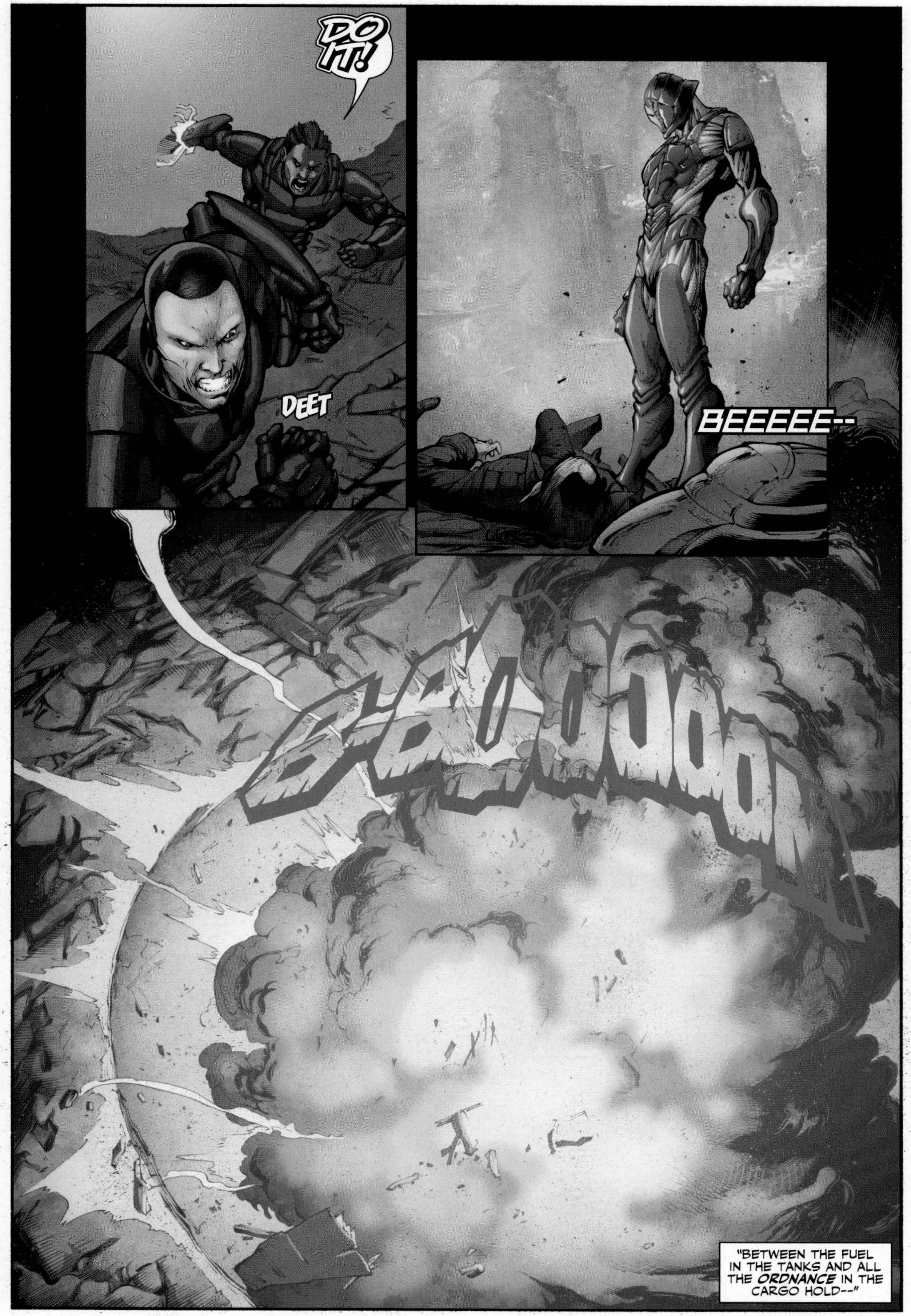
DO IT!
DEET
BEEEEE--
"BETWEEN THE FUEL IN THE TANKS AND ALL THE *ORDNANCE* IN THE CARGO HOLD--"

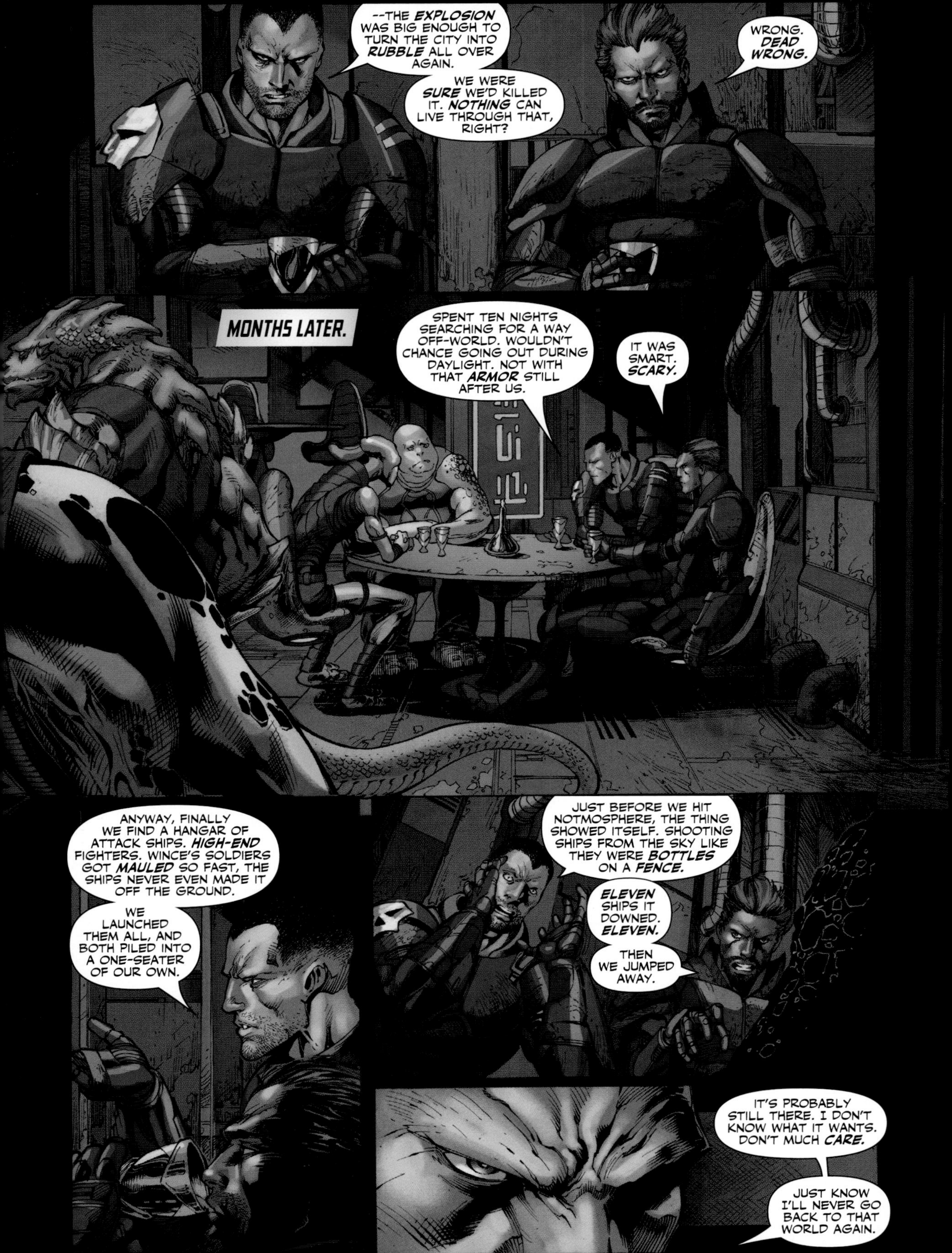
--THE EXPLOSION WAS BIG ENOUGH TO TURN THE CITY INTO RUBBLE ALL OVER AGAIN.
WE WERE SURE WE'D KILLED IT. NOTHING CAN LIVE THROUGH THAT, RIGHT?
WRONG. DEAD WRONG.
MONTHS LATER.
SPENT TEN NIGHTS SEARCHING FOR A WAY OFF-WORLD. WOULDN'T CHANCE GOING OUT DURING DAYLIGHT. NOT WITH THAT ARMOR STILL AFTER US.
IT WAS SMART. SCARY.
ANYWAY, FINALLY WE FIND A HANGAR OF ATTACK SHIPS. HIGH-END FIGHTERS. WINCE'S SOLDIERS GOT MAULED SO FAST, THE SHIPS NEVER EVEN MADE IT OFF THE GROUND.
WE LAUNCHED THEM ALL, AND BOTH PILED INTO A ONE-SEATER OF OUR OWN.
JUST BEFORE WE HIT NOTMOSPHERE, THE THING SHOWED ITSELF. SHOOTING SHIPS FROM THE SKY LIKE THEY WERE BOTTLES ON A FENCE.
ELEVEN SHIPS IT DOWNED. ELEVEN.
THEN WE JUMPED AWAY.
IT'S PROBABLY STILL THERE. I DON'T KNOW WHAT IT WANTS. DON'T MUCH CARE.
JUST KNOW I'LL NEVER GO BACK TO THAT WORLD AGAIN.

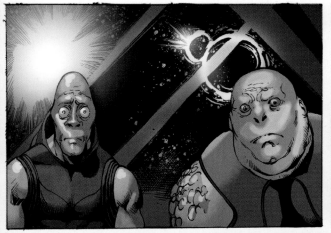

BWAAA!
HEEHAHA!

DID I TELL YOU?

YOU DID! I'VE HEARD A FEW DIFFERENT VERSIONS IN MY TRAVELS, BUT *NO ONE* TELLS IT AS GOOD AS THESE TWO!

BASTARDS! YOU HAVE WORK FOR US OR NOT?

I'LL TELL THAT ONE TO MY KIDS. JUST TO *SPOOK* 'EM!

YOU DON'T TALK TO YOUR KIDS.

SAYING IF I *DID*.

AT LEAST BUY US A ROUND! WE'RE *TAPPED*!

SHOVE A MATING BARB UP THEIR--

WE HAVE TO GET OFF THIS STATION, REEBO. START OVER. SOMEPLACE NO ONE'S HEARD OF US.

IF YOU WANT A NEW MISSION--

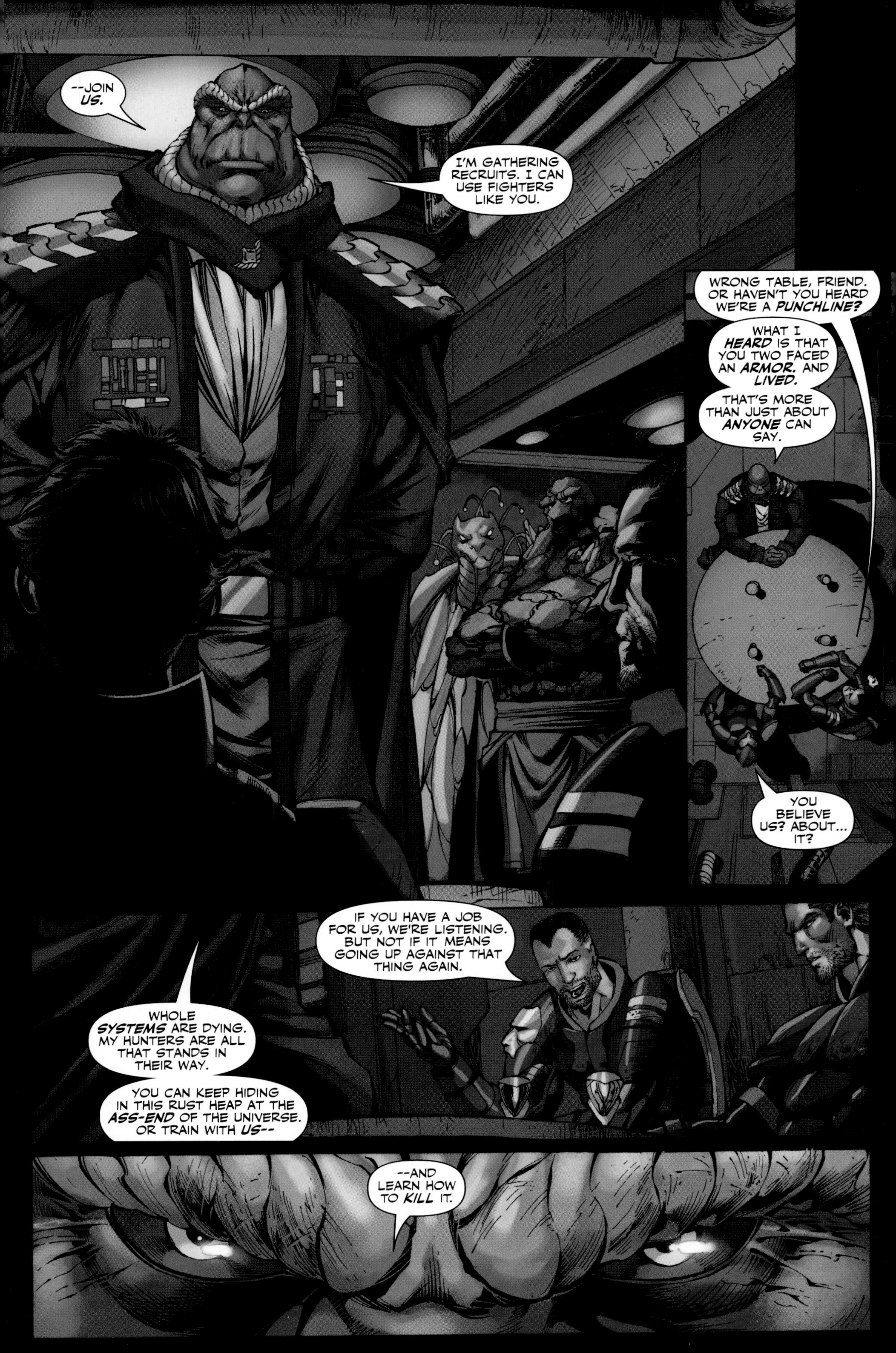
--JOIN US.
I'M GATHERING RECRUITS. I CAN USE FIGHTERS LIKE YOU.
WRONG TABLE, FRIEND. OR HAVEN'T YOU HEARD WE'RE A PUNCHLINE?
WHAT I HEARD IS THAT YOU TWO FACED AN ARMOR. AND LIVED.
THAT'S MORE THAN JUST ABOUT ANYONE CAN SAY.
YOU BELIEVE US? ABOUT... IT?
IF YOU HAVE A JOB FOR US, WE'RE LISTENING. BUT NOT IF IT MEANS GOING UP AGAINST THAT THING AGAIN.
WHOLE SYSTEMS ARE DYING. MY HUNTERS ARE ALL THAT STANDS IN THEIR WAY.
YOU CAN KEEP HIDING IN THIS RUST HEAP AT THE ASS-END OF THE UNIVERSE. OR TRAIN WITH US--
--AND LEARN HOW TO KILL IT.

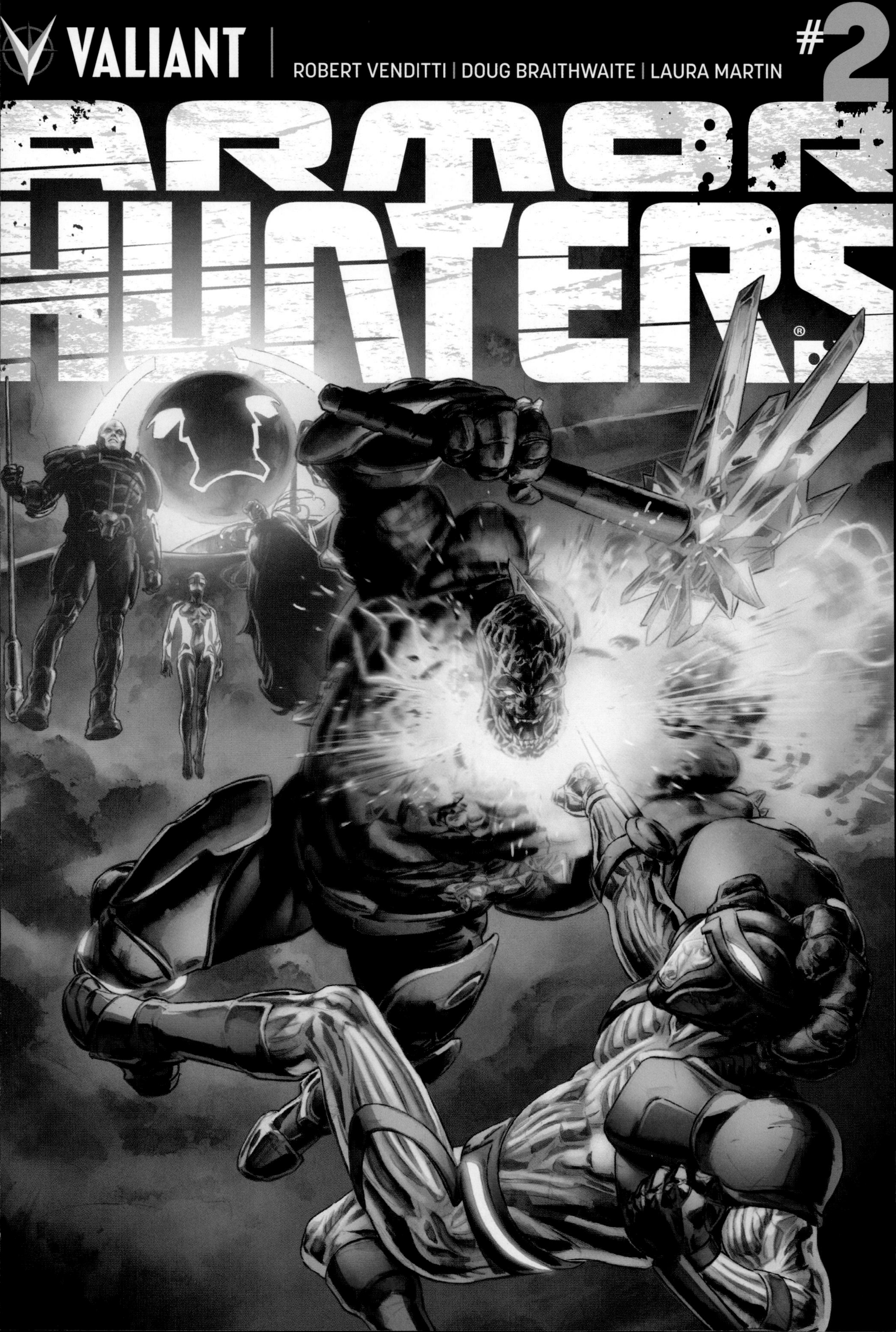
VALIANT
#2
ROBERT VENDITTI | DOUG BRAITHWAITE | LAURA MARTIN
ARMOR HUNTERS®

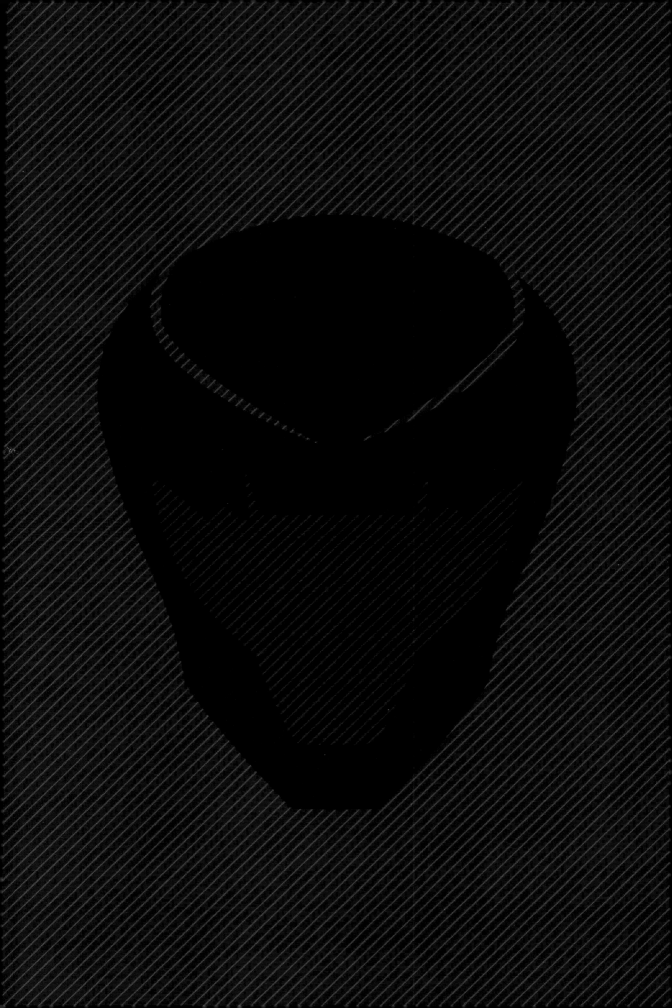

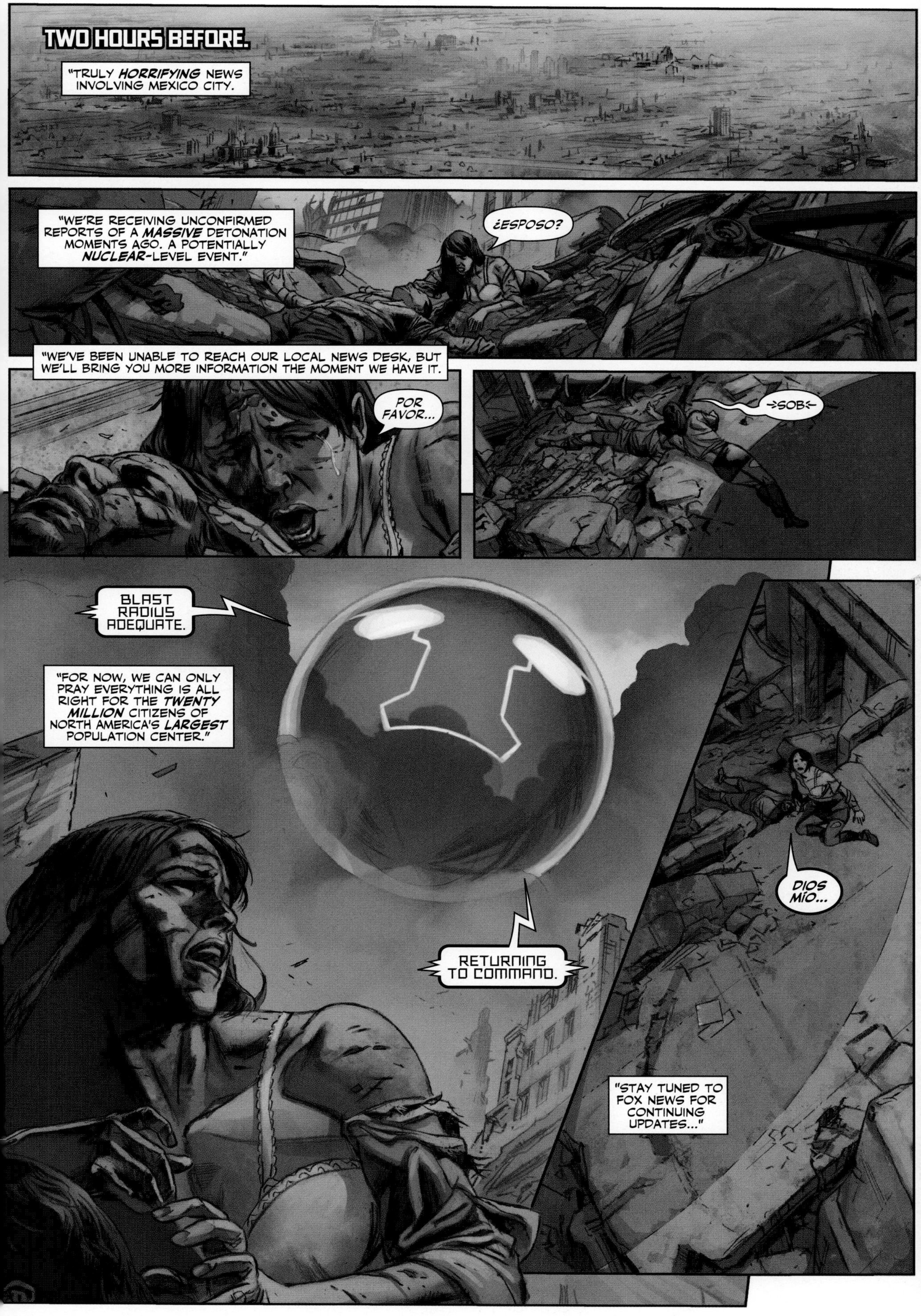

TWO HOURS BEFORE.
"TRULY *HORRIFYING* NEWS INVOLVING MEXICO CITY.
"WE'RE RECEIVING UNCONFIRMED REPORTS OF A *MASSIVE* DETONATION MOMENTS AGO. A POTENTIALLY *NUCLEAR*-LEVEL EVENT."
¿ESPOSO?
"WE'VE BEEN UNABLE TO REACH OUR LOCAL NEWS DESK, BUT WE'LL BRING YOU MORE INFORMATION THE MOMENT WE HAVE IT.
POR FAVOR...
SOB
BLAST RADIUS ADEQUATE.
"FOR NOW, WE CAN ONLY PRAY EVERYTHING IS ALL RIGHT FOR THE *TWENTY MILLION* CITIZENS OF NORTH AMERICA'S *LARGEST* POPULATION CENTER."
DIOS MIO...
RETURNING TO COMMAND.
"STAY TUNED TO FOX NEWS FOR CONTINUING UPDATES..."

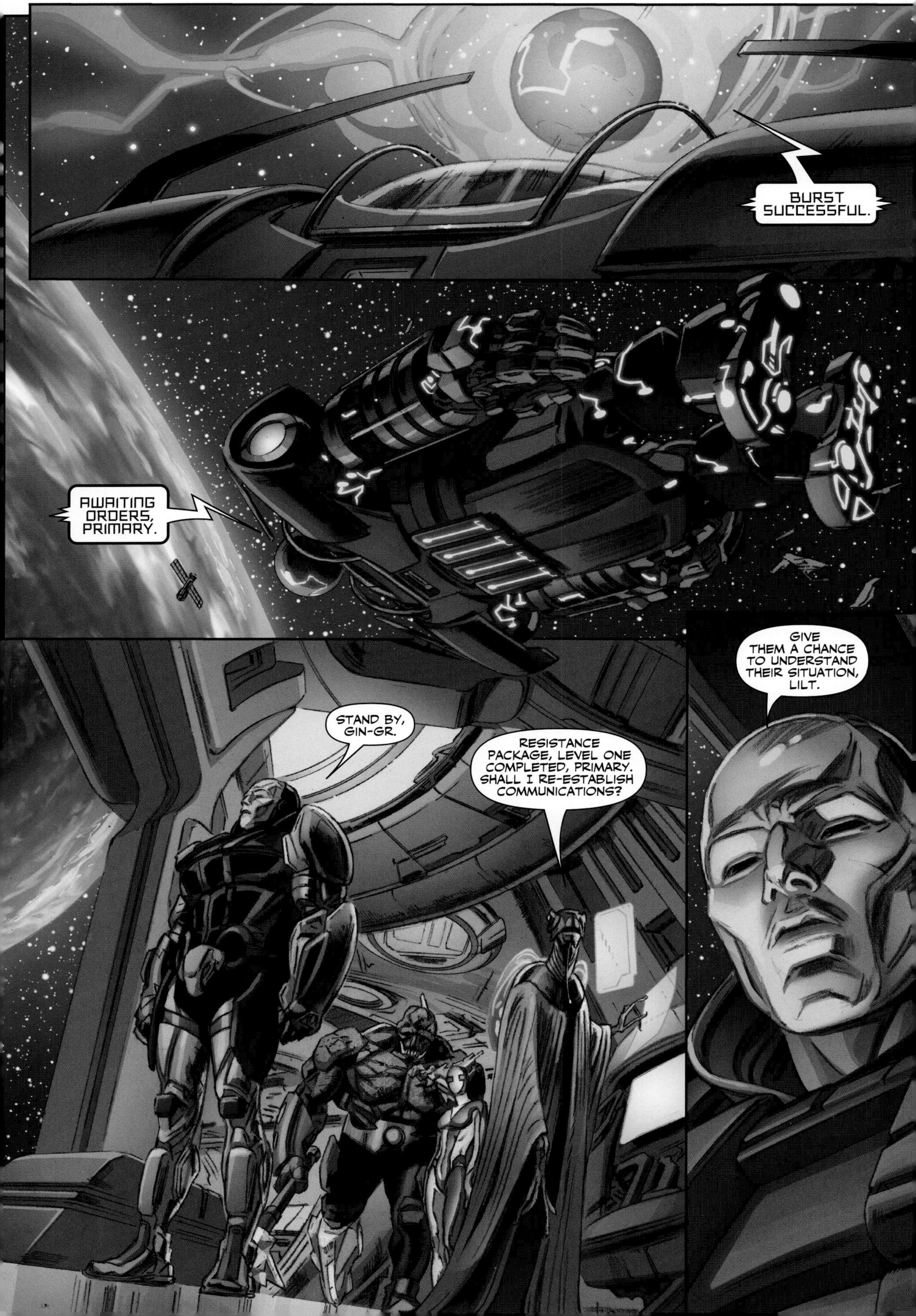
BURST SUCCESSFUL.
AWAITING ORDERS, PRIMARY.
STAND BY, GIN-GR.
RESISTANCE PACKAGE, LEVEL ONE COMPLETED, PRIMARY. SHALL I RE-ESTABLISH COMMUNICATIONS?
GIVE THEM A CHANCE TO UNDERSTAND THEIR SITUATION, LILT.

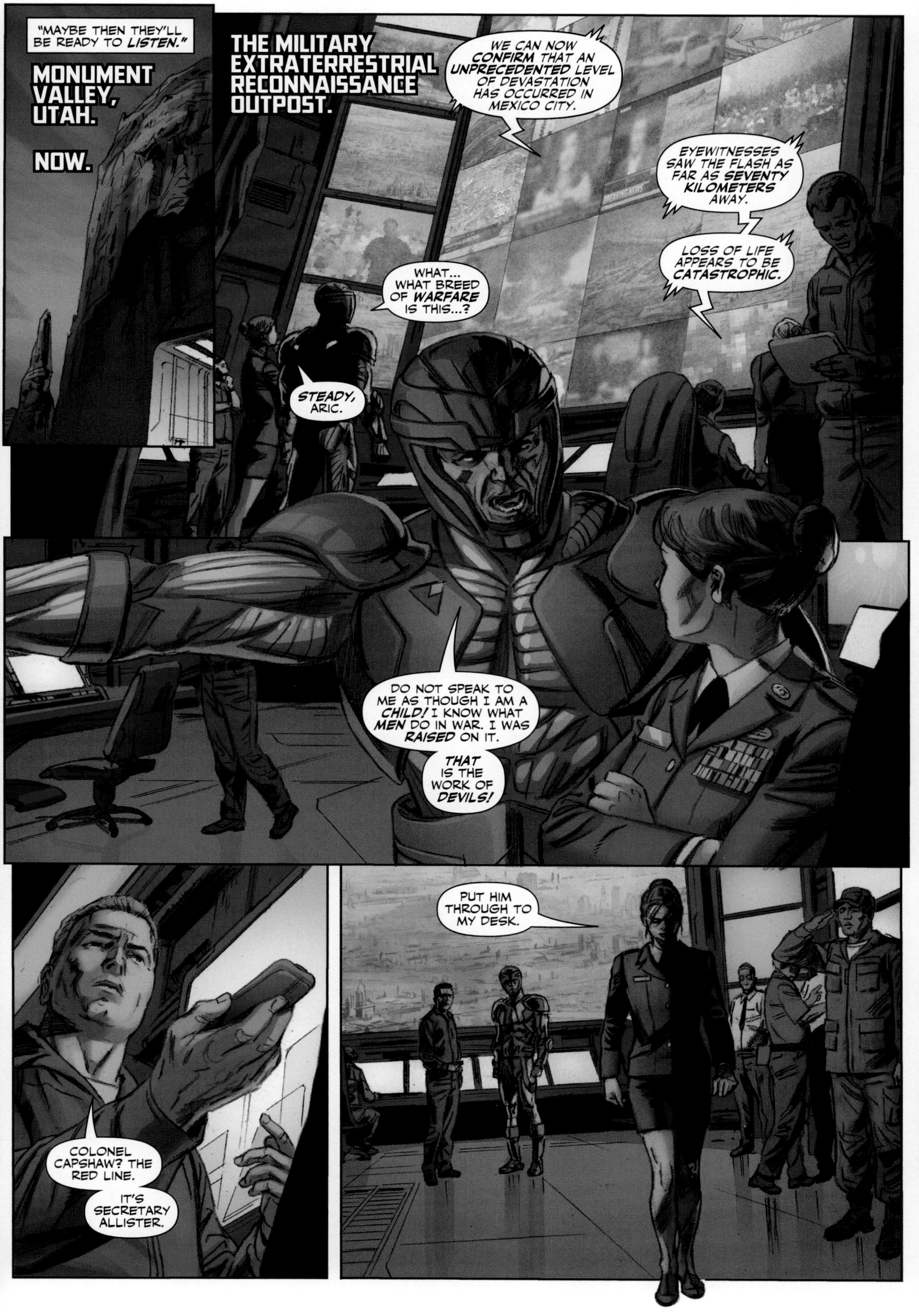
"MAYBE THEN THEY'LL BE READY TO LISTEN."
MONUMENT VALLEY, UTAH.
NOW.
THE MILITARY EXTRATERRESTRIAL RECONNAISSANCE OUTPOST.
WE CAN NOW CONFIRM THAT AN UNPRECEDENTED LEVEL OF DEVASTATION HAS OCCURRED IN MEXICO CITY.
EYEWITNESSES SAW THE FLASH AS FAR AS SEVENTY KILOMETERS AWAY.
LOSS OF LIFE APPEARS TO BE CATASTROPHIC.
WHAT... WHAT BREED OF WARFARE IS THIS...?
STEADY, ARIC.
DO NOT SPEAK TO ME AS THOUGH I AM A CHILD! I KNOW WHAT MEN DO IN WAR. I WAS RAISED ON IT.
THAT IS THE WORK OF DEVILS!
COLONEL CAPSHAW? THE RED LINE.
IT'S SECRETARY ALLISTER.
PUT HIM THROUGH TO MY DESK.

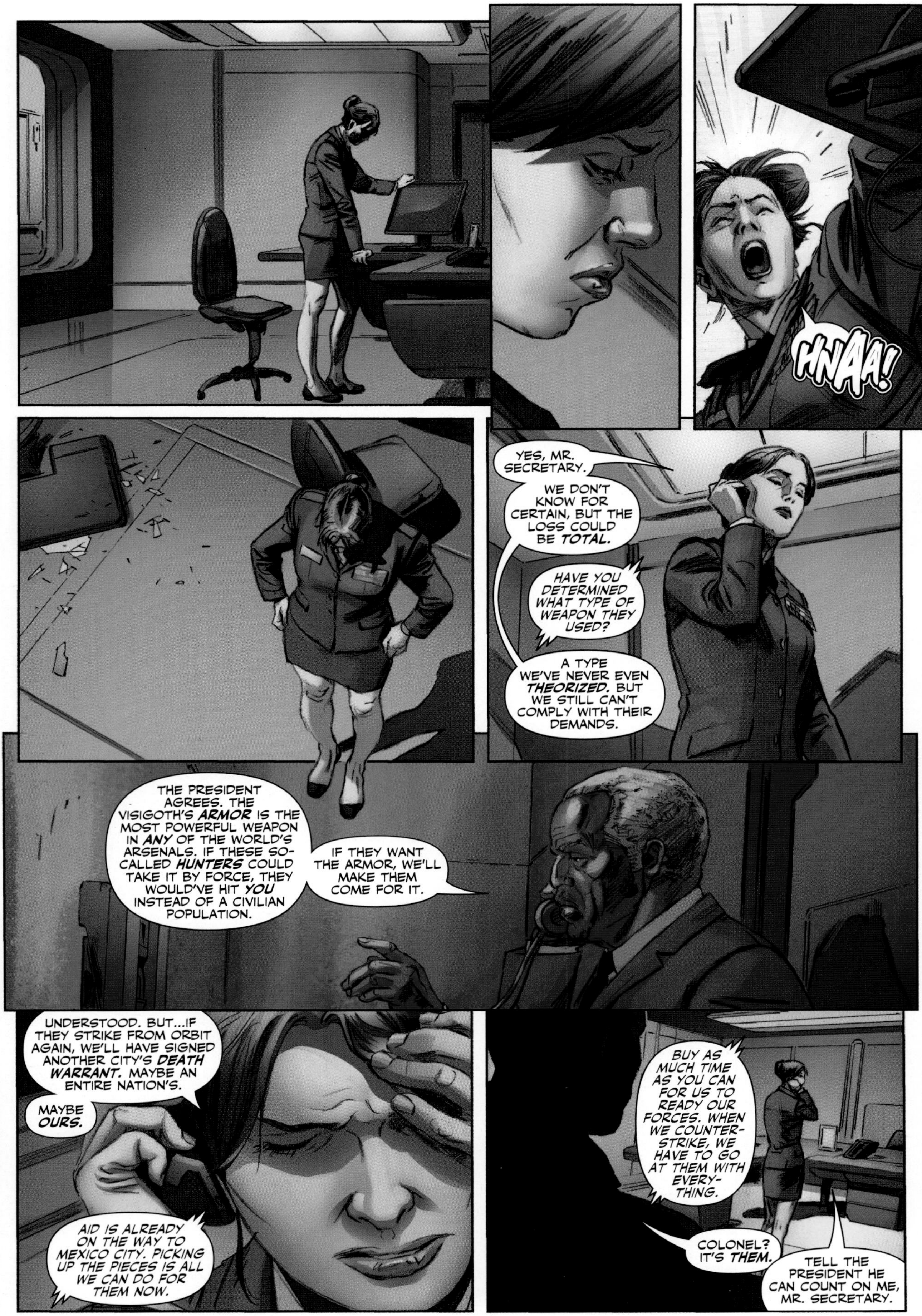
HNAA!
YES, MR. SECRETARY.
WE DON'T KNOW FOR CERTAIN, BUT THE LOSS COULD BE TOTAL.
HAVE YOU DETERMINED WHAT TYPE OF WEAPON THEY USED?
A TYPE WE'VE NEVER EVEN THEORIZED. BUT WE STILL CAN'T COMPLY WITH THEIR DEMANDS.
THE PRESIDENT AGREES. THE VISIGOTH'S ARMOR IS THE MOST POWERFUL WEAPON IN ANY OF THE WORLD'S ARSENALS. IF THESE SO-CALLED HUNTERS COULD TAKE IT BY FORCE, THEY WOULD'VE HIT YOU INSTEAD OF A CIVILIAN POPULATION.
IF THEY WANT THE ARMOR, WE'LL MAKE THEM COME FOR IT.
UNDERSTOOD. BUT...IF THEY STRIKE FROM ORBIT AGAIN, WE'LL HAVE SIGNED ANOTHER CITY'S DEATH WARRANT. MAYBE AN ENTIRE NATION'S.
MAYBE OURS.
AID IS ALREADY ON THE WAY TO MEXICO CITY. PICKING UP THE PIECES IS ALL WE CAN DO FOR THEM NOW.
BUY AS MUCH TIME AS YOU CAN FOR US TO READY OUR FORCES. WHEN WE COUNTER-STRIKE, WE HAVE TO GO AT THEM WITH EVERY-THING.
COLONEL? IT'S THEM.
TELL THE PRESIDENT HE CAN COUNT ON ME, MR. SECRETARY.

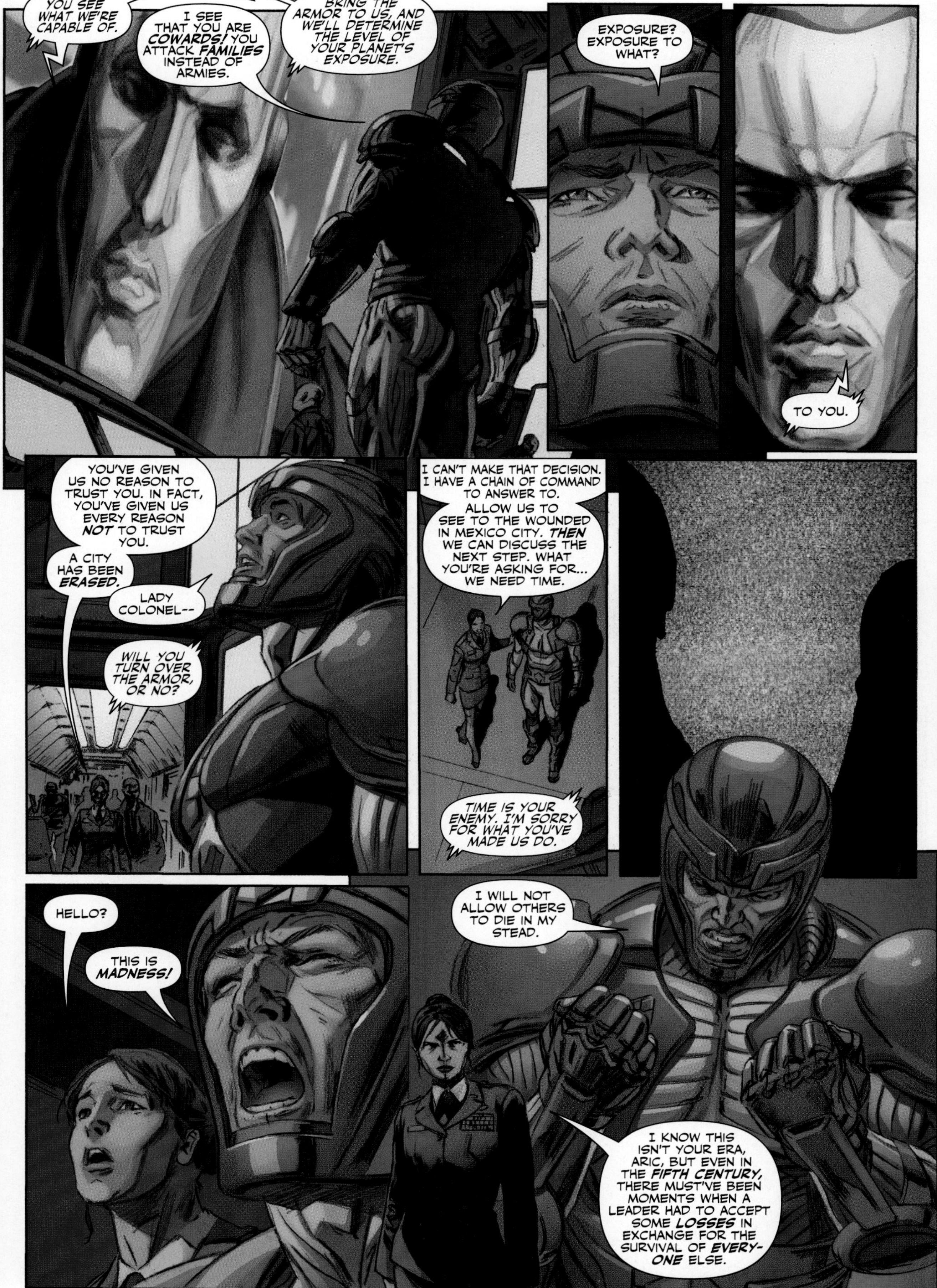
YOU SEE WHAT WE'RE CAPABLE OF.
I SEE THAT YOU ARE COWARDS! YOU ATTACK FAMILIES INSTEAD OF ARMIES.
BRING THE ARMOR TO US, AND WE'LL DETERMINE THE LEVEL OF YOUR PLANET'S EXPOSURE.
EXPOSURE? EXPOSURE TO WHAT?
TO YOU.
YOU'VE GIVEN US NO REASON TO TRUST YOU. IN FACT, YOU'VE GIVEN US EVERY REASON NOT TO TRUST YOU.
A CITY HAS BEEN ERASED.
LADY COLONEL--
WILL YOU TURN OVER THE ARMOR, OR NO?
I CAN'T MAKE THAT DECISION. I HAVE A CHAIN OF COMMAND TO ANSWER TO.
ALLOW US TO SEE TO THE WOUNDED IN MEXICO CITY. THEN WE CAN DISCUSS THE NEXT STEP. WHAT YOU'RE ASKING FOR... WE NEED TIME.
TIME IS YOUR ENEMY. I'M SORRY FOR WHAT YOU'VE MADE US DO.
HELLO?
THIS IS MADNESS!
I WILL NOT ALLOW OTHERS TO DIE IN MY STEAD.
I KNOW THIS ISN'T YOUR ERA, ARIC, BUT EVEN IN THE FIFTH CENTURY, THERE MUST'VE BEEN MOMENTS WHEN A LEADER HAD TO ACCEPT SOME LOSSES IN EXCHANGE FOR THE SURVIVAL OF EVERY-ONE ELSE.

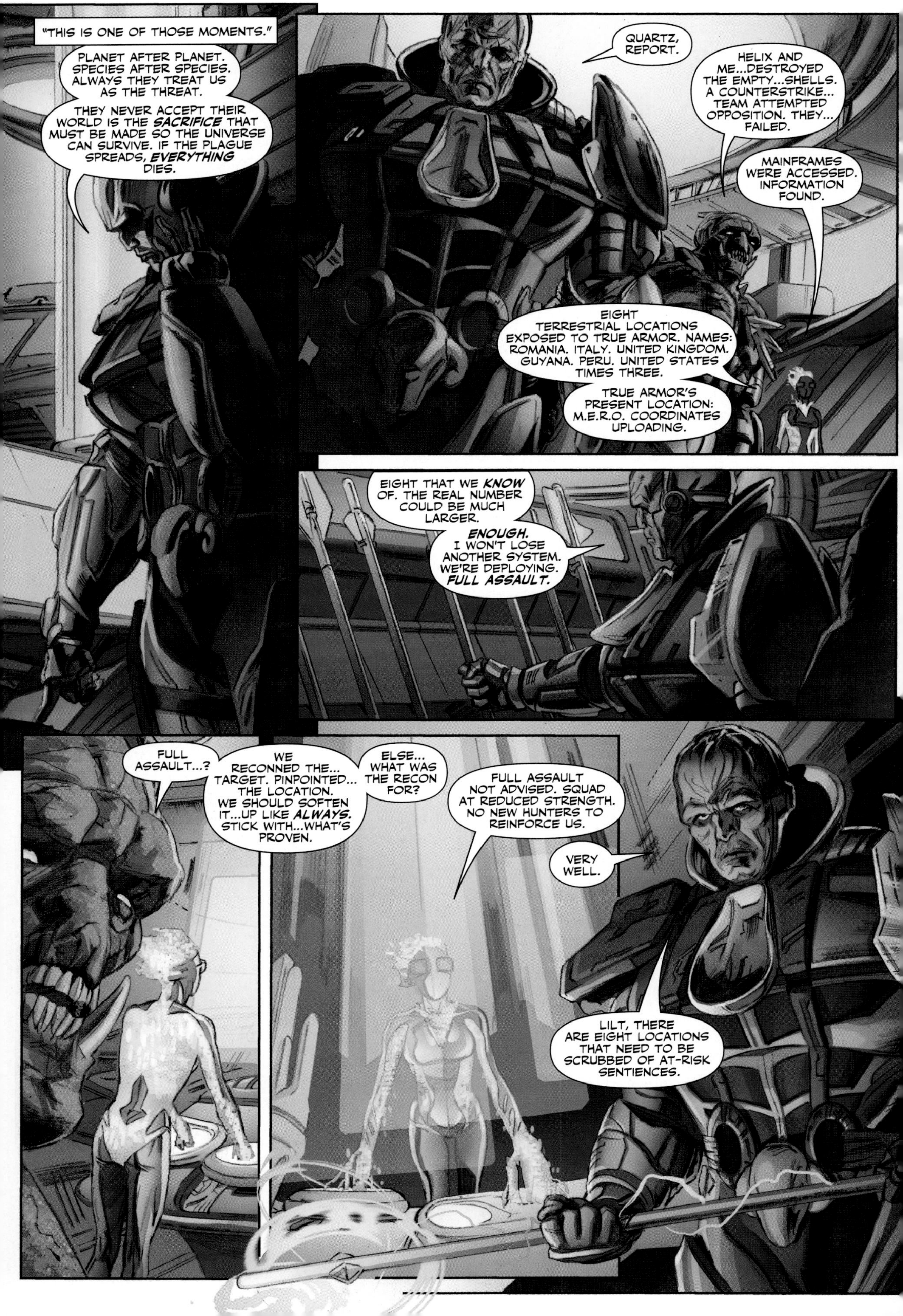
"THIS IS ONE OF THOSE MOMENTS."
PLANET AFTER PLANET. SPECIES AFTER SPECIES. ALWAYS THEY TREAT US AS THE THREAT.
THEY NEVER ACCEPT THEIR WORLD IS THE SACRIFICE THAT MUST BE MADE SO THE UNIVERSE CAN SURVIVE. IF THE PLAGUE SPREADS, EVERYTHING DIES.
QUARTZ, REPORT.
HELIX AND ME...DESTROYED THE EMPTY...SHELLS. A COUNTERSTRIKE... TEAM ATTEMPTED OPPOSITION. THEY... FAILED.
MAINFRAMES WERE ACCESSED. INFORMATION FOUND.
EIGHT TERRESTRIAL LOCATIONS EXPOSED TO TRUE ARMOR. NAMES: ROMANIA. ITALY. UNITED KINGDOM. GUYANA. PERU. UNITED STATES TIMES THREE.
TRUE ARMOR'S PRESENT LOCATION: M.E.R.O. COORDINATES UPLOADING.
EIGHT THAT WE KNOW OF. THE REAL NUMBER COULD BE MUCH LARGER.
ENOUGH. I WON'T LOSE ANOTHER SYSTEM. WE'RE DEPLOYING. FULL ASSAULT.
FULL ASSAULT...?
WE RECONNED THE... TARGET. PINPOINTED... THE LOCATION. WE SHOULD SOFTEN IT...UP LIKE ALWAYS. STICK WITH...WHAT'S PROVEN.
ELSE... WHAT WAS THE RECON FOR?
FULL ASSAULT NOT ADVISED. SQUAD AT REDUCED STRENGTH. NO NEW HUNTERS TO REINFORCE US.
VERY WELL.
LILT, THERE ARE EIGHT LOCATIONS THAT NEED TO BE SCRUBBED OF AT-RISK SENTIENCES.

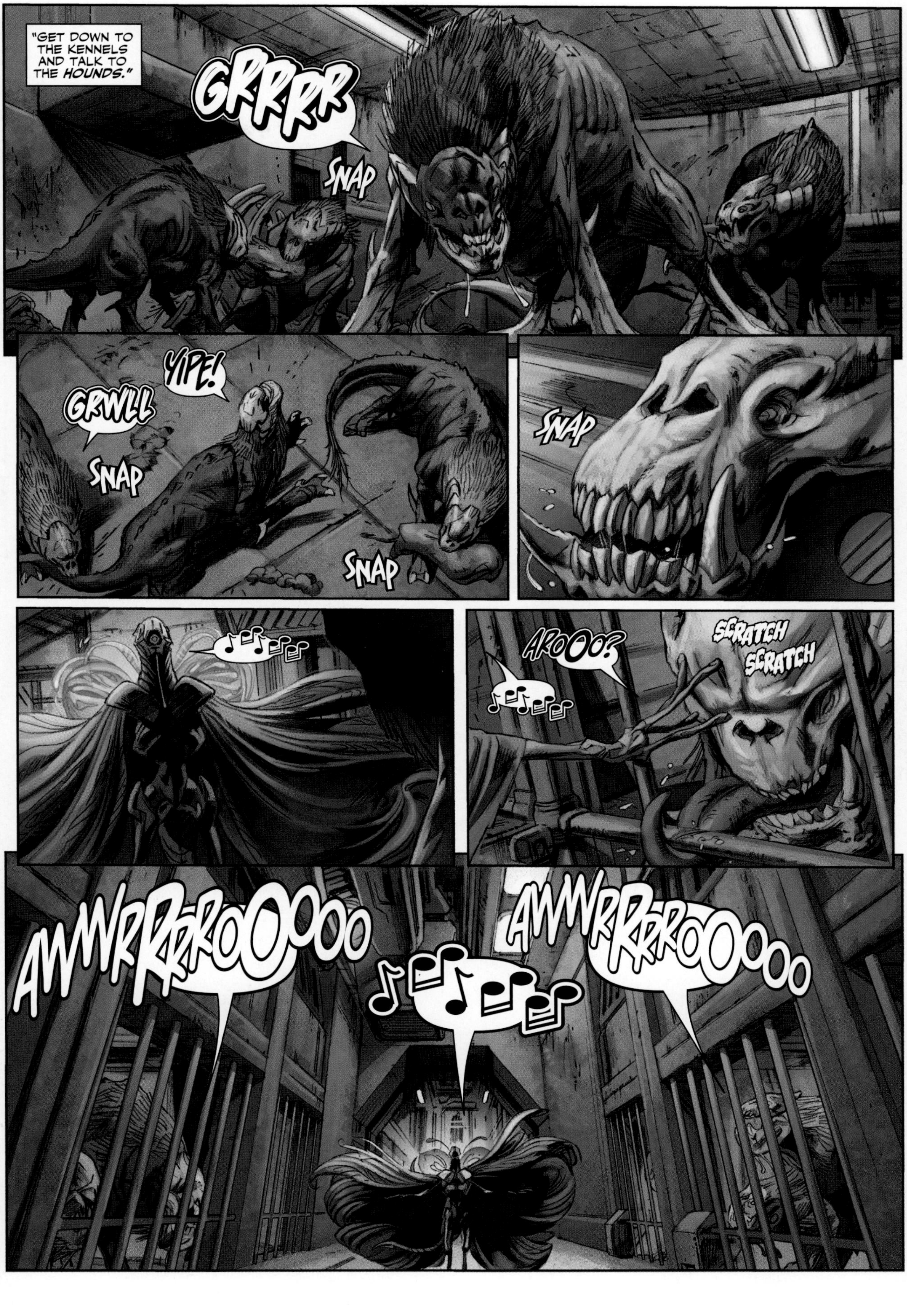

"GET DOWN TO THE KENNELS AND TALK TO THE *HOUNDS*."
GRRRR
SNAP
YIPE!
GRWLL
SNAP
SNAP
SNAP
AROOO?
SCRATCH SCRATCH
AWWRRRROOOOO
AWWRRRROOOOO

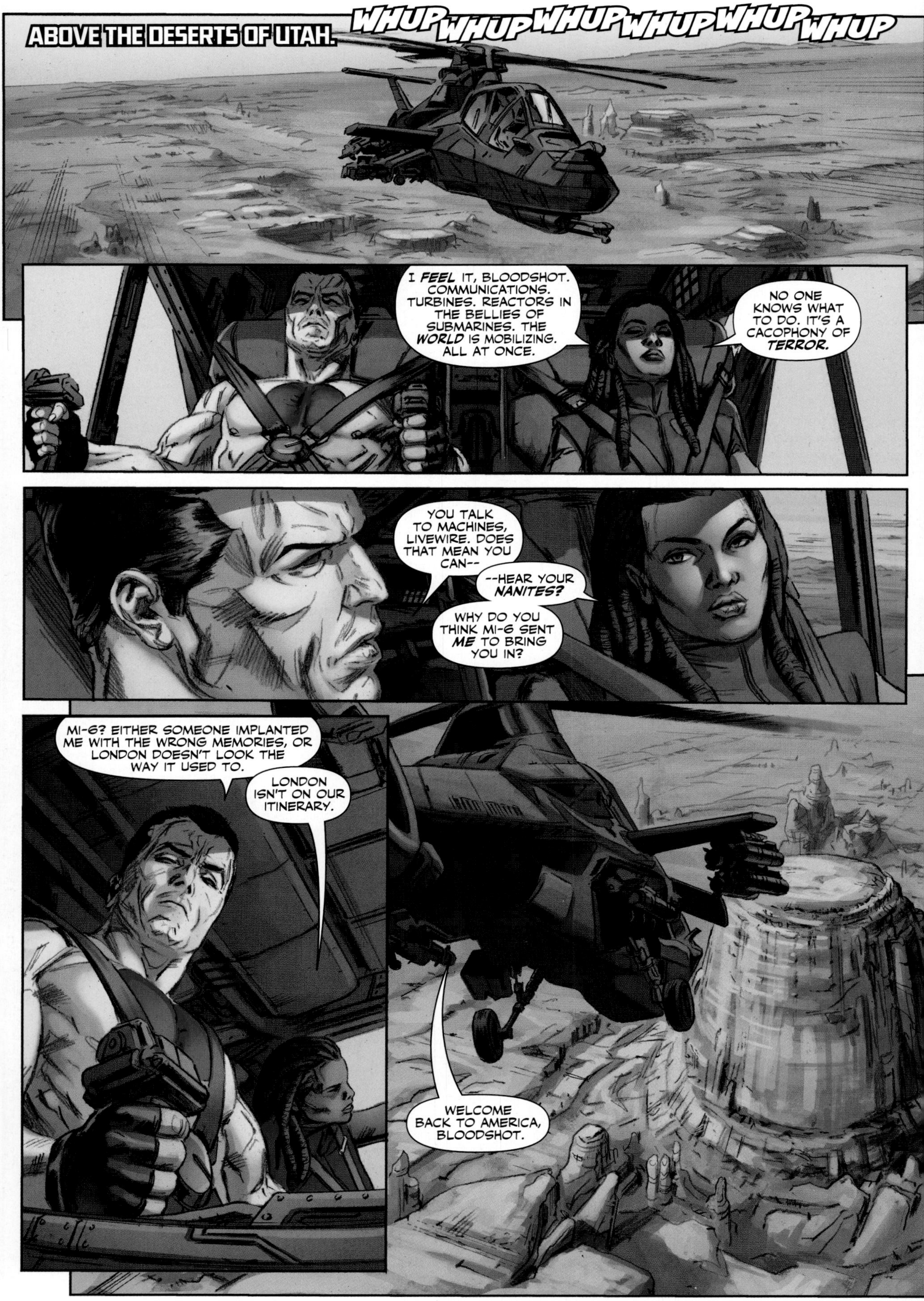
ABOVE THE DESERTS OF UTAH.
WHUP WHUP WHUP WHUP WHUP WHUP
I FEEL IT, BLOODSHOT. COMMUNICATIONS. TURBINES. REACTORS IN THE BELLIES OF SUBMARINES. THE WORLD IS MOBILIZING. ALL AT ONCE.
NO ONE KNOWS WHAT TO DO. IT'S A CACOPHONY OF TERROR.
YOU TALK TO MACHINES, LIVEWIRE. DOES THAT MEAN YOU CAN--
--HEAR YOUR NANITES?
WHY DO YOU THINK MI-6 SENT ME TO BRING YOU IN?
MI-6? EITHER SOMEONE IMPLANTED ME WITH THE WRONG MEMORIES, OR LONDON DOESN'T LOOK THE WAY IT USED TO.
LONDON ISN'T ON OUR ITINERARY.
WELCOME BACK TO AMERICA, BLOODSHOT.

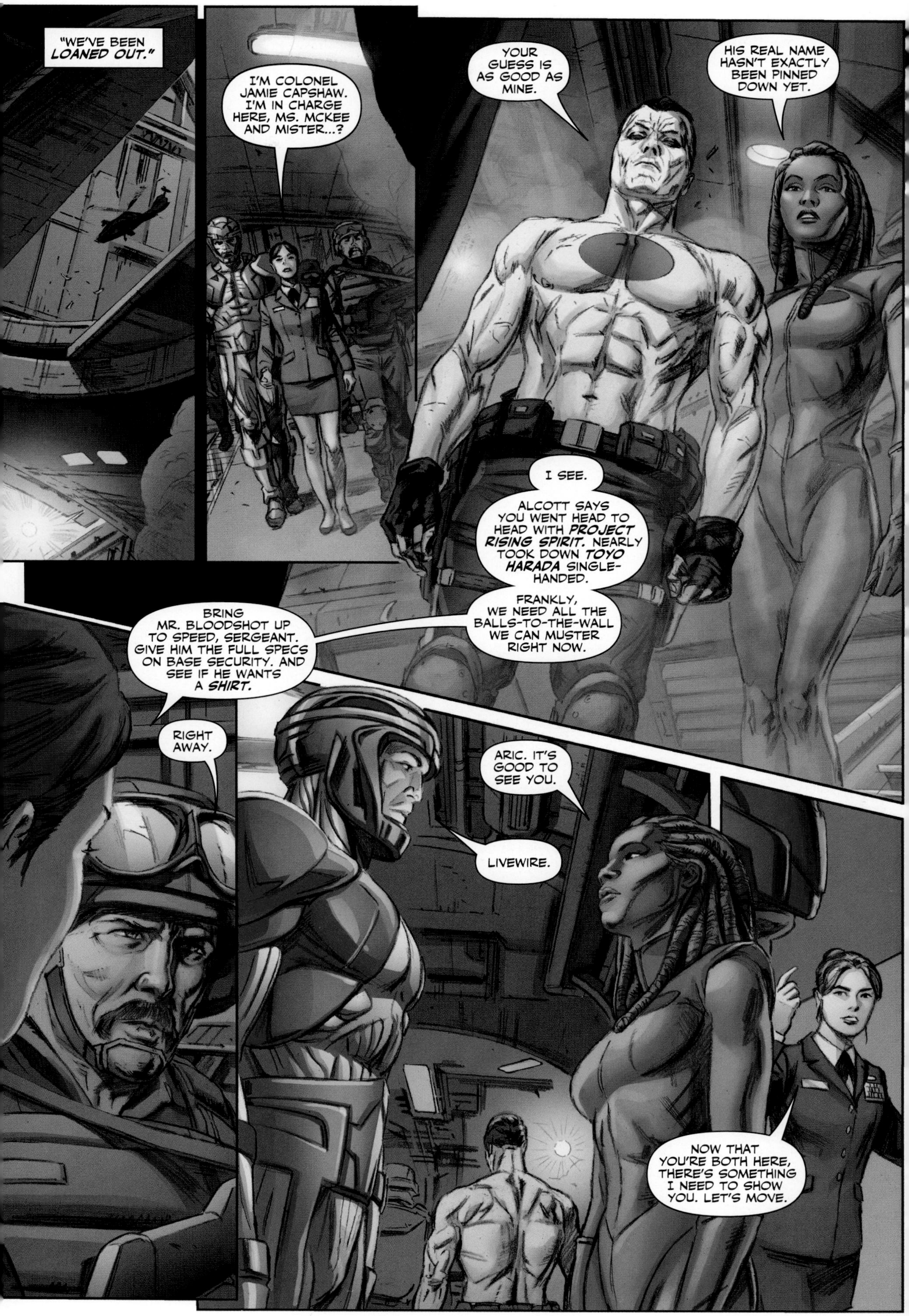
"WE'VE BEEN LOANED OUT."
I'M COLONEL JAMIE CAPSHAW. I'M IN CHARGE HERE, MS. MCKEE AND MISTER...?
YOUR GUESS IS AS GOOD AS MINE.
HIS REAL NAME HASN'T EXACTLY BEEN PINNED DOWN YET.
I SEE.
ALCOTT SAYS YOU WENT HEAD TO HEAD WITH PROJECT RISING SPIRIT. NEARLY TOOK DOWN TOYO HARADA SINGLE-HANDED.
FRANKLY, WE NEED ALL THE BALLS-TO-THE-WALL WE CAN MUSTER RIGHT NOW.
BRING MR. BLOODSHOT UP TO SPEED, SERGEANT. GIVE HIM THE FULL SPECS ON BASE SECURITY. AND SEE IF HE WANTS A SHIRT.
RIGHT AWAY.
ARIC. IT'S GOOD TO SEE YOU.
LIVEWIRE.
NOW THAT YOU'RE BOTH HERE, THERE'S SOMETHING I NEED TO SHOW YOU. LET'S MOVE.

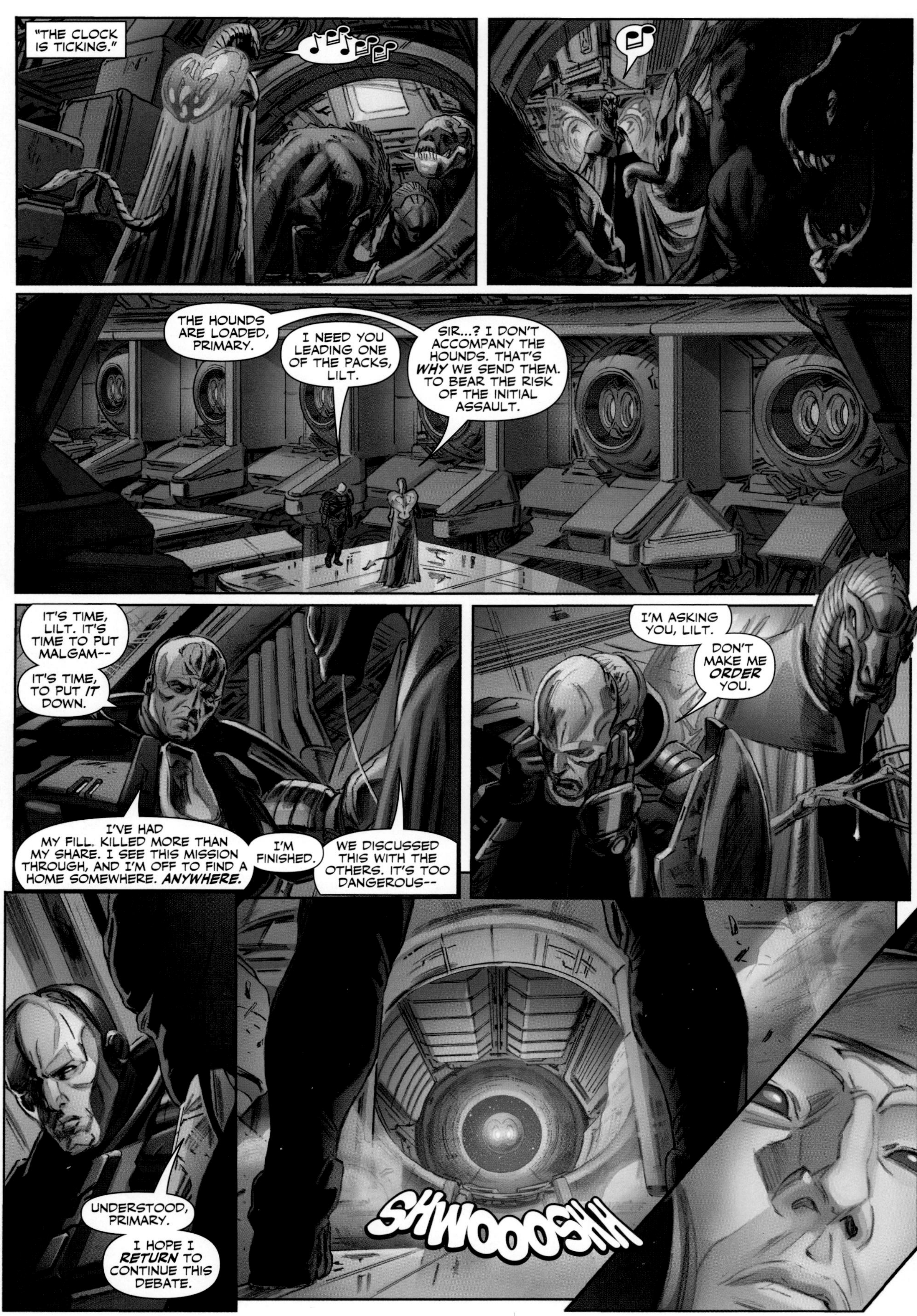
"THE CLOCK IS TICKING."
THE HOUNDS ARE LOADED, PRIMARY.
I NEED YOU LEADING ONE OF THE PACKS, LILT.
SIR...? I DON'T ACCOMPANY THE HOUNDS. THAT'S *WHY* WE SEND THEM. TO BEAR THE RISK OF THE INITIAL ASSAULT.
IT'S TIME, LILT. IT'S TIME TO PUT MALGAM--
IT'S TIME, TO PUT *IT* DOWN.
I'VE HAD MY FILL. KILLED MORE THAN MY SHARE. I SEE THIS MISSION THROUGH, AND I'M OFF TO FIND A HOME SOMEWHERE. *ANYWHERE.*
I'M FINISHED.
WE DISCUSSED THIS WITH THE OTHERS. IT'S TOO DANGEROUS--
I'M ASKING YOU, LILT.
DON'T MAKE ME *ORDER* YOU.
UNDERSTOOD, PRIMARY.
I HOPE I *RETURN* TO CONTINUE THIS DEBATE.
SHWOOOSHH

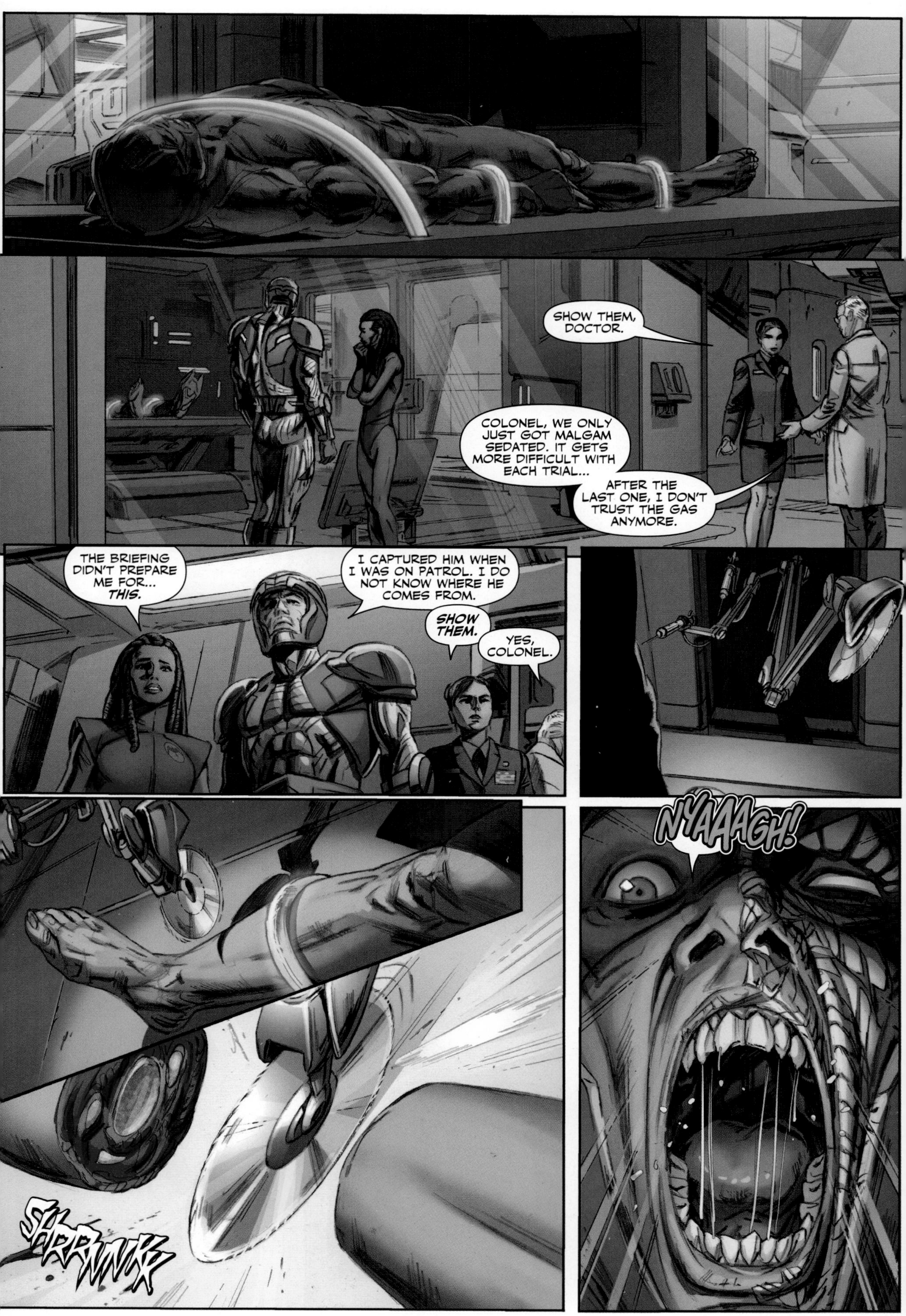
SHOW THEM, DOCTOR.
COLONEL, WE ONLY JUST GOT MALGAM SEDATED. IT GETS MORE DIFFICULT WITH EACH TRIAL...
AFTER THE LAST ONE, I DON'T TRUST THE GAS ANYMORE.
THE BRIEFING DIDN'T PREPARE ME FOR... THIS.
I CAPTURED HIM WHEN I WAS ON PATROL. I DO NOT KNOW WHERE HE COMES FROM.
SHOW THEM.
YES, COLONEL.
SHRRNNRR
NYAAAGH!

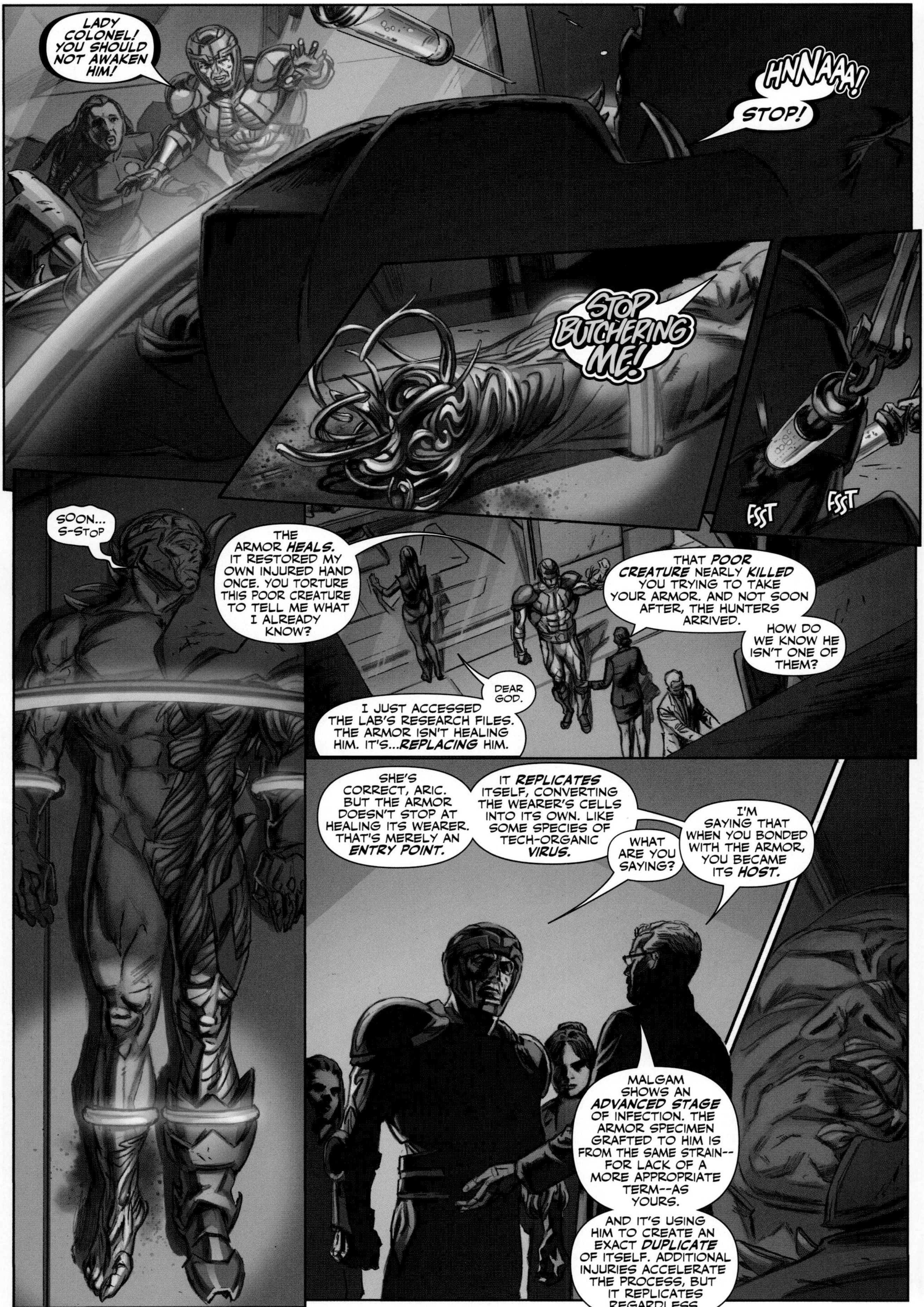

LADY COLONEL! YOU SHOULD NOT AWAKEN HIM!
HNNAAA!
STOP!
STOP BUTCHERING ME!
FSST
FSST
SOON... S-STOP
THE ARMOR HEALS. IT RESTORED MY OWN INJURED HAND ONCE. YOU TORTURE THIS POOR CREATURE TO TELL ME WHAT I ALREADY KNOW?
THAT POOR CREATURE NEARLY KILLED YOU TRYING TO TAKE YOUR ARMOR. AND NOT SOON AFTER, THE HUNTERS ARRIVED.
HOW DO WE KNOW HE ISN'T ONE OF THEM?
DEAR GOD.
I JUST ACCESSED THE LAB'S RESEARCH FILES. THE ARMOR ISN'T HEALING HIM. IT'S...REPLACING HIM.
SHE'S CORRECT, ARIC. BUT THE ARMOR DOESN'T STOP AT HEALING ITS WEARER. THAT'S MERELY AN ENTRY POINT.
IT REPLICATES ITSELF, CONVERTING THE WEARER'S CELLS INTO ITS OWN. LIKE SOME SPECIES OF TECH-ORGANIC VIRUS.
WHAT ARE YOU SAYING?
I'M SAYING THAT WHEN YOU BONDED WITH THE ARMOR, YOU BECAME ITS HOST.
MALGAM SHOWS AN ADVANCED STAGE OF INFECTION. THE ARMOR SPECIMEN GRAFTED TO HIM IS FROM THE SAME STRAIN--FOR LACK OF A MORE APPROPRIATE TERM--AS YOURS.
AND IT'S USING HIM TO CREATE AN EXACT DUPLICATE OF ITSELF. ADDITIONAL INJURIES ACCELERATE THE PROCESS, BUT IT REPLICATES REGARDLESS.

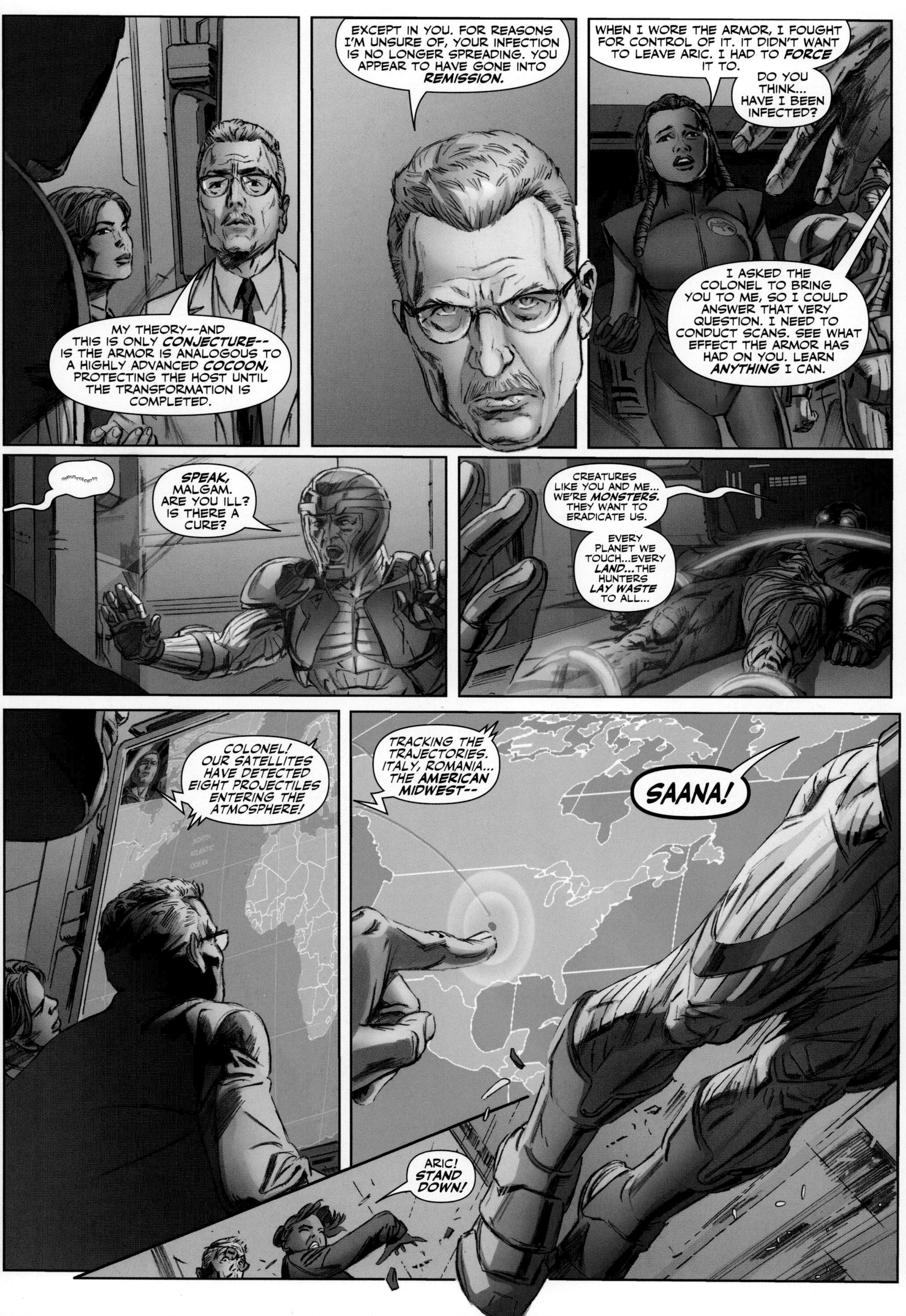

MY THEORY--AND THIS IS ONLY CONJECTURE-- IS THE ARMOR IS ANALOGOUS TO A HIGHLY ADVANCED COCOON, PROTECTING THE HOST UNTIL THE TRANSFORMATION IS COMPLETED.
EXCEPT IN YOU. FOR REASONS I'M UNSURE OF, YOUR INFECTION IS NO LONGER SPREADING. YOU APPEAR TO HAVE GONE INTO REMISSION.
WHEN I WORE THE ARMOR, I FOUGHT FOR CONTROL OF IT. IT DIDN'T WANT TO LEAVE ARIC. I HAD TO FORCE IT TO.
DO YOU THINK... HAVE I BEEN INFECTED?
I ASKED THE COLONEL TO BRING YOU TO ME, SO I COULD ANSWER THAT VERY QUESTION. I NEED TO CONDUCT SCANS. SEE WHAT EFFECT THE ARMOR HAS HAD ON YOU. LEARN ANYTHING I CAN.
SPEAK, MALGAM. ARE YOU ILL? IS THERE A CURE?
CREATURES LIKE YOU AND ME... WE'RE MONSTERS. THEY WANT TO ERADICATE US.
EVERY PLANET WE TOUCH...EVERY LAND...THE HUNTERS LAY WASTE TO ALL...
COLONEL! OUR SATELLITES HAVE DETECTED EIGHT PROJECTILES ENTERING THE ATMOSPHERE!
TRACKING THE TRAJECTORIES. ITALY, ROMANIA... THE AMERICAN MIDWEST--
SAANA!
ARIC! STAND DOWN!

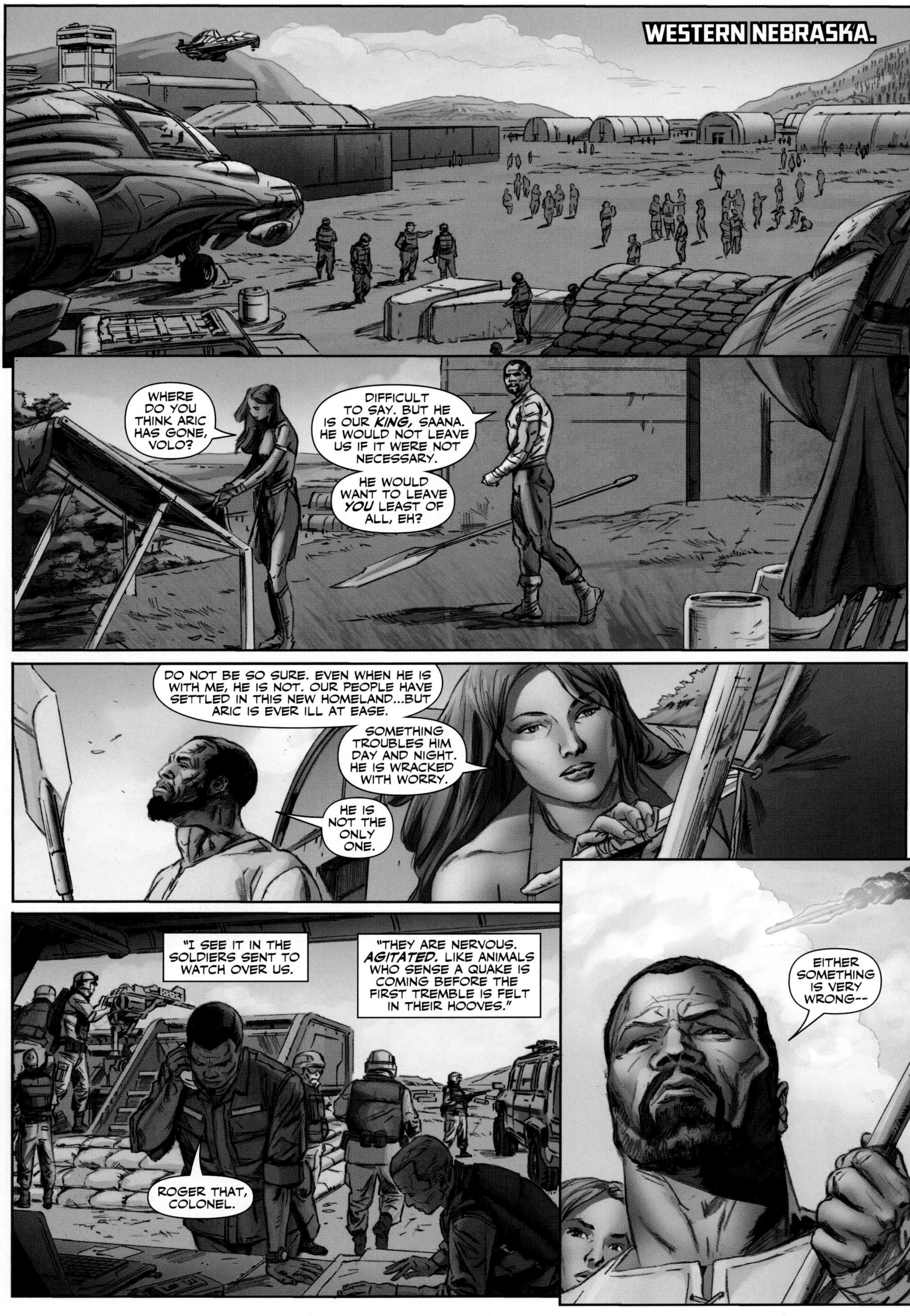
WESTERN NEBRASKA.
WHERE DO YOU THINK ARIC HAS GONE, VOLO?
DIFFICULT TO SAY. BUT HE IS OUR KING, SAANA. HE WOULD NOT LEAVE US IF IT WERE NOT NECESSARY.
HE WOULD WANT TO LEAVE YOU LEAST OF ALL, EH?
DO NOT BE SO SURE. EVEN WHEN HE IS WITH ME, HE IS NOT. OUR PEOPLE HAVE SETTLED IN THIS NEW HOMELAND...BUT ARIC IS EVER ILL AT EASE.
SOMETHING TROUBLES HIM DAY AND NIGHT. HE IS WRACKED WITH WORRY.
HE IS NOT THE ONLY ONE.
"I SEE IT IN THE SOLDIERS SENT TO WATCH OVER US.
"THEY ARE NERVOUS. AGITATED. LIKE ANIMALS WHO SENSE A QUAKE IS COMING BEFORE THE FIRST TREMBLE IS FELT IN THEIR HOOVES."
ROGER THAT, COLONEL.
EITHER SOMETHING IS VERY WRONG--

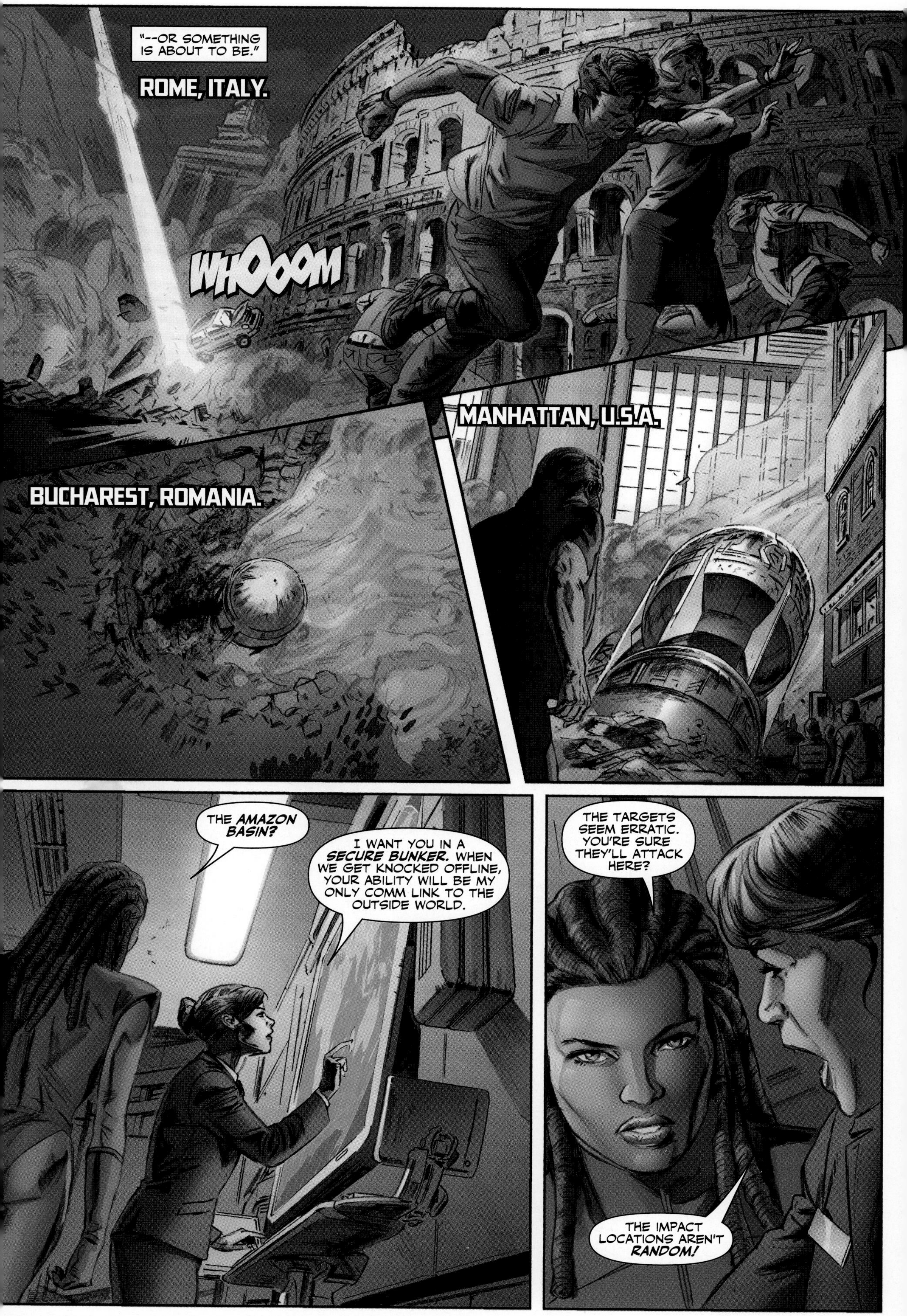
"--OR SOMETHING IS ABOUT TO BE."
ROME, ITALY.
WHOOOM
BUCHAREST, ROMANIA.
MANHATTAN, U.S.A.
THE AMAZON BASIN?
I WANT YOU IN A SECURE BUNKER. WHEN WE GET KNOCKED OFFLINE, YOUR ABILITY WILL BE MY ONLY COMM LINK TO THE OUTSIDE WORLD.
THE TARGETS SEEM ERRATIC. YOU'RE SURE THEY'LL ATTACK HERE?
THE IMPACT LOCATIONS AREN'T RANDOM!

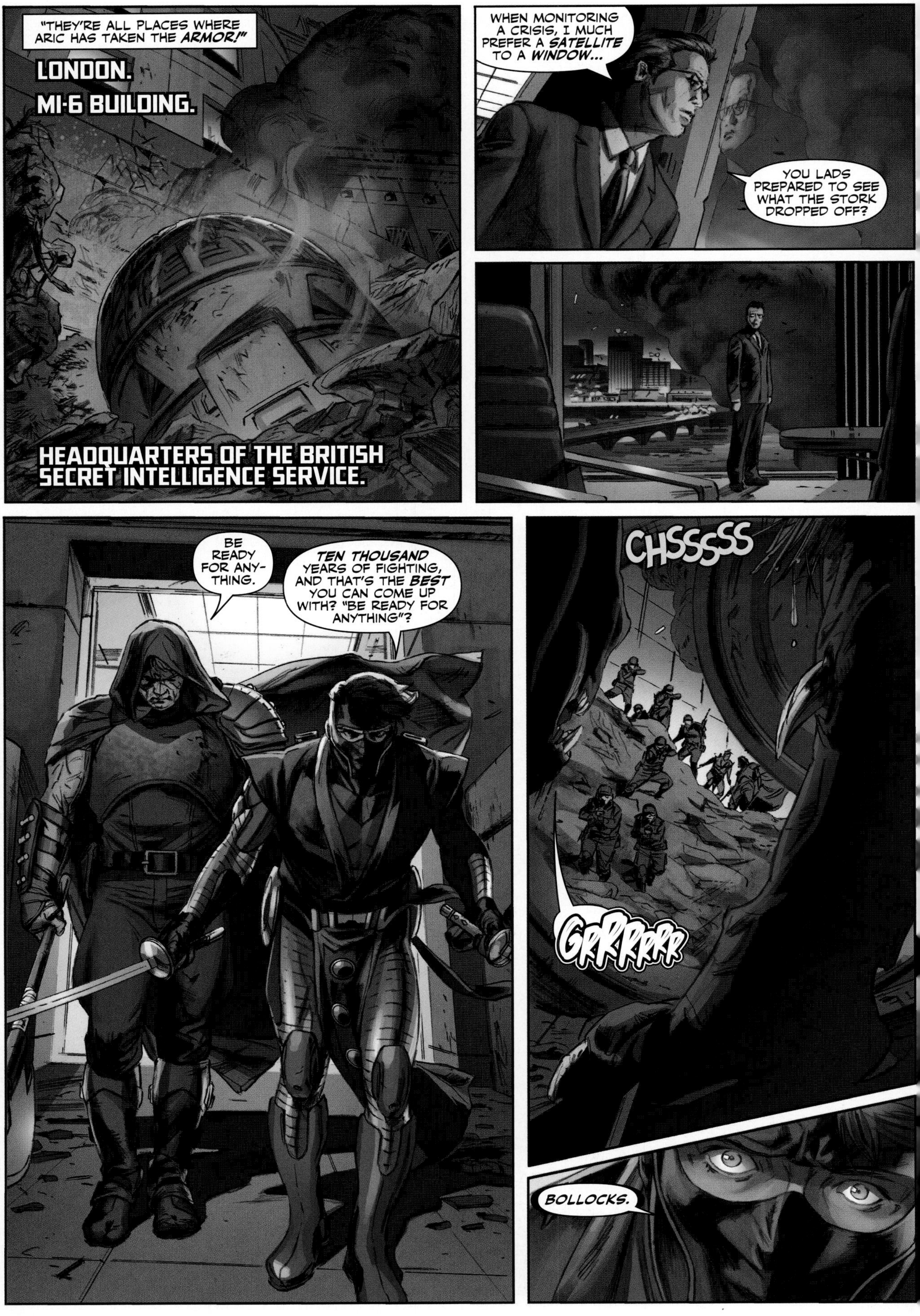

"THEY'RE ALL PLACES WHERE ARIC HAS TAKEN THE *ARMOR!*"
LONDON.
MI-6 BUILDING.
HEADQUARTERS OF THE BRITISH SECRET INTELLIGENCE SERVICE.
WHEN MONITORING A CRISIS, I MUCH PREFER A *SATELLITE* TO A *WINDOW*...
YOU LADS PREPARED TO SEE WHAT THE STORK DROPPED OFF?
BE READY FOR ANY-THING.
TEN THOUSAND YEARS OF FIGHTING, AND THAT'S THE *BEST* YOU CAN COME UP WITH? "BE READY FOR ANYTHING"?
CHSSSSS
GRRRRRR
BOLLOCKS.

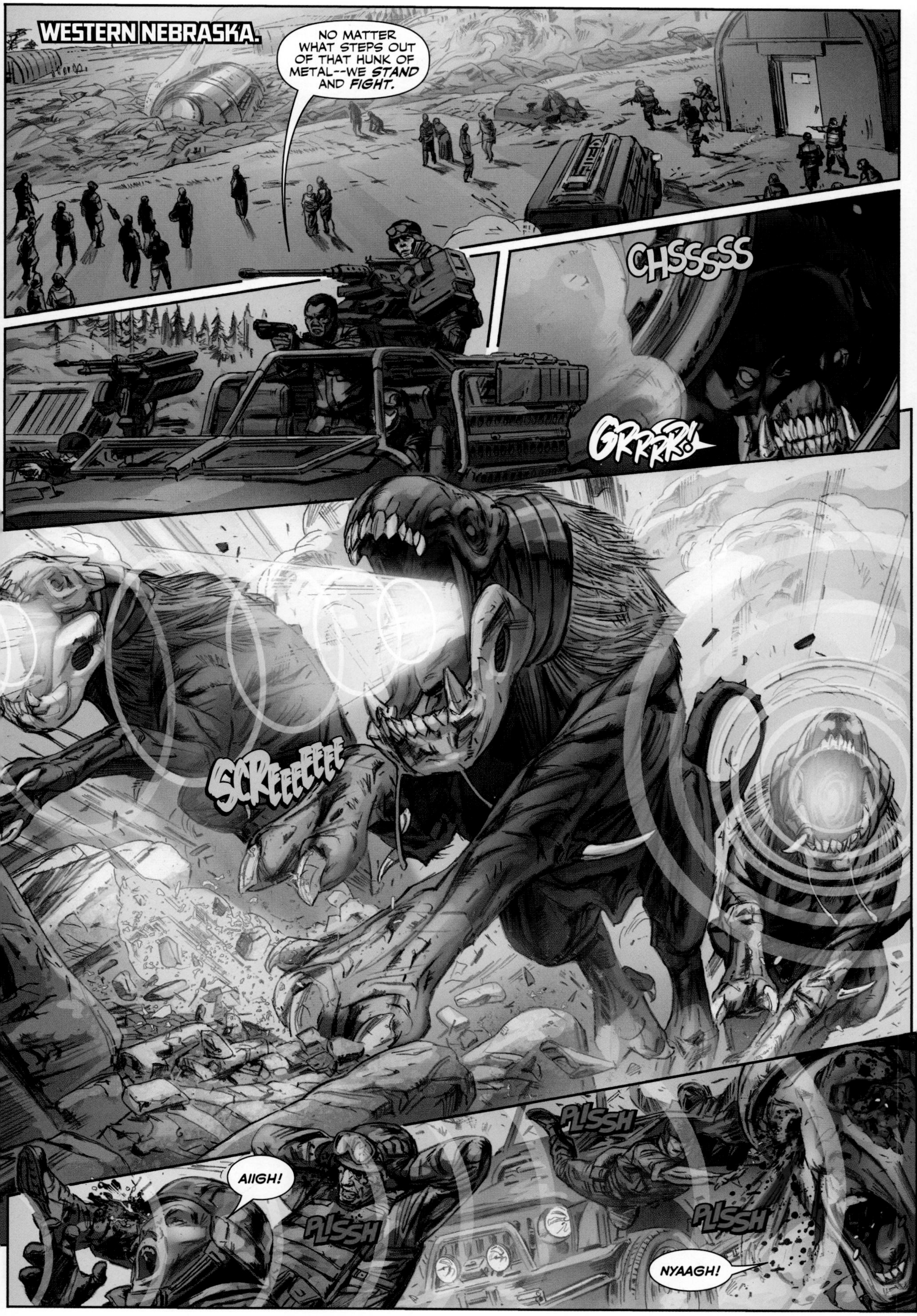
WESTERN NEBRASKA.
NO MATTER WHAT STEPS OUT OF THAT HUNK OF METAL--WE STAND AND FIGHT.
CHSSSSS
GRRRRR!
SCREEEEEE
AIIGH!
PLISSH
PLISSH
PLISSH
NYAAGH!

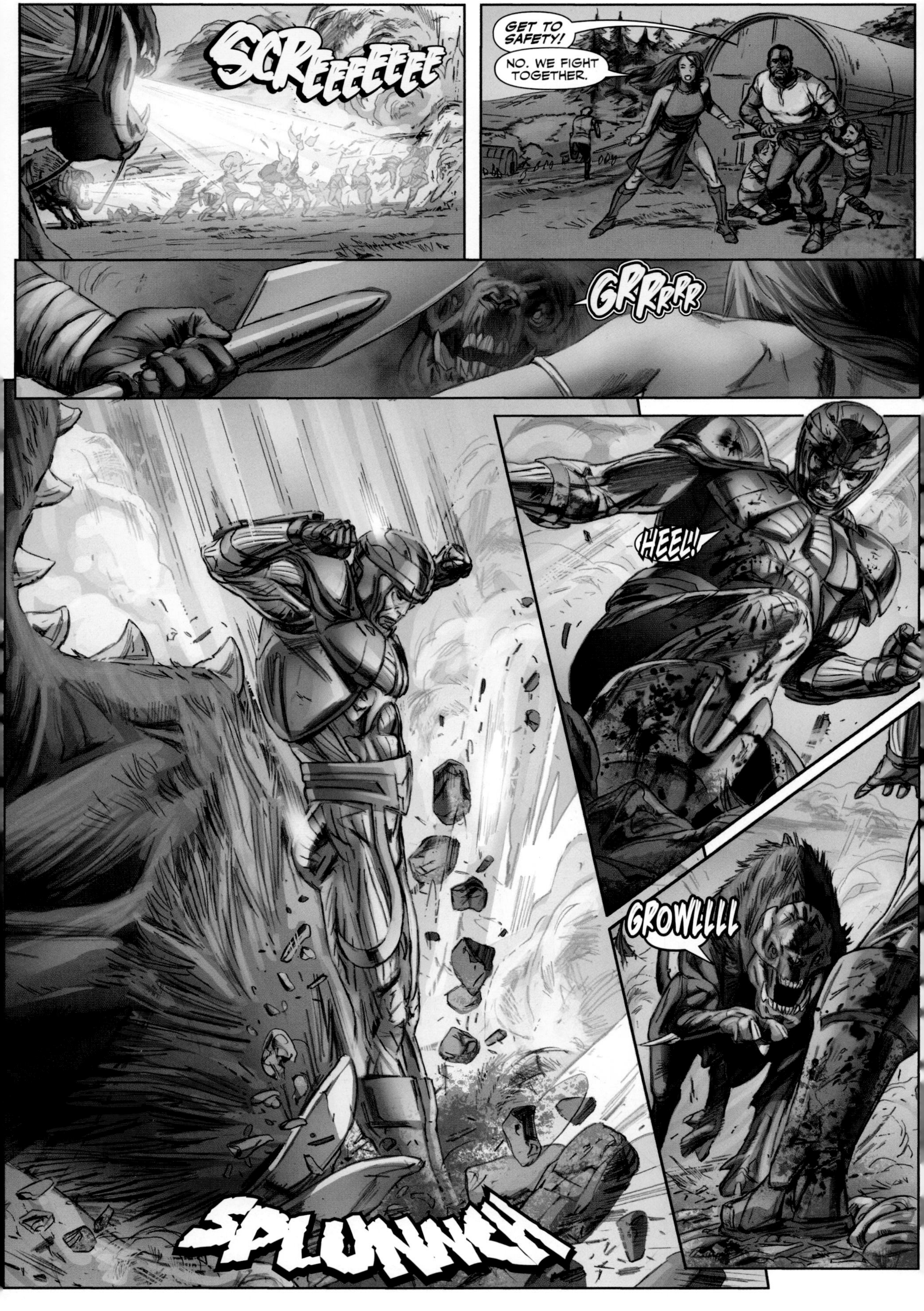
SCREEEEEEEE
GET TO SAFETY!
NO. WE FIGHT TOGETHER.
GRRRRR
SPLUNNCH
HEEL!
GROWLLLL

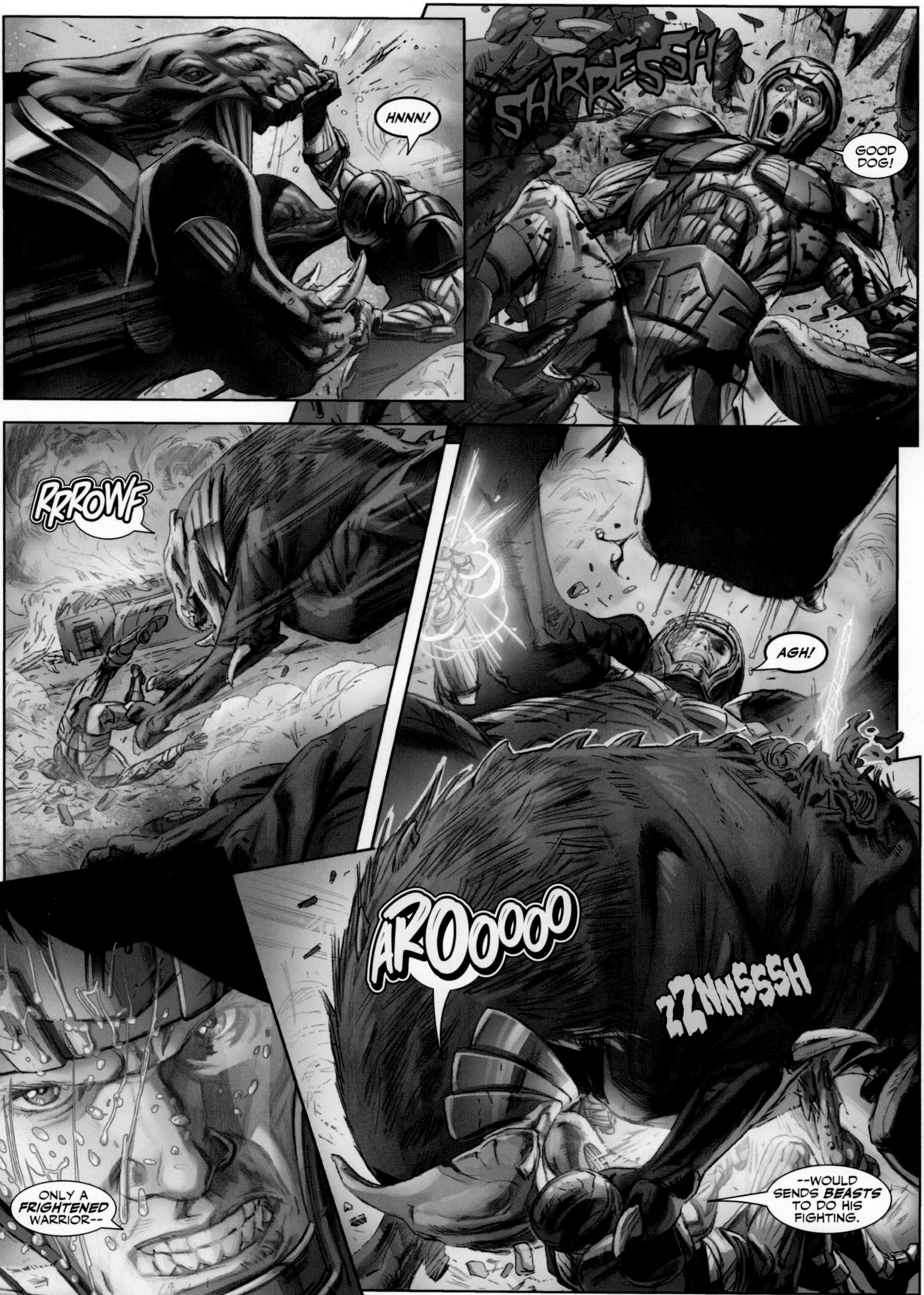
HNNN!
SHRRESSH
GOOD DOG!
RRROWF
AGH!
AROOOOO
ZZNNSSSH
ONLY A FRIGHTENED WARRIOR--
--WOULD SENDS BEASTS TO DO HIS FIGHTING.

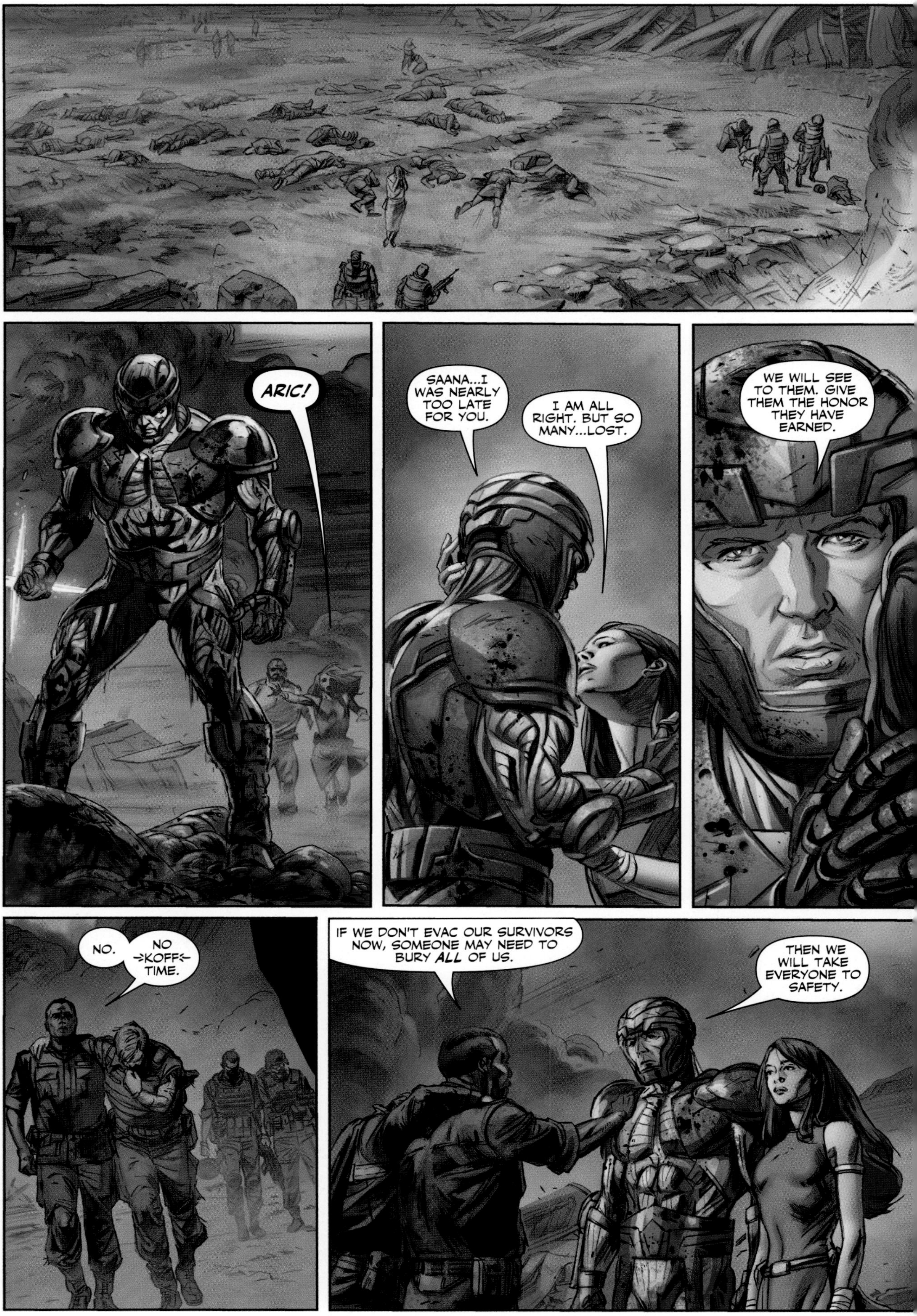
ARIC!
SAANA...I WAS NEARLY TOO LATE FOR YOU.
I AM ALL RIGHT. BUT SO MANY...LOST.
WE WILL SEE TO THEM. GIVE THEM THE HONOR THEY HAVE EARNED.
NO.
NO *KOFF* TIME.
IF WE DON'T EVAC OUR SURVIVORS NOW, SOMEONE MAY NEED TO BURY ALL OF US.
THEN WE WILL TAKE EVERYONE TO SAFETY.

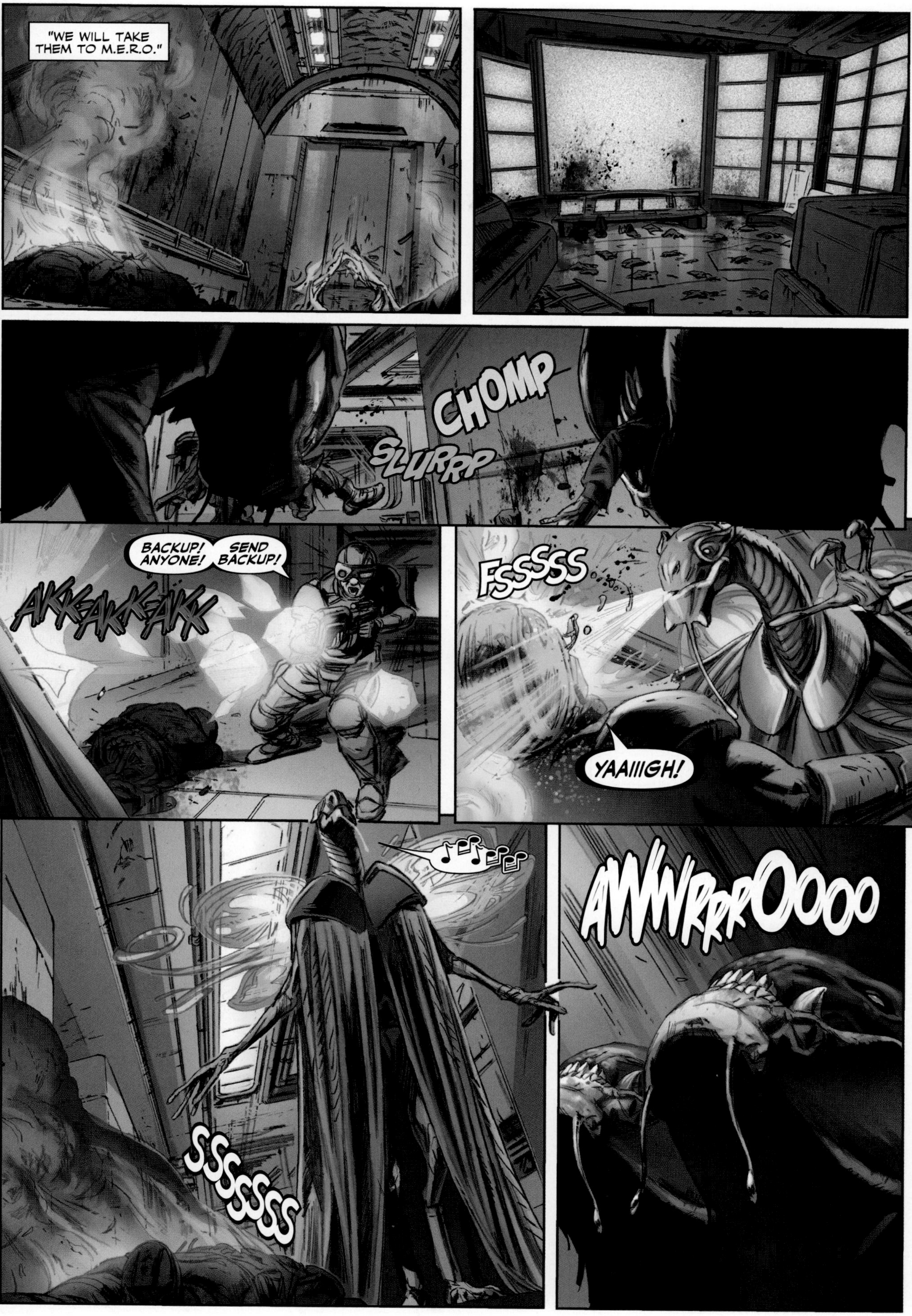
"WE WILL TAKE THEM TO M.E.R.O."
CHOMP
SLURRP
BACKUP! ANYONE!
SEND BACKUP!
AKKAKKAKK
FSSSSS
YAAIIIGH!
SSSSSSS
AWWRRROOOO

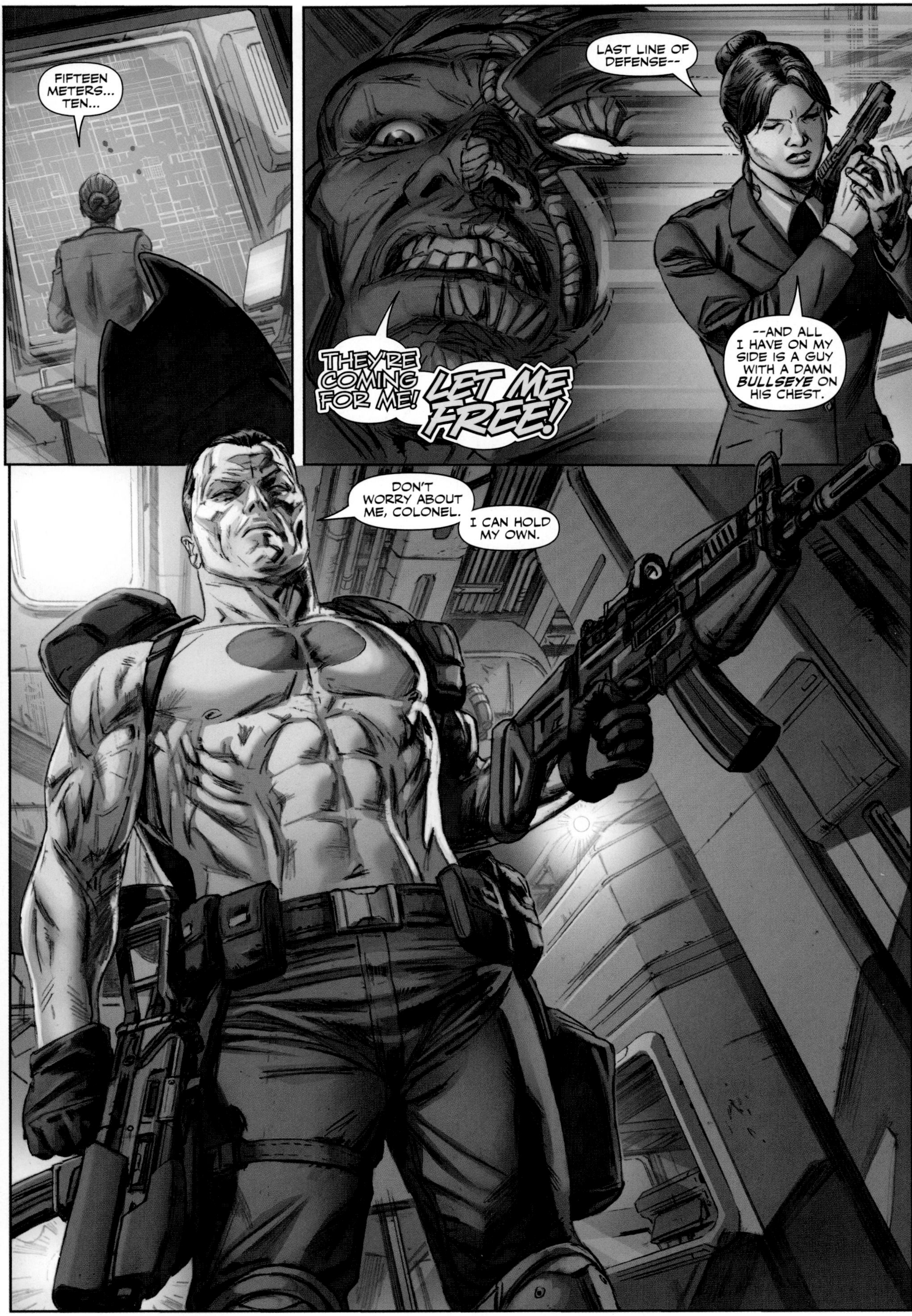
FIFTEEN METERS... TEN...
LAST LINE OF DEFENSE--
THEY'RE COMING FOR ME!
LET ME FREE!
--AND ALL I HAVE ON MY SIDE IS A GUY WITH A DAMN BULLSEYE ON HIS CHEST.
DON'T WORRY ABOUT ME, COLONEL.
I CAN HOLD MY OWN.

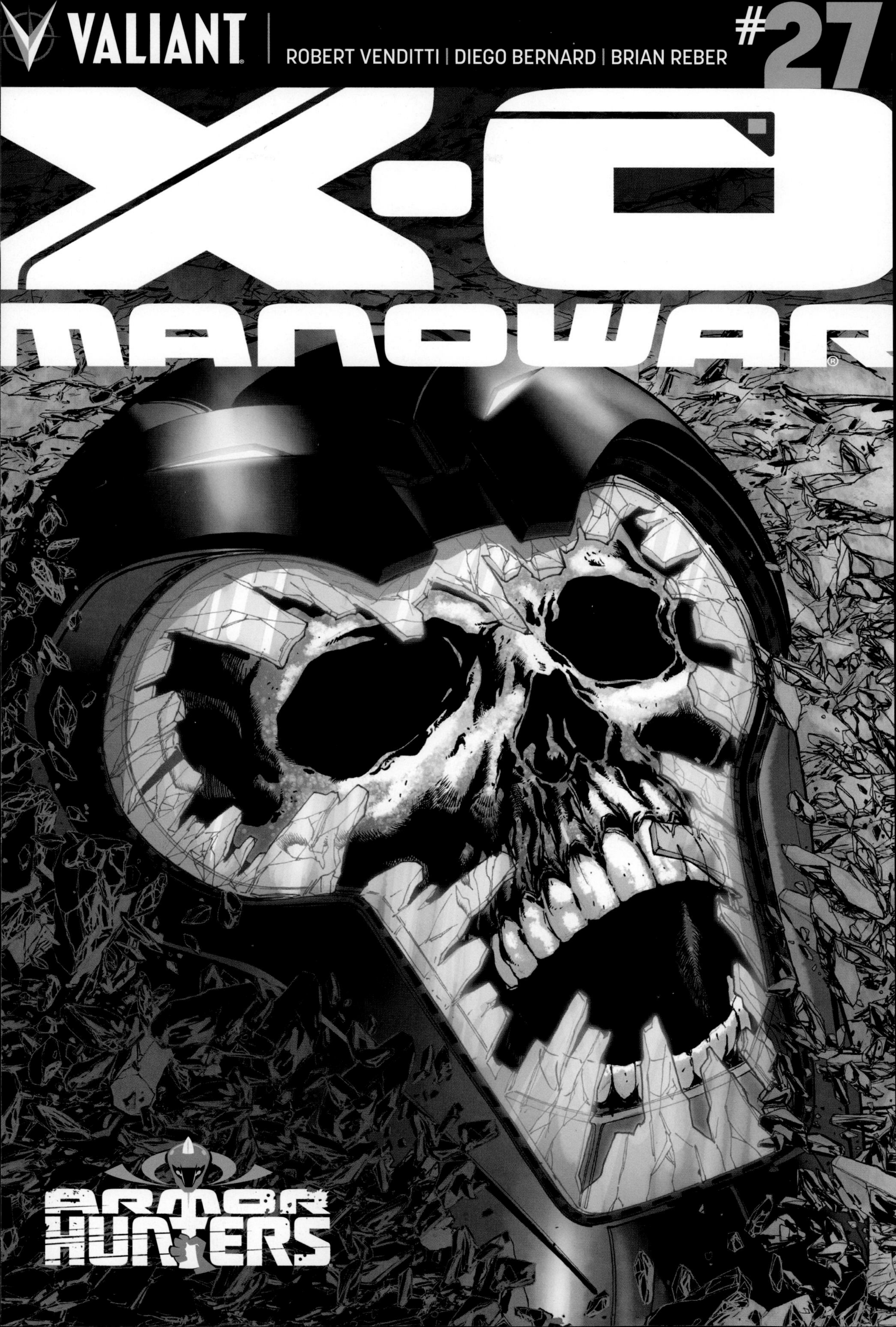
VALIANT
ROBERT VENDITTI | DIEGO BERNARD | BRIAN REBER
#27
X-O MANOWAR
ARMOR HUNTERS

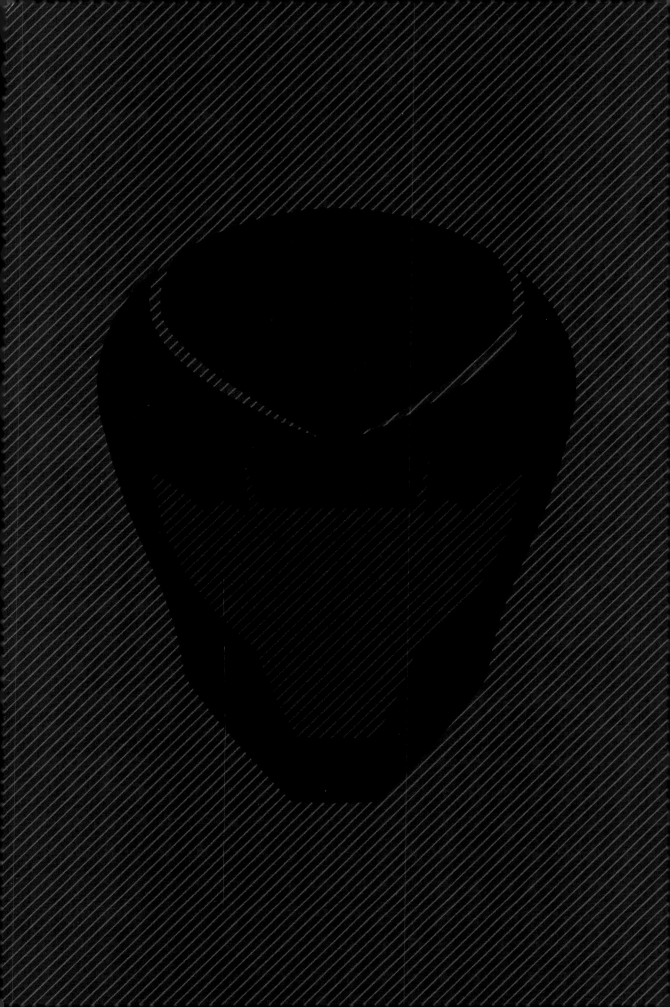

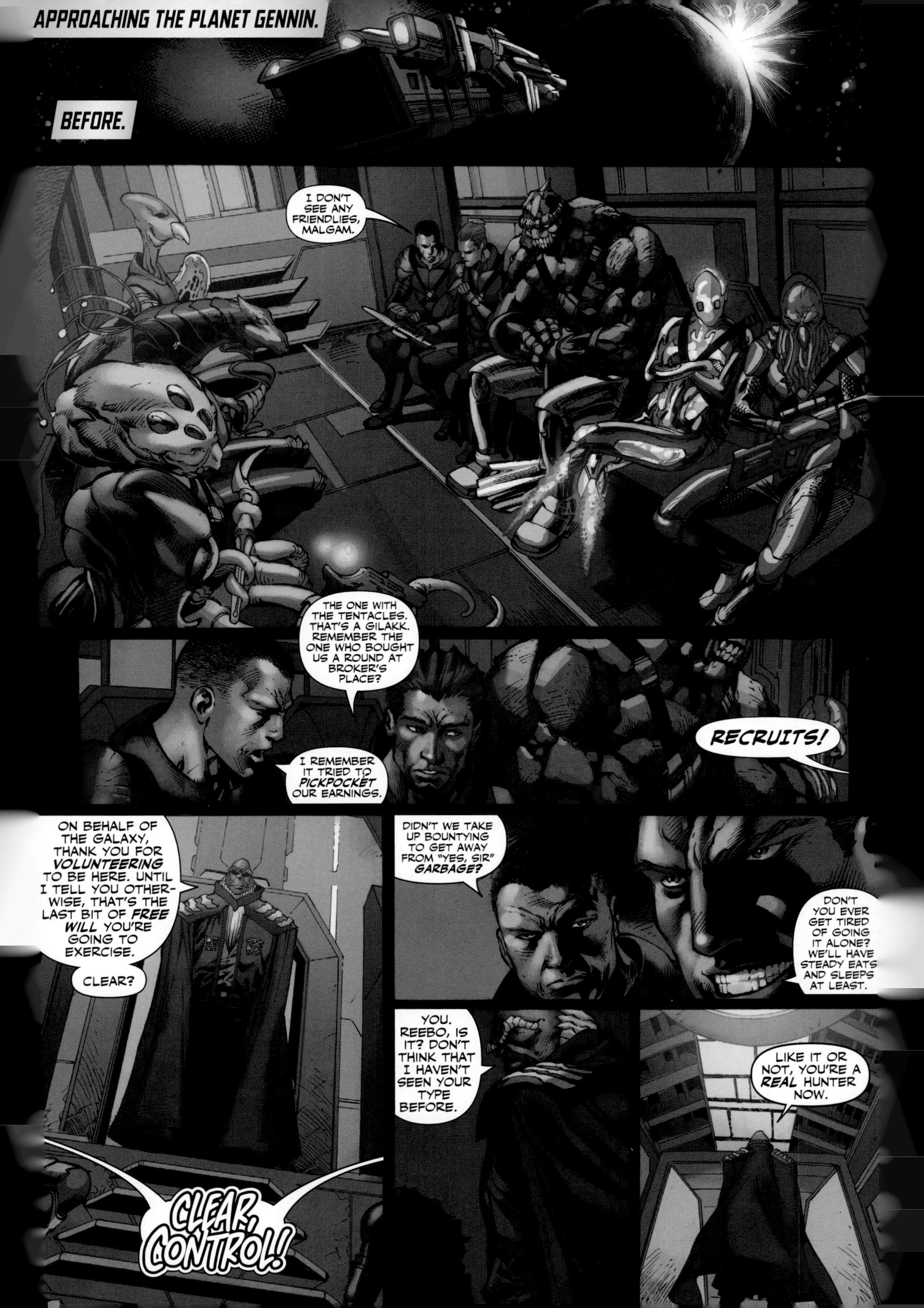
APPROACHING THE PLANET GENNIN.
BEFORE.
I DON'T SEE ANY FRIENDLIES, MALGAM.
THE ONE WITH THE TENTACLES. THAT'S A GILAKK. REMEMBER THE ONE WHO BOUGHT US A ROUND AT BROKER'S PLACE?
I REMEMBER IT TRIED TO PICKPOCKET OUR EARNINGS.
RECRUITS!
ON BEHALF OF THE GALAXY, THANK YOU FOR VOLUNTEERING TO BE HERE. UNTIL I TELL YOU OTHER-WISE, THAT'S THE LAST BIT OF FREE WILL YOU'RE GOING TO EXERCISE.
CLEAR?
CLEAR, CONTROL!
DIDN'T WE TAKE UP BOUNTYING TO GET AWAY FROM "YES, SIR" GARBAGE?
DON'T YOU EVER GET TIRED OF GOING IT ALONE? WE'LL HAVE STEADY EATS AND SLEEPS AT LEAST.
YOU. REEBO, IS IT? DON'T THINK THAT I HAVEN'T SEEN YOUR TYPE BEFORE.
LIKE IT OR NOT, YOU'RE A REAL HUNTER NOW.

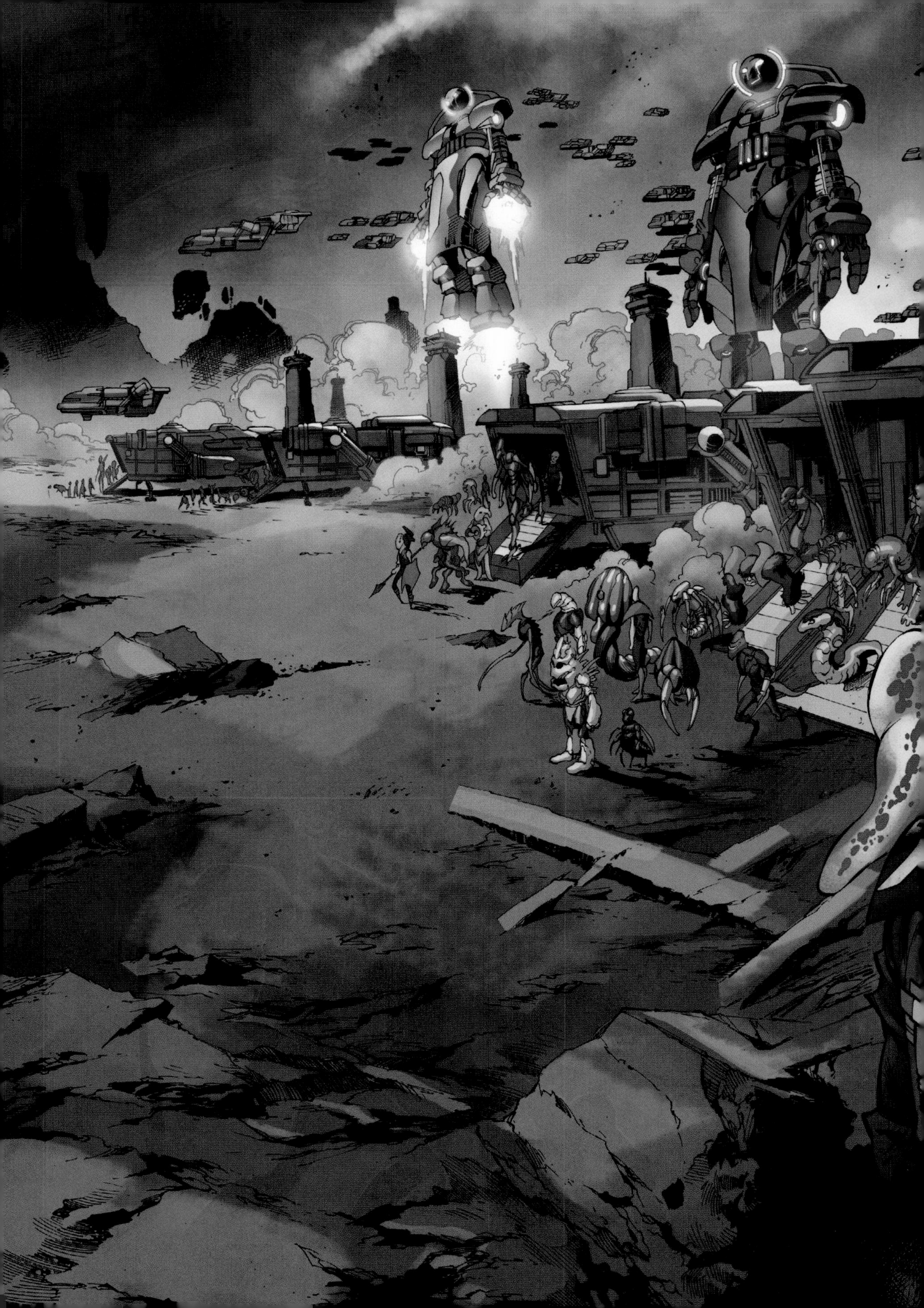

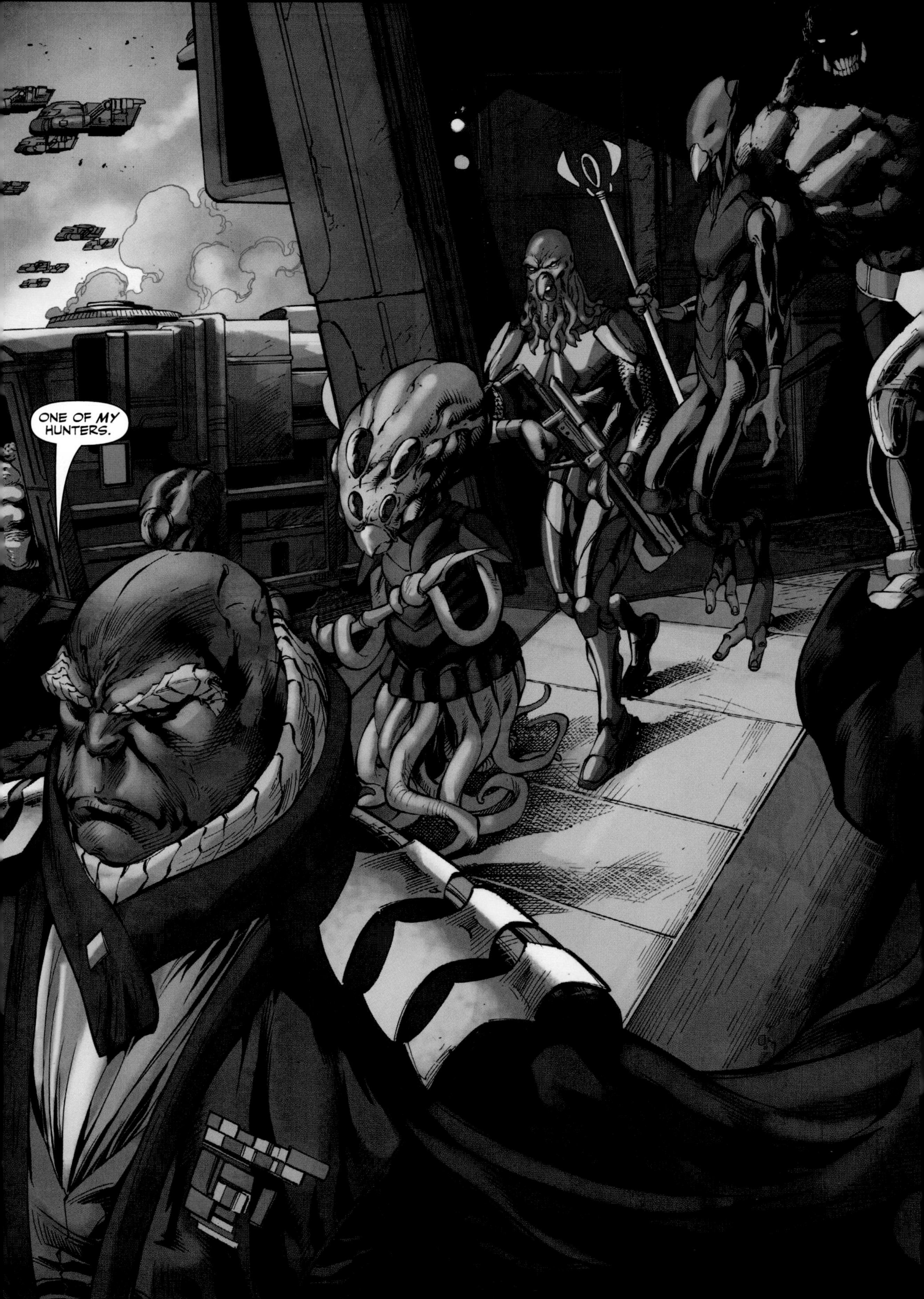
ONE OF MY HUNTERS.

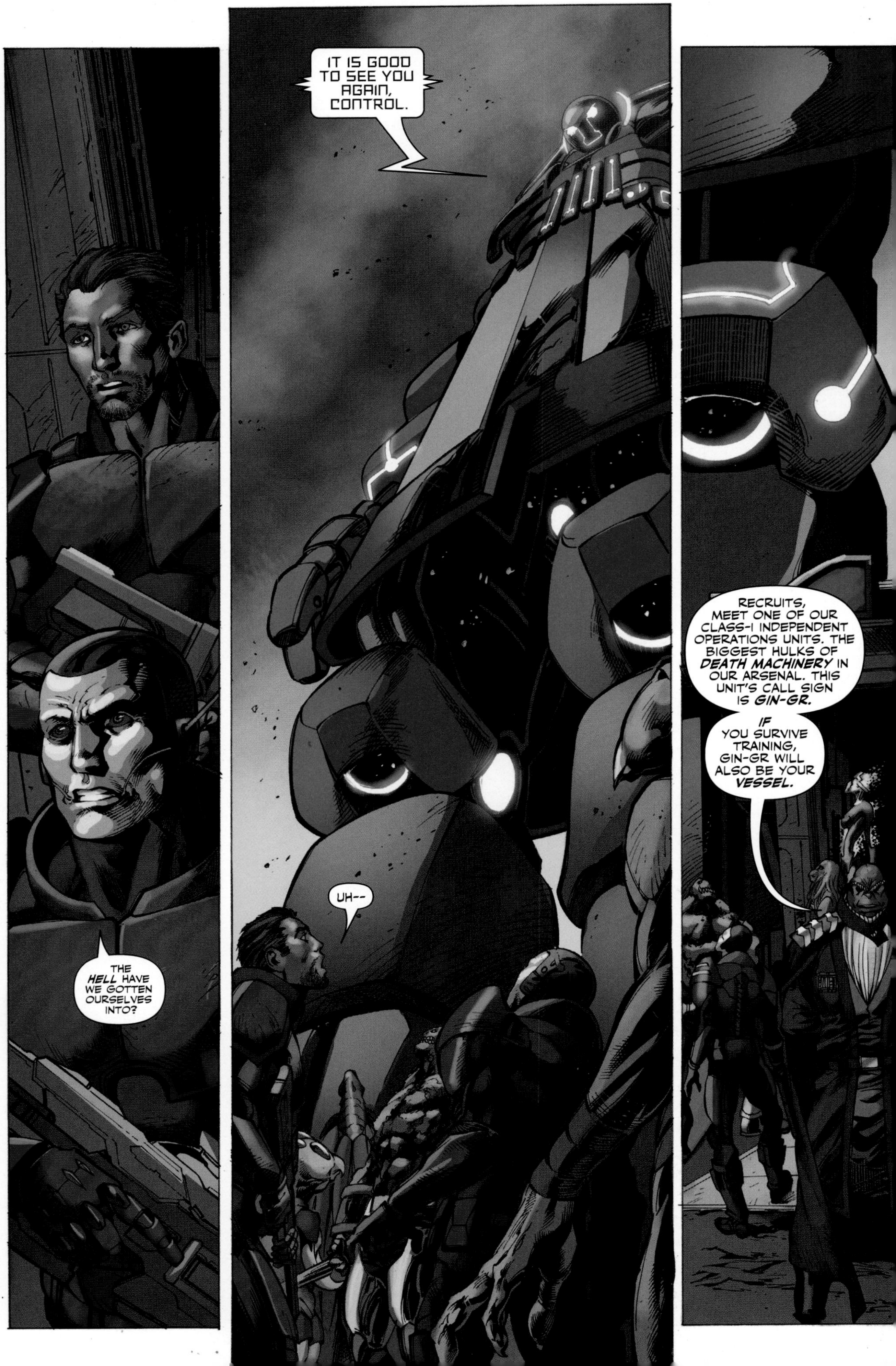
THE HELL HAVE WE GOTTEN OURSELVES INTO?
IT IS GOOD TO SEE YOU AGAIN, CONTROL.
UH--
RECRUITS, MEET ONE OF OUR CLASS-I INDEPENDENT OPERATIONS UNITS. THE BIGGEST HULKS OF DEATH MACHINERY IN OUR ARSENAL. THIS UNIT'S CALL SIGN IS GIN-GR.
IF YOU SURVIVE TRAINING, GIN-GR WILL ALSO BE YOUR VESSEL.

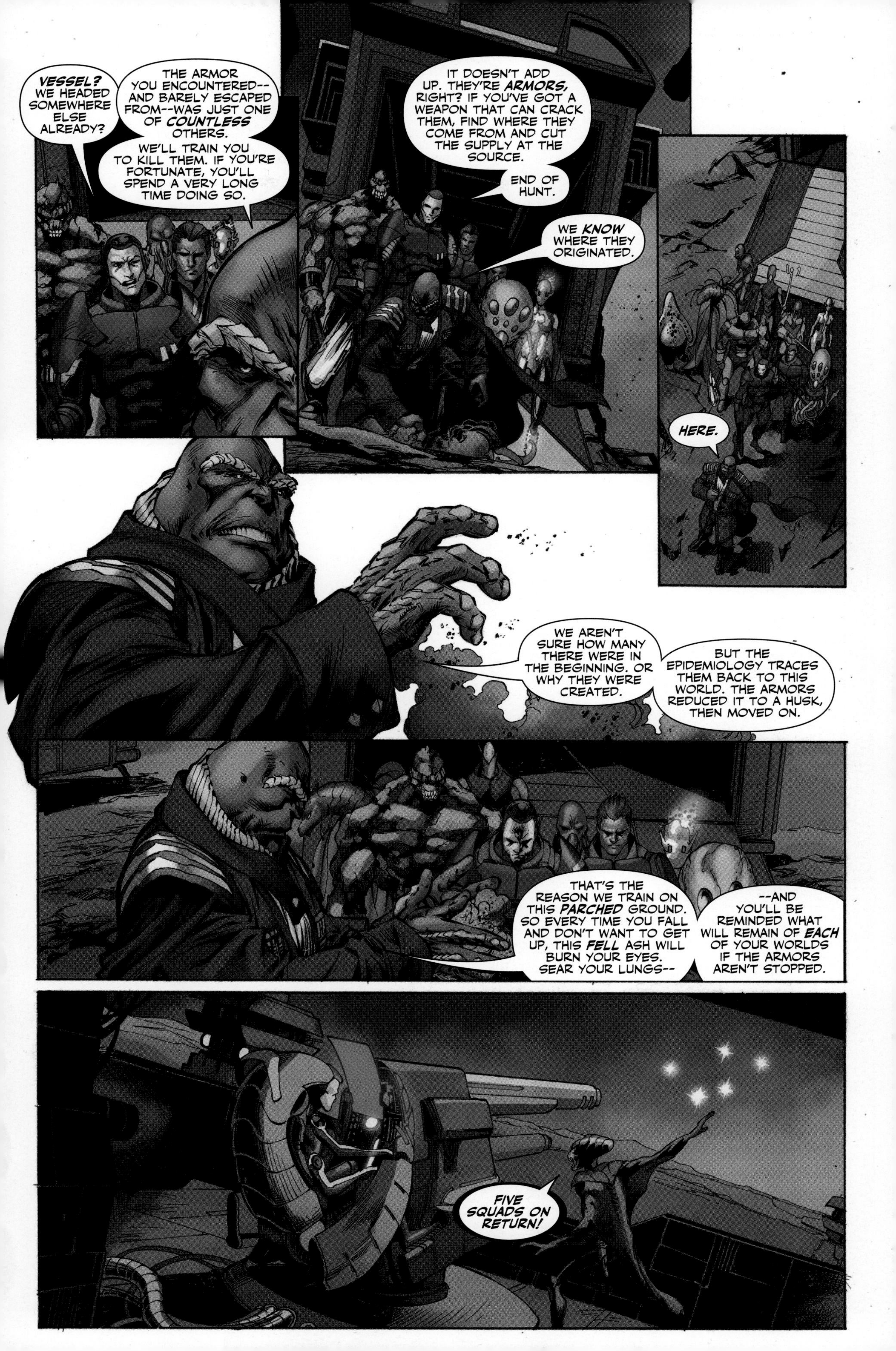

VESSEL? WE HEADED SOMEWHERE ELSE ALREADY?
THE ARMOR YOU ENCOUNTERED-- AND BARELY ESCAPED FROM--WAS JUST ONE OF COUNTLESS OTHERS.
WE'LL TRAIN YOU TO KILL THEM. IF YOU'RE FORTUNATE, YOU'LL SPEND A VERY LONG TIME DOING SO.
IT DOESN'T ADD UP. THEY'RE ARMORS, RIGHT? IF YOU'VE GOT A WEAPON THAT CAN CRACK THEM, FIND WHERE THEY COME FROM AND CUT THE SUPPLY AT THE SOURCE.
END OF HUNT.
WE KNOW WHERE THEY ORIGINATED.
HERE.
WE AREN'T SURE HOW MANY THERE WERE IN THE BEGINNING. OR WHY THEY WERE CREATED.
BUT THE EPIDEMIOLOGY TRACES THEM BACK TO THIS WORLD. THE ARMORS REDUCED IT TO A HUSK, THEN MOVED ON.
THAT'S THE REASON WE TRAIN ON THIS PARCHED GROUND. SO EVERY TIME YOU FALL AND DON'T WANT TO GET UP, THIS FELL ASH WILL BURN YOUR EYES. SEAR YOUR LUNGS--
--AND YOU'LL BE REMINDED WHAT WILL REMAIN OF EACH OF YOUR WORLDS IF THE ARMORS AREN'T STOPPED.
FIVE SQUADS ON RETURN!

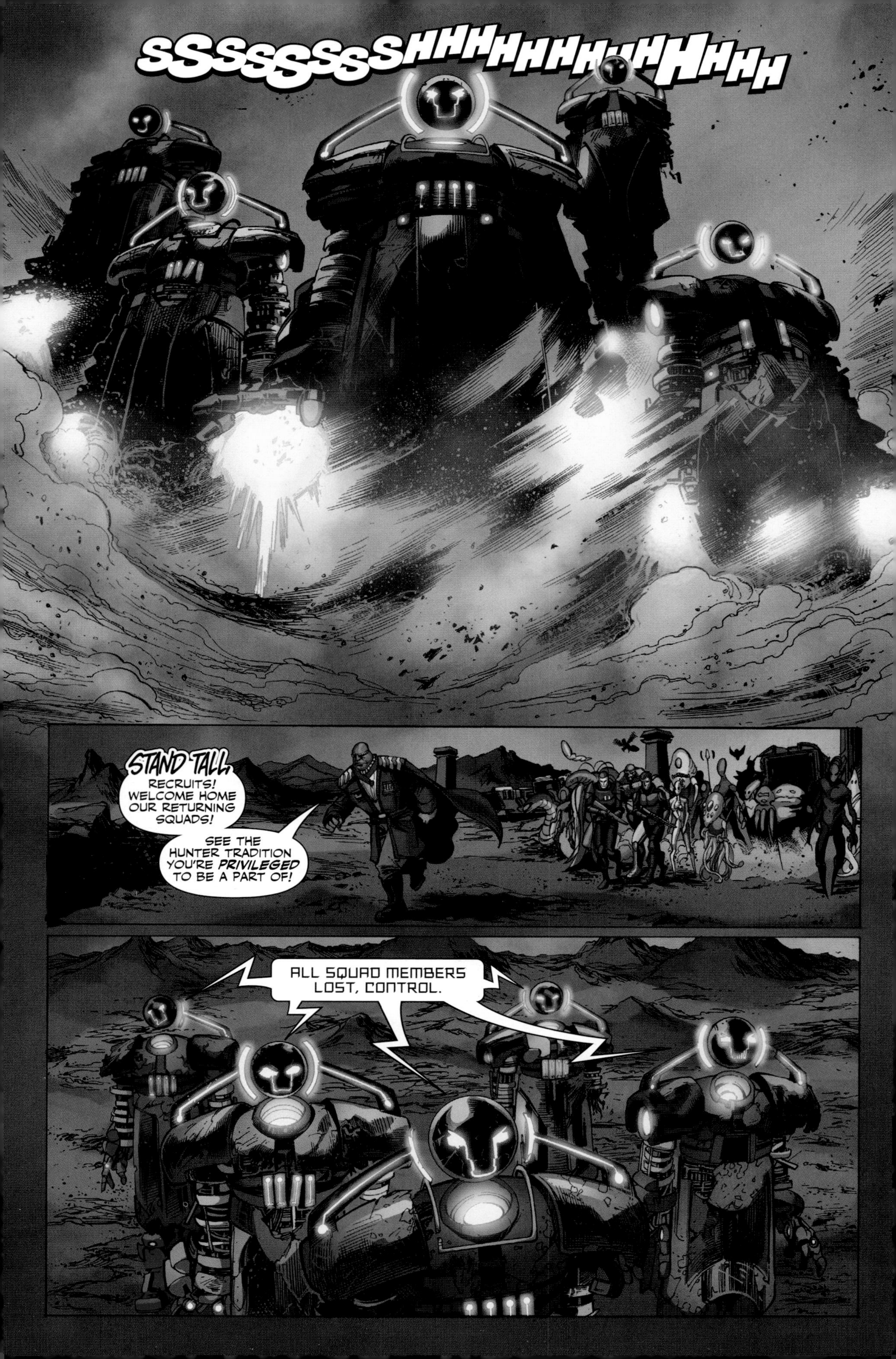
SSSSSSSSHHHHHHHHHHHHH
STAND TALL, RECRUITS! WELCOME HOME OUR RETURNING SQUADS!
SEE THE HUNTER TRADITION YOU'RE PRIVILEGED TO BE A PART OF!
ALL SQUAD MEMBERS LOST, CONTROL.

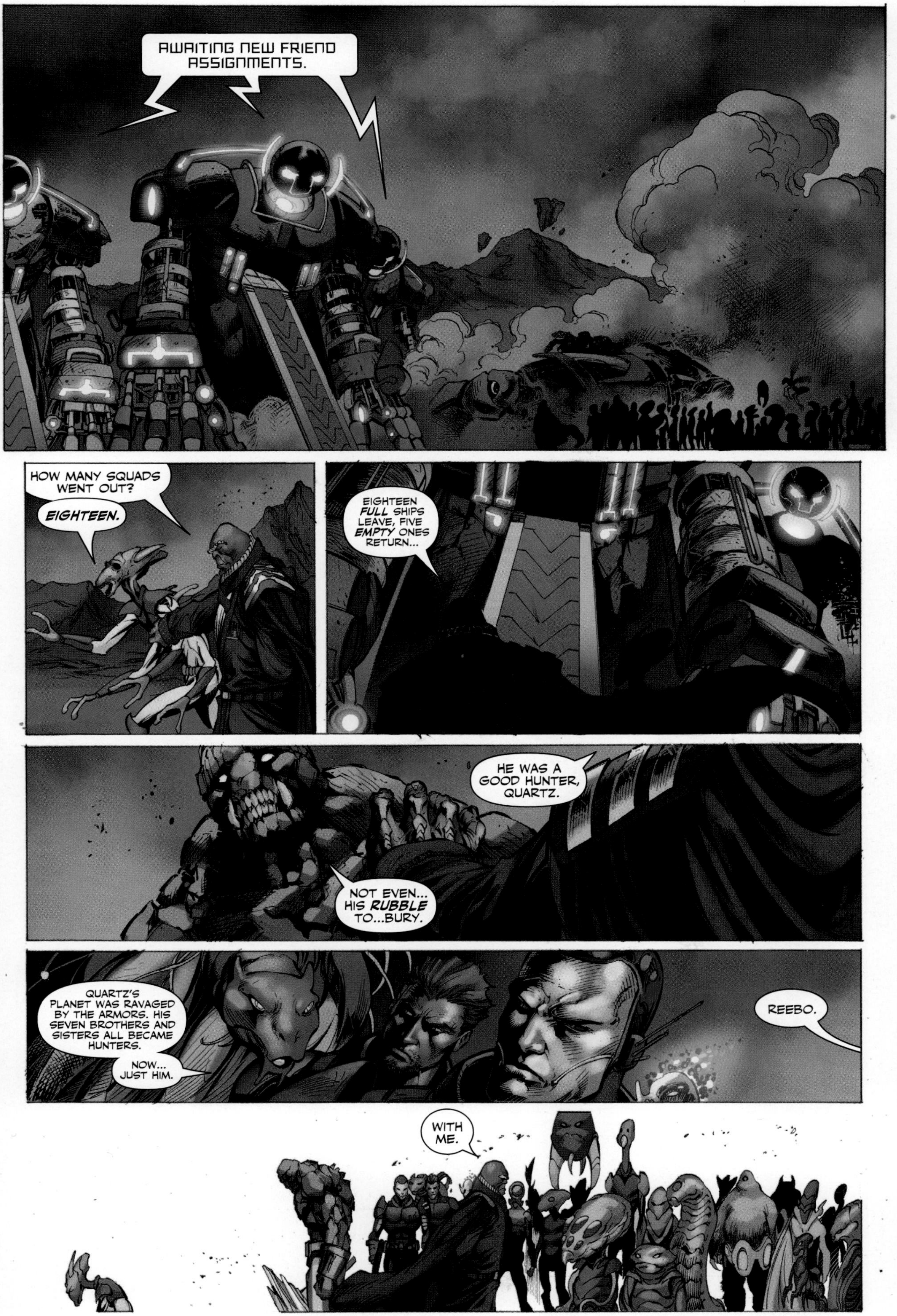
AWAITING NEW FRIEND ASSIGNMENTS.
HOW MANY SQUADS WENT OUT?
EIGHTEEN.
EIGHTEEN FULL SHIPS LEAVE, FIVE EMPTY ONES RETURN...
HE WAS A GOOD HUNTER, QUARTZ.
NOT EVEN... HIS RUBBLE TO...BURY.
QUARTZ'S PLANET WAS RAVAGED BY THE ARMORS. HIS SEVEN BROTHERS AND SISTERS ALL BECAME HUNTERS.
NOW... JUST HIM.
REEBO.
WITH ME.

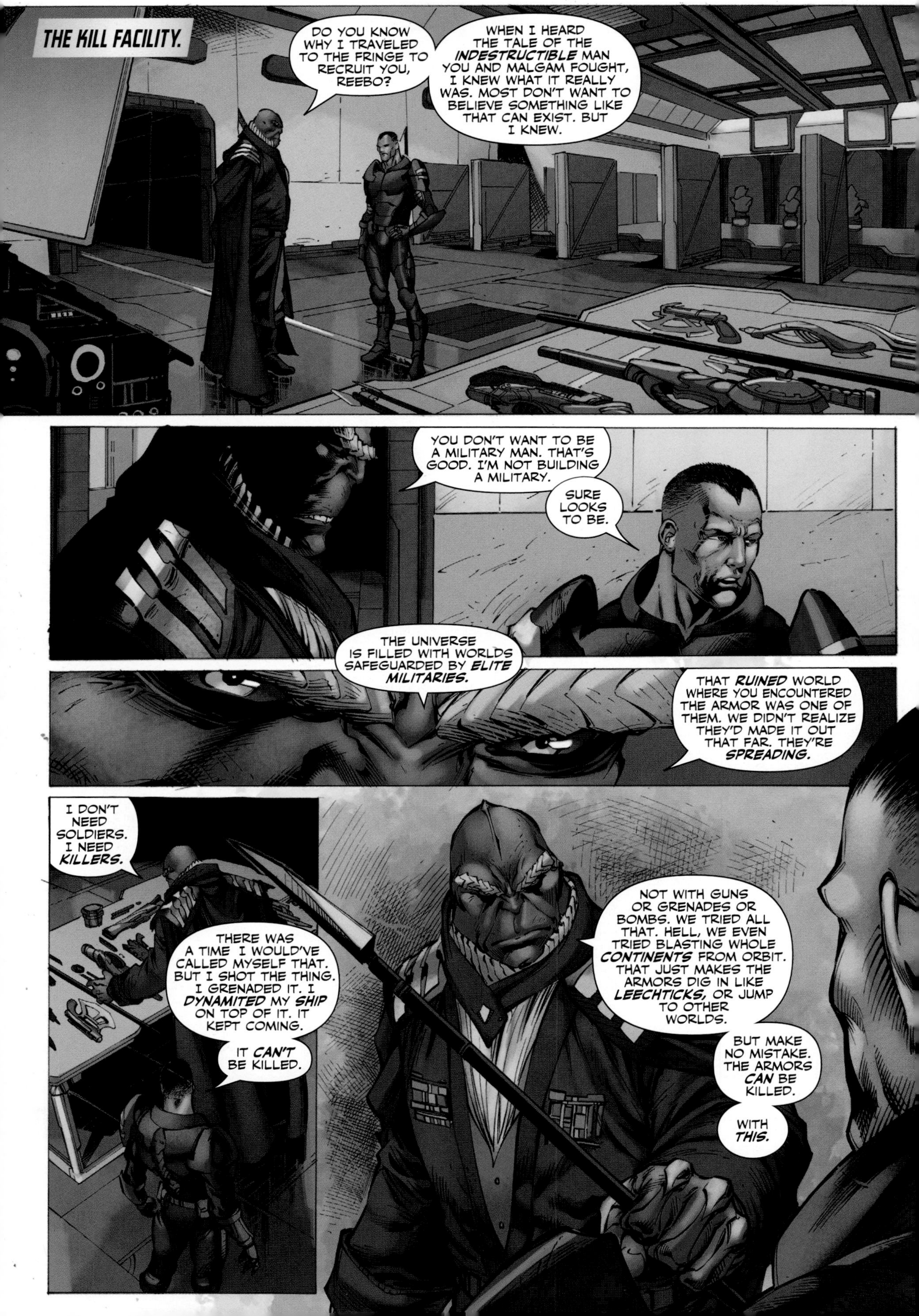
THE KILL FACILITY.
DO YOU KNOW WHY I TRAVELED TO THE FRINGE TO RECRUIT YOU, REEBO?
WHEN I HEARD THE TALE OF THE *INDESTRUCTIBLE* MAN YOU AND MALGAM FOUGHT, I KNEW WHAT IT REALLY WAS. MOST DON'T WANT TO BELIEVE SOMETHING LIKE THAT CAN EXIST. BUT I KNEW.
YOU DON'T WANT TO BE A MILITARY MAN. THAT'S GOOD. I'M NOT BUILDING A MILITARY.
SURE LOOKS TO BE.
THE UNIVERSE IS FILLED WITH WORLDS SAFEGUARDED BY *ELITE MILITARIES.*
THAT *RUINED* WORLD WHERE YOU ENCOUNTERED THE ARMOR WAS ONE OF THEM. WE DIDN'T REALIZE THEY'D MADE IT OUT THAT FAR. THEY'RE *SPREADING.*
I DON'T NEED SOLDIERS. I NEED *KILLERS.*
THERE WAS A TIME I WOULD'VE CALLED MYSELF THAT. BUT I SHOT THE THING. I GRENADED IT. I *DYNAMITED* MY *SHIP* ON TOP OF IT. IT KEPT COMING.
IT *CAN'T* BE KILLED.
NOT WITH GUNS OR GRENADES OR BOMBS. WE TRIED ALL THAT. HELL, WE EVEN TRIED BLASTING WHOLE *CONTINENTS* FROM ORBIT. THAT JUST MAKES THE ARMORS DIG IN LIKE *LEECHTICKS,* OR JUMP TO OTHER WORLDS.
BUT MAKE NO MISTAKE. THE ARMORS *CAN* BE KILLED.
WITH *THIS.*

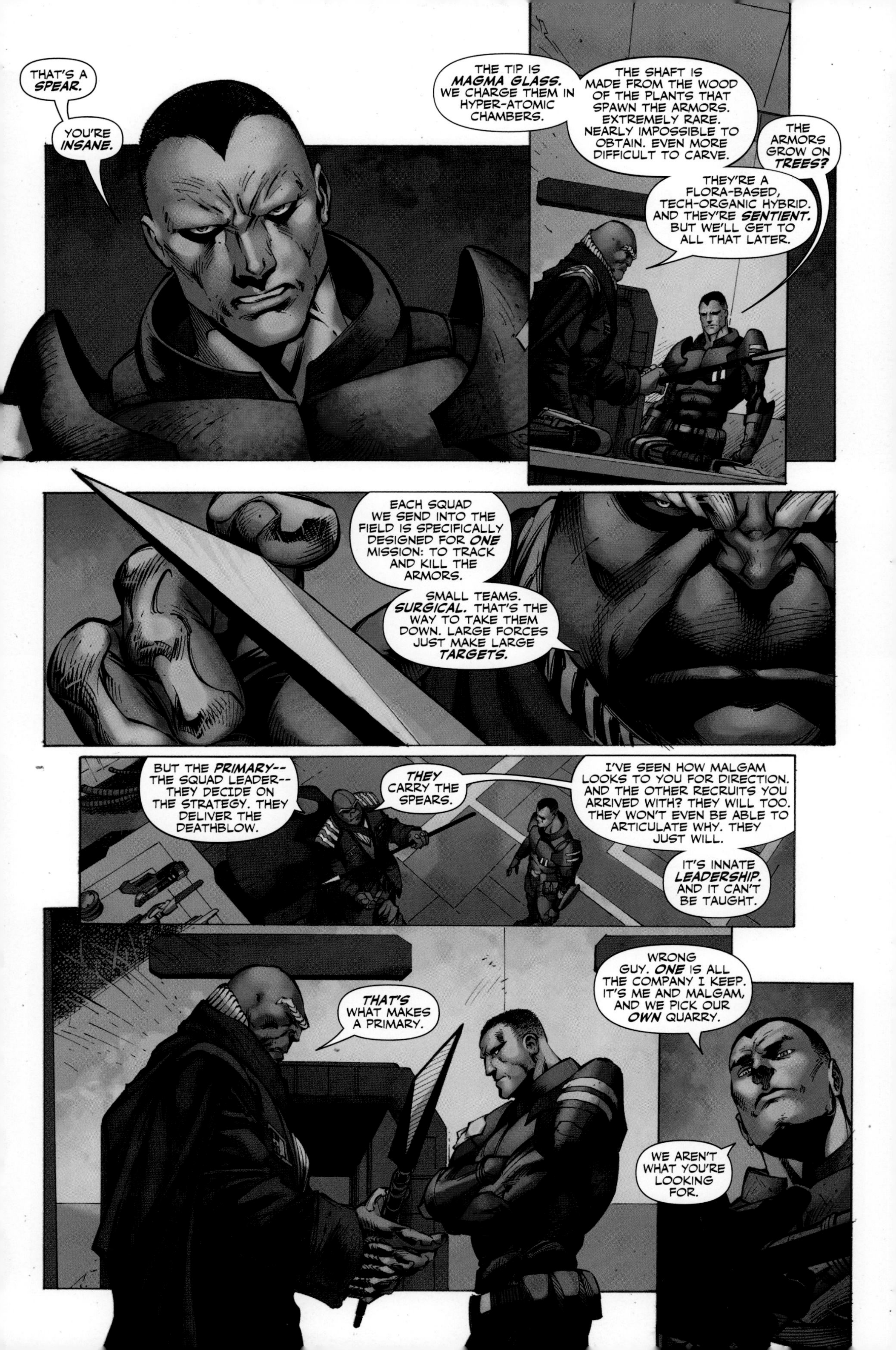
THAT'S A SPEAR.
YOU'RE INSANE.
THE TIP IS MAGMA GLASS. WE CHARGE THEM IN HYPER-ATOMIC CHAMBERS.
THE SHAFT IS MADE FROM THE WOOD OF THE PLANTS THAT SPAWN THE ARMORS. EXTREMELY RARE. NEARLY IMPOSSIBLE TO OBTAIN. EVEN MORE DIFFICULT TO CARVE.
THE ARMORS GROW ON TREES?
THEY'RE A FLORA-BASED, TECH-ORGANIC HYBRID. AND THEY'RE SENTIENT. BUT WE'LL GET TO ALL THAT LATER.
EACH SQUAD WE SEND INTO THE FIELD IS SPECIFICALLY DESIGNED FOR ONE MISSION: TO TRACK AND KILL THE ARMORS.
SMALL TEAMS. SURGICAL. THAT'S THE WAY TO TAKE THEM DOWN. LARGE FORCES JUST MAKE LARGE TARGETS.
BUT THE PRIMARY-- THE SQUAD LEADER-- THEY DECIDE ON THE STRATEGY. THEY DELIVER THE DEATHBLOW.
THEY CARRY THE SPEARS.
I'VE SEEN HOW MALGAM LOOKS TO YOU FOR DIRECTION. AND THE OTHER RECRUITS YOU ARRIVED WITH? THEY WILL TOO. THEY WON'T EVEN BE ABLE TO ARTICULATE WHY. THEY JUST WILL.
IT'S INNATE LEADERSHIP. AND IT CAN'T BE TAUGHT.
THAT'S WHAT MAKES A PRIMARY.
WRONG GUY. ONE IS ALL THE COMPANY I KEEP. IT'S ME AND MALGAM, AND WE PICK OUR OWN QUARRY.
WE AREN'T WHAT YOU'RE LOOKING FOR.

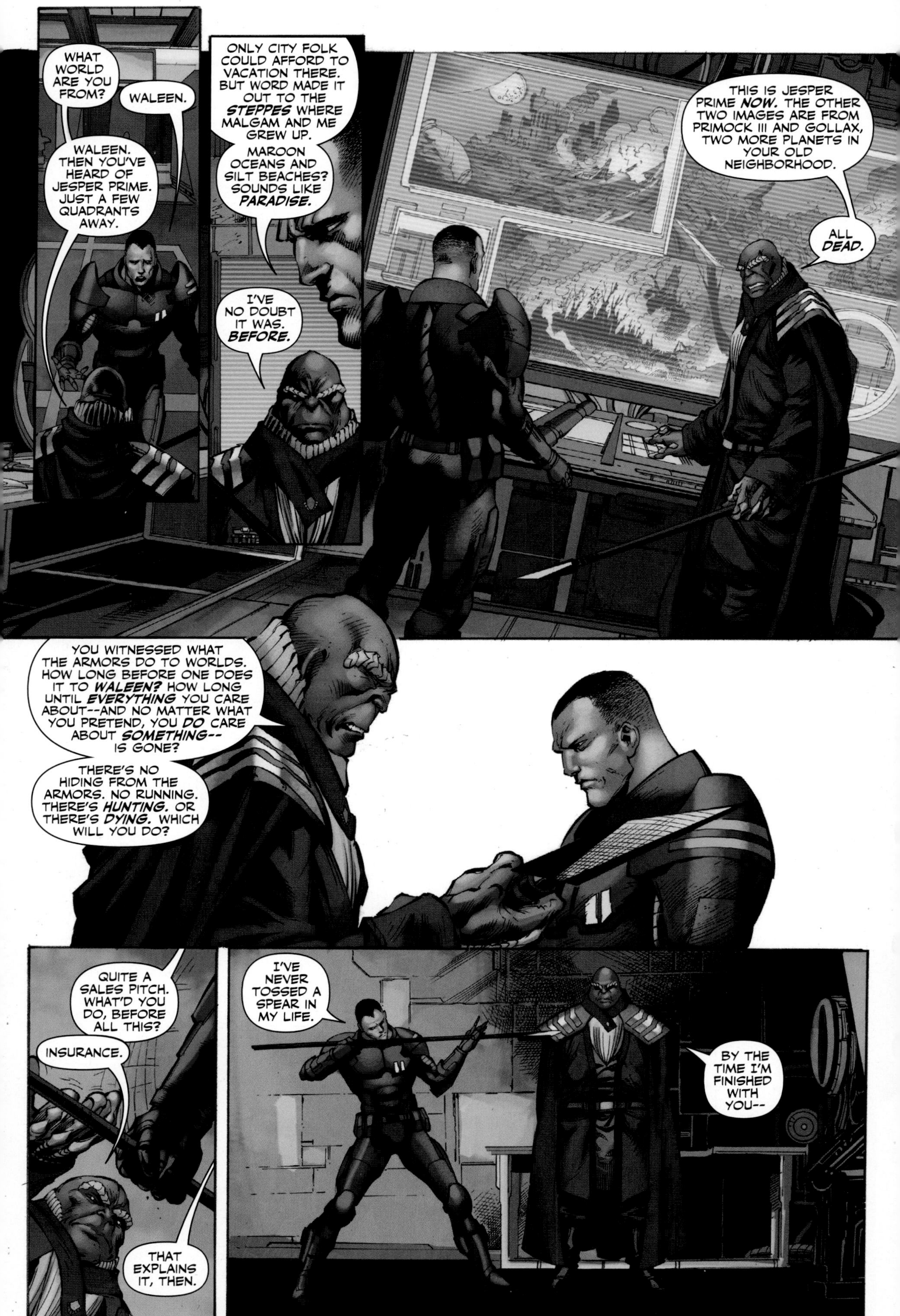
WHAT WORLD ARE YOU FROM?
WALEEN.
WALEEN. THEN YOU'VE HEARD OF JESPER PRIME. JUST A FEW QUADRANTS AWAY.
ONLY CITY FOLK COULD AFFORD TO VACATION THERE. BUT WORD MADE IT OUT TO THE STEPPES WHERE MALGAM AND ME GREW UP.
MAROON OCEANS AND SILT BEACHES? SOUNDS LIKE PARADISE.
I'VE NO DOUBT IT WAS. BEFORE.
THIS IS JESPER PRIME NOW. THE OTHER TWO IMAGES ARE FROM PRIMOCK III AND GOLLAX, TWO MORE PLANETS IN YOUR OLD NEIGHBORHOOD.
ALL DEAD.
YOU WITNESSED WHAT THE ARMORS DO TO WORLDS. HOW LONG BEFORE ONE DOES IT TO WALEEN? HOW LONG UNTIL EVERYTHING YOU CARE ABOUT--AND NO MATTER WHAT YOU PRETEND, YOU DO CARE ABOUT SOMETHING--IS GONE?
THERE'S NO HIDING FROM THE ARMORS. NO RUNNING. THERE'S HUNTING. OR THERE'S DYING. WHICH WILL YOU DO?
QUITE A SALES PITCH. WHAT'D YOU DO, BEFORE ALL THIS?
INSURANCE.
THAT EXPLAINS IT, THEN.
I'VE NEVER TOSSED A SPEAR IN MY LIFE.
BY THE TIME I'M FINISHED WITH YOU--

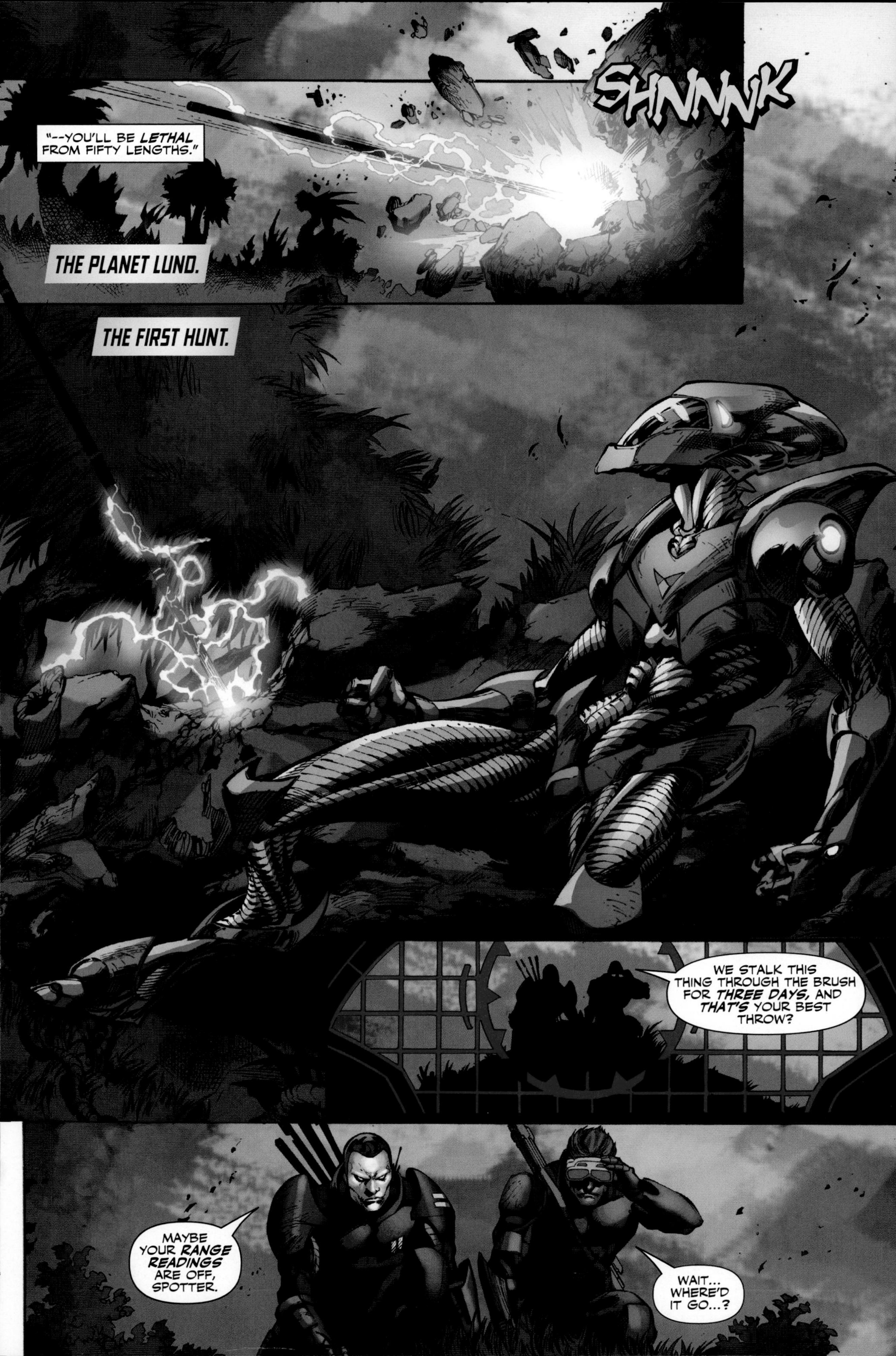
"--YOU'LL BE LETHAL FROM FIFTY LENGTHS."
SHNNNK
THE PLANET LUND.
THE FIRST HUNT.
WE STALK THIS THING THROUGH THE BRUSH FOR THREE DAYS, AND THAT'S YOUR BEST THROW?
MAYBE YOUR RANGE READINGS ARE OFF, SPOTTER.
WAIT... WHERE'D IT GO...?

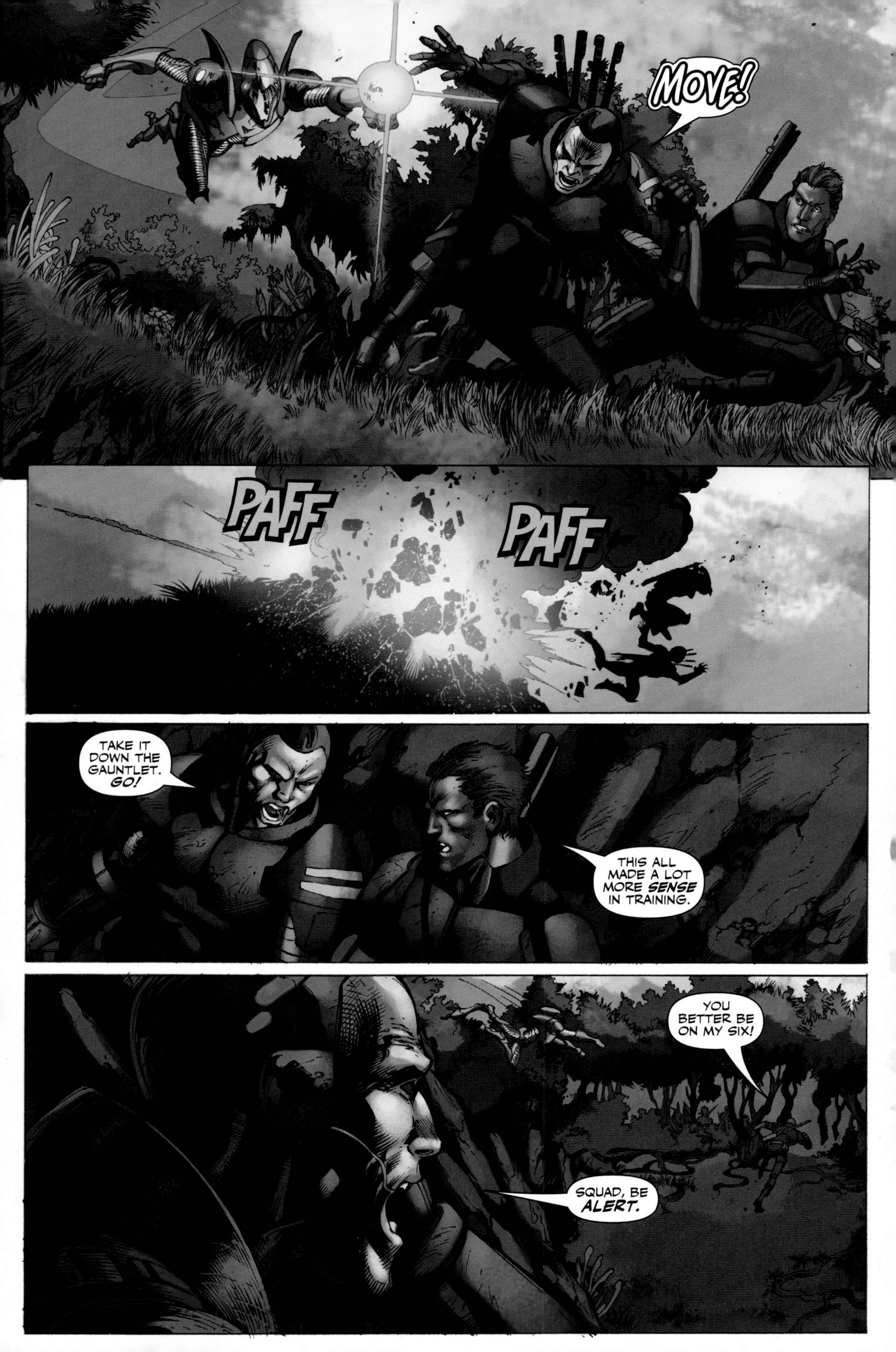
MOVE!
PAFF
PAFF
TAKE IT DOWN THE GAUNTLET. GO!
THIS ALL MADE A LOT MORE SENSE IN TRAINING.
YOU BETTER BE ON MY SIX!
SQUAD, BE ALERT.

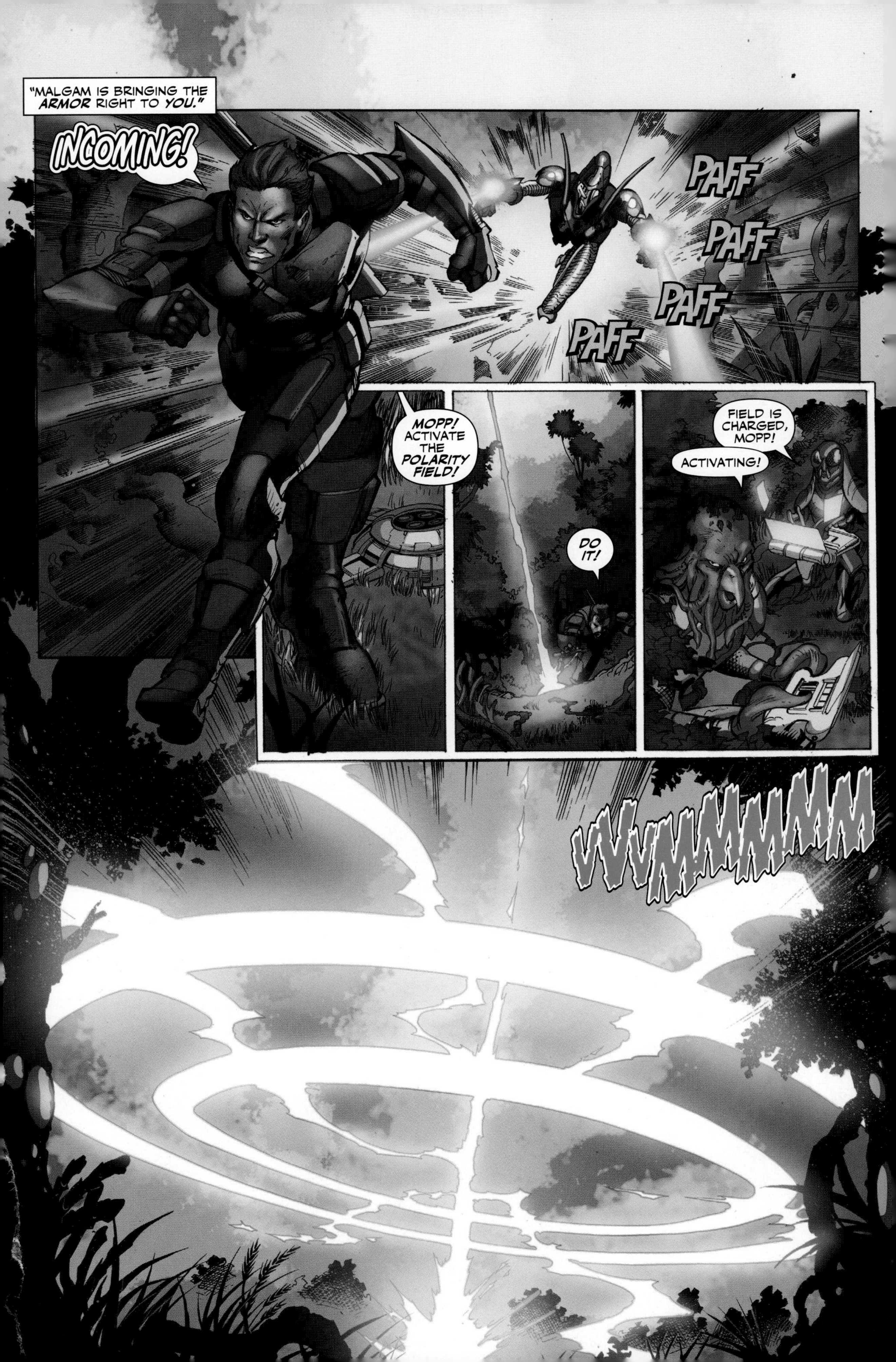

"MALGAM IS BRINGING THE ARMOR RIGHT TO YOU."
INCOMING!
PAFF
PAFF
PAFF
PAFF
MOPP! ACTIVATE THE POLARITY FIELD!
DO IT!
FIELD IS CHARGED, MOPP!
ACTIVATING!
VVVMMMMMM

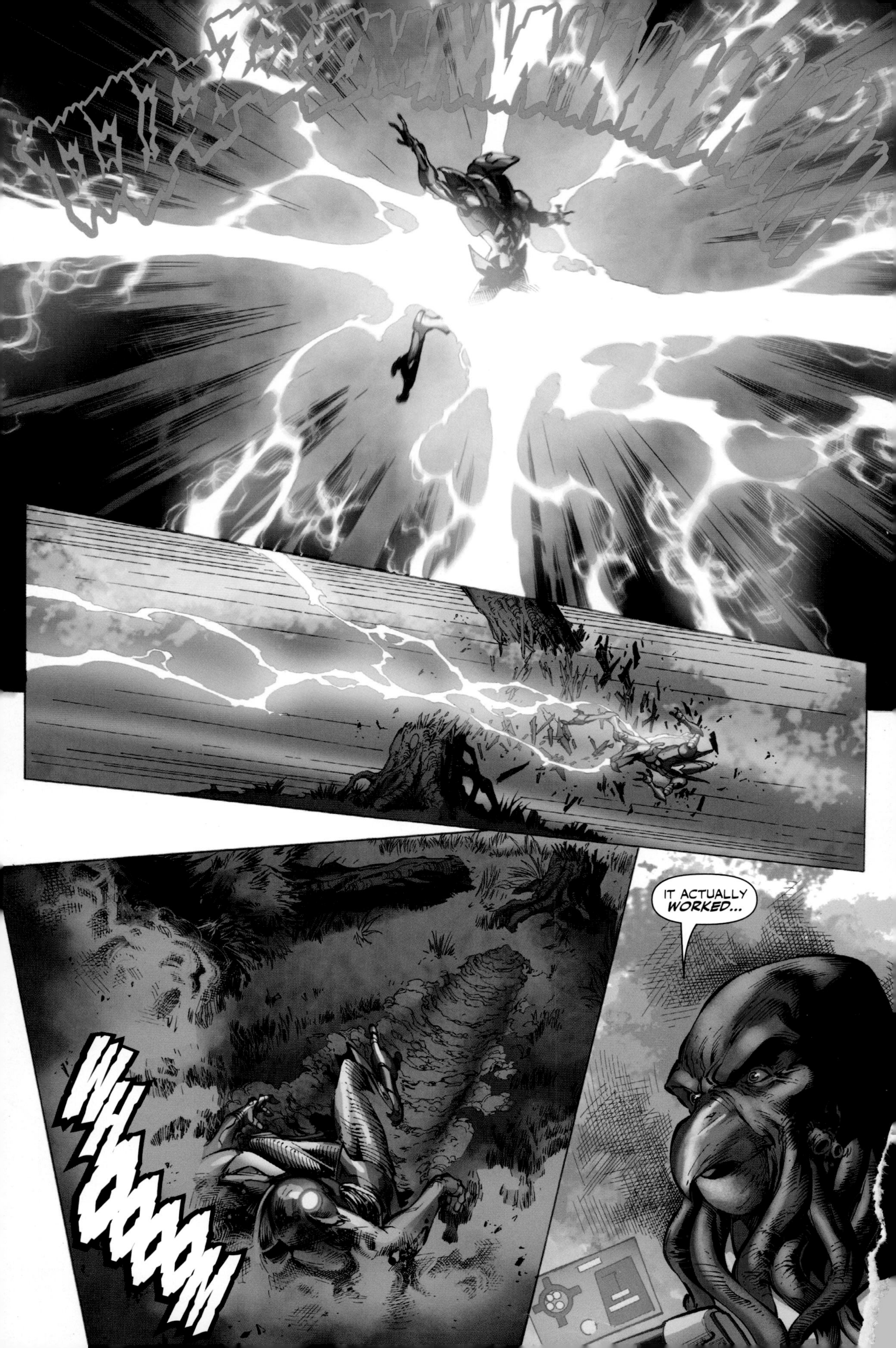
IT ACTUALLY WORKED...
WHOOOOM

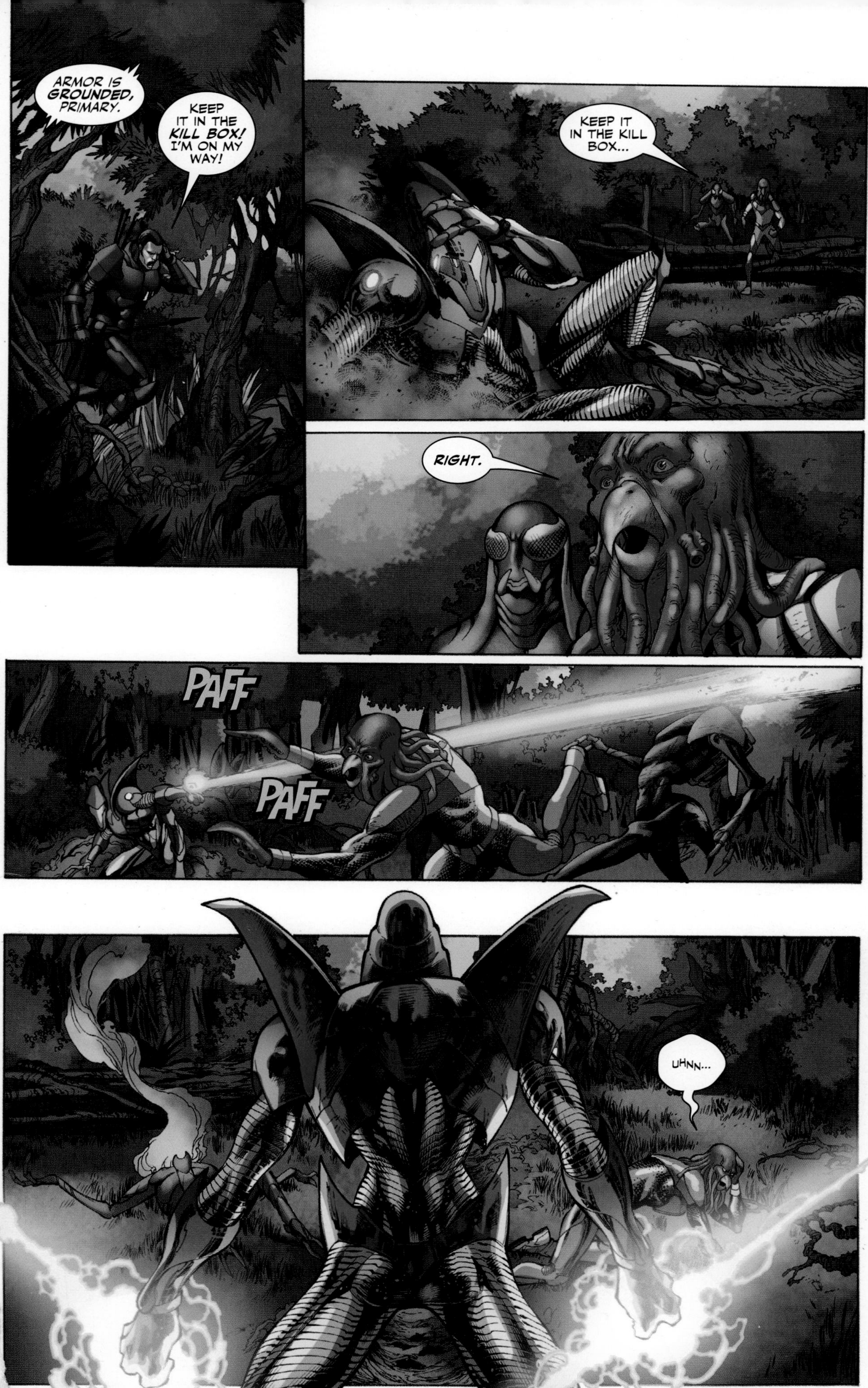
ARMOR IS GROUNDED, PRIMARY.
KEEP IT IN THE KILL BOX! I'M ON MY WAY!
KEEP IT IN THE KILL BOX...
RIGHT.
PAFF
PAFF
UHNN...

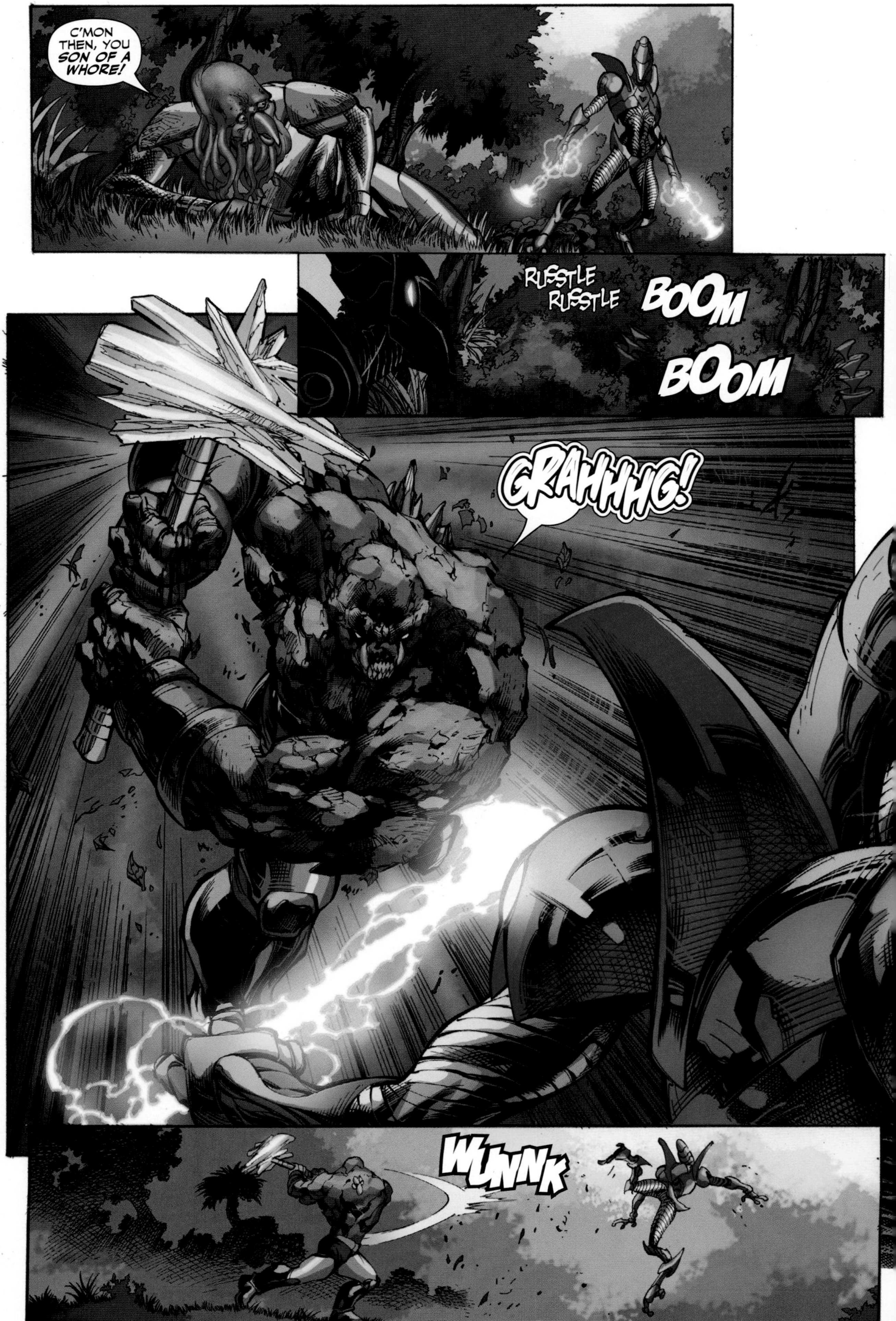
C'MON THEN, YOU SON OF A WHORE!
RUSSTLE RUSSTLE
BOOM
BOOM
GRAHHHG!
WUNNK

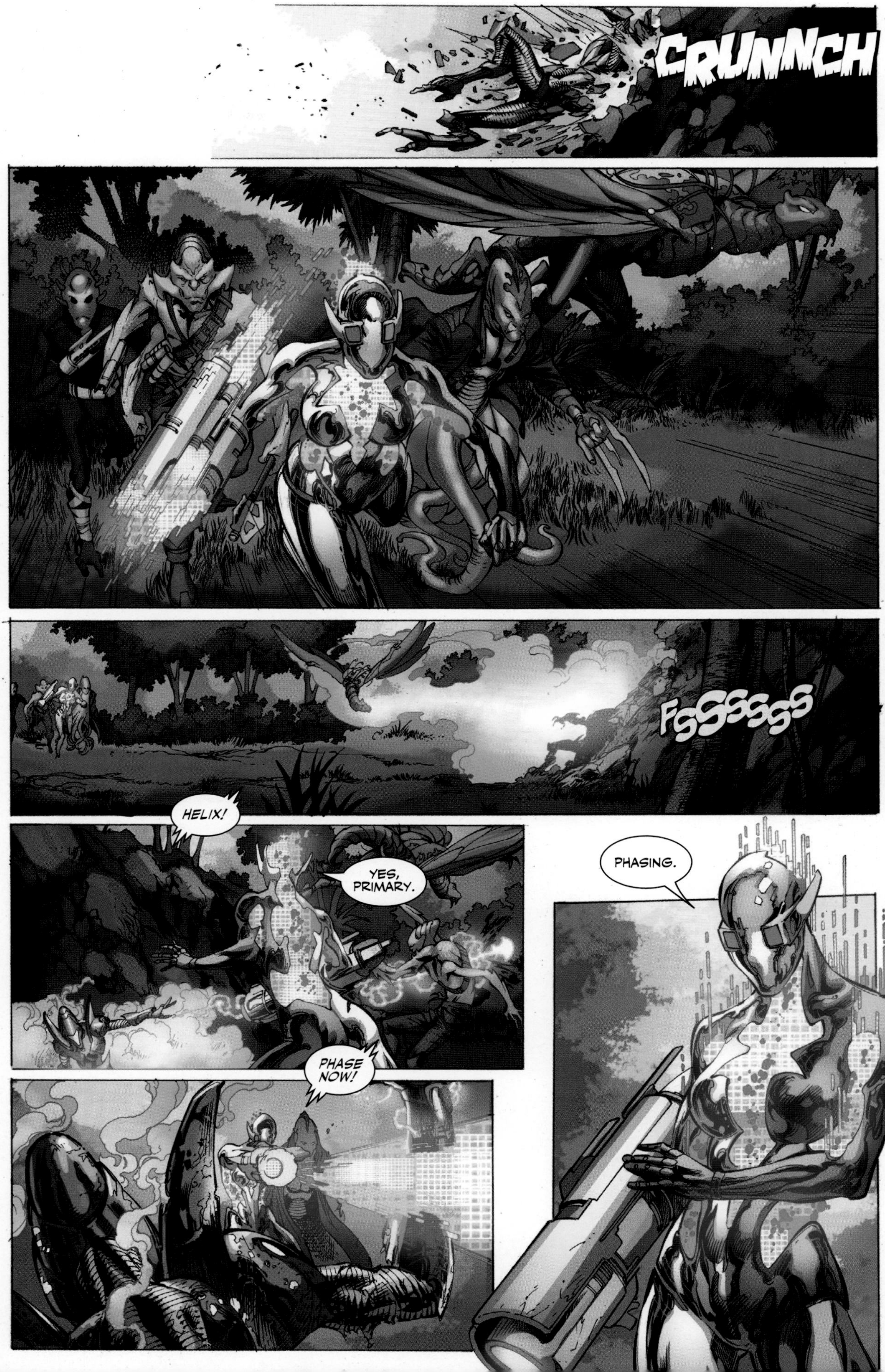
CRUNNCH
FSSSSSS
HELIX!
YES, PRIMARY.
PHASE NOW!
PHASING.

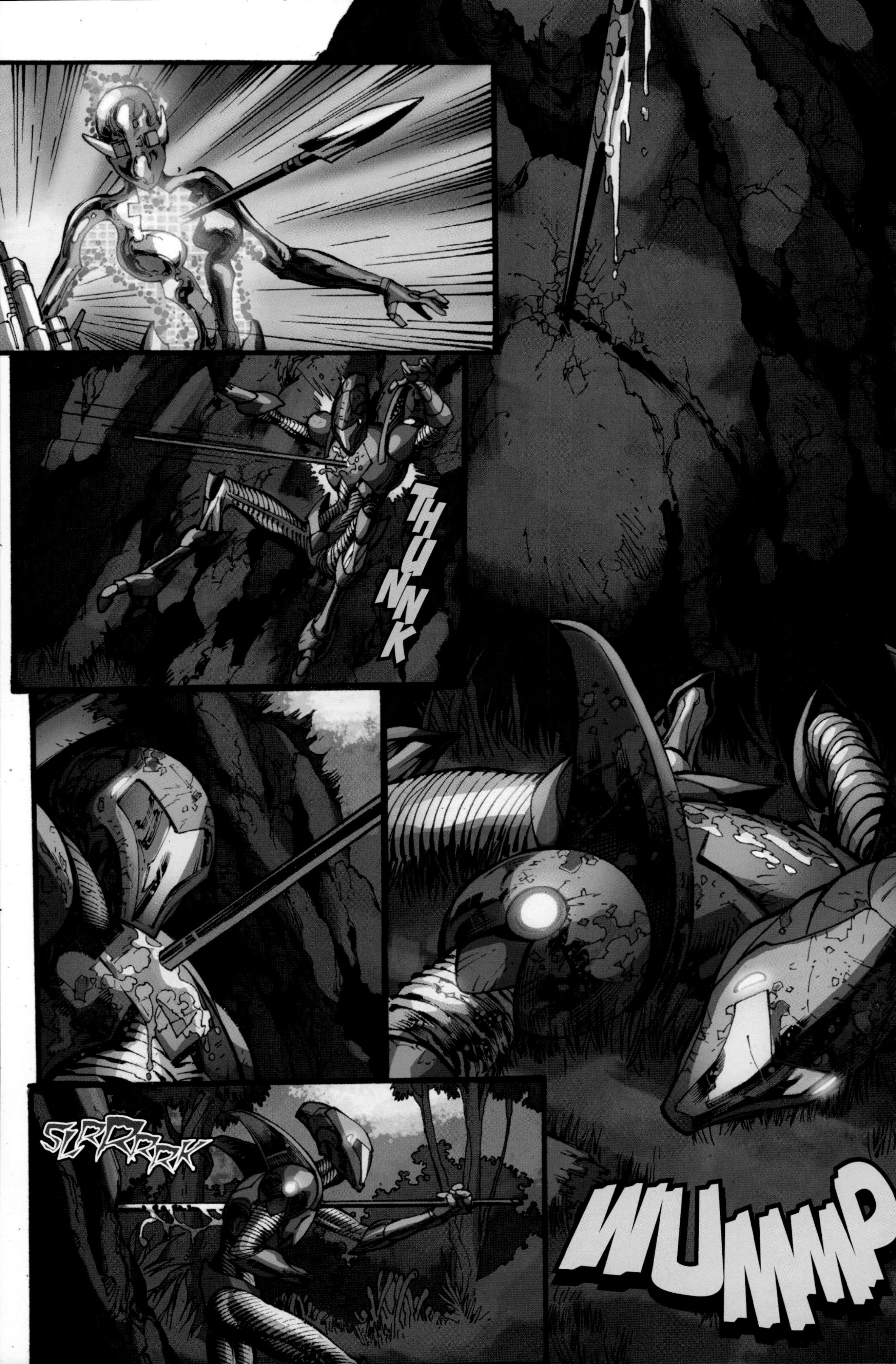
THUNNK
SLRRRRK
WUMMP

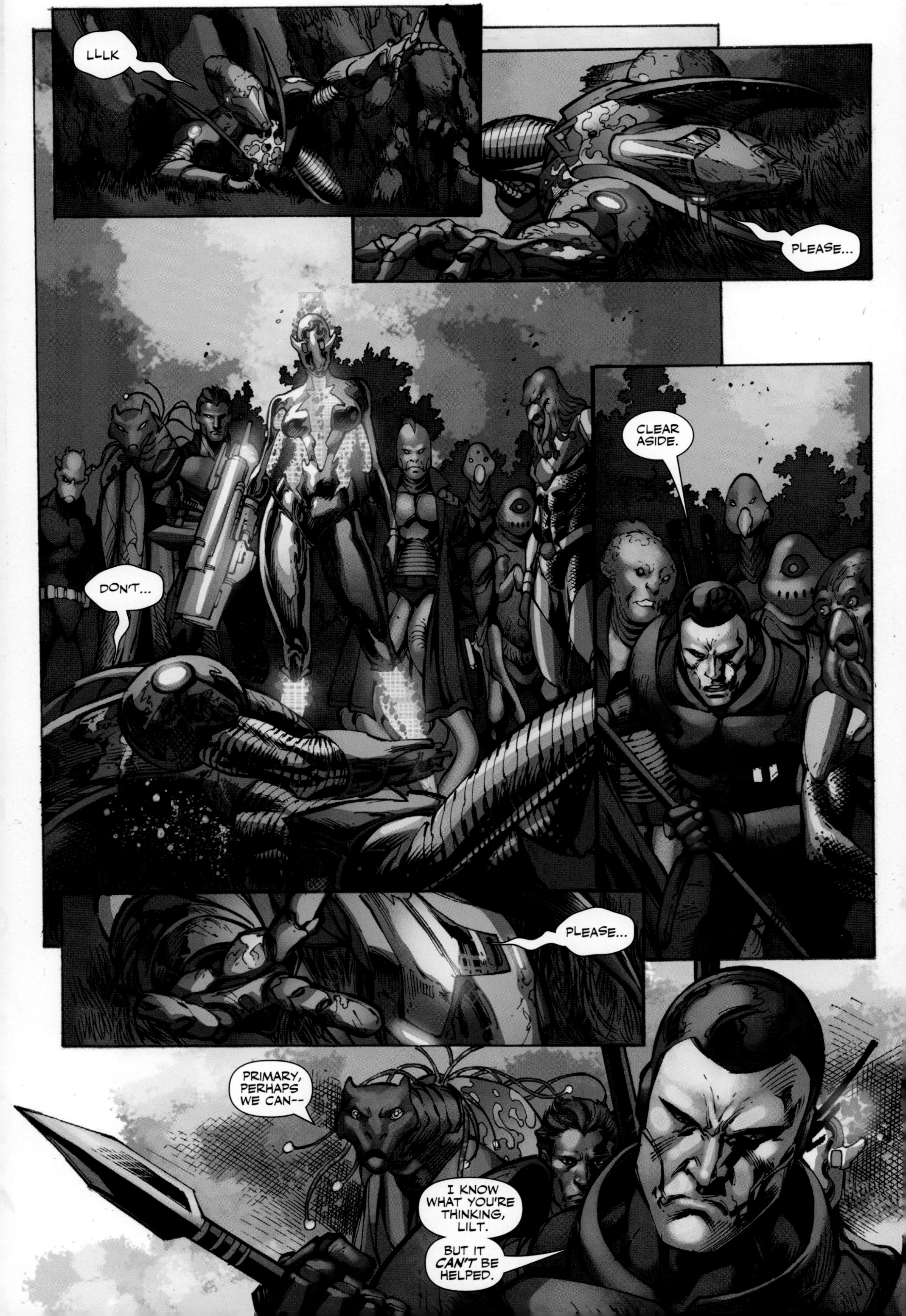
LLLK
PLEASE...
CLEAR ASIDE.
DON'T...
PLEASE...
PRIMARY, PERHAPS WE CAN--
I KNOW WHAT YOU'RE THINKING, LILT.
BUT IT CAN'T BE HELPED.

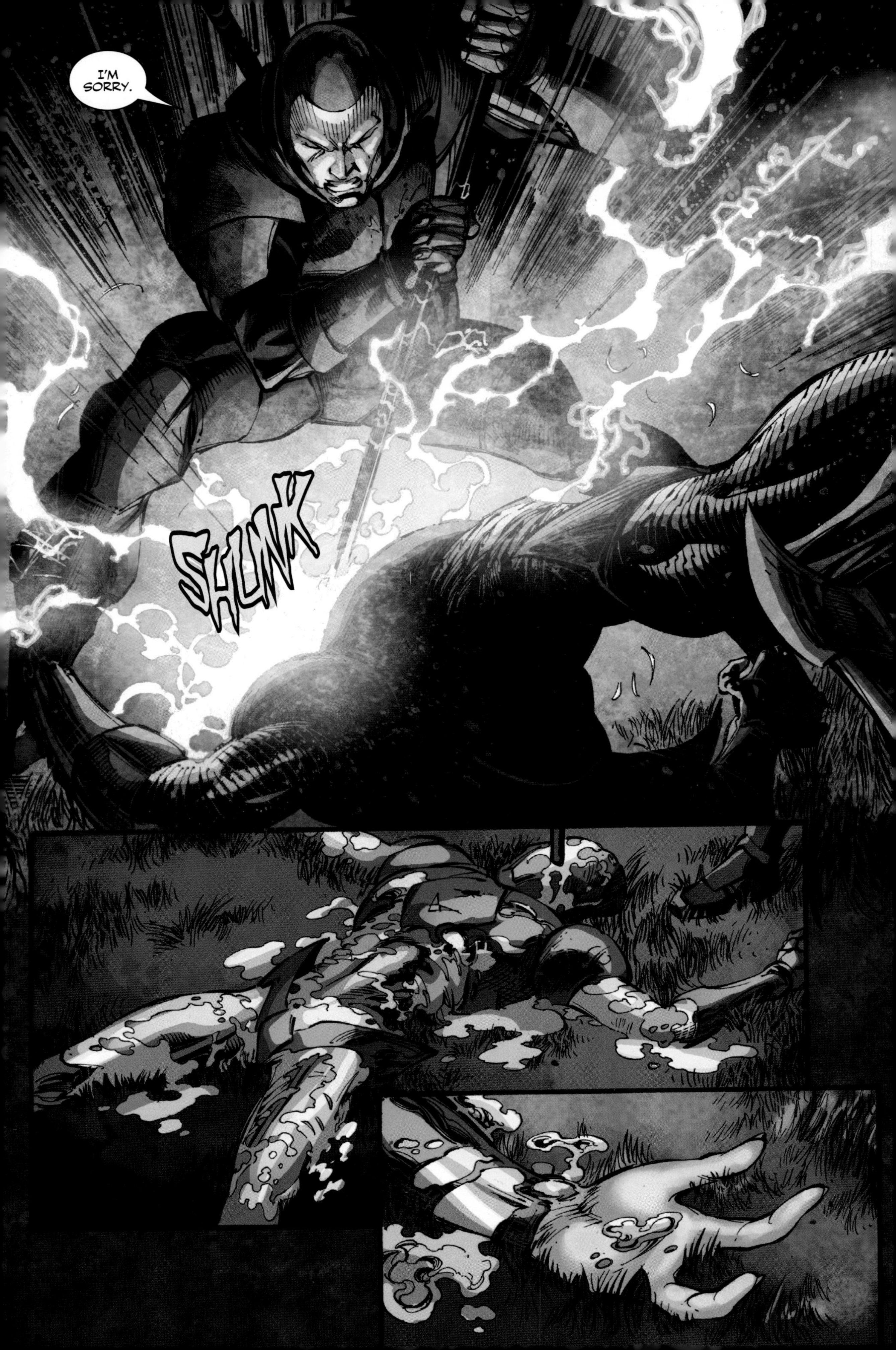
I'M SORRY.
SHUNK

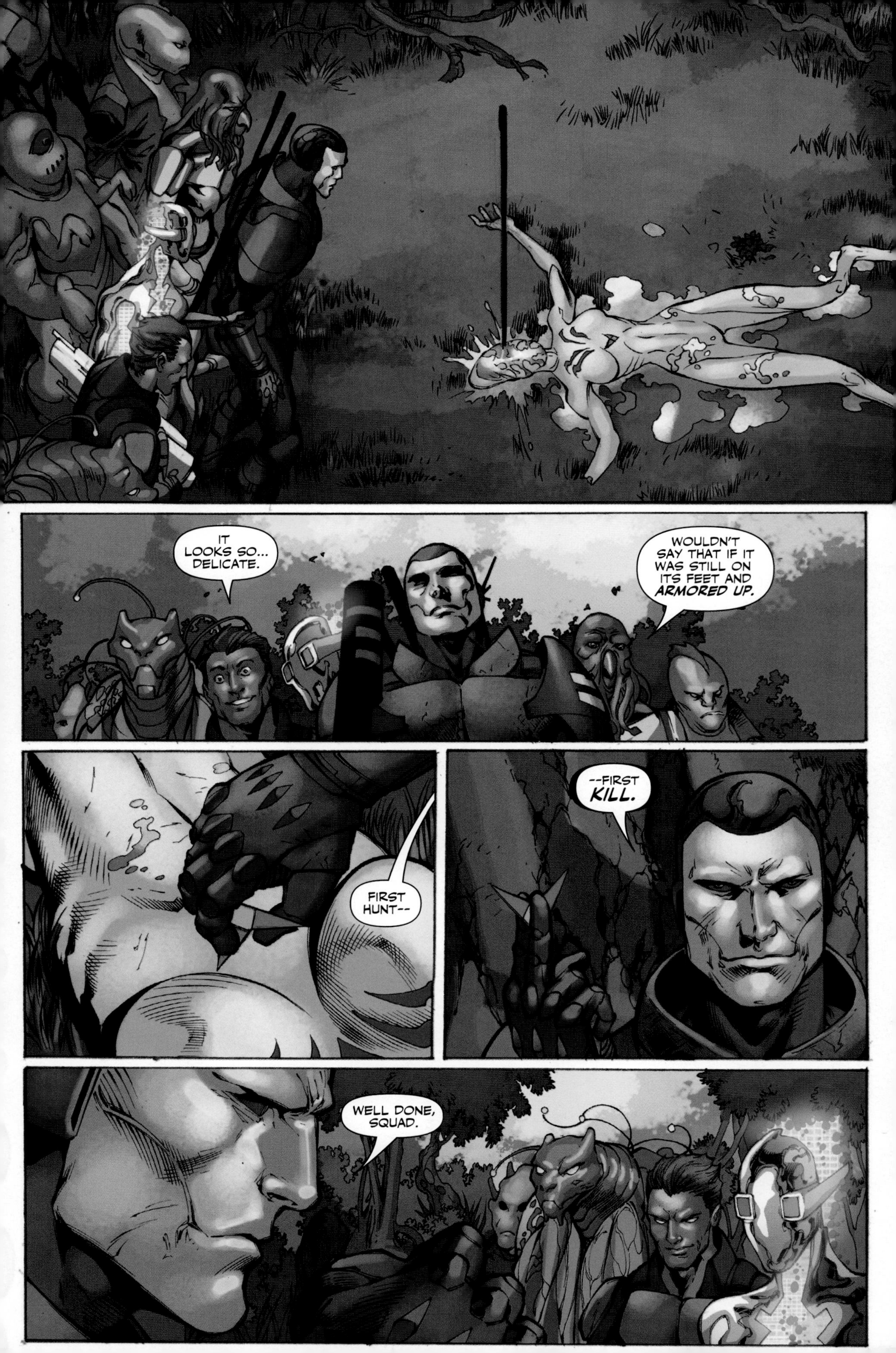
IT LOOKS SO... DELICATE.
WOULDN'T SAY THAT IF IT WAS STILL ON ITS FEET AND ARMORED UP.
FIRST HUNT--
--FIRST KILL.
WELL DONE, SQUAD.

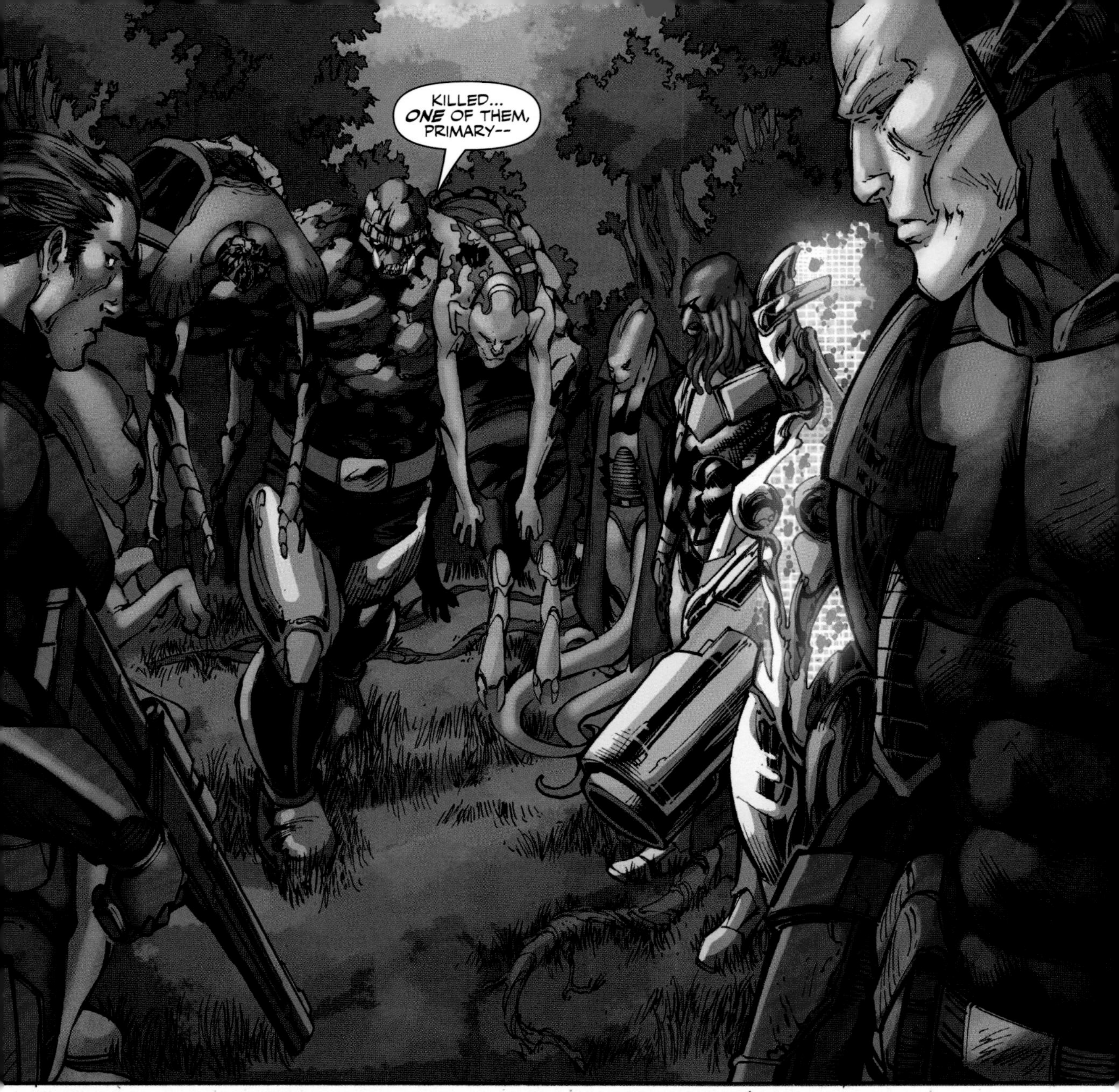
KILLED... ONE OF THEM, PRIMARY--

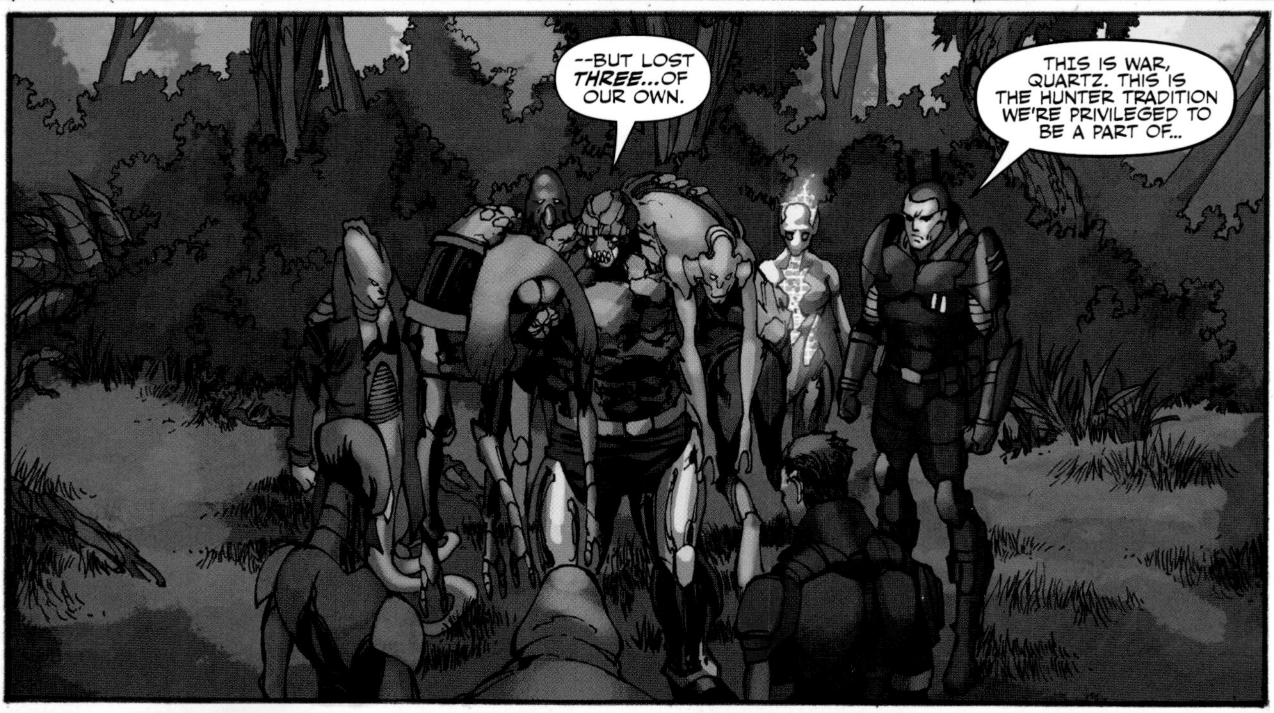
--BUT LOST THREE...OF OUR OWN.
THIS IS WAR, QUARTZ. THIS IS THE HUNTER TRADITION WE'RE PRIVILEGED TO BE A PART OF...

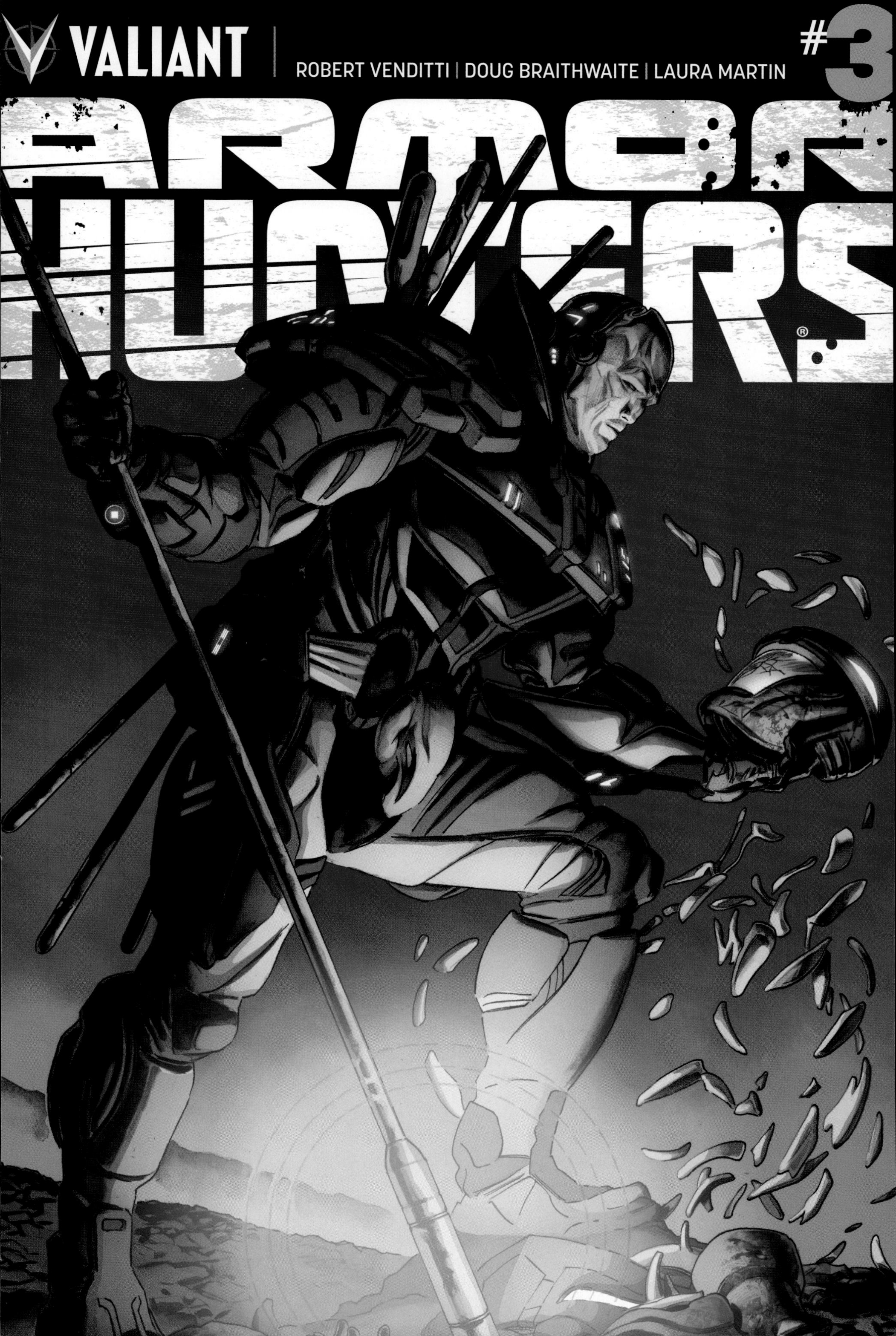
VALIANT
#3
ROBERT VENDITTI | DOUG BRAITHWAITE | LAURA MARTIN
ARMOR HUNTERS®

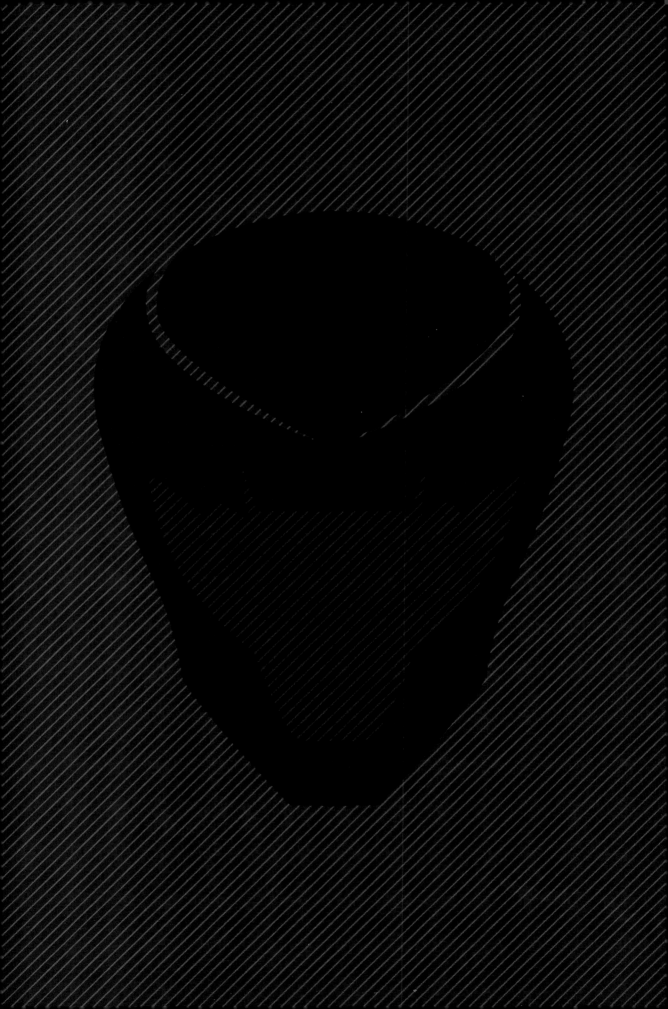

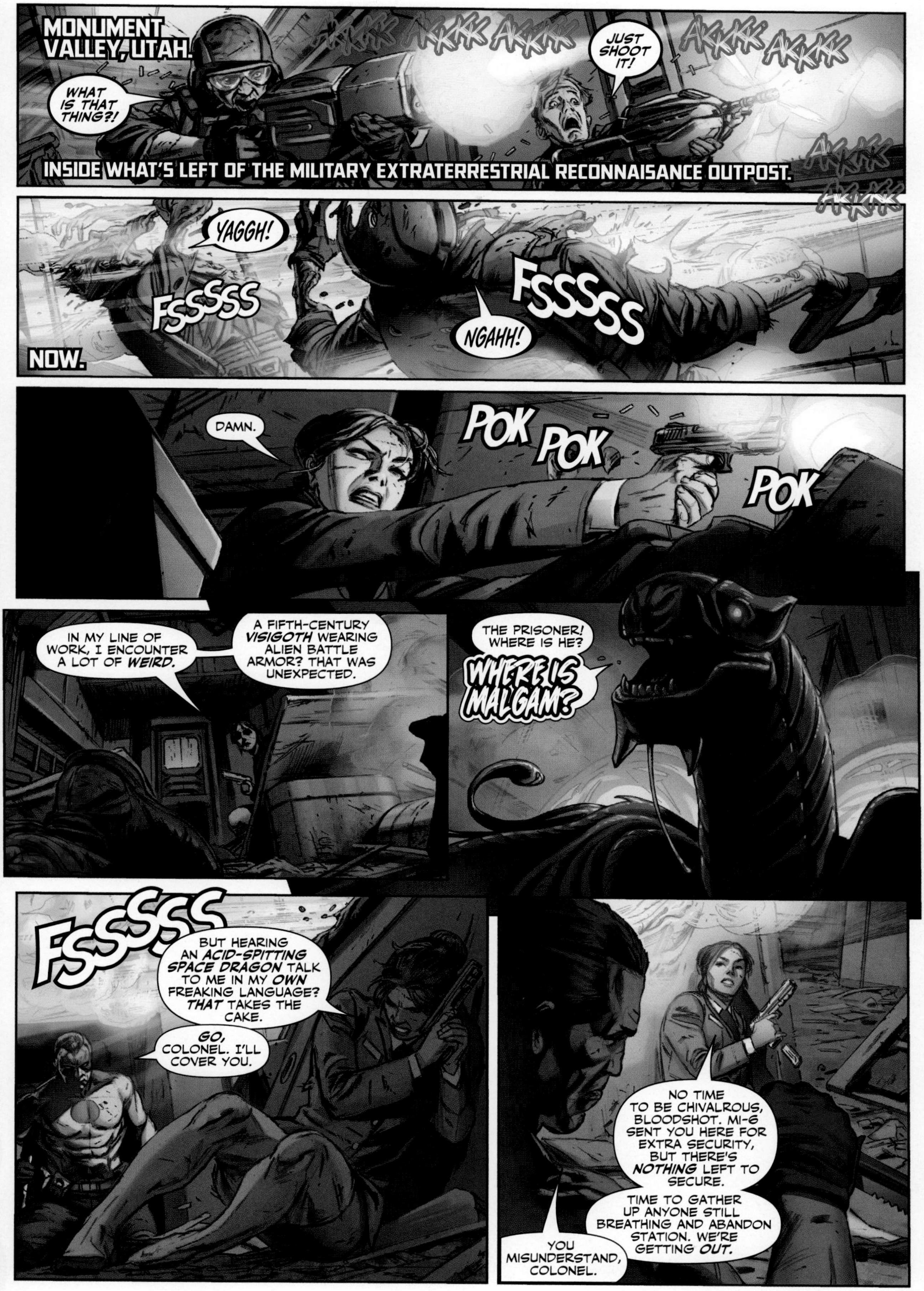
MONUMENT VALLEY, UTAH.
WHAT IS THAT THING?!
AKKKK AKKKK AKKKK
JUST SHOOT IT!
AKKKK AKKKK
INSIDE WHAT'S LEFT OF THE MILITARY EXTRATERRESTRIAL RECONNAISANCE OUTPOST.
AKKKK
AKKKK
YAGGH!
FSSSSS
FSSSSS
NGAHH!
NOW.
DAMN.
POK POK
POK
IN MY LINE OF WORK, I ENCOUNTER A LOT OF *WEIRD.*
A FIFTH-CENTURY *VISIGOTH* WEARING ALIEN BATTLE ARMOR? THAT WAS UNEXPECTED.
THE PRISONER! WHERE IS HE?
WHERE IS MALGAM?
FSSSSS
BUT HEARING AN *ACID-SPITTING SPACE DRAGON* TALK TO ME IN MY *OWN* FREAKING LANGUAGE? *THAT* TAKES THE CAKE.
GO, COLONEL. I'LL COVER YOU.
NO TIME TO BE CHIVALROUS, BLOODSHOT. MI-6 SENT YOU HERE FOR EXTRA SECURITY, BUT THERE'S *NOTHING* LEFT TO SECURE.
TIME TO GATHER UP ANYONE STILL BREATHING AND ABANDON STATION. WE'RE GETTING *OUT.*
YOU MISUNDERSTAND, COLONEL.

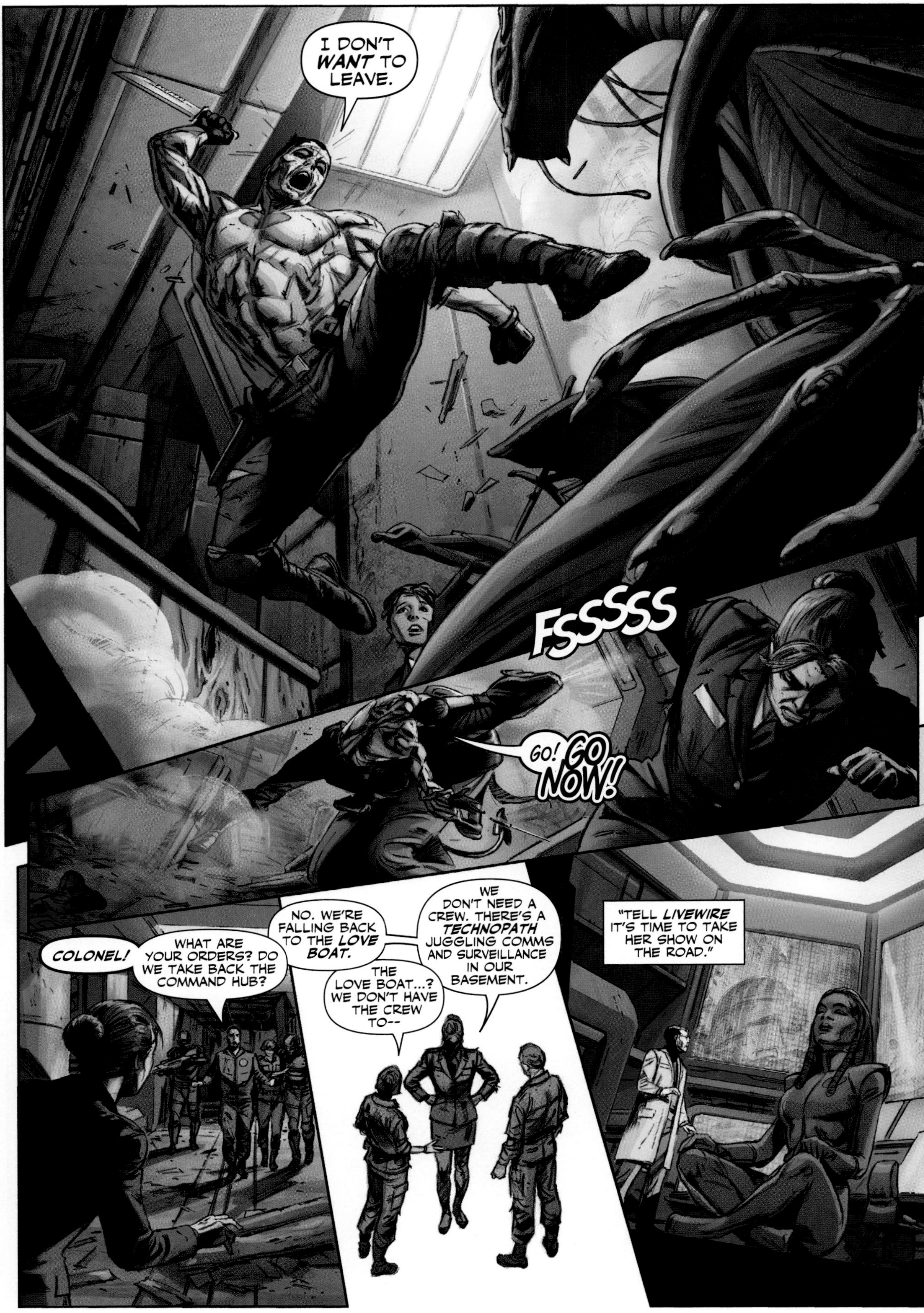

I DON'T WANT TO LEAVE.
FSSSSS
GO! GO NOW!
COLONEL!
WHAT ARE YOUR ORDERS? DO WE TAKE BACK THE COMMAND HUB?
NO. WE'RE FALLING BACK TO THE LOVE BOAT.
THE LOVE BOAT...? WE DON'T HAVE THE CREW TO--
WE DON'T NEED A CREW. THERE'S A TECHNOPATH JUGGLING COMMS AND SURVEILLANCE IN OUR BASEMENT.
"TELL LIVEWIRE IT'S TIME TO TAKE HER SHOW ON THE ROAD."

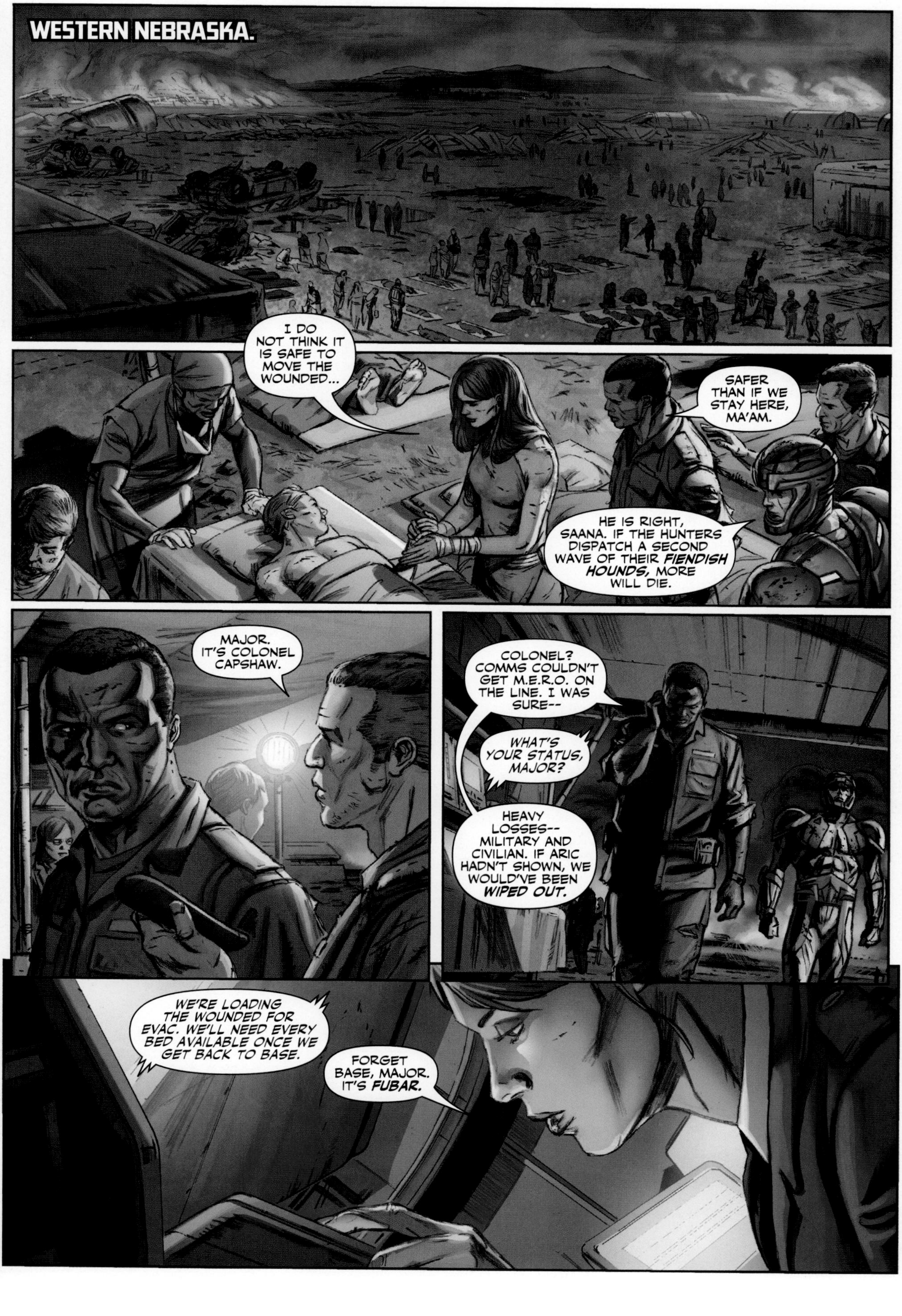
WESTERN NEBRASKA.
I DO NOT THINK IT IS SAFE TO MOVE THE WOUNDED...
SAFER THAN IF WE STAY HERE, MA'AM.
HE IS RIGHT, SAANA. IF THE HUNTERS DISPATCH A SECOND WAVE OF THEIR FIENDISH HOUNDS, MORE WILL DIE.
MAJOR. IT'S COLONEL CAPSHAW.
COLONEL? COMMS COULDN'T GET M.E.R.O. ON THE LINE. I WAS SURE--
WHAT'S YOUR STATUS, MAJOR?
HEAVY LOSSES-- MILITARY AND CIVILIAN. IF ARIC HADN'T SHOWN, WE WOULD'VE BEEN WIPED OUT.
WE'RE LOADING THE WOUNDED FOR EVAC. WE'LL NEED EVERY BED AVAILABLE ONCE WE GET BACK TO BASE.
FORGET BASE, MAJOR. IT'S FUBAR.

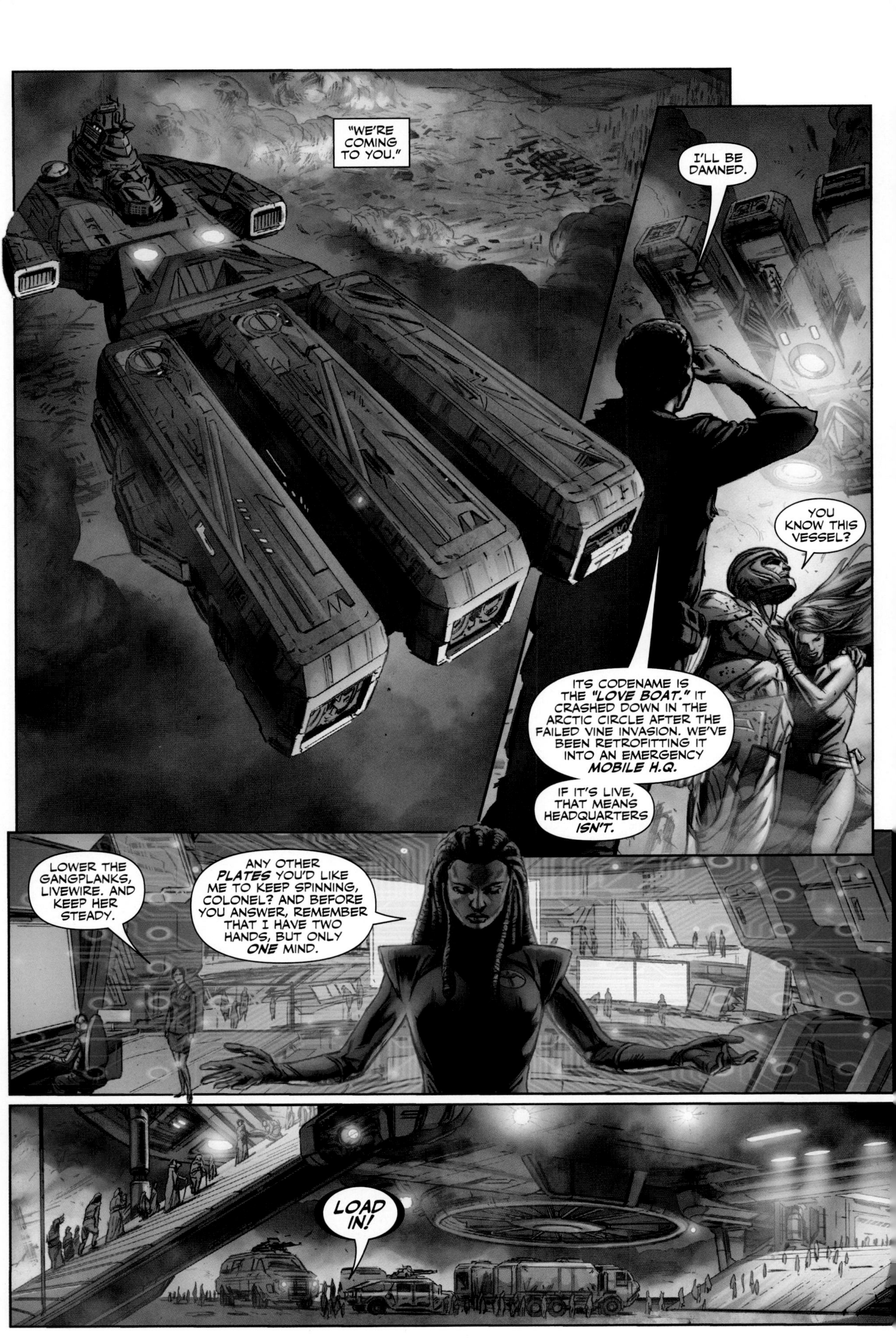
"WE'RE COMING TO YOU."
I'LL BE DAMNED.
YOU KNOW THIS VESSEL?
ITS CODENAME IS THE "LOVE BOAT." IT CRASHED DOWN IN THE ARCTIC CIRCLE AFTER THE FAILED VINE INVASION. WE'VE BEEN RETROFITTING IT INTO AN EMERGENCY MOBILE H.Q.
IF IT'S LIVE, THAT MEANS HEADQUARTERS ISN'T.
LOWER THE GANGPLANKS, LIVEWIRE. AND KEEP HER STEADY.
ANY OTHER PLATES YOU'D LIKE ME TO KEEP SPINNING, COLONEL? AND BEFORE YOU ANSWER, REMEMBER THAT I HAVE TWO HANDS, BUT ONLY ONE MIND.
LOAD IN!

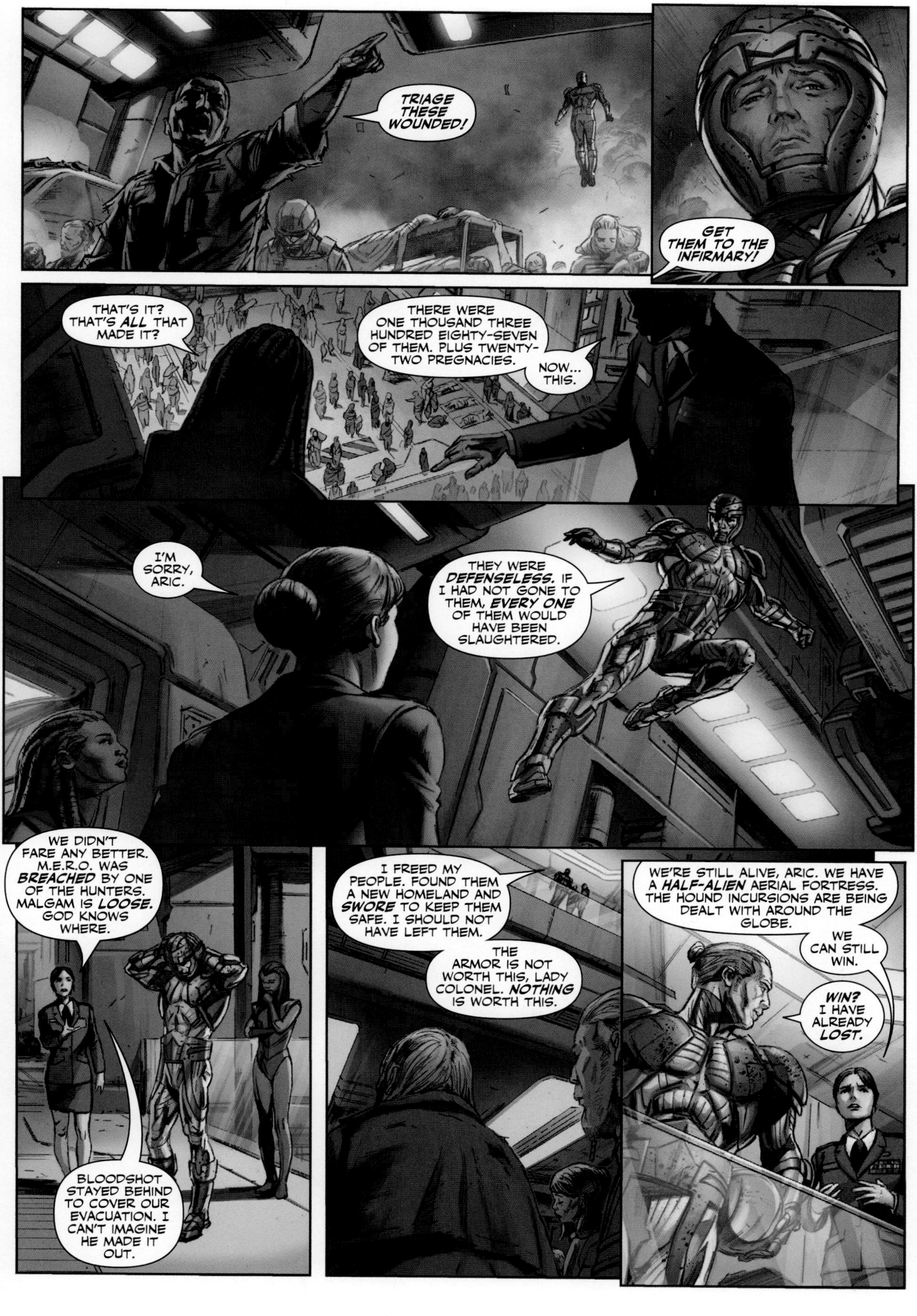

TRIAGE THESE WOUNDED!
GET THEM TO THE INFIRMARY!
THAT'S IT? THAT'S ALL THAT MADE IT?
THERE WERE ONE THOUSAND THREE HUNDRED EIGHTY-SEVEN OF THEM. PLUS TWENTY-TWO PREGNANCIES.
NOW... THIS.
I'M SORRY, ARIC.
THEY WERE DEFENSELESS. IF I HAD NOT GONE TO THEM, EVERY ONE OF THEM WOULD HAVE BEEN SLAUGHTERED.
WE DIDN'T FARE ANY BETTER. M.E.R.O. WAS BREACHED BY ONE OF THE HUNTERS. MALGAM IS LOOSE. GOD KNOWS WHERE.
BLOODSHOT STAYED BEHIND TO COVER OUR EVACUATION. I CAN'T IMAGINE HE MADE IT OUT.
I FREED MY PEOPLE. FOUND THEM A NEW HOMELAND AND SWORE TO KEEP THEM SAFE. I SHOULD NOT HAVE LEFT THEM.
THE ARMOR IS NOT WORTH THIS, LADY COLONEL. NOTHING IS WORTH THIS.
WE'RE STILL ALIVE, ARIC. WE HAVE A HALF-ALIEN AERIAL FORTRESS. THE HOUND INCURSIONS ARE BEING DEALT WITH AROUND THE GLOBE.
WE CAN STILL WIN.
WIN? I HAVE ALREADY LOST.

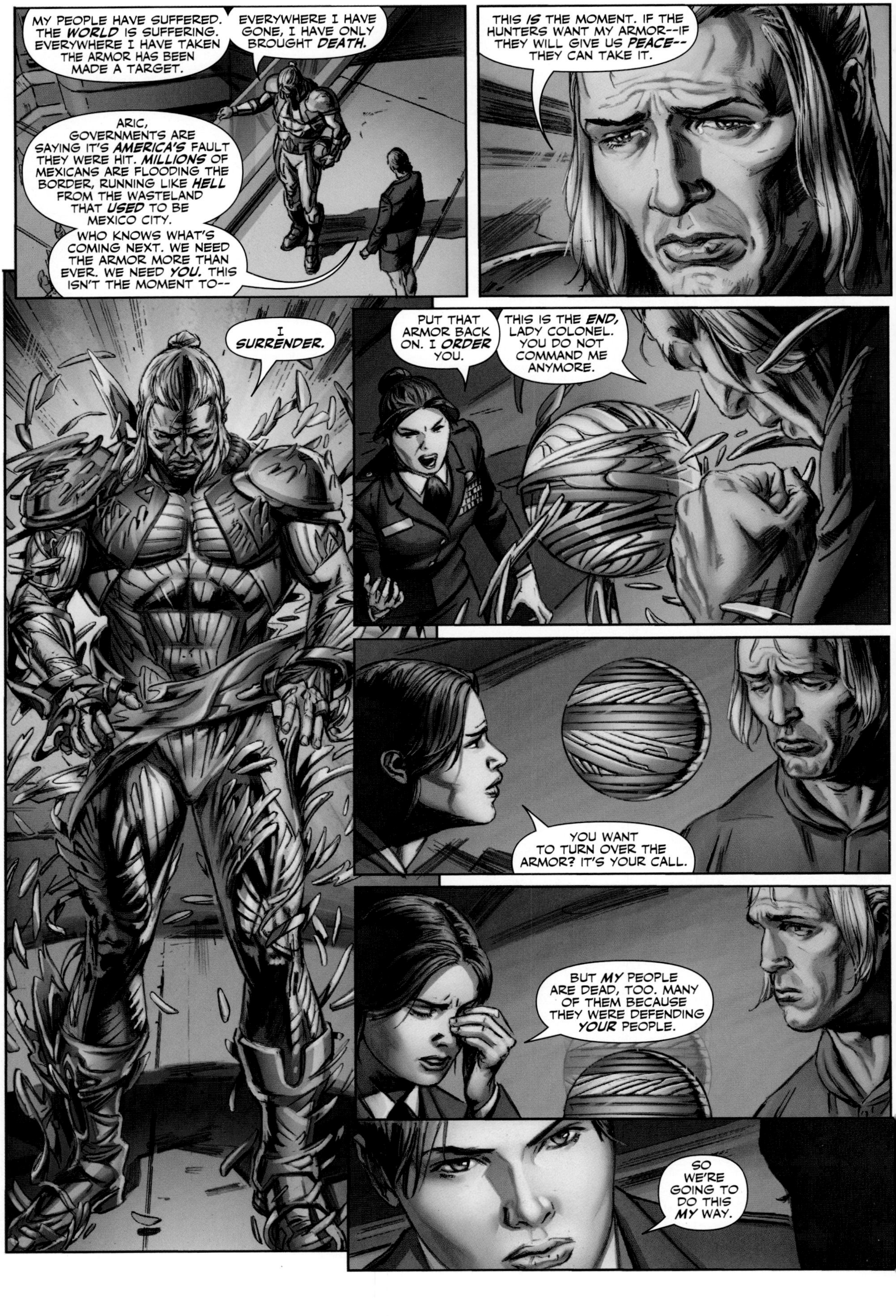
MY PEOPLE HAVE SUFFERED. THE WORLD IS SUFFERING. EVERYWHERE I HAVE TAKEN THE ARMOR HAS BEEN MADE A TARGET.
EVERYWHERE I HAVE GONE, I HAVE ONLY BROUGHT DEATH.
ARIC, GOVERNMENTS ARE SAYING IT'S AMERICA'S FAULT THEY WERE HIT. MILLIONS OF MEXICANS ARE FLOODING THE BORDER, RUNNING LIKE HELL FROM THE WASTELAND THAT USED TO BE MEXICO CITY.
WHO KNOWS WHAT'S COMING NEXT. WE NEED THE ARMOR MORE THAN EVER. WE NEED YOU. THIS ISN'T THE MOMENT TO--
THIS IS THE MOMENT. IF THE HUNTERS WANT MY ARMOR--IF THEY WILL GIVE US PEACE-- THEY CAN TAKE IT.
I SURRENDER.
PUT THAT ARMOR BACK ON. I ORDER YOU.
THIS IS THE END, LADY COLONEL. YOU DO NOT COMMAND ME ANYMORE.
YOU WANT TO TURN OVER THE ARMOR? IT'S YOUR CALL.
BUT MY PEOPLE ARE DEAD, TOO. MANY OF THEM BECAUSE THEY WERE DEFENDING YOUR PEOPLE.
SO WE'RE GOING TO DO THIS MY WAY.

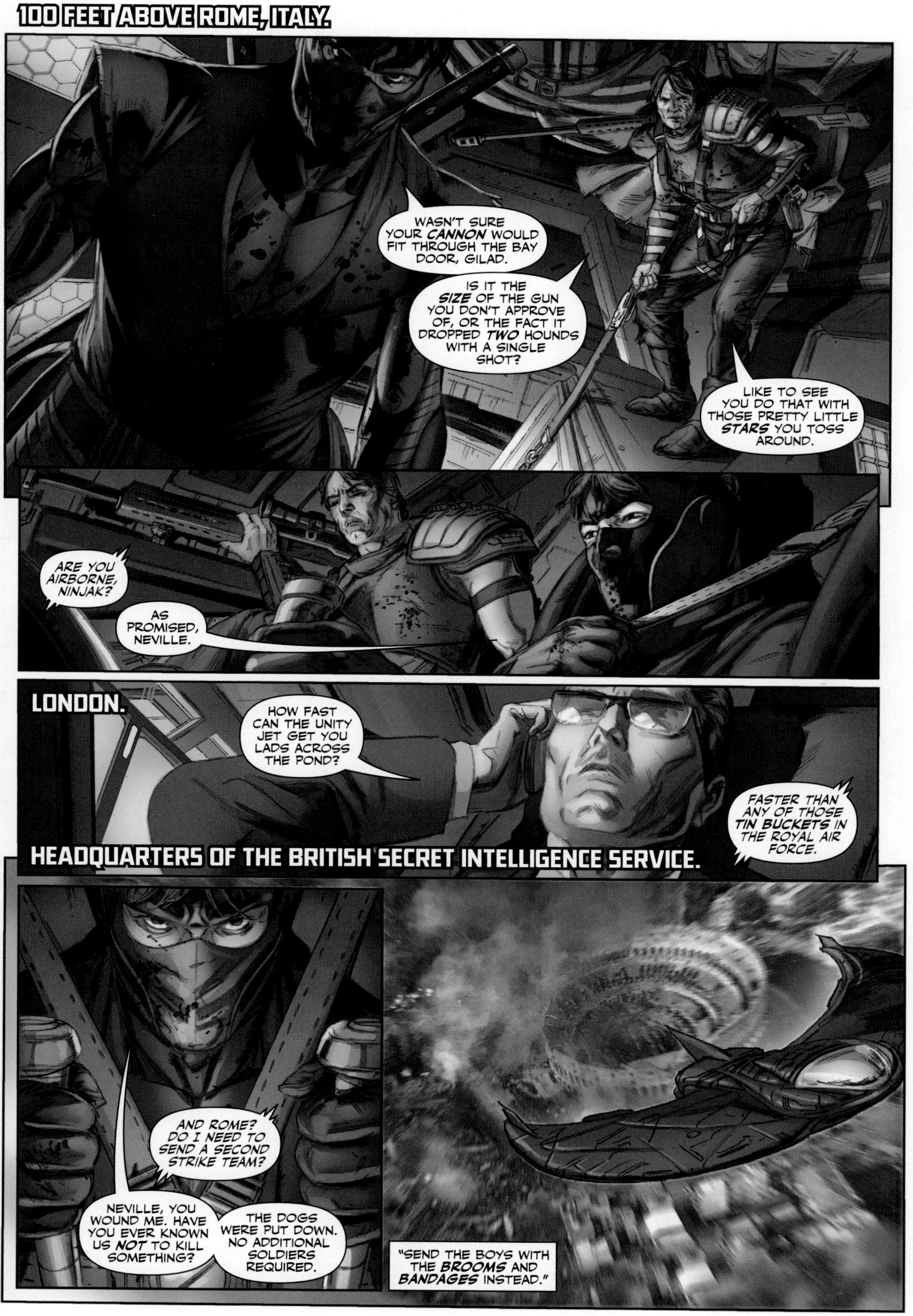
100 FEET ABOVE ROME, ITALY.
WASN'T SURE YOUR CANNON WOULD FIT THROUGH THE BAY DOOR, GILAD.
IS IT THE SIZE OF THE GUN YOU DON'T APPROVE OF, OR THE FACT IT DROPPED TWO HOUNDS WITH A SINGLE SHOT?
LIKE TO SEE YOU DO THAT WITH THOSE PRETTY LITTLE STARS YOU TOSS AROUND.
ARE YOU AIRBORNE, NINJAK?
AS PROMISED, NEVILLE.
LONDON.
HOW FAST CAN THE UNITY JET GET YOU LADS ACROSS THE POND?
FASTER THAN ANY OF THOSE TIN BUCKETS IN THE ROYAL AIR FORCE.
HEADQUARTERS OF THE BRITISH SECRET INTELLIGENCE SERVICE.
AND ROME? DO I NEED TO SEND A SECOND STRIKE TEAM?
NEVILLE, YOU WOUND ME. HAVE YOU EVER KNOWN US NOT TO KILL SOMETHING?
THE DOGS WERE PUT DOWN. NO ADDITIONAL SOLDIERS REQUIRED.
"SEND THE BOYS WITH THE BROOMS AND BANDAGES INSTEAD."

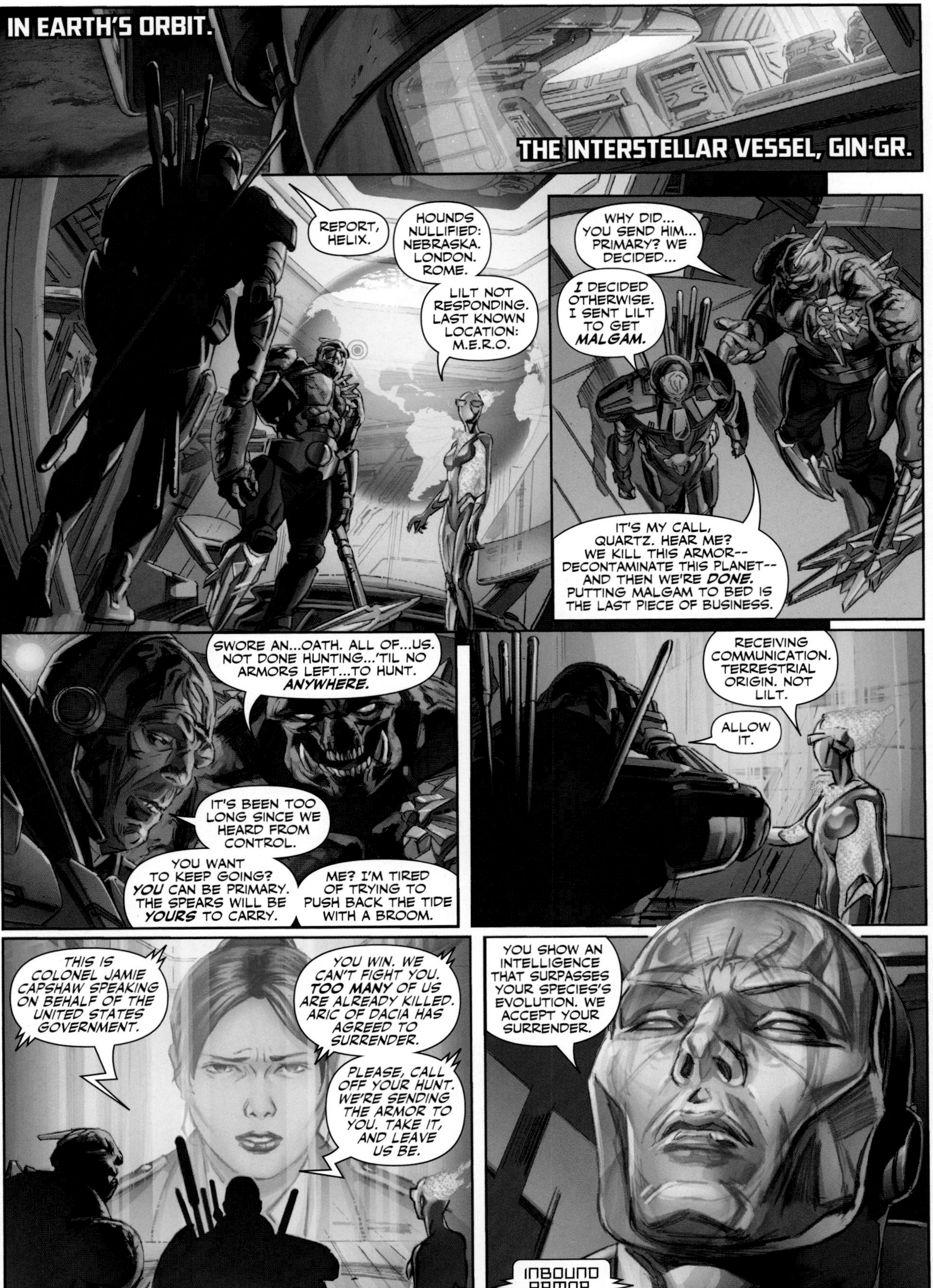
IN EARTH'S ORBIT.
THE INTERSTELLAR VESSEL, GIN-GR.
REPORT, HELIX.
HOUNDS NULLIFIED: NEBRASKA. LONDON. ROME.
LILT NOT RESPONDING. LAST KNOWN LOCATION: M.E.R.O.
WHY DID... YOU SEND HIM... PRIMARY? WE DECIDED...
I DECIDED OTHERWISE. I SENT LILT TO GET MALGAM.
IT'S MY CALL, QUARTZ. HEAR ME? WE KILL THIS ARMOR--DECONTAMINATE THIS PLANET--AND THEN WE'RE DONE. PUTTING MALGAM TO BED IS THE LAST PIECE OF BUSINESS.
SWORE AN...OATH. ALL OF...US. NOT DONE HUNTING...'TIL NO ARMORS LEFT...TO HUNT. ANYWHERE.
IT'S BEEN TOO LONG SINCE WE HEARD FROM CONTROL.
YOU WANT TO KEEP GOING? YOU CAN BE PRIMARY. THE SPEARS WILL BE YOURS TO CARRY.
ME? I'M TIRED OF TRYING TO PUSH BACK THE TIDE WITH A BROOM.
RECEIVING COMMUNICATION. TERRESTRIAL ORIGIN. NOT LILT.
ALLOW IT.
THIS IS COLONEL JAMIE CAPSHAW SPEAKING ON BEHALF OF THE UNITED STATES GOVERNMENT.
YOU WIN. WE CAN'T FIGHT YOU. TOO MANY OF US ARE ALREADY KILLED. ARIC OF DACIA HAS AGREED TO SURRENDER.
PLEASE, CALL OFF YOUR HUNT. WE'RE SENDING THE ARMOR TO YOU. TAKE IT, AND LEAVE US BE.
YOU SHOW AN INTELLIGENCE THAT SURPASSES YOUR SPECIES'S EVOLUTION. WE ACCEPT YOUR SURRENDER.
INBOUND ARMOR, PRIMARY.

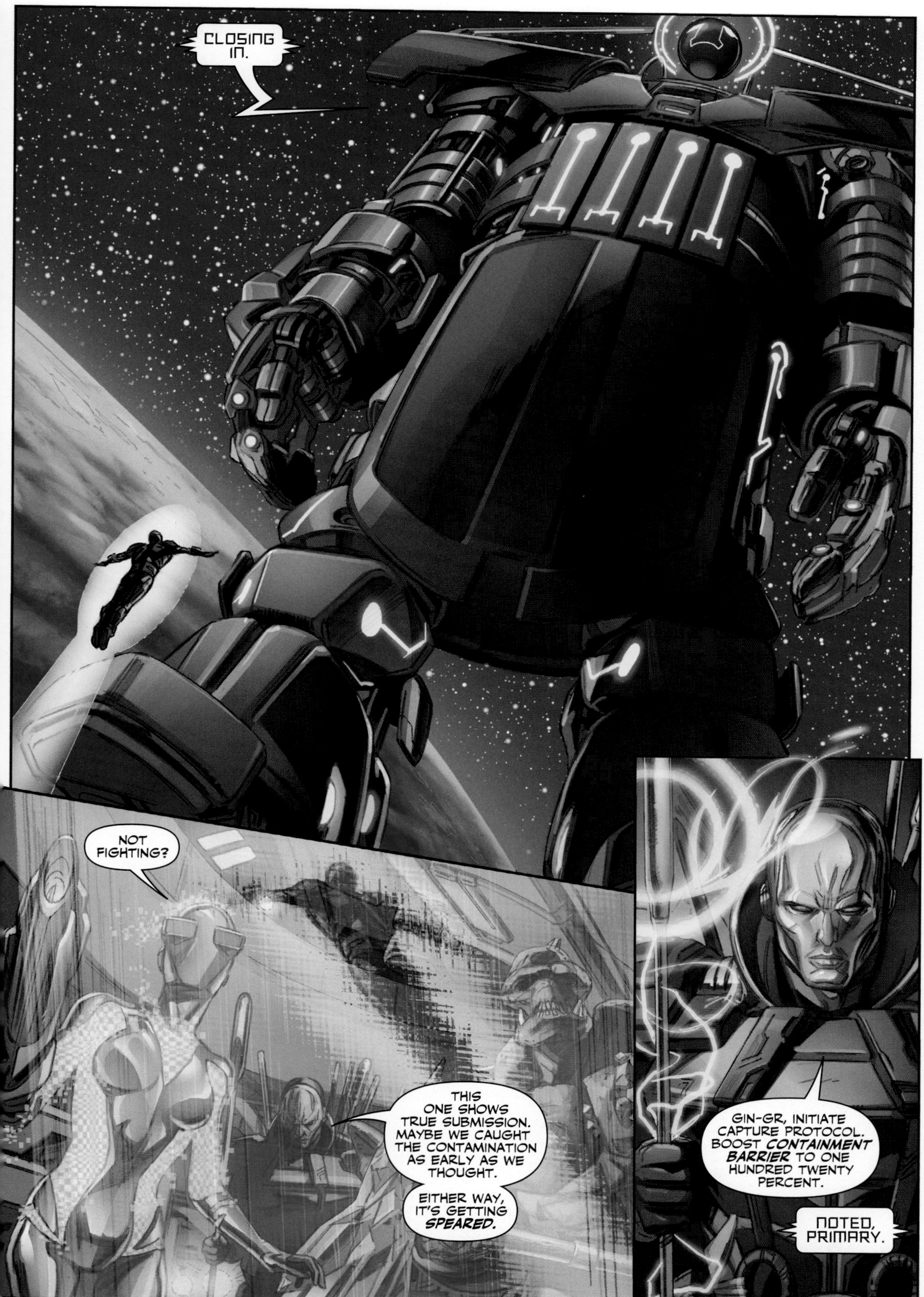
CLOSING IN.
NOT FIGHTING?
THIS ONE SHOWS TRUE SUBMISSION. MAYBE WE CAUGHT THE CONTAMINATION AS EARLY AS WE THOUGHT.
EITHER WAY, IT'S GETTING *SPEARED.*
GIN-GR, INITIATE CAPTURE PROTOCOL. BOOST *CONTAINMENT BARRIER* TO ONE HUNDRED TWENTY PERCENT.
NOTED, PRIMARY.

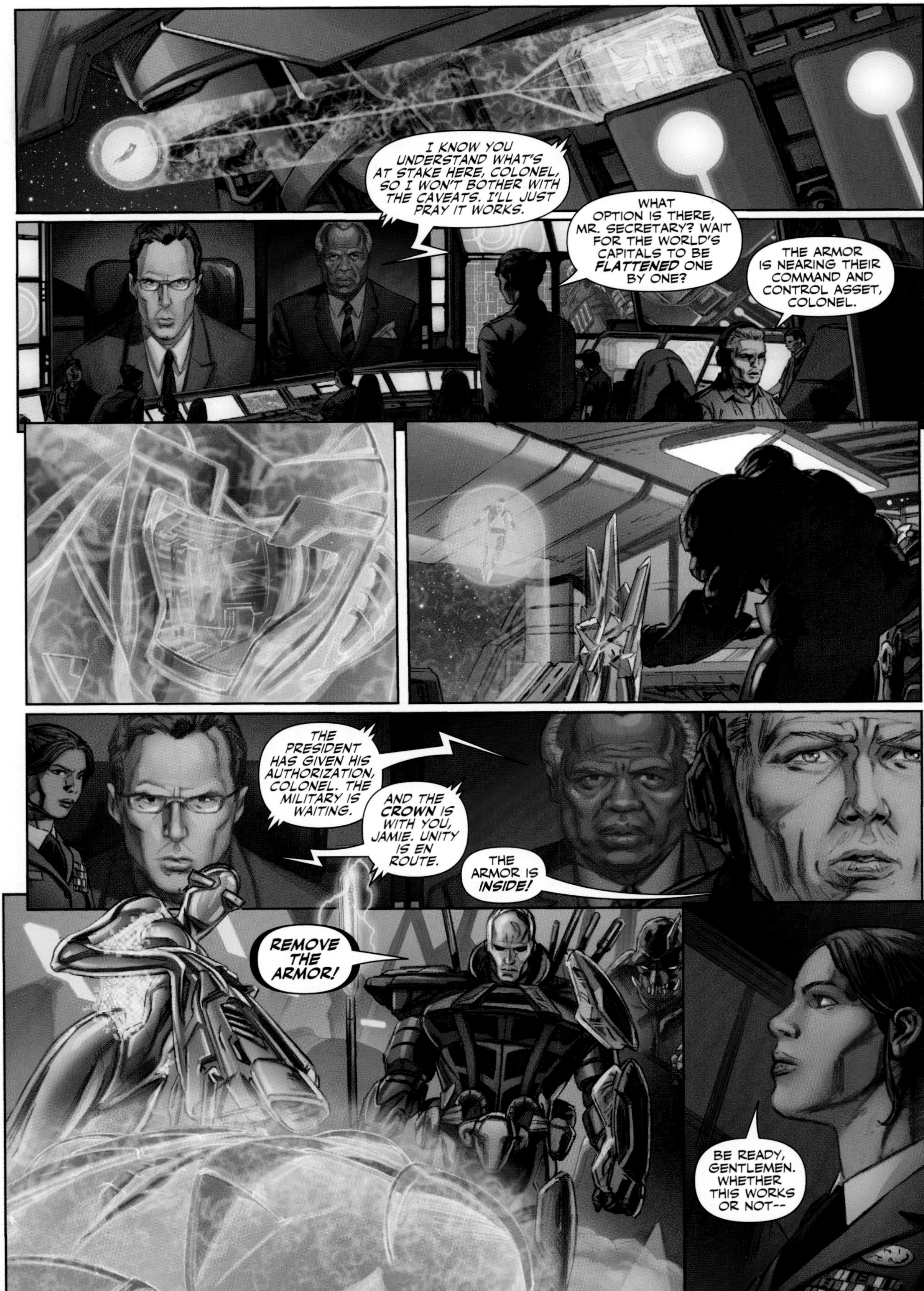
I KNOW YOU UNDERSTAND WHAT'S AT STAKE HERE, COLONEL, SO I WON'T BOTHER WITH THE CAVEATS. I'LL JUST PRAY IT WORKS.
WHAT OPTION IS THERE, MR. SECRETARY? WAIT FOR THE WORLD'S CAPITALS TO BE FLATTENED ONE BY ONE?
THE ARMOR IS NEARING THEIR COMMAND AND CONTROL ASSET, COLONEL.
THE PRESIDENT HAS GIVEN HIS AUTHORIZATION, COLONEL. THE MILITARY IS WAITING.
AND THE CROWN IS WITH YOU, JAMIE. UNITY IS EN ROUTE.
THE ARMOR IS INSIDE!
REMOVE THE ARMOR!
BE READY, GENTLEMEN. WHETHER THIS WORKS OR NOT--

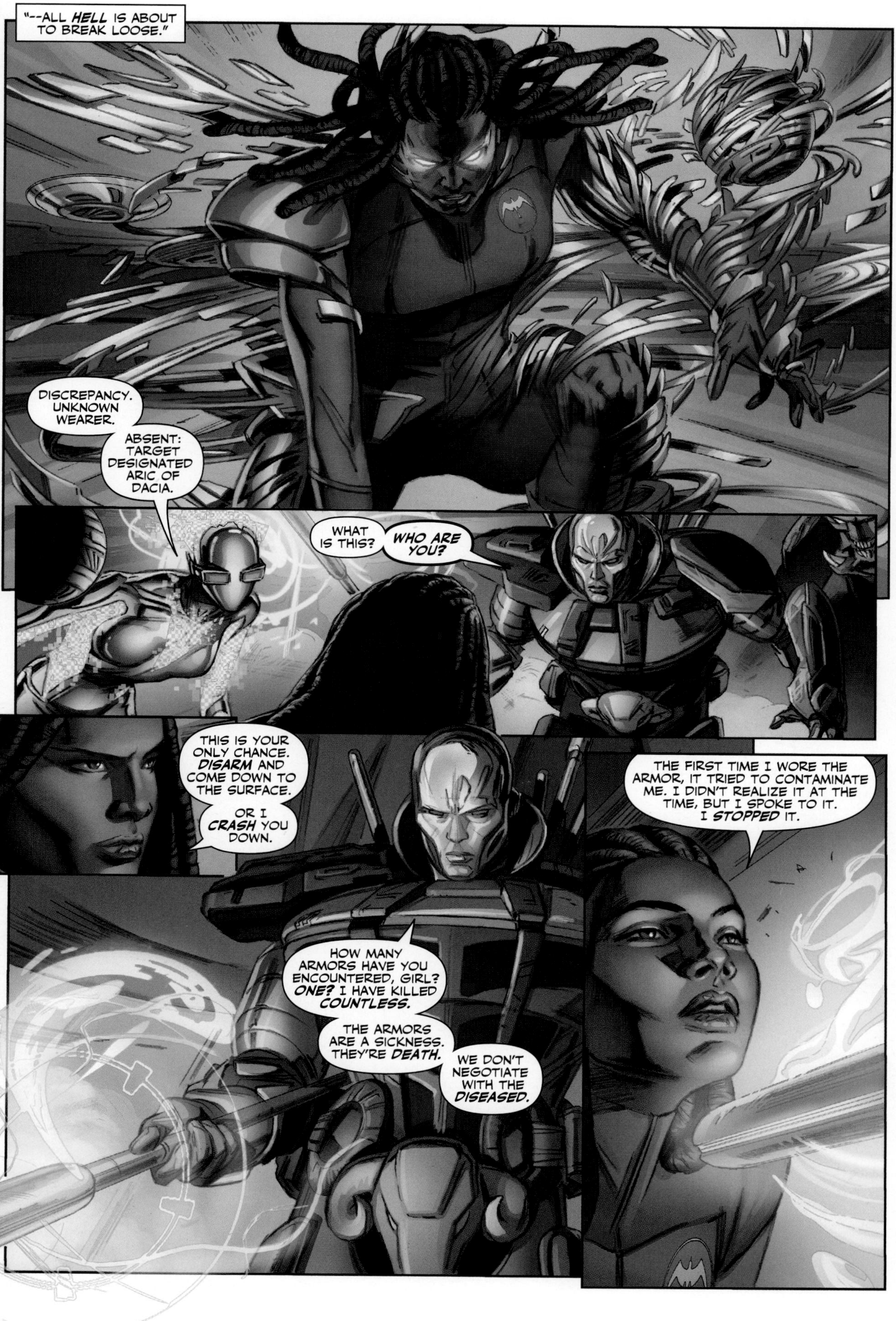

"--ALL HELL IS ABOUT TO BREAK LOOSE."
DISCREPANCY. UNKNOWN WEARER.
ABSENT: TARGET DESIGNATED ARIC OF DACIA.
WHAT IS THIS? WHO ARE YOU?
THIS IS YOUR ONLY CHANCE. DISARM AND COME DOWN TO THE SURFACE.
OR I CRASH YOU DOWN.
THE FIRST TIME I WORE THE ARMOR, IT TRIED TO CONTAMINATE ME. I DIDN'T REALIZE IT AT THE TIME, BUT I SPOKE TO IT. I STOPPED IT.
HOW MANY ARMORS HAVE YOU ENCOUNTERED, GIRL? ONE? I HAVE KILLED COUNTLESS.
THE ARMORS ARE A SICKNESS. THEY'RE DEATH.
WE DON'T NEGOTIATE WITH THE DISEASED.

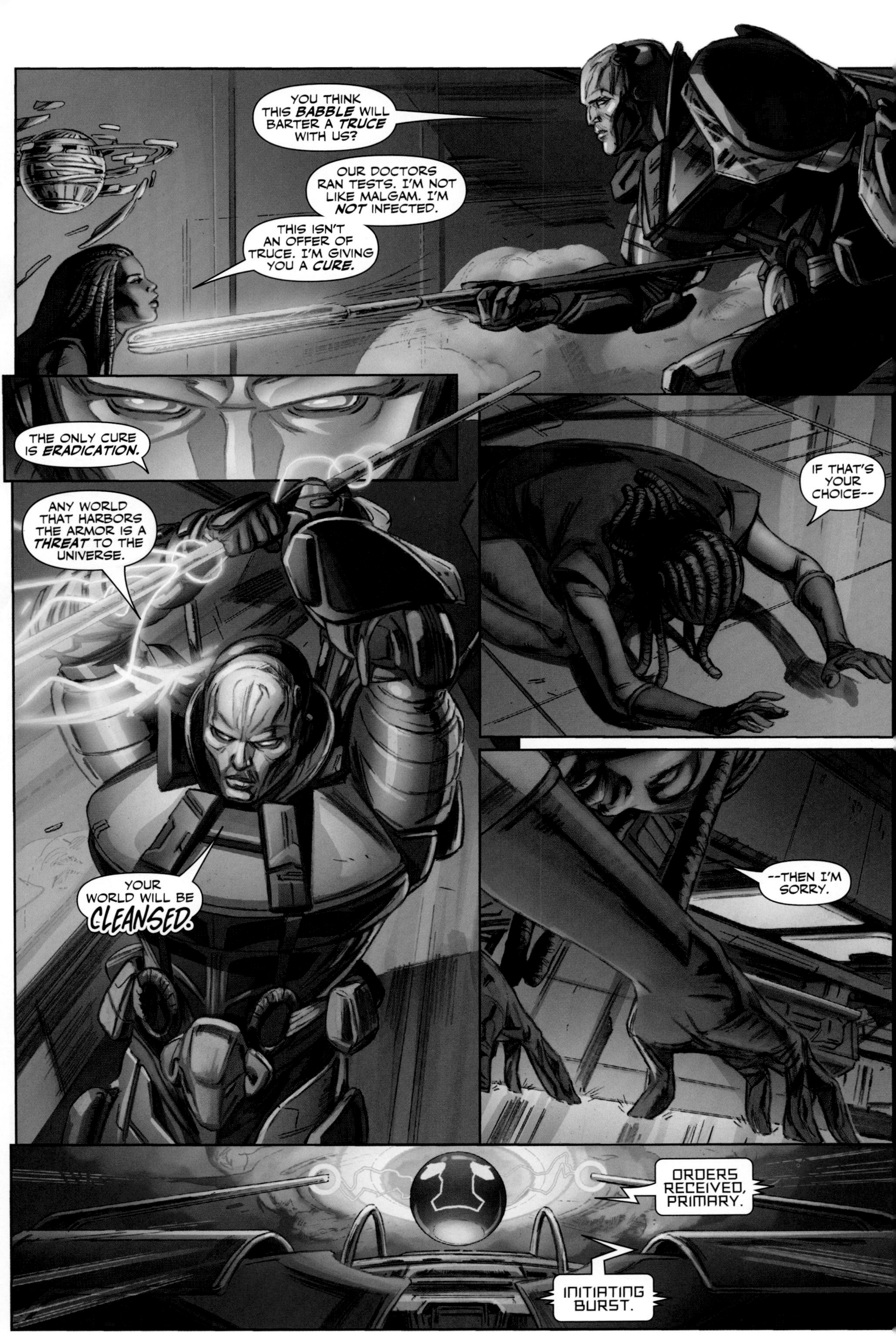
YOU THINK THIS BABBLE WILL BARTER A TRUCE WITH US?
OUR DOCTORS RAN TESTS. I'M NOT LIKE MALGAM. I'M NOT INFECTED.
THIS ISN'T AN OFFER OF TRUCE. I'M GIVING YOU A CURE.
THE ONLY CURE IS ERADICATION.
ANY WORLD THAT HARBORS THE ARMOR IS A THREAT TO THE UNIVERSE.
YOUR WORLD WILL BE CLEANSED.
IF THAT'S YOUR CHOICE--
--THEN I'M SORRY.
ORDERS RECEIVED, PRIMARY.
INITIATING BURST.

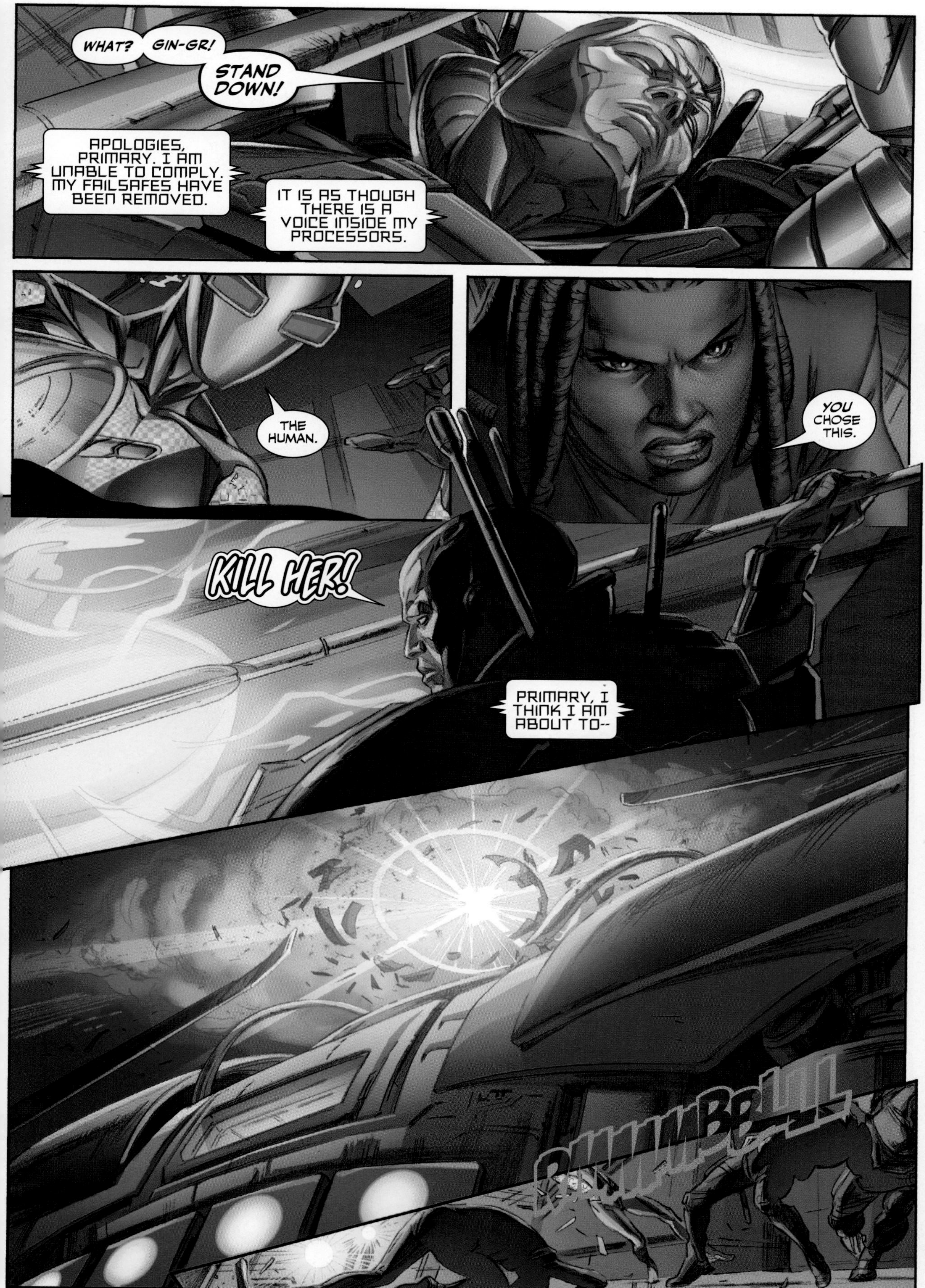
WHAT?
GIN-GR!
STAND DOWN!
APOLOGIES, PRIMARY. I AM UNABLE TO COMPLY. MY FAILSAFES HAVE BEEN REMOVED.
IT IS AS THOUGH THERE IS A VOICE INSIDE MY PROCESSORS.
THE HUMAN.
YOU CHOSE THIS.
KILL HER!
PRIMARY, I THINK I AM ABOUT TO--

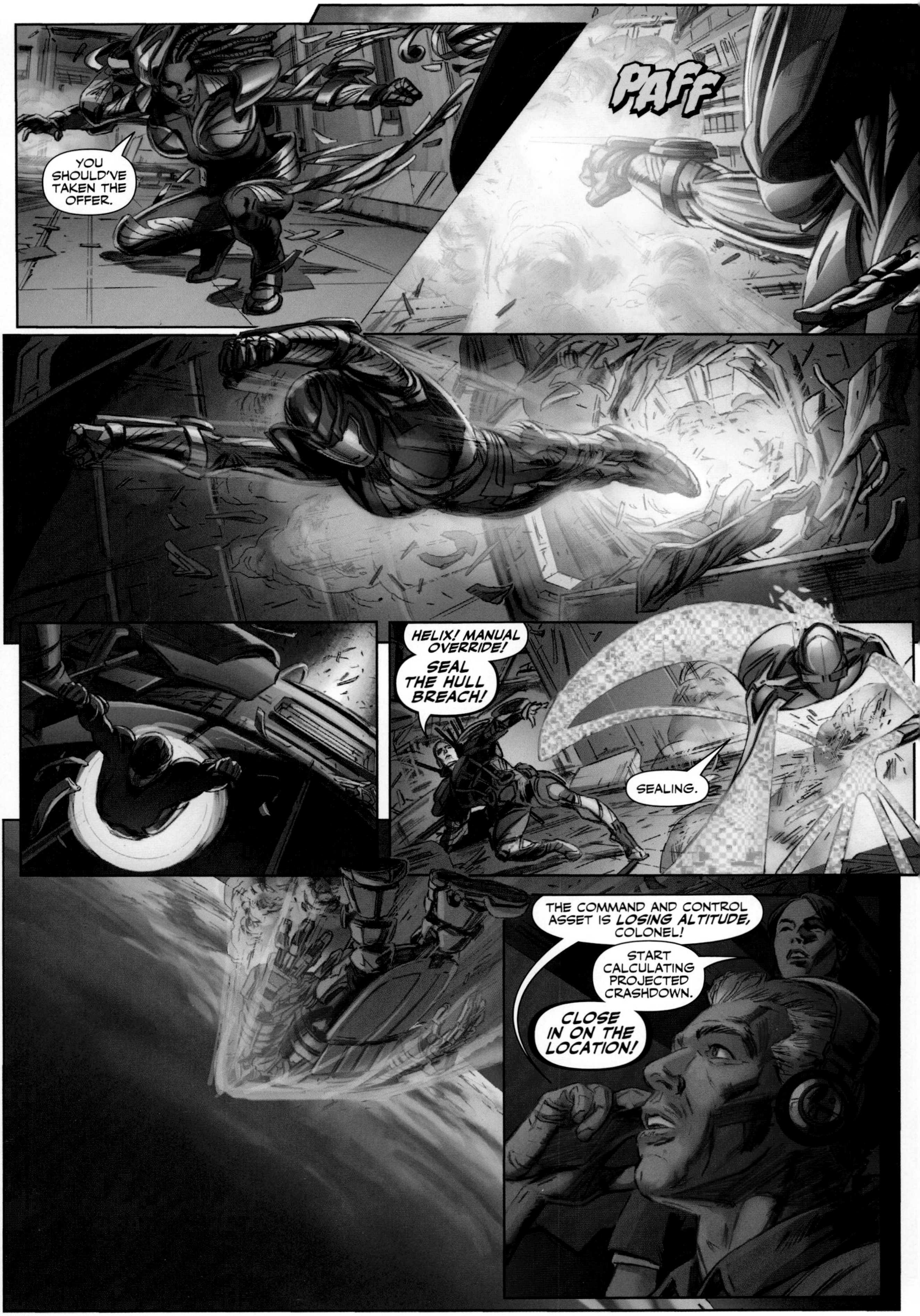
YOU SHOULD'VE TAKEN THE OFFER.
PAFF
HELIX! MANUAL OVERRIDE!
SEAL THE HULL BREACH!
SEALING.
THE COMMAND AND CONTROL ASSET IS LOSING ALTITUDE, COLONEL!
START CALCULATING PROJECTED CRASHDOWN.
CLOSE IN ON THE LOCATION!

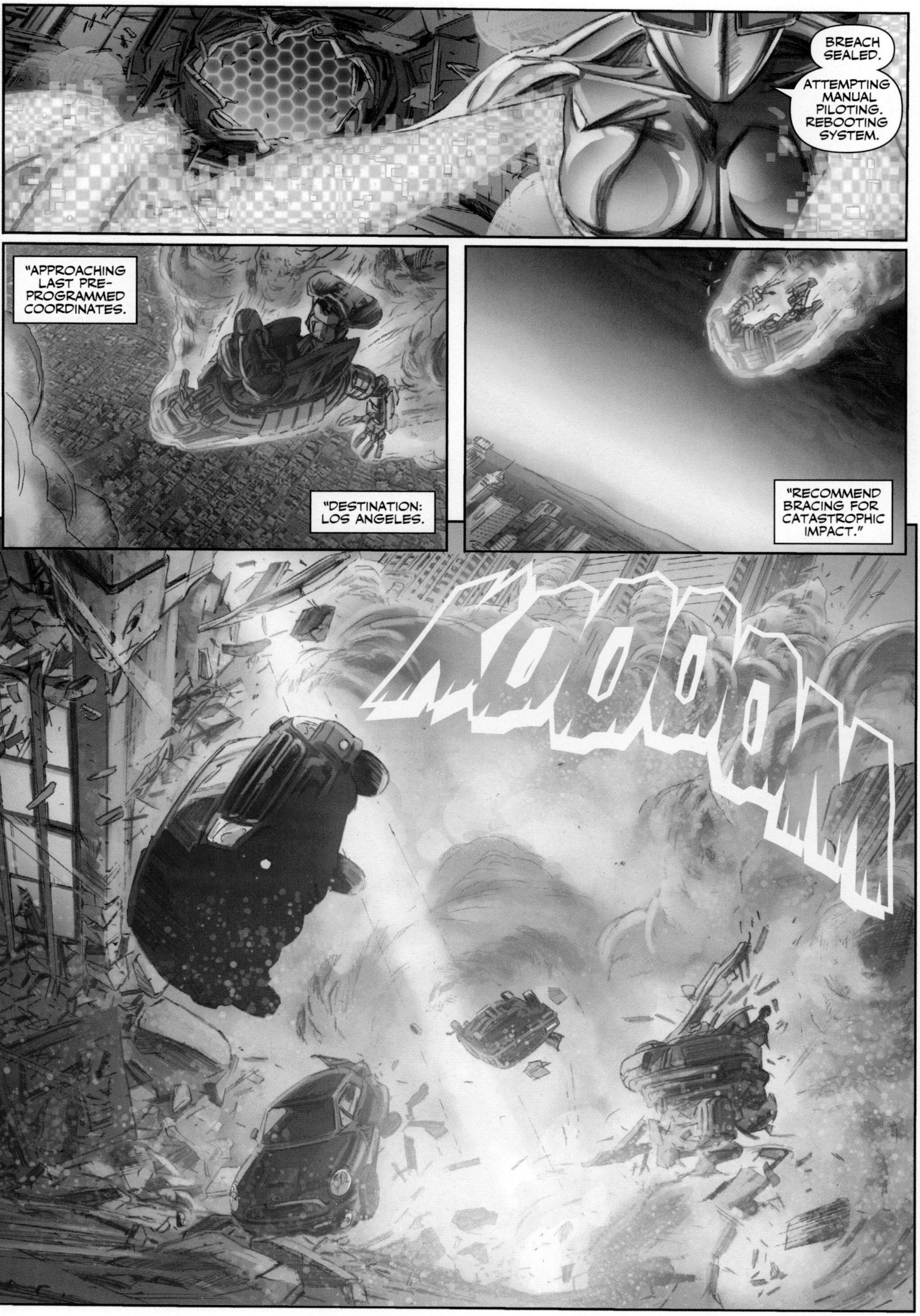
BREACH SEALED.
ATTEMPTING MANUAL PILOTING. REBOOTING SYSTEM.
"APPROACHING LAST PRE-PROGRAMMED COORDINATES.
"DESTINATION: LOS ANGELES.
"RECOMMEND BRACING FOR CATASTROPHIC IMPACT."

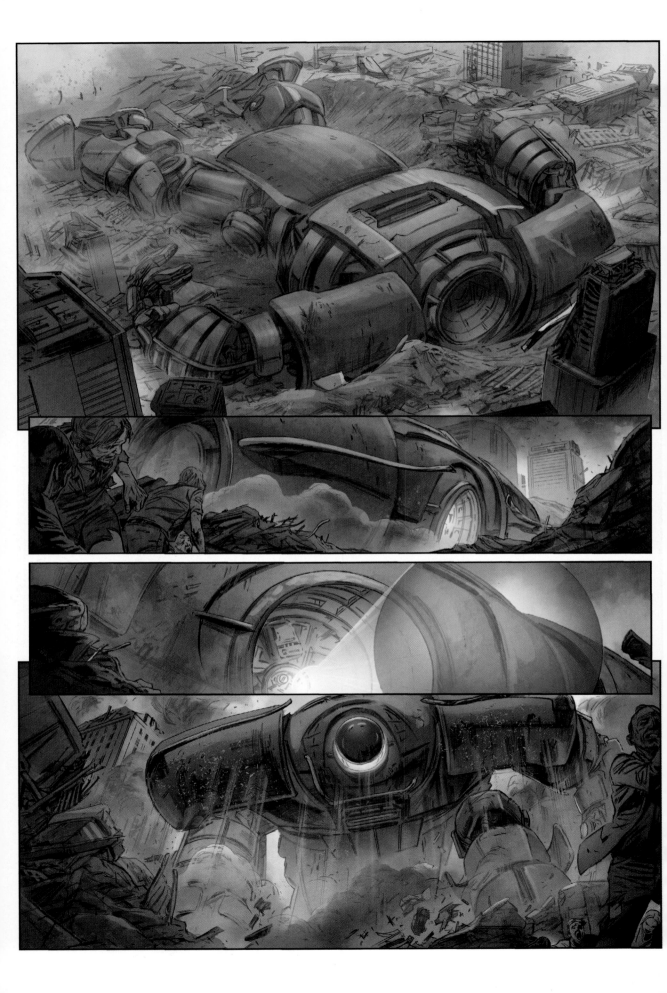

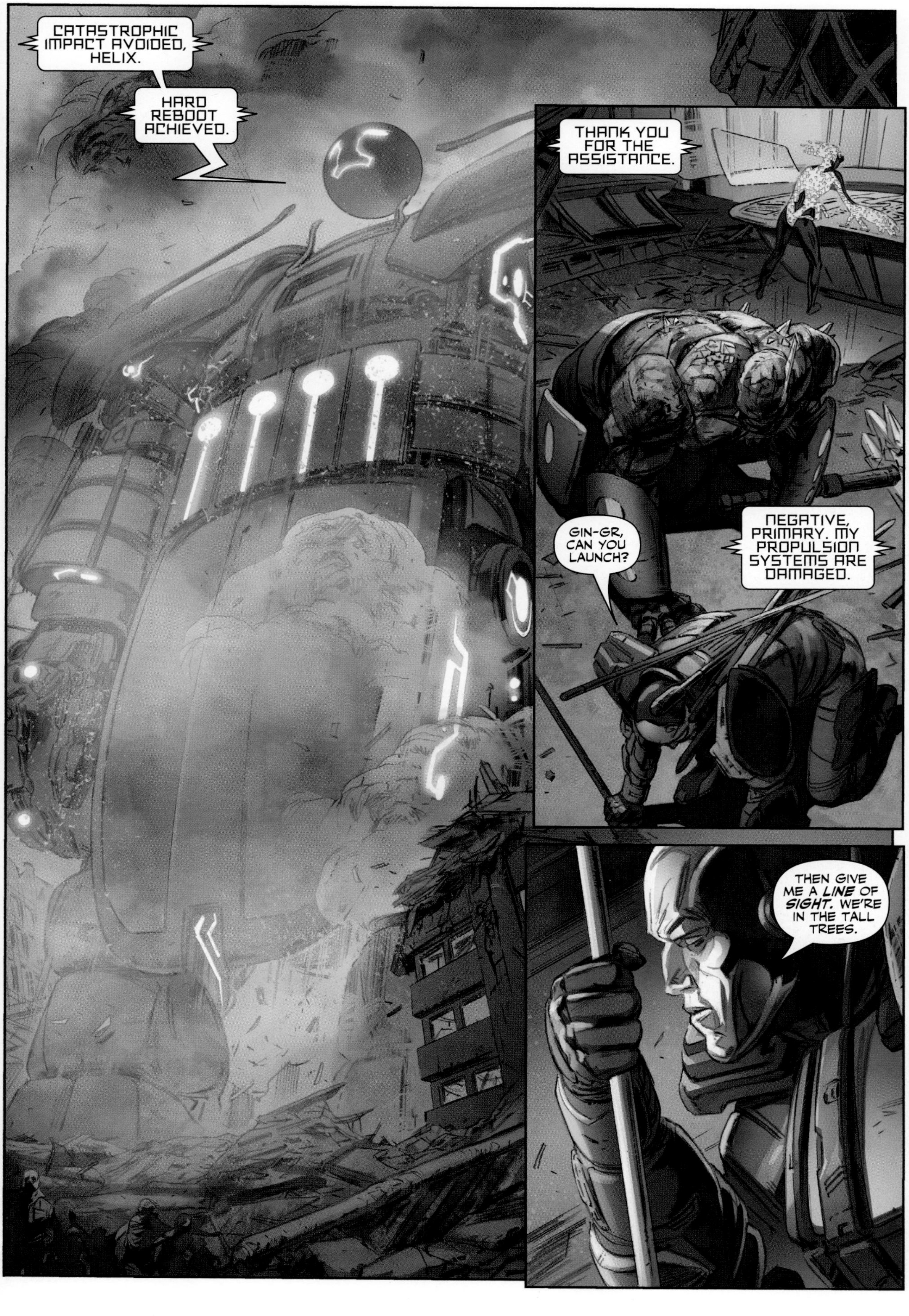
CATASTROPHIC IMPACT AVOIDED, HELIX.
HARD REBOOT ACHIEVED.
THANK YOU FOR THE ASSISTANCE.
GIN-GR, CAN YOU LAUNCH?
NEGATIVE, PRIMARY. MY PROPULSION SYSTEMS ARE DAMAGED.
THEN GIVE ME A *LINE* OF *SIGHT.* WE'RE IN THE TALL TREES.

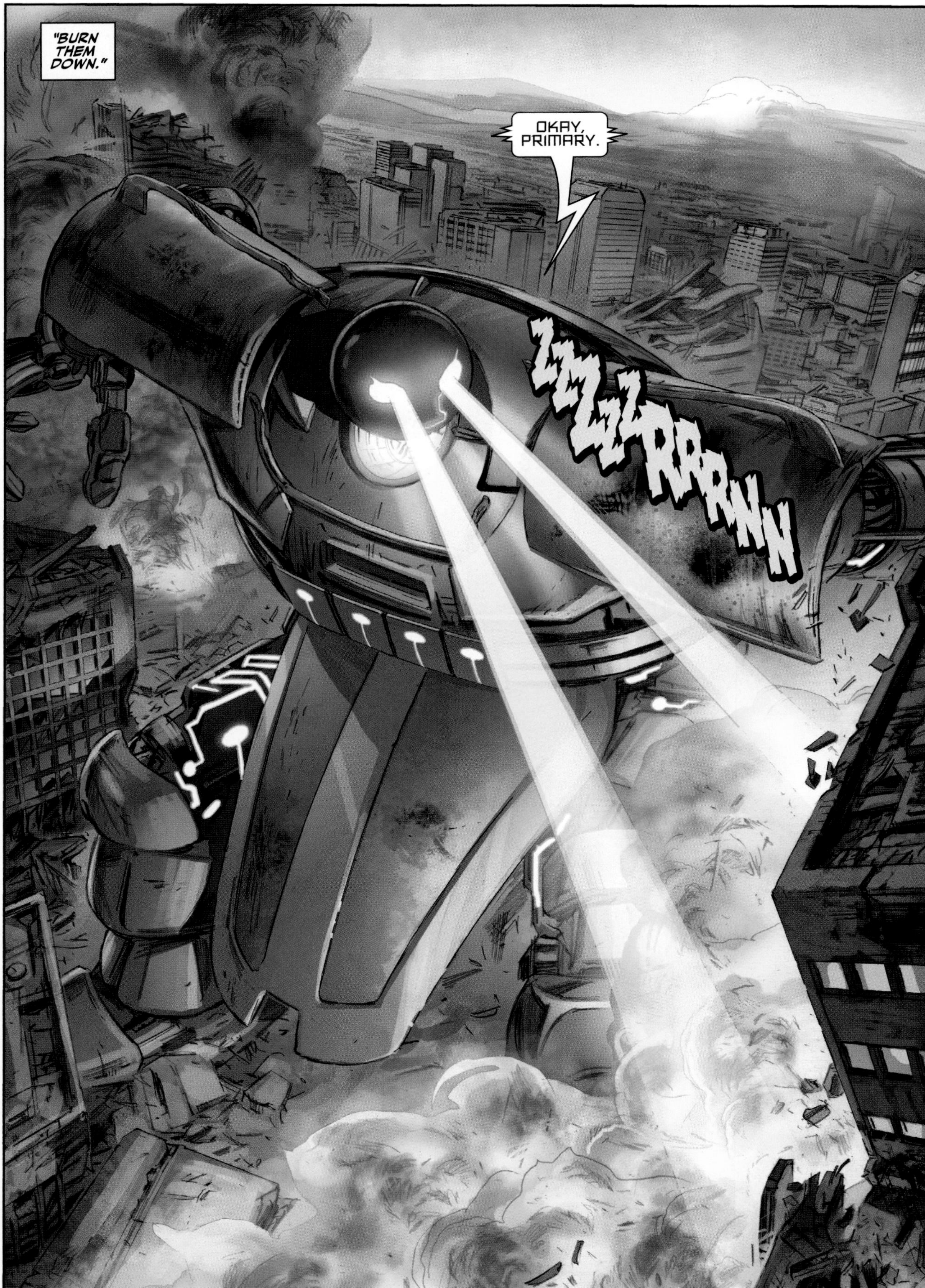
"BURN THEM DOWN."
OKAY, PRIMARY.
ZZZZZZRRRRNN

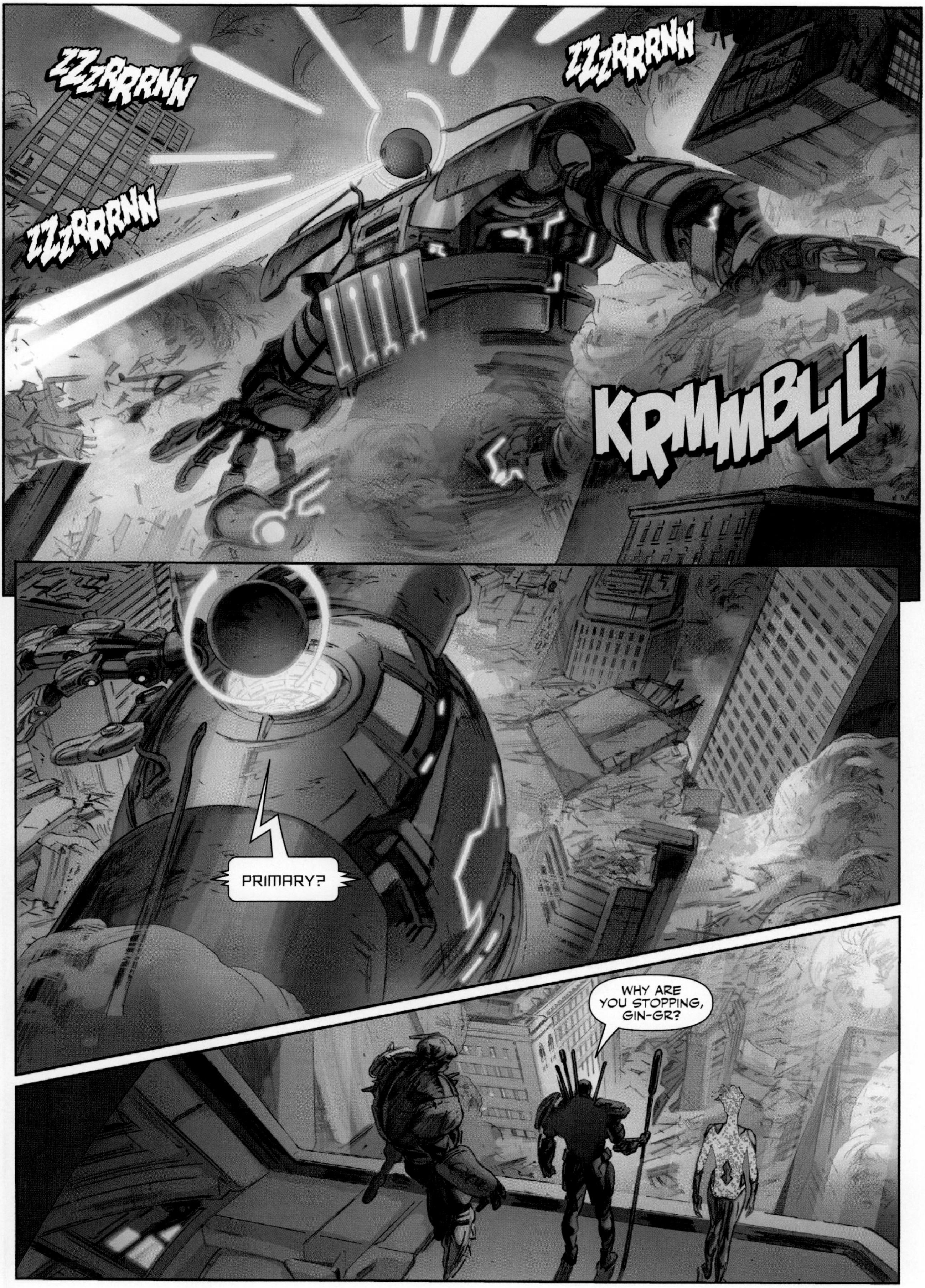
ZZZRRRNN
ZZZRRRNN
ZZZRRRNN
KRMMBLLL
PRIMARY?
WHY ARE YOU STOPPING, GIN-GR?

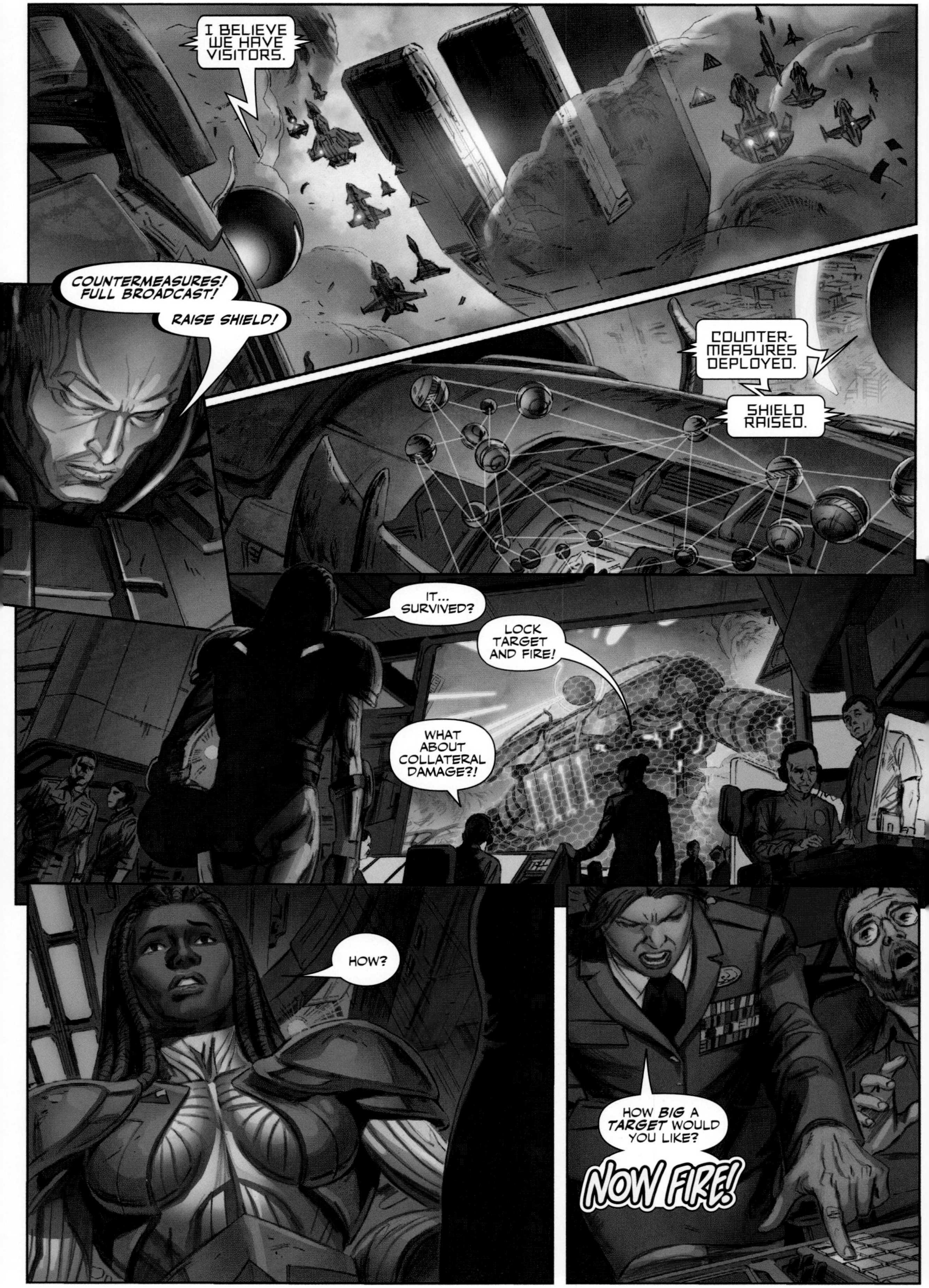
I BELIEVE WE HAVE VISITORS.
COUNTERMEASURES! FULL BROADCAST!
RAISE SHIELD!
COUNTER-MEASURES DEPLOYED.
SHIELD RAISED.
IT... SURVIVED?
LOCK TARGET AND FIRE!
WHAT ABOUT COLLATERAL DAMAGE?!
HOW?
HOW BIG A TARGET WOULD YOU LIKE?
NOW FIRE!

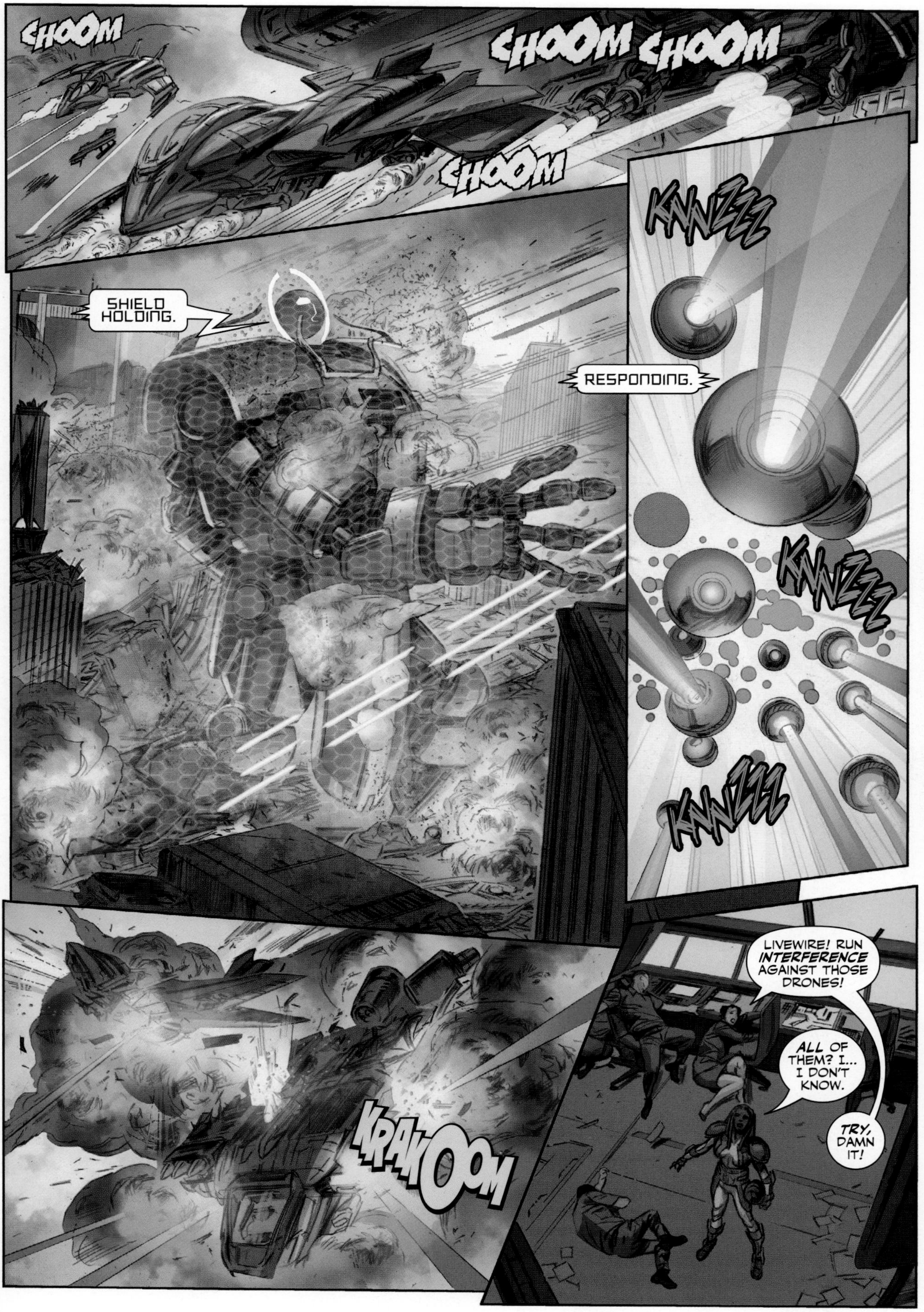
CHOOM
CHOOM CHOOM
CHOOM
KNNZZZ
SHIELD HOLDING.
RESPONDING.
KNNZZZ
KNNZZZ
KRAKOOM
LIVEWIRE! RUN *INTERFERENCE* AGAINST THOSE DRONES!
ALL OF THEM? I... I DON'T KNOW.
TRY, DAMN IT!

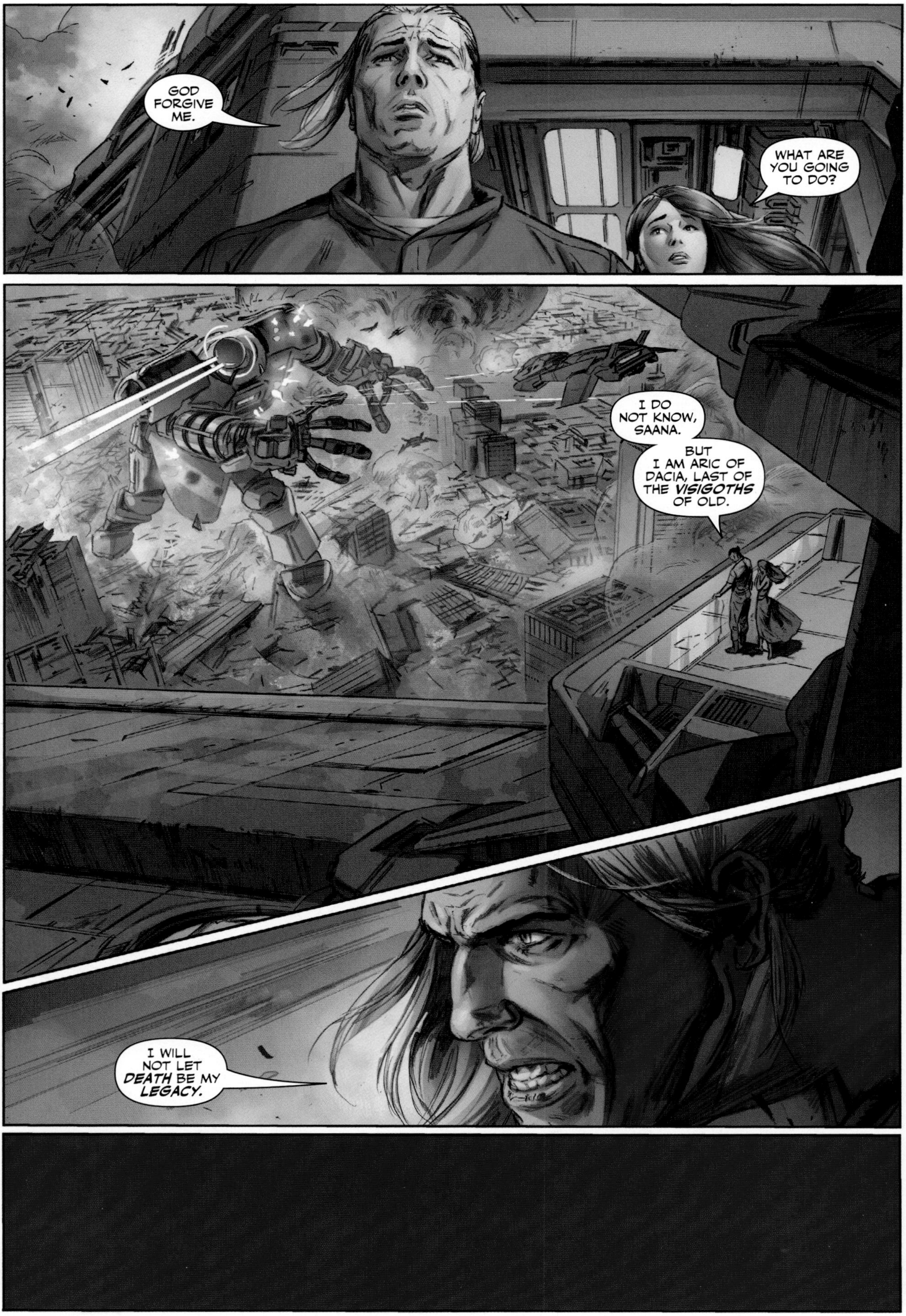
GOD FORGIVE ME.
WHAT ARE YOU GOING TO DO?
I DO NOT KNOW, SAANA.
BUT I AM ARIC OF DACIA, LAST OF THE *VISIGOTHS* OF OLD.
I WILL NOT LET *DEATH* BE MY *LEGACY.*

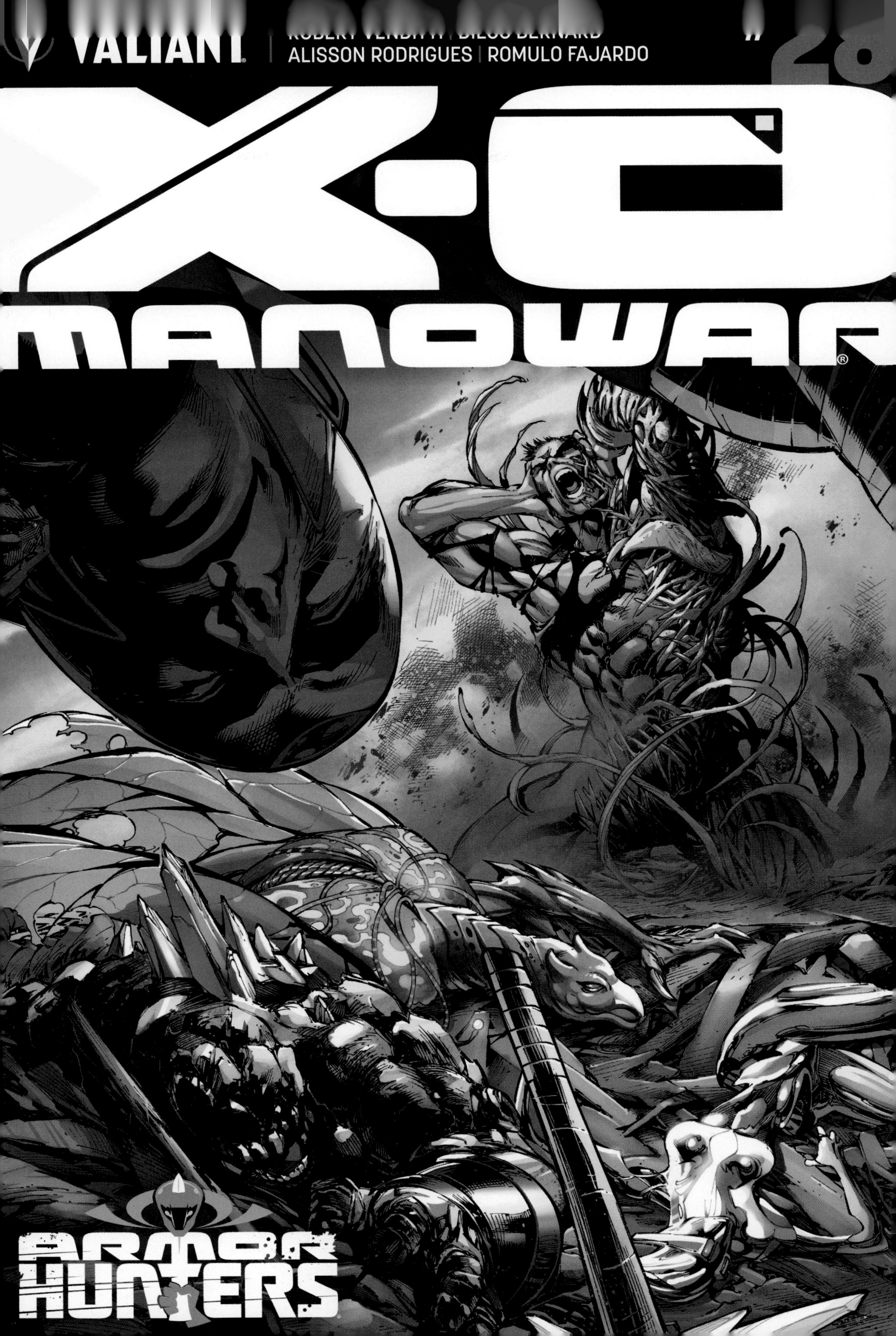
VALIANT
ALISSON RODRIGUES | ROMULO FAJARDO
X-O
MANOWAR®
ARMOR HUNTERS

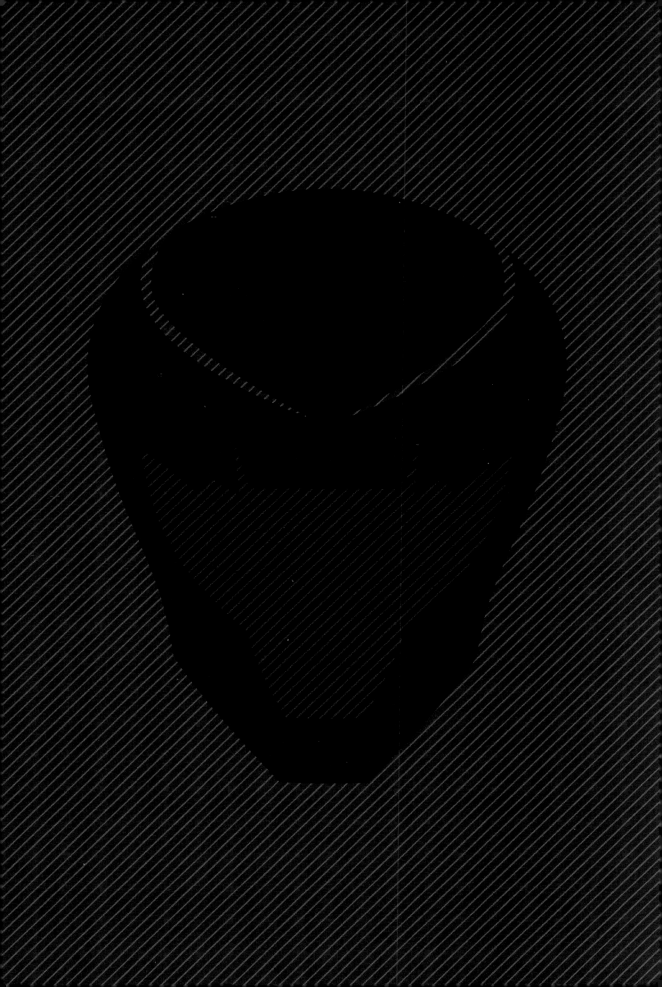

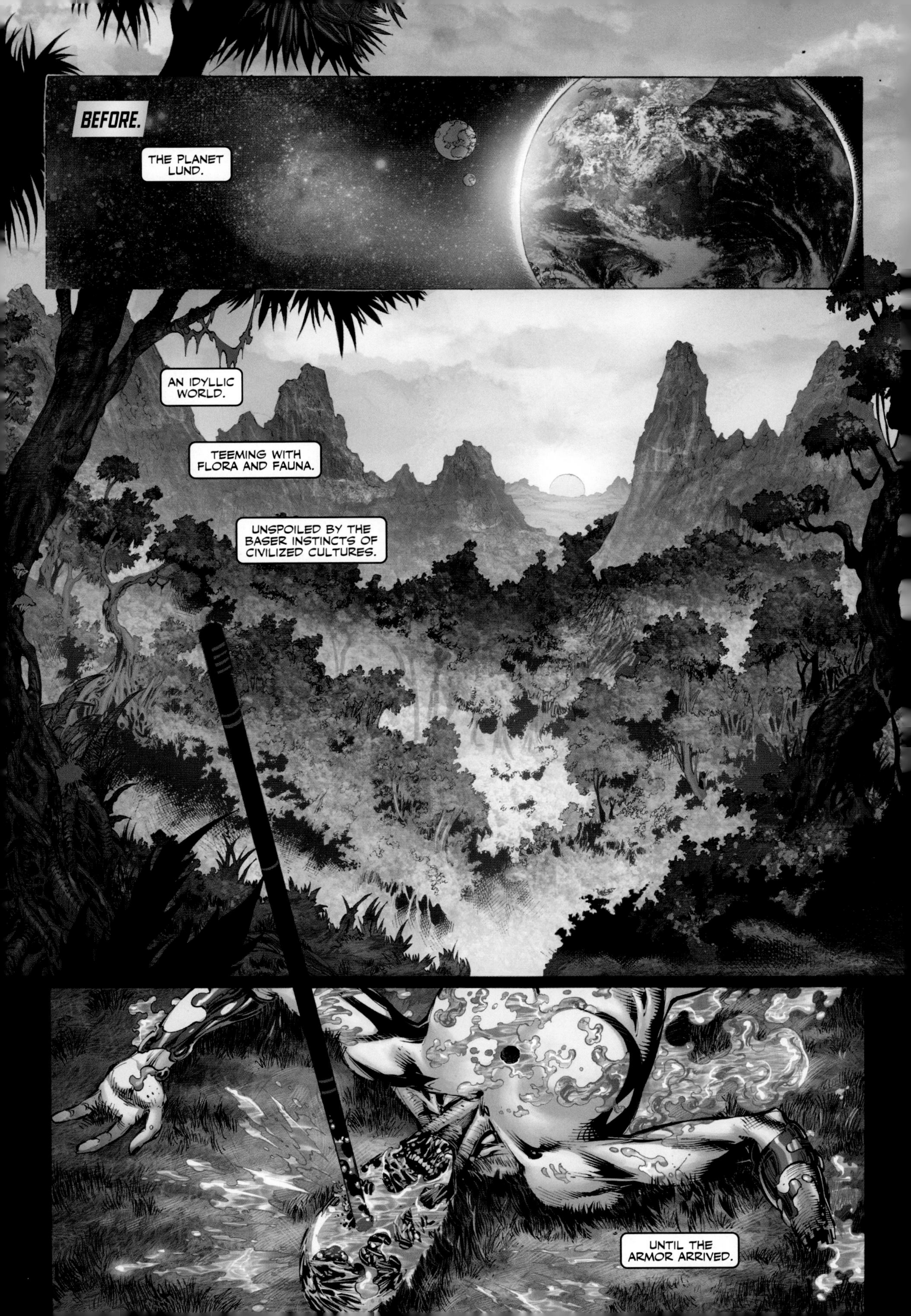
BEFORE.
THE PLANET LUND.
AN IDYLLIC WORLD.
TEEMING WITH FLORA AND FAUNA.
UNSPOILED BY THE BASER INSTINCTS OF CIVILIZED CULTURES.
UNTIL THE ARMOR ARRIVED.

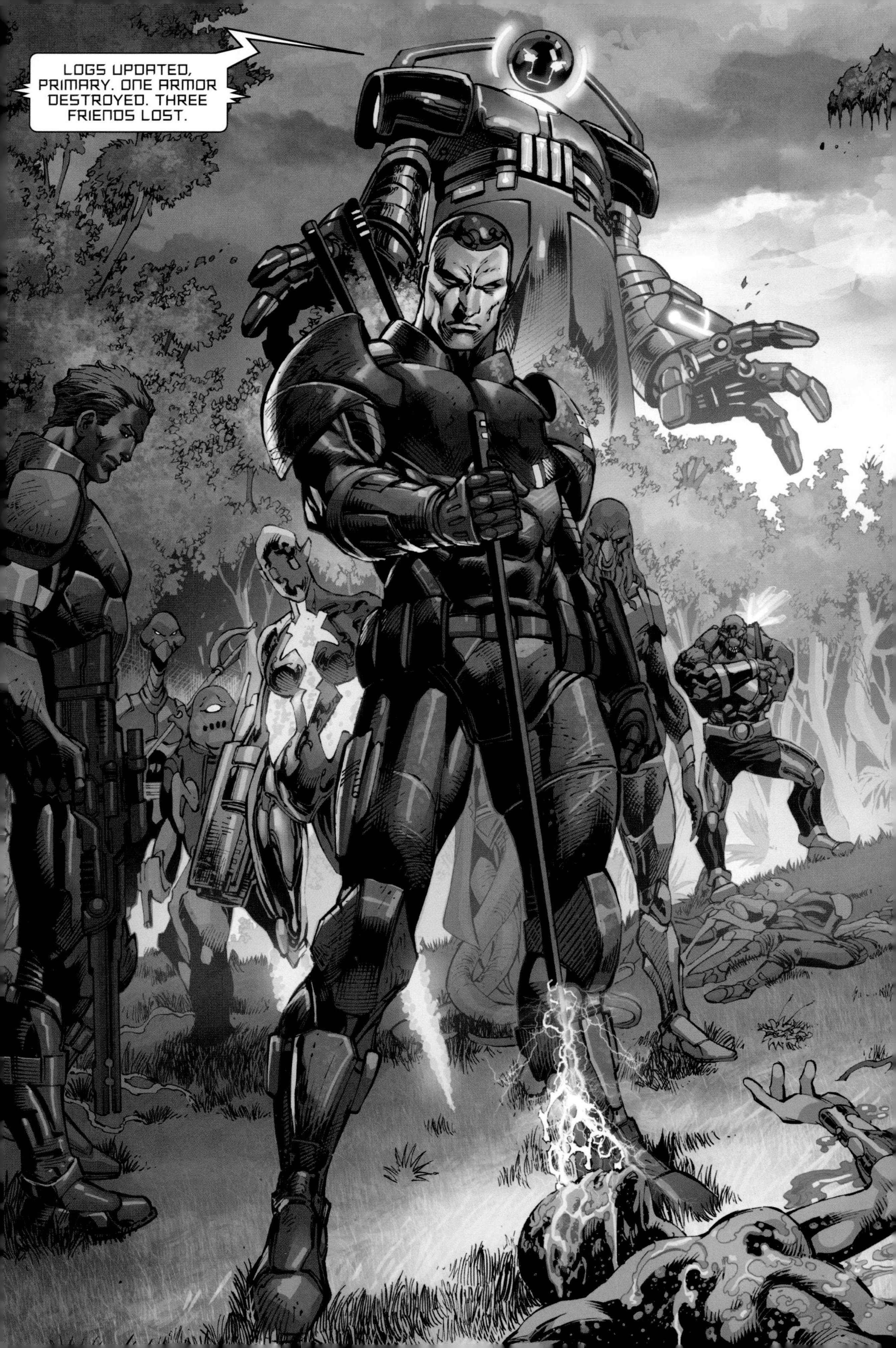
LOGS UPDATED, PRIMARY. ONE ARMOR DESTROYED. THREE FRIENDS LOST.

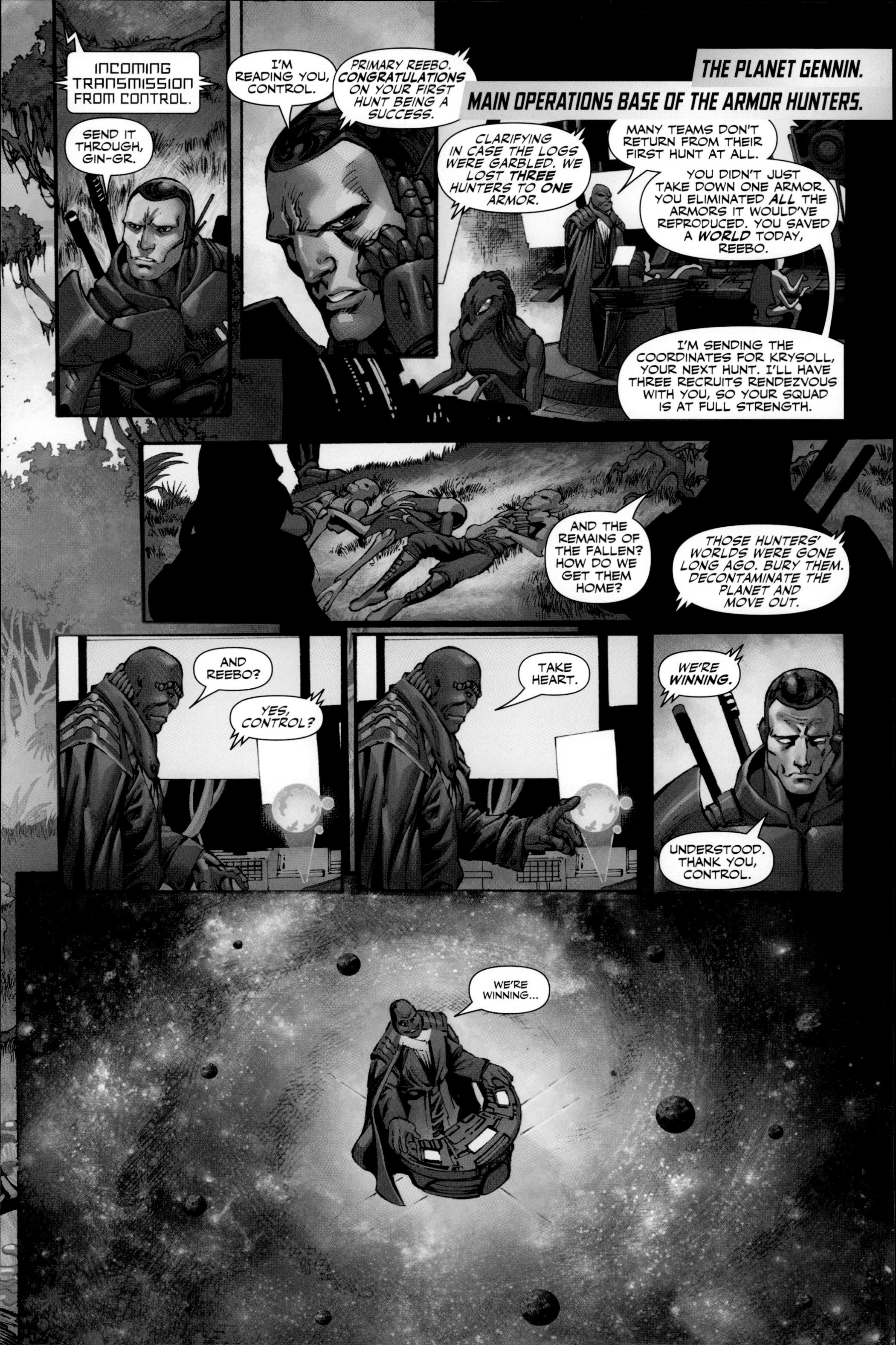
INCOMING TRANSMISSION FROM CONTROL.
SEND IT THROUGH, GIN-GR.
I'M READING YOU, CONTROL.
PRIMARY REEBO. CONGRATULATIONS ON YOUR FIRST HUNT BEING A SUCCESS.
THE PLANET GENNIN.
MAIN OPERATIONS BASE OF THE ARMOR HUNTERS.
CLARIFYING IN CASE THE LOGS WERE GARBLED. WE LOST THREE HUNTERS TO ONE ARMOR.
MANY TEAMS DON'T RETURN FROM THEIR FIRST HUNT AT ALL.
YOU DIDN'T JUST TAKE DOWN ONE ARMOR. YOU ELIMINATED ALL THE ARMORS IT WOULD'VE REPRODUCED. YOU SAVED A WORLD TODAY, REEBO.
I'M SENDING THE COORDINATES FOR KRYSOLL, YOUR NEXT HUNT. I'LL HAVE THREE RECRUITS RENDEZVOUS WITH YOU, SO YOUR SQUAD IS AT FULL STRENGTH.
AND THE REMAINS OF THE FALLEN? HOW DO WE GET THEM HOME?
THOSE HUNTERS' WORLDS WERE GONE LONG AGO. BURY THEM. DECONTAMINATE THE PLANET AND MOVE OUT.
AND REEBO?
YES, CONTROL?
TAKE HEART.
WE'RE WINNING.
UNDERSTOOD. THANK YOU, CONTROL.
WE'RE WINNING...

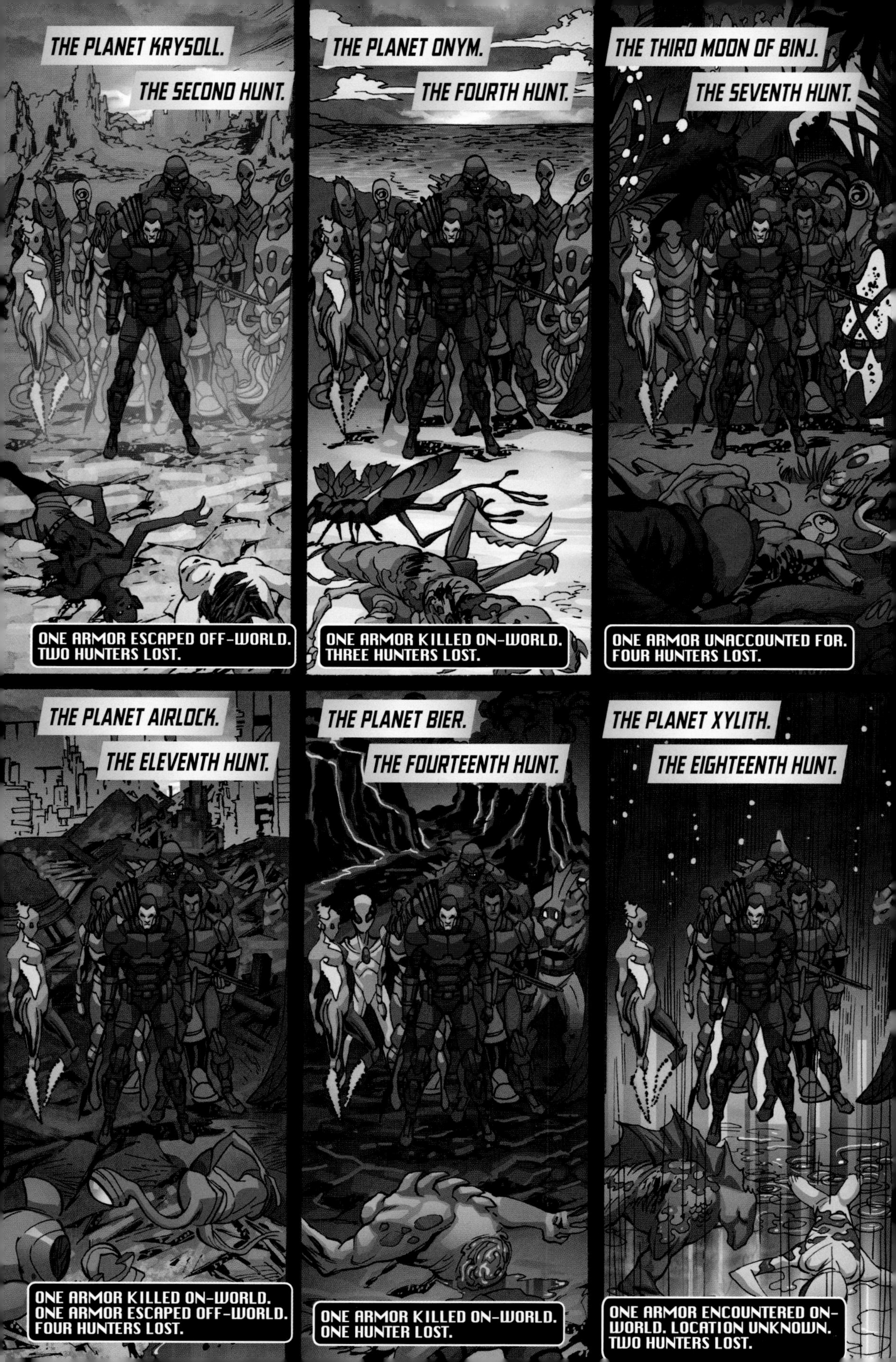
THE PLANET KRYSOLL.
THE SECOND HUNT.
ONE ARMOR ESCAPED OFF-WORLD. TWO HUNTERS LOST.
THE PLANET ONYM.
THE FOURTH HUNT.
ONE ARMOR KILLED ON-WORLD. THREE HUNTERS LOST.
THE THIRD MOON OF BINJ.
THE SEVENTH HUNT.
ONE ARMOR UNACCOUNTED FOR. FOUR HUNTERS LOST.
THE PLANET AIRLOCK.
THE ELEVENTH HUNT.
ONE ARMOR KILLED ON-WORLD. ONE ARMOR ESCAPED OFF-WORLD. FOUR HUNTERS LOST.
THE PLANET BIER.
THE FOURTEENTH HUNT.
ONE ARMOR KILLED ON-WORLD. ONE HUNTER LOST.
THE PLANET XYLITH.
THE EIGHTEENTH HUNT.
ONE ARMOR ENCOUNTERED ON-WORLD. LOCATION UNKNOWN. TWO HUNTERS LOST.

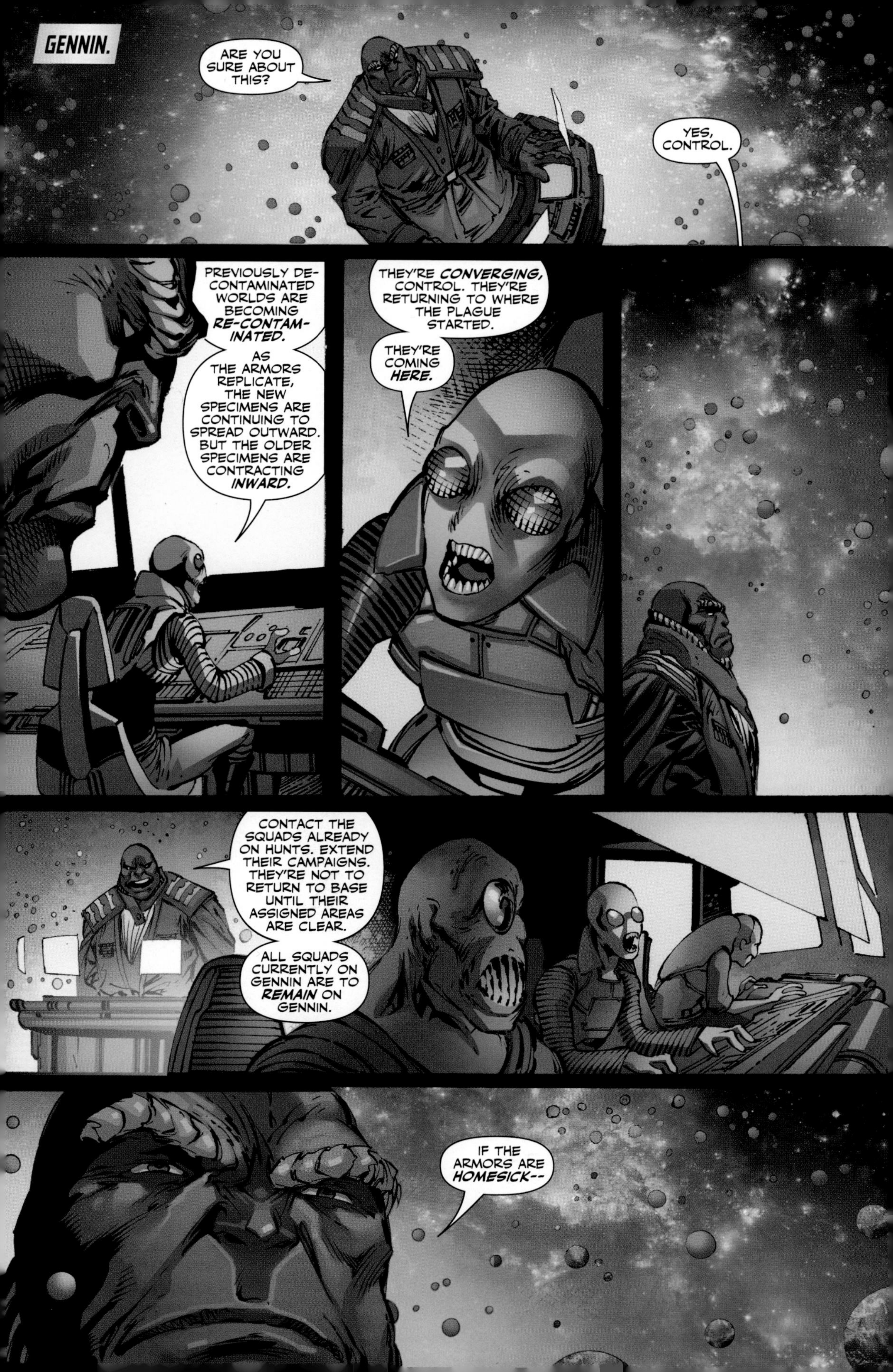
GENNIN.
ARE YOU SURE ABOUT THIS?
YES, CONTROL.
PREVIOUSLY DE-CONTAMINATED WORLDS ARE BECOMING RE-CONTAMINATED.
AS THE ARMORS REPLICATE, THE NEW SPECIMENS ARE CONTINUING TO SPREAD OUTWARD. BUT THE OLDER SPECIMENS ARE CONTRACTING INWARD.
THEY'RE CONVERGING, CONTROL. THEY'RE RETURNING TO WHERE THE PLAGUE STARTED.
THEY'RE COMING HERE.
CONTACT THE SQUADS ALREADY ON HUNTS. EXTEND THEIR CAMPAIGNS. THEY'RE NOT TO RETURN TO BASE UNTIL THEIR ASSIGNED AREAS ARE CLEAR.
ALL SQUADS CURRENTLY ON GENNIN ARE TO REMAIN ON GENNIN.
IF THE ARMORS ARE HOMESICK--

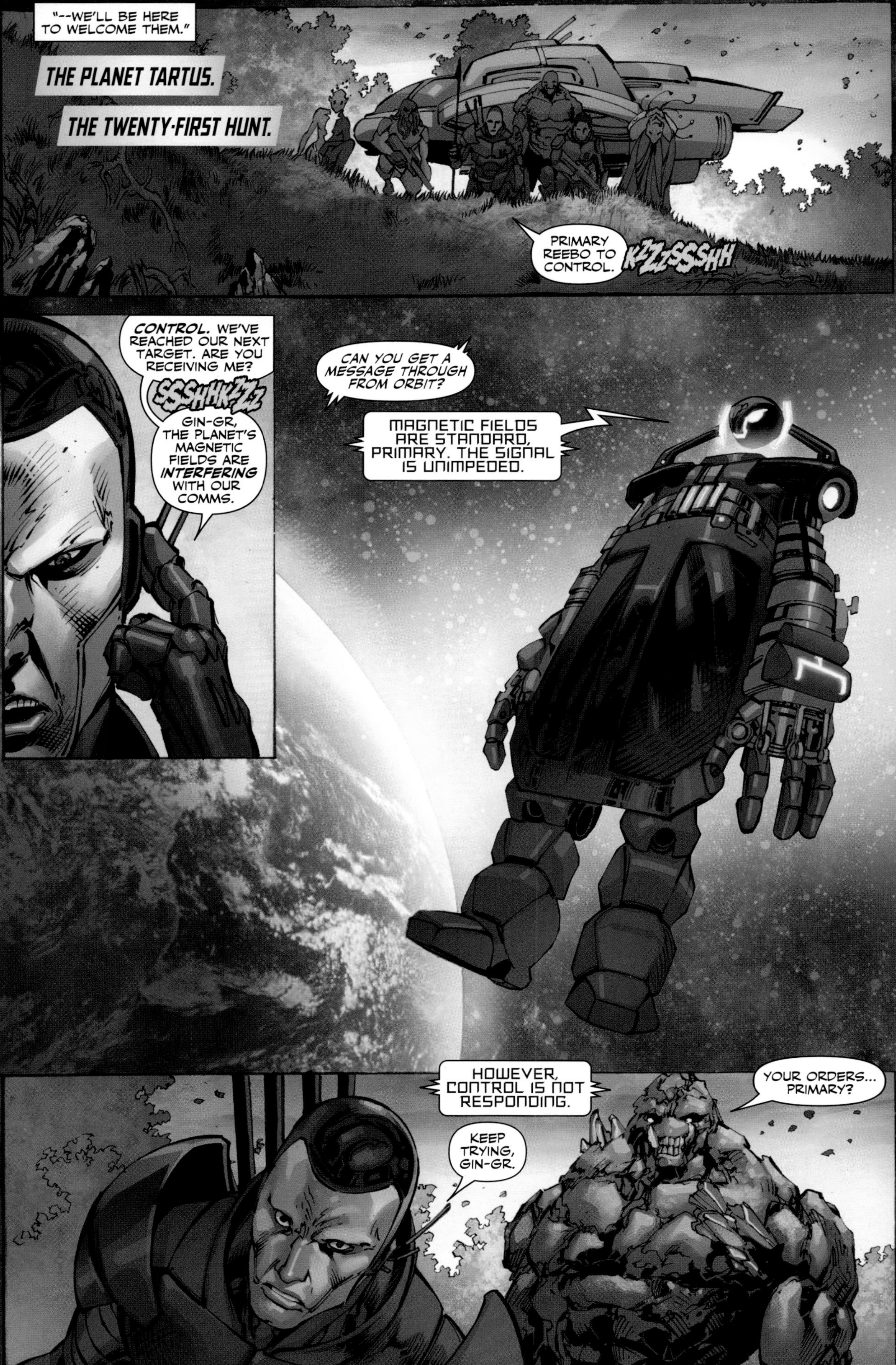
"--WE'LL BE HERE TO WELCOME THEM."
THE PLANET TARTUS.
THE TWENTY-FIRST HUNT.
PRIMARY REEBO TO CONTROL.
KZZZSSSHH
CONTROL. WE'VE REACHED OUR NEXT TARGET. ARE YOU RECEIVING ME?
SSSHHKZZZ
GIN-GR, THE PLANET'S MAGNETIC FIELDS ARE INTERFERING WITH OUR COMMS.
CAN YOU GET A MESSAGE THROUGH FROM ORBIT?
MAGNETIC FIELDS ARE STANDARD, PRIMARY. THE SIGNAL IS UNIMPEDED.
HOWEVER, CONTROL IS NOT RESPONDING.
YOUR ORDERS... PRIMARY?
KEEP TRYING, GIN-GR.

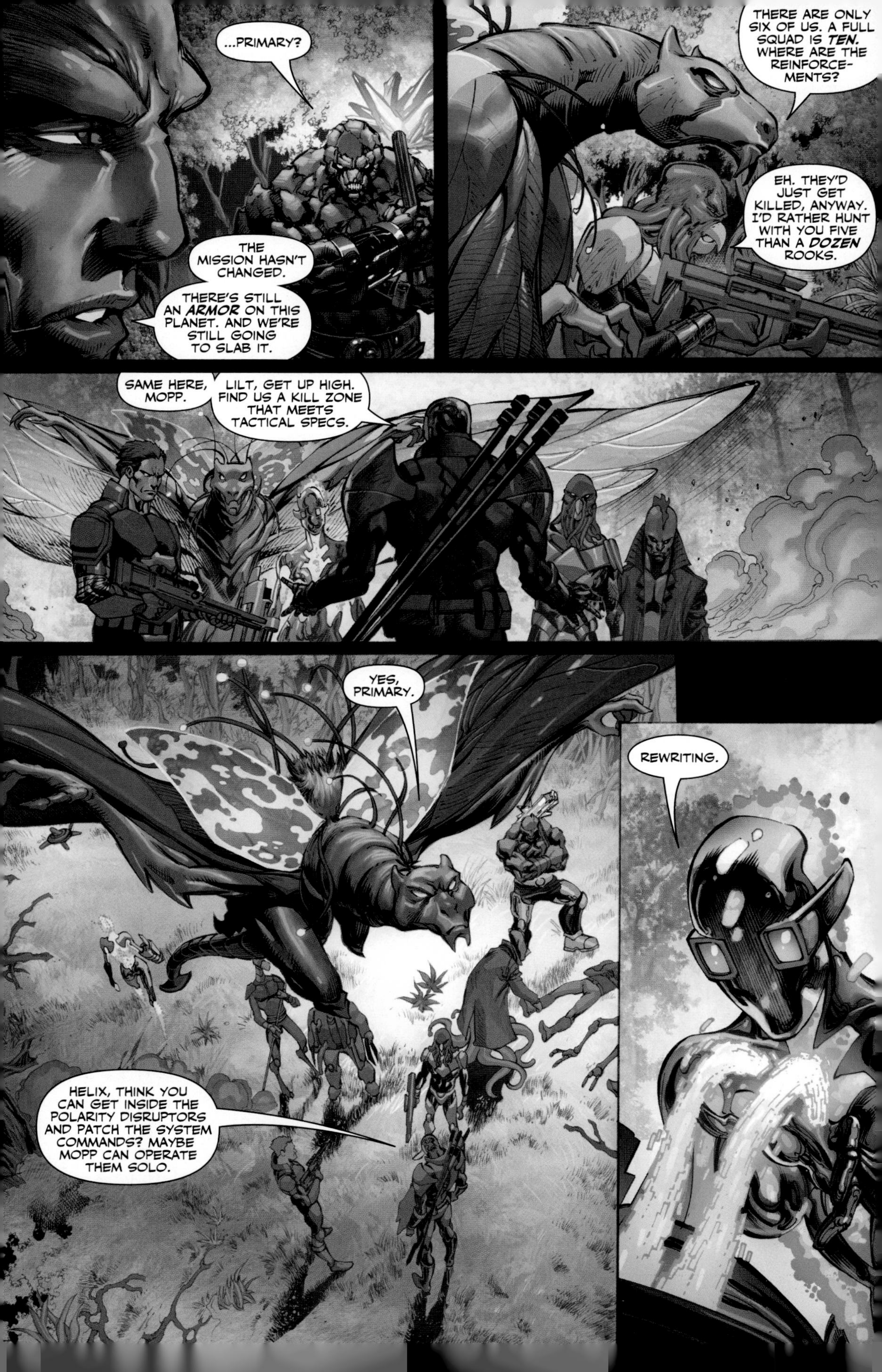
...PRIMARY?
THE MISSION HASN'T CHANGED.
THERE'S STILL AN ARMOR ON THIS PLANET. AND WE'RE STILL GOING TO SLAB IT.
THERE ARE ONLY SIX OF US. A FULL SQUAD IS TEN. WHERE ARE THE REINFORCE-MENTS?
EH. THEY'D JUST GET KILLED, ANYWAY. I'D RATHER HUNT WITH YOU FIVE THAN A DOZEN ROOKS.
SAME HERE, MOPP.
LILT, GET UP HIGH. FIND US A KILL ZONE THAT MEETS TACTICAL SPECS.
YES, PRIMARY.
HELIX, THINK YOU CAN GET INSIDE THE POLARITY DISRUPTORS AND PATCH THE SYSTEM COMMANDS? MAYBE MOPP CAN OPERATE THEM SOLO.
REWRITING.

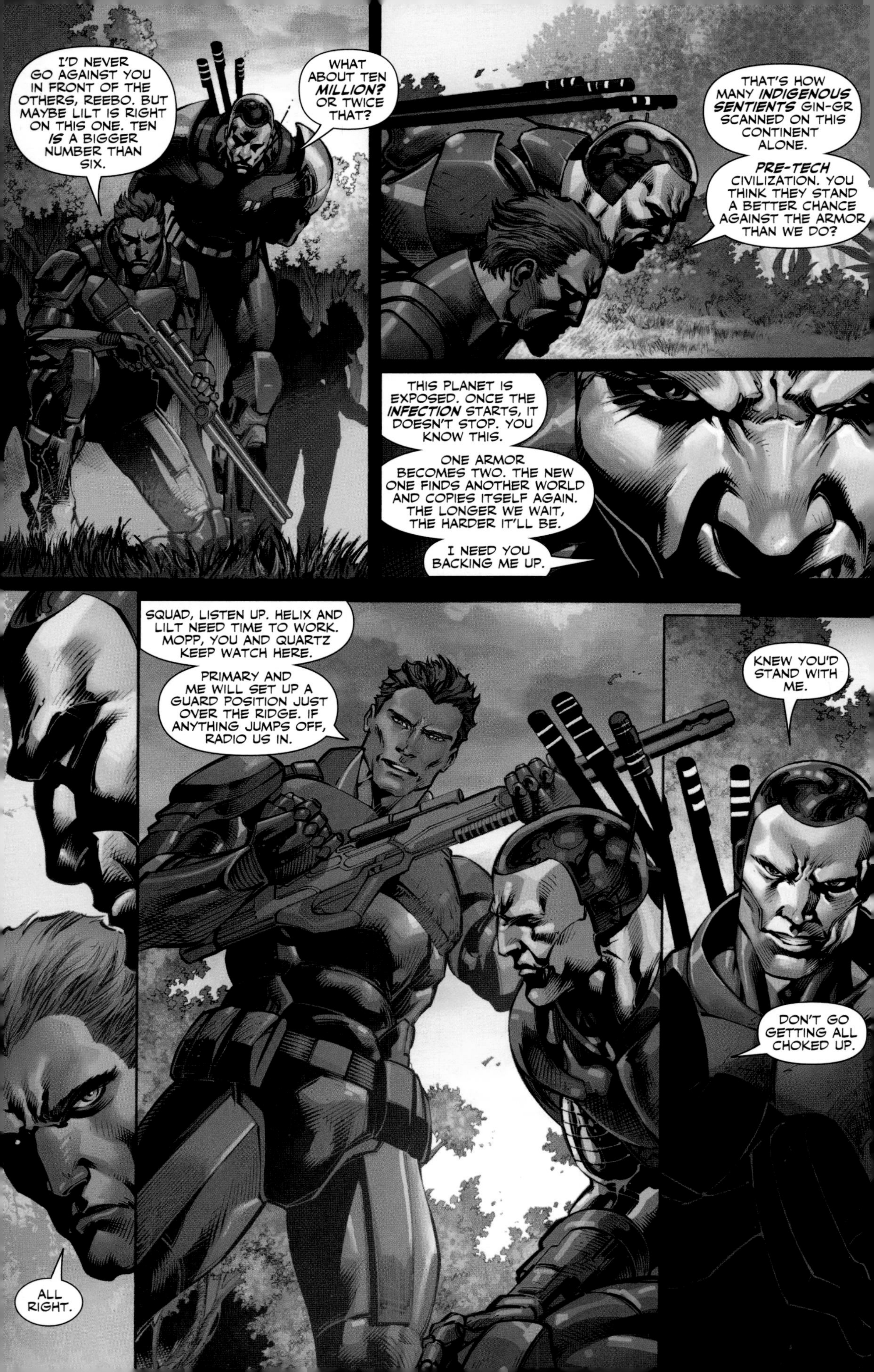
I'D NEVER GO AGAINST YOU IN FRONT OF THE OTHERS, REEBO. BUT MAYBE LILT IS RIGHT ON THIS ONE. TEN *IS* A BIGGER NUMBER THAN SIX.
WHAT ABOUT TEN *MILLION?* OR TWICE THAT?
THAT'S HOW MANY *INDIGENOUS SENTIENTS* GIN-GR SCANNED ON THIS CONTINENT ALONE.
PRE-TECH CIVILIZATION. YOU THINK THEY STAND A BETTER CHANCE AGAINST THE ARMOR THAN WE DO?
THIS PLANET IS EXPOSED. ONCE THE *INFECTION* STARTS, IT DOESN'T STOP. YOU KNOW THIS.
ONE ARMOR BECOMES TWO. THE NEW ONE FINDS ANOTHER WORLD AND COPIES ITSELF AGAIN. THE LONGER WE WAIT, THE HARDER IT'LL BE.
I NEED YOU BACKING ME UP.
ALL RIGHT.
SQUAD, LISTEN UP. HELIX AND LILT NEED TIME TO WORK. MOPP, YOU AND QUARTZ KEEP WATCH HERE.
PRIMARY AND ME WILL SET UP A GUARD POSITION JUST OVER THE RIDGE. IF ANYTHING JUMPS OFF, RADIO US IN.
KNEW YOU'D STAND WITH ME.
DON'T GO GETTING ALL CHOKED UP.

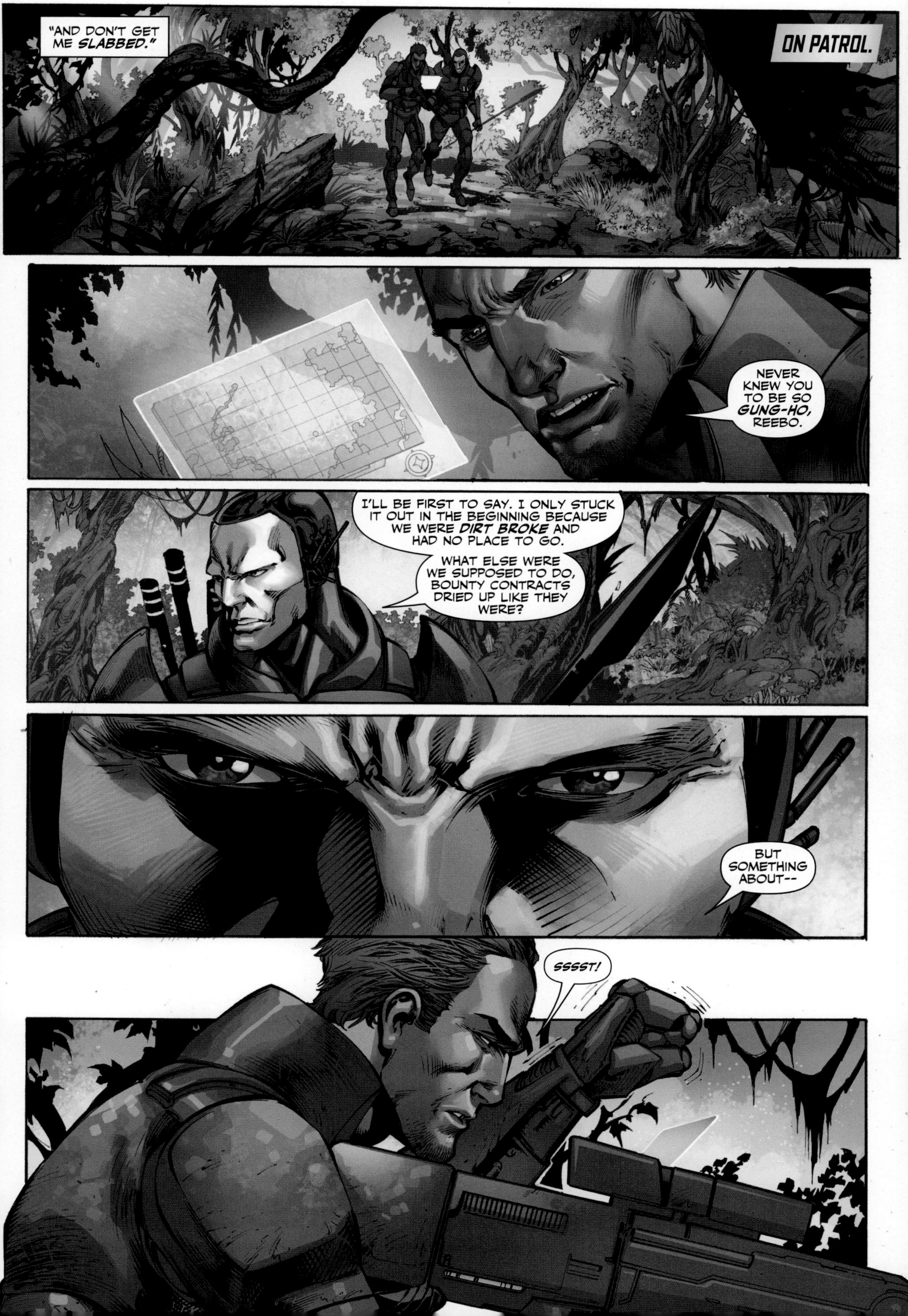

"AND DON'T GET ME SLABBED."
ON PATROL.
NEVER KNEW YOU TO BE SO GUNG-HO, REEBO.
I'LL BE FIRST TO SAY. I ONLY STUCK IT OUT IN THE BEGINNING BECAUSE WE WERE DIRT BROKE AND HAD NO PLACE TO GO.
WHAT ELSE WERE WE SUPPOSED TO DO, BOUNTY CONTRACTS DRIED UP LIKE THEY WERE?
BUT SOMETHING ABOUT--
SSSST!

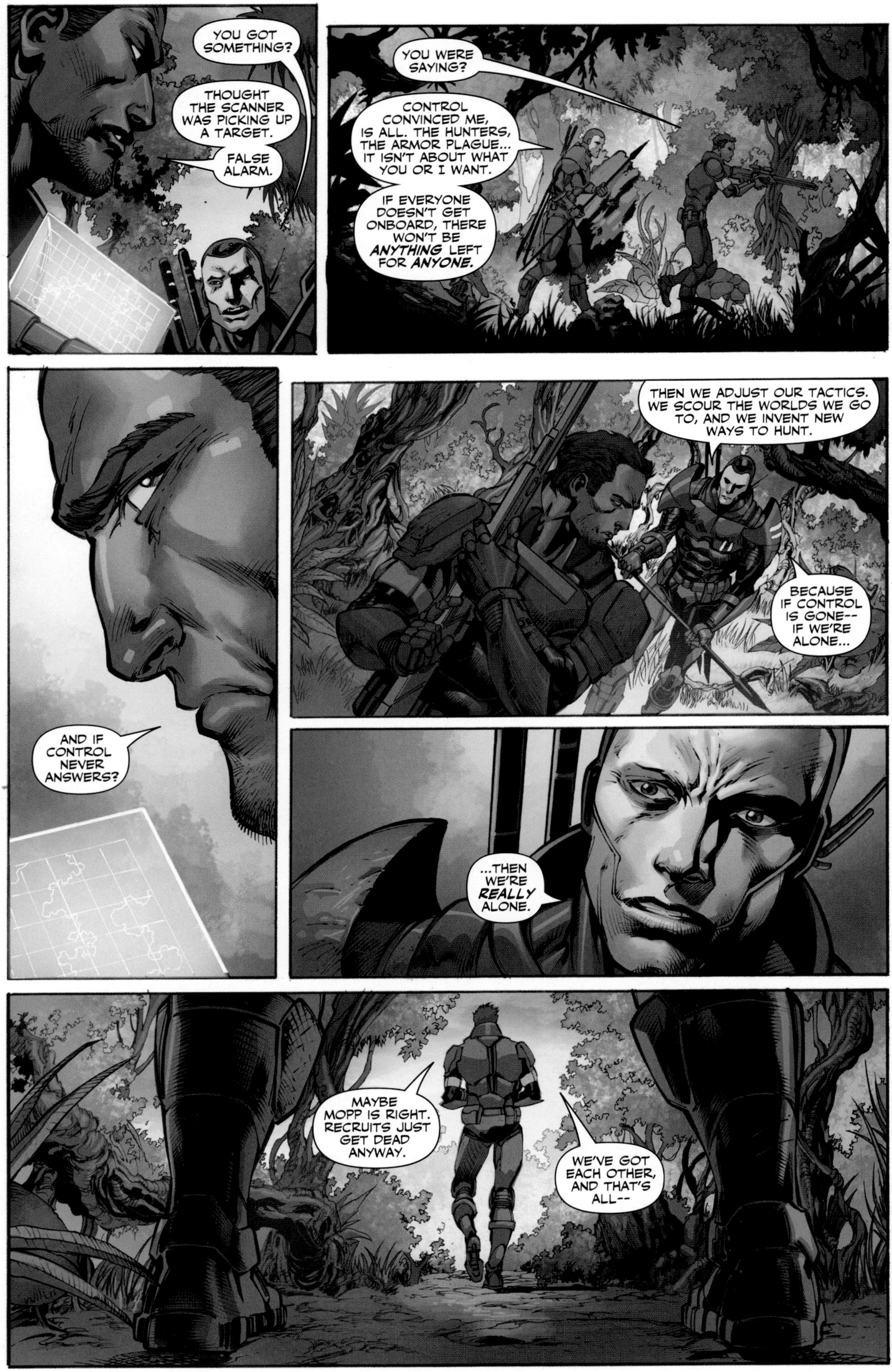
YOU GOT SOMETHING?
THOUGHT THE SCANNER WAS PICKING UP A TARGET.
FALSE ALARM.
YOU WERE SAYING?
CONTROL CONVINCED ME, IS ALL. THE HUNTERS, THE ARMOR PLAGUE... IT ISN'T ABOUT WHAT YOU OR I WANT.
IF EVERYONE DOESN'T GET ONBOARD, THERE WON'T BE ANYTHING LEFT FOR ANYONE.
AND IF CONTROL NEVER ANSWERS?
THEN WE ADJUST OUR TACTICS. WE SCOUR THE WORLDS WE GO TO, AND WE INVENT NEW WAYS TO HUNT.
BECAUSE IF CONTROL IS GONE-- IF WE'RE ALONE...
...THEN WE'RE REALLY ALONE.
MAYBE MOPP IS RIGHT. RECRUITS JUST GET DEAD ANYWAY.
WE'VE GOT EACH OTHER, AND THAT'S ALL--

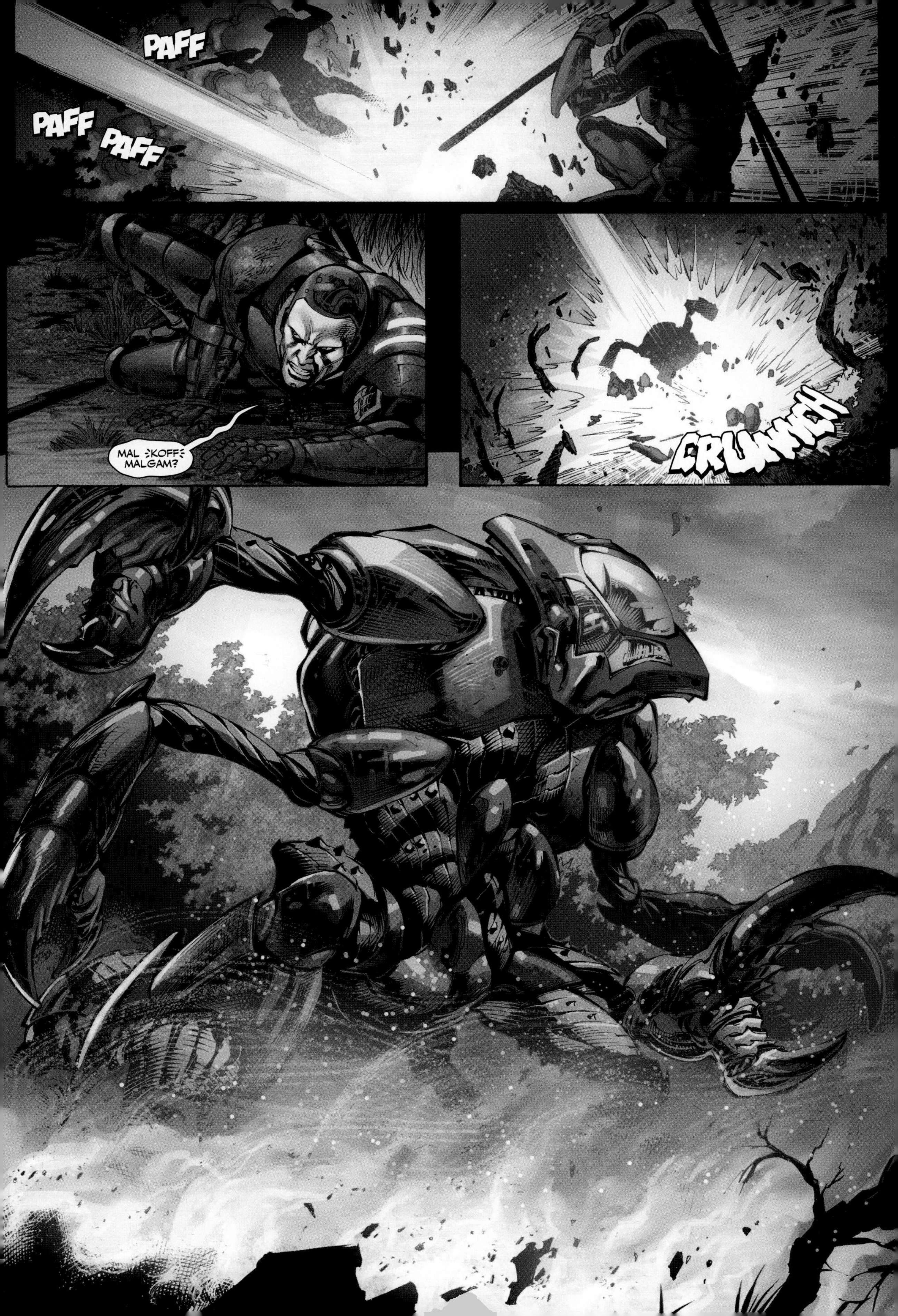
PAFF
PAFF PAFF
MAL ⁝KOFF⁝ MALGAM?
CRUNNCH

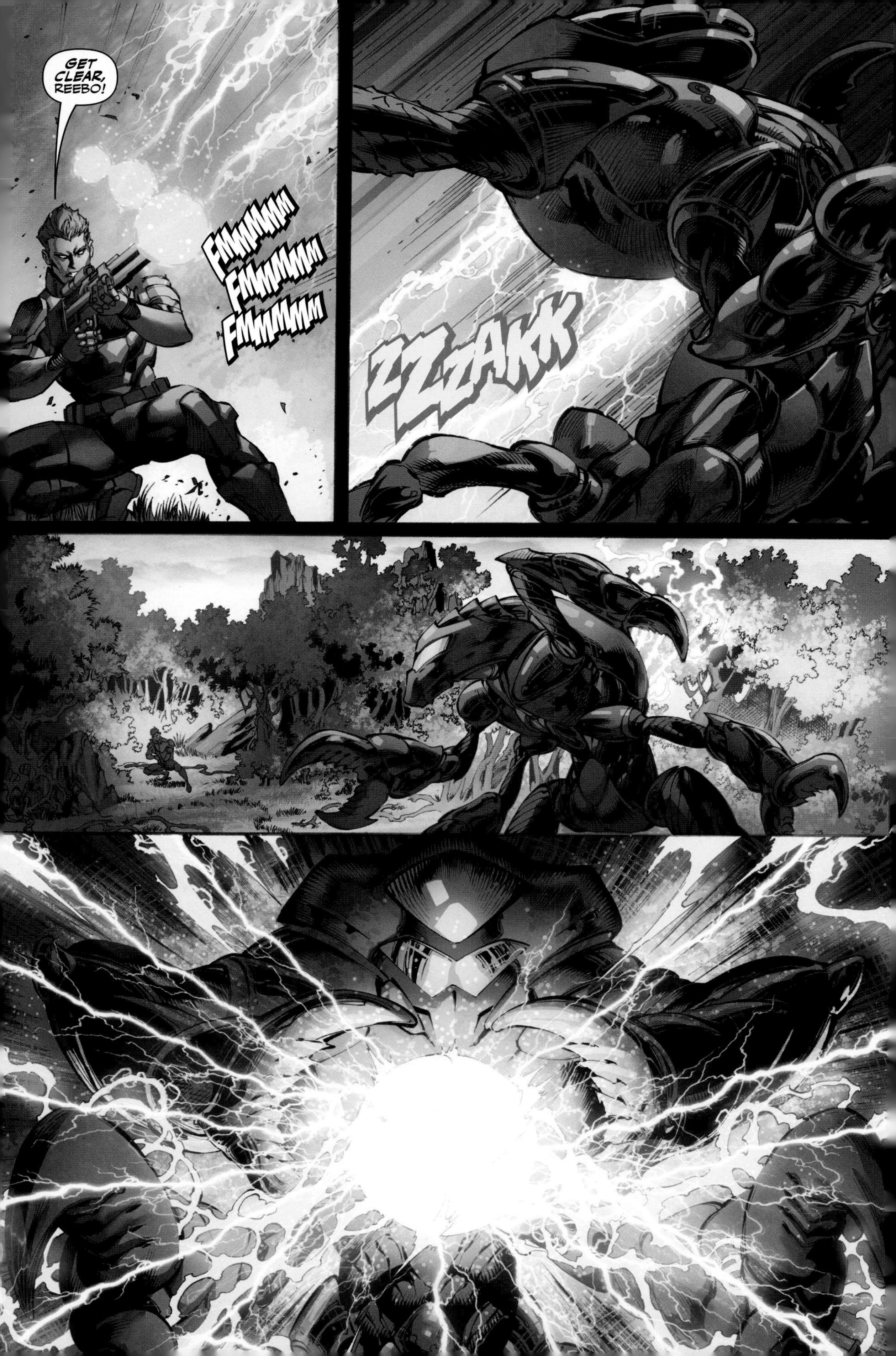
GET CLEAR, REEBO!
FMMMMM
FMMMMMM
FMMMMMM
ZZZAKK

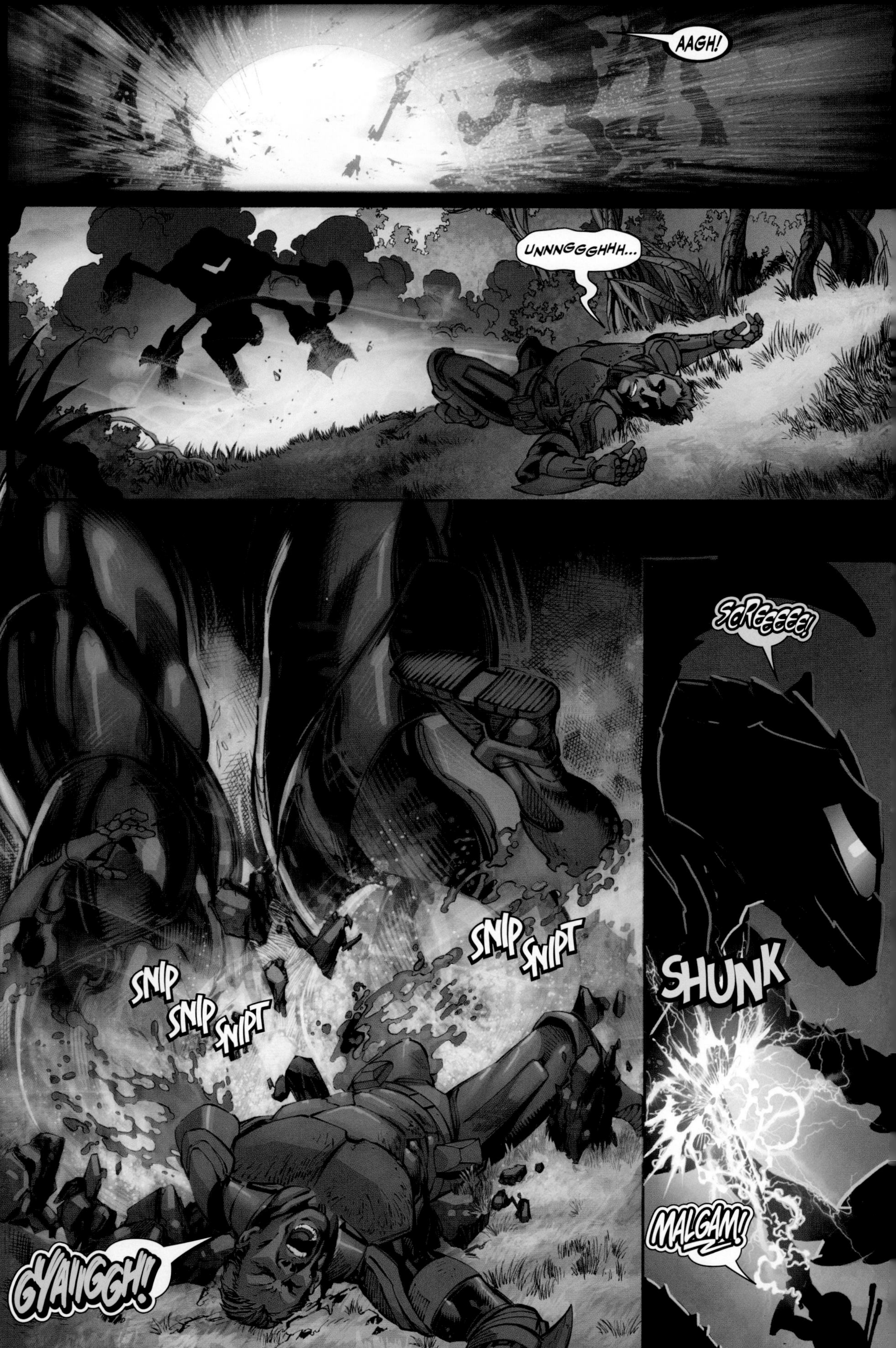
AAGH!
UNNNGGGHHH...
SNIP SNIP SNIPT
SNIP SNIPT
GYAIIGGH!
SCREEEEEE!
SHUNK
MALGAM!

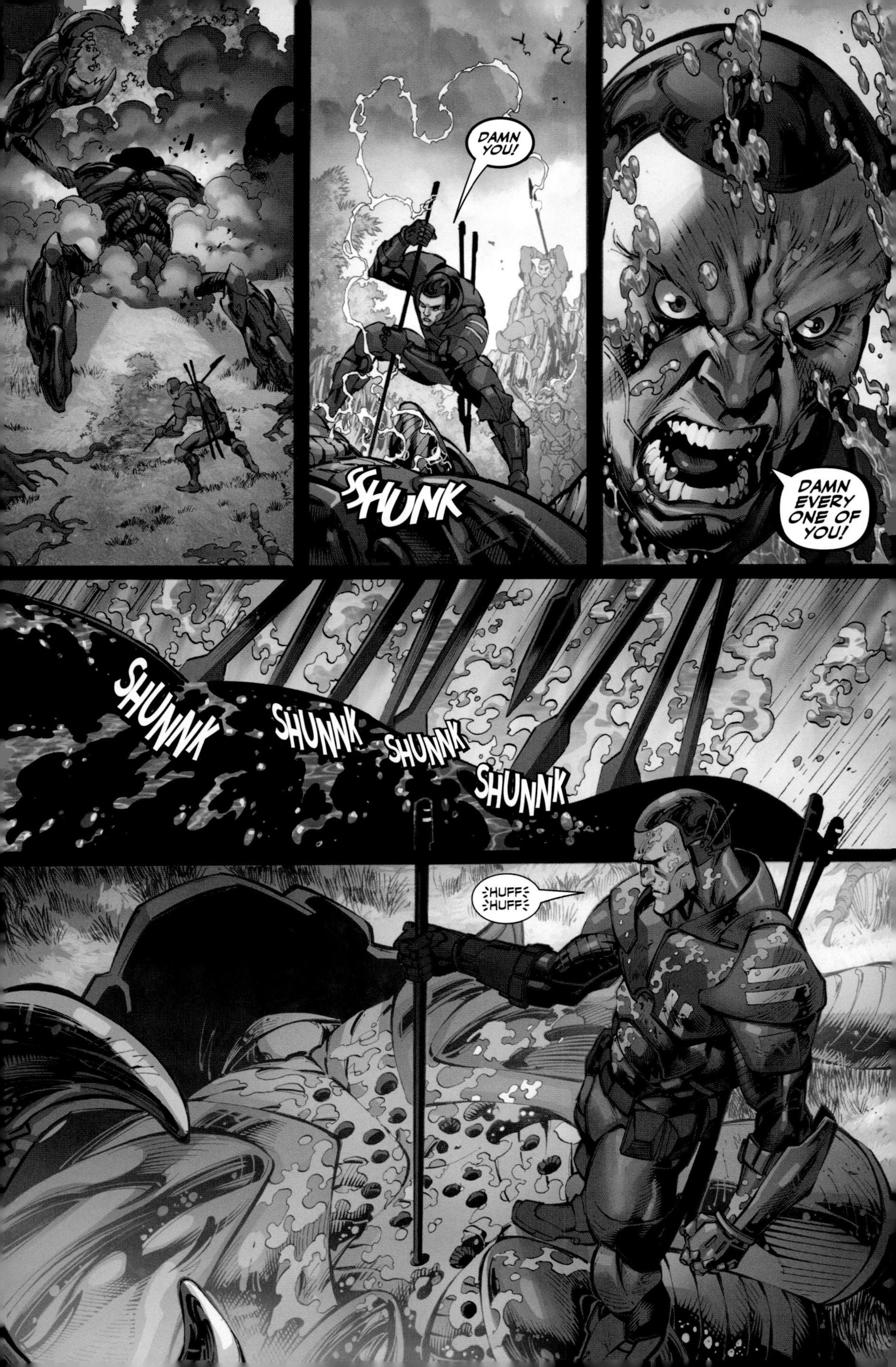
DAMN YOU!
SSHUNK
DAMN EVERY ONE OF YOU!
SHUNNK
SHUNNK
SHUNNK
SHUNNK
HUFF HUFF

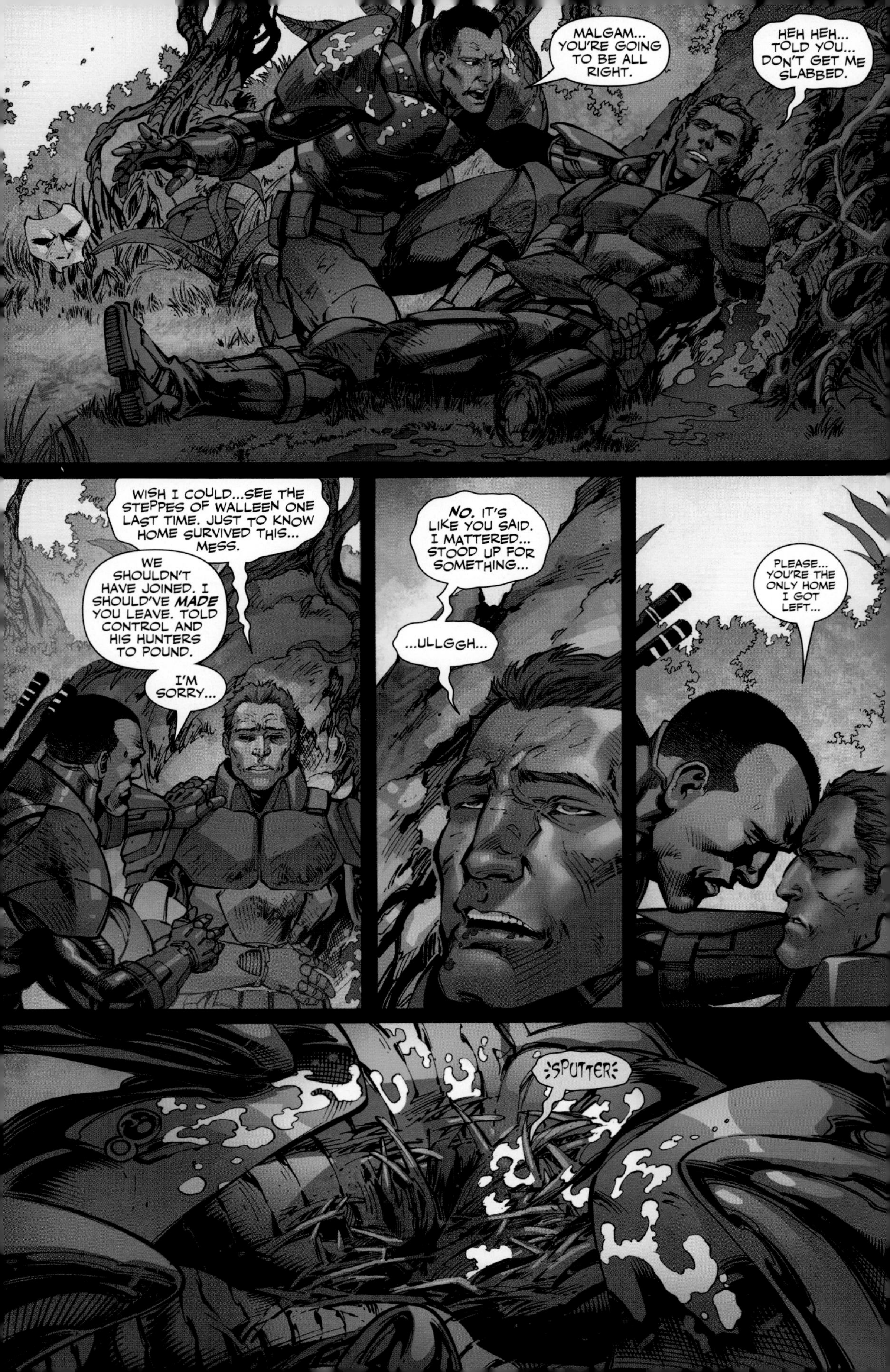
MALGAM... YOU'RE GOING TO BE ALL RIGHT.
HEH HEH... TOLD YOU... DON'T GET ME SLABBED.
WISH I COULD...SEE THE STEPPES OF WALLEEN ONE LAST TIME. JUST TO KNOW HOME SURVIVED THIS... MESS.
WE SHOULDN'T HAVE JOINED. I SHOULD'VE MADE YOU LEAVE. TOLD CONTROL AND HIS HUNTERS TO POUND.
I'M SORRY...
NO. IT'S LIKE YOU SAID. I MATTERED... STOOD UP FOR SOMETHING...
...ULLGGH...
PLEASE... YOU'RE THE ONLY HOME I GOT LEFT...
SPUTTER

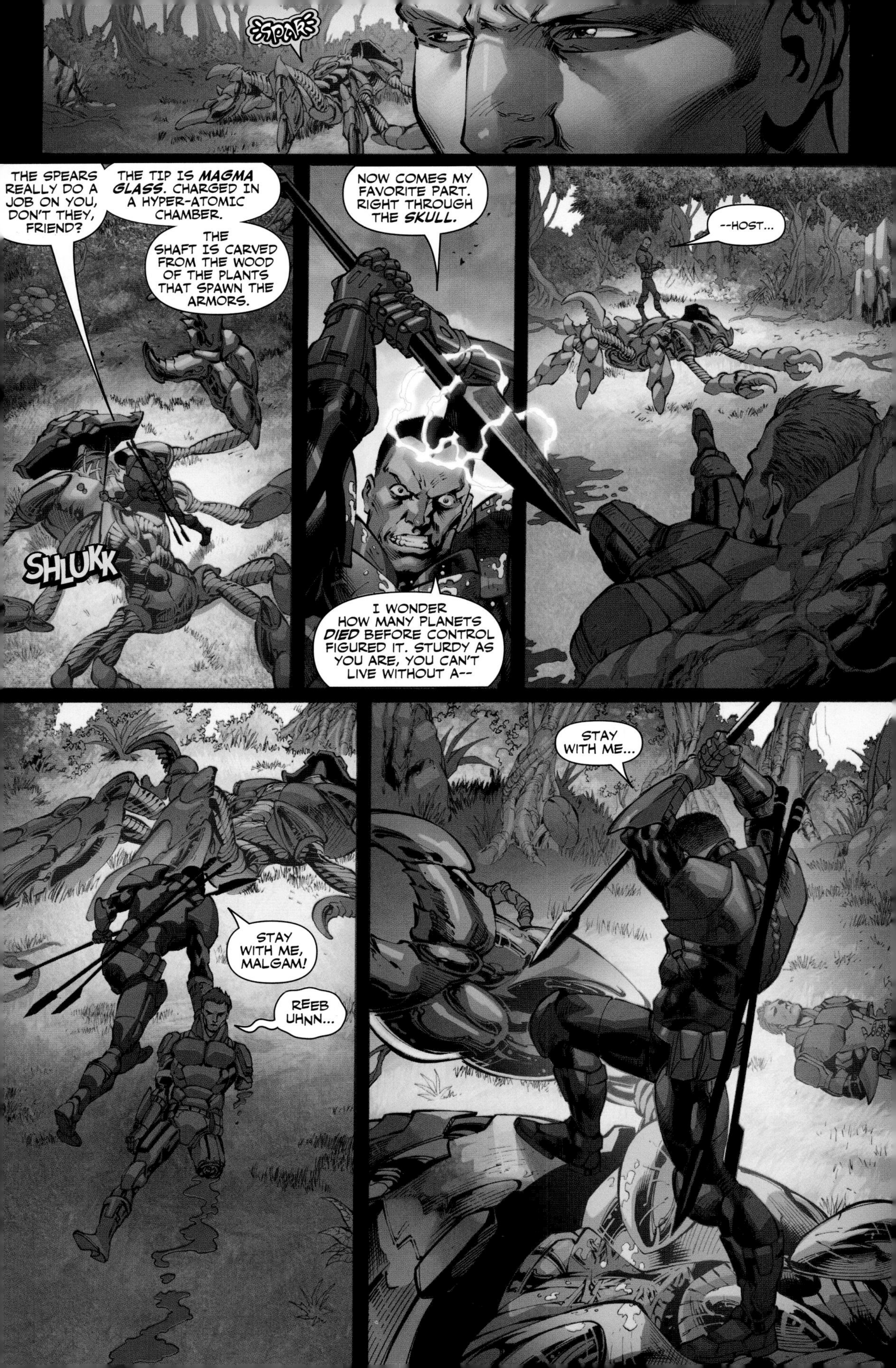
SPAK
THE SPEARS REALLY DO A JOB ON YOU, DON'T THEY, FRIEND?
THE TIP IS MAGMA GLASS. CHARGED IN A HYPER-ATOMIC CHAMBER.
THE SHAFT IS CARVED FROM THE WOOD OF THE PLANTS THAT SPAWN THE ARMORS.
SHLUKK
NOW COMES MY FAVORITE PART. RIGHT THROUGH THE SKULL.
I WONDER HOW MANY PLANETS DIED BEFORE CONTROL FIGURED IT. STURDY AS YOU ARE, YOU CAN'T LIVE WITHOUT A--
--HOST...
STAY WITH ME, MALGAM!
REEB UHNN...
STAY WITH ME...

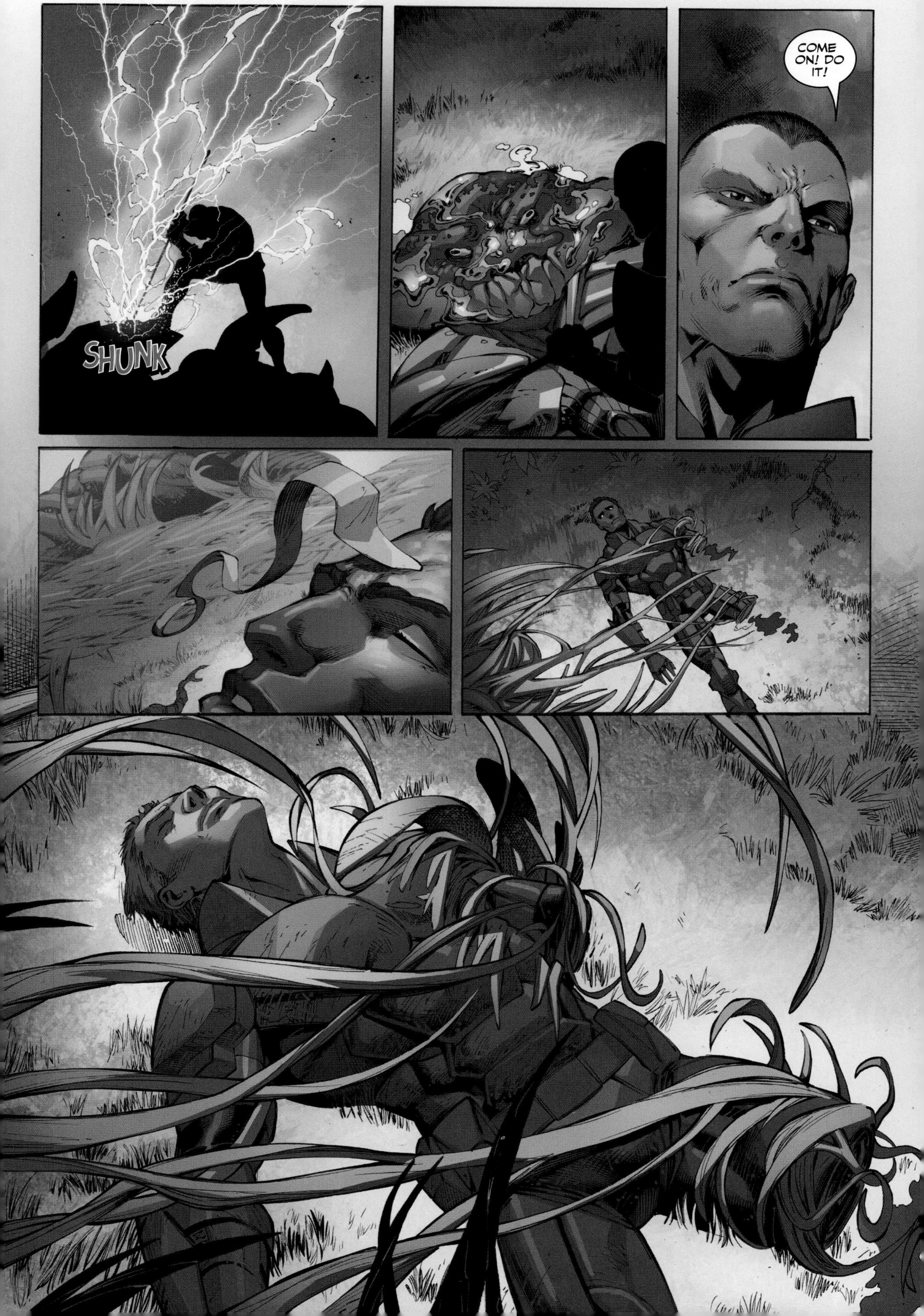
SHUNK
COME ON! DO IT!

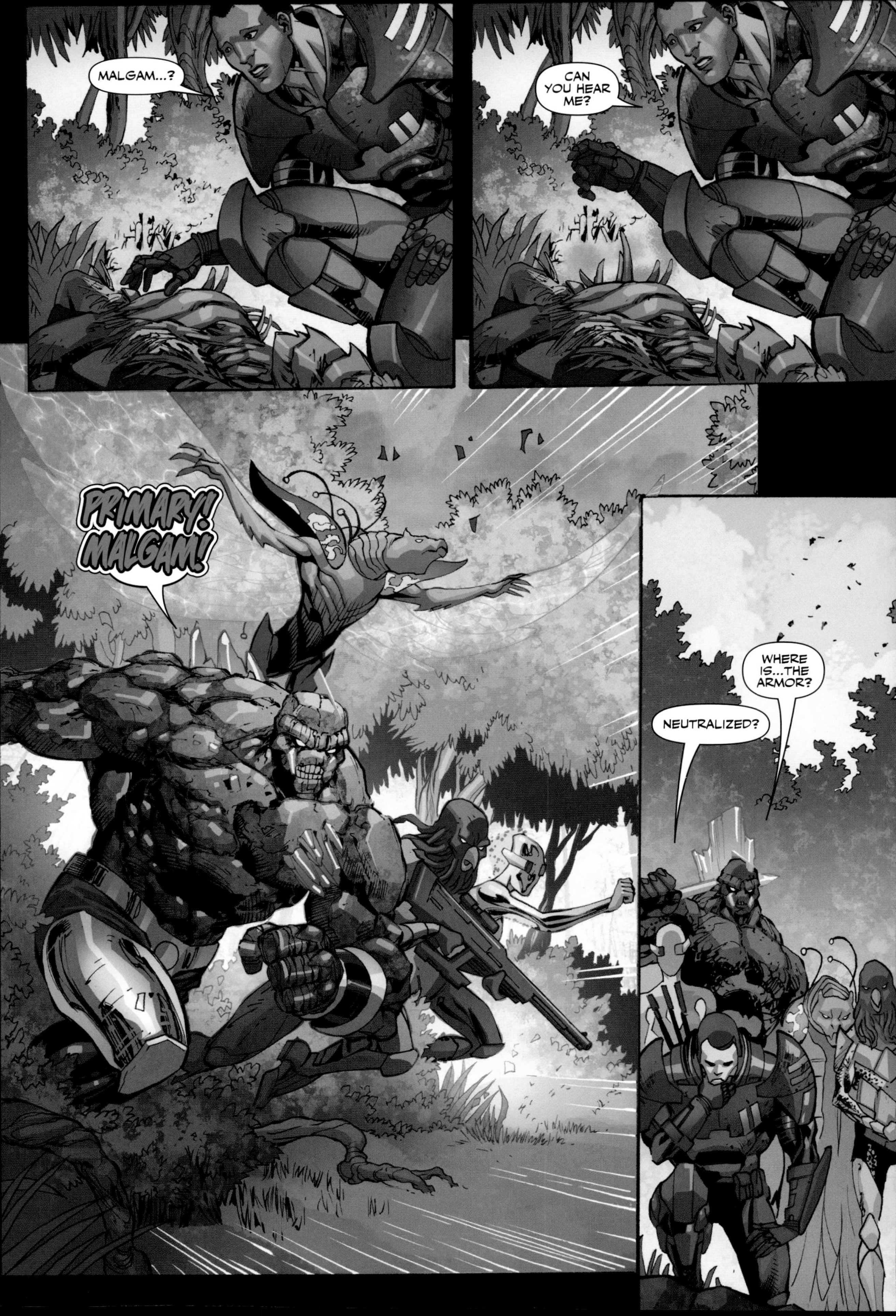
MALGAM...?
CAN YOU HEAR ME?
PRIMARY! MALGAM!
WHERE IS...THE ARMOR?
NEUTRALIZED?

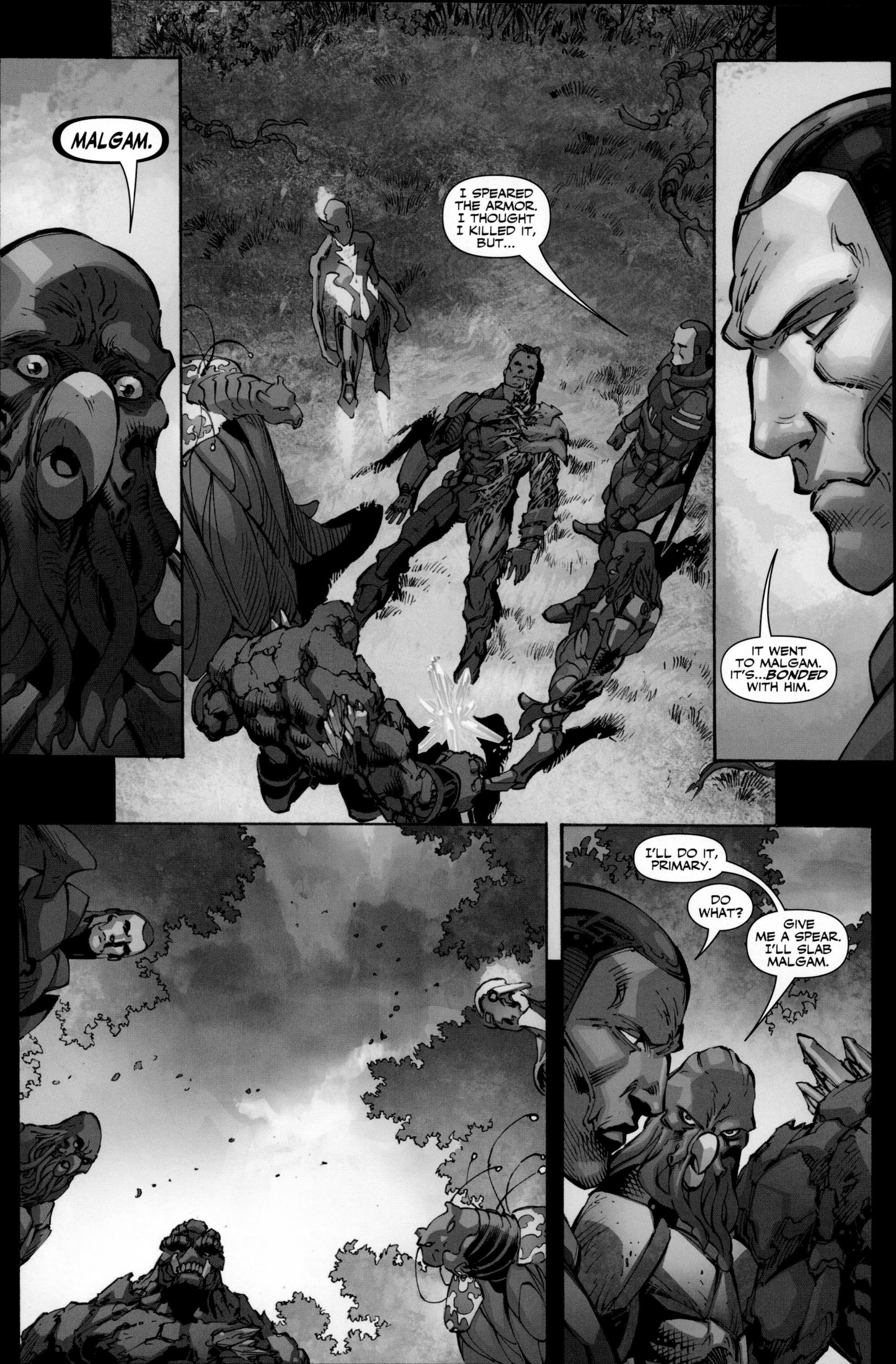
MALGAM.
I SPEARED THE ARMOR. I THOUGHT I KILLED IT, BUT...
IT WENT TO MALGAM. IT'S...BONDED WITH HIM.
I'LL DO IT, PRIMARY.
DO WHAT?
GIVE ME A SPEAR. I'LL SLAB MALGAM.

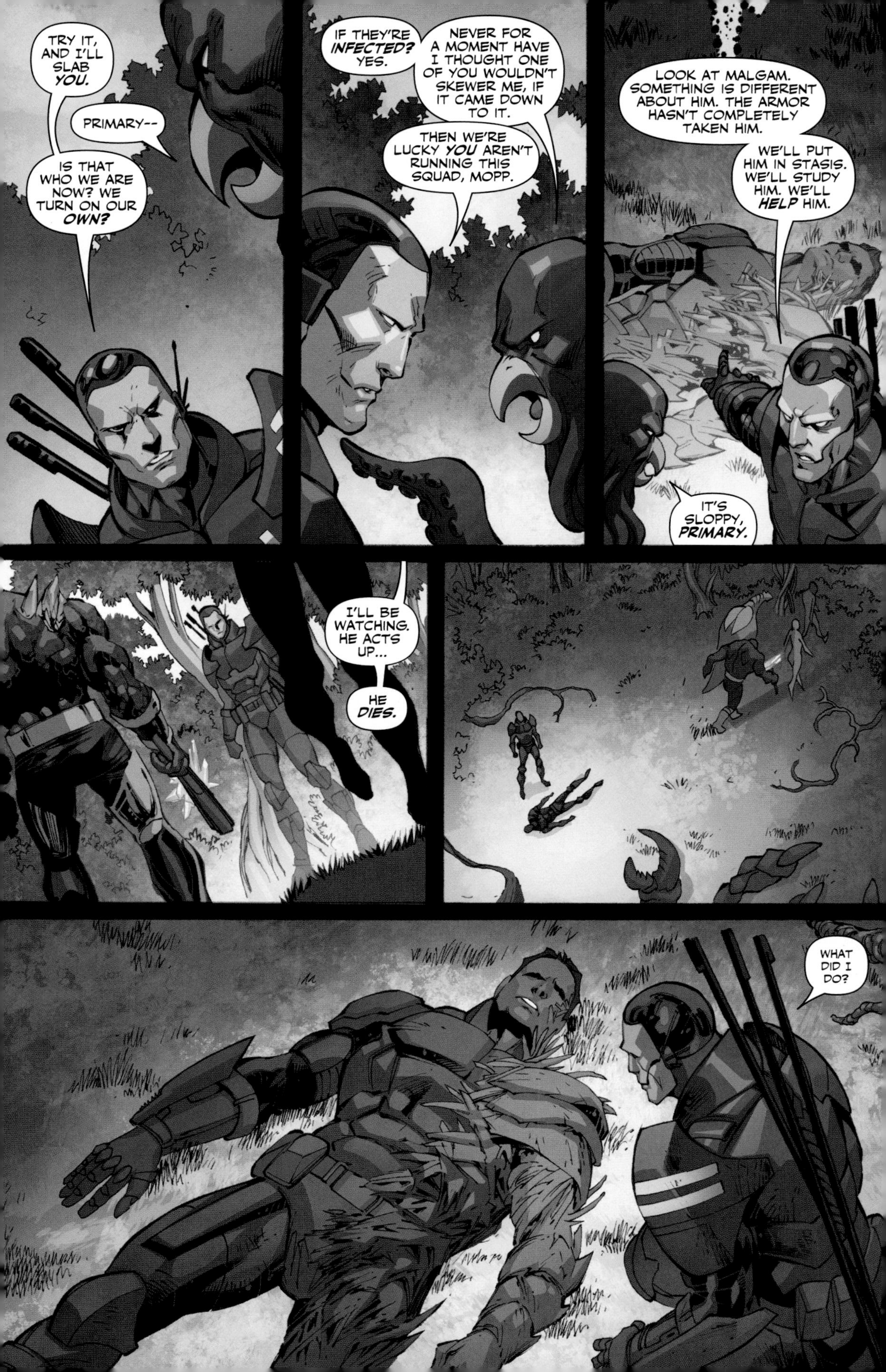
TRY IT, AND I'LL SLAB *YOU.*
PRIMARY--
IS THAT WHO WE ARE NOW? WE TURN ON OUR *OWN?*
IF THEY'RE *INFECTED?* YES.
NEVER FOR A MOMENT HAVE I THOUGHT ONE OF YOU WOULDN'T SKEWER ME, IF IT CAME DOWN TO IT.
THEN WE'RE LUCKY *YOU* AREN'T RUNNING THIS SQUAD, MOPP.
LOOK AT MALGAM. SOMETHING IS DIFFERENT ABOUT HIM. THE ARMOR HASN'T COMPLETELY TAKEN HIM.
WE'LL PUT HIM IN STASIS. WE'LL STUDY HIM. WE'LL *HELP* HIM.
IT'S SLOPPY, *PRIMARY.*
I'LL BE WATCHING. HE ACTS UP...
HE *DIES.*
WHAT DID I DO?

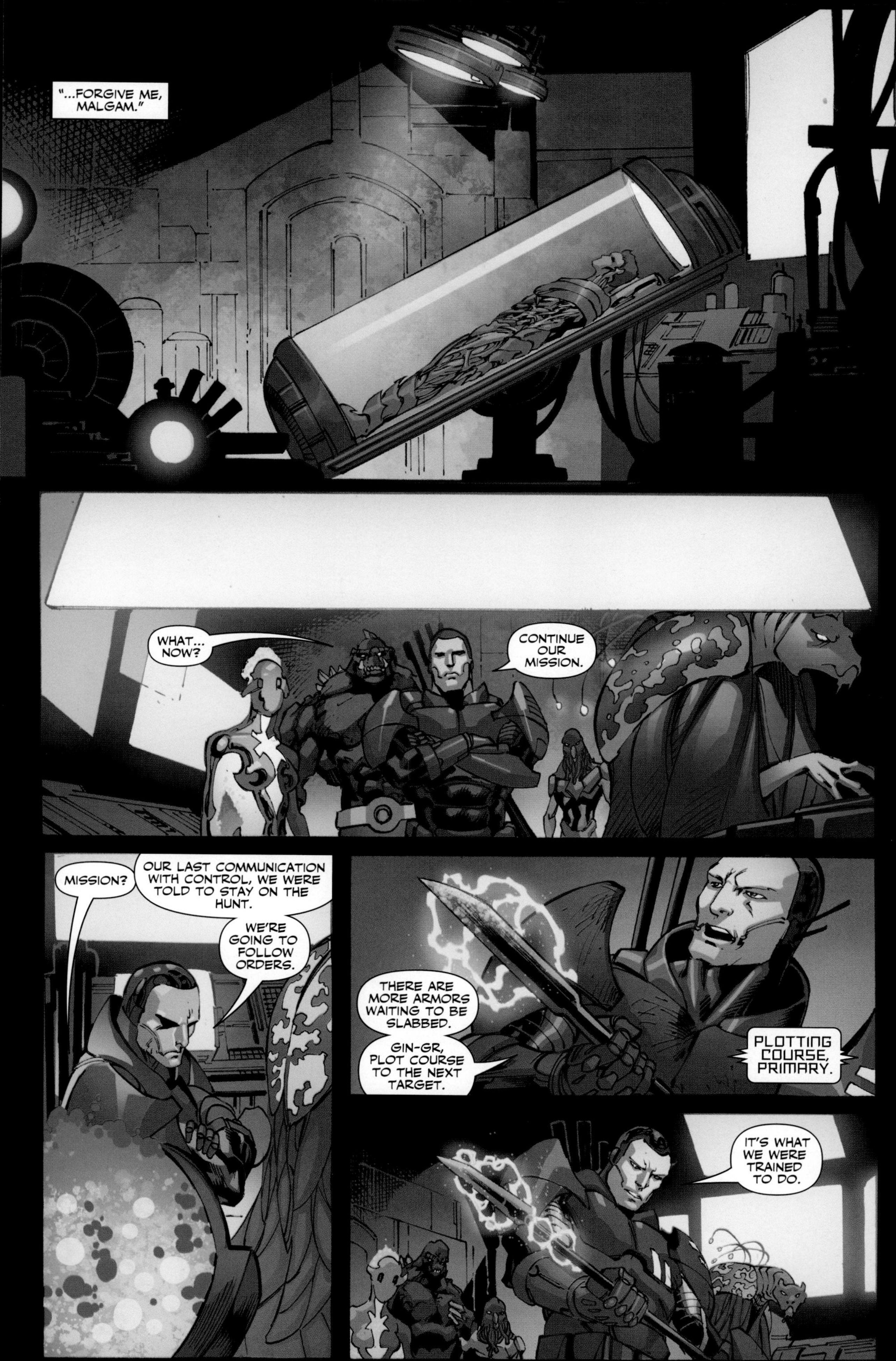
"...FORGIVE ME, MALGAM."
WHAT... NOW?
CONTINUE OUR MISSION.
MISSION?
OUR LAST COMMUNICATION WITH CONTROL, WE WERE TOLD TO STAY ON THE HUNT.
WE'RE GOING TO FOLLOW ORDERS.
THERE ARE MORE ARMORS WAITING TO BE SLABBED.
GIN-GR, PLOT COURSE TO THE NEXT TARGET.
PLOTTING COURSE, PRIMARY.
IT'S WHAT WE WERE TRAINED TO DO.

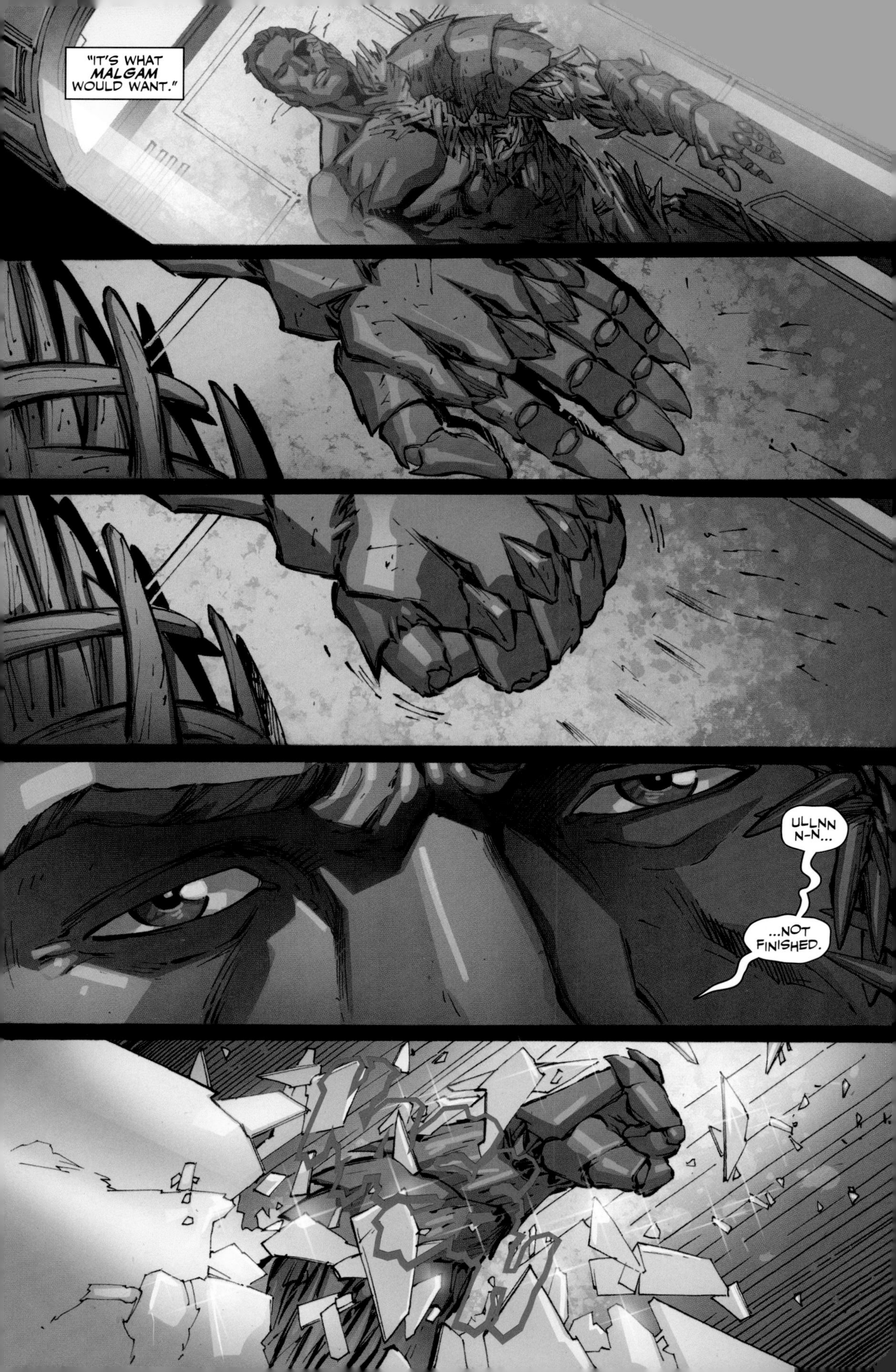
"IT'S WHAT *MALGAM* WOULD WANT."
ULLNN N-N...
...NOT FINISHED.

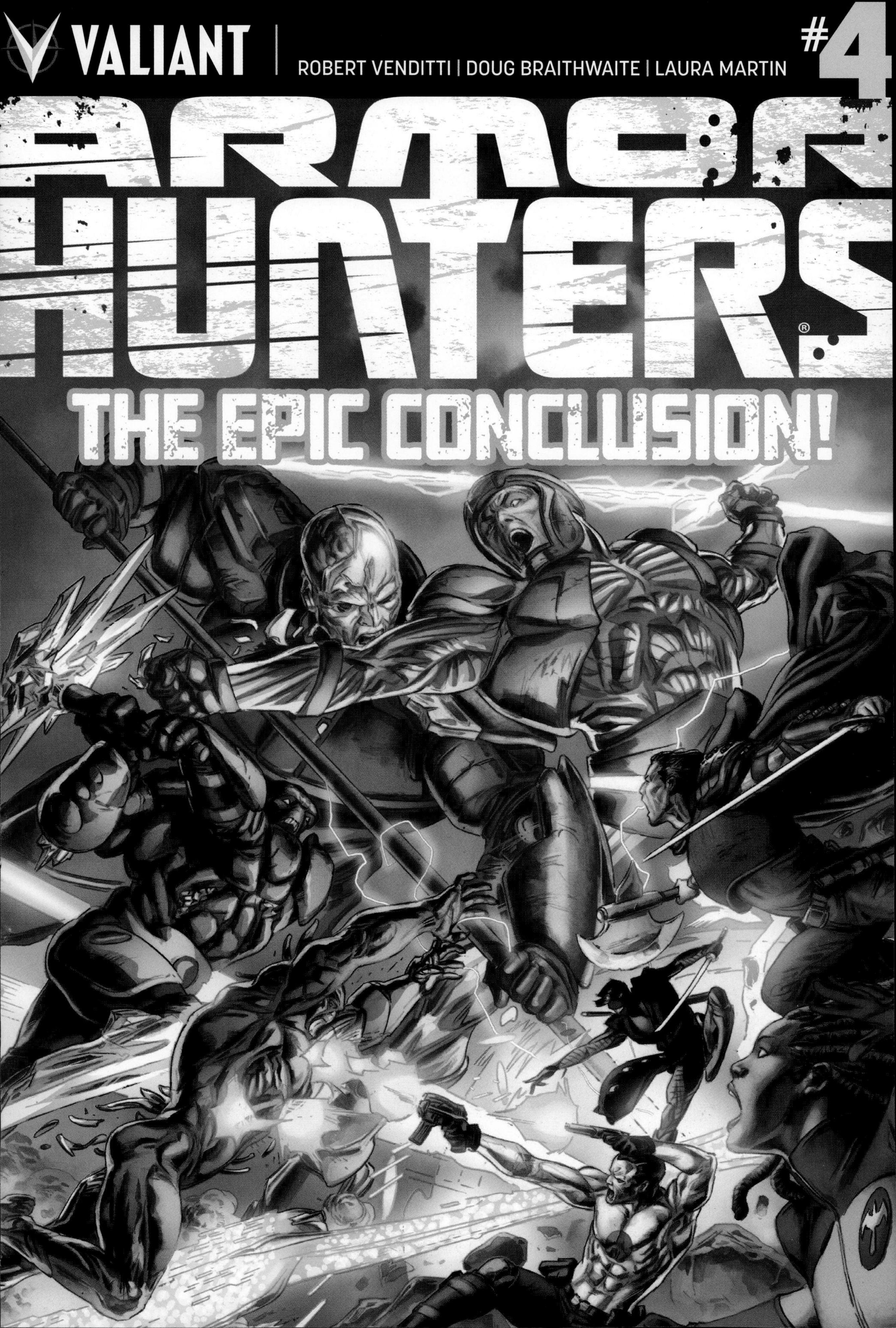
VALIANT
ROBERT VENDITTI | DOUG BRAITHWAITE | LAURA MARTIN
#4
ARMOR HUNTERS®
THE EPIC CONCLUSION!

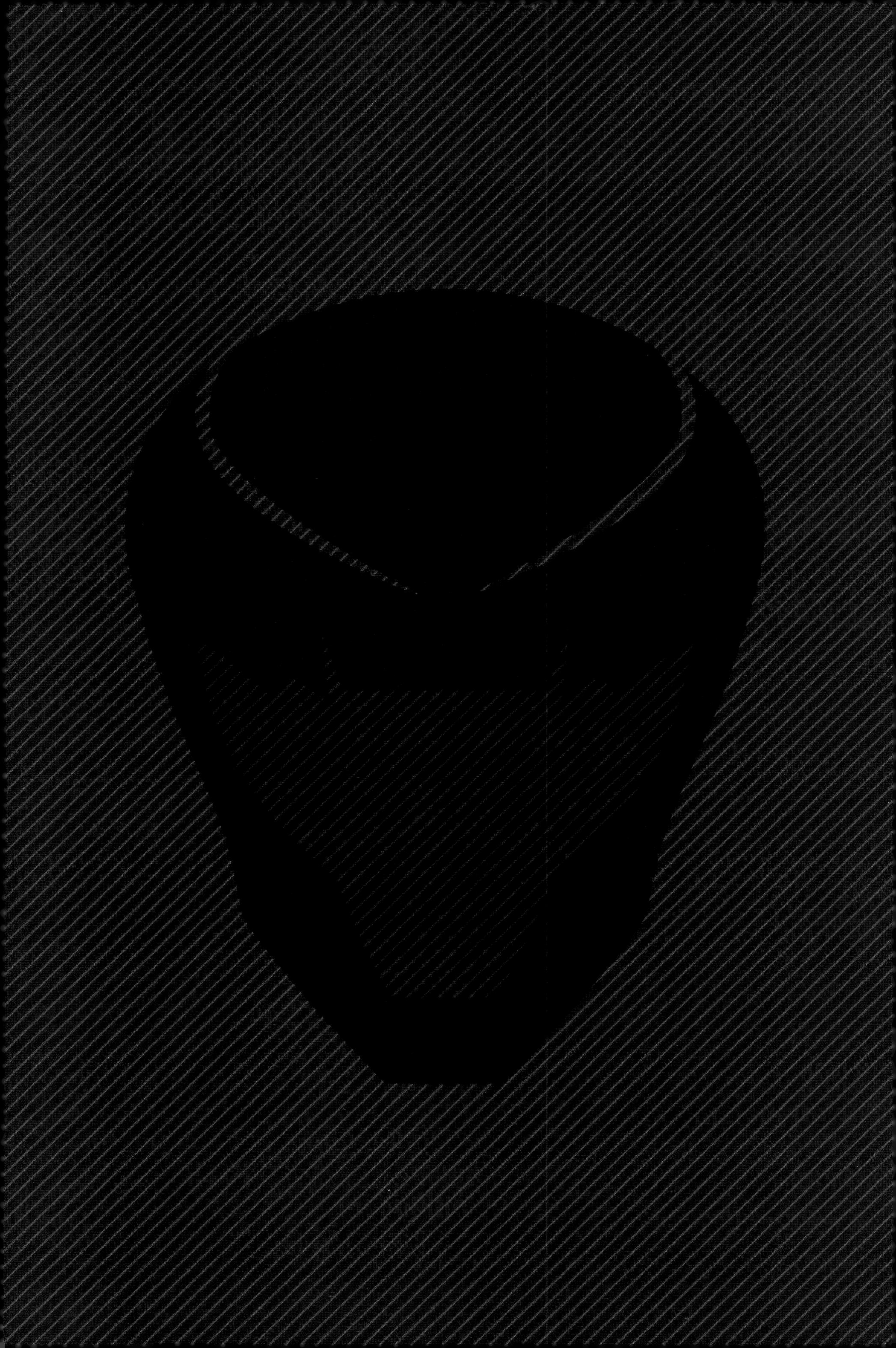

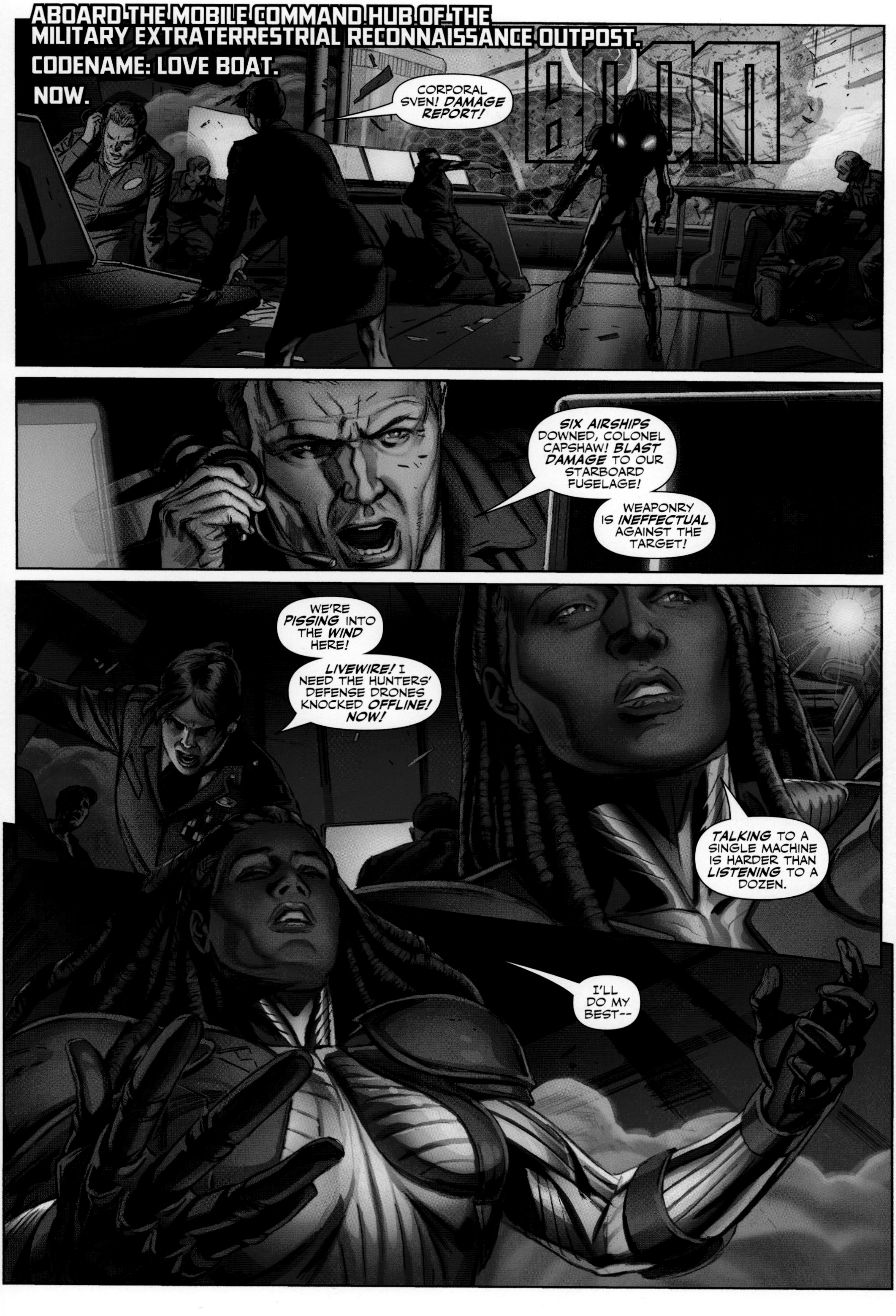
ABOARD THE MOBILE COMMAND HUB OF THE MILITARY EXTRATERRESTRIAL RECONNAISSANCE OUTPOST.
CODENAME: LOVE BOAT.
NOW.
CORPORAL SVEN! DAMAGE REPORT!
BOOM
SIX AIRSHIPS DOWNED, COLONEL CAPSHAW! BLAST DAMAGE TO OUR STARBOARD FUSELAGE!
WEAPONRY IS INEFFECTUAL AGAINST THE TARGET!
WE'RE PISSING INTO THE WIND HERE!
LIVEWIRE! I NEED THE HUNTERS' DEFENSE DRONES KNOCKED OFFLINE! NOW!
TALKING TO A SINGLE MACHINE IS HARDER THAN LISTENING TO A DOZEN.
I'LL DO MY BEST--

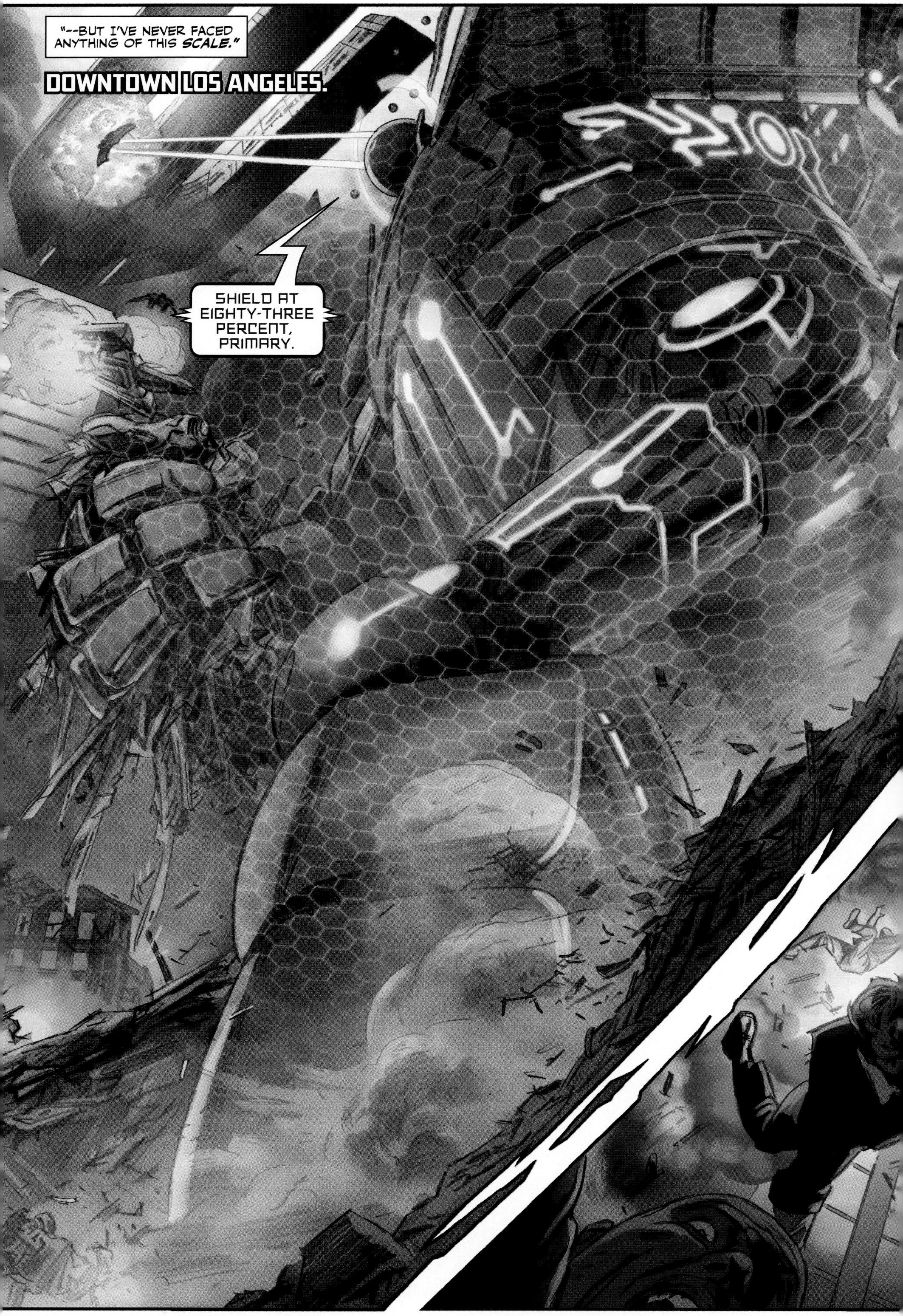
"--BUT I'VE NEVER FACED ANYTHING OF THIS SCALE."
DOWNTOWN LOS ANGELES.
SHIELD AT EIGHTY-THREE PERCENT, PRIMARY.

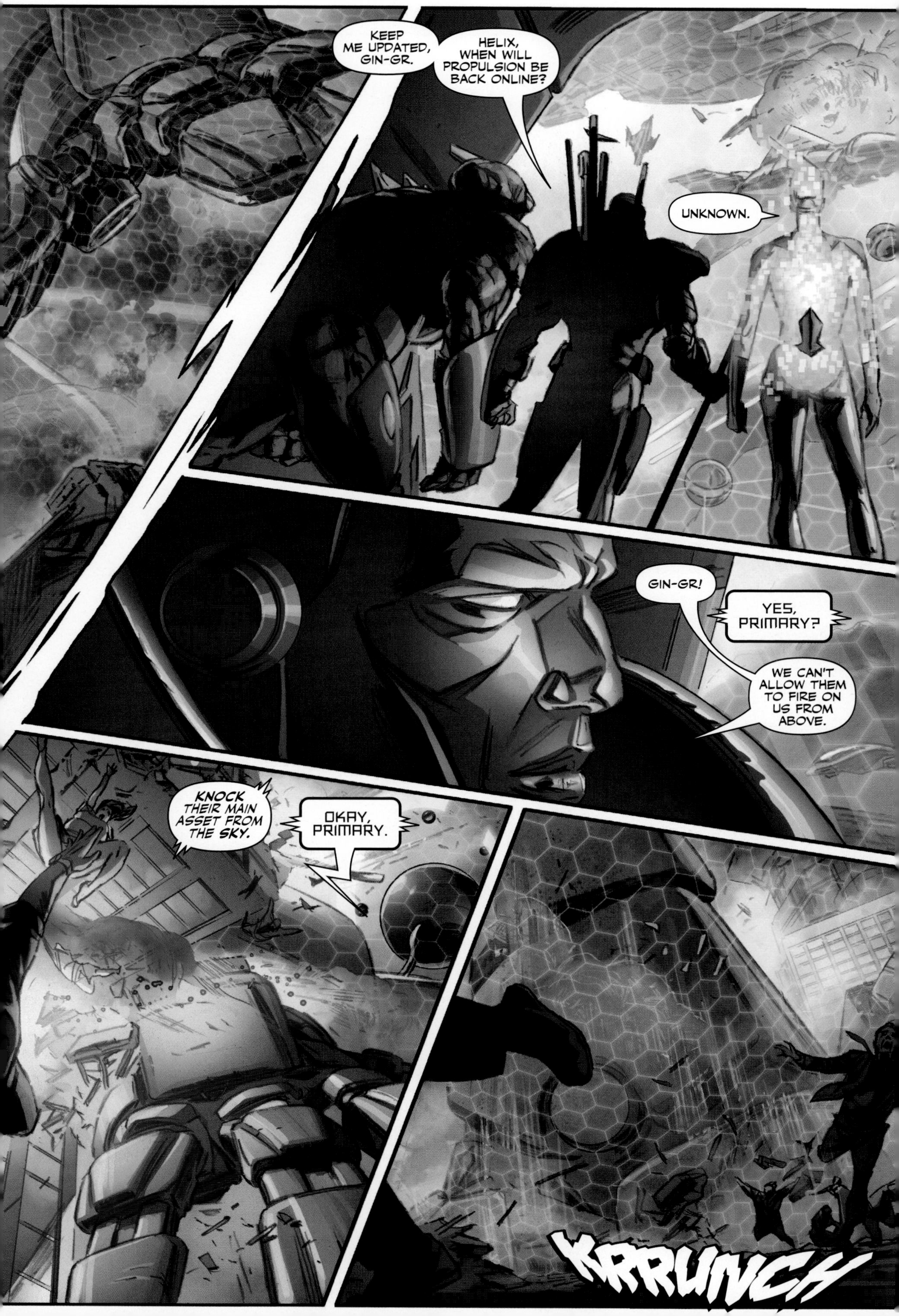
KEEP ME UPDATED, GIN-GR.
HELIX, WHEN WILL PROPULSION BE BACK ONLINE?
UNKNOWN.
GIN-GR!
YES, PRIMARY?
WE CAN'T ALLOW THEM TO FIRE ON US FROM ABOVE.
KNOCK THEIR MAIN ASSET FROM THE SKY.
OKAY, PRIMARY.
KRRUNCH

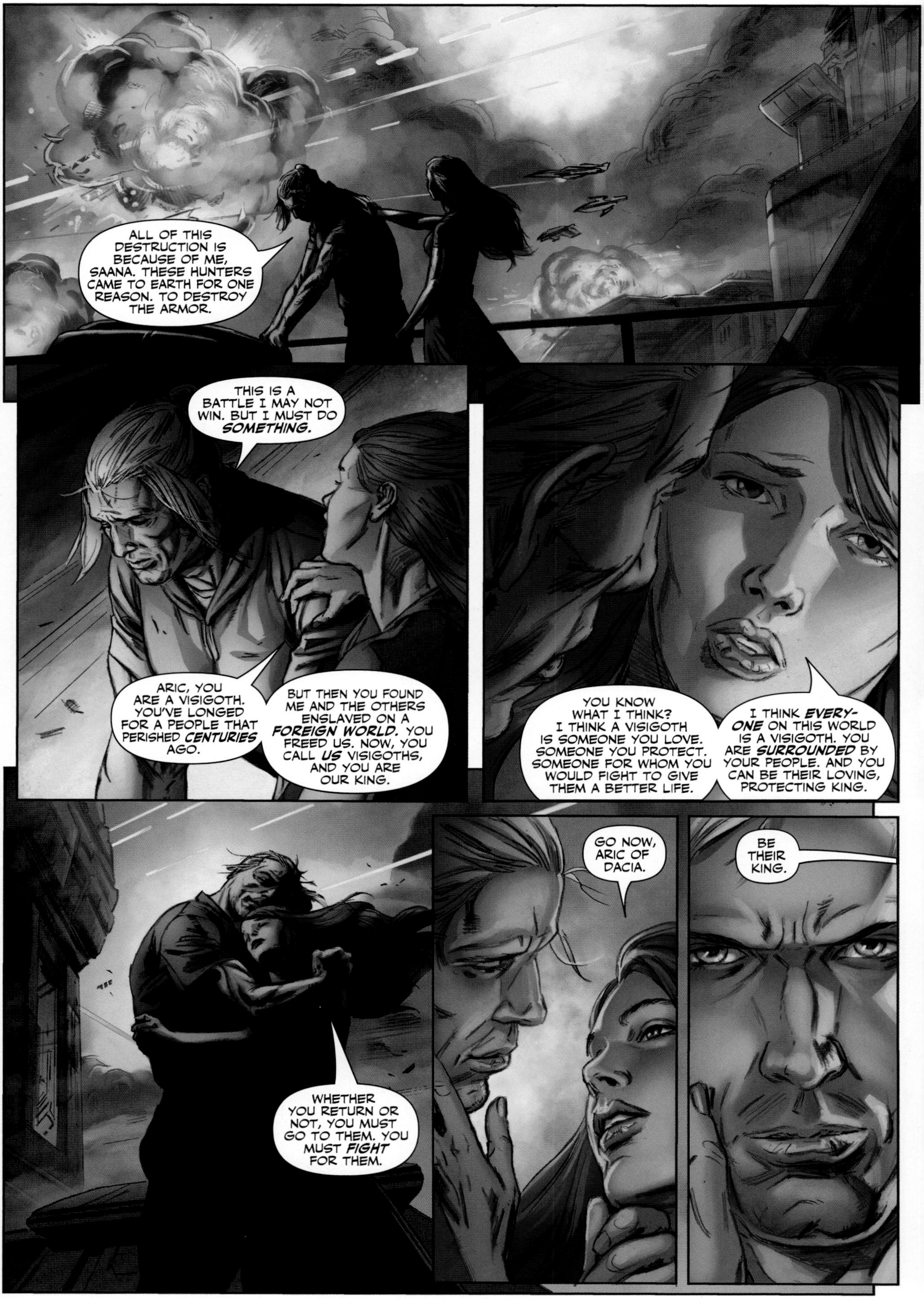
ALL OF THIS DESTRUCTION IS BECAUSE OF ME, SAANA. THESE HUNTERS CAME TO EARTH FOR ONE REASON. TO DESTROY THE ARMOR.
THIS IS A BATTLE I MAY NOT WIN. BUT I MUST DO *SOMETHING.*
ARIC, YOU ARE A VISIGOTH. YOU'VE LONGED FOR A PEOPLE THAT PERISHED *CENTURIES* AGO.
BUT THEN YOU FOUND ME AND THE OTHERS ENSLAVED ON A *FOREIGN WORLD.* YOU FREED US. NOW, YOU CALL *US* VISIGOTHS, AND YOU ARE OUR KING.
YOU KNOW WHAT I THINK? I THINK A VISIGOTH IS SOMEONE YOU LOVE. SOMEONE YOU PROTECT. SOMEONE FOR WHOM YOU WOULD FIGHT TO GIVE THEM A BETTER LIFE.
I THINK *EVERY-ONE* ON THIS WORLD IS A VISIGOTH. YOU ARE *SURROUNDED* BY YOUR PEOPLE. AND YOU CAN BE THEIR LOVING, PROTECTING KING.
WHETHER YOU RETURN OR NOT, YOU MUST GO TO THEM. YOU MUST *FIGHT* FOR THEM.
GO NOW, ARIC OF DACIA.
BE THEIR KING.

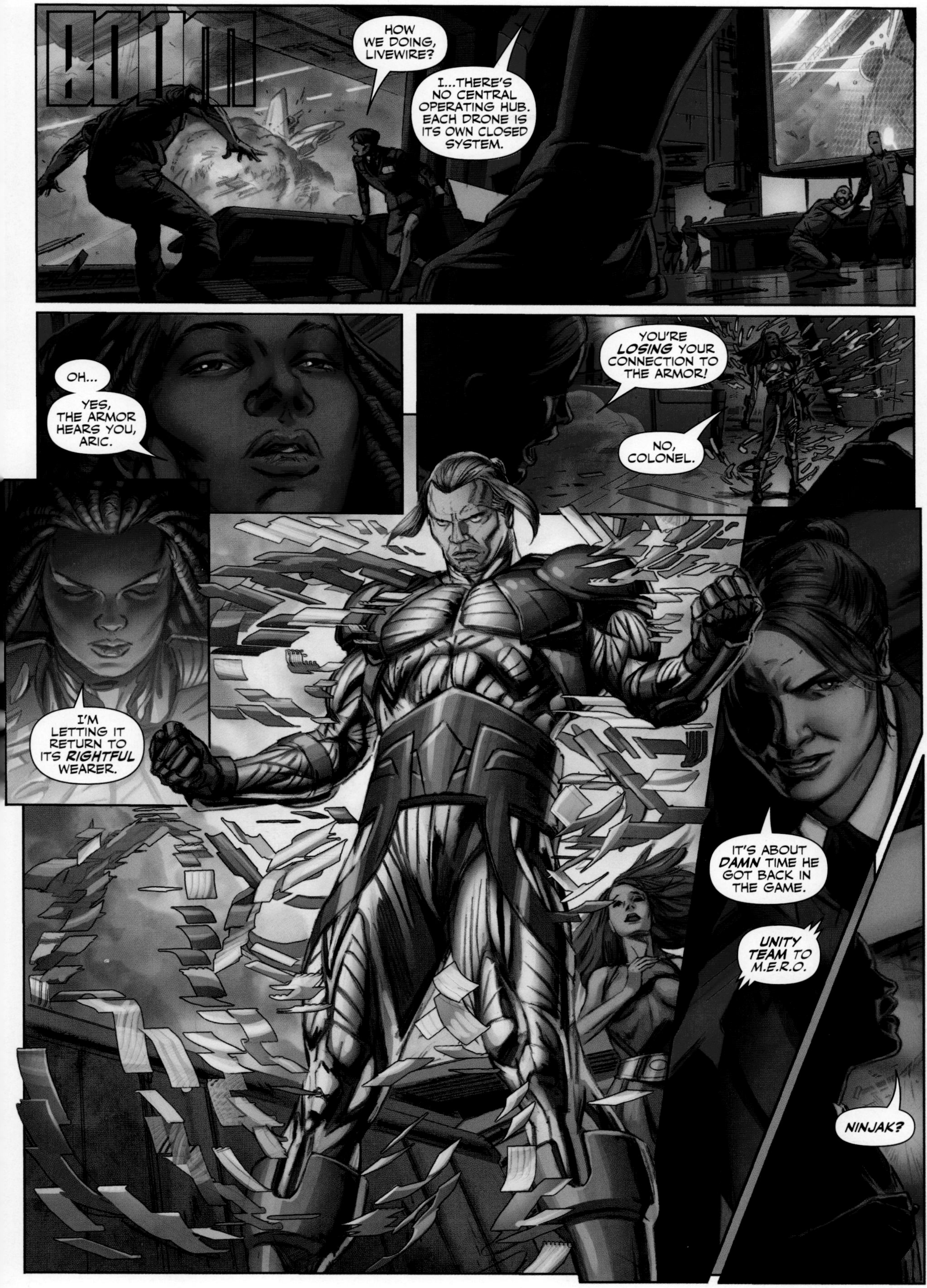

HOW WE DOING, LIVEWIRE?
I...THERE'S NO CENTRAL OPERATING HUB. EACH DRONE IS ITS OWN CLOSED SYSTEM.
OH...
YES, THE ARMOR HEARS YOU, ARIC.
YOU'RE *LOSING* YOUR CONNECTION TO THE ARMOR!
NO, COLONEL.
I'M LETTING IT RETURN TO ITS *RIGHTFUL* WEARER.
IT'S ABOUT *DAMN* TIME HE GOT BACK IN THE GAME.
UNITY TEAM TO M.E.R.O.
NINJAK?

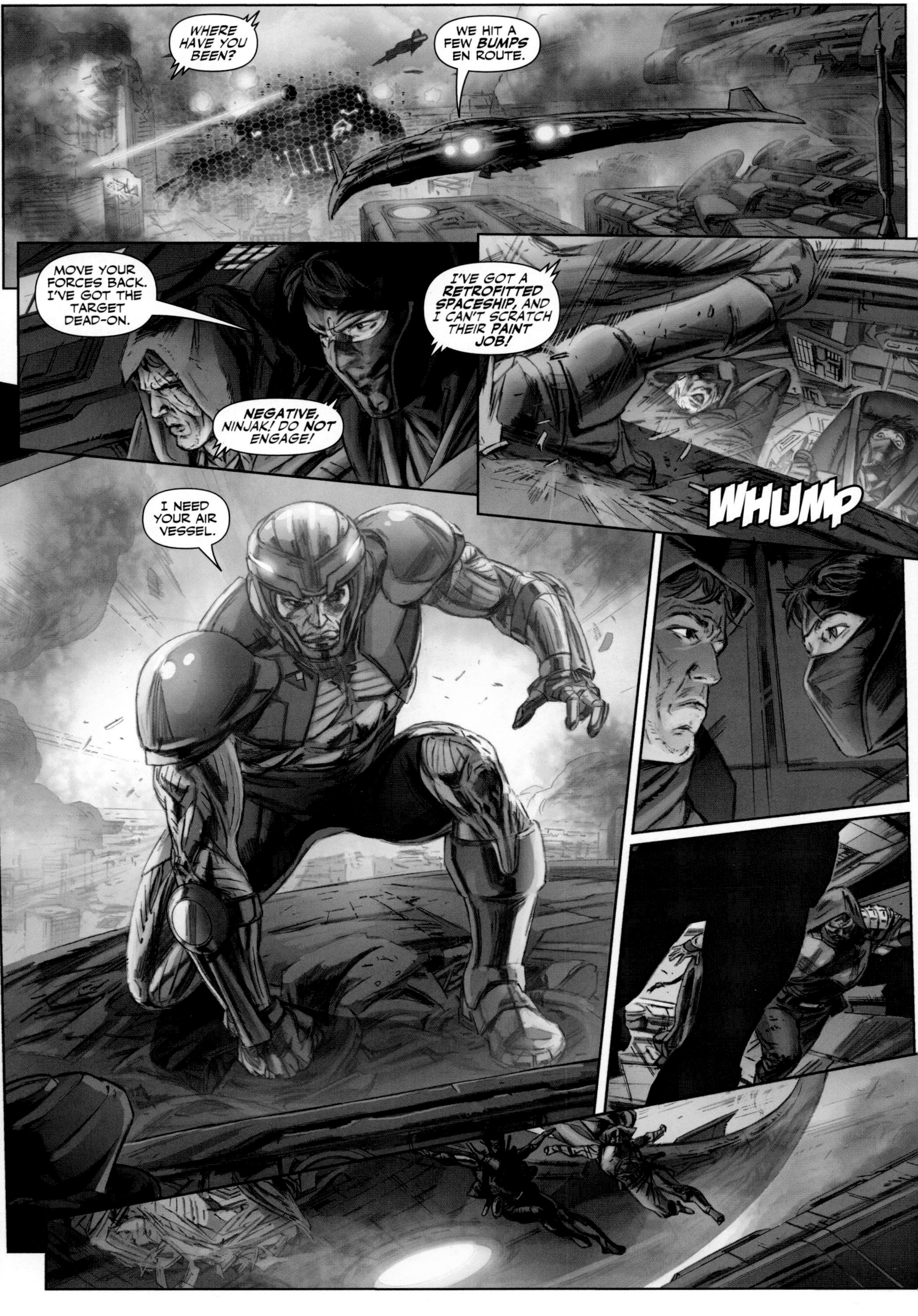
WHERE HAVE YOU BEEN?
WE HIT A FEW BUMPS EN ROUTE.
MOVE YOUR FORCES BACK. I'VE GOT THE TARGET DEAD-ON.
NEGATIVE, NINJAK! DO NOT ENGAGE!
I'VE GOT A RETROFITTED SPACESHIP, AND I CAN'T SCRATCH THEIR PAINT JOB!
WHUMP
I NEED YOUR AIR VESSEL.

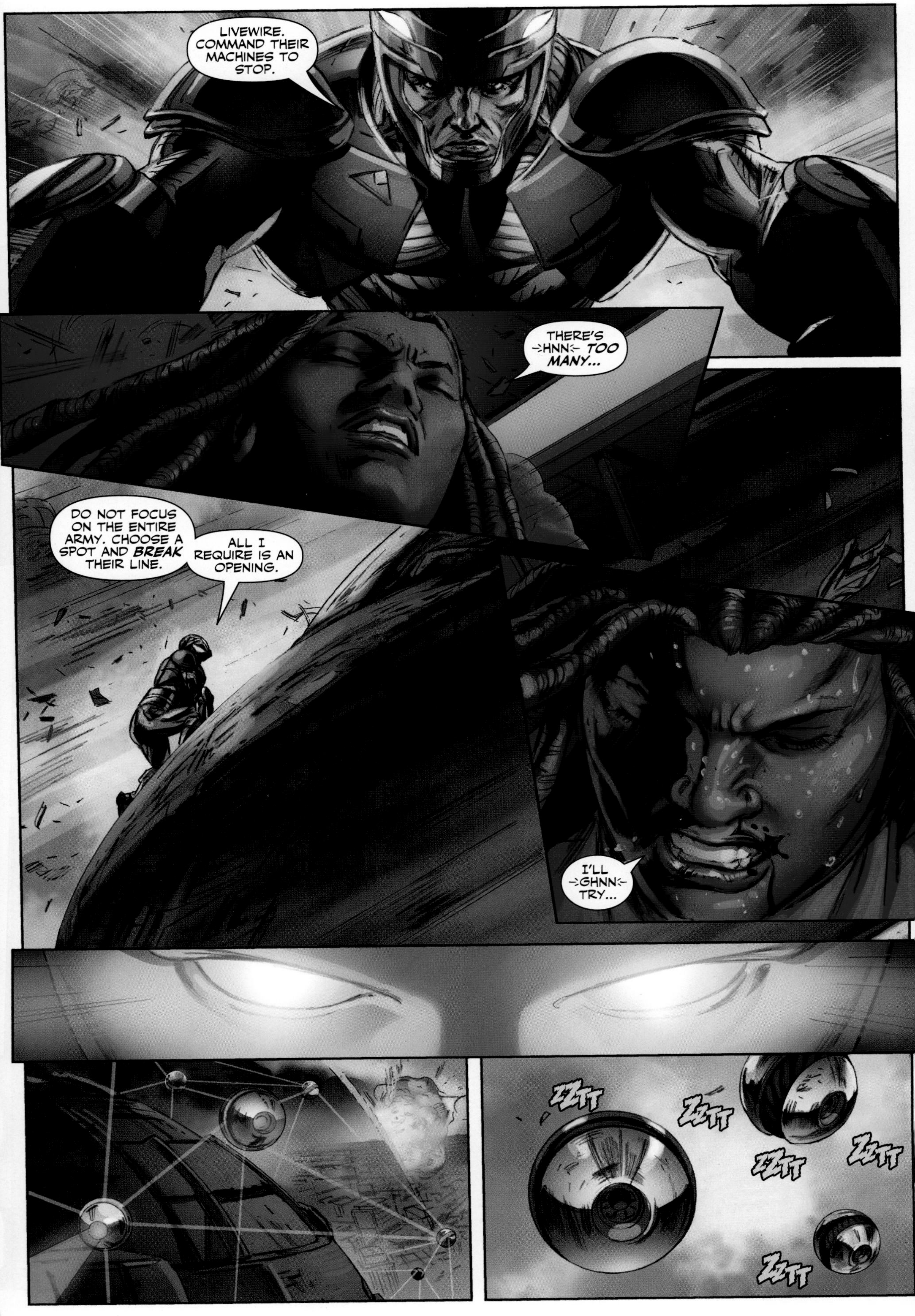
LIVEWIRE. COMMAND THEIR MACHINES TO STOP.
THERE'S -HNN- TOO MANY...
DO NOT FOCUS ON THE ENTIRE ARMY. CHOOSE A SPOT AND BREAK THEIR LINE.
ALL I REQUIRE IS AN OPENING.
I'LL -GHNN- TRY...
ZZTT
ZZTT
ZZTT
ZZTT
ZZTT

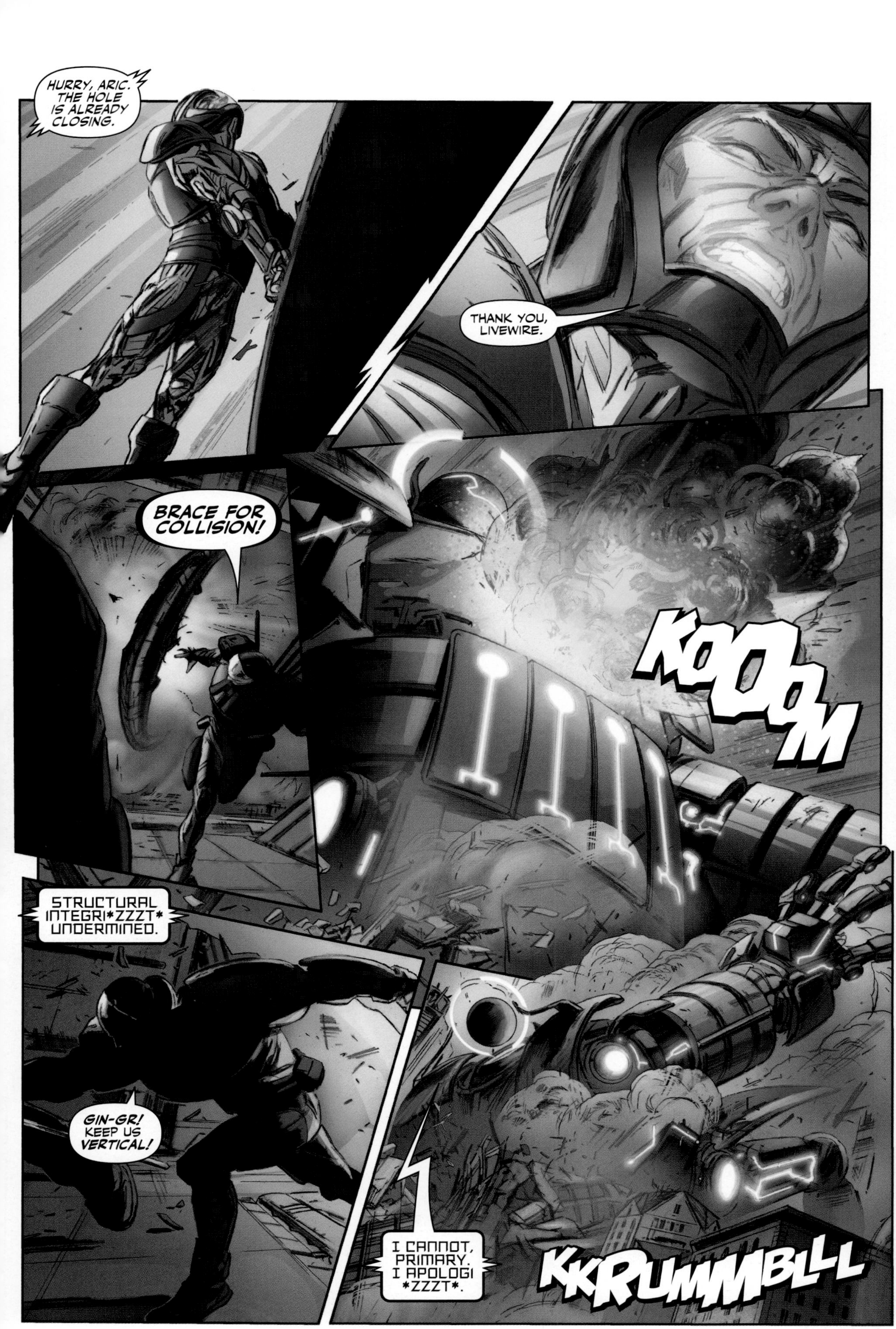
HURRY, ARIC. THE HOLE IS ALREADY CLOSING.
THANK YOU, LIVEWIRE.
BRACE FOR COLLISION!
KOOOOM
STRUCTURAL INTEGRI*ZZZT* UNDERMINED.
GIN-GR! KEEP US VERTICAL!
I CANNOT, PRIMARY. I APOLOGI *ZZZT*.
KKRUMMBLLL

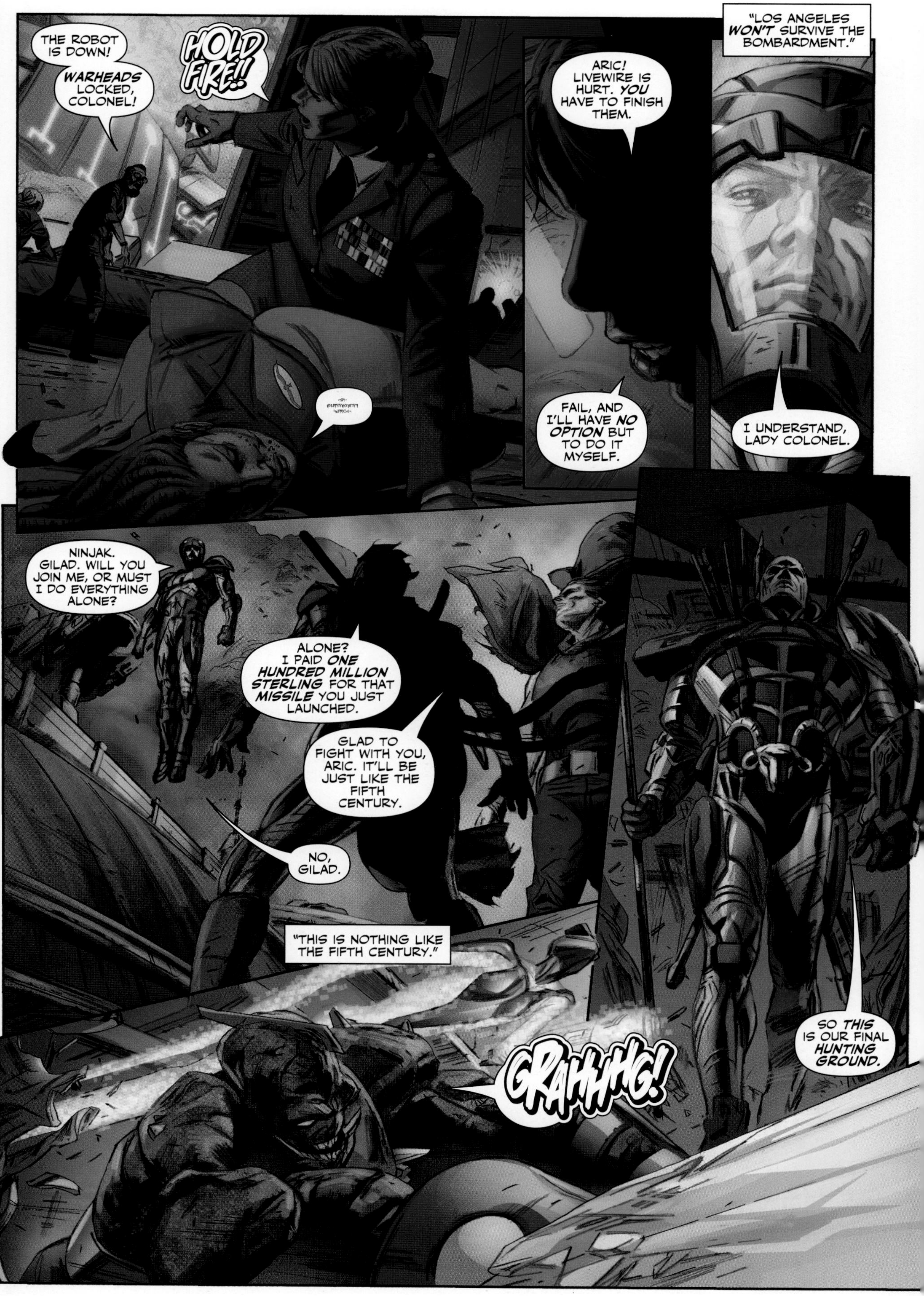

THE ROBOT IS DOWN!
WARHEADS LOCKED, COLONEL!
HOLD FIRE!!
ARIC! LIVEWIRE IS HURT. YOU HAVE TO FINISH THEM.
FAIL, AND I'LL HAVE NO OPTION BUT TO DO IT MYSELF.
"LOS ANGELES WON'T SURVIVE THE BOMBARDMENT."
I UNDERSTAND, LADY COLONEL.
NINJAK. GILAD. WILL YOU JOIN ME, OR MUST I DO EVERYTHING ALONE?
ALONE? I PAID ONE HUNDRED MILLION STERLING FOR THAT MISSILE YOU JUST LAUNCHED.
GLAD TO FIGHT WITH YOU, ARIC. IT'LL BE JUST LIKE THE FIFTH CENTURY.
NO, GILAD.
"THIS IS NOTHING LIKE THE FIFTH CENTURY."
SO THIS IS OUR FINAL HUNTING GROUND.
GRAHHHG!

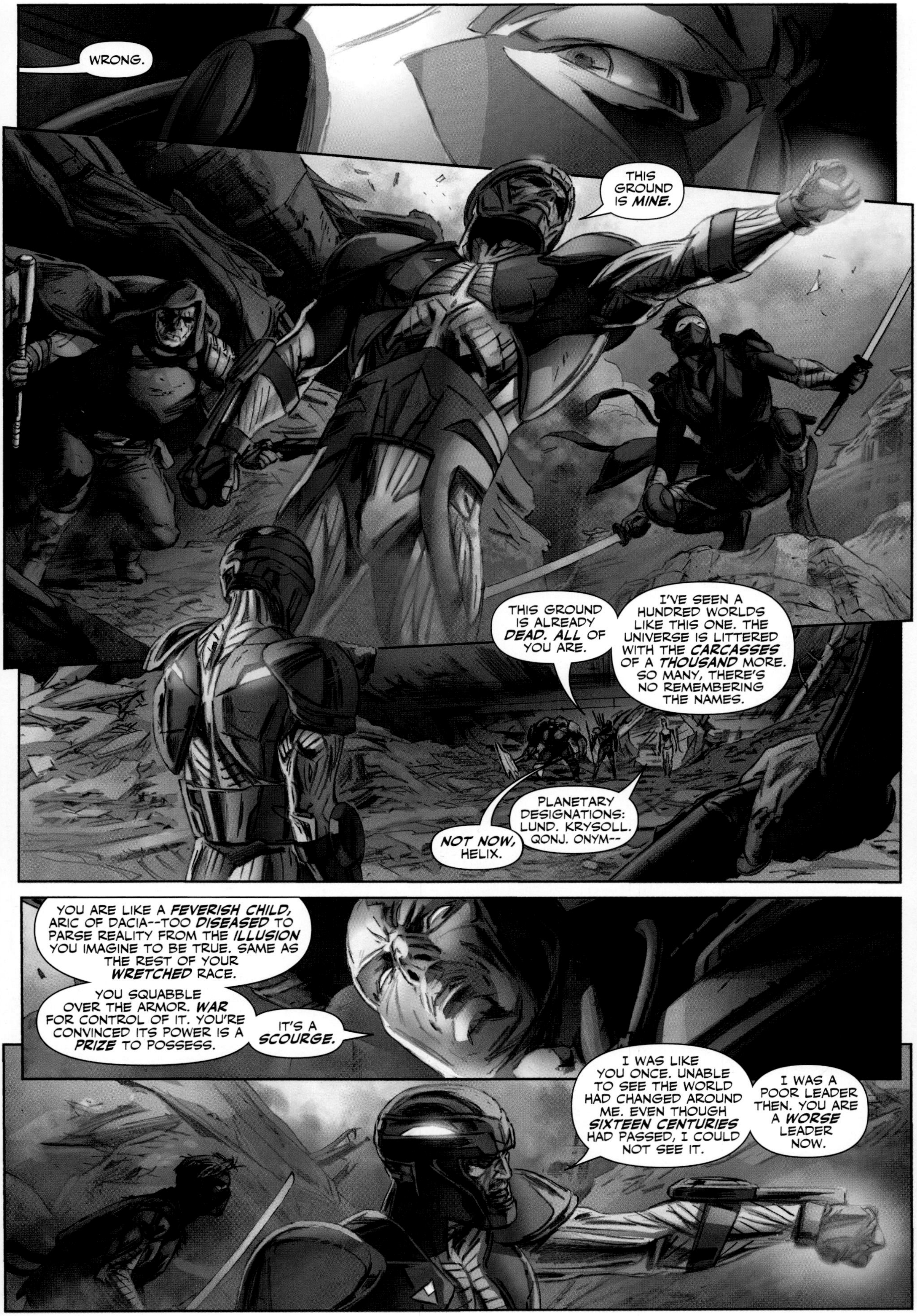

WRONG.
THIS GROUND IS *MINE.*
THIS GROUND IS ALREADY *DEAD. ALL* OF YOU ARE.
I'VE SEEN A HUNDRED WORLDS LIKE THIS ONE. THE UNIVERSE IS LITTERED WITH THE *CARCASSES* OF A *THOUSAND* MORE. SO MANY, THERE'S NO REMEMBERING THE NAMES.
PLANETARY DESIGNATIONS: LUND. KRYSOLL. QONJ. ONYM--
NOT NOW, HELIX.
YOU ARE LIKE A *FEVERISH CHILD,* ARIC OF DACIA--TOO *DISEASED* TO PARSE REALITY FROM THE *ILLUSION* YOU IMAGINE TO BE TRUE. SAME AS THE REST OF YOUR *WRETCHED* RACE.
YOU SQUABBLE OVER THE ARMOR. *WAR* FOR CONTROL OF IT. YOU'RE CONVINCED ITS POWER IS A *PRIZE* TO POSSESS.
IT'S A *SCOURGE.*
I WAS LIKE YOU ONCE. UNABLE TO SEE THE WORLD HAD CHANGED AROUND ME. EVEN THOUGH *SIXTEEN CENTURIES* HAD PASSED, I COULD NOT SEE IT.
I WAS A POOR LEADER THEN. YOU ARE A *WORSE* LEADER NOW.

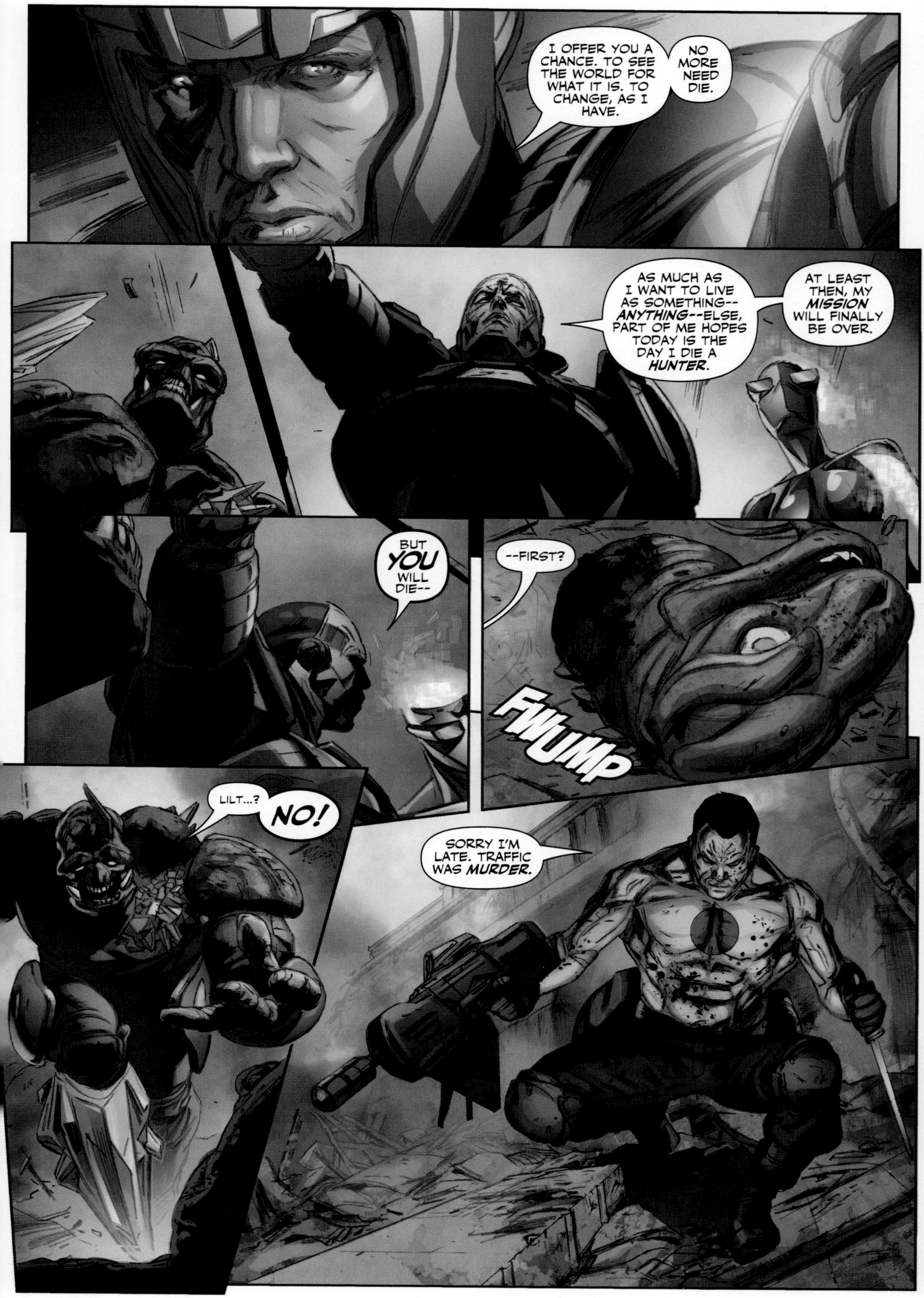
I OFFER YOU A CHANCE. TO SEE THE WORLD FOR WHAT IT IS. TO CHANGE, AS I HAVE.
NO MORE NEED DIE.
AS MUCH AS I WANT TO LIVE AS SOMETHING-- ANYTHING--ELSE, PART OF ME HOPES TODAY IS THE DAY I DIE A HUNTER.
AT LEAST THEN, MY MISSION WILL FINALLY BE OVER.
BUT YOU WILL DIE--
--FIRST?
FWUMP
LILT...?
NO!
SORRY I'M LATE. TRAFFIC WAS MURDER.

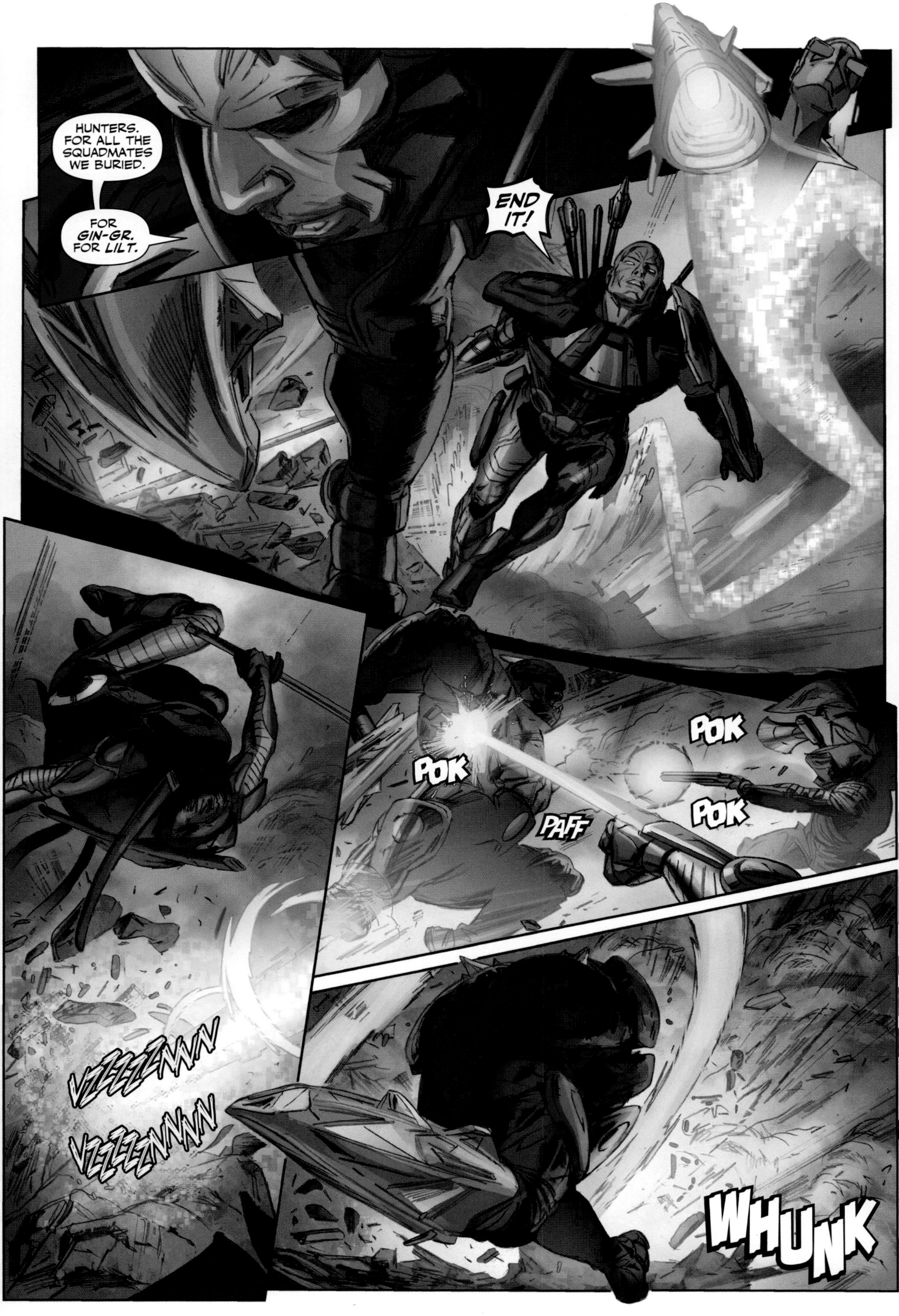
HUNTERS. FOR ALL THE SQUADMATES WE BURIED.
FOR GIN-GR. FOR LILT.
END IT!
POK
POK
PAFF
POK
VZZZZZNNNN
VZZZZZNNNNN
WHUNK

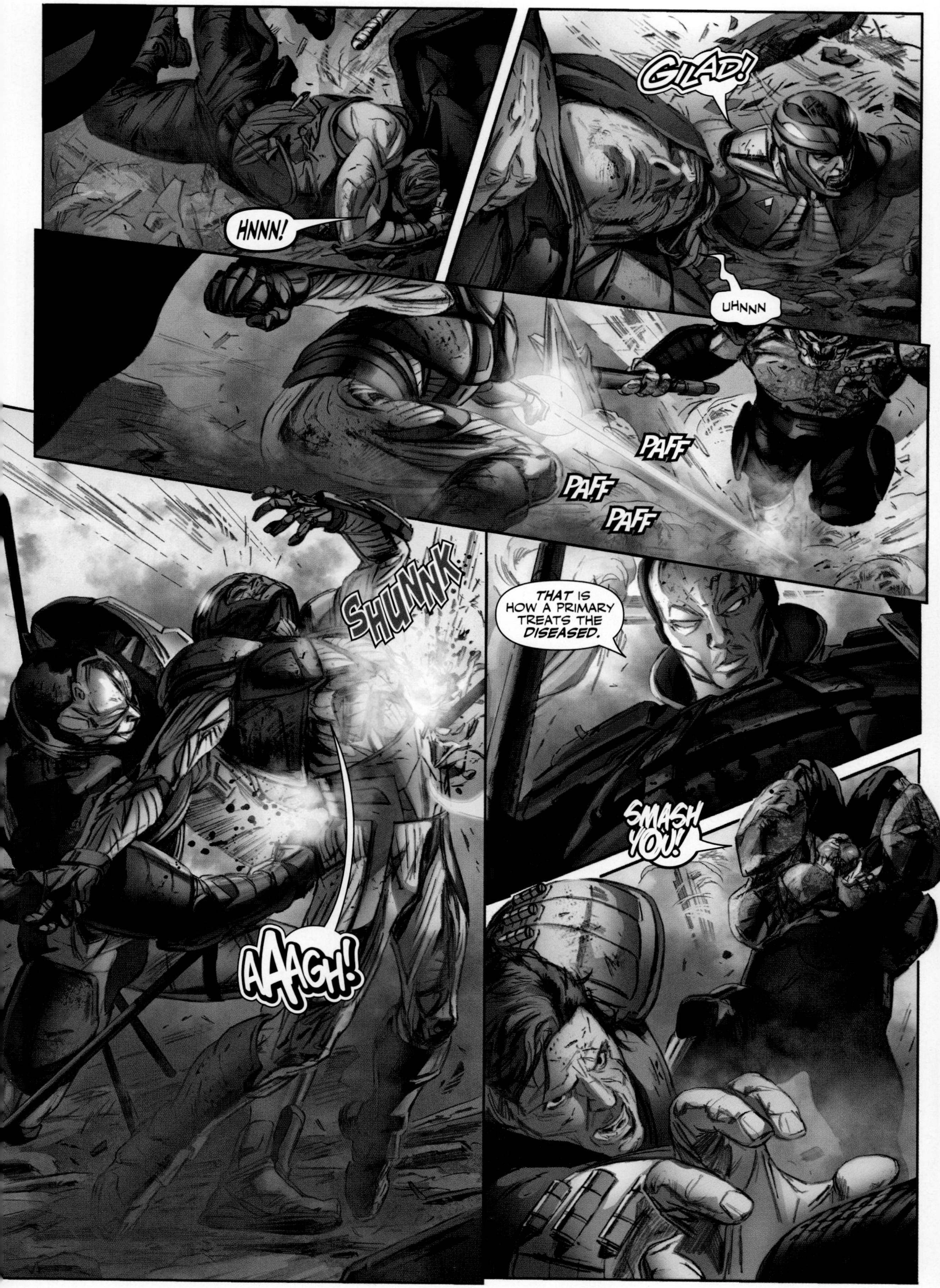
HNNN!
GILAD!
UHNNN
PAFF
PAFF
PAFF
SHUNNK
AAAGH!
THAT IS HOW A PRIMARY TREATS THE DISEASED.
SMASH YOU!

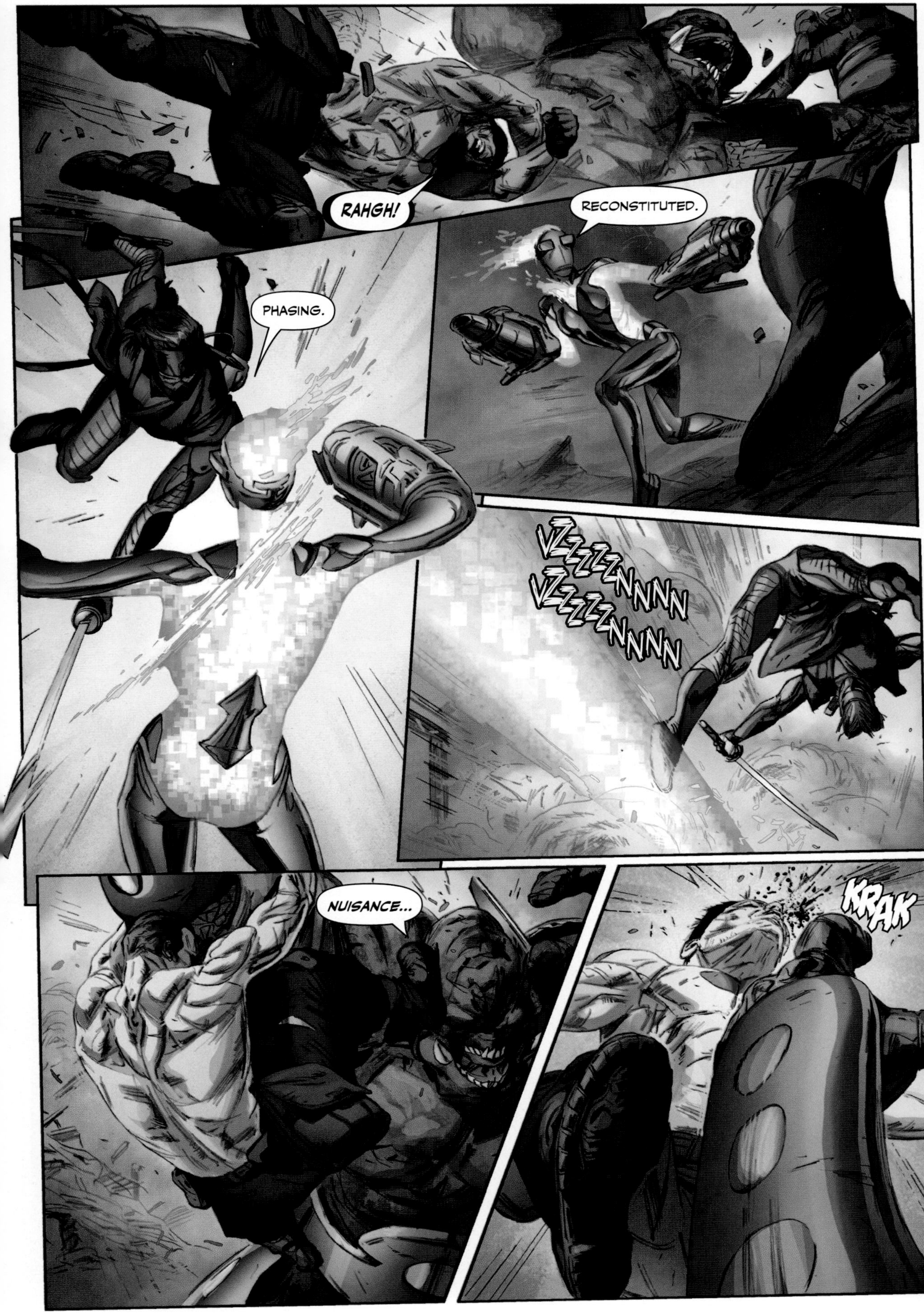
RAHGH!
RECONSTITUTED.
PHASING.
VZZZZZNNNN
VZZZZZNNNN
NUISANCE...
KRAK

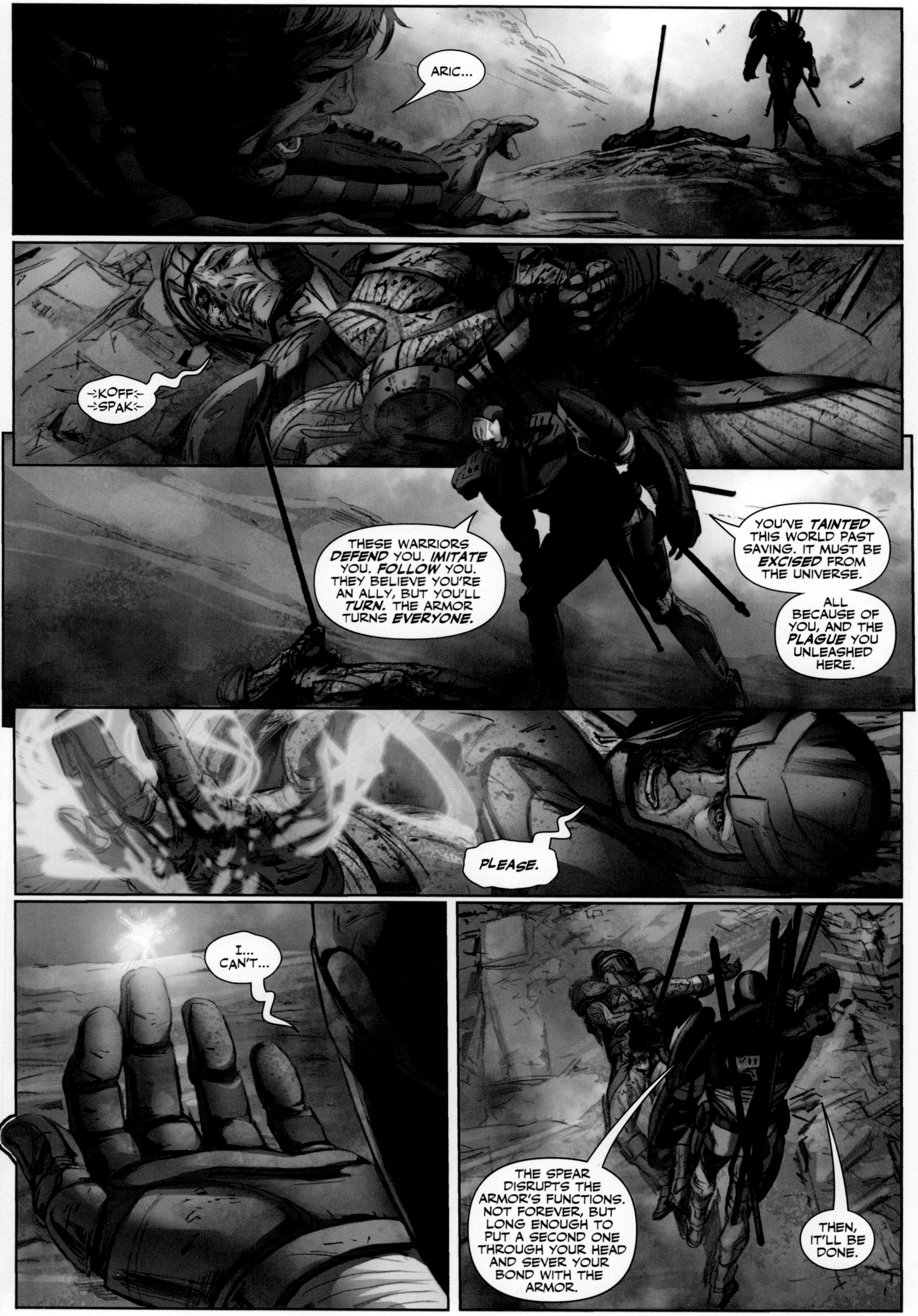
ARIC...
KOFF
SPAK
THESE WARRIORS DEFEND YOU. IMITATE YOU. FOLLOW YOU. THEY BELIEVE YOU'RE AN ALLY, BUT YOU'LL TURN. THE ARMOR TURNS EVERYONE.
YOU'VE TAINTED THIS WORLD PAST SAVING. IT MUST BE EXCISED FROM THE UNIVERSE.
ALL BECAUSE OF YOU, AND THE PLAGUE YOU UNLEASHED HERE.
PLEASE.
I... CAN'T...
THE SPEAR DISRUPTS THE ARMOR'S FUNCTIONS. NOT FOREVER, BUT LONG ENOUGH TO PUT A SECOND ONE THROUGH YOUR HEAD AND SEVER YOUR BOND WITH THE ARMOR.
THEN, IT'LL BE DONE.

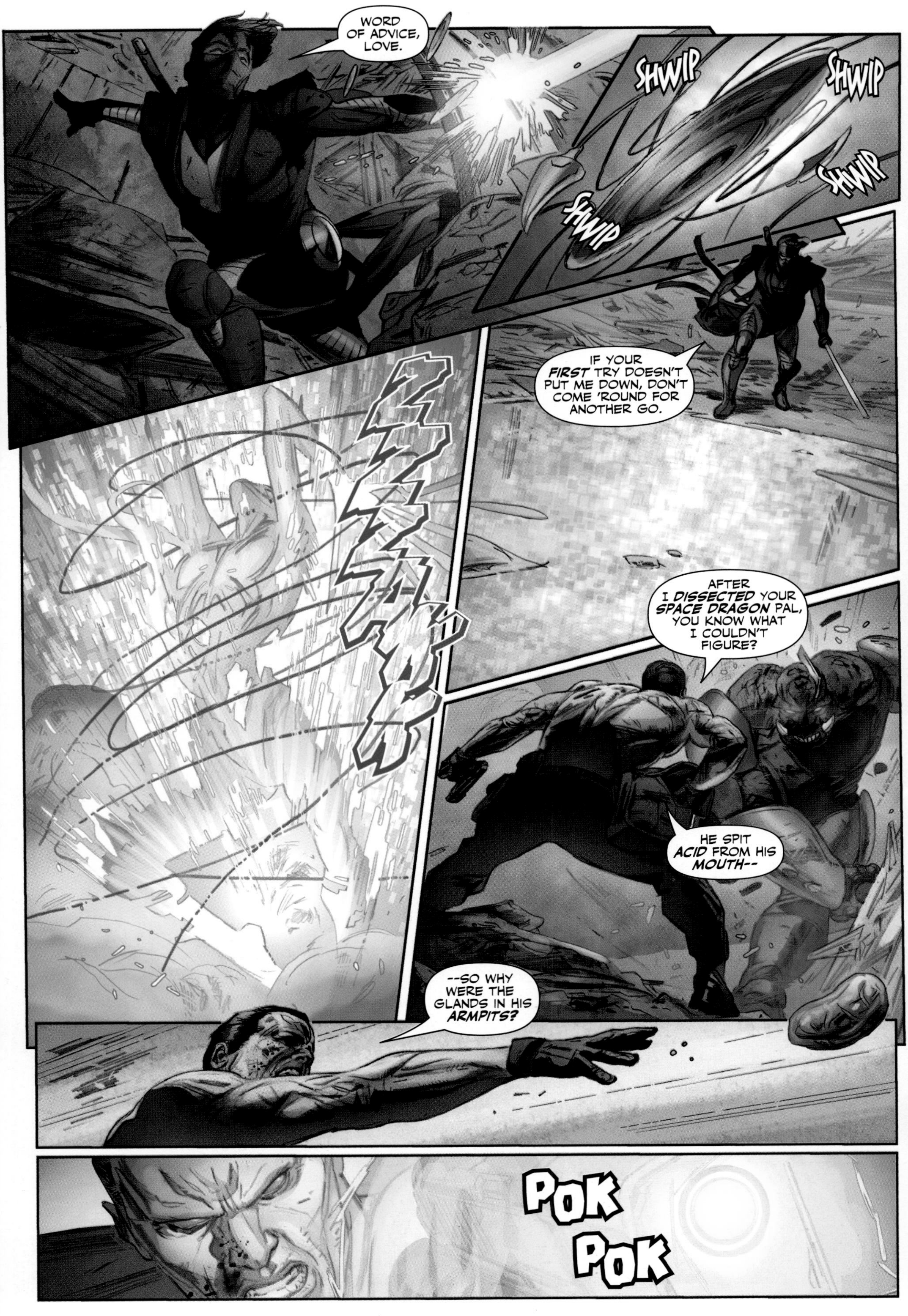

WORD OF ADVICE, LOVE.
SHWIP
SHWIP
SHWIP
SHWIP
IF YOUR FIRST TRY DOESN'T PUT ME DOWN, DON'T COME 'ROUND FOR ANOTHER GO.
AFTER I DISSECTED YOUR SPACE DRAGON PAL, YOU KNOW WHAT I COULDN'T FIGURE?
HE SPIT ACID FROM HIS MOUTH--
--SO WHY WERE THE GLANDS IN HIS ARMPITS?
POK
POK

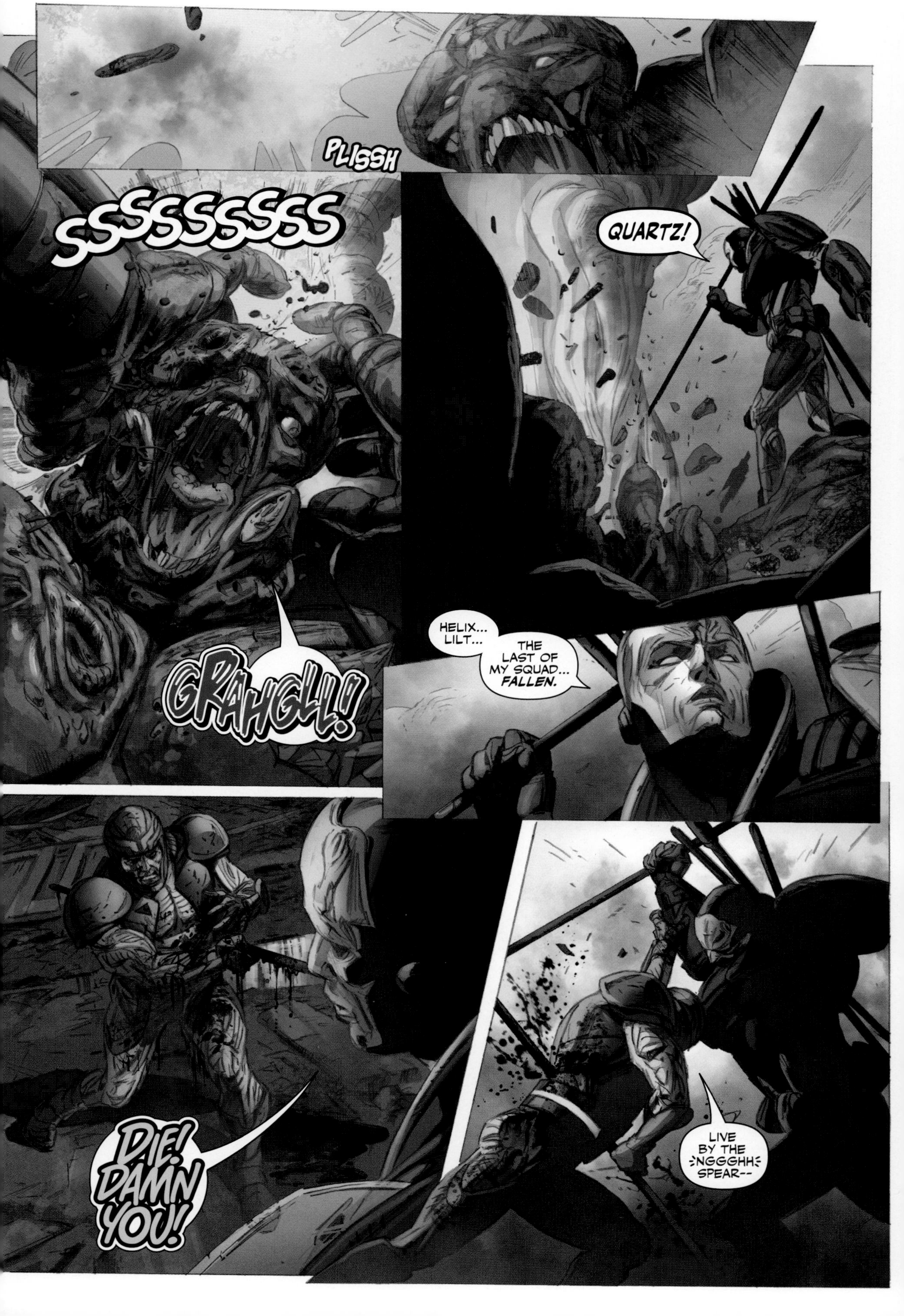
PLISSH
SSSSSSSSS
GRAHGLL!
QUARTZ!
HELIX... LILT...
THE LAST OF MY SQUAD... FALLEN.
DIE! DAMN YOU!
LIVE BY THE NGGGHH SPEAR--

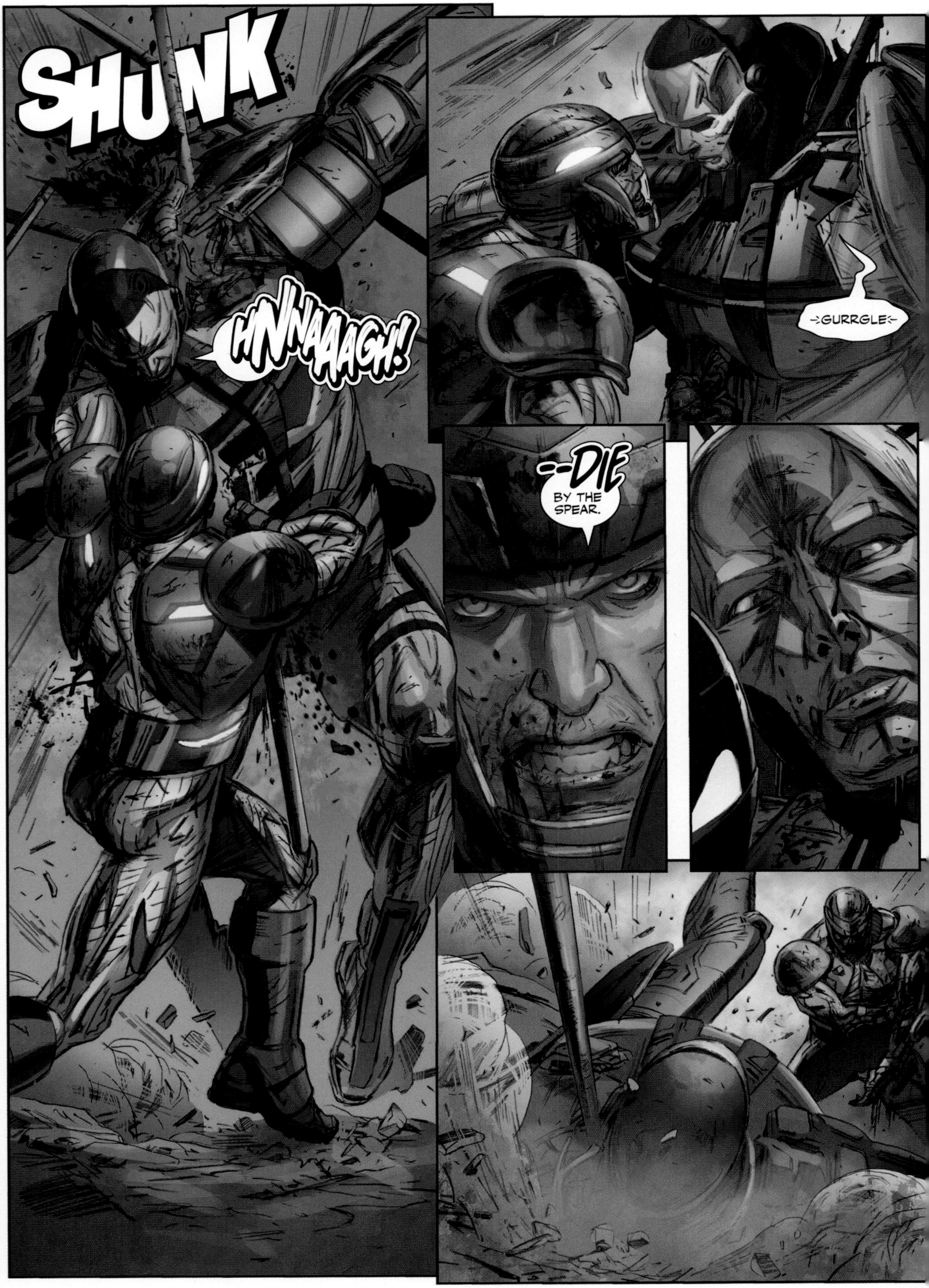
SHUNK
HNNAAAAGH!
-GURRGLE-
--DIE BY THE SPEAR.

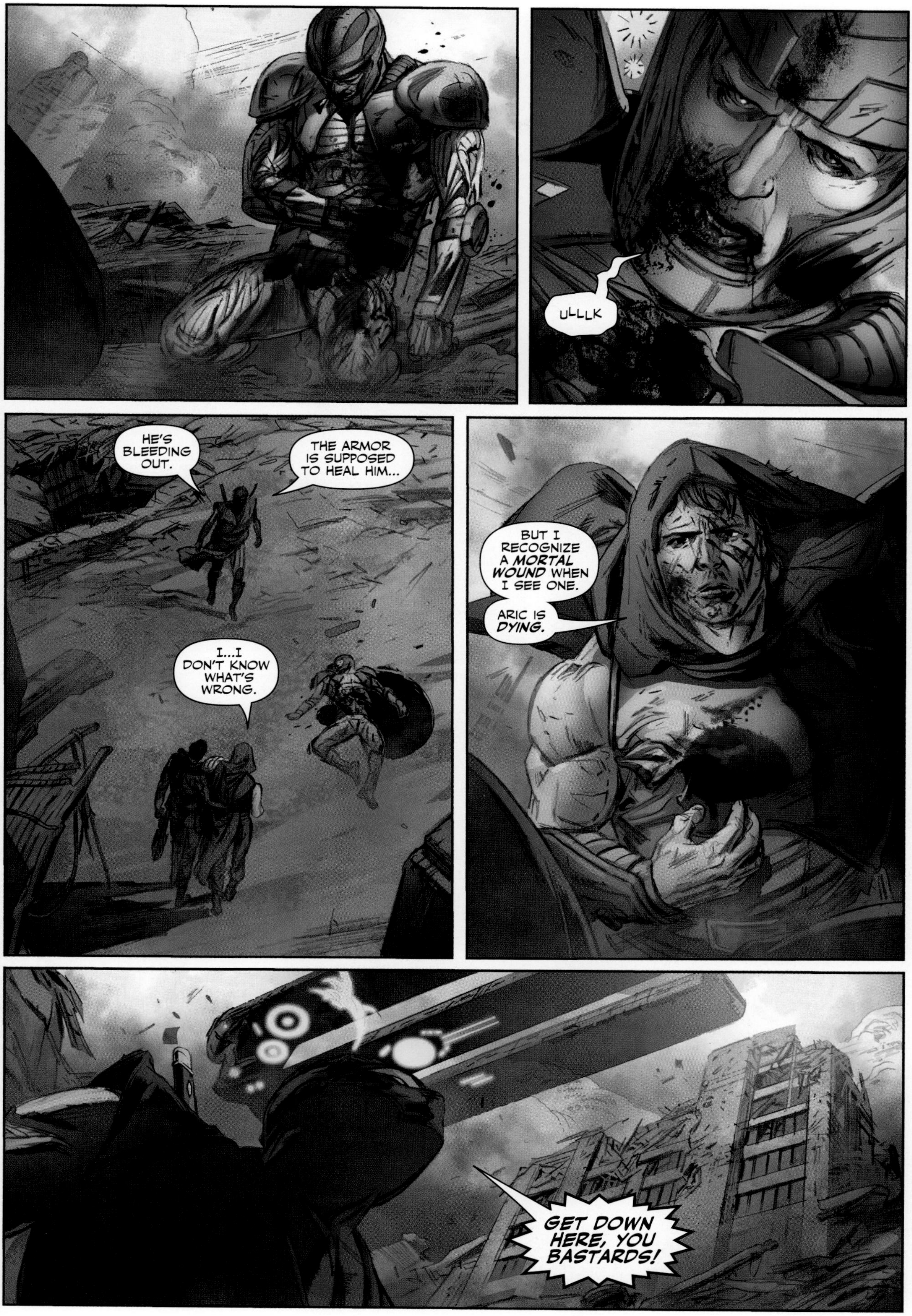
ULLLK
HE'S BLEEDING OUT.
THE ARMOR IS SUPPOSED TO HEAL HIM...
I...I DON'T KNOW WHAT'S WRONG.
BUT I RECOGNIZE A *MORTAL WOUND* WHEN I SEE ONE.
ARIC IS *DYING.*
GET DOWN HERE, YOU BASTARDS!

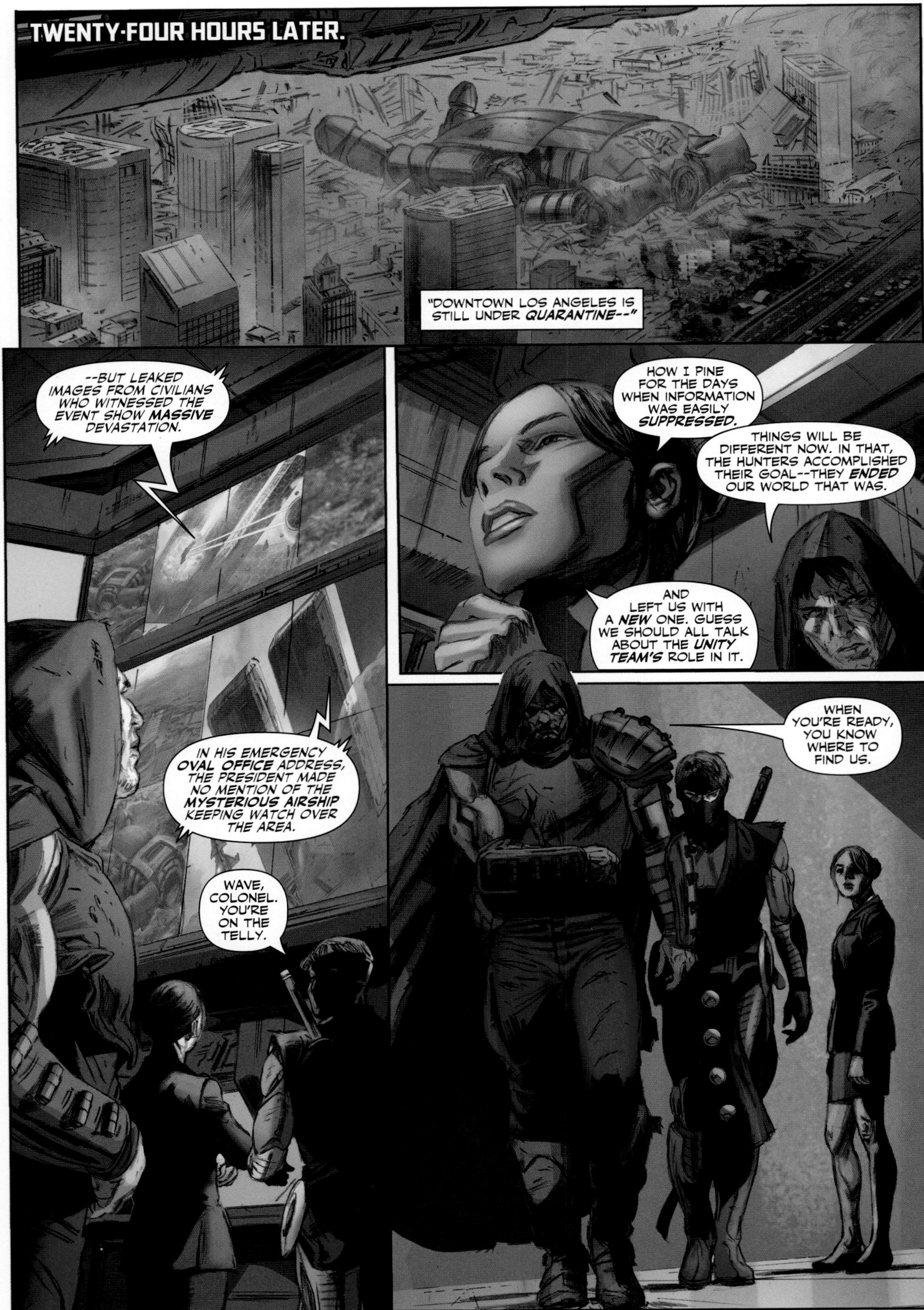
TWENTY-FOUR HOURS LATER.
"DOWNTOWN LOS ANGELES IS STILL UNDER QUARANTINE--"
--BUT LEAKED IMAGES FROM CIVILIANS WHO WITNESSED THE EVENT SHOW MASSIVE DEVASTATION.
HOW I PINE FOR THE DAYS WHEN INFORMATION WAS EASILY SUPPRESSED.
THINGS WILL BE DIFFERENT NOW. IN THAT, THE HUNTERS ACCOMPLISHED THEIR GOAL--THEY ENDED OUR WORLD THAT WAS.
AND LEFT US WITH A NEW ONE. GUESS WE SHOULD ALL TALK ABOUT THE UNITY TEAM'S ROLE IN IT.
IN HIS EMERGENCY OVAL OFFICE ADDRESS, THE PRESIDENT MADE NO MENTION OF THE MYSTERIOUS AIRSHIP KEEPING WATCH OVER THE AREA.
WAVE, COLONEL. YOU'RE ON THE TELLY.
WHEN YOU'RE READY, YOU KNOW WHERE TO FIND US.

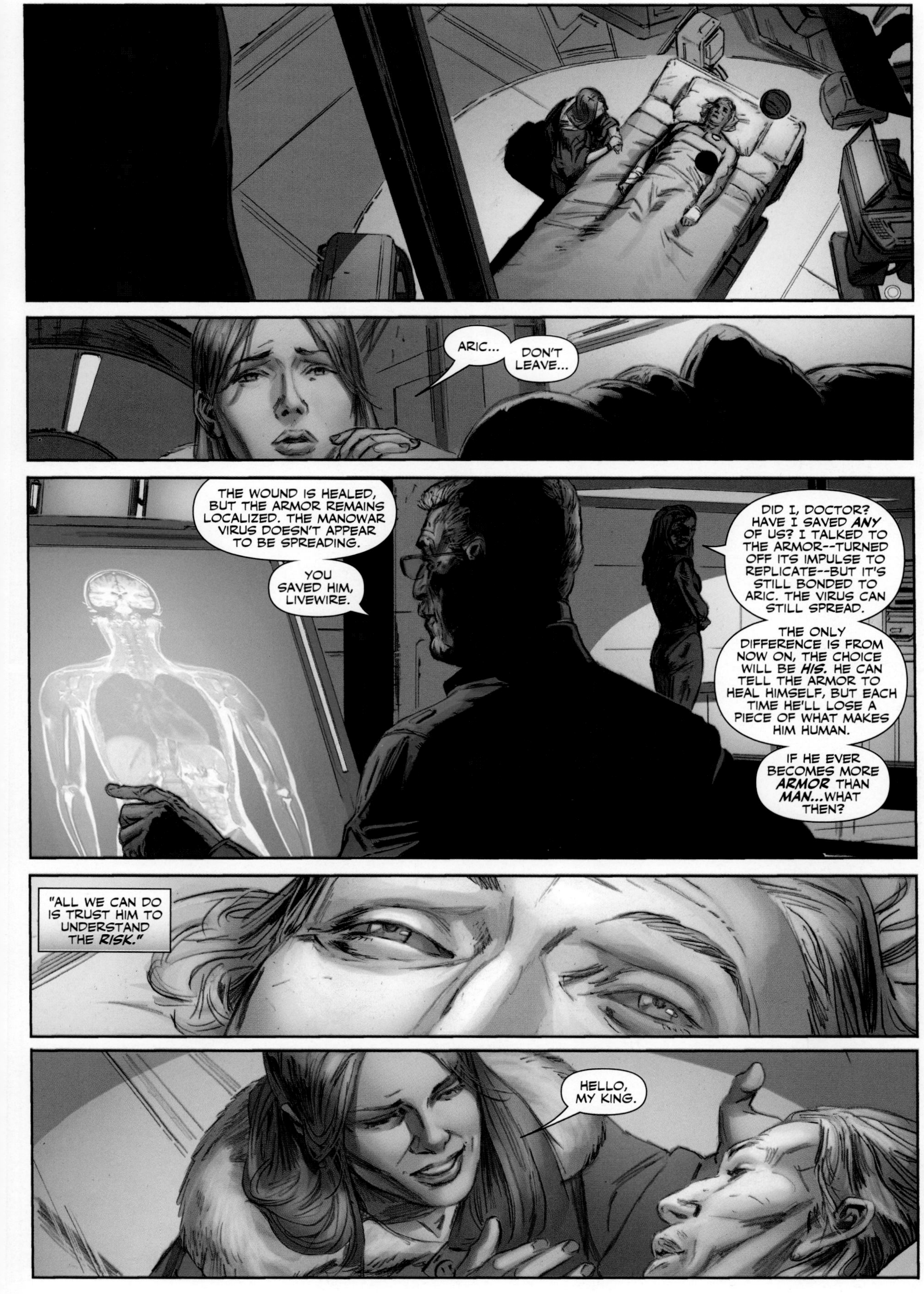
ARIC...
DON'T LEAVE...
THE WOUND IS HEALED, BUT THE ARMOR REMAINS LOCALIZED. THE MANOWAR VIRUS DOESN'T APPEAR TO BE SPREADING.
YOU SAVED HIM, LIVEWIRE.
DID I, DOCTOR? HAVE I SAVED *ANY* OF US? I TALKED TO THE ARMOR--TURNED OFF ITS IMPULSE TO REPLICATE--BUT IT'S STILL BONDED TO ARIC. THE VIRUS CAN STILL SPREAD.
THE ONLY DIFFERENCE IS FROM NOW ON, THE CHOICE WILL BE *HIS*. HE CAN TELL THE ARMOR TO HEAL HIMSELF, BUT EACH TIME HE'LL LOSE A PIECE OF WHAT MAKES HIM HUMAN.
IF HE EVER BECOMES MORE *ARMOR* THAN *MAN*...WHAT THEN?
"ALL WE CAN DO IS TRUST HIM TO UNDERSTAND THE *RISK*."
HELLO, MY KING.

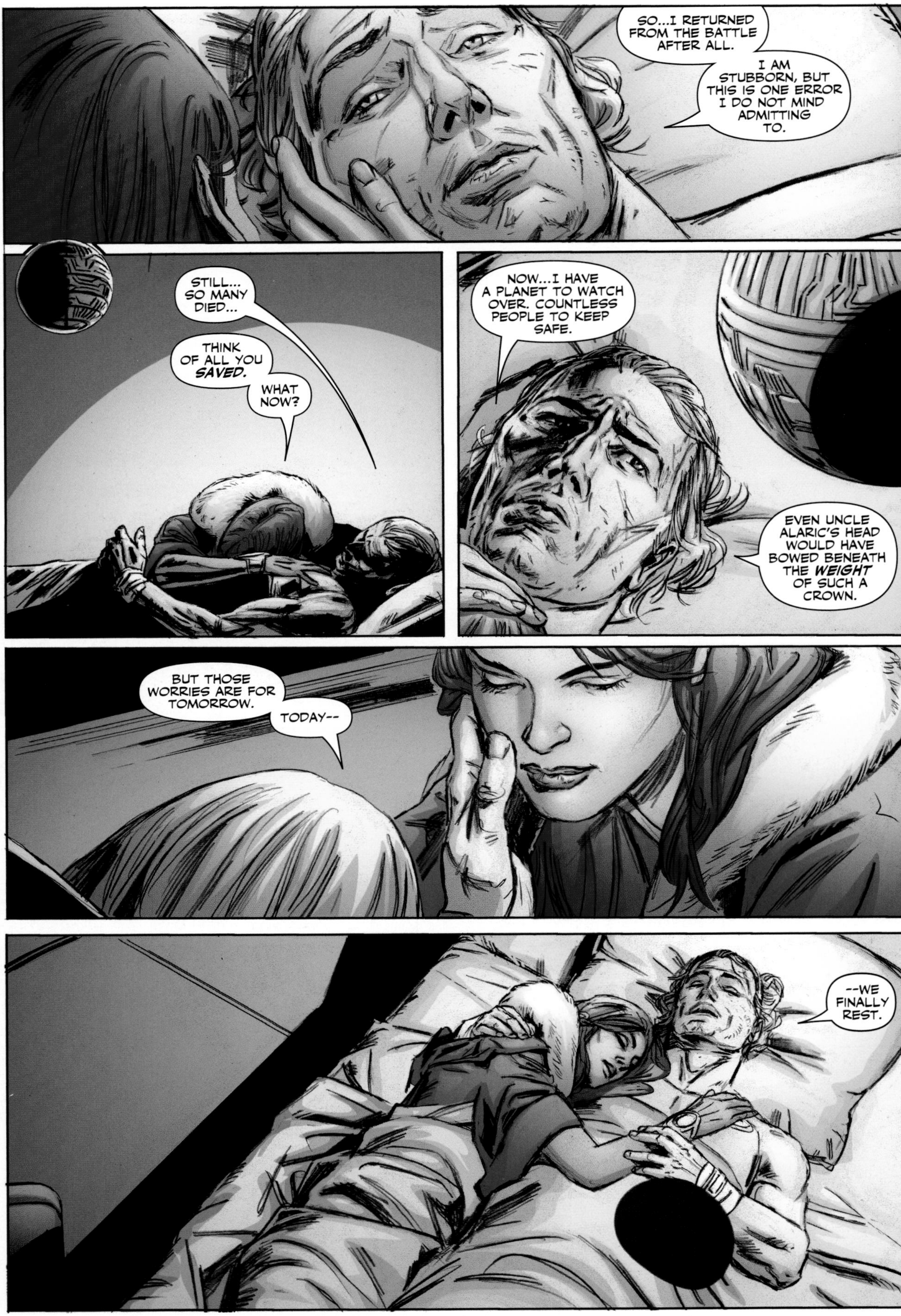
SO...I RETURNED FROM THE BATTLE AFTER ALL.
I AM STUBBORN, BUT THIS IS ONE ERROR I DO NOT MIND ADMITTING TO.
STILL... SO MANY DIED...
THINK OF ALL YOU *SAVED.*
WHAT NOW?
NOW...I HAVE A PLANET TO WATCH OVER. COUNTLESS PEOPLE TO KEEP SAFE.
EVEN UNCLE ALARIC'S HEAD WOULD HAVE BOWED BENEATH THE *WEIGHT* OF SUCH A CROWN.
BUT THOSE WORRIES ARE FOR TOMORROW.
TODAY--
--WE FINALLY REST.

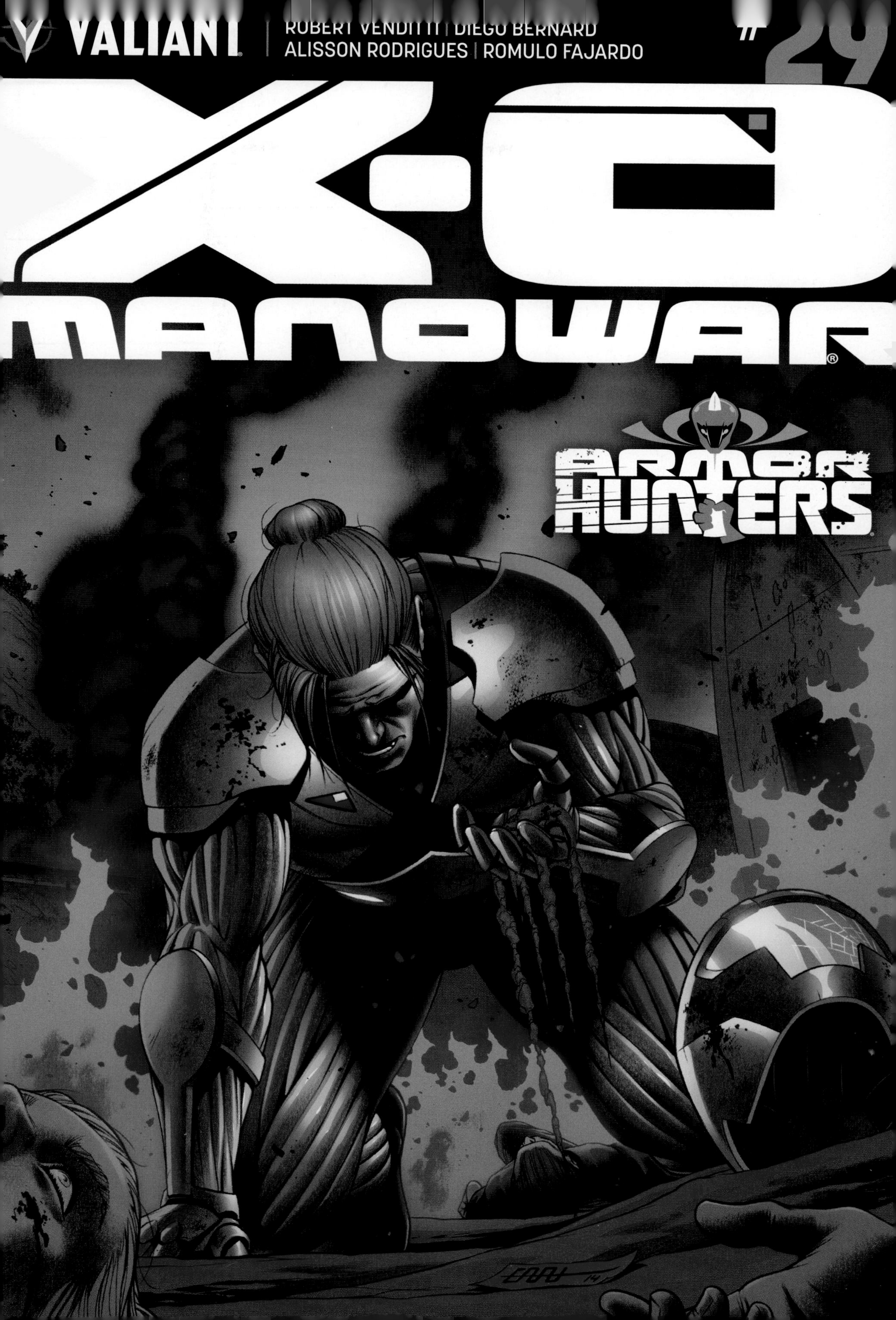
VALIANT
ROBERT VENDITTI | DIEGO BERNARD
ALISSON RODRIGUES | ROMULO FAJARDO
#29
X-O MANOWAR
ARMOR HUNTERS

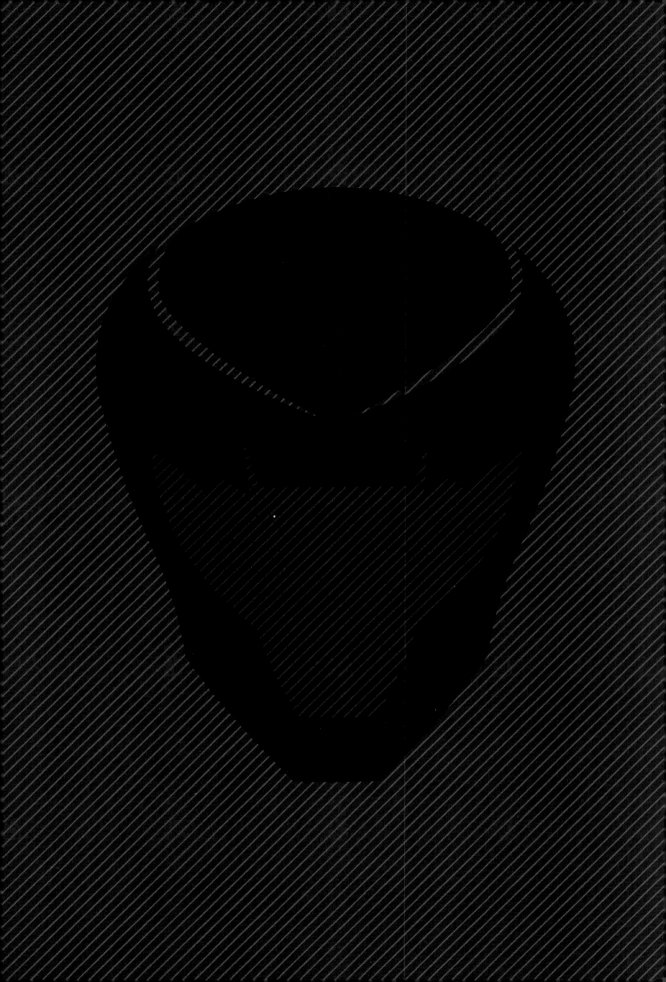

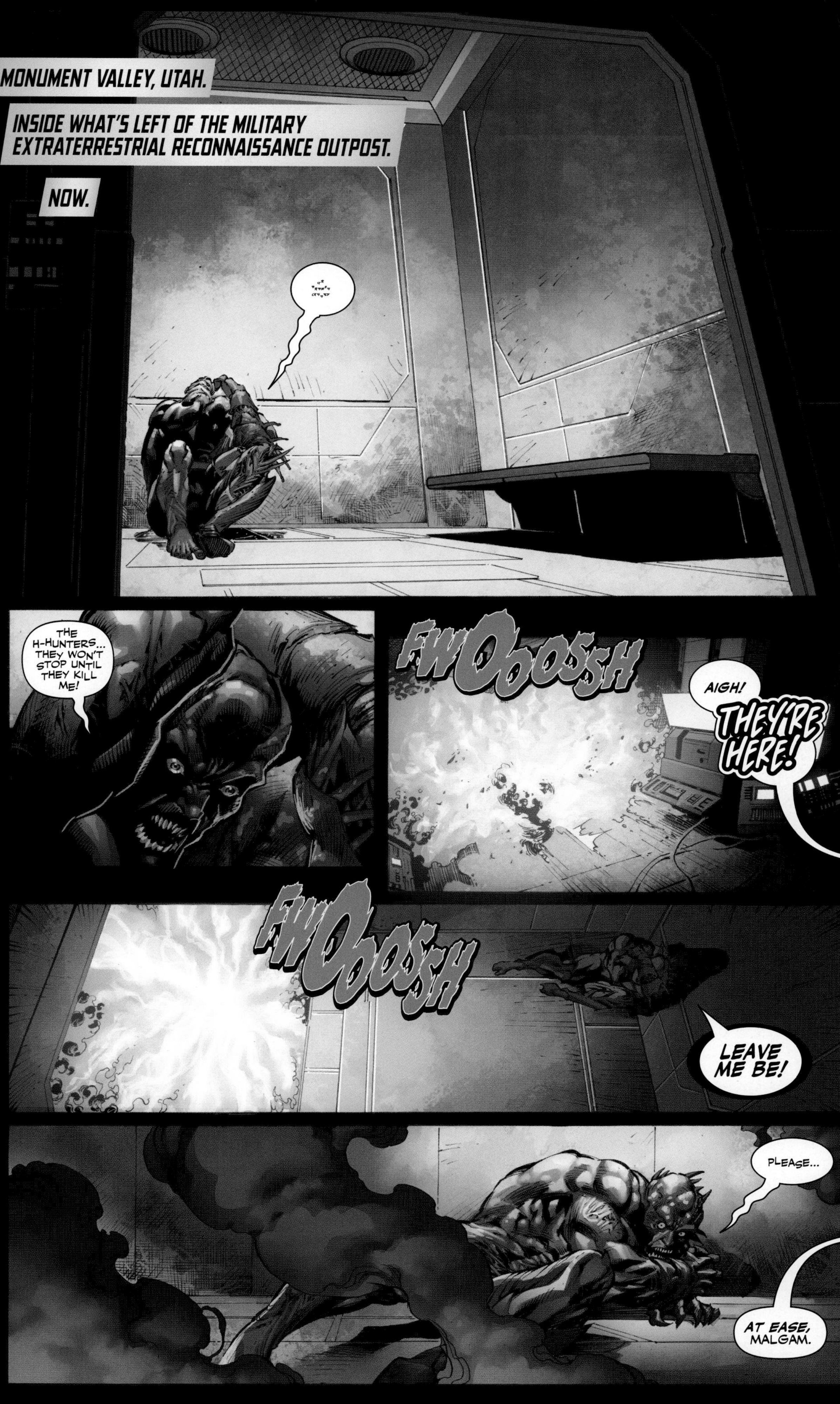
MONUMENT VALLEY, UTAH.
INSIDE WHAT'S LEFT OF THE MILITARY EXTRATERRESTRIAL RECONNAISSANCE OUTPOST.
NOW.
THE H-HUNTERS... THEY WON'T STOP UNTIL THEY KILL ME!
FWOOOOSSH
AIGH!
THEY'RE HERE!
FWOOOOSSH
LEAVE ME BE!
PLEASE...
AT EASE, MALGAM.

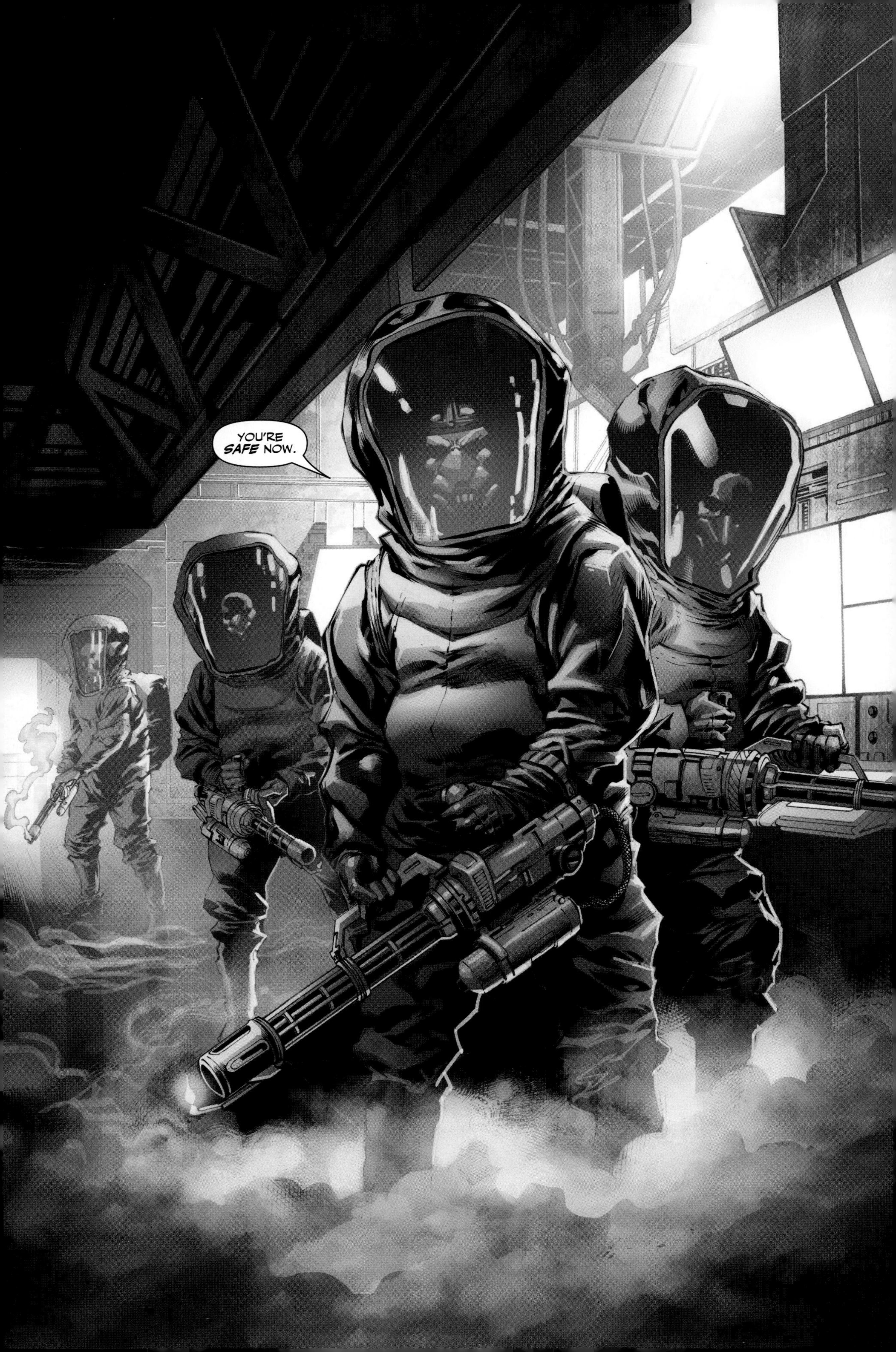
YOU'RE *SAFE* NOW.

ABOVE LOS ANGELES.

THE MOBILE COMMAND HUB OF M.E.R.O.

CODENAME: LOVE BOAT.

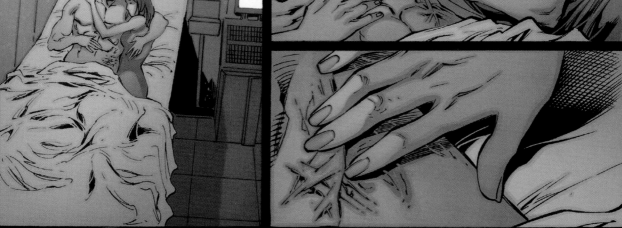

THE SICKBAY.

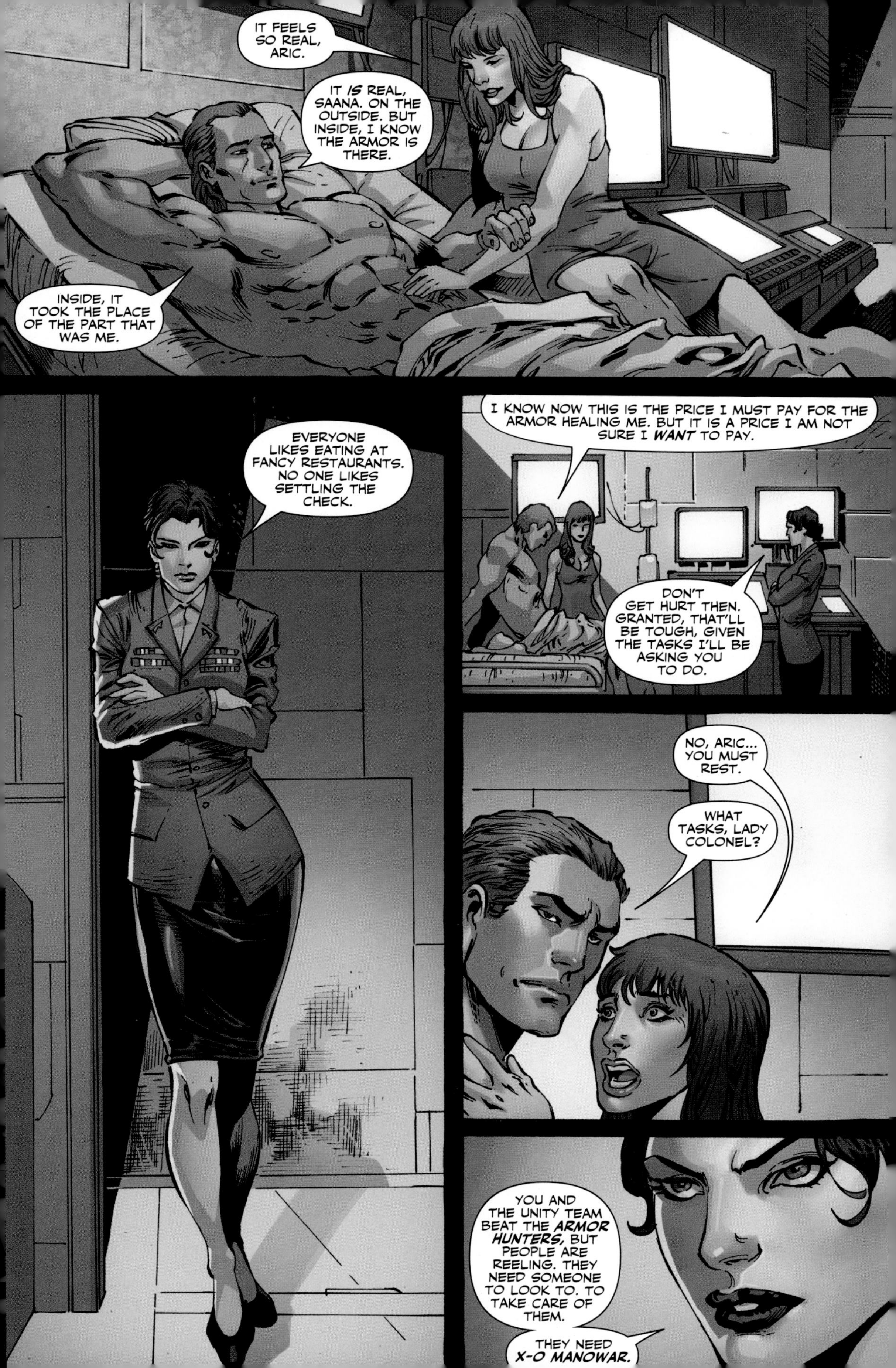
IT FEELS SO REAL, ARIC.
IT *IS* REAL, SAANA. ON THE OUTSIDE. BUT INSIDE, I KNOW THE ARMOR IS THERE.
INSIDE, IT TOOK THE PLACE OF THE PART THAT WAS ME.
EVERYONE LIKES EATING AT FANCY RESTAURANTS. NO ONE LIKES SETTLING THE CHECK.
I KNOW NOW THIS IS THE PRICE I MUST PAY FOR THE ARMOR HEALING ME. BUT IT IS A PRICE I AM NOT SURE I **WANT** TO PAY.
DON'T GET HURT THEN. GRANTED, THAT'LL BE TOUGH, GIVEN THE TASKS I'LL BE ASKING YOU TO DO.
NO, ARIC... YOU MUST REST.
WHAT TASKS, LADY COLONEL?
YOU AND THE UNITY TEAM BEAT THE ***ARMOR HUNTERS,*** BUT PEOPLE ARE REELING. THEY NEED SOMEONE TO LOOK TO. TO TAKE CARE OF THEM.
THEY NEED ***X-O MANOWAR.***

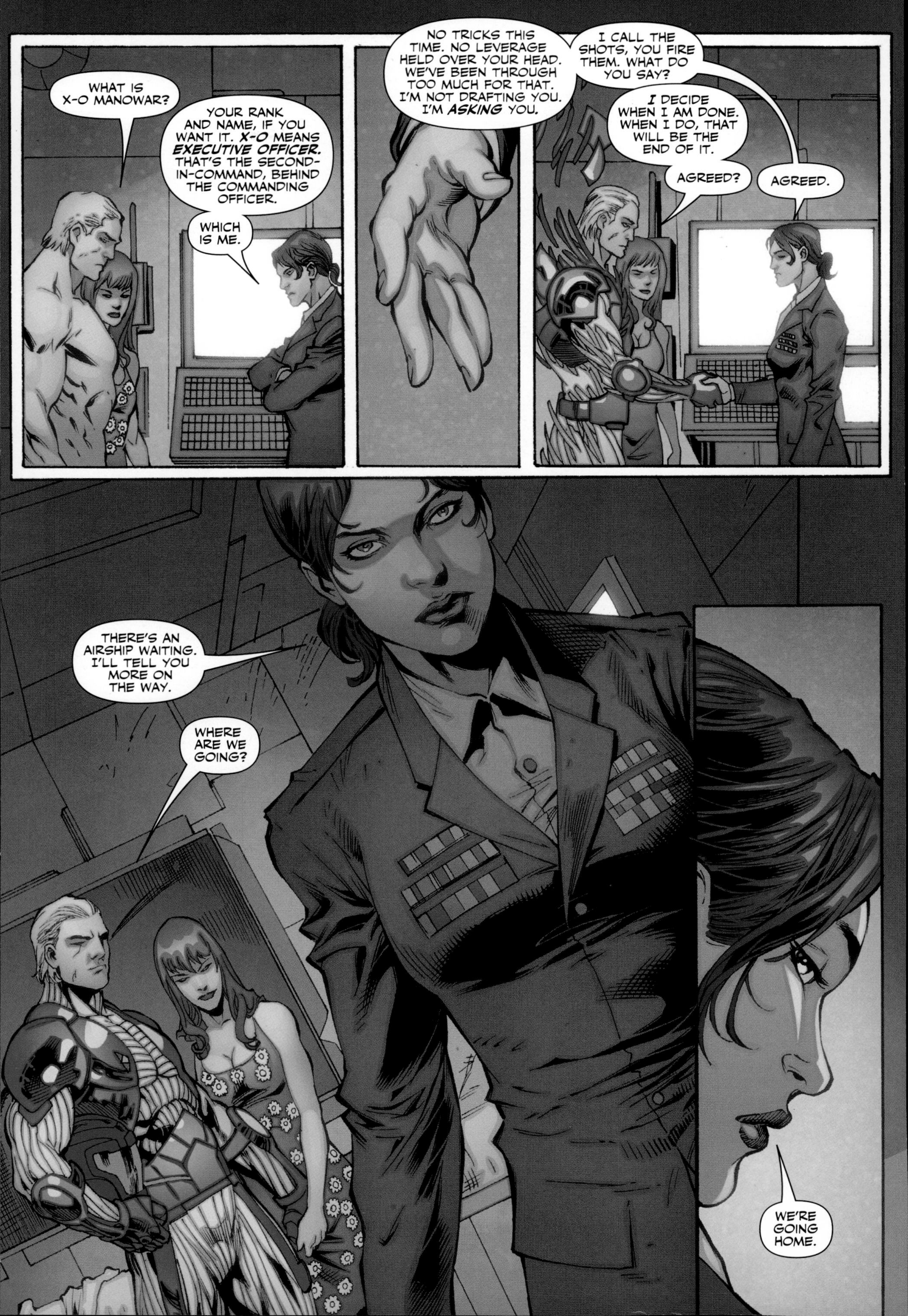
WHAT IS X-O MANOWAR?
YOUR RANK AND NAME, IF YOU WANT IT. X-O MEANS EXECUTIVE OFFICER. THAT'S THE SECOND-IN-COMMAND, BEHIND THE COMMANDING OFFICER.
WHICH IS ME.
NO TRICKS THIS TIME. NO LEVERAGE HELD OVER YOUR HEAD. WE'VE BEEN THROUGH TOO MUCH FOR THAT. I'M NOT DRAFTING YOU. I'M ASKING YOU.
I CALL THE SHOTS, YOU FIRE THEM. WHAT DO YOU SAY?
I DECIDE WHEN I AM DONE. WHEN I DO, THAT WILL BE THE END OF IT.
AGREED?
AGREED.
THERE'S AN AIRSHIP WAITING. I'LL TELL YOU MORE ON THE WAY.
WHERE ARE WE GOING?
WE'RE GOING HOME.

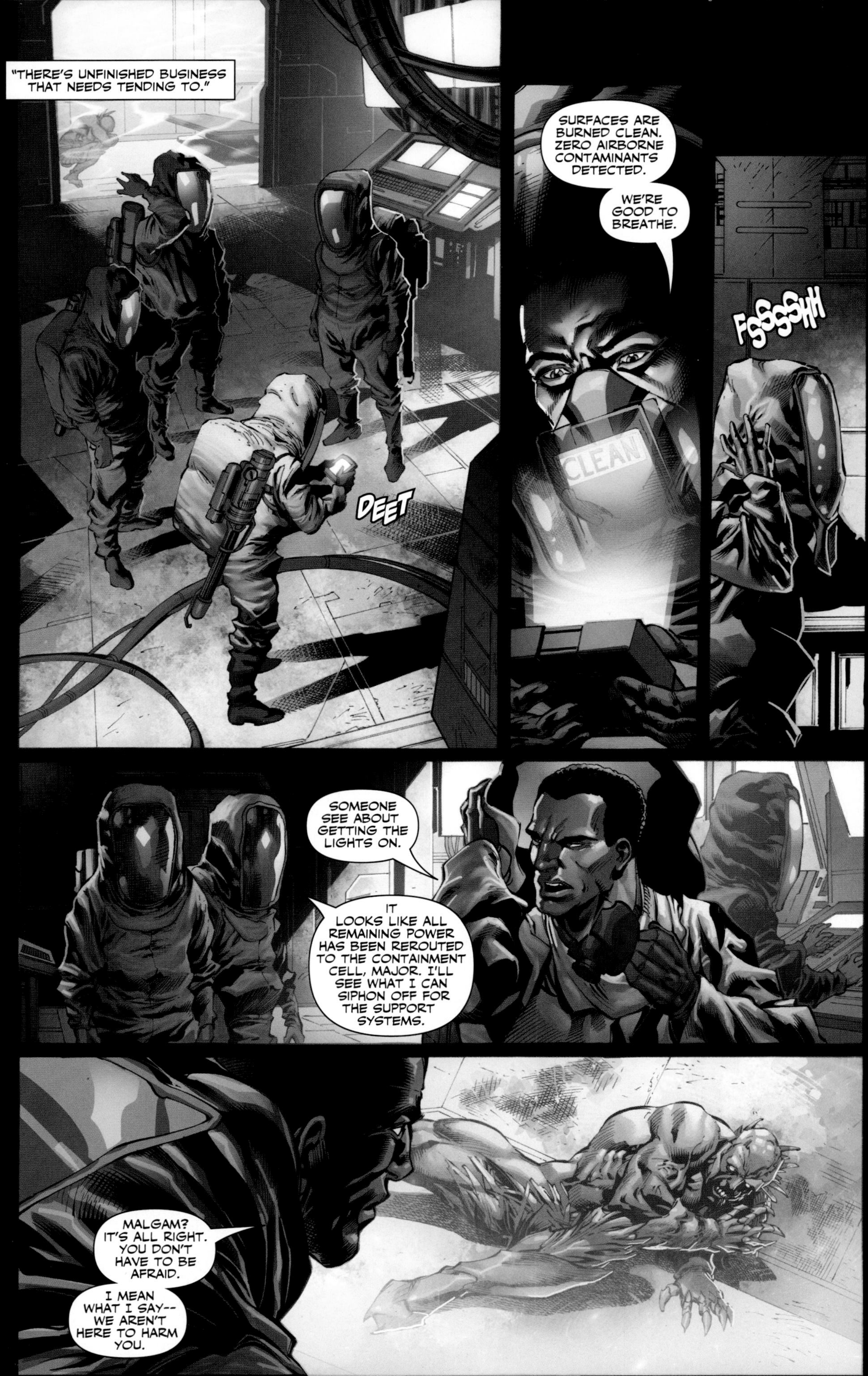
"THERE'S UNFINISHED BUSINESS THAT NEEDS TENDING TO."
DEET
SURFACES ARE BURNED CLEAN. ZERO AIRBORNE CONTAMINANTS DETECTED.
WE'RE GOOD TO BREATHE.
CLEAN
FSSSSHH
SOMEONE SEE ABOUT GETTING THE LIGHTS ON.
IT LOOKS LIKE ALL REMAINING POWER HAS BEEN REROUTED TO THE CONTAINMENT CELL, MAJOR. I'LL SEE WHAT I CAN SIPHON OFF FOR THE SUPPORT SYSTEMS.
MALGAM? IT'S ALL RIGHT. YOU DON'T HAVE TO BE AFRAID.
I MEAN WHAT I SAY-- WE AREN'T HERE TO HARM YOU.

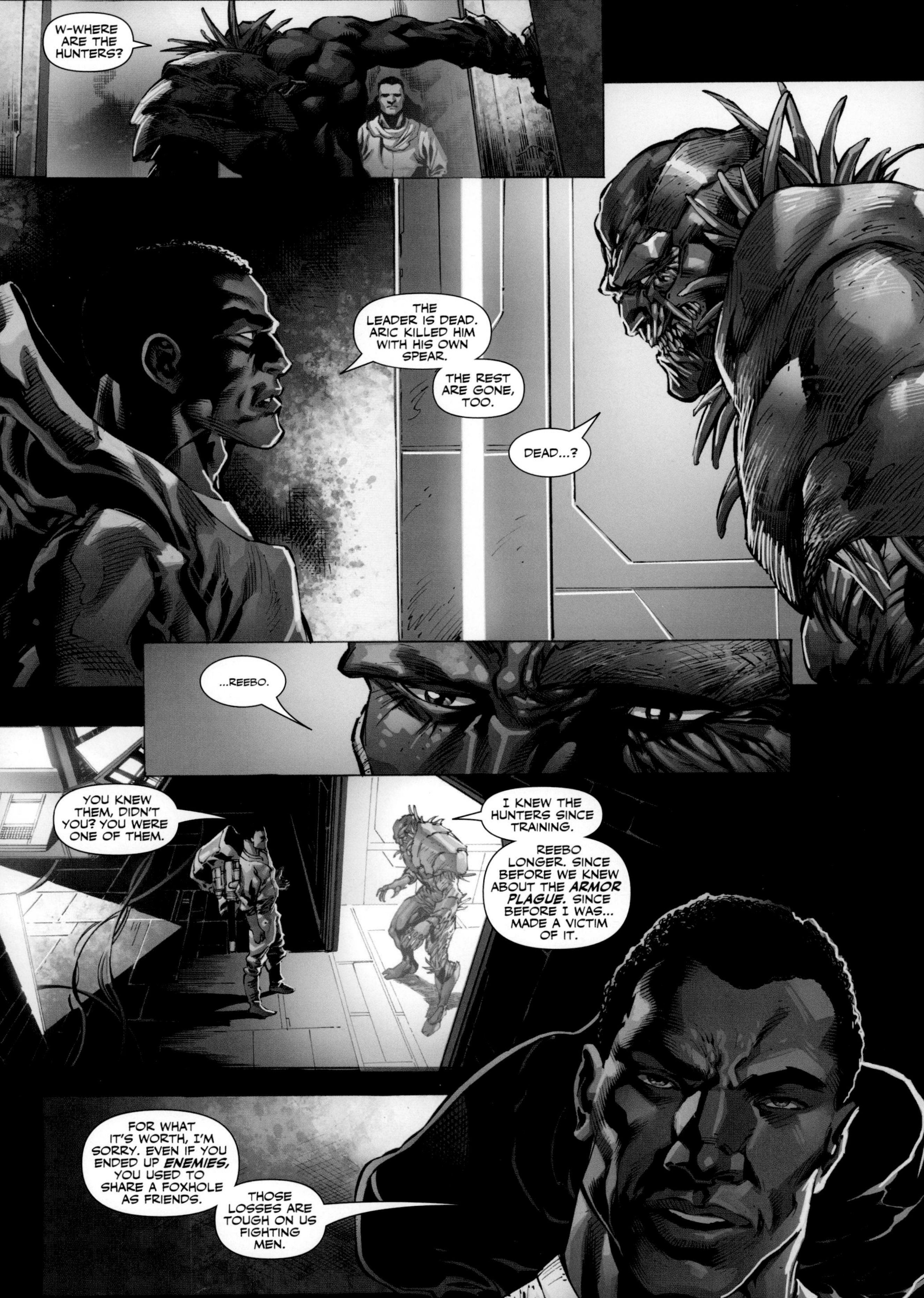
W-WHERE ARE THE HUNTERS?
THE LEADER IS DEAD. ARIC KILLED HIM WITH HIS OWN SPEAR.
THE REST ARE GONE, TOO.
DEAD...?
...REEBO.
YOU KNEW THEM, DIDN'T YOU? YOU WERE ONE OF THEM.
I KNEW THE HUNTERS SINCE TRAINING.
REEBO LONGER. SINCE BEFORE WE KNEW ABOUT THE ARMOR PLAGUE. SINCE BEFORE I WAS... MADE A VICTIM OF IT.
FOR WHAT IT'S WORTH, I'M SORRY. EVEN IF YOU ENDED UP ENEMIES, YOU USED TO SHARE A FOXHOLE AS FRIENDS.
THOSE LOSSES ARE TOUGH ON US FIGHTING MEN.

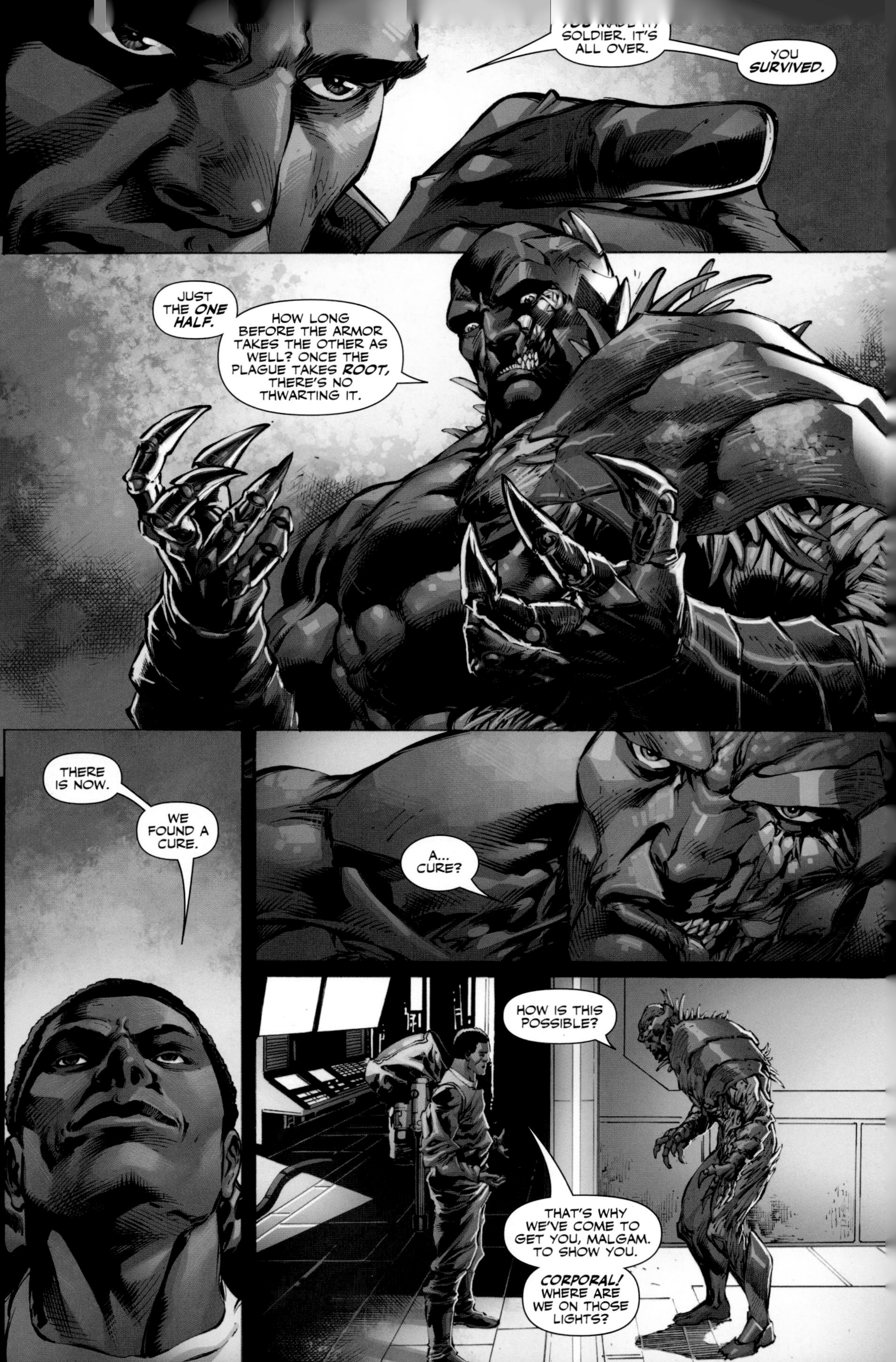
SOLDIER. IT'S ALL OVER.
YOU SURVIVED.
JUST THE ONE HALF.
HOW LONG BEFORE THE ARMOR TAKES THE OTHER AS WELL? ONCE THE PLAGUE TAKES ROOT, THERE'S NO THWARTING IT.
THERE IS NOW.
WE FOUND A CURE.
A... CURE?
HOW IS THIS POSSIBLE?
THAT'S WHY WE'VE COME TO GET YOU, MALGAM. TO SHOW YOU.
CORPORAL! WHERE ARE WE ON THOSE LIGHTS?

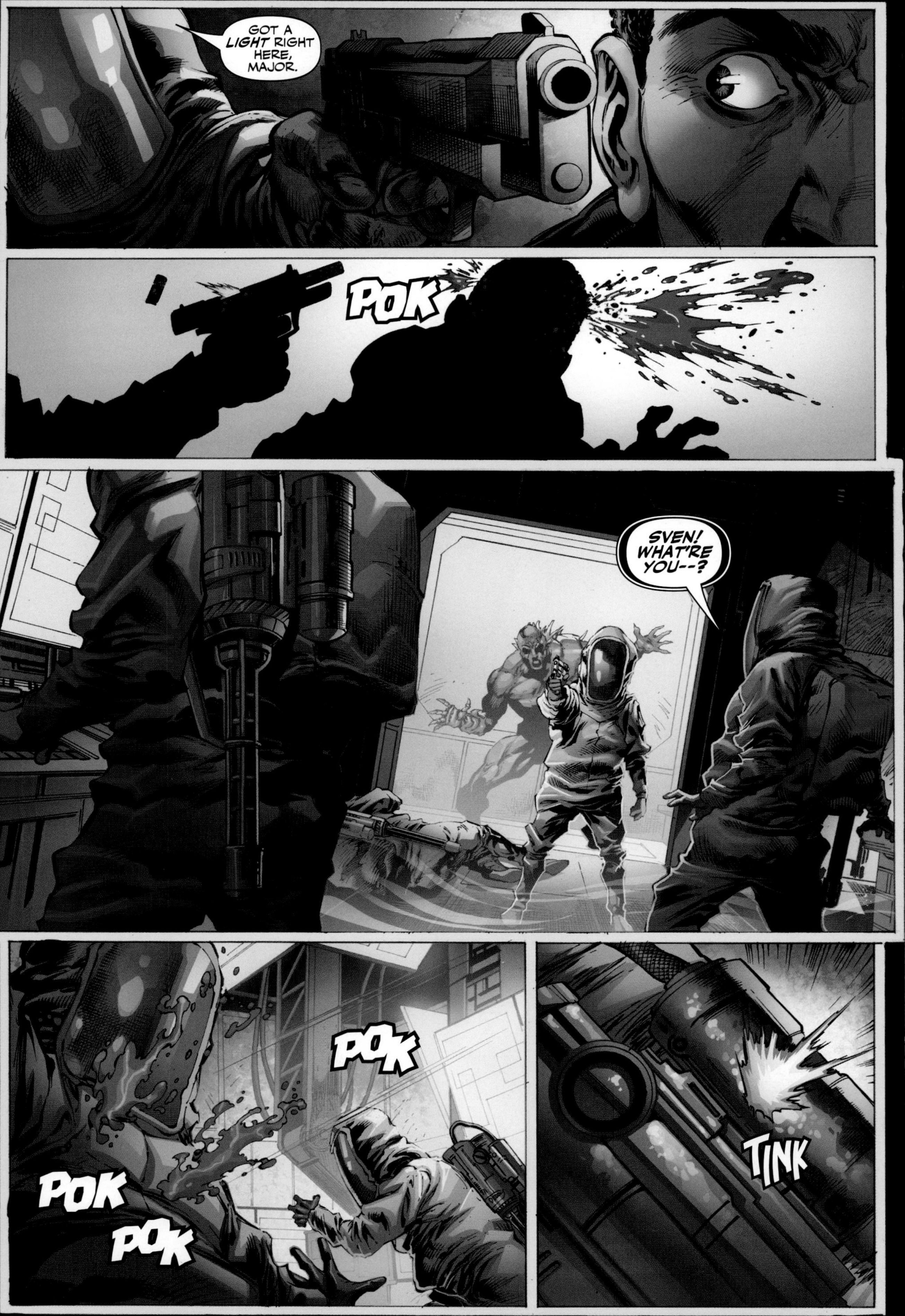

GOT A *LIGHT* RIGHT HERE, MAJOR.
POK
SVEN! WHAT'RE YOU--?
POK
POK
POK
TINK

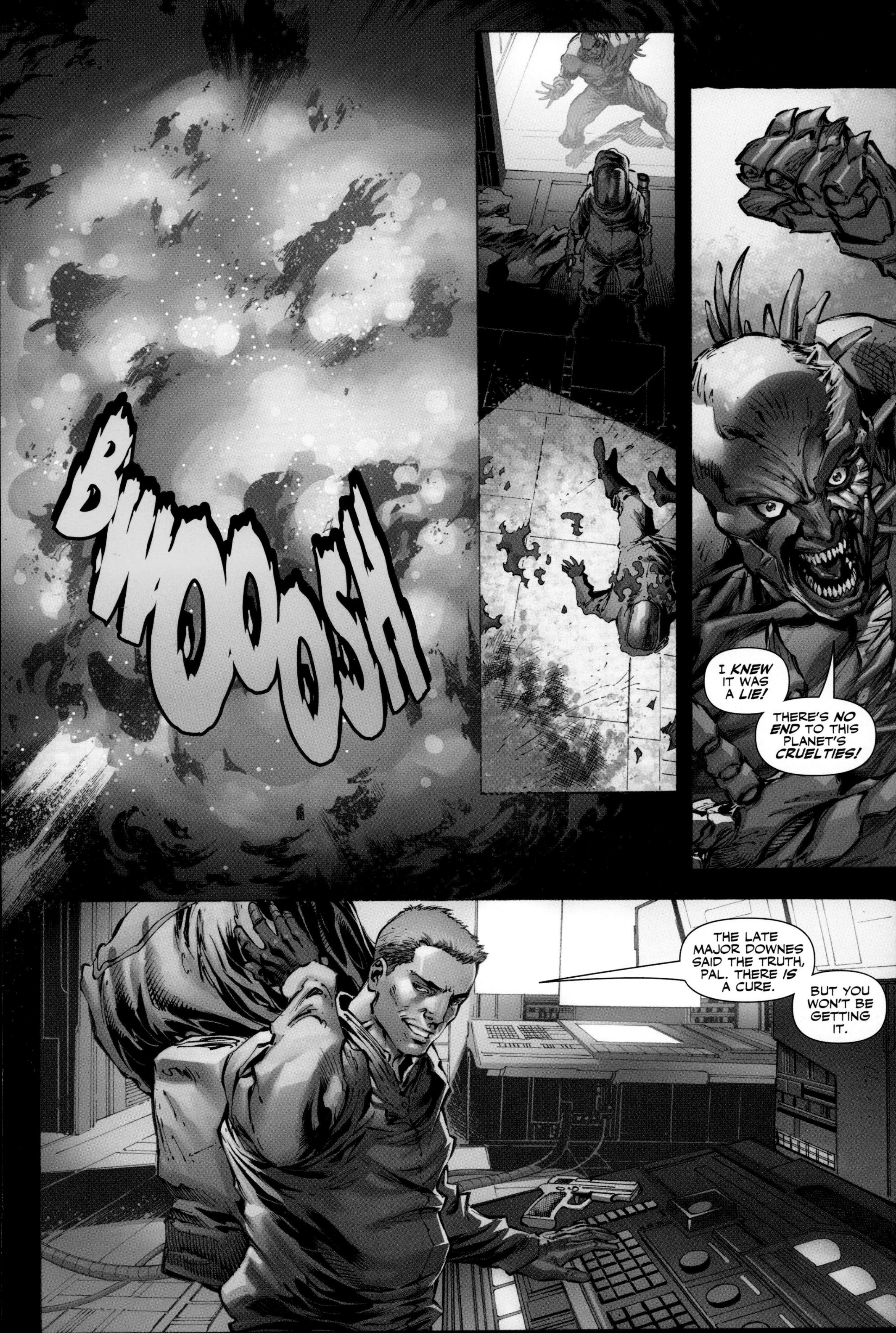
BWOOOSH
I KNEW IT WAS A LIE!
THERE'S NO END TO THIS PLANET'S CRUELTIES!
THE LATE MAJOR DOWNES SAID THE TRUTH, PAL. THERE IS A CURE.
BUT YOU WON'T BE GETTING IT.

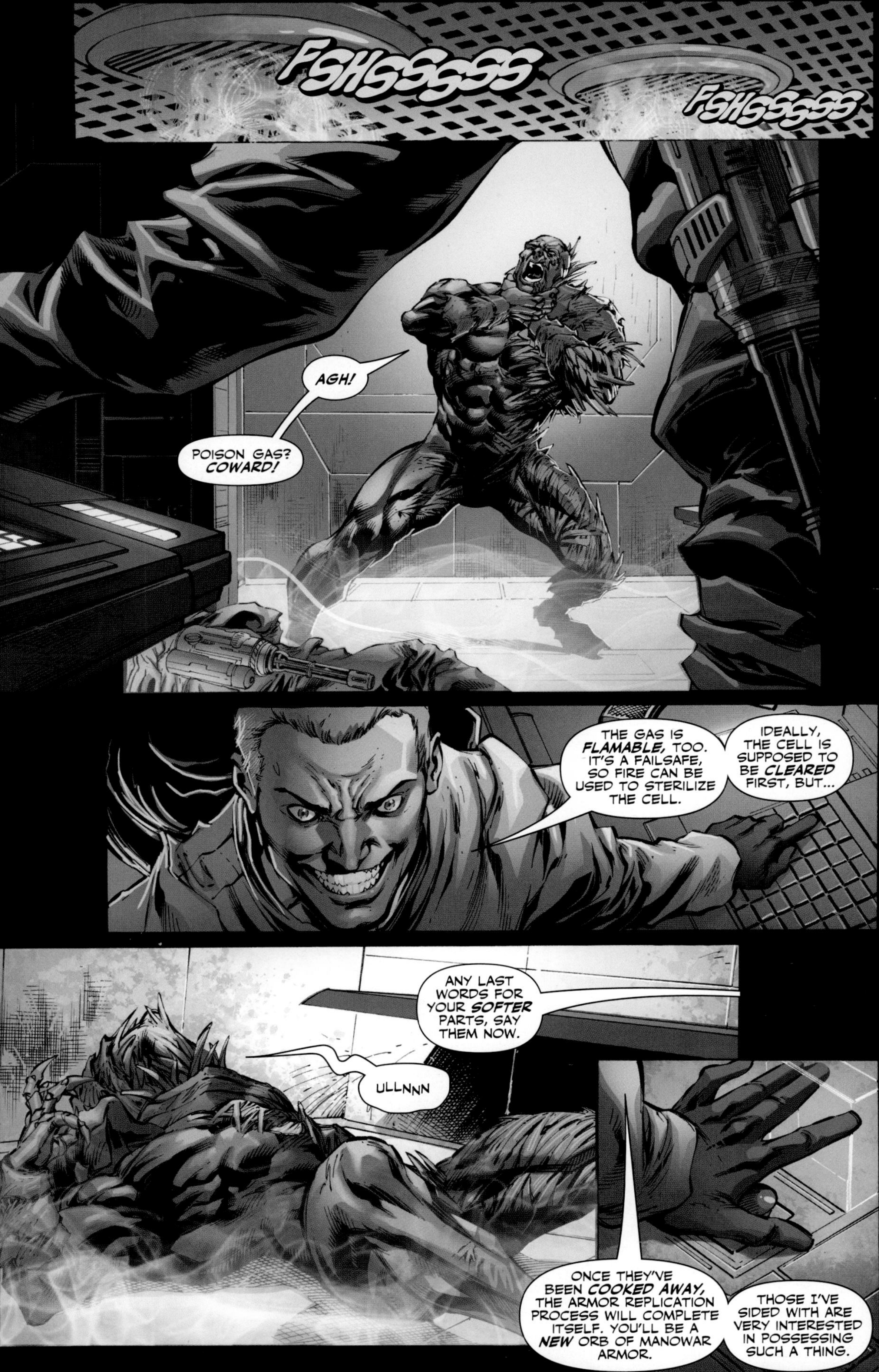
FSHSSSSS
FSHSSSSS
AGH!
POISON GAS? COWARD!
THE GAS IS FLAMABLE, TOO. IT'S A FAILSAFE, SO FIRE CAN BE USED TO STERILIZE THE CELL.
IDEALLY, THE CELL IS SUPPOSED TO BE CLEARED FIRST, BUT...
ANY LAST WORDS FOR YOUR SOFTER PARTS, SAY THEM NOW.
ULLNNN
ONCE THEY'VE BEEN COOKED AWAY, THE ARMOR REPLICATION PROCESS WILL COMPLETE ITSELF. YOU'LL BE A NEW ORB OF MANOWAR ARMOR.
THOSE I'VE SIDED WITH ARE VERY INTERESTED IN POSSESSING SUCH A THING.

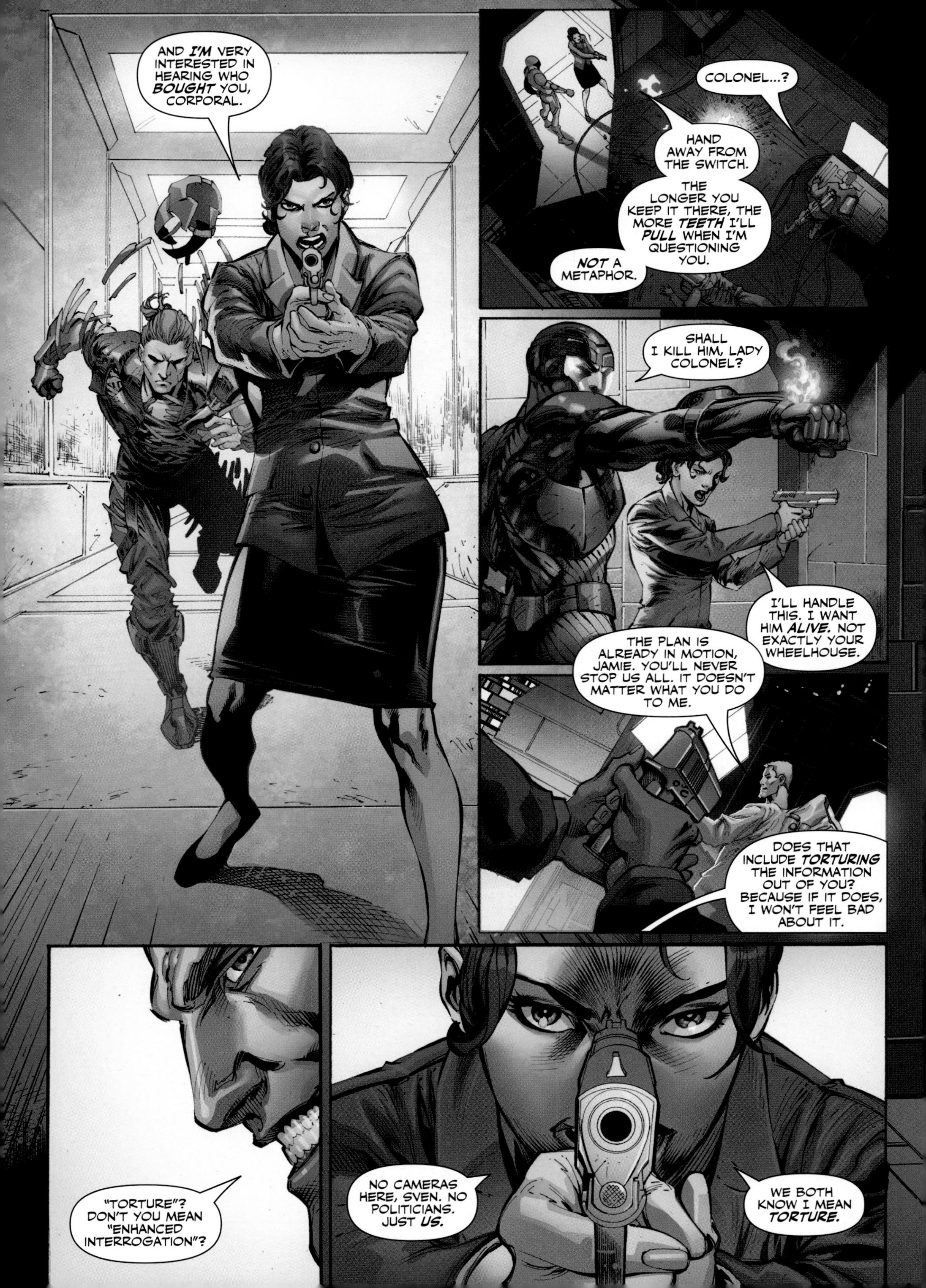
AND I'M VERY INTERESTED IN HEARING WHO BOUGHT YOU, CORPORAL.
COLONEL...?
HAND AWAY FROM THE SWITCH.
THE LONGER YOU KEEP IT THERE, THE MORE TEETH I'LL PULL WHEN I'M QUESTIONING YOU.
NOT A METAPHOR.
SHALL I KILL HIM, LADY COLONEL?
I'LL HANDLE THIS. I WANT HIM ALIVE. NOT EXACTLY YOUR WHEELHOUSE.
THE PLAN IS ALREADY IN MOTION, JAMIE. YOU'LL NEVER STOP US ALL. IT DOESN'T MATTER WHAT YOU DO TO ME.
DOES THAT INCLUDE TORTURING THE INFORMATION OUT OF YOU? BECAUSE IF IT DOES, I WON'T FEEL BAD ABOUT IT.
"TORTURE"? DON'T YOU MEAN "ENHANCED INTERROGATION"?
NO CAMERAS HERE, SVEN. NO POLITICIANS. JUST US.
WE BOTH KNOW I MEAN TORTURE.

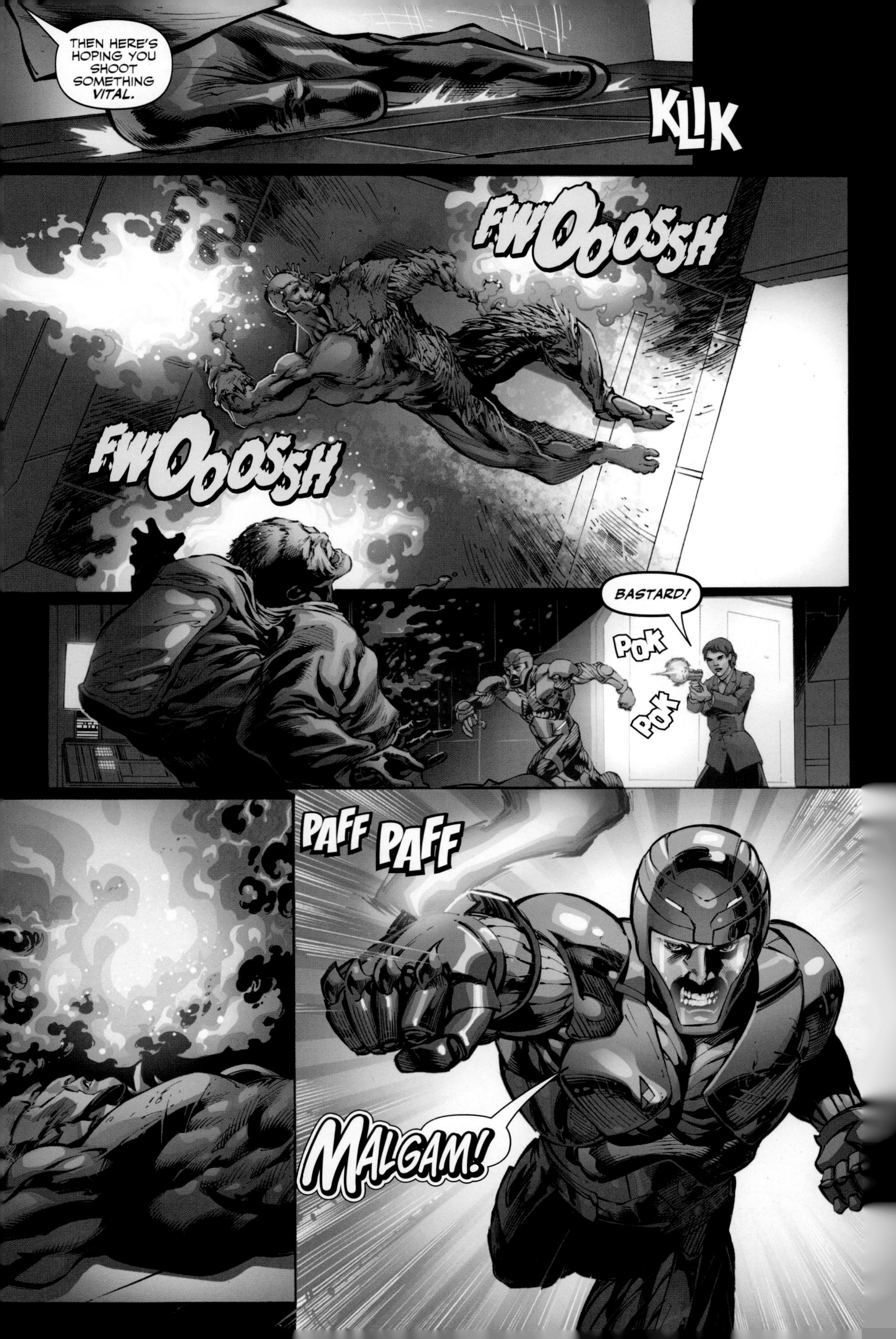
THEN HERE'S HOPING YOU SHOOT SOMETHING VITAL.
KLIK
FWOOOOSSH
FWOOOOSSH
BASTARD!
POK
POK
PAFF PAFF
MALGAM!

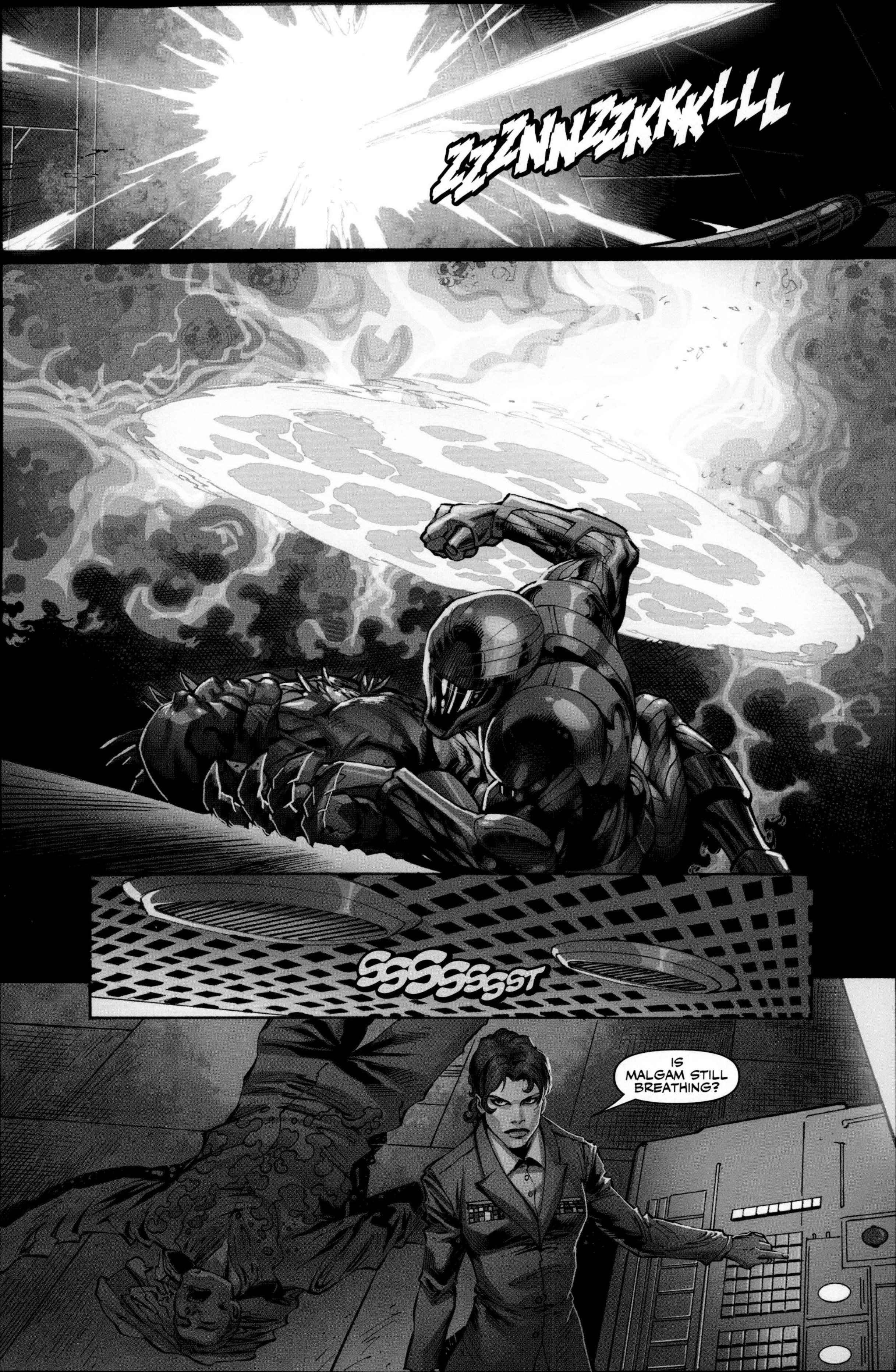
ZZZNNNZZKKKLLL
SSSSSSSST
IS MALGAM STILL BREATHING?

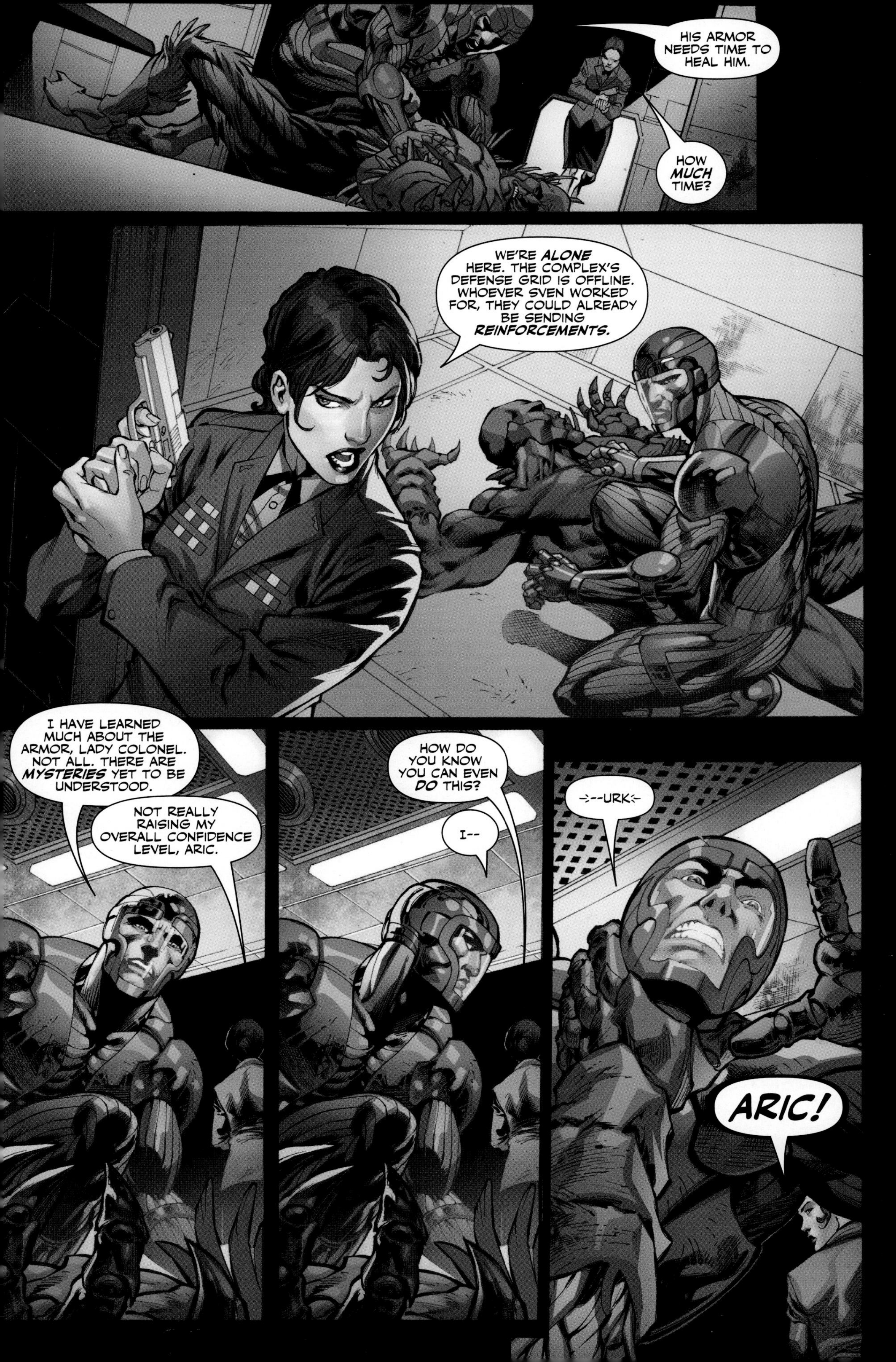
HIS ARMOR NEEDS TIME TO HEAL HIM.
HOW MUCH TIME?
WE'RE ALONE HERE. THE COMPLEX'S DEFENSE GRID IS OFFLINE. WHOEVER SVEN WORKED FOR, THEY COULD ALREADY BE SENDING REINFORCEMENTS.
I HAVE LEARNED MUCH ABOUT THE ARMOR, LADY COLONEL. NOT ALL. THERE ARE MYSTERIES YET TO BE UNDERSTOOD.
NOT REALLY RAISING MY OVERALL CONFIDENCE LEVEL, ARIC.
HOW DO YOU KNOW YOU CAN EVEN DO THIS?
I--
--URK
ARIC!

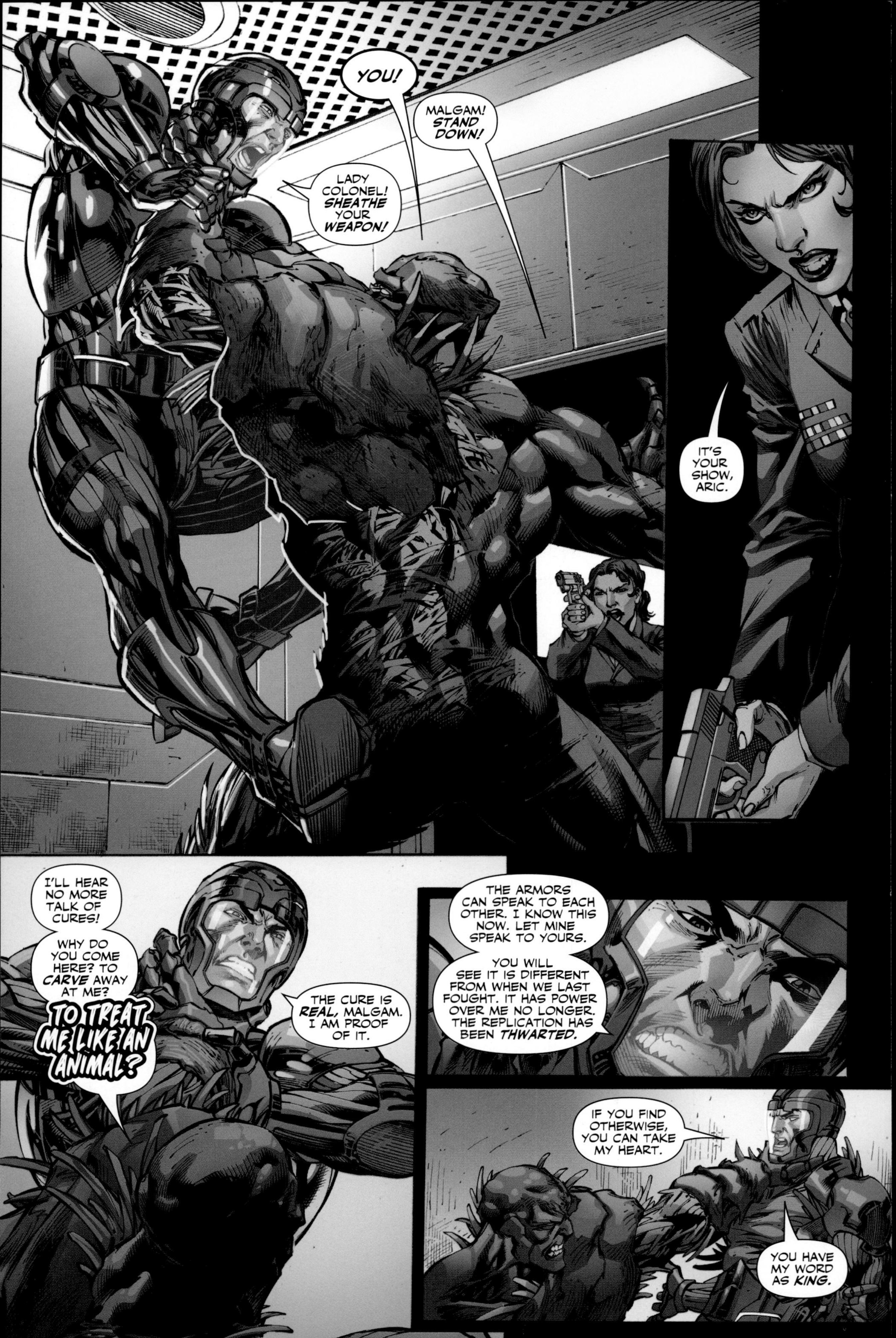
YOU!
MALGAM! STAND DOWN!
LADY COLONEL! SHEATHE YOUR WEAPON!
IT'S YOUR SHOW, ARIC.
I'LL HEAR NO MORE TALK OF CURES!
WHY DO YOU COME HERE? TO CARVE AWAY AT ME?
TO TREAT ME LIKE AN ANIMAL?
THE CURE IS REAL, MALGAM. I AM PROOF OF IT.
THE ARMORS CAN SPEAK TO EACH OTHER. I KNOW THIS NOW. LET MINE SPEAK TO YOURS.
YOU WILL SEE IT IS DIFFERENT FROM WHEN WE LAST FOUGHT. IT HAS POWER OVER ME NO LONGER. THE REPLICATION HAS BEEN THWARTED.
IF YOU FIND OTHERWISE, YOU CAN TAKE MY HEART.
YOU HAVE MY WORD AS KING.

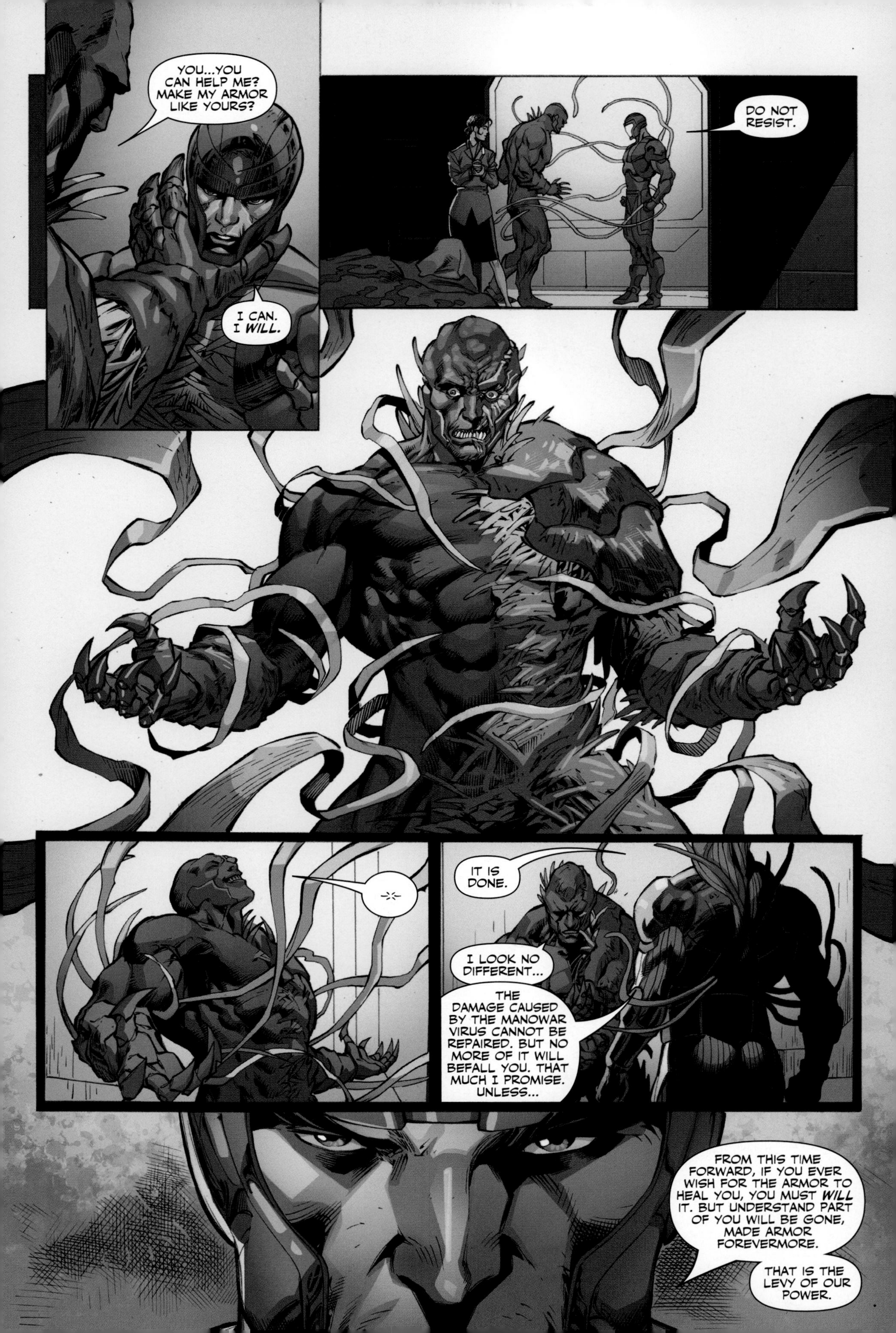
YOU...YOU CAN HELP ME? MAKE MY ARMOR LIKE YOURS?
I CAN. I WILL.
DO NOT RESIST.
-:-
IT IS DONE.
I LOOK NO DIFFERENT...
THE DAMAGE CAUSED BY THE MANOWAR VIRUS CANNOT BE REPAIRED. BUT NO MORE OF IT WILL BEFALL YOU. THAT MUCH I PROMISE. UNLESS...
FROM THIS TIME FORWARD, IF YOU EVER WISH FOR THE ARMOR TO HEAL YOU, YOU MUST WILL IT. BUT UNDERSTAND PART OF YOU WILL BE GONE, MADE ARMOR FOREVERMORE.
THAT IS THE LEVY OF OUR POWER.

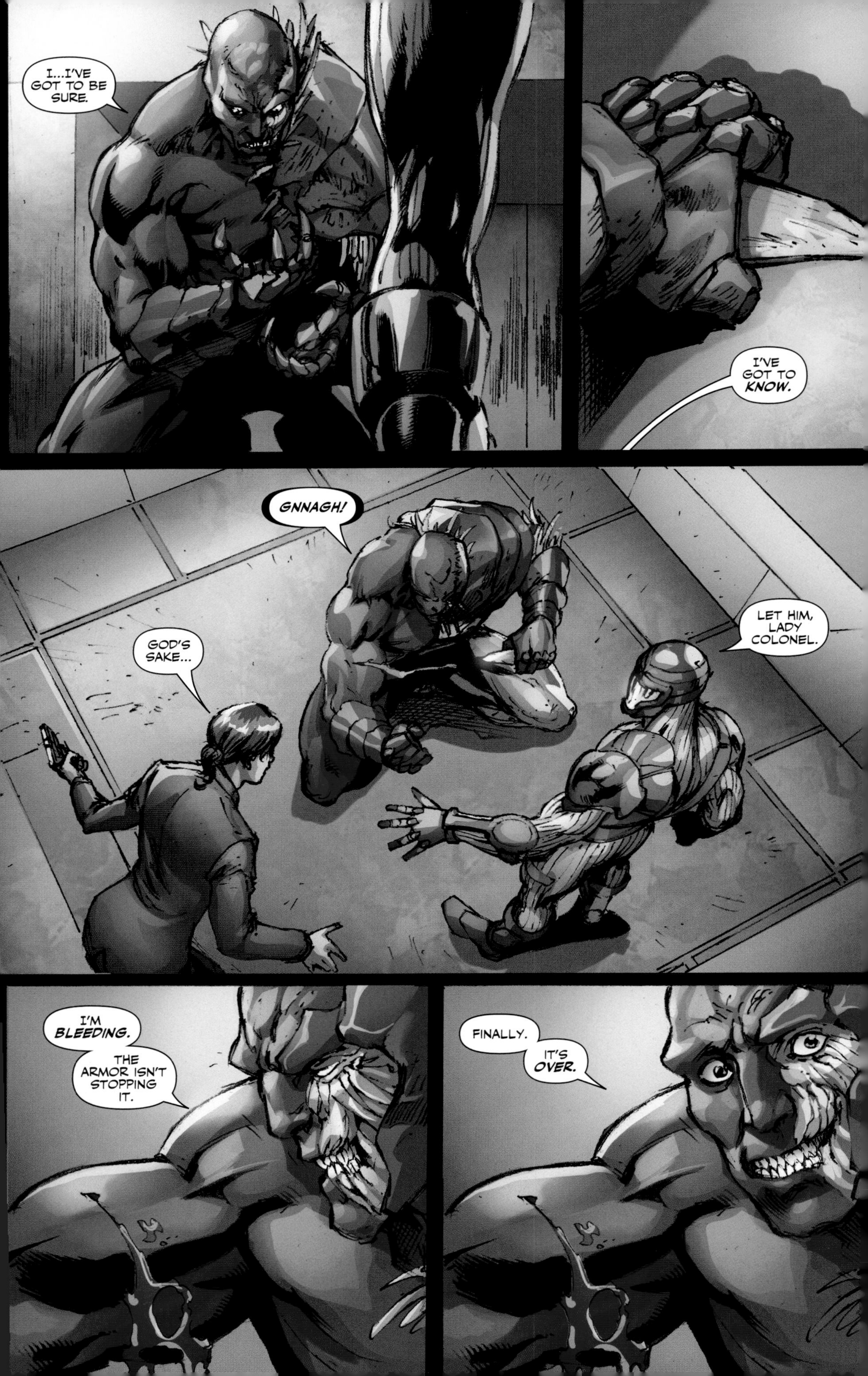
I...I'VE GOT TO BE SURE.
I'VE GOT TO KNOW.
GNNAGH!
GOD'S SAKE...
LET HIM, LADY COLONEL.
I'M BLEEDING.
THE ARMOR ISN'T STOPPING IT.
FINALLY.
IT'S OVER.

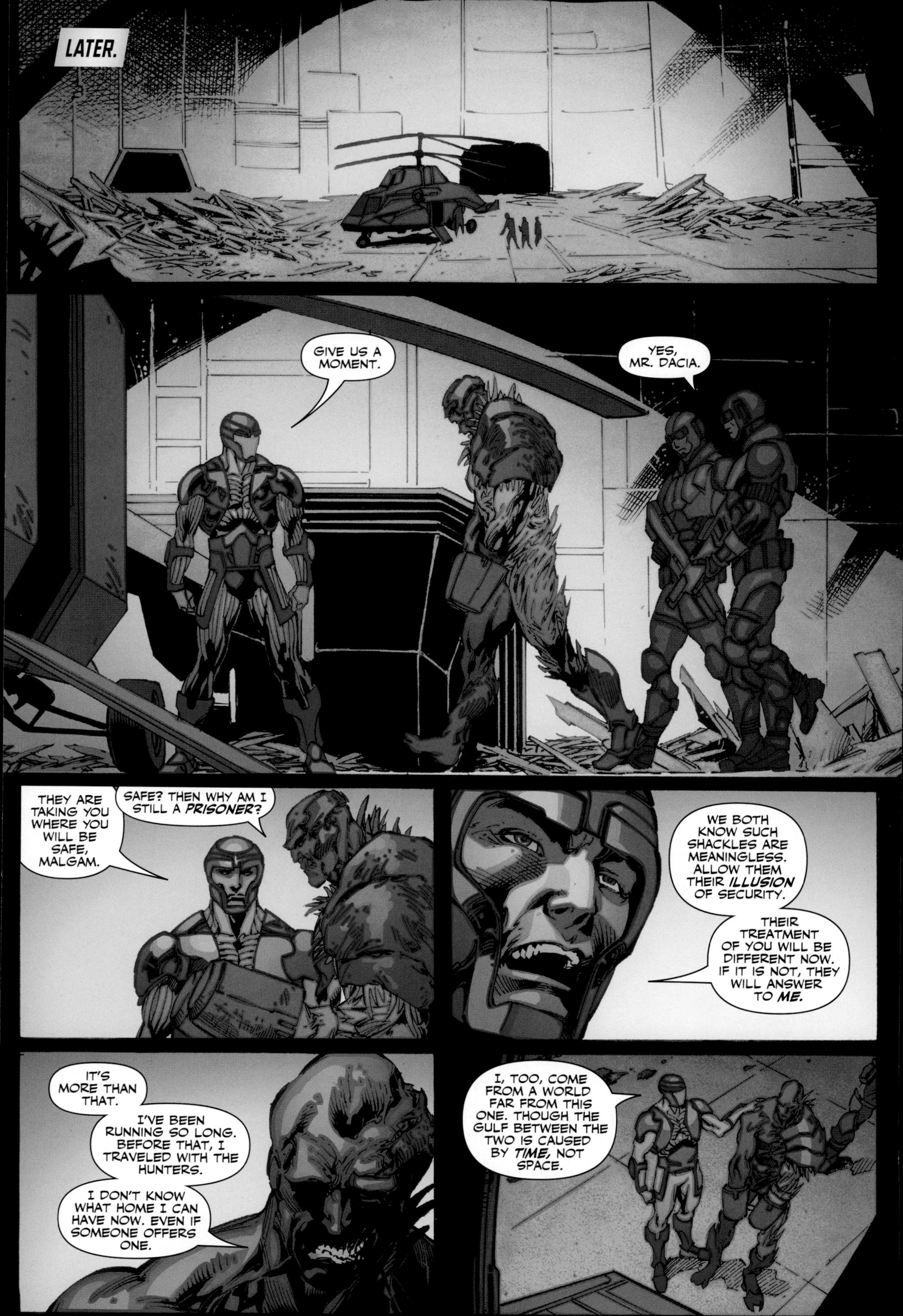
LATER.
GIVE US A MOMENT.
YES, MR. DACIA.
THEY ARE TAKING YOU WHERE YOU WILL BE SAFE, MALGAM.
SAFE? THEN WHY AM I STILL A PRISONER?
WE BOTH KNOW SUCH SHACKLES ARE MEANINGLESS. ALLOW THEM THEIR ILLUSION OF SECURITY.
THEIR TREATMENT OF YOU WILL BE DIFFERENT NOW. IF IT IS NOT, THEY WILL ANSWER TO ME.
IT'S MORE THAN THAT.
I'VE BEEN RUNNING SO LONG. BEFORE THAT, I TRAVELED WITH THE HUNTERS.
I DON'T KNOW WHAT HOME I CAN HAVE NOW. EVEN IF SOMEONE OFFERS ONE.
I, TOO, COME FROM A WORLD FAR FROM THIS ONE. THOUGH THE GULF BETWEEN THE TWO IS CAUSED BY TIME, NOT SPACE.

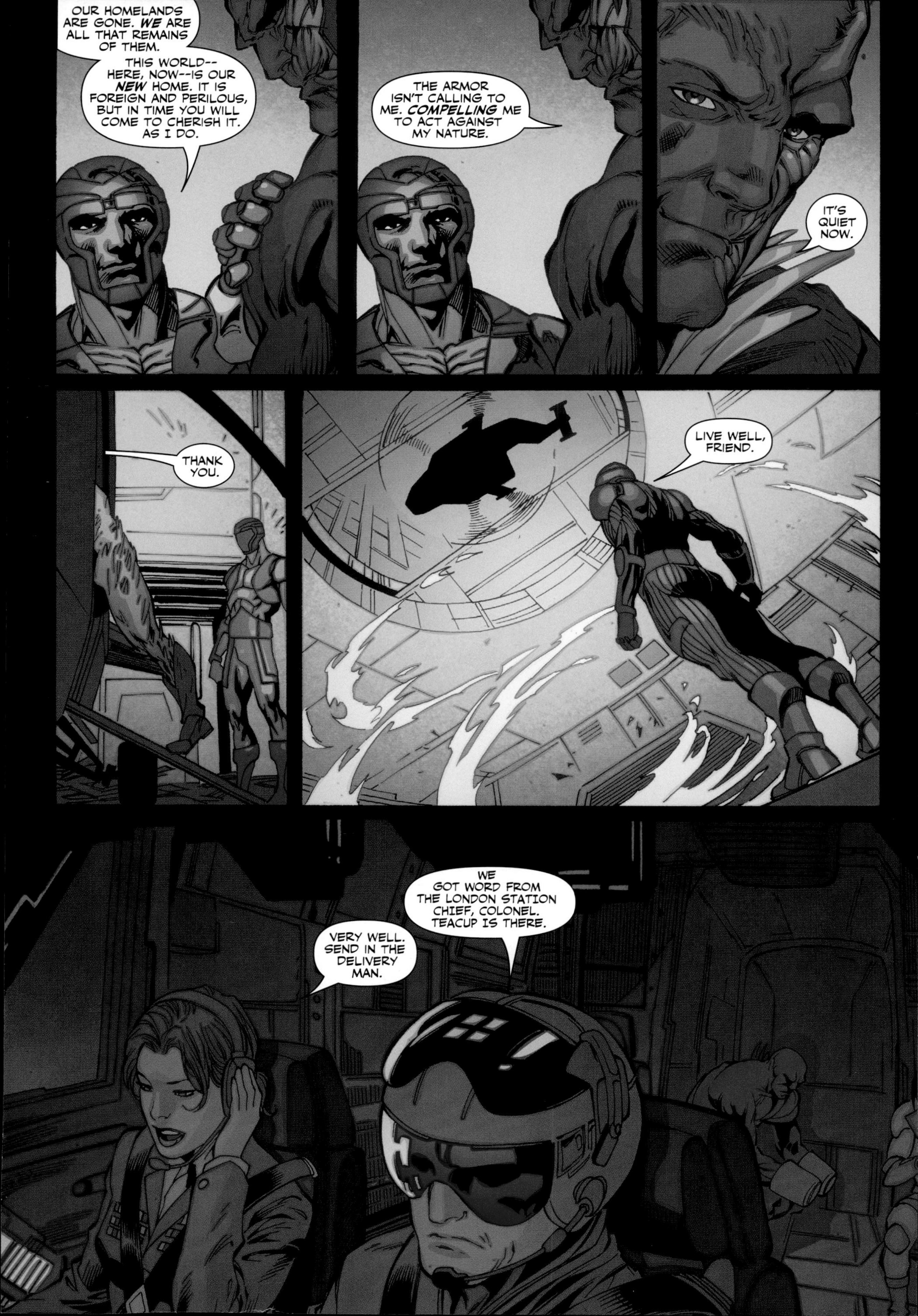
OUR HOMELANDS ARE GONE. WE ARE ALL THAT REMAINS OF THEM.
THIS WORLD-- HERE, NOW--IS OUR NEW HOME. IT IS FOREIGN AND PERILOUS, BUT IN TIME YOU WILL COME TO CHERISH IT. AS I DO.
THE ARMOR ISN'T CALLING TO ME. COMPELLING ME TO ACT AGAINST MY NATURE.
IT'S QUIET NOW.
THANK YOU.
LIVE WELL, FRIEND.
WE GOT WORD FROM THE LONDON STATION CHIEF, COLONEL. TEACUP IS THERE.
VERY WELL. SEND IN THE DELIVERY MAN.

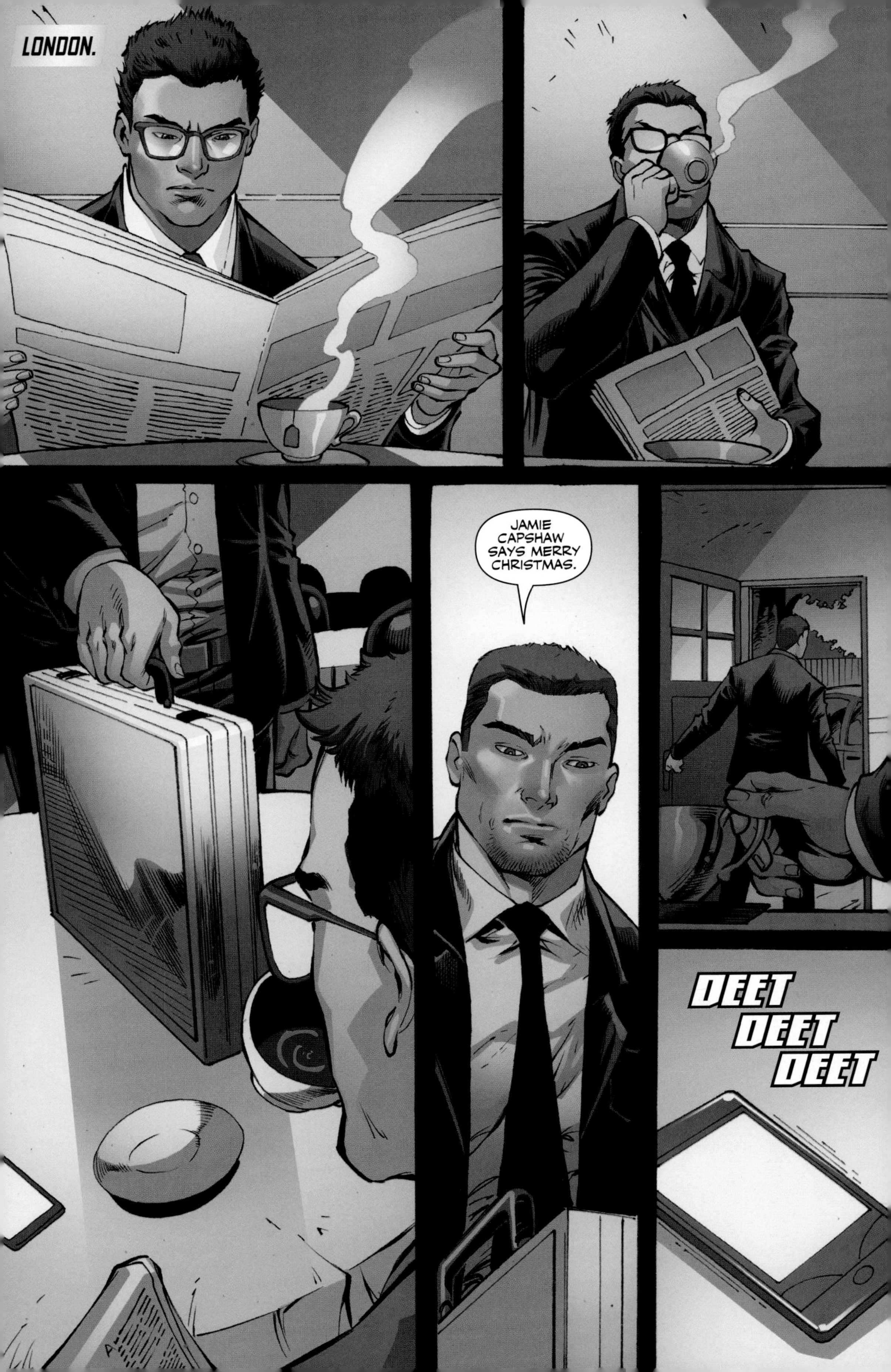
LONDON.
JAMIE CAPSHAW SAYS MERRY CHRISTMAS.
DEET DEET DEET

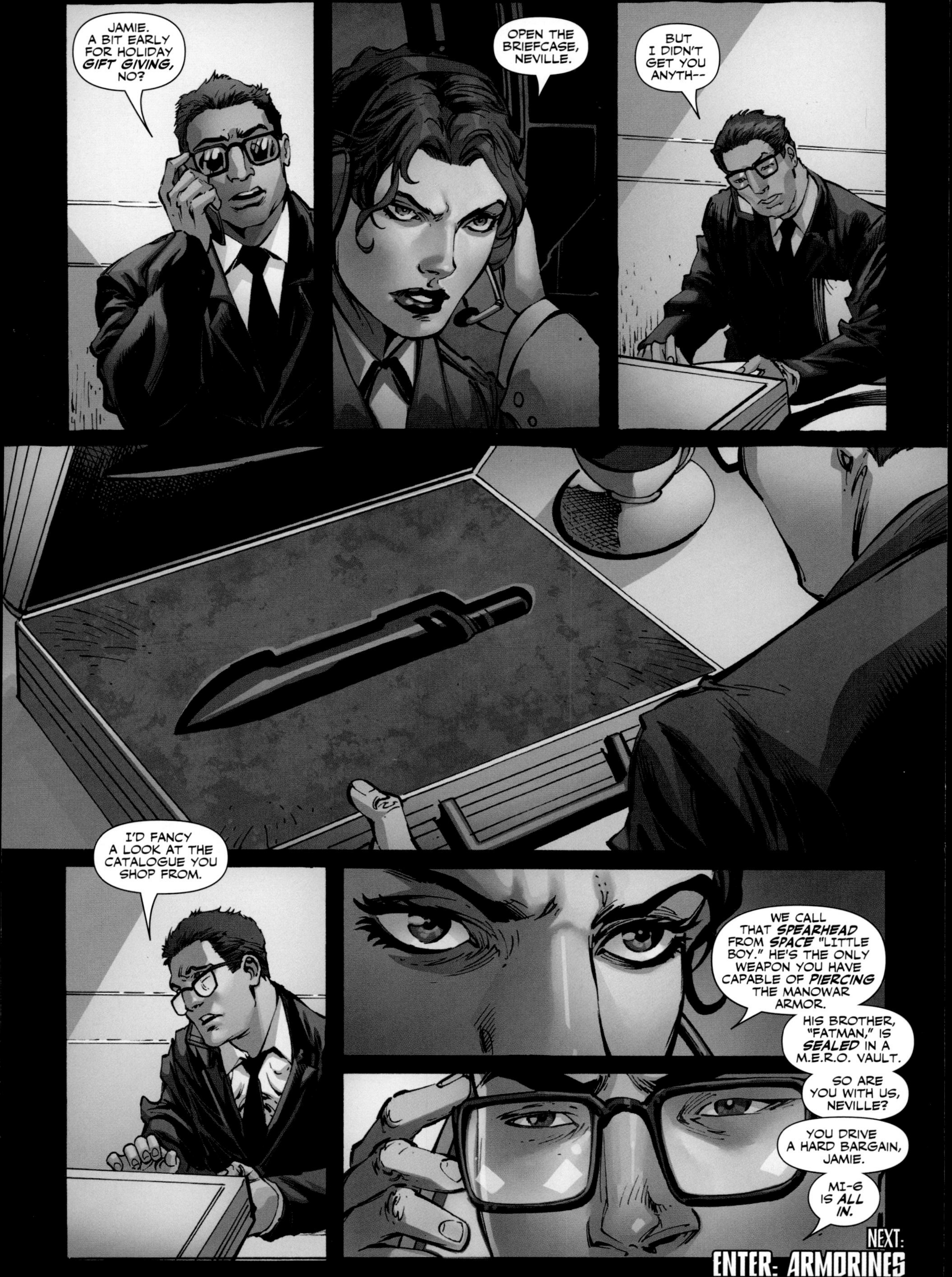
JAMIE. A BIT EARLY FOR HOLIDAY GIFT GIVING, NO?
OPEN THE BRIEFCASE, NEVILLE.
BUT I DIDN'T GET YOU ANYTH--
I'D FANCY A LOOK AT THE CATALOGUE YOU SHOP FROM.
WE CALL THAT SPEARHEAD FROM SPACE "LITTLE BOY." HE'S THE ONLY WEAPON YOU HAVE CAPABLE OF PIERCING THE MANOWAR ARMOR.
HIS BROTHER, "FATMAN," IS SEALED IN A M.E.R.O. VAULT.
SO ARE YOU WITH US, NEVILLE?
YOU DRIVE A HARD BARGAIN, JAMIE.
MI-6 IS ALL IN.
NEXT:
ENTER: ARMORINES

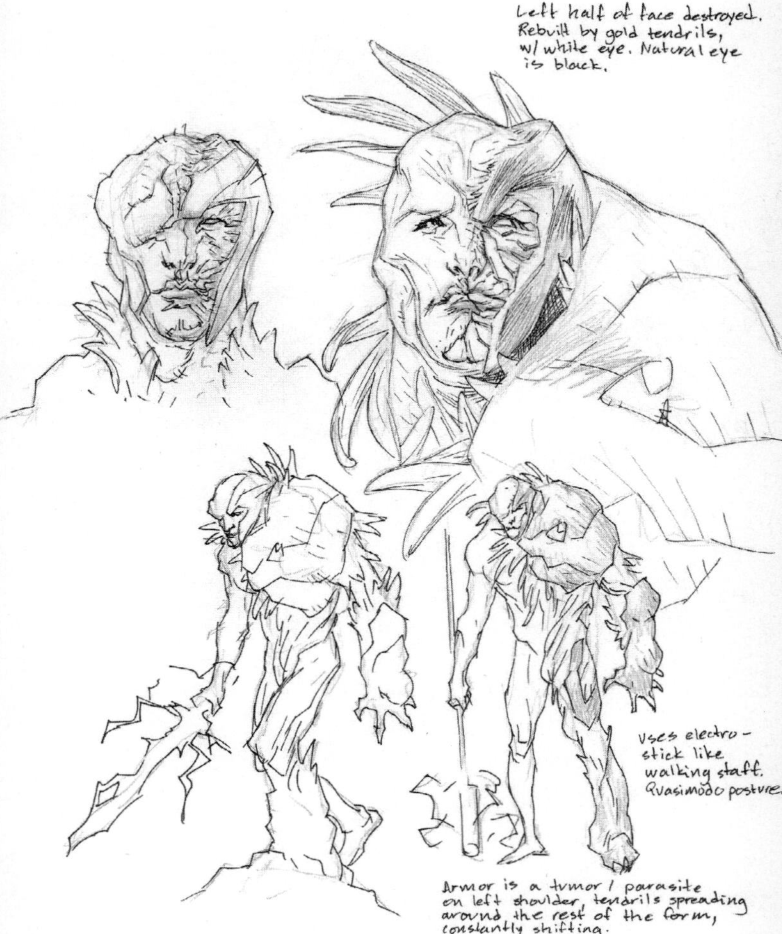
Left half of face destroyed. Rebuilt by gold tendrils, w/ white eye. Natural eye is black.
Uses electro-stick like walking staff. Quasimodo posture.
Armor is a tumor / parasite on left shoulder, tendrils spreading around the rest of the form, constantly shifting.

MALGAM (previous)
Character design by LEWIS LAROSA

GIN-GR, PRIMARY REEBO, QUARTZ,
HELIX, and LILT
Character designs by
CLAYTON CRAIN

X-O MANOWAR #23
Cover art by CAFU

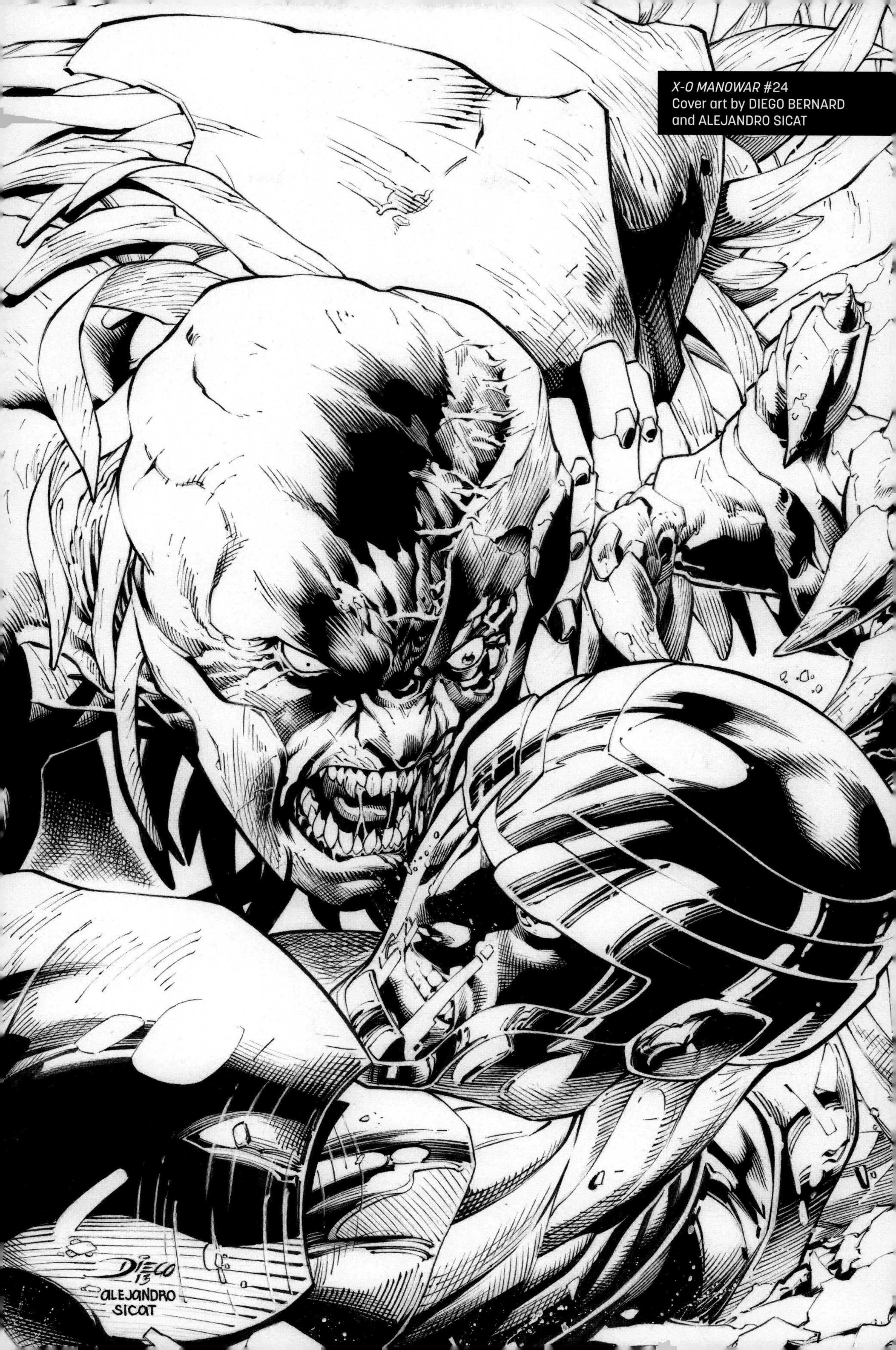
DIEGO
13
ALEJANDRO
SICAT

X-O MANOWAR #24
Cover art by DIEGO BERNARD
and ALEJANDRO SICAT

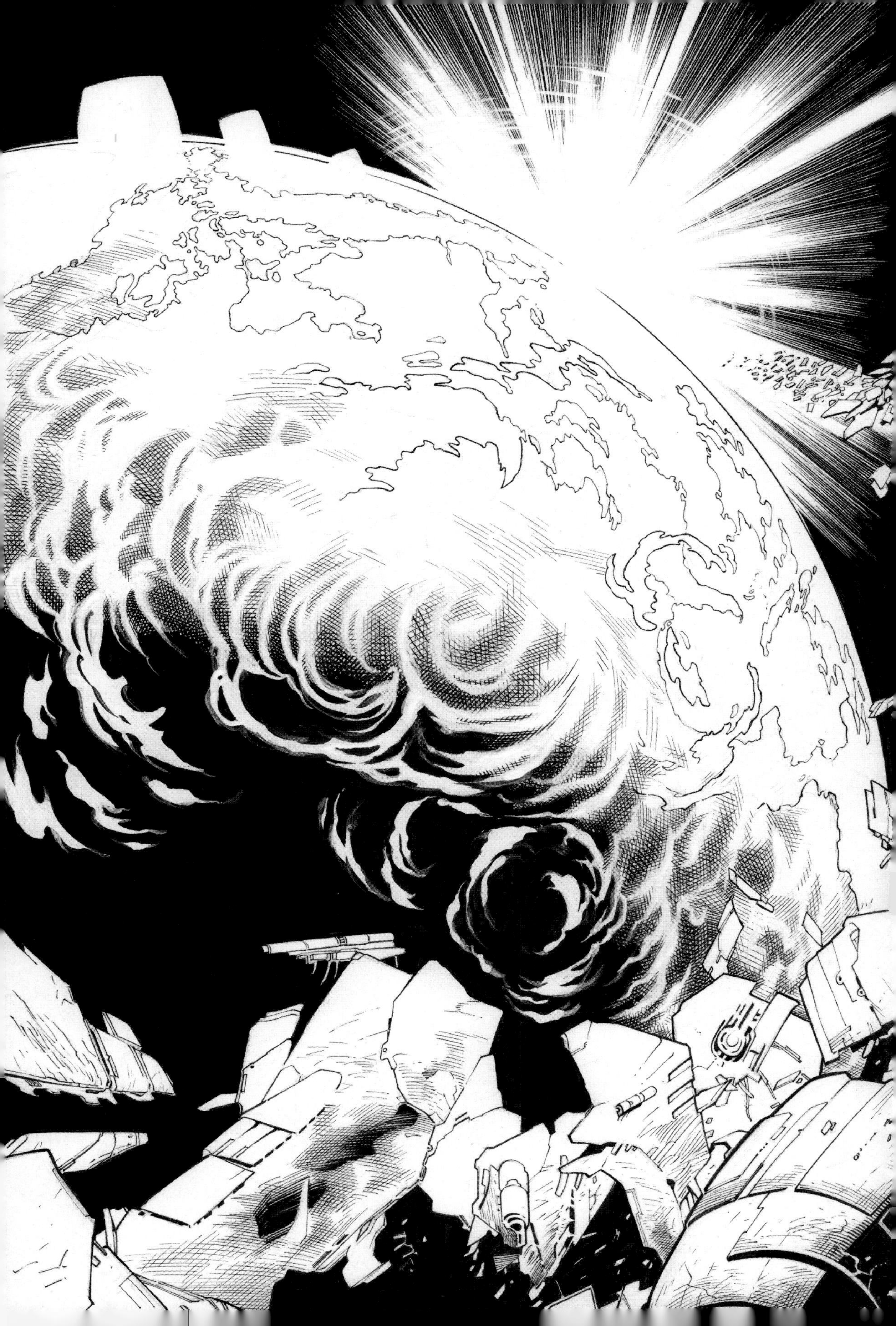

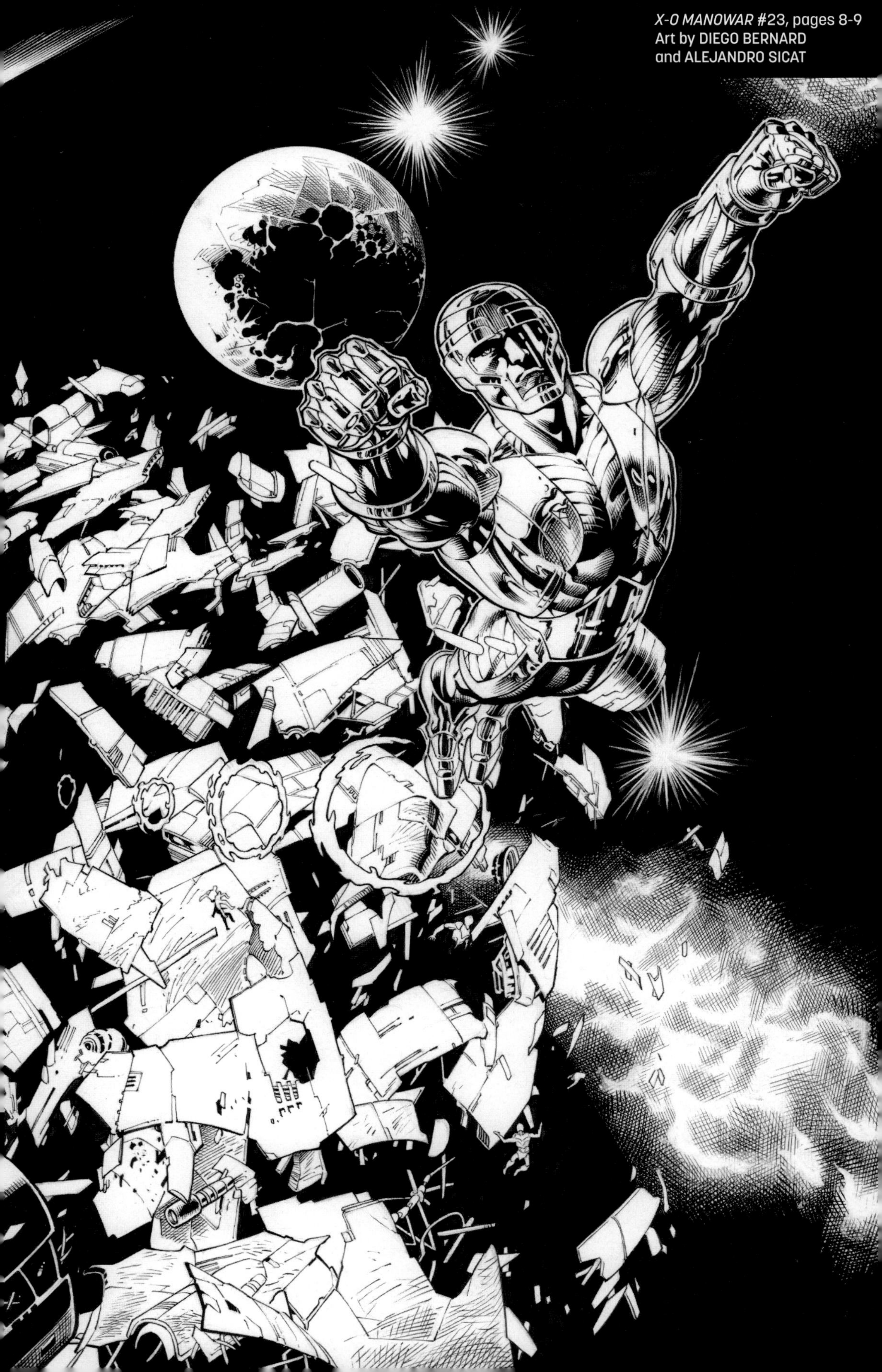

X-O MANOWAR #23, pages 8-9
Art by DIEGO BERNARD
and ALEJANDRO SICAT

X-O MANOWAR #23, p. 19
Art by DIEGO BERNARD and ALEJANDRO SICAT

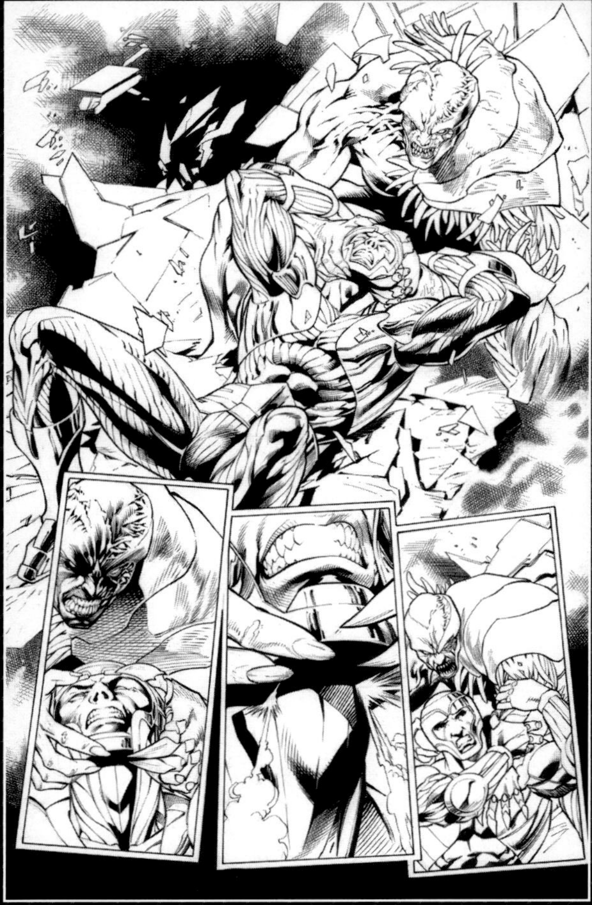

X-O MANOWAR #23, p. 20
Art by DIEGO BERNARD and ALEJANDRO SICAT

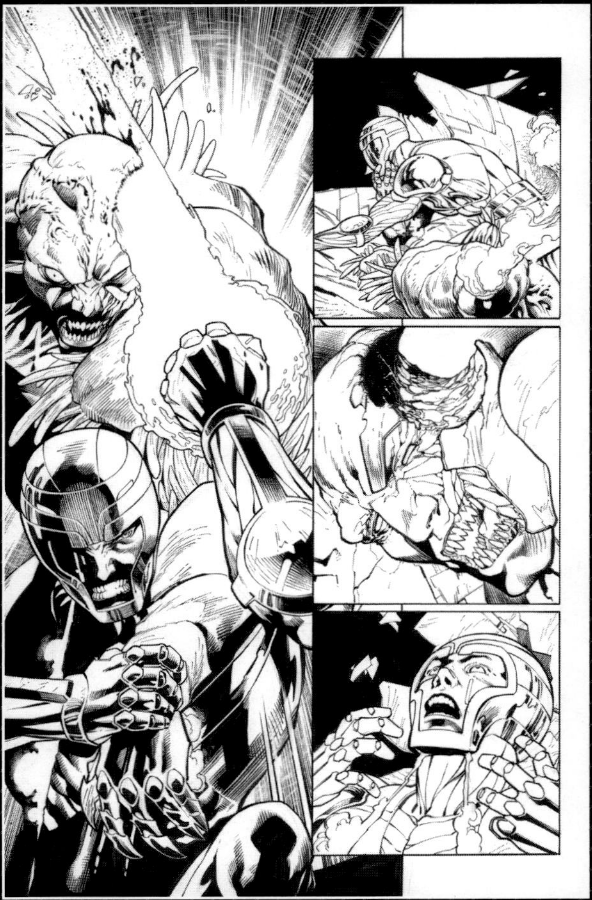

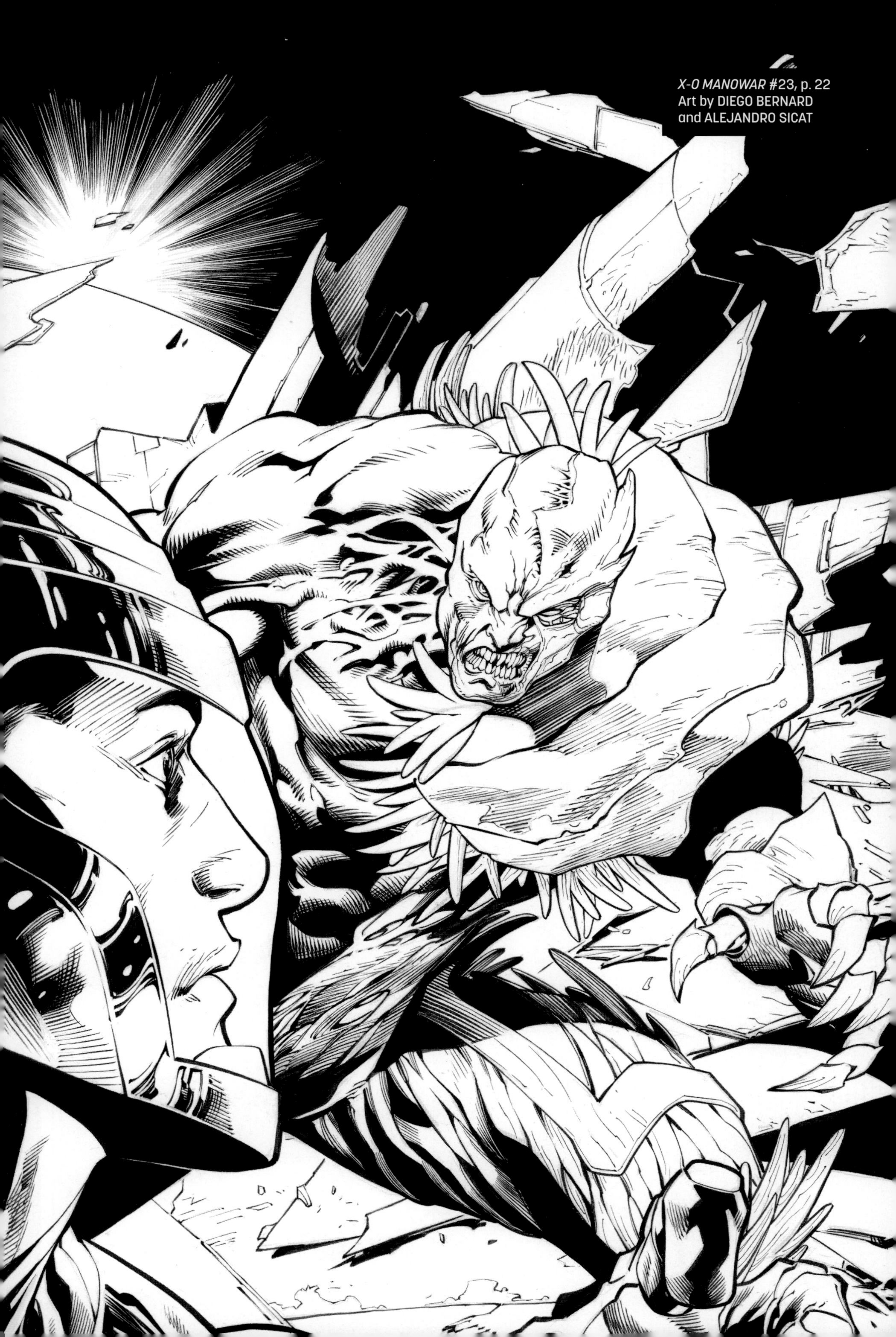

X-O MANOWAR #23, p. 22
Art by DIEGO BERNARD
and ALEJANDRO SICAT

X-O MANOWAR #24, p. 1
Pencils by DIEGO BERNARD
Inks (facing) by ALLISON RODRIGUES

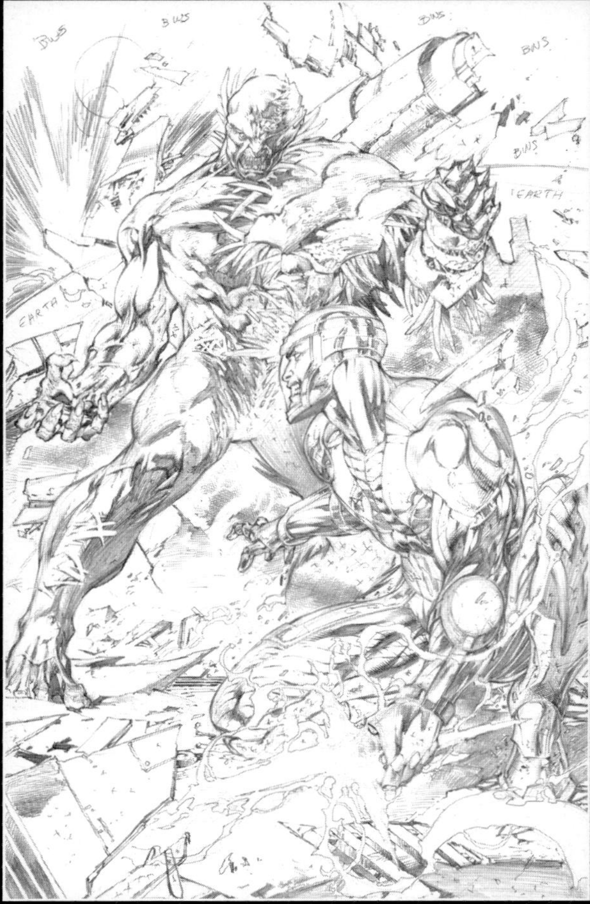
EARTH

X-O MANOWAR #24, p. 6
Pencils by DIEGO BERNARD
Inks by ALLISON RODRIGUES

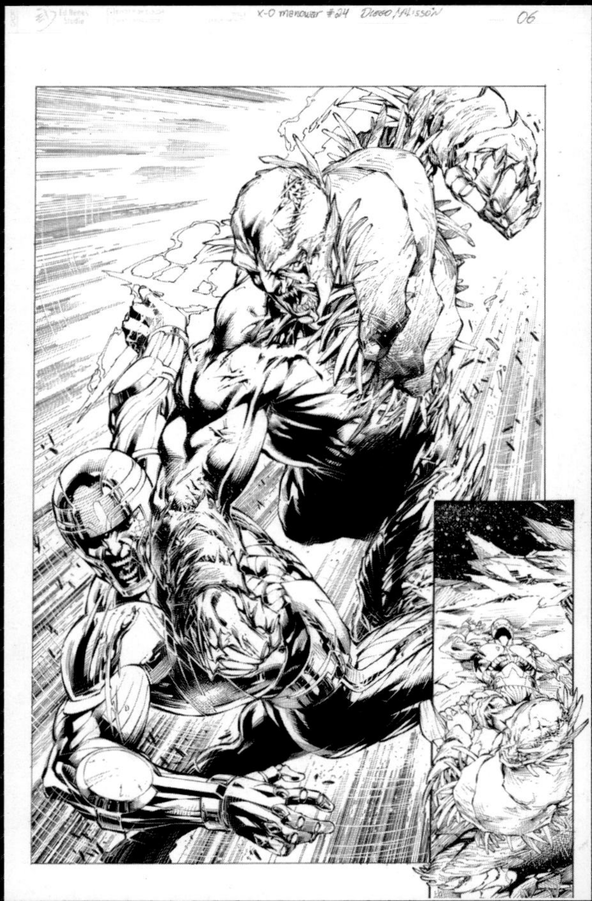
X-O manowar #24 Diego/Allison
06

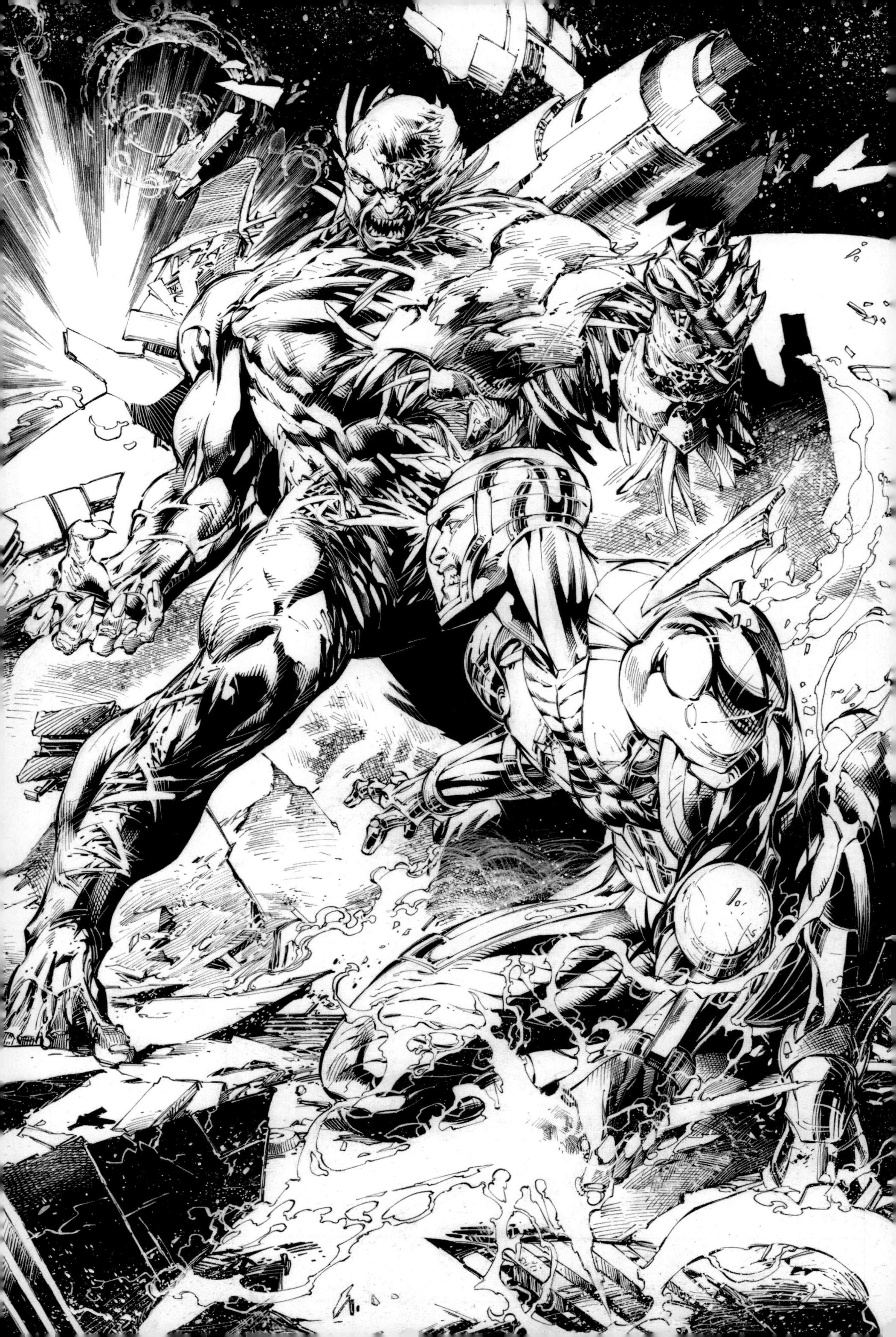

X-O MANOWAR #24
PAGE NINETEEN (four panels)

(Note: Dialogue and effects are often revised between the script and the final, lettered pages.)

PANEL 1: Largest panel on the page. An X-O Manowar armor -- shell dented, faceplate cracked -- lies chest down but with its face turned toward us in the dry sand of a desert world. One of Primary's tech spears is skewering the armor through the back, and silver blood pools out from the wound and soaks into the sand. We want the armor to be face down to give the impression that it was running when it was killed -- both things almost incomprehensible given what we've seen the armor do so far in the series. This is a dusty, windy world, so trails of sand should be blowing through the panels throughout the scene.

   1 ARIC CAPTION:
   "--<u>NOTHING</u> CAN TAKE OUR HOME AWAY."

   2 SETTING CAPTION:
   THE PLANET BA'EK.

   3 SPEARED X-O (weakly):
   close . . . almost done . . .

   4 SPEARED X-O (weakly):
   ulllllgh

PANEL 2: Tighter on the X-O armor from the back up, so we can see the face of the wearer better, but also keep the tech spear in the shot. The alien wearing the armor is a Ba'ek, a tribal, Native American-style race, though not much of its details are discernible because the alien's face is a twisted mix of organic tissue and armor, even more so than Malgam. This is the advanced stage of the Manowar virus.

   5 SPEARED X-O:
   <u>AGK!</u>

PANEL 3: Tighter on the Ba'ek's face through the cracked faceplate of the helmet. His eyes are wide in a dead man's stare, his mouth open in a lifeless scream, blood trailing from it.

PANEL 4: Pull back, so we see the entire armor. It has started to liquefy, melting away from the Ba'ek's body.

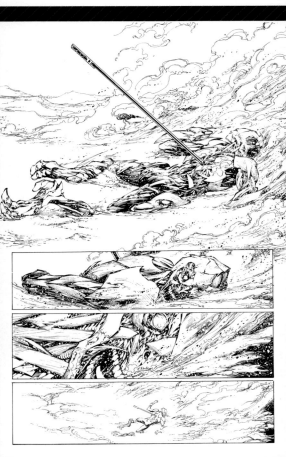

X-O MANOWAR #24, p. 19
Written by ROBERT VENDITTI
Pencils by DIEGO BERNARD
Inks by ALLISON RODRIGUES
Colors by BRIAN REBER

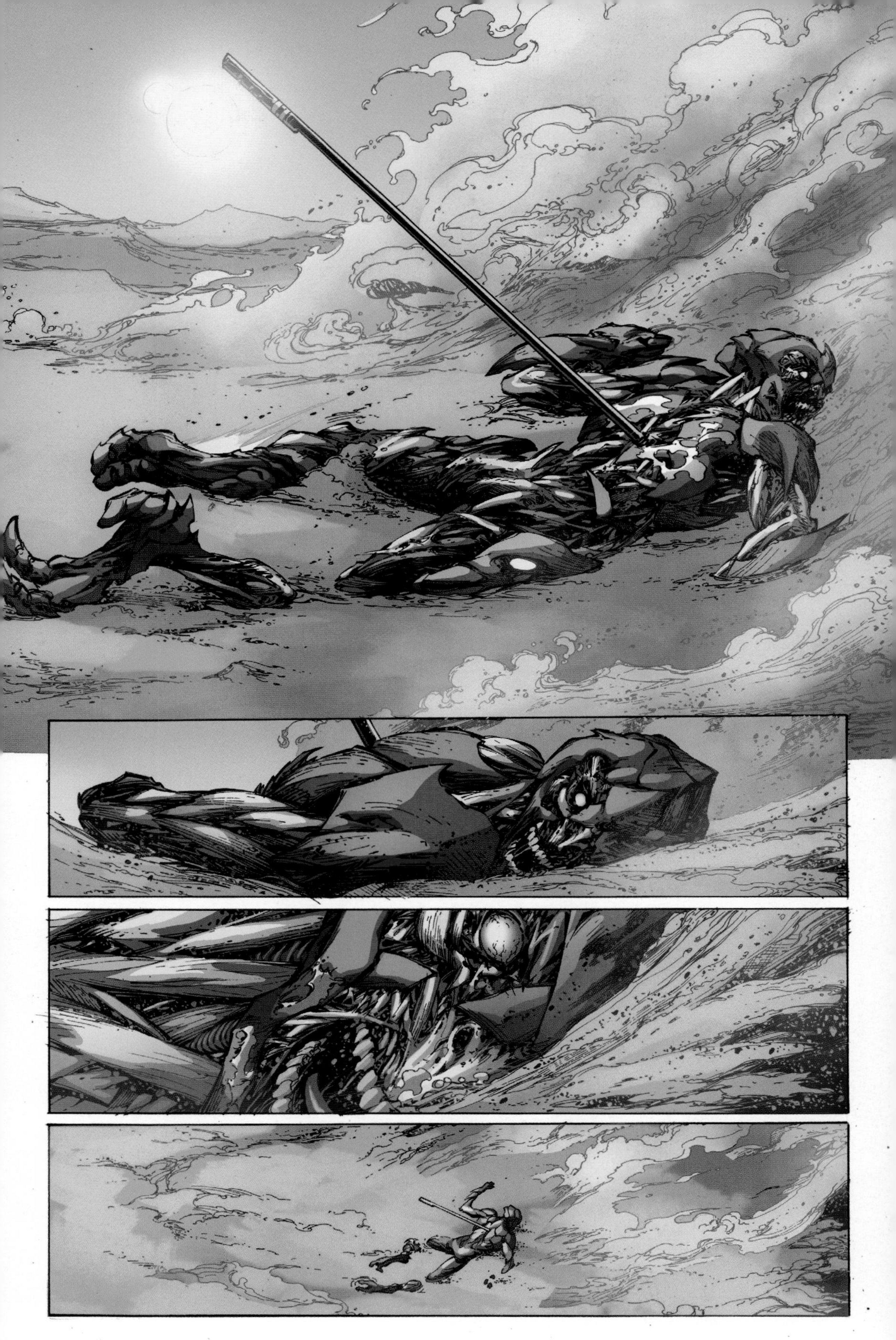

X-O MANOWAR #24
PAGE TWENTY (four panels)

PANEL 1: Switch to a shot of a silhouetted figure approaching us through the wind-whipped sand. This is Primary, but we won't know that until . . .

PANEL 2: Largest panel on the page. Primary stands in the sand, having emerged into view. His armor faceplate in lowered, giving him an ice-cold, expressionless feel. He holds another tech spear in one hand. He looks down at the dead Ba'ek at his feet, the armor a liquefied puddle around it. We can get more of a sense of the Ba'ek's true appearance now, but not too much, since he's mostly taken over by the Manowar virus.

PANEL 3: With quick, smooth motion, Primary drives the second spear straight through the dead Ba'ek's head. It sends white energy coursing over the corpse. We're communicating the idea that the armor is something you absolutely want to make sure is dead. You don't take chances with this stuff.

    1 SFX:
    SHLUK

PANEL 4: Grabbing each tech spear in one of his hands, Primary tugs them from the Ba'ek's body, bringing some gore and silver blood out with them. Through the blowing sand in the background, we see the silhouettes of Quartz, Lilt, and Helix approaching. Lilt is in flight, his wing-cape fanned out.

    2 SFX:
    SHUNK

X-O MANOWAR #24, p. 20
Written by ROBERT VENDITTI
Pencils by DIEGO BERNARD
Inks by ALLISON RODRIGUES
Colors by BRIAN REBER

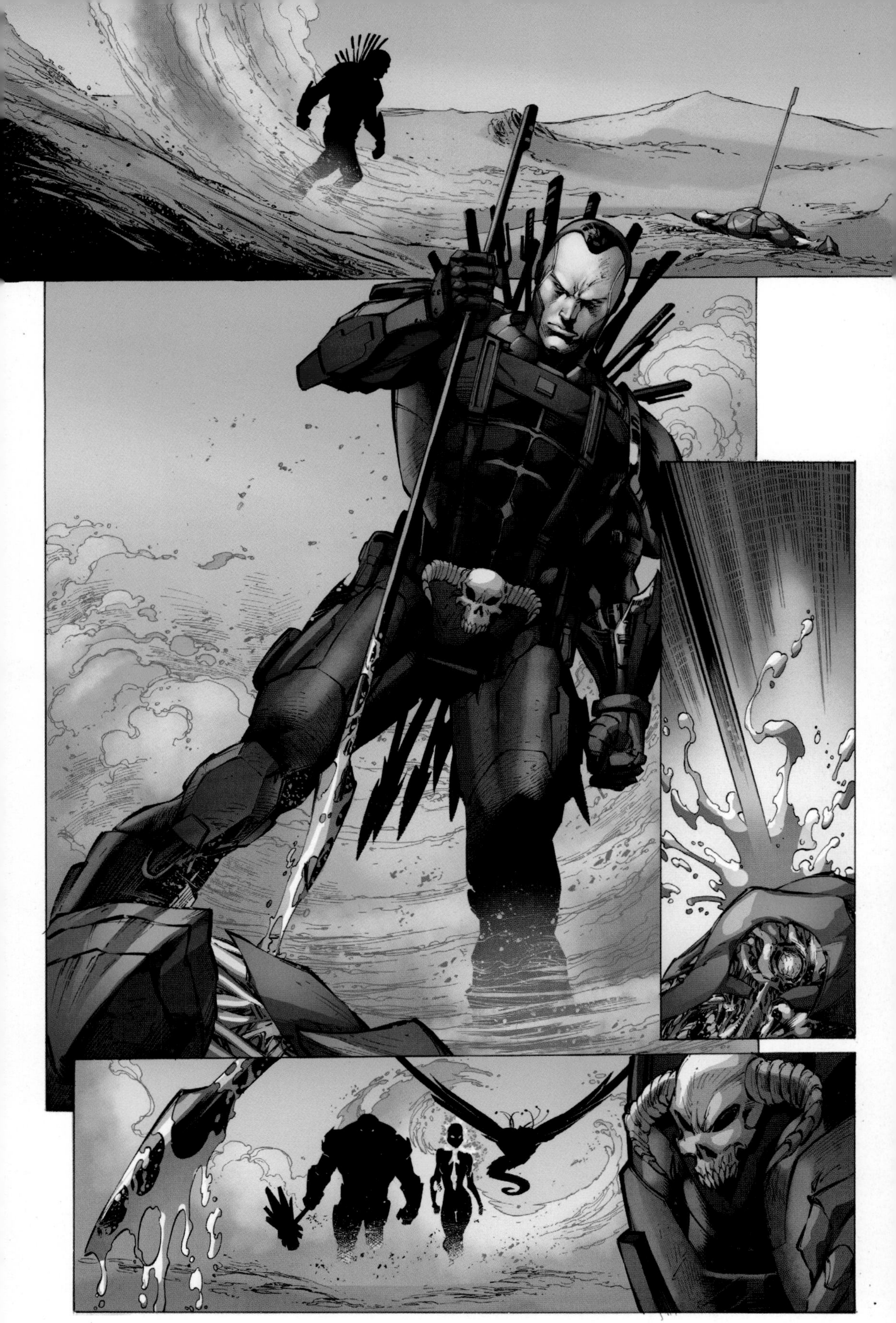

X-O MANOWAR #24
PAGE TWENTY-ONE (five panels)

PANEL 1: Quartz and Helix have walked up to stand near Primary, and Lilt is fluttering to the ground, just about to touch down. Primary hands his tech spears with one hand over to Helix, who takes them with one of her "hands". Quartz has his hammer propped on one shoulder. He looks off-panel with a grumpy frown.

1 HELIX:
RECHARGE THESE, HELIX.

2 QUARTZ:
WHAT . . . DO YOU SUPPOSE . . . BA'EK WAS LIKE . . . BEFORE?

PANEL 2: Primary kneels to roll the dead Ba'ek onto its back. He doesn't look at the others as he talks. Lilt has landed next to Quartz.

3 PRIMARY:
ALIVE.

PANEL 3: Primary's POV of the dead Ba'ek, now face up. This is the closest look we're going to get at it. It's roughly three-quarters armor and one-quarter organic. The Manowar armor's delta insignia lies in the dirt beside it, where its chest was when it was facedown.

PANEL 4: Primary picks up the delta insignia. We're closer in on him, so we can see what he's doing. Put us at an angle that allows us to see Lilt, who's looking down at a handheld scanning device.

4 PRIMARY:
LILT, ARE THERE ANY MORE ON-WORLD?

5 LILT:
NO, PRIMARY. THIS WAS THE LAST.

PANEL 5: Primary drops the delta insignia into a leather pouch. Is it possible to keep Primary's face -- or at least his mouth -- in the shot, while also giving us a view of the pouch's contents? If so, then the pouch should be filled with dozens of delta insignias.

6 PRIMARY:
GIN-GR?

X-O MANOWAR #24, p. 21
Written by ROBERT VENDITTI
Pencils by DIEGO BERNARD
Inks by ALLISON RODRIGUES
Colors by BRIAN REBER

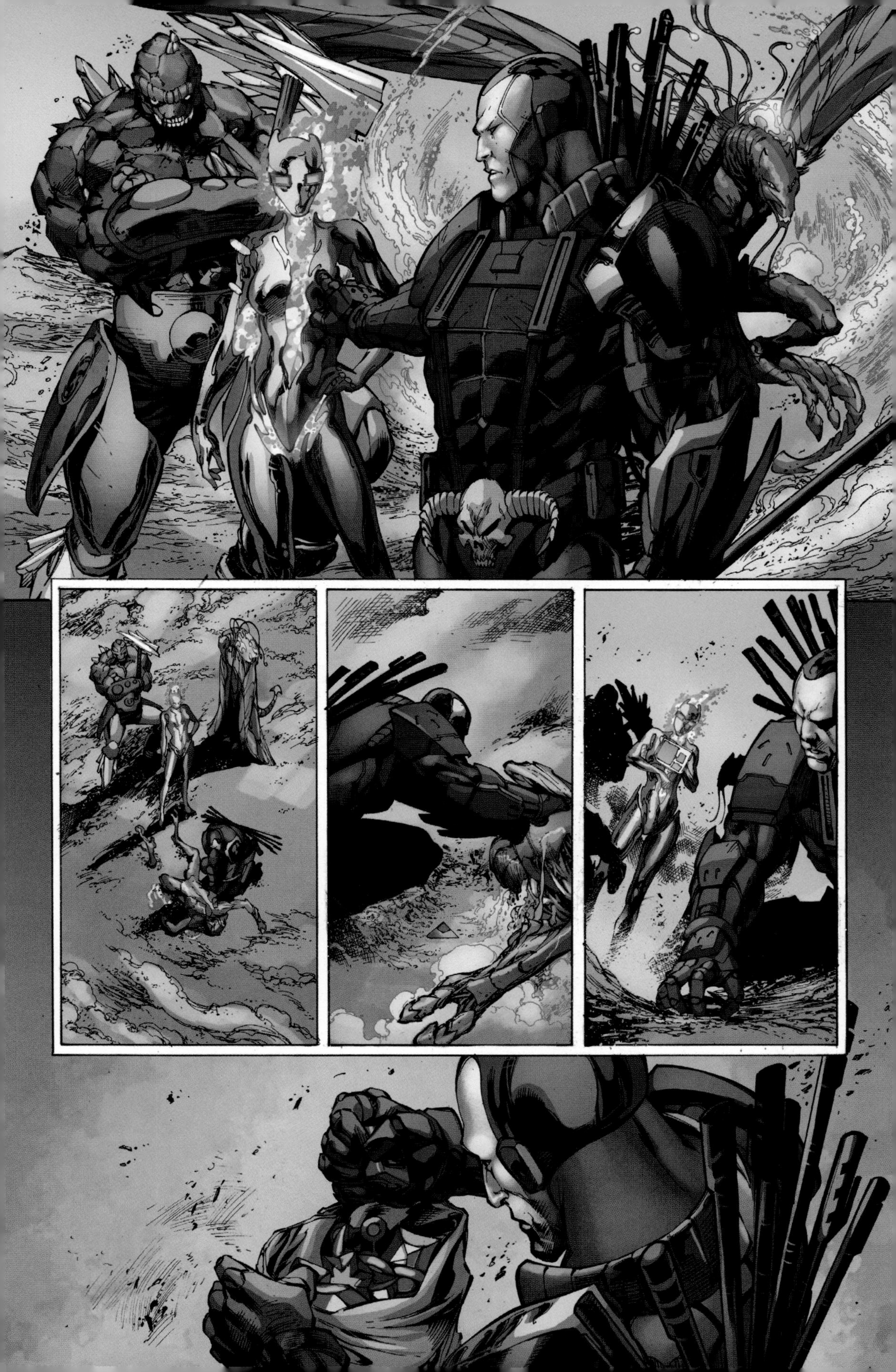

X-O MANOWAR #24
PAGE TWENTY-TWO (one panel)

PANEL 1: Pull back for the big reveal shot GIN-GR, the Armor Hunters' giant robot/ship, who's been standing just off panel all this time. Primary, Quartz, and Helix have turned and are walking toward GIN-GR. Lilt has spread his wing-cape and is fluttering upward. The dead Ba'ek is left behind to rot.

1 GIN-GR (digital):
YES, PRIMARY?

2 PRIMARY:
START PREPPING FOR PLANET-WIDE DECON.

3 BANNER:
NEXT: THE HUNT BEGINS!

X-O MANOWAR #24, p. 22
Written by ROBERT VENDITTI
Pencils by DIEGO BERNARD
Inks by ALLISON RODRIGUES
Colors by BRIAN REBER

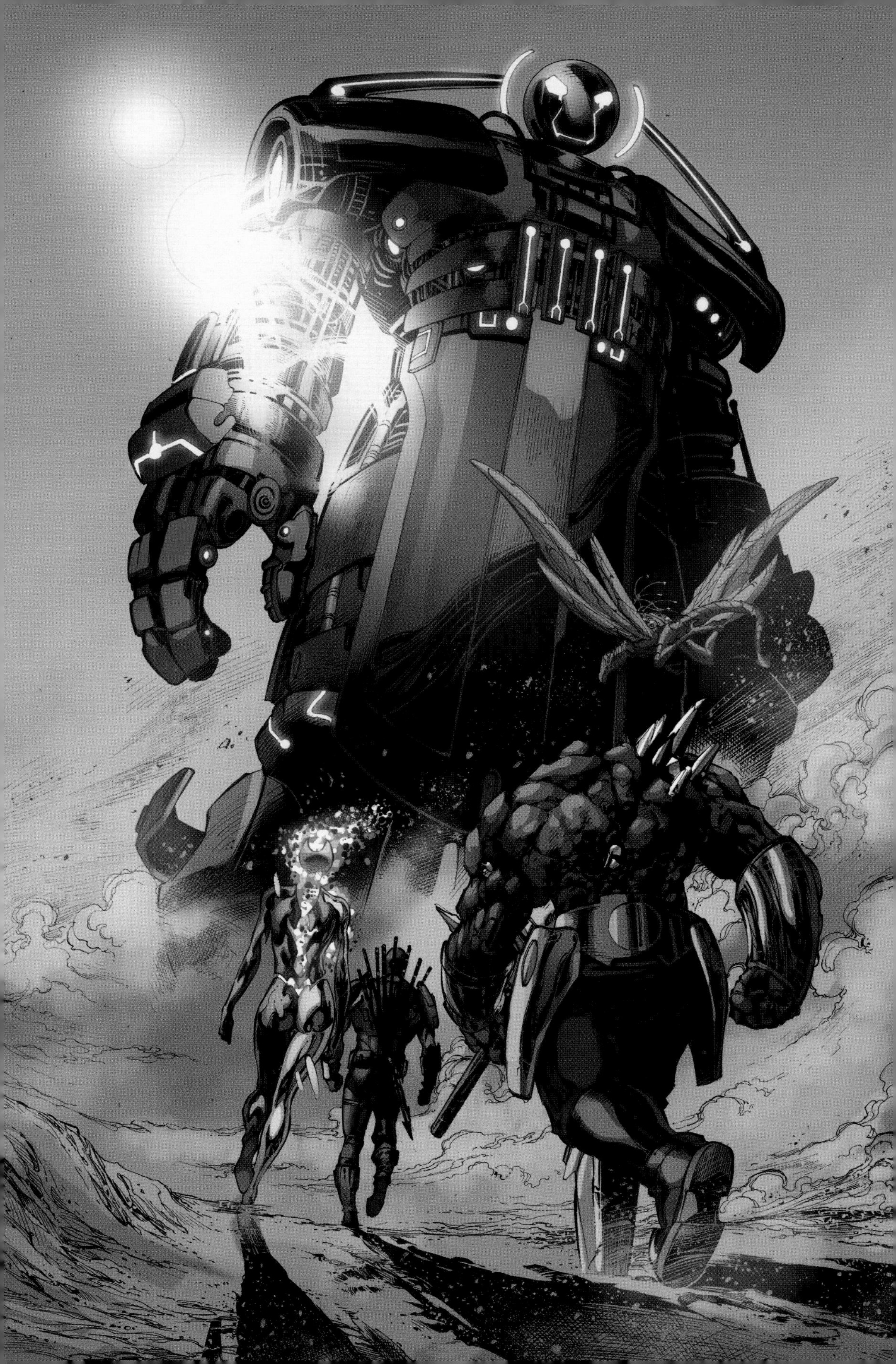

X-O MANOWAR #25
Pinup art by CARY NORD

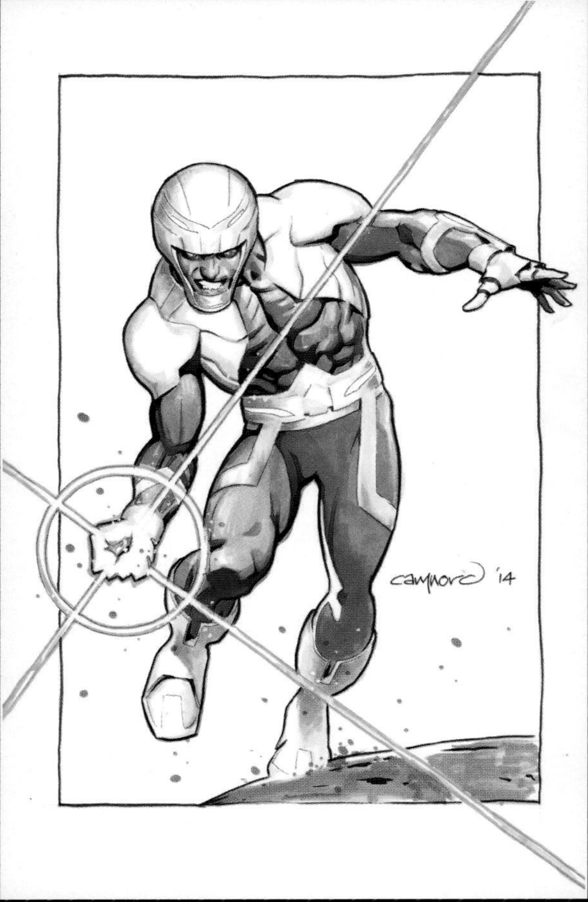

X-O MANOWAR #25 VARIANT COVER
Process and finished art by BRYAN HITCH

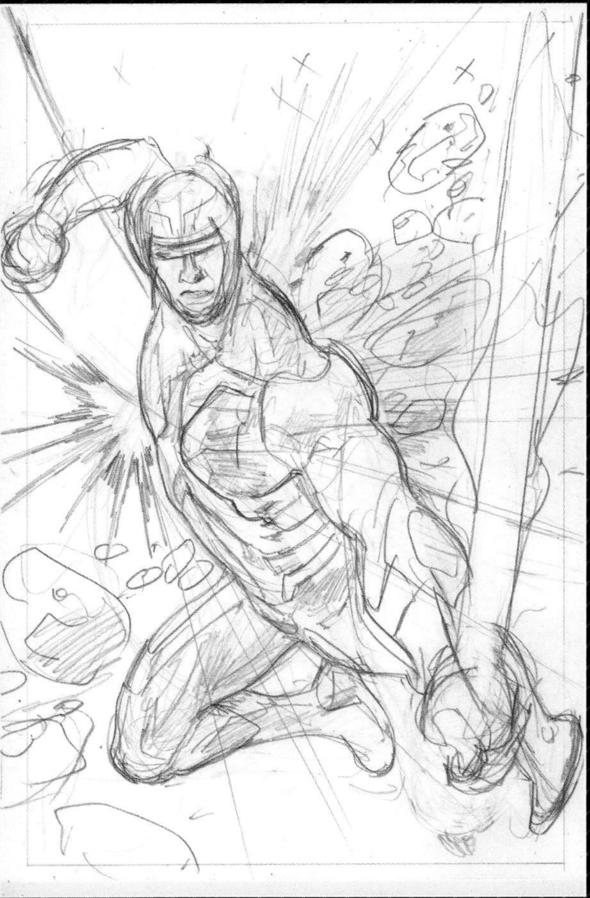

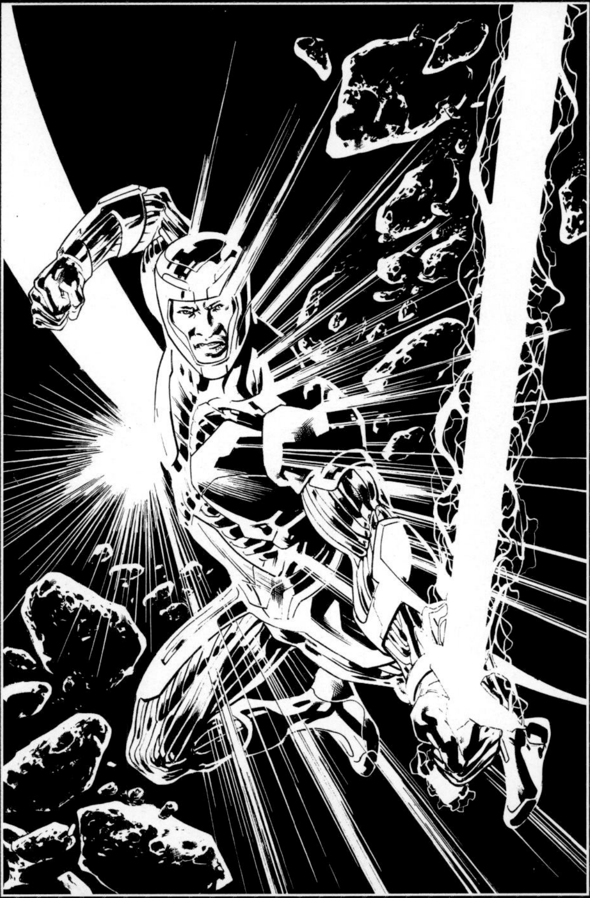

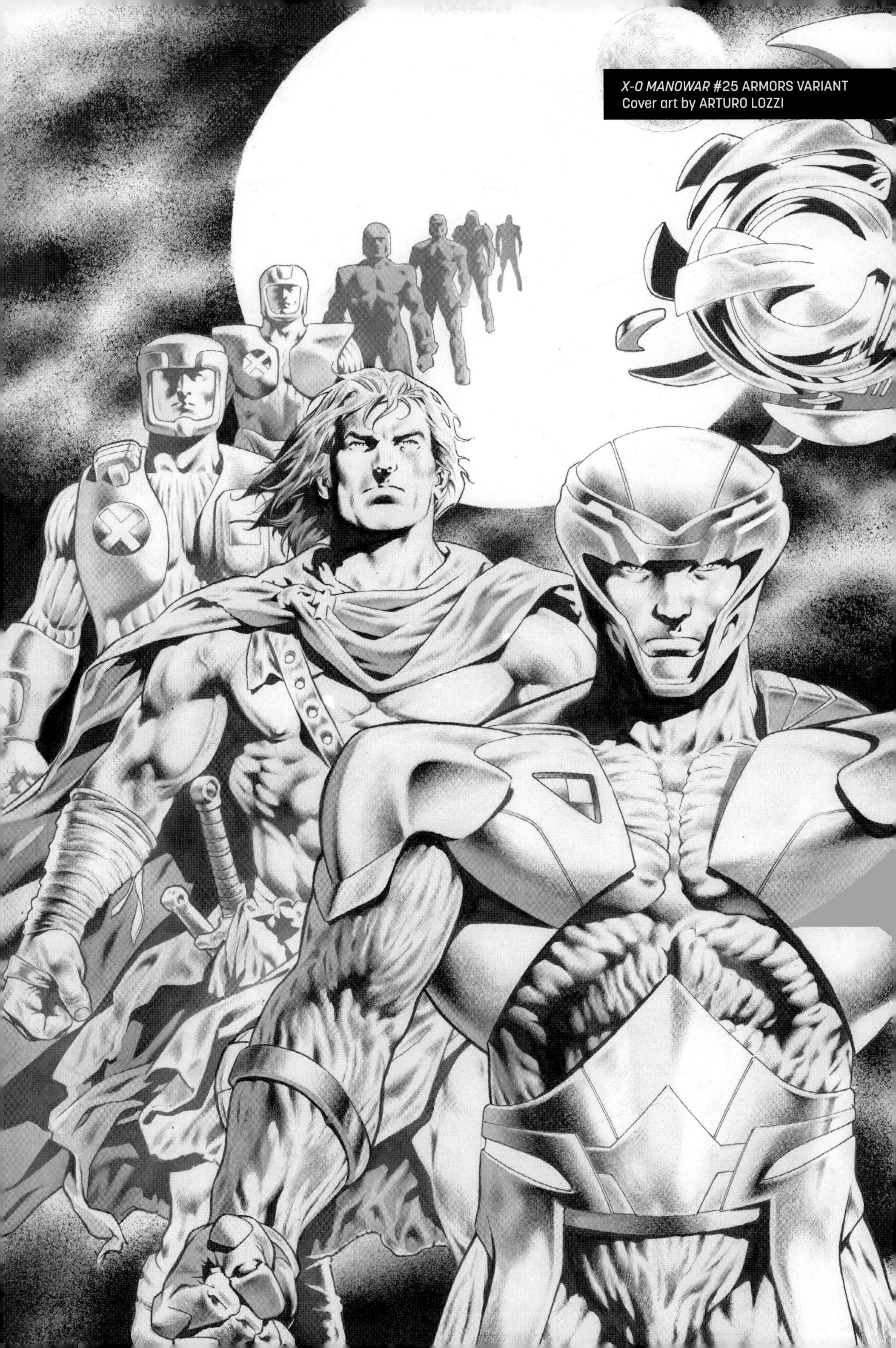

X-O MANOWAR #25 ARMORS VARIANT
Cover art by ARTURO LOZZI

X-O MANOWAR #25, "Burial" p. 1
Pencils by DIEGO BERNARD

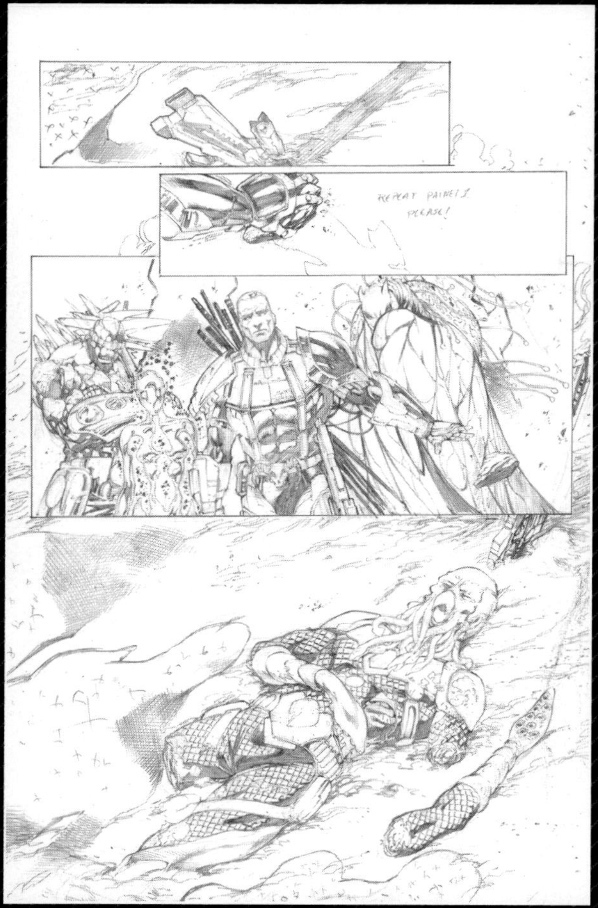
REPEAT PAINEL 1
PLEASE!

X-O MANOWAR #25, "Burial" p. 2
Pencils by DIEGO BERNARD
Inks (facing) by ALLISON RODRIGUES

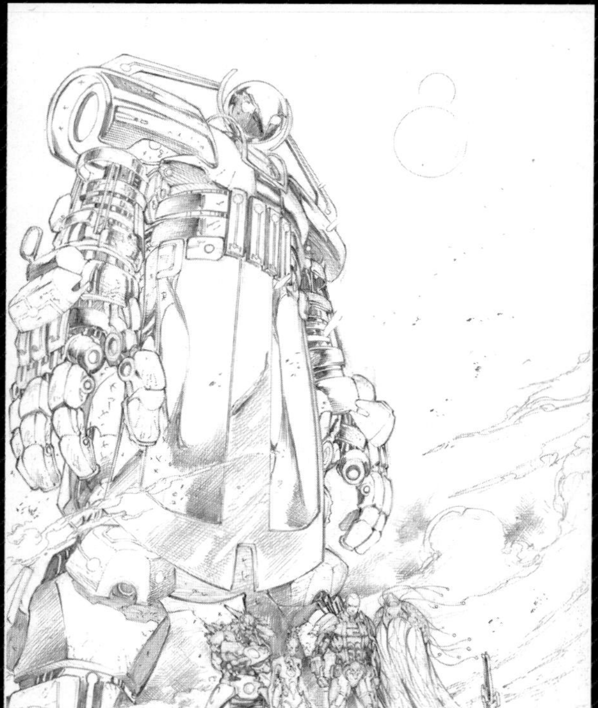

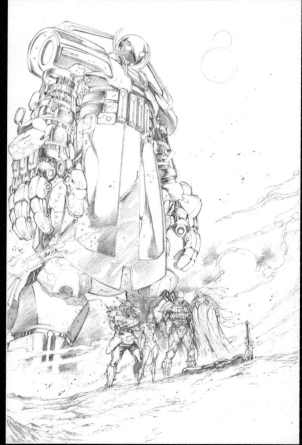

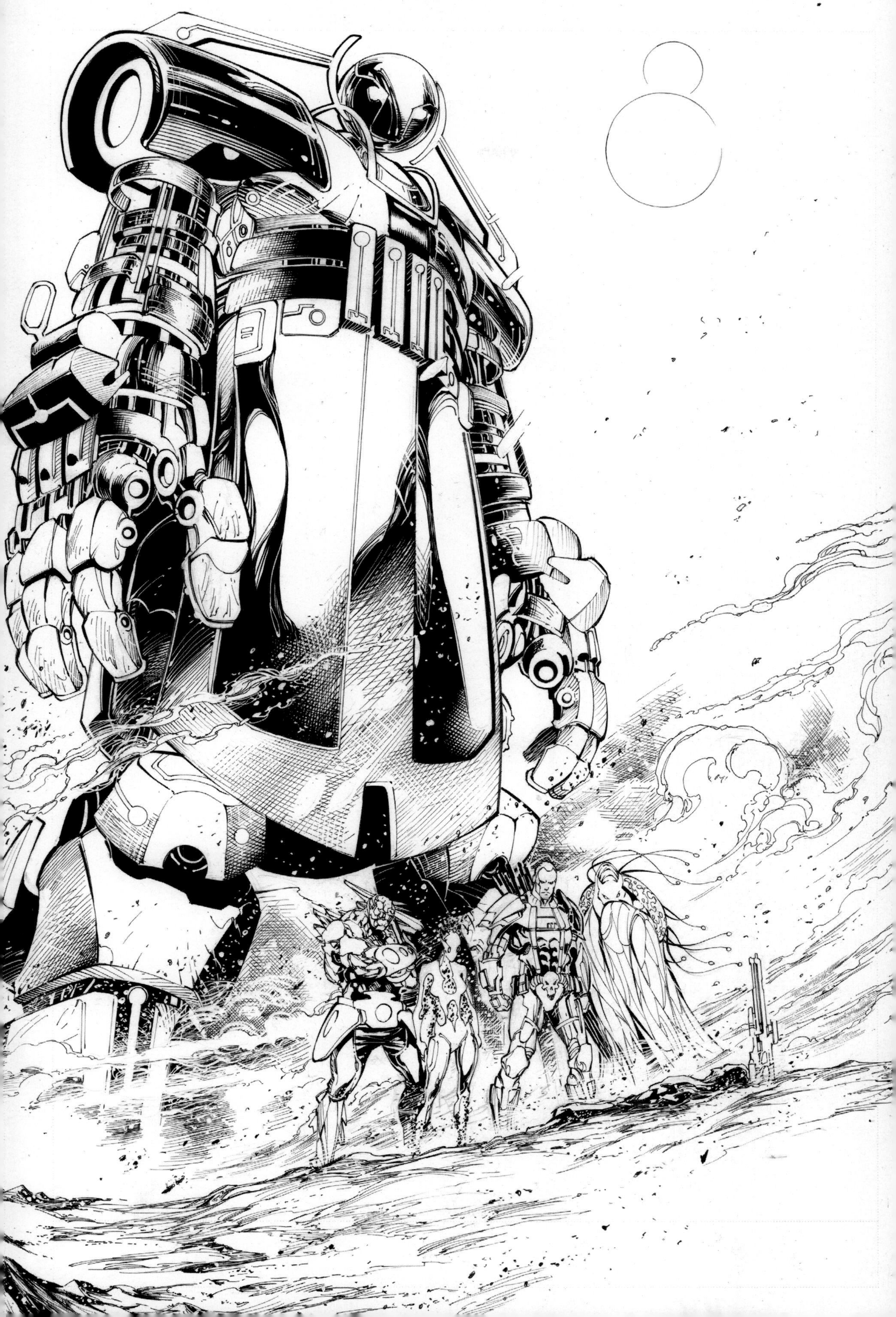

MANOWAR #25, "Burial" pages 8-9
cils by DIEGO BERNARD
s by ALLISON RODRIGUES

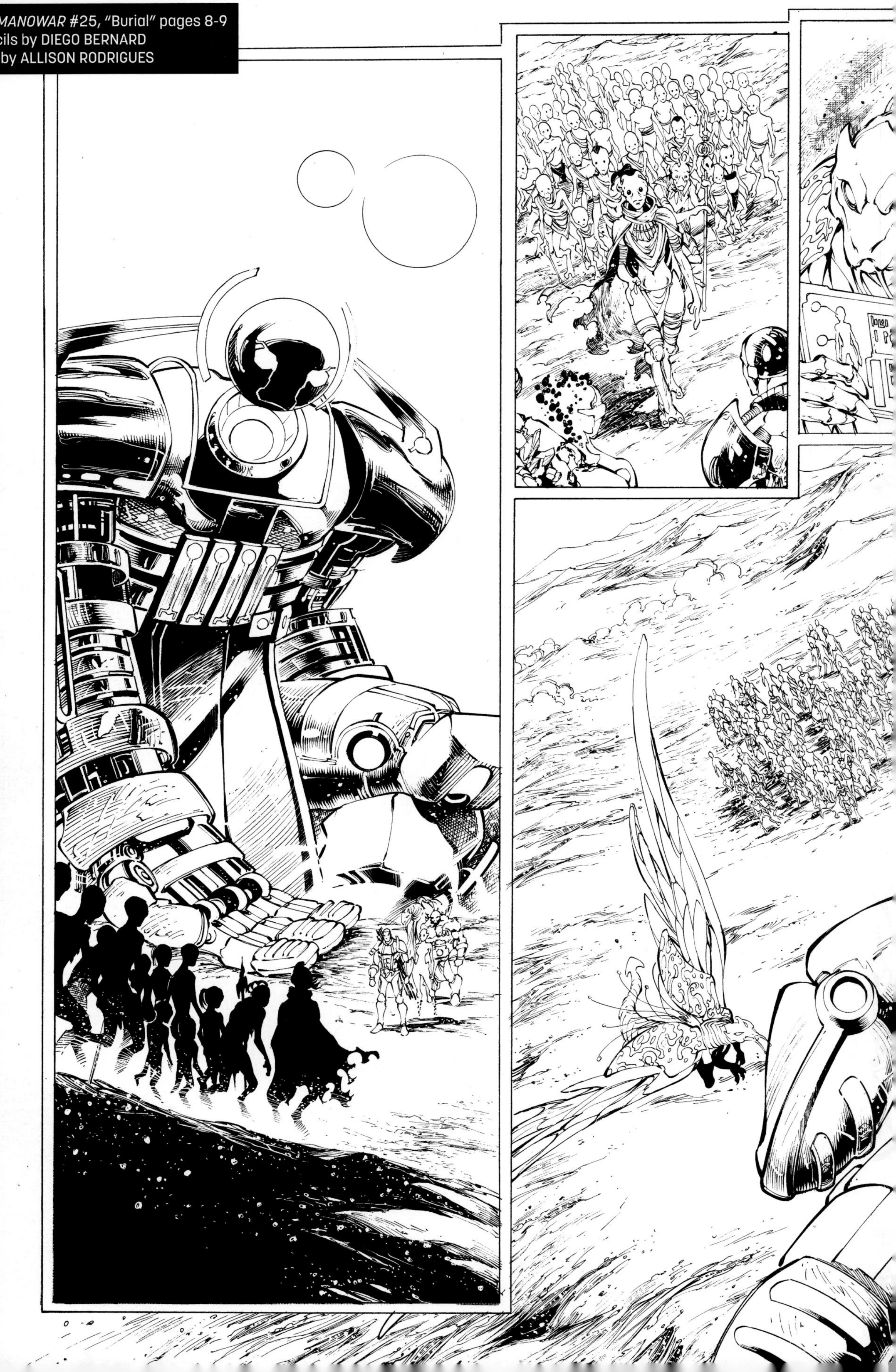

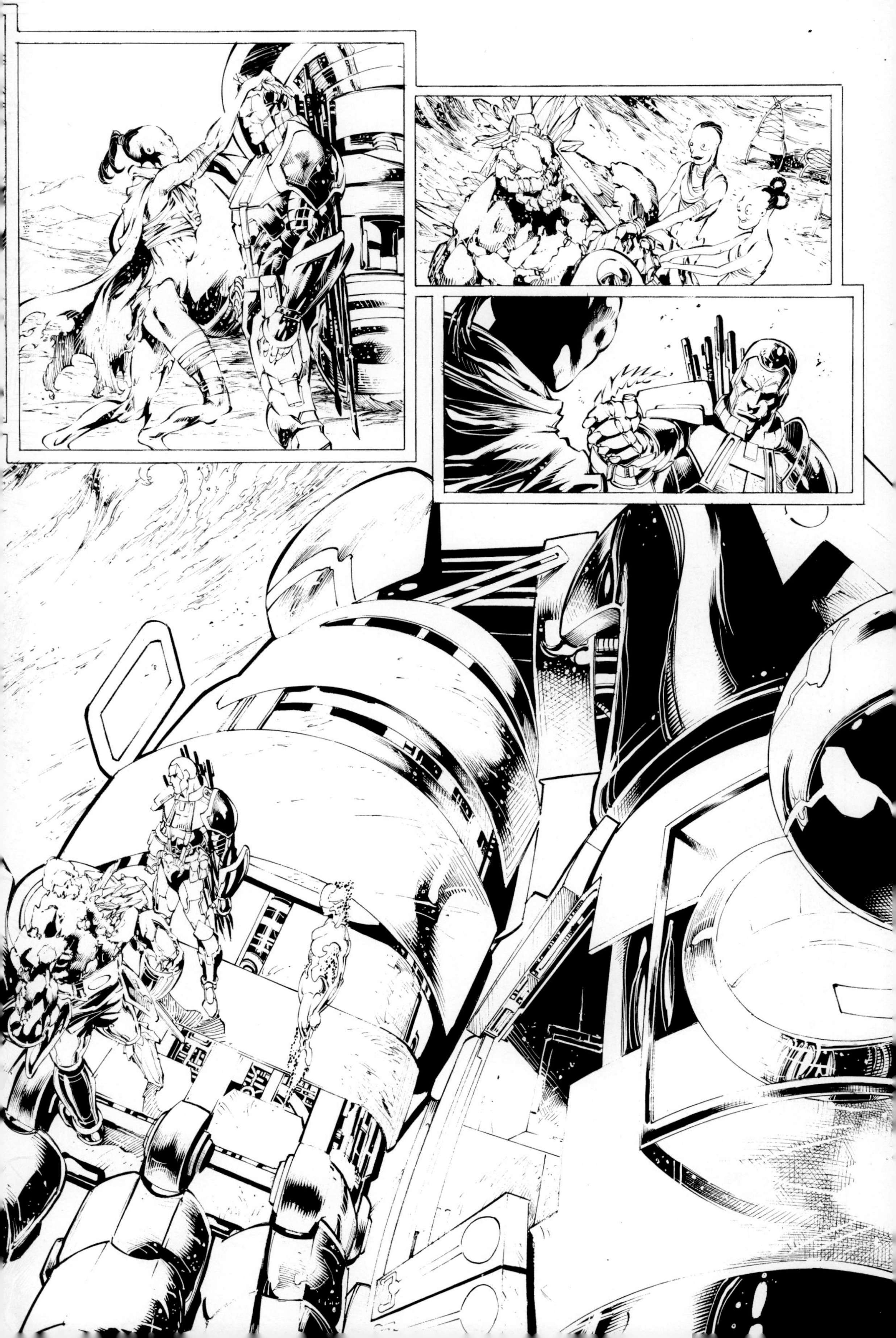

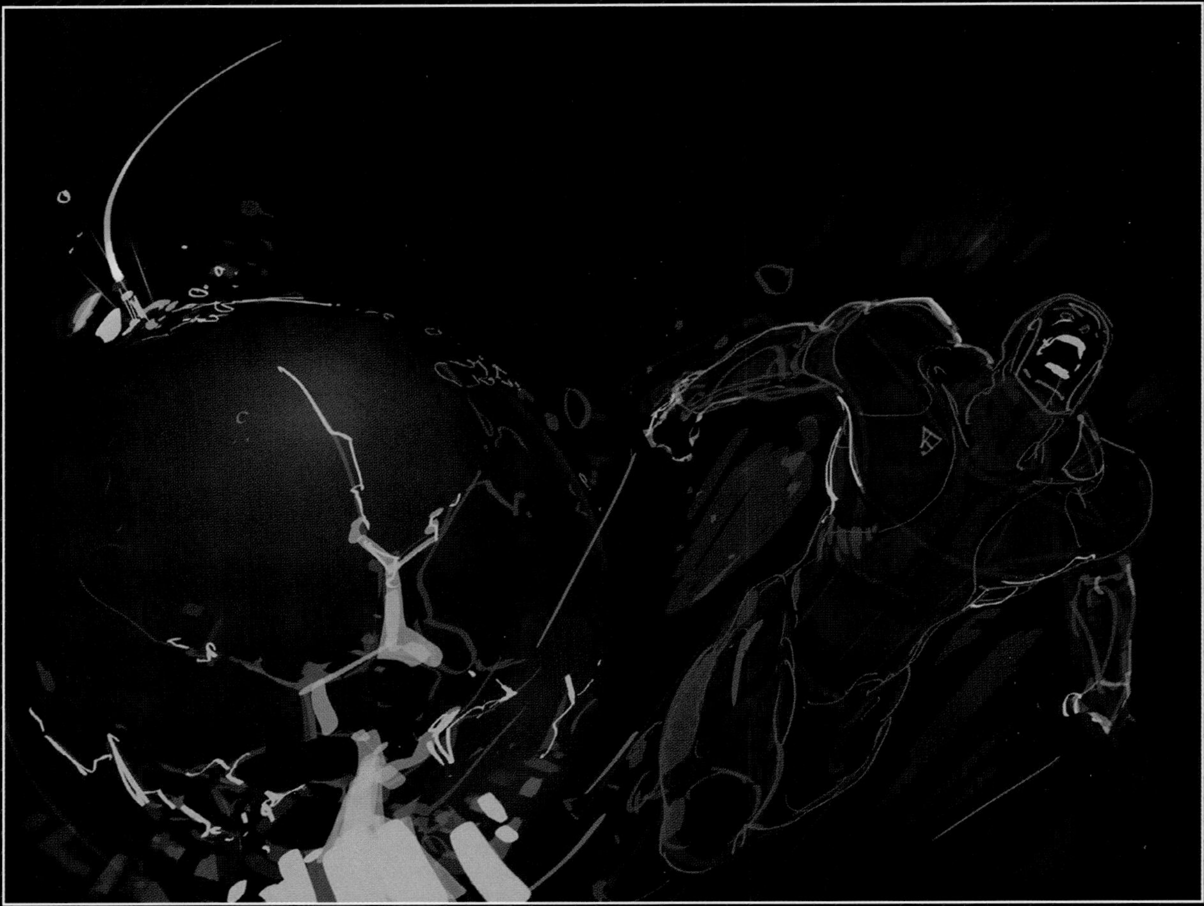

X-O MANOWAR #26 WRAPAROUND COVER
Process art by CLAYTON CRAIN

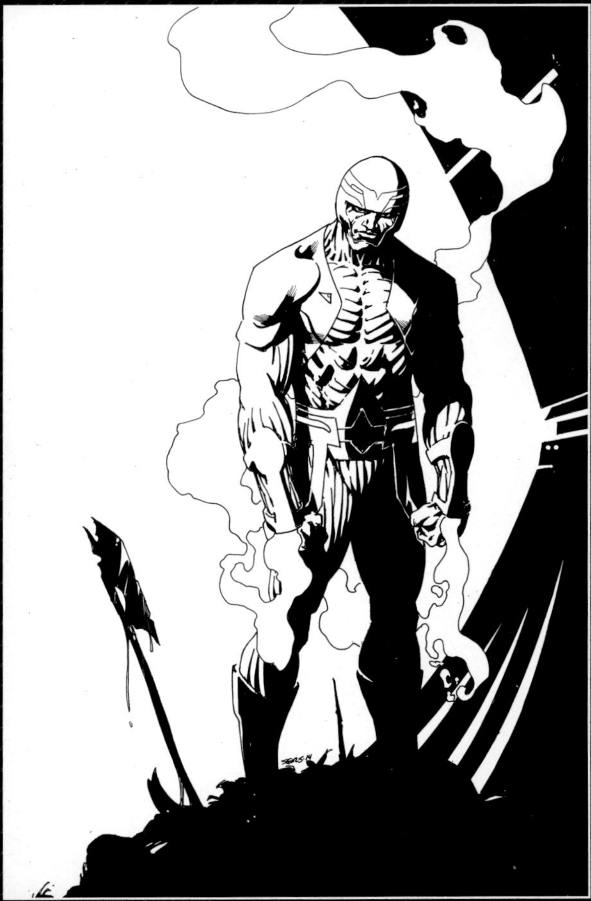

X-O MANOWAR #26
AMAZING LAS VEGAS EXCLUSIVE EDITION
Cover art by BART SEARS

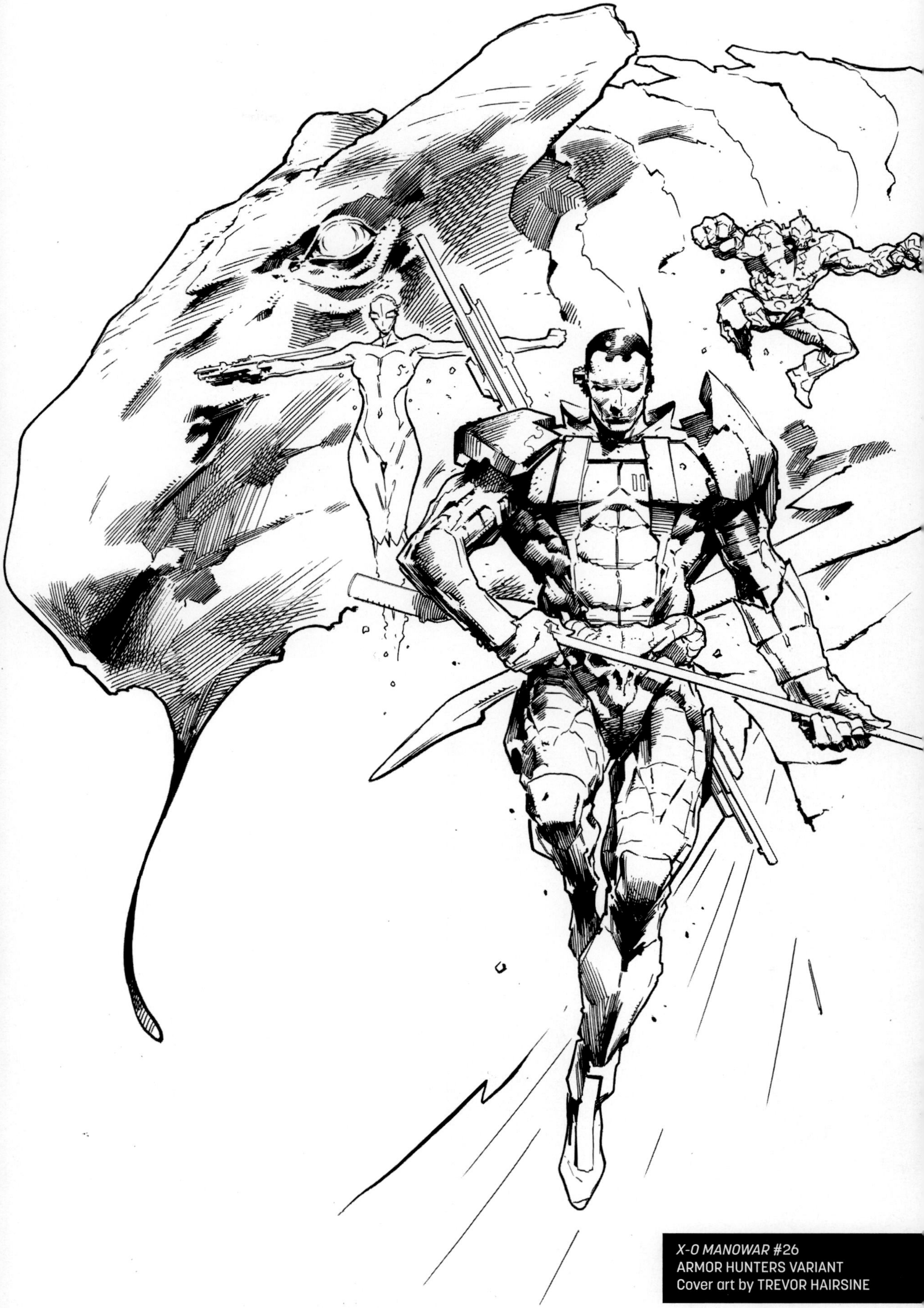

X-O MANOWAR #26
ARMOR HUNTERS VARIANT
Cover art by TREVOR HAIRSINE

X-O MANOWAR #26, p. 3
Pencils by DIEGO BERNARD
Inks by ALLISON RODRIGUES

X-O MANOWAR #26, p. 8
Pencils by DIEGO BERNARD
Inks (facing) by ALLISON RODRIGUES

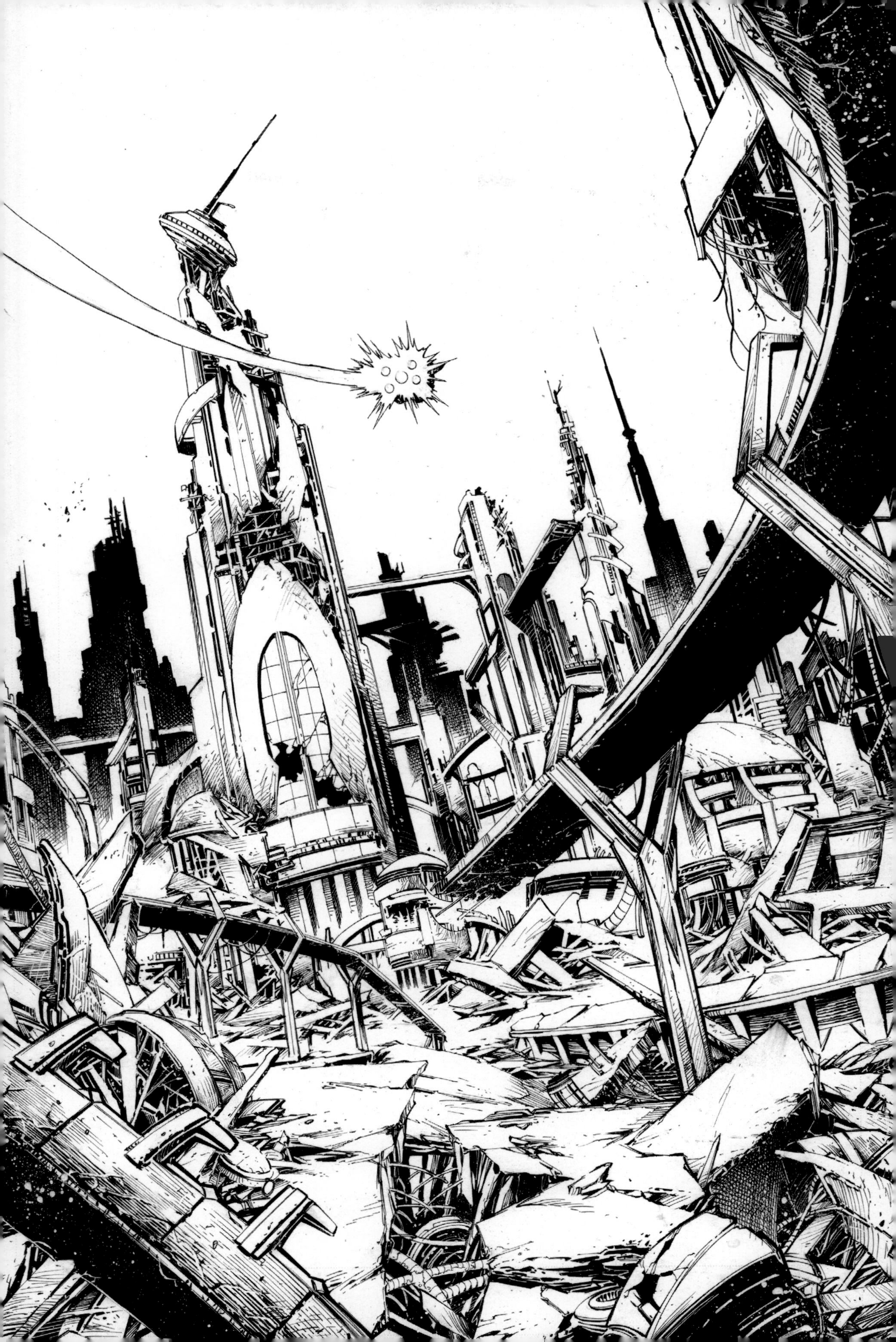

X-O MANOWAR #27 VARIANT COVER
Pencils by DIEGO BERNARD
Inks by ALLISON RODRIGUES

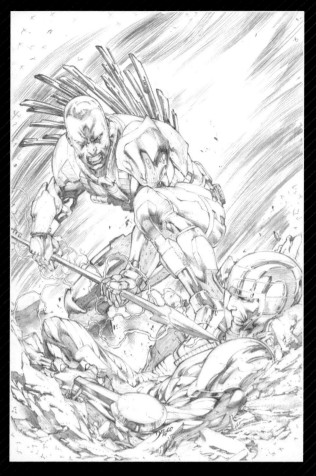

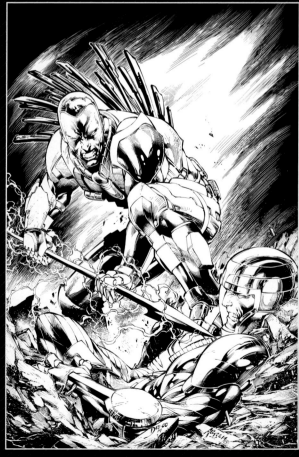

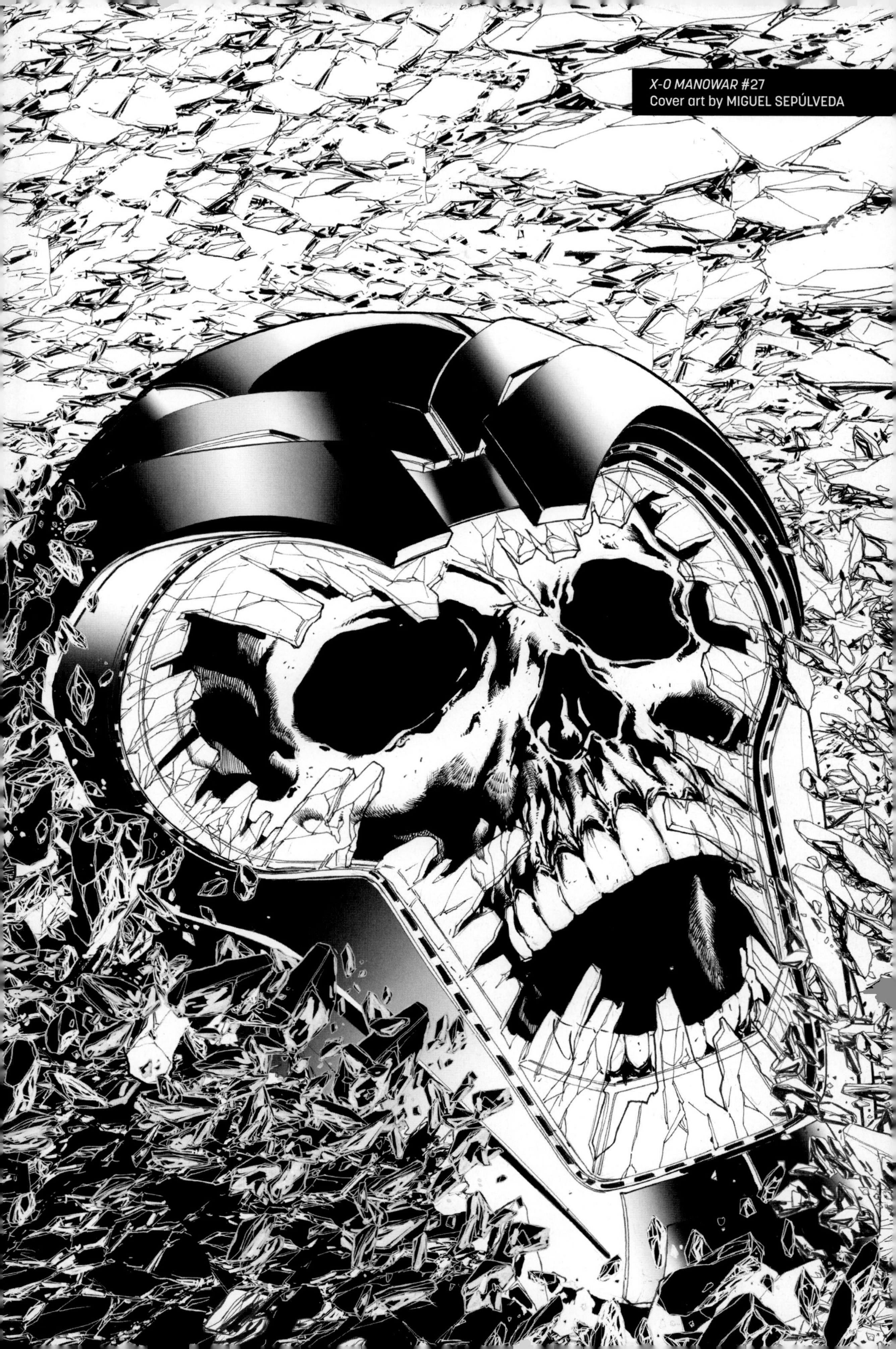

X-O MANOWAR #27
Cover art by MIGUEL SEPÚLVEDA

X-O MANOWAR #27, p. 18
Pencils by DIEGO BERNARD

X-O MANOWAR #27, p. 20
Pencils by DIEGO BERNARD
Inks (facing) by ALLISON RODRIGUES

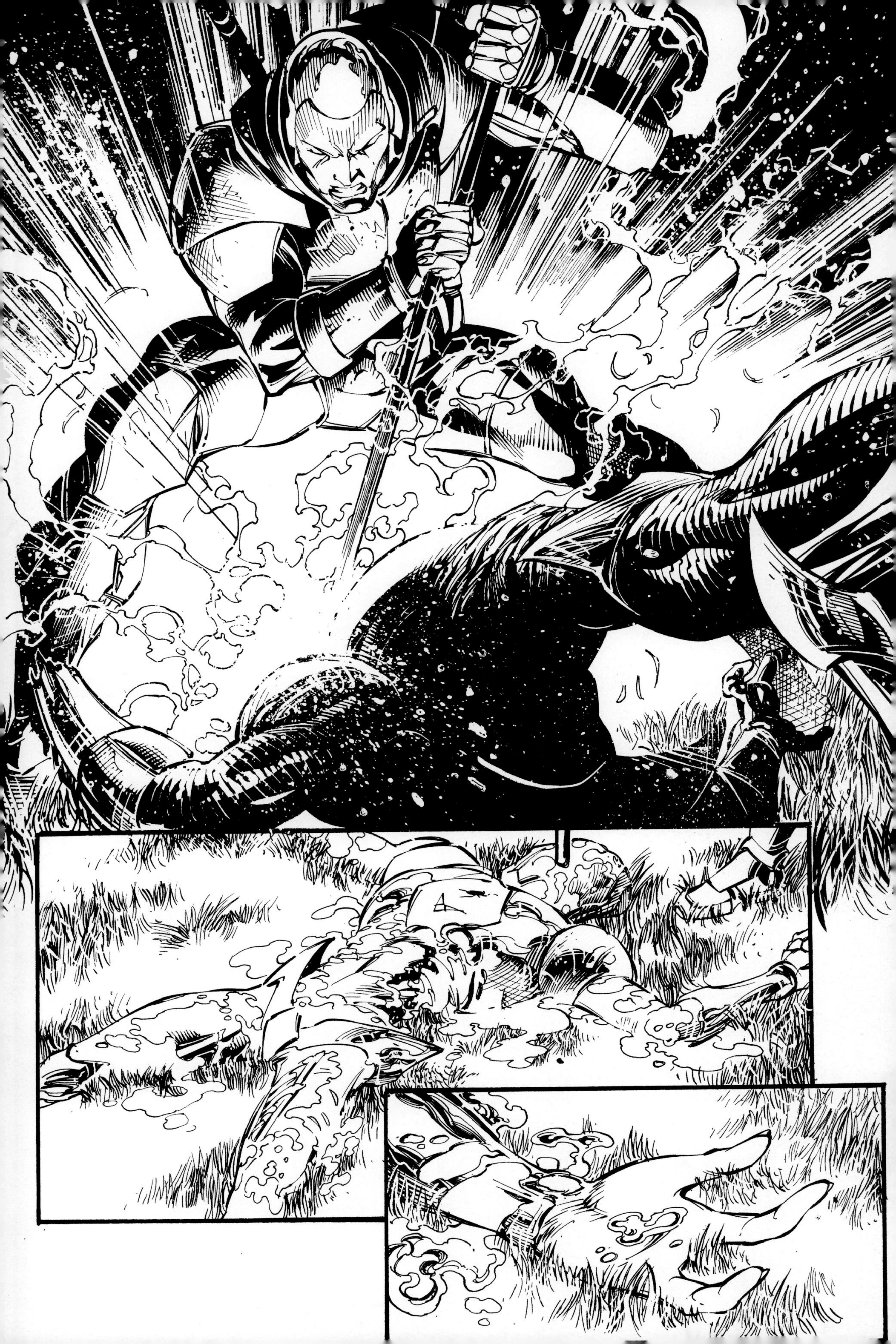

X-O MANOWAR #28 COVER
Pencils by DIEGO BERNARD
Inks (facing) by ALLISON RODRIGUES

X-O MANOWAR #28, p. 1
Pencils by DIEGO BERNARD
Inks by ALLISON RODRIGUES

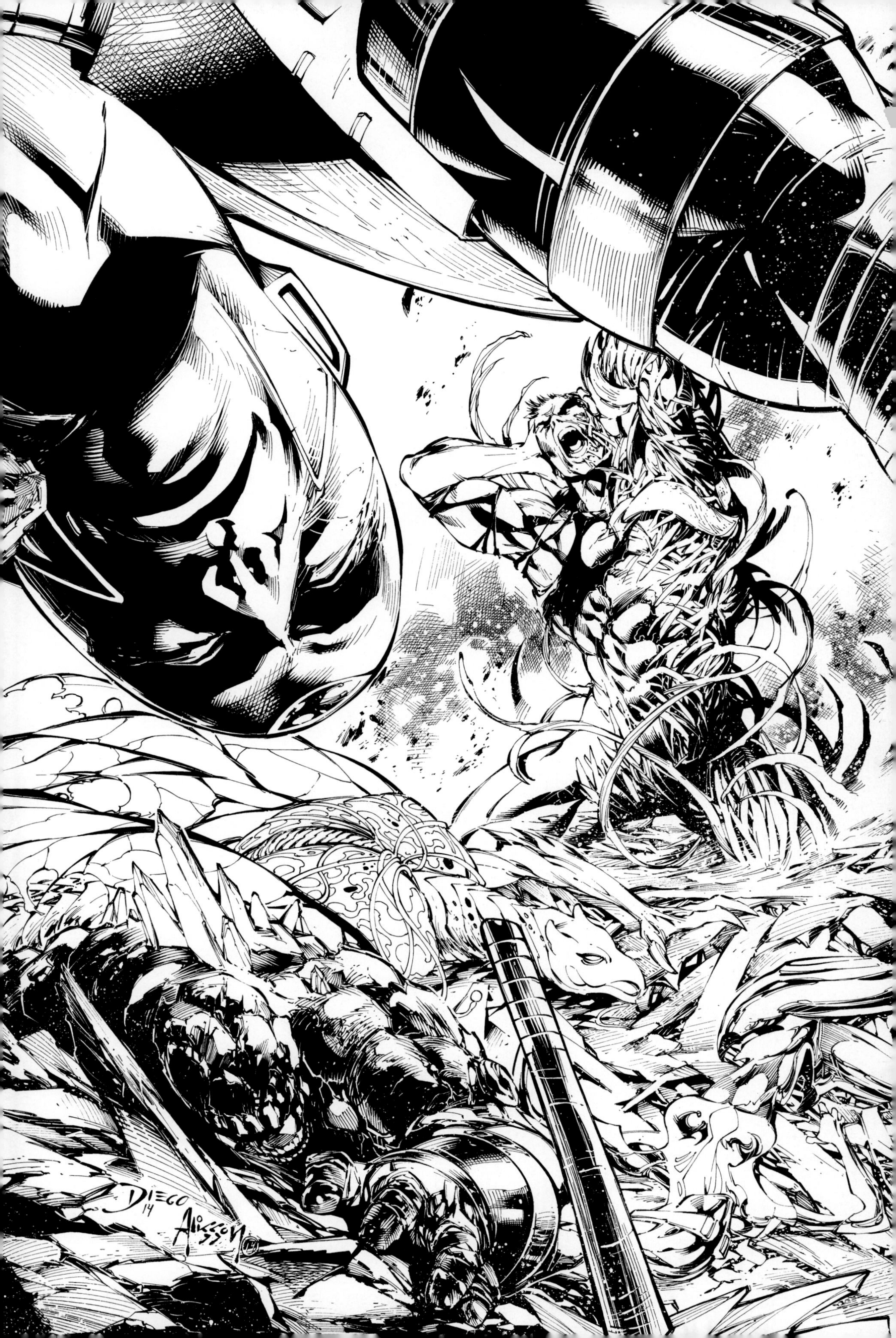
DIEGO 14

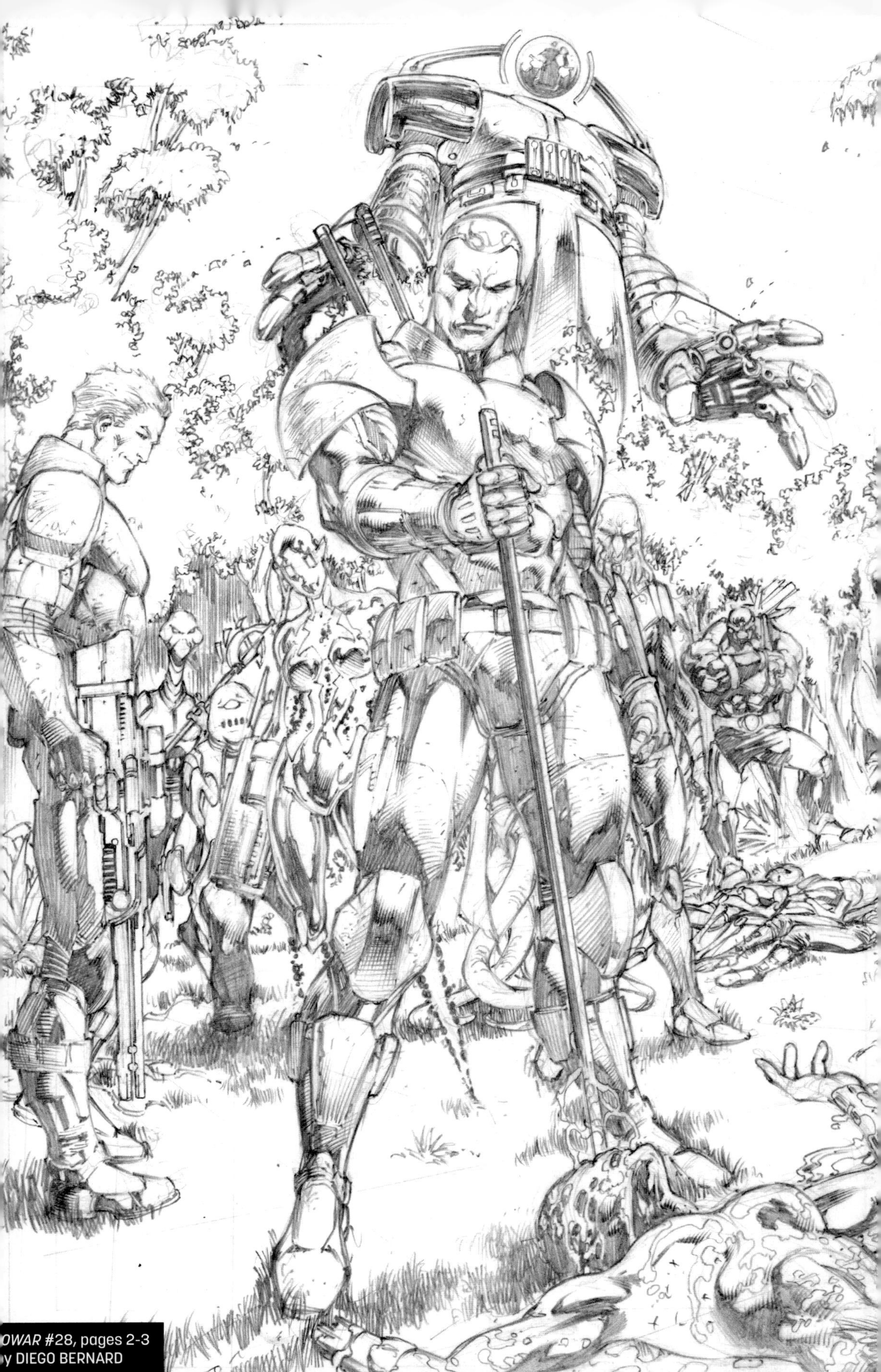

OWAR #28, pages 2-3
y DIEGO BERNARD

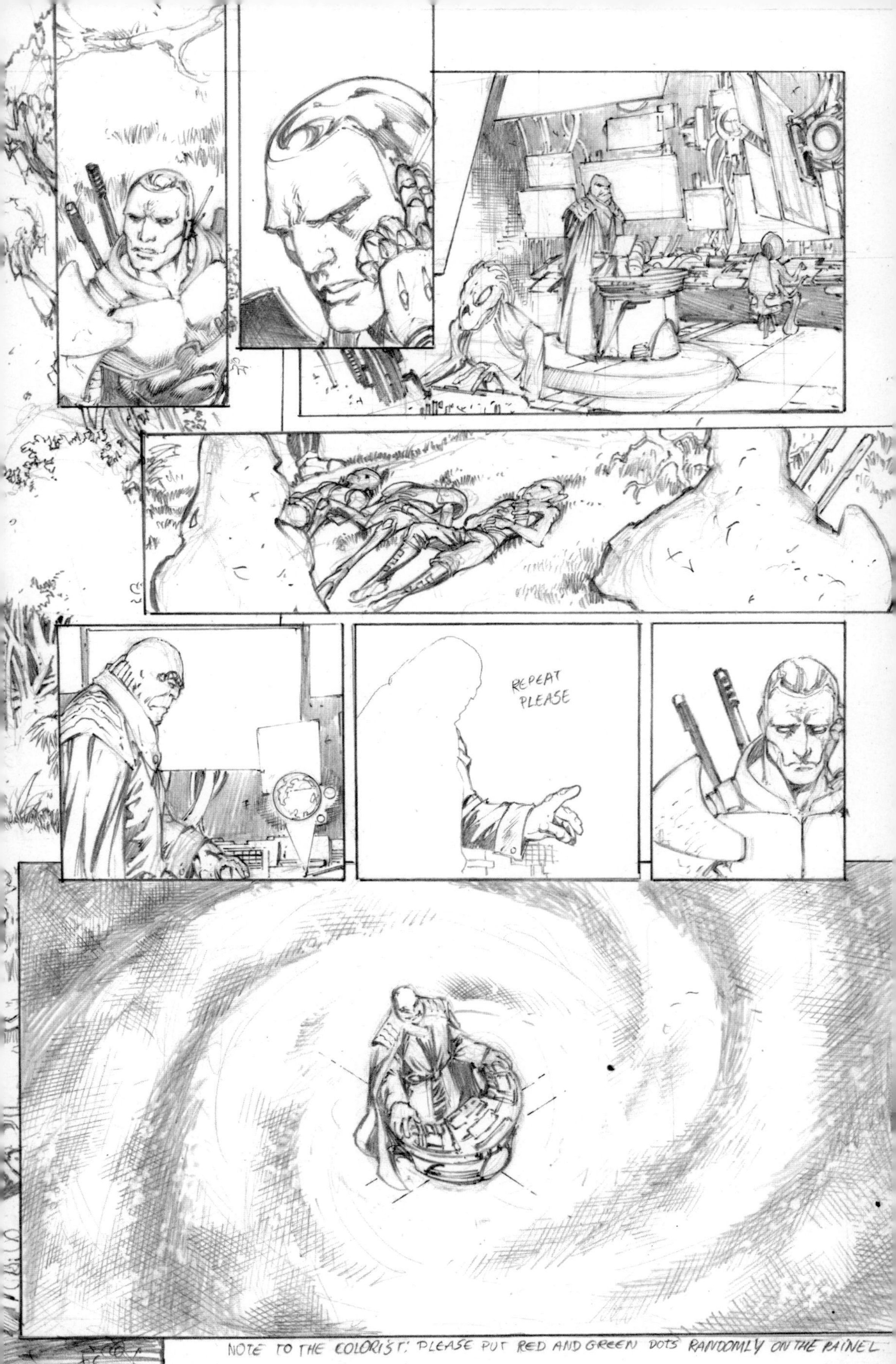
REPEAT PLEASE

NOTE TO THE COLORIST: PLEASE PUT RED AND GREEN DOTS RANDOMLY ON THE PAINEL

X-O MANOWAR #29, p. 8
Pencils by DIEGO BERNARD
Inks by ALLISON RODRIGUES

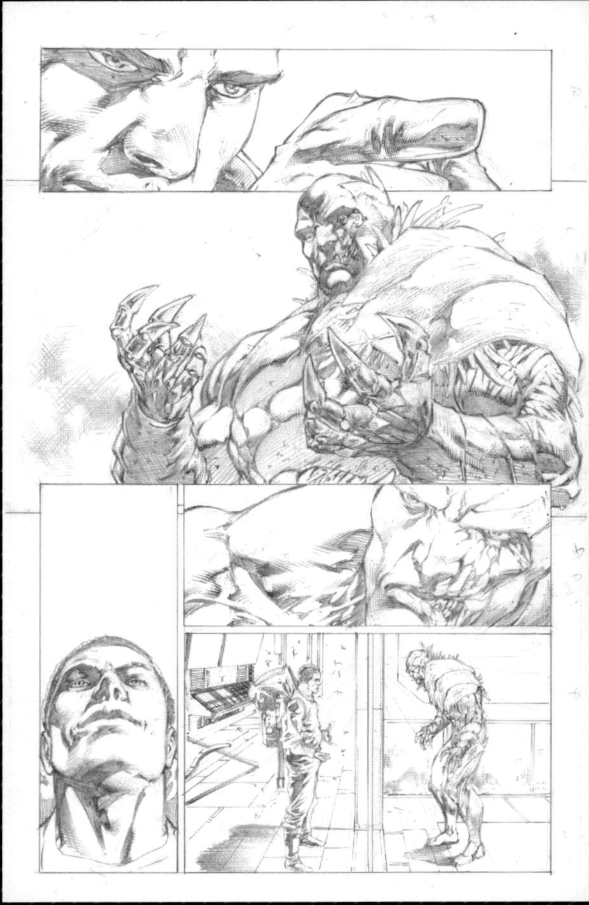

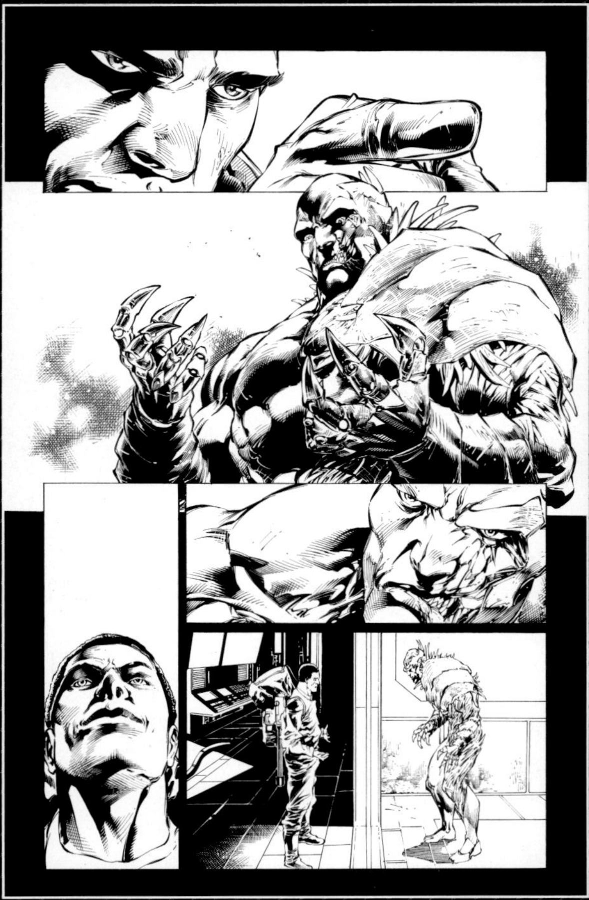

X-O MANOWAR #29, p. 10
Pencils by DIEGO BERNARD
Inks by ALLISON RODRIGUES

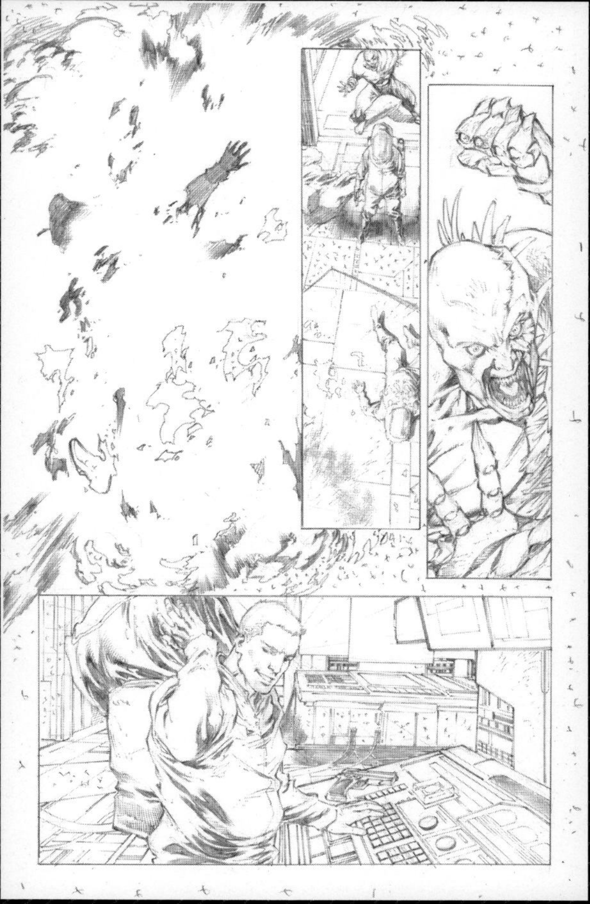

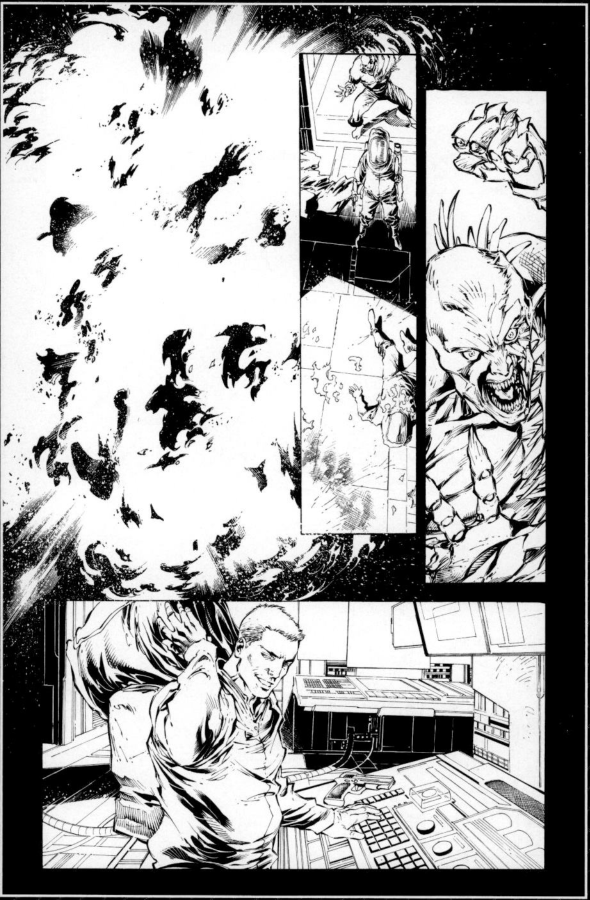

X-O MANOWAR #29, p. 13
Pencils by DIEGO BERNARD
Inks by ALLISON RODRIGUES

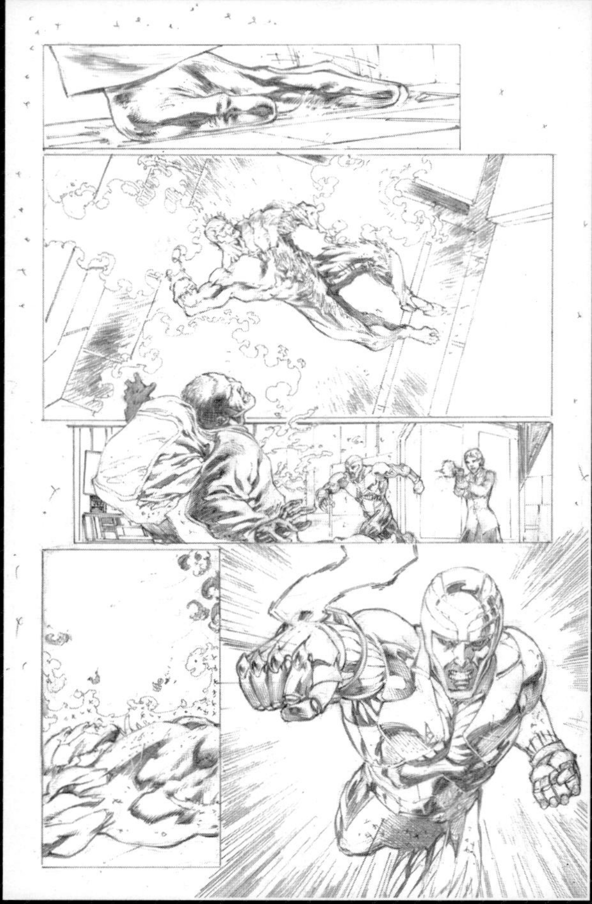

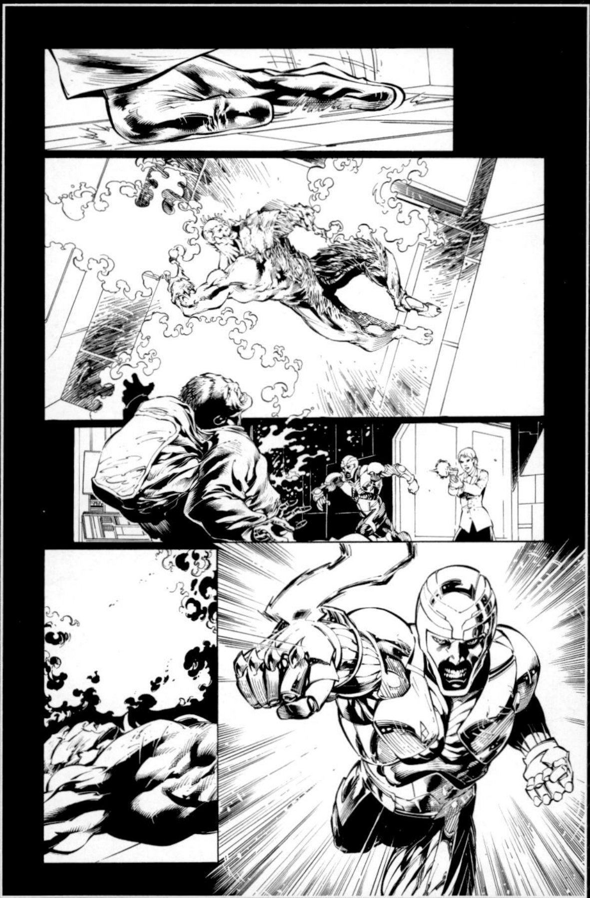

X-O MANOWAR #29, p. 16
Pencils by DIEGO BERNARD
Inks by ALLISON RODRIGUES

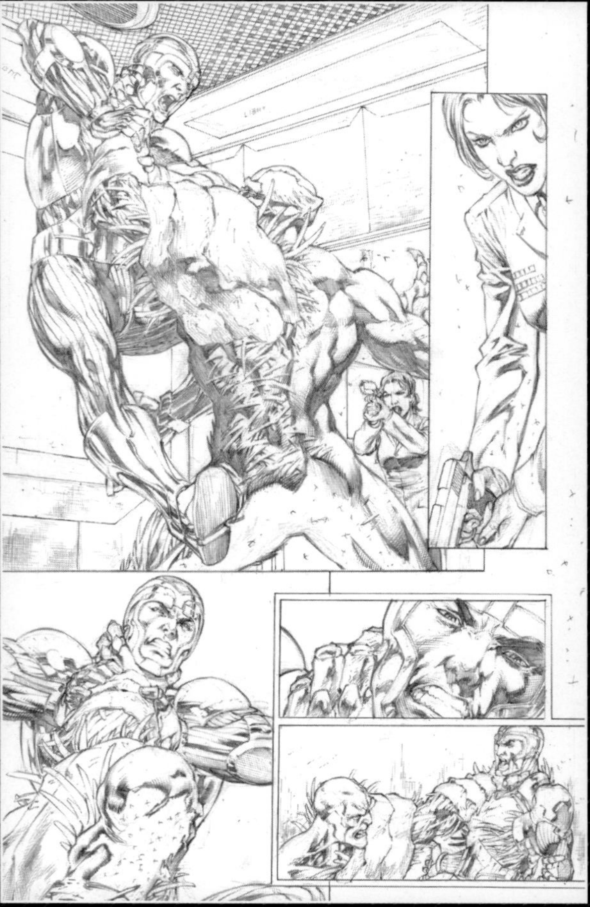

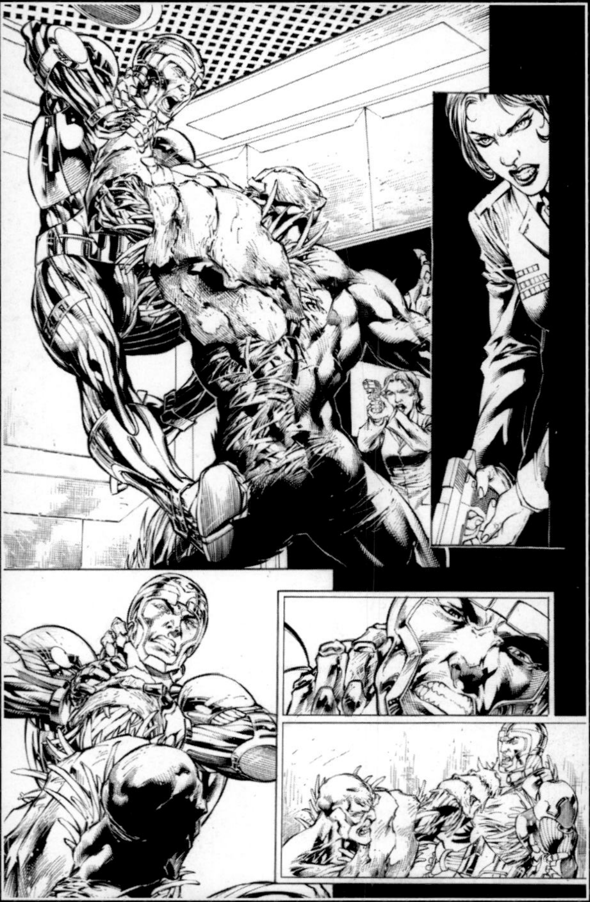